BARBAROSSA DERAILED

THE BATTLE FOR SMOLENSK 10 JULY–10 SEPTEMBER 1941
Volume 3

The Documentary Companion
Tables, Orders and Reports Prepared by Participating Red Army Forces

David M. Glantz

Helion & Company

Dedication

To my wife, Mary Ann, without whose assistance and loyal support, this and
other books could not be written

Helion & Company Limited
26 Willow Road
Solihull
West Midlands
B91 1UE
England
Tel. 0121 705 3393
Fax 0121 711 4075
Email: info@helion.co.uk
Website: www.helion.co.uk
Twitter: @helionbooks
Visit our blog http://blog.helion.co.uk/

Published by Helion & Company 2014

Designed and typeset by Farr out Publications, Wokingham, Berkshire
Cover designed by Paul Hewitt, Battlefield Design (www.battlefield-design.co.uk)
Printed by Gutenberg Press Limited, Tarxien, Malta

Text and maps © David M. Glantz 2014

ISBN 978 1 909982 11 6

British Library Cataloguing-in-Publication Data.
A catalogue record for this book is available from the British Library.

For details of other military history titles published by Helion & Company Limited contact
the above address, or visit our website: http://www.helion.co.uk.

We always welcome receiving book proposals from prospective authors.

Contents

List of Archival Maps

List of Tables

Abbreviations

German

a) Listed in order of unit size

AG	army group
A	army
Pz A	panzer army
AC	army corps
MotC	motorized corps
ID	infantry division
PzD	panzer division
MotD	motorized division
CavD	cavalry division
MtnD	mountain division
Sec. D	security division
IB	infantry brigade
PzB	panzer brigade
AR	artillery regiment
IR	infantry regiment
PzR	panzer regiment
EngR	engineer regiment
MotR	motorized regiment
MtrcR	motorcycle regiment
Bn	battalion
EngBn	engineer battalion
Co	company
Btry	battery

b) Listed alphabetically by abbreviation

A	army
AC	army corps
AG	army group
AR	artillery regiment
Bn	battalion
Btry	battery
CavD	cavalry division
Co	company
EngBn	engineer battalion
EngR	engineer regiment
IB	infantry brigade
ID	infantry division
IR	infantry regiment
MotC	motorized corps
MotD	motorized division
MotR	motorized regiment
MtnD	mountain division
MtrcR	motorcycle regiment
Pz A	panzer army
PzB	panzer brigade
PzD	panzer division
PzR	panzer regiment
Sec. D	security division

Soviet

a) Listed in order of unit size

A	army
MC	mechanized corps
RC	rifle corps
CG	cavalry group
RD	rifle division
TD	tank division
MD	motorized division
MRD	motorized rifle division
CD	cavalry division
DNO	People's militia division
BAD	bomber aviation division
FAD	fighter aviation division
MAD	mixed aviation division
RB	rifle brigade
TB	tank brigade
MRB	motorized rifle brigade
FR	fortified region
RR	rifle regiment
AR	artillery regiment
ATR	antitank artillery regiment
CAR	corps artillery regiment
GAR	gun artillery regiment
HAR	howitzer artillery regiment
MtrR	mortar regiment

TR	tank regiment	MAD	mixed aviation division
MRR	motorized rifle regiment	MC	mechanized corps
CR	cavalry regiment	MD	motorized division
RAS	reconnaissance aviation squadron	MRB	motorized rifle brigade
		MRD	motorized rifle division
RBn	rifle battalion	MRR	motorized rifle regiment
TBn	tank battalion	MtrR	mortar regiment
AABn	antiaircraft artillery battalion	RAS	reconnaissance aviation squadron
ATBn	antitank battalion	RB	rifle brigade
AutoBn	automobile battalion	RBn	rifle battalion
BEPO	armored train	RC	rifle corps
Bn	battalion	RD	rifle division
Co	company	RR	rifle regiment
Btry	battery	Sep.	separate
Gds.	guards	TB	tank brigade
Sep.	separate	TBn	tank battalion
G (as a prefix with any abbrev.) guards		TD	tank division
		TR	tank regiment

b) Listed alphabetically by abbreviation

A	army
AABn	antiaircraft artillery battalion
AR	artillery regiment
ATBn	antitank battalion
ATR	antitank artillery regiment
AutoBn	automobile battalion
BAD	bomber aviation division
BEPO	armored train
Bn	battalion
Btry	battery
CAR	corps artillery regiment
CD	cavalry division
CG	cavalry group
Co	company
CR	cavalry regiment
DNO	People's Militia division
FAD	fighter aviation division
FR	fortified region
G (as a prefix with any abbrev.) guards	
GAR	gun artillery regiment
Gds.	guards
HAR	howitzer artillery regiment

Preface

This book, the *Documentary Companion* to *Barbarossa Derailed*, is the third volume in a planned four-volume set investigating the nature and consequences of the Battle for Smolensk, a series of military operations which took place in the Smolensk region of central Russia during the period from 10 July to 10 September 1941. The struggle as a whole began three weeks after Adolf Hitler's Third German Reich commenced its invasion of Josef Stalin's Soviet Union on 22 June 1941. Code-named Operation Barbarossa, the German invasion sought to defeat and destroy the Soviet Union's Red Army, overthrow Stalin's Communist regime, conquer large portions of the Soviet Union, and exploit these regions for the benefit of Nazi Germany. The ten weeks of fighting in the Smolensk region pitted the forces of German Army Group Center against the forces of the Red Army's Western Main Direction Command, initially, the Red Army's Western Front, but, subsequently, its Central, Reserve, and Briansk Fronts. As such, the battles involved over 900,000 German troops, supported by about 2,000 tanks, against roughly 1.2 million Soviet soldiers, supported by as many as 500 tanks.

During the over 60 years since war's end, most memoirists and military historians viewed the battles in the Smolensk region during July, August, and early September 1941 as little more than bothersome "bumps in the road" of an otherwise seamless offensive operation code-named Barbarossa. Hitler's *Wehrmacht* [Armed Forces] commenced Operation Barbarossa on 22 June 1941 along a massive front extending from the Barents Sea southward to the Black Sea. Employing time-honored Blitzkrieg strategy and the tactics of high-speed panzer thrusts, the invading German forces smashed the Red Army's forces defending the western border regions of Stalin's Soviet Union in a matter of weeks. Thereafter, they spread out northeastward and eastward into the Soviet Union's vast strategic depths.

The battle for Smolensk proper began on 10 July 1941, when the forces of Field Marshal Fedor von Bock's Army Group Center crossed the Western Dvina and Dnepr Rivers and, in accordance with Plan Barbarossa, began a rapid exploitation operation eastward toward the city of Smolensk. The battle ended on 10 September 1941, the date when Army Group Center's Second Army and Second Panzer Group began their southward advance which culminated in the encirclement and destruction of its Southwestern Front in the Kiev region, one of the Red Army's most infamous wartime defeats. Therefore, the battle for Smolensk constituted the ten-week-long struggle for possession of and victory in the Smolensk region.

Unlike previous histories of the fighting in Russia during the summer of 1941, this is a strictly "documentary" study. This is so, first and foremost, because, for the first time since the end of the Soviet-German War, this study exploits "ground truth," specifically, the daily strategic, operational, and tactical records of the forces that participated in the fighting. Therefore, this study is also unique, because most histories of the Soviet-German War, in general, or its component operations, in particular, have lacked the sound basis of "ground truth." It is especially important since the struggle in the Smolensk region during the high summer of 1941 has also generated considerable controversy. In particular, this controversy involves heated debate over the wisdom of the decision by Adolf Hitler, Germany's dictator, to delay Army Group Center's advance on Moscow from early September to early October 1941 for the sake of destroying large Red Army forces fighting in the Kiev region.

This study has to be "documentary" in nature because it challenges conventional wisdom, which maintains that the fighting in the Smolensk region was nothing more than a "bump in the road" to Moscow. In sharp contrast, on the basis of these fresh archival materials, this study argues that the battle for Smolensk was much larger-scale than previously believed, it damaged Army Group Center far more than previously thought, and, ultimately, it contributed significantly to the army group's embarrassing defeat at the gates of Moscow in early December 1941. Finally, the study is also "documentary" because it restores a significant "forgotten battle" to the historical record, specifically, the Red Army's massive September counteroffensive in the Smolensk region.

Since this study relies heavily on "ground truth" to describe the fighting and reach its conclusions, its structure and contents rests heavily on the sound "shoulders" of extensive and direct documentation. Therefore, the first two volumes contain an unvarnished narrative of the course and outcome of military operations in the Smolensk region based largely on paraphrased versions of period directives, orders, reports, and critiques prepared by the headquarters of the forces which participated in the operations. In particular, these include documents prepared by the respective High Command (OKW and *Stavka*) and headquarters down to army and, sometimes, division level.

Because accuracy is absolutely essential to validate the study's many conclusions, this *Documentary Companion* contains unexpurgated and accurate literal translations of virtually all of the documents paraphrased in the two narrative volumes. These are referenced in the text of the volume's narrative by parenthetical notes citing the appropriate appendix and specific document number within each appendix. The inclusion of these documents is critically important for two cogent reasons. First, the verbatim documents are necessary to confirm the accuracy of the study's contents. Second, the structure and contents of these directives, orders, reports, and critiques, as well as the language used, provide uniquely personal portraits of the commanders who prepared them. Specifically, the crispness, conciseness, logic, and wording of these documents, or lack thereof, reflects the intelligence, skill, and effectiveness of the leaders (or absence thereof), as well as such less tangible but equally important personal traits such as their egos, their ruthlessness, and their morale. In addition, for essential context, the *Companion* also includes ten key documents (directives and orders) prepared by the German High Command of the Armed Forces (OKW), High Command of the Ground Forces (OKH), and Army Group Center, which gave shape and form to the Germans' Barbarossa offensive.

Since the extremely detailed contents of the two-volume-narrative and *Documentary Companion* must be studied as well as read, maps are absolutely vital to understanding the strategic and operational "flow" of the battle. Therefore, this *Companion* supplements the 201 operational and regional maps included in the narrative volumes with eleven archival maps taken from the collections of documents compiled by the Red Army General Staff upon which this study is based.

Considering the vast amounts of fresh archival materials upon which this study is based, I must give special thanks to the government of the Russian Federation, which has released the documents essential for its creation. More important still, in light of the considerable work necessary to prepare these volumes, as in the past, my wife Mary Ann, deserves immense credit for editing and proofing of these volumes.

In the last analysis, however, I alone am responsible for any errors found in these volumes, either in fact or translation.

David M. Glantz
Carlisle, Pennsylvania

Corrections to Volume Two

To ensure compatibility between the two narrative volumes and the *Documentary Companion*, the following corrections are necessary to the marginal annotations in Volume two of the narrative:

- Page 141 – change R, 21 to R, 1.
- Page 142 – change R, 22 to R, 2.
- Page 196 – change S, 20 to S, 17.
- Page 218 – change S, 24 to S, 23.
- Page 243 – change S, 32 to S, 35 and change S, 34 to S, 33.
- Page 283 – change S, 48-51 to S, 48, 51, 49, and 50.
- Page 421, note 4, ln. 4 – change "Impossibility of" to "Necessity for"
- Appendix U, which pertains to the operations by *Armeegruppe* Guderian and the Briansk Front's Roslavl'-Novozybkov offensive, is split into three parts associated with three distinct periods of time.
- Page 493 – Add "See Volume 3 (Documents) U, 77.

Appendix A

The Composition, Dispositions, Command Cadre, and Armored Strength of Mechanized Corps Supporting the Western Front in July 1941

- **5th Mechanized Corps** (Trans-Baikal Military District)
  - **Commander** – Major General of Tank Forces Il'ia Prokof'evich Alekseenko.
  - **Composition**:
    - 13th Tank Division – Colonel Fedor Ustinovich Grachev (killed in action in mid-July 1941).
    - 17th Tank Division – Colonel Ivan Petrovich Korchagin.
    - 109th Motorized Division – Colonel Nikolai Ivanovich Sidorenko.
  - **Mobilization assignment** – 16th Army, Western TVD.
  - **Actual deployments**:
    - 25 May-26 June 1941 – deployed with 16th Army to Ostrug, Iziaslavl', and Shepetovka, Kiev Special Military District.
    - 26-29 June 1941 – deployed with 16th Army to Orsha in the Western Front.
    - 4 July 1941 – reassigned to the Western Front's 20th Army.
    - 5 July 1941 – attacked toward Lepel' under 20th Army's control in coordination with 7th Mechanized Corps.
    - 19 July 1941 – 109th Motorized Division became 109th Rifle Division and, later, 304th Rifle Division.
    - 10 August 1941 – 13th Tank Division was destroyed and disbanded.
    - Late August 1941 – 17th Tank Division was severely damaged in the Smolensk encirclement and converted into 126th Tank Brigade.
  - **Strength on 6 July 1941**
    - Headquarters – 7 tanks (BT) and 12 armored cars.
    - 13th Tank Division – 441 tanks (7 KV, 10 T-34, 238 BT, 112 T-26, 26 KhT, and 48 T-37/38 models) and 97 armored cars. 77 BT-7 and 32 T-26 tanks on 10 July.
    - 17th Tank Division – 413 tanks (237 BT, 130 T-26, 35 KhT, and 11 T-37/38) and 74 armored cars.
    - 109th Motorized Division – 113 tanks (all BT) and 11 armored cars.
    - 8th Motorcycle Regiment – 19 armored cars.
    - Total – 974 tanks (7 KV, 10 T-34, 595 BT, 242 T-26, 61 KhT, and 59 T-37/38 models) and 213 armored cars.

- **7th Mechanized Corps** (Moscow Military District)
  - **Commander** – Major General Vasilii Ivanovich Vinogradov.
  - **Composition**:
    - 14th Tank Division – Colonel Ivan Dmitrievich Vasil'ev.
    - 18th Tank Division – Major General of Tank Forces Feodor Timofeevich Rezimov.
    - 1st Motorized Division – Colonel Iakov Grigor'evich Kreizer.
  - **Mobilization assignment** – Strategic Reserve.
  - **Actual deployments**:
    - 24 June 1941 – dispatched to Viaz'ma.
    - 26 June – sent to Smolensk and Orsha under 13th Army's control.
    - 26 June – deployed to Orsha under 20th Army's control.
    - 28 June – transferred to Rudnia under 20th Army's control to block the German advance on Smolensk.
    - 5 July – attacked toward Lepel' under 20th Army's control in cooperation with 5th Mechanized Corps.
  - **Strength on 6 July 1941**
    - 14th Tank Division – 293 tanks (24 KV, 29 T-34, 179 BT, 20 T-26, 17 KhT, and 24 T-37/38 models) and 55 armored cars.
    - 18th Tank Division – 272 tanks (10 KV, 11 BT, 193 T-26, 54 KhT, and 3 T-37/38 models) and 46 armored cars.
    - 9th Motorcycle Regiment – 17 armored cars.
    - 251st Separate Signal Battalion – 6 tanks (all BT).
    - <u>Total</u> – 571 tanks (34 KV, 29 T-34, 196 BT, 269 T-26, 71 KhT, and 27 T-37/38 models) and 118 armored cars.
    - 1st Motorized Division (operated separately from 7th Mechanized Corps after 5 July) – 229 tanks (205 BT and 24 T-37/38 models) and 39 armored cars.
- **17th Mechanized Corps** (Minsk, Western Front)
  - **Commander** – Major General Mikhail Petrovich Petrov.
  - **Composition**:
    - 27th Tank Division – Colonel Aleksei Osipovich Akhmanov.
    - 36th Tank Division – Colonel Sergei Zakharovich Miroshnikov.
    - 209th Motorized Division – Colonel Aleksei Il'ich Murav'ev.
  - **Deployments**
    - 4 July – ordered to the Bobruisk region with 204th Airborne Brigade and 56th Rifle Division.
    - 5 July – subordinated to 21st Army.
    - Late July – withdrawn to the Sukhinichi region under 4th Army and incorporated into 27th Tank Division.
    - 1 August – converted into 147th Tank Brigade.
  - **Strength on 7 July 1941** – no armored vehicles.
- **20th Mechanized Corps** (Baranovichi, Western Front)
  - **Commander** – Major General Andrei Grigor'evich Nikitin, Major General of Tank Forces Nikolai Denisovich Vedeneev on 21 July 1941.
  - **Composition**:
    - 26th Tank Division – Major General Viktor Timofeevich Obukhov.

  ✧ 38th Tank Division – Colonel Sergei Ivanovich Kapustin.
  ✧ 210th Motorized Division.
- **Deployments**:
  ✧ 22-27 June – fought in the vicinity of Minsk.
  ✧ 9-27 July – fought and destroyed in the Mogilev encirclement, with 100-200 men escaping on 27-28 July.
- **Strength on 7 July 1941**
  ✧ 26th Tank Division – 3,000 men and 3 152mm howitzers.
  ✧ 38th Tank Division – 3,800 men and 5 guns.
  ✧ 210th Motorized Division – 5,000 men and 9 guns.
  ✧ Total – 12,000 men and 27 guns, but no tanks.
- **23rd Mechanized Corps** (Orel Military District)
  - **Commander** – Major General Mikhail Akimovich Miasnikov.
  - **Composition**:
    ✧ 48th Tank Division – Colonel Dmitrii Iakovlevich Iakovlev.
    ✧ 51st Tank Division – Colonel Grigorii Georgievich Chernov.
    ✧ 220th Motorized Division – Major General Nikifor Gordeevich Khoruzhenko.
  - **Mobilization assignment** – Strategic Reserve.
  - **Actual deployments**:
    ✧ 27 June 1941 – assigned to 24th Army, which was deploying westward from the Siberian Military District.
    ✧ 1 July – assigned to the Western Front's 19th Army to replace 25th Mechanized Corps and deployed to Vitebsk and Liozno region.
    ✧ 10 July – 51st Tank Division was assigned to 31st Army, but its replacement, 57th Tank Division, never arrived.
    ✧ 11 July – dispatched to the Mogil'no and Berezino region in 19th Army's reserve.
  - **Strength on 29 June 1941**
    ✧ 48th Tank Division – 104 tanks (3-T-34 and 101 T-26 models).
    ✧ 57th Tank Division – unknown.
    ✧ 220th Motorized Division – unknown.
    ✧ Total – 413 tanks (21 KVs and T-34 models).
- **25th Mechanized Corps** (Khar'kov Military District)
  - **Commander** – Major General Semen Moiseevich Krivoshein.
  - **Composition**:
    ✧ 50th Tank Division – Colonel Boris Sergeevich Bakharov.
    ✧ 55th Tank Division – Colonel Vasilii Mikhailovich Badanov.
    ✧ 219th Motorized Division – Major General Pavel Petrovich Korzun.
  - **Mobilization assignment** – Strategic Reserve.
  - **Actual deployments**:
    ✧ 24-29 June 1941 – deployed by rail to the Kiev region.
    ✧ 30 June – assigned to 19th Army in Kiev region.
    ✧ 3-8 July – transferred by rail to the Novozybkov region under 21st Army's control.
    ✧ 13 July – prepared to counterattack toward Bykhov and Bobruisk with 21st Army.

- **+ Strength on 1 July 1941**
  - ◇ 50th Tank Division – Unknown.
  - ◇ 55th Tank Division – Unknown.
  - ◇ <u>Total</u> – 163 tanks (6 BTs and 157 T-26 models), reinforced by 64 T-34 tanks by 13 July.
- **26th Mechanized Corps** (North Caucasus Military District)
  - **+ Commander** – Major General Nikolai Iakovlevich Kirichenko.
  - **+ Composition**
    - ◇ 52nd Tank Division – Colonel Grigorii Mikhailovich Mikhailov.
    - ◇ 56th Tank Division – Colonel Ivan Dmitrievich Illarionov.
    - ◇ 103rd Motorized Division – Major General Grigorii Timofeevich Timofeev, Lieutenant Colonel V. P Sokolov on 22 July, and Major General Ivan Ivanovich Birichev on 11 August.
  - **+ Mobilization assignment** – Strategic Reserve.
  - **+ Actual deployments**
    - ◇ 28-29 June – dispatched to the Kiev region with 19th Army, but diverted to 24th Army on 13 July.
    - ◇ 8-16 July – disbanded, with 52nd and 56th Tank Divisions converted to 101st and 102nd Tank Divisions and 103rd Motorized Division to 103rd Tank Division, all in 24th Army's reserve.
  - **+ Strength on 7 July** – unknown.
- **27th Mechanized Corps** (Central Asian Military District)
  - **+ Commander** – Major General Ivan Efimovich Petrov.
  - **+ Composition**:
    - ◇ 9th Tank Division – Colonel Vasilii Gerasimovich Burkov.
    - ◇ 53rd Tank Division – Colonel Aleksei Stepanovich Beloglazov.
    - ◇ 221st Motorized Division – Colonel Gersh Moiseevich Roitenberg.
  - **+ Mobilization assignment** – Strategic Reserve.
  - **+ Actual deployments**:
    - ◇ 25 June – received alert order for deployment to the West beginning on 4 July.
    - ◇ 27 June – began rail movement to Voronezh.
    - ◇ 10 July – assigned to 28th Army and began moving to the Kirov region.
    - ◇ 11-15 July – disbanded, with 9th Tank Division converted into 104th Tank Division, 53rd Tank Division into 105th Tank Division, and 221st Motorized Division into 106th Tank Division. All were located in the Spas-Demensk region subordinate to 28th Army.
    - ◇ 19 July – 106th Tank Division was renamed 106th Motorized Division and moved to the Smolensk region.
  - **+ Strength on 15 July 1941**
    - ◇ 104th Tank Division – 208 tanks (50 BT-7, 19 BT-5, 3 BT-2, and 136 T-26 models) and 51 armored cars.
    - ◇ 53rd Tank Division – unknown.
    - ◇ <u>Total</u> – unknown.

Note: KhT means chemical [*khimicheskii*] tanks equipped with flamethrowers or smoke generators.

Sources: Evgenii Drig, *Mekhanizirovnnye korpusa RKKA v boiu: Istorii avtobronetankovykh voisk Krasnoi Armii v 1940-1941 godakh* [The RKKA's Mechanized Corps in Battle: A history of the auto-armored forces of the Red Army in 1940-1941] (Moscow: Transkniga, 2005); and Il'ia Moshchansky and Ivan Khokhlov, "Protivostoianie: Smolenskoe srazhenie, 10 iiulia-10 sentiabria 1941 goda, chast' 1" [Confrontation: the Battle of Smolensk, 10 July-10 September 1941, part 1], in *Voennaia letopis'* [Military chronicle], 3, 2003, 4-7.

Appendix B

The Western Front's Lepel' Counterstroke, 6-9 July 1941

German 1. The High Command of the Ground Forces (OKH), the General Staff's Order No. 31554/41 to Army Group Center, 25 June 1941

25 June 1941

The High Command of the Ground Forces [OKH]
General Staff. Operations Department
Order No. 31554/41. Secret

To: Army Group Center
After reaching the region north and south of Minsk, the following missions are placed before the Second and Third Panzer Groups:

1. Frustrate attempts by enemy groupings encircled in the regions between Belostok and Minsk to penetrate to the eastern, southeastern, and northeastern directions until the units of the army corps approach.

2. Capture crossings over the Dnepr River in the Mogilev and Orsha regions and across the Western Dvina River in the Vitebsk and Polotsk region with rapid advances of combat capable forward units and at the same time create conditions for further offensives of the panzer groups toward the eastern and northeastern directions.

3. Bring up all formation of the panzer groups that have lagged behind to the Minsk region and also move up fuel, ammunition, and food supply groups which are absolutely necessary for further offensives.

The pause, which has arisen in connection with this in the offensive operations of the panzer groups' main forces must be as brief as possible.

A further advance of the panzer groups on the eastern and northeastern axes can be implemented only with the agreement of the High Command of the Ground Forces [OKH].

The High Command of the Ground Forces

Source: *Sbornik voenno-istoricheskikh materialov Velikoi Otechestvennoi voiny, vypusk 18* [Collection of military-historical materials of the Great Patriotic War, issue 18] (Moscow: Voenizdat, 1960), 227. Prepared by the Military-Historical Department of the Military-Scientific Directorate of the Red Army General Staff and classified secret.

German 2. The High Command of the Ground Forces (OKH), the General Staff's Order No. 16457/41 to Army Group Center, 26 June 1941

26 June 1941

The High Command of the Ground Forces [OKH

General Staff. Operations Department
Order No. 16457/41. Secret

To: Army Group Center
1. In order to prevent the escape of Russian forces from the pocket which has formed in the region east of Belostok, Army Group Center will close the encirclement ring from the east by committing Ninth Army's 28th and 161st Infantry Divisions in the Petski region and advancing Fourth Army's infantry divisions into the region southeast of Volkovysk.

While taking into account the situation which has arisen in the grouping of Ninth Army's forces, it is necessary for V Army Corps to move eastward through Lida and to the north and VI Army Corps to cover Vilnius and the Kaunas-Vilnius railroad. The army's main forces will move eastward south of Vilnius.

In deploying Second and Third Panzer Groups' forces, envisage the Barbarossa directive and make no changes whatsoever. All infantry formations not occupied in the encirclement operation in the Belostok region, will be brought forward to the Minsk region to free up the panzer groups for fulfilling further missions.

2. After completing the encirclement in the Belostok region and the link up of Second and Third Panzer Groups' forces in the Minsk region, [do the following]:

a) The formations, which have been fulfilling the mission of encircling the enemy forces in the Belostok region, will be subordinated to the orders of the commander of Army Group Center's Second Army, with the mission to destroy the Belostok grouping as rapidly as possible. The formations, which have been freed up, will come under the command of the army group.

b) Second and Third Panzer Groups and the formations of Fourth Army, which have not been participating in the fighting for encircling the enemy forces in the Belostok region, will be combined under the command of Fourth Army for further offensives, together with Ninth Army, in the general direction toward the east. The date of the beginning of the offensive of forces from the Minsk region will be specified by an order of the High Command of the Ground Forces [OKH].

Second Army is subordinated to Army Group Center.

The command of Army Group Center will create a new command and control organization for the forces calculated such that it corresponds to the situation and can be implemented in timely fashion.

In accordance with an order of the General Staff, transfer Fourth Army's rear services to Second Army for creating an intermediate supply point in the Minsk region as a supply base of the panzer groups during the time they are developing their offensive.

The High Command of the Ground Forces

Source: *Sbornik voenno-istoricheskikh materialov Velikoi Otechestvennoi voiny, vypusk 18* [Collection of military-historical materials of the Great Patriotic War, issue 18] (Moscow: Voenizdat, 1960), 228. Prepared by the Military-Historical Department of the Military-Scientific Directorate of the Red Army General Staff and classified secret.

German 3. The High Command of the Ground Forces (OKH), the General Staff's Order No. 31574/41 to Army Group Center, 30 June 1941

30 June 1941

The High Command of the Ground Forces [OKH
General Staff. Operations Department
Order No. 31574/41. Secret

To Army Group Center
As an addition to the High Command of the Ground Forces' Order No. 31554 of 25 June 1941, take into account that, for conducting the operation toward Smolensk, the rapid capture of crossings on the Dnepr – in the Rogachev, Mogilev, and Orsha regions and on the Western Dvina – in the Vitebsk and Polotsk regions will be of the most decisive importance.

The command of Army Group Center must report when and with which forces it will be possible to carry this out.

The High Command of the Ground Forces

Source: *Sbornik voenno-istoricheskikh materialov Velikoi Otechestvennoi voiny, vypusk 18* [Collection of military-historical materials of the Great Patriotic War, issue 18] (Moscow: Voenizdat, 1960), 229. Prepared by the Military-Historical Department of the Military-Scientific Directorate of the Red Army General Staff and classified secret.

German 4. The High Command of the Ground Forces (OKH), the General Staff's Order No. 40406/41 to Army Group Center, 3 July 1941

3 July 1941

The High Command of the Ground Forces [OKH
General Staff. Operations Department
Order No. 40406/41. Secret

To: Army Group Center
After reaching the Opochka and Ostrov regions, the mobile formations of Army Group Center will form groups in the region west of the Velikie Luki low ground, Lake Il'men', and south of the Lake Il'men' and Lake Pskov line so that, having protected their flank between Velikie Luki and Lake Il'men' and, if possible, between Lake Il'men and Lake Chud, they can conduct an offensive.

Mission:

a) Seize the sector of terrain between Lake Chud and the Gulf of Narva; and

b) Capture the territory between the Gulf of Finland and Lake Ladoga and, at the same time, complete encircling Leningrad from the southwest, south, and east.

An OKH order concerning the commencement of an offensive northward through the Lake I'lmen' and Lake Pskov line will follow.

The High Command of the Ground Forces

Source: *Sbornik voenno-istoricheskikh materialov Velikoi Otechestvennoi voiny, vypusk 18* [Collection of military-historical materials of the Great Patriotic War, issue 18] (Moscow: Voenizdat, 1960), 229. Prepared by the Military-Historical Department of the Military-Scientific Directorate of the Red Army General Staff and classified secret.

1. Directive No. 16 of the Military Council of the Western Front of 4 July 1941 on a Defense of the *Front's* Forces along the Polotsk and Western Dvina and Dnepr River Lines and on the Preparation of a Counterstroke by 7th and 5th Mechanized Corps toward Ostrovno and Senno.

Directive No. 16 of the Headquarters of the Western Front,
Gnezdovo, 2315 hours on 4 July 1941

First. The enemy is concentrating up to two tank and one-two motorized divisions along the Lepel' axis for a future attack in the general direction of Vitebsk or Porkhov.

Second. The Western Front will firmly defend the Polotsk Fortified Region, Western Dvina River, Senno, and Orsha line, and further along the Dnepr River and prevent an enemy penetration to the north and east.

Third. 22nd Army, in its present composition, but without 128th and 153rd Rifle Divisions, will firmly defend the Polotsk Fortified Region and the line of the Western Dvina River up to Beshenkovichi, inclusively, and prevent the enemy from reaching the right bank of the Western Dvina River. Burn the bridge at Beshenkovichi.

Boundary on the left: (incl [inclusive].) Vitebsk, Beshenkovichi, and Lepel'.

Fourth. 20th Army, consisting of 61st Rifle Corps (110th and 172nd Rifle Divisions), 69th Rifle Corps (73rd, 229th, and 233rd Rifle Divisions), 18th, 53rd, 137th, 128th, and 153rd Rifle Divisions, and 7th and 5th Mechanized Corps, will create a strong antitank defense along the Beshenkovichi, Senno, Mon'kovo, Orsha, and Shklov line after reinforcing the Senno region with a battalion of tanks, with five KV tanks. Move 229th Rifle Division to the (incl.) Senno and Mon'kovo line.

Prepare a counterstroke with 7th and 5th Mechanized Corps, in cooperation with aviation, along the Ostrovno and Senno axes and, for that purpose, concentrate 7th Mechanized Corps in the Liozno region [32 kilometers southeast of Vitebsk] and 5th Mechanized Corps in the Devino, Staiki Station, and Orekhovsk region [8-16 kilometers north of Orsha]. Develop success with 7th Mechanized Corps along the Kamen' and Kublichi axis [westward south of the Western Dvina River] and with 5th Mechanized Corps toward Lepel'.

The 1st Motorized Rifle Division, reinforced by a tank regiment, will attack toward Borisov to seize crossings over the Berezina River. If successful, the mechanized units will exploit their attack northward toward Dokshchitsy [87 kilometers northwest of Borisov].

20th Army's command post – Kliukovka.

Boundary on the left: Pochinok, Shklov, and Cherven'.

Fifth. 21st Army, in its present composition, will firmly defend the Dnepr River line. On the night of 5 July 1941, destroy separate groups of enemy tanks and motorized infantry east of Bobruisk by the bold actions of detachments in the direction of Bobruisk, blow up all bridges, and burn the forests in regions of enemy tank operations.

Sixth. The VVS [Air Forces] of the *front*. The 23rd Composite Aviation Division will be re-subordinated to the commander of 20th Army for immediate cooperation with the forces on the field of battle. The *front's* remaining air forces will:

1. Prevent enemy forces from crossing to the right bank of the Western Dvina River and an enemy penetration to Orsha; and

2. On the night of 5 July 1941, burn the forests in the Lepel', Glubokoe, and Dokshchitsy regions.

The Commander of the Forces of the Western Front,
      Marshal of the Soviet Union Timoshenko
The Member of the Military Council of the Western Front, L. Mekhlis
The Chief of Staff of the Western Front, Lieutenant General Malandin.

Source: "Direktiva Voennogo Soveta Zapadnogo fronta No. 16 ot 4 iiulia 1941 g. na oboronu voisk fronta na rubezhe Polotsk, rr. Zap. Dvina i Dnepr i podgotovku kontrudara 7-m i 5-m. mekhanizirovannymi korpusami v napravlenii Ostrovno, Senno" [Directive No. 16 of the Military Council of the Western Front of 4 July 1941 on a defense of the *front's* forces along the Polotsk and Western Dvina and Dnepr River lines and on the preparation of a counterstroke by 7th and 5th Mechanized Corps toward Ostrovno and Senno], in *Sbornik boevykh dokumentov Velikoi Otechestvennoi voiny, vypusk 35* [Collection of combat documents of the Great Patriotic War, Issue 35] (Moscow: Voenizdat, 1955), 107. Prepared by the Military-Scientific Directorate of the General Staff and classified secret. Hereafter cited as *SBDVOV*, with appropriate issue, date, and page(s).

2. Report by the Commander of 20th Army to the People's Commissar of Defense of the USSR of 5 July 1941 about the Missions in the Counterattack of 5th and 7th Mechanized Corps toward Lepel' (see Map 1).

To the People's Commissar of Defense
Marshal of the Soviet Union S. K. Timoshenko
0030 hours on 5 July 1941

In fulfillment of your order, 20th Army, consisting of 5th and 7th Mechanized Corps, 115th Separate Tank Regiment, and units of 128th, 153rd, 229th, 233rd, 73rd, 18th, and 137th Rifle Divisions are preparing an attack against the flank and rear of the main enemy grouping operating along the Polotsk axis, in which:

1. 7th Mechanized Corps, concentrated in the Vorony, Krynki Station, and Khomeny region on the night of 4-5 July 1941, upon receipt of a special order, will conduct an attack toward Beshenkovichi and Lepel' and reach the Kublichi, (incl.) Lepel', and Kamen' region; subsequently, the corps will conduct an attack against the flank and rear of the enemy's main Polotsk mechanized grouping.

2. 5th Mechanized Corps, concentrated in the Vysokoe, Selitse, and Osinovka Station region, upon receipt of a special order, will conduct an attack toward Senno and Lepel'. The corps will reach the Liudchitsy (10 kilometers southeast of Lepel'), Krasnoluchna, and Lukoml' regions. Subsequently, conduct an attack through Lepel' to Glubokoe and through Zembin to Dokshchitsy.

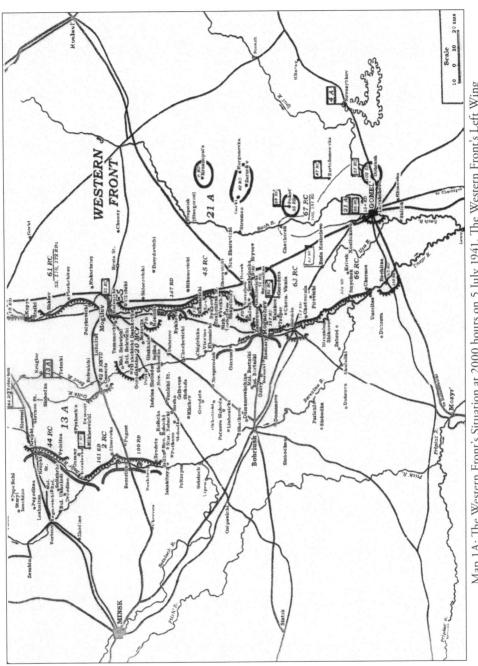

Map 1A: The Western Front's Situation at 2000 hours on 5 July 1941. The Western Front's Left Wing

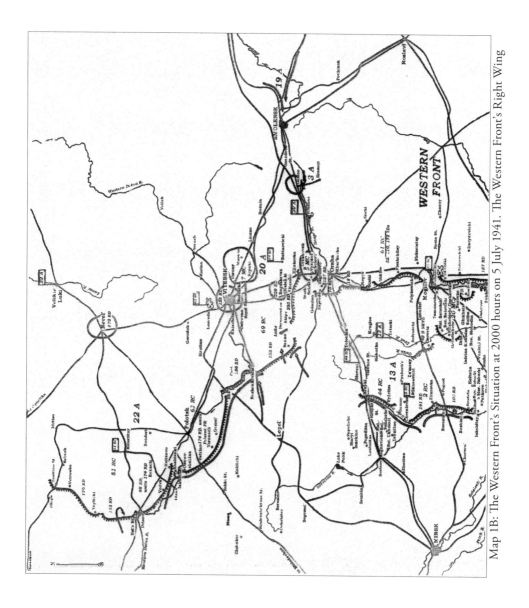

Map 1B: The Western Front's Situation at 2000 hours on 5 July 1941. The Western Front's Right Wing

The boundary between the mechanized corps – Bogushevskoe, Senno, and Lepel' (all for 5th Mechanized Corps).

3. 1st Motorized Rifle Division, with 115th Tank Regiment, will hold onto its positions along the Bobr River and, upon receipt of a special order, conduct a counterattack toward Borisov.

4. 69th Rifle Corps (153rd, 233rd, and 229th Rifle Divisions) will hold onto its positions along the Vitebsk and (incl.) Staiki line and prepare to move separate regiments and battalions, with artillery, forward behind 7th Mechanized Corps.

5. 61st Rifle Corps (73rd, 137th, and 18th Rifle Divisions) will hold onto its positions along the Staiki Station and (incl.) Shklov line and prepare to move separate regiments with artillery forward behind 5th Mechanized Corps and 1st Motorized Rifle Division.

6. The mechanized corps and separate detachments of the rifle corps will be ready to attack by 0600 hours on 5 July 1941.

7. 13th Army has been ordered to hold onto its positions along the Berezina River at all costs.

8. Responsible delegates, personally instructed by me, have been sent to the headquarters of the corps and divisions at 2200 hours on 4 July to transmit instructions and verify the readiness of the formations for the attack.

The Commander of 20th Army, Lieutenant General Kurochkin
The Member of the Military Council, Corps Commissar Semenovsky
The Chief of Staff of the army, Major General Korneev

Source: "Donesenie komanduiushchego 20-i armii Narodnomu Komissaru Oborony Soiuza SSR ot 5 iiulia 1941 g. o zadachakh na kontrudara 5-go i 7-go Mekhanizirovannykh Korpusakh v napravlenii Lepel'" [Report of the commander of 20th Army to the People's Commissar of Defense of the USSR of 5 July 1941 about the missions in the counterattack of 5th and 7th Mechanized Corps toward Lepel'], in *SBDVOV, vypusk 33* [Issue 33] (Moscow: Voenizdat, 1957), 80.

Appendix C

Army Group Center's Advance on Smolensk and the Timoshenko "Counteroffensive," 10-15 July 1941

German 5. Army Group Center's Order on the Further Conduct of Operations, 14 July 1941

14 July 1941

Order on the Further Conduct of Operations

1. Army Group Center, before conducting further operations as indicated in Plan Barbarossa, remains with the mission to smash the opposing enemy, seize the territory southeast and northeast of Smolensk, and destroy the Russians' remaining combat-capable units. Only after this can the question arise about further offensive operations into the depths of Russian territory. An order about that will follow additionally.

2. Fourth Panzer Army will attack according to the order up to the line from south of El'nia to the high ground east of Iartsevo with Second Panzer Group and to the sector between Iartsevo and Belyi and, later, to Nevel' with Third Panzer Group. Conduct reconnaissance toward Velikie Luki.

The army group command will make provision for the commitment of LVII Motorized Corps into combat toward Belyi or toward Toropets.

Second Panzer Group, after reaching the region southeast of Smolensk, will regroup its forces so that they can attack toward the south and southeast upon receipt of a special order.

3. Second and Ninth Armies will follow right after the panzer groups across the Dnepr and Western Dvina River, Second Army up to the Krichev, Khislavichi, and Smolensk line and Ninth Army up to the Smolensk, Baevo, and Velikie Luki line.

Second Army's XXXXIII Army Corps (the army group's reserve) will advance behind the right wing.

4. The boundary line between Second Panzer Group and Second Army, on the one hand, and with Third Panzer Group and Ninth Army, on the other hand, are as before up to Senno and further to the road junction (25 kilometers west of Smolensk), Smolensk, and the Smolensk-Viaz'ma railroad line.

5. Leave Second Army's 258th and 268th Divisions and Ninth Army's 256th Division for clearing out the region west of the Berezina, Lepel', Polotsk, and Western Dvina line. Inform the army group command of their missions and deployment areas.

6. Second and Ninth Armies' units, which are attached to the panzer groups for forcing the Dnepr and Western Dvina Rivers, will be returned to their armies upon reaching the lines indicated in the order.

26

7. The army group command will take up positions in the region north of Borisov.

The Command of Army Group Center

Source: *Sbornik voenno-istoricheskikh materialov Velikoi Otechestvennoi voiny, vypusk 18* [Collection of military-historical materials of the Great Patriotic War, issue 18] (Moscow: Voenizdat, 1960), 230. Prepared by the Military-Historical Department of the Military-Scientific Directorate of the Red Army General Staff and classified secret.

1. Intelligence Summary No. 28 of the Headquarters of the Western Front at 0800 hours on 10 July about the Combat Operations of the Enemy

Intelligence Summary No. 28 of the Headquarters of the Western Front
at 0800 hours on 10 July 1941
1:500,000 scale map

First. During the day on 9 July and overnight on 9-10 July, the enemy along the Lepel'-Vitebsk axis forced the Western Dvina River with large motor-mechanized and infantry units (up to two AC) and captured the city of Vitebsk.

Along the Bobruisk axis, after concentrating a large grouping, he is preparing to force the Dnepr River.

Along the Borisov axis – there is fighting of a local nature with large enemy motorized units.

Second. The Sebezh axis.

During the second half of the day and overnight on 9-10 July, the enemy conducted fierce fighting with a force of up to three infantry divisions (3rd, 28th, and 121st IDs) and a panzer regiment, supported by aviation. He captured Sebezh and reached the Sebezh, Lake Osveiskoe, and Ust'e front (7 kilometers southwest of Drissa) with his main forces.

Third. The Polotsk axis.

During the day on 9 July, the enemy fought along the Borkovichi and Polotsk front with a force of up two divisions (14th MotD and 51st ID) and one panzer division, supported by aviation.

Fourth. The Lepel'-Vitebsk axis.

The enemy forced the Western Dvina River in the Ulla and Beshenkovichi sector with the forces of 8th [sic] and 39th ACs (motorized), developed the attack toward Sirotino and Vitebsk, and reached the Zabor'e, Obol', Sirotino, and Vitebsk front by first light on 10 July.

The withdrawal of the enemy from the Senno region (28 kilometers southeast of Beshenkovichi), which was noted on 8 July, was an evasive maneuver by enemy motor-mechanized units away from the fighting until reserves approached from the depths.

On 9 July large enemy motor-mechanized units were fighting west of Senno, while protecting their left flank with strong antitank regions [strong points] along the Chernogost'e, Ozera, and Novoselki line and supporting actions by bombers, dive-bombers, and heavy artillery.

Fifth. The Borisov axis.

The enemy, consisting of 4th AC (4th and 10th MotDs, 18th PzD, and units of 7th PzD), fought along our intermediate Kokhanovo (33 kilometers west of Orsha) and Drut' River line. The enemy lost a considerable number of tanks and personnel as a result of the fighting. He was advancing toward Shklov with separate detachments consisting of up to a battalion of motorized infantry, up to a company of tanks, one-two battalions of artillery, and a sapper subunit in each, and, simultaneously, was carrying out a regrouping of forces from the Borisov region toward Mogilev.

Sixth. The Bobruisk axis.

During the day on 9 July and the night of 9-10 July, the enemy has continued concentrating large forces from 24th AC (motorized), consisting of 3rd and 4th PzDs, a motorized division, and 265th ID, on the western bank of the Dnepr River in the Vishchin (15 kilometers northeast of Rogachev), Rogachev, Zhlobin, and Proskurin regions and, while conducting artillery fire against our units, was preparing crossings in the Zborovo [8 kilometers north of Rogachev], Zadrut'e [5 kilometers south of Rogachev], Zhlobin, and Proskurin sector by the end of the day on 9 July and the night of 9-10 July.

Conclusions

We have noted that the main effort of the enemy's operations is along the Lepel'-Vitebsk axis, and concentrations of large groupings – are along the Bobruisk axis, where we can expect him to cross the Dnepr River in the near future.

Along the Borisov axis, while fighting along our intermediate line, the enemy is approaching the Dnepr River

Along the Sebezh axis, the enemy is continuing to capture the Sebezh region.

> The Chief of Staff of the Western Front, Lieutenant General Malandin
> The Chief of the Intelligence Department of the Western Front,
>   Colonel Korneev

Source: "Razvedyvatel'naia svodka shtaba Zapadnogo fronta No. 28 k 8 chasam 10 iiulia 1941 g. o boevykh deistviiakh protivnika" [Intelligence Summary No. 28 of the headquarters of the Western Front at 0800 hours on 10 July about the combat operations of the enemy], in *SBDVOV, vypusk* 37 [Issue 37] (Moscow: Voenizdat, 1957), 80-81.

2. Operational Summary No. 33 of the Headquarters of the Western Front at 2000 hours on 11 July 1941 about the Combat Actions of the *Front's* Forces

Operational Summary No. 33 of the Headquarters of the Western Front
at 2000 hours on 11 July 1941
1:500,000 scale map

First. During the day, the *front's* forces continued fighting with attacking enemy units in the Sebezh, Osveia, Borkovichi, Gorodok, Vitebsk, Barsuki Station, and Borkolobovo regions, while directing their main efforts on the liquidation of the enemy's advancing Vitebsk grouping.

Second. 22nd Army [Ershakov]. The army's units fought intense defensive battles along its entire front, having before it units of 8th and 39th ACs.

51st RC: 170th RD attacked with its right wing at 1000 hours on 11 July, and its left wing is fighting along its previous positions;

112th RD, while holding off numerically superior enemy forces in the Volyntsy region on its left wing, was conducting intense fighting with enemy tanks penetrating from Iukhovichi toward Kliastitsy at 1000 hours on 11 July;

98th Rifle Division, while repelling enemy attempts to force the Drissa River, is occupying its previous positions; and

126th Rifle Division is engaged in defensive fighting along the Ignatovo and Kulikovo line.

51st Corps' headquarters – Kliastitsy.

62nd RC: 174th Rifle Division was occupying its previous positions at 1000 hours on 11 July. The enemy did not conduct active operations on the division's front.

186th Rifle Division's 238th Regiment is attacking toward Lovsha Station, and the regiment's forward units are fighting fiercely in the vicinity of Lovsha Station.

The remaining units of 186th Rifle Division have been concentrated in the Prudok and Bobrovshchina region (14 kilometers east of Trudy).

62nd Corps' headquarters – Trudy

Third. 19th Army [Konev] has been conducting intense fighting for Vitebsk, but the results of the battle still remain undetermined. The remaining units are continuing their concentration.

Of the 350 trains that arrived on 11 July, 130 trains have been unloaded.

7th MC and 153rd, 186th, and 50th RDs are being subordinated to the army.

19th Army's headquarters – Rudnia.

Fourth. 20th Army [Kurochkin], while withdrawing the mechanized corps [20th] behind the front lines, conducted defensive fighting in its previous positions

The enemy group which has been crossing at Kopys is being beaten back.

The [enemy force of] up to two battalions of infantry with tanks that have been forcing the Dnepr north of Shklov is being driven back by a counterattack by our units, and 15 enemy tanks have been left behind on the battlefield.

19th and 153rd RDs and 7th MC are being re-subordinated from 20th Army to the commander of 19th Army.

Fifth. 13th Army [Remezov]. During the day on 11 July, the army was holding onto its positions in the Shklov and Novyi Bykhov sector and fighting with enemy units penetrating in the Barsuki Station and Barkalabovo region, while continuing to concentrate its approaching units.

61st RC is holding onto the Shklov, Mogilev, and Buinichi line, while conducting reinforced reconnaissance north of Shklov, where an enemy force of up to two battalions conducted an attack on the morning of 11 July, and small groups of infantry and individual tanks forced the Dnepr.

53rd RD is holding on to the Shklov and Pleshchitsy line, while conducting reconnaissance north of Shklov. At 1200 hours the enemy forced the Dnepr River, 2 kilometers north of Pleshchitsy, with a force of up to two battalions with tanks. A counterattack by 61st RC's units threw them back to the river, and the enemy suffered heavy losses and lost 15 tanks.

110th RD – along the Pleshchnitsy and Shapochitsy defensive line.

172nd RD is defending the Mogilev bridgehead fortifications and strengthening the defensive sector along the eastern bank of the Dnepr River in the Shapochitsy and Buinichi sector. The Shklov bridge has been blown up.

61st Corps' headquarters – the forest south of Evdokimovichi.

45th RC. During the day on 11 July, the corps fought with enemy units crossing in the Barsuki and Borkolobovo region.

The enemy is holding on to the Sidorovichi and Sladiuki region and the forest to the south and is concentrating reserves in the Borkolobovo region.

148th RD is continuing its concentration and, simultaneously, fighting with crossing enemy.

187th RD fought with crossing enemy units during the day.

137th RD, after completing its march, was concentrating in the Sukhari and Pridantsy region on 10 July.

45th Corps' headquarters – the forest northwest of Chervonnyi and Osevets.

20th MC was extracted from combat during the day for its withdrawal behind the front for rest and refitting.

13th Army's headquarters – the Chausy region.

Sixth. 21st Army [Gerasimenko]. While continuing its concentration, was holding onto its previous lines at 1330 hours on 11 July.

The enemy did not display any active operations before the army's front.

102nd RD and 63rd and 67th RC – positions unchanged.

66th RC – 232nd RD and 110th RR, 53rd RD, after completing their regrouping, occupied the (incl.) Streshin and Belyi Bereg line, with 110th RR in the (incl.) Streshin and mouth of the Berezina sector.

75th RD – no new information.

Corps' headquarters – Teleshi.

28th MtnRD has concentrated in the Bragin region.

25th MC – 55th TD and 219th MRD continued their concentration in previous regions. 50th TD – unchanged.

25th Corps' headquarters – Novozybkov.

16th MC is being concentrated in the Mozyr' region (a motorized rifle regiment and the rear services of 15th TD arrived by 11 July).

Armored Trains [BEPO] Nos. 51 and 52, cooperating with the detachment of Colonel Kurmashev, engaged in fighting in the Starushki Station, Rabkor Station, and Ratmirovichi region. Kurmashev's detachment destroyed up to 30 enemy tanks and armored vehicles from 7 through 9 July.

21st Army's headquarters – Gomel'

Seventh. 4th Army [Sandalov]. The army's units finished regrouping in refitting regions and are continuing strengthening of defensive positions in its regions.

During the day on 10 July, enemy aircraft bombed the Chausy, Propoisk, and Krichev regions and, as a result, 25 men were killed and 4 wounded in 42nd RD.

Eighth. The VVS of the *front*. During the second half of the day on 10 July, 3 enemy aircraft were shot down in air combat, and 8 aircraft were destroyed on the ground. Our losses: 1 aircraft shot down, and 4 aircraft did not return to their airfields.

The Chief of Staff of the Western Front. Lieutenant General Malandin
The Chief of the Operations Department, Major General Semenov

Source: "Operativnaia svodka shtaba Zapadnogo fronta No. 33 k 2000 chasam 11 iiulia 1941 g. o boevykh deistviiakh voisk fronta" [Operational Summary No. 33 of the headquarters of the Western Front at 2000 hours on 11 July 1941 about the combat actions of the *front's* forces], in *SBDVOV*, issue 37, 84-85.

3. Order of the Commander of the Western Front's Forces of 11 July 1941 to the Commander of the Forces of 21st Army on the Tying Down of Enemy Combat Operations with Mobile Detachments

To the Commander of 21st Army
2020 hours on 11 July 1941

The enemy is displaying no activity on 21st Army's front and, while not encountering any energetic actions from our side, is maneuvering with his mobile units to other places, while conducting attacks toward Mogilev.

I order:

1. Tie down the operations of the enemy and force him to fear the possibilities of our attacks.

2. Dispatch mobile detachments with sappers, antitank guns, and tank destroyer commands for operations in the direction of Zborovo, Chigirinka, Gorodishche, Zhlobin, Parichi, and Bobruisk.

3. Assign the [following] missions to the detachments: the destruction of enemy tanks, the disorganization of his rear, the destruction of transport, communications, radio transmitters, warehouses, and so forth, the destruction of supply routes, and the emplacement of mine traps.

Assign to the detachments operating toward Zborov and Gorodishche the mission to disrupt activity along the Bobruisk and Mogilev highway and wreck the enemy crossing in the vicinity of Bykhov Station.

The detachments sent toward Bobruisk will disorganize the rear and provisioning of the enemy's Zhlobin group and, if possible, blow up the bridges at Bobruisk and destroy aircraft on their airfields.

4. Organize radio posts for receipt of reports from the detachments.

5. Prepare an operation and keep units in readiness for a surprise seizure of Bobruisk and Parichi.

Timoshenko, Malandin

Source: "Prikaz komanduiushchego voiskami Zapadnogo fronta ot 11 iiulia 1941 g. komanduiushchemu voiskami 21-i Armii na skovyvanie boevykh deistvii protivnika podvizhnymi otriadami" [Order of the commander of the Western Front's forces of 11 July 1941 to the commander of the forces of 21st Army on the tying down of enemy combat operations with mobile detachments], in *SBDVOV*, issue 37, 86-87.

4. Combat Instructions of the Headquarters of the Main Command of the Western Direction of 12 July 1941 to the Commanders of the Forces of 19th and 22nd Armies about the Combined Conduct of Attacks against the Enemy in the Vitebsk Region

Iakubovshchina [Western Direction headquarters]   Top Secret

To Konev and Ershakov:

The Commander-in-Chief orders:

1. Together with Ershakov, attack the enemy in the Vitebsk region on 12 July and throw him back behind the line of the Polotsk-Vitebsk road.

2. Ershakov will conduct his attack at 0800 hours on 12 July toward Selo Station; and Konev – Vitebsk and Kniazhitsa Station.

Support Konev's attack with 1-2 battalions of tanks.

3. The mission being given to the VVS [Air Forces] at 0800 hours is to protect [cover] the area of operations of the attacking forces.

4. Establish Konev's headquarters in Iakuboshchina, and get your command and control right.

5. Put your forces in order.

6. Comrade Konev must bear in mind that 134th RD has unloaded in the Smolensk region, and 127th RD has unloaded 14 trains in the Smolensk region.

Prepare antitank positions along the Moshna River line with the forces from the arriving trains, paying special attention to the direction of the road to Smolensk.

Report your course of operations every 3 hours.

> Malandin
> No. 1012, issued at 0300 hours on 12 July and 0705 hours on 12 July

Source: "Boevoe rasporiazhenie shtaba Glavnogo Komandovaniia Zapadnogo Napravleniia ot 12 iiulia 1941 g. komanduiushchim voiskami 19-i i 22-i Armii o sovmestnom nanesenii udara po protivnika v raione Vitebsk" [Combat instructions of the headquarters of the Main Command of the Western Direction of 12 July 1941 about the combined delivery of attacks on the enemy in the Vitebsk region], in *SBDVOV*, issue 37, 24-25.

5. Combat Order No. 060 of the Commander-in-Chief of the Western Direction's Forces of 12 July 1941 on an Offensive (see Map 2)

Order No. 060 to the Western Direction's Forces
12 July 1941

1. The enemy, having concentrated 8th [sic] and 39th Panzer Corps in Vitebsk and up to a panzer corps along the Mogilev axis, forced the Western Dvina and Dnepr Rivers and is developing his offensive toward Velizh and Gorki.

2. The mission of the *front* is to destroy the penetrating enemy by combined operations with 22nd, 19th, and 20th Armies, in cooperation with aviation, and, after capturing the city of Vitebsk, dig in along the front of the Idritsa and Polotsk FRs, Sirotino, Khiazhitsa Station, Shilki, Orsha, and farther along the Dnepr River.

Begin the offensive at 0800 hours on 13 July 1941.

3. 22nd Army [Ershakov], while holding firmly to the existing front on its right wing and the Polotsk FR, will go over to the attack from the Voikhany Station and

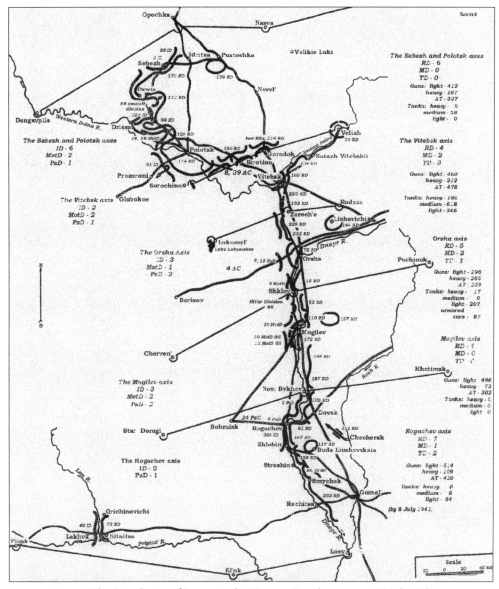

Map 2: The Correlation of Forces in the Western Front's sector on 12 July 1941

Gorodok front with the forces of 214th and 186th RDs, with 56th HAR, 390th HAR, 102nd ATBn, and 46th MAD, and, while delivering the main attack toward Vitebsk, will reach the Sirotino and Kniazhitsa Station line, where it will firmly dig in.

Boundary on the left – (incl.) Velizh, Ulanovichi, and Beshenkovichi.

4. 19th Army [Konev], while holding off the enemy group penetrating toward Velizh, will attack from the Shumovshchina and Vorony line toward Vitebsk with the forces of 7th MC, 162nd RD. 220th MD, 399th HAR, and 11th MAD, with the mission of capturing the city of Vitebsk. Reach the Voroshily and Pushkari line the end of the day, where you will dig in and firmly defend that line.

Boundary on the left – Iartsevo, Zabolotinka Station, and Beshenkovichi (all points inclusive for 20th Army).

5. 20th Army [Kurochkin] will destroy the enemy penetrating to the eastern bank of the Dnepr River by active operations on its left wing and firmly dig in along the Bogushevsk and Dnepr River line. With the main grouping on your right wing, attack toward Ostrovno with the forces of 5th MC and 153rd and 229th RDs, with 57th TD (without 115th TR), and 23rd AD, to assist the successful offensive by 19th Army. Reach and dig in along the Pavlovichi, Shilki, and Bogushevsk line by day's end.

Boundary on the left – as before.

6. 13th Army [Remezov], within its present boundaries, will destroy the enemy units penetrating to the eastern bank of the Dnepr River and firmly defend the Dnepr River line.

7. 21st Army [F. I. Kuznetsov] will go over to the attack from the Rogachev and Zhlobin front toward Bobruisk with the forces of 63rd RC (61st, 167th, and 154th RDs) and toward Shatsilki and Parichi with 232nd RD, with the mission of capturing the city of Bobruisk and the Parichi region. Simultaneously, destroy the enemy grouping operating along the Bykhov axis by attacking from the Taimonovo and Shapchitsy regions toward Komarichi and Bykhov with 102nd and 187th RDs.

Move 117th RD forward to the Rogachev and Zhlobin front along the eastern bank of the Dnepr River for the protection of the Rogachev and Zhlobin axis.

8. The VVS of the *front*. Missions:

1. Inflict air strikes on the enemy in the Gorodok, Ostrovno, and Vitebsk regions at 0730 hours on 13 July, while operating chiefly against enemy artillery and tanks.

2. Detect enemy centers of resistance along the routes of movement of our forces by timely observation from the air and strike them immediately.

3. Protect the ground forces against enemy air strikes.

4. Employ the long-range bomber aviation corps for strikes against the enemy in the Gorodok, Vitebsk, Beshenkovichi, and Shklov region.

5. Send army aviation completely for strikes in cooperation with the ground forces.

> The Commander-in-Chief of the Western Direction,
>   Marshal of the Soviet Union S. Timoshenko
> The Member of the Military Council [signed]
> The Chief of Staff of the Western Direction,
>   Lieutenant General Malandin

Source: "Boevoi prikaz Glavnokomanduiushchego voiskami Zapadnogo napravleniia No. 060 ot 12 iiulia 1941 g na nastuplenie" [Combat Order No. 060 of the commander-in-chief of the Western Direction's forces of 12 July 1941 on an offensive], in *SBDVOV*, issue 37, 23-24.

6. Combat Order No. 03/op of the Commander of 21st Army's Forces of 13 July 1941 on the Capture of Bobruisk and Parichi

Combat Order No. 30/op, Headquarters, 21st Army, Gomel'
1:500,000 scale map
0241 hours on 13 July 1941

1. The enemy, having concentrated 8th and 39th Panzer Corps in Vitebsk and up to a tank corps on the Mogilev axis, forced the Western Dvina and Dnepr Rivers and is developing an attack on Velizh and Gorki.

2. 21st Army will go over to the attack, with the mission of capturing Bobruisk and Parichi and destroy the enemy grouping operating along the Bykhov axis by simultaneous attacks from the Taimonovo and Shapchitsy region toward Komarichi.

3. 67th RC (102nd, 151st, and 187th RDs), with 696th ATR and 15th MtrBn, will firmly protect the left wing of the army along the Zimnitsa and Novyi Bykhov front from the north and will attack at 0800 hours on 13 July with its main forces toward Shapchitsy, Komarichi, and Bykhov and destroy the enemy grouping operating along the Bykhov axis. Quickly close the front, cutting the enemy tanks off from their infantry.

Boundary on the left – Shirki, (incl.) Gadilovichi, and Chigirinka (35 kilometers west of Novyi Bykhov).

4. 63rd RC (61st, 167th, and 154th RDs), with 387th HAR, 318th HAR (High-Power), and 5th and 6th MtrBns, will go over to the attack from the Rogachev and Zhlobin front.

Mission – in cooperation with 66th RC, destroy the enemy Rogachev and Zhlobin grouping and seize Bobruisk. Subsequently, be prepared for an attack toward the north. The corps will begin the attack with its main forces at 1700 hours on 13 July.

Boundary on the left – Lopatino, Streshin, (incl.) Parichi, and further along the Berezina River.

5. 66th RC (232nd and 75th RDs), with 51st and 52nd BEPOs, will firmly hold on to its positions along the eastern bank of the Lan' River with 75th RD and attack along the western bank of the Berezina River with its main forces. Mission – capture Bobruisk and cut the enemy's deep reserves off from their units at the front and prevent the movement of enemy reserves from west to east from Bobruisk, while destroying his forces in piecemeal fashion.

Jumping-off positions of 232nd RD – Iakimovskoe and Strakovichi.

6. The commander of 117th RD, with 110th RR, 36th LAR, and 537th CAR, will be moved to the eastern bank of the Dnepr River in the Zborovo, Rogachev, Zhlobin, Streshin, and mouth of the Berezina River sector to protect the army's offensive.

7. 25th MC (50th TD and 219th MRD), having concentrated 219th MRD in the Rudnia, Borkhov, and Pribor region (15-25 kilometers west of Gomel') and

50th TD in the region it occupies, will be prepared to develop the attack along the Bykhov and Bobruisk axes.

8. The commanders of the corps will capture the western bank of the Dnepr River in the Novyi Bykhov, Shapchitsy, Zborovo, Rogachev, and Zhlobin regions overnight on 12-13 July and prepare crossing for the attack by the main forces.

9. The VVS of the army will have [the following] missions beginning on the morning of 13 July:

a) Bomb enemy crossings over the Dnepr River at Bykhov;

b) Destroy enemy aircraft on the Bobruisk airfield;

c) Protect the crossings of the army on the Dnepr River; and

d) In cooperation with the ground forces of 67th and 63rd RCs, destroy the enemy on the battlefield.

10. The commanders of units and formations will organize the destruction of enemy tanks by artillery fire.

Stop cowardice and panic on the spot.

> The Commander of the forces of 21st Army, Colonel General Kuznetsov
> The Member of the Military Council, Division Commissar [left blank]
> The Chief of Staff of 21st Army, Major General Gordov

Source: "Boevoi prikaz komanduiushchego voiskami 21-i Armii No. 03/op ot 13 iiulia 1941 g. na ovladenie Bobruisk, Parichi" [Combat order no. 03/op of the commander of 21st Army's forces of 13 July 1941 on the capture of Bobruisk and Parichi], in *SBDVOV*, issue 37, 284-285.

7. Excerpt from Operational Summary No. 37 of the Headquarters of the Western Front at 2000 hours on 13 July 1941 about the Combat Actions of the *Front's* Forces

Operational Summary No. 37 of the Headquarters of the Western Front
at 2000 hours on 13 July 1941
1: 500,000 scale map

Fourth. 20th Army. Having thrown back the enemy infantry at Bogushevskoe and Kopys', [the army] restored the previous situation on the evening of 12 July and overnight on 12-13 July. Beginning on the morning of 13 July, the units of the army are fighting with uncoordinated groups of tanks and motorized infantry, which have penetrated into the depths of the defense

69th RC, having thrown the enemy back, occupied a defense:

153rd RD – along the eastern bank of the Luchesa River on the Vorony, Zabolotinka Station, and Griada front;

229th RD – (incl.) Griada, Luchi, and Bogushevskoe; and

233rd RD – Kolen'ki and Staiki Station.

20th RC, having pressed the enemy behind the Dnepr River, is occupying:

73rd RD – the Selekta and (incl.) Orsha line; and

18th RD – along the eastern bank of the Dnepr River in the southeastern outskirts of Orsha and Kopys' line.

2nd RC is fighting with enemy, which has reached the rifle corps' flank and rear in the forested region west of Gorki.

The positions of the corps' units are being verified.

5th MC, together with 69th RC, was fighting during the day on 13 July to liquidate the enemy in the Sofievka region, while covering the automobile road in the Vysokoe region with one battalion.

The results of the fighting are being clarified.

57th TD is concentrating in the Gusino region.

144th RD, while holding onto crossings over the Dnepr River, is cooperating with 1st MRD in the destruction of a group of enemy in the Kobryn' and Lenino sector south of the Dnepr River.

Fifth. 13th Army was fighting with enemy units penetrating in the Shklov and Bykhov Station region during the day on 13 July.

61st RC, together with units of 20th MC, under heavy pressure by large enemy motor-mechanized forces penetrating in the Shklov region, withdrew its right wing and is holding on to the Sas'kovka and Novyi Prudki line and farther along the eastern bank of the Dnepr River to Buinichi.

53rd RD, which was defending the Shklov and Pleshchitsy line and was subjected to the enemy's main attack, withdrew; the positions of its units are still unknown.

20th MC went over to the attack from the Sos'kovka and Nichiporovichi line toward Bel' at 0500 hours on 13 July and, after advancing 2 kilometers, was stopped by enemy artillery and aviation.

> Corps' headquarters – Ekhany.
> The Chief of Staff of the Western Front. Lieutenant General Malandin
> The Chief of the Operations Department, Major General Semenov

Source: "Operativnaia svodka shtaba Zapadnogo fronta No. 37 k 2000 chasam 13 iiulia 1941 g. o boevykh deistviiakh voisk fronta" [Operational Summary No. 37 of the headquarters of the Western Front at 2000 hours on 13 July 1941 about the combat actions of the *front's* forces], in Ibid., 89-91.

8. Report by the Commander-in-Chief of the Western Direction's Forces of 13 July 1941 to the *Stavka* of the High Command about the Combat Operations of the Western Front's Forces on 12 and 13 July 1941

To Comrade Stalin
To Comrade Zhukov
1: 500,000 scale map
13 July 1941

The enemy conducted uninterrupted attacks along the entire Western Front, except 21st Army, during the course of 12 and 13 July 1941.

After bitter fighting with great losses, the enemy succeeded in capturing Vitebsk on 12 July and forced the Dnepr River in the direction of Shklov and Bykhov; the enemy attacks along the remaining front were beaten off.

22nd Army is holding on to the Idritsa region and the Polotsk FR.

Along the Pribytki axis (10 kilometers west of Tolmachevskaia), the enemy, with a force of up to two infantry regiments, pushed 98th RD back. Along the Vitebsk axis, fighting is going for Gorodok with varying success.

19th Army, after suffering great losses in the fighting for Vitebsk, withdrew to the southern bank of the Western Dvina River and, from the morning of 13 July, is conducting an offensive toward Vitebsk with 162nd RD and 220th MD. The offensive is taking place in difficult conditions, that is, 19th Army succeeded in concentrating only two rifle divisions. The enemy has penetrated into 19th Army's rear with small groups in the Velizh and Liozno region.

20th Army has liquidated the enemy penetration at Kopys with night operations and, together with the units of 13th Army, is continuing operations to liquidate the enemy penetration in the Shklov region. Since the morning of 13 July, the right-wing 153rd and 29th RDs are conducting an offensive toward Ostrovno to envelop Vitebsk, in cooperation with its seizure by 19th Army's forces.

13th Army repelled attacks by the enemy in the Shklov, Bykhov, and Zarech'e region on 12 July. Crack enemy units – 11th and 30th SS Divisions, are operating along this axis. The forward tank units of 11th SS ID succeeded in penetrating into the Gorki region from the Shklov region with heavy losses by the end of the day on 12 July; and, at the remaining crossings, fighting is going on in the immediate vicinity of the crossings. The commander of 13th Army, Remezov, has been wounded.

21st Army launched an offensive along the Rogachev and Chigirinka, Zhlobin and Bobruisk, and Rechitsa and Parichi axes on the morning of 13 July. The offensive is developing successfully.

The *front's* reserves – 4th Army and 6th, 42nd, 143rd, and 55th RDs – in the process of filling out and re-organizing – are occupying rear positions along the Pronia River in the Chausy and Propoisk front.

The VVS conducted a strong strike against the enemy in the Vitebsk region on the morning of 13 July and are continuing systematic actions against columns of enemy operating in that region.

Simultaneously, the enemy crossings at Shklov are being destroyed by air strikes, and enemy tank columns in the Gorki region are being subjected to constant attacks.

I have decided:

1) 22nd, 19th, and 20th Armies, reinforced by aviation, will capture Vitebsk with active operations by day's end on 13 July and restore the front along the Sirotino, Kniazhitsa Station, and Luchesa River line.

2) 20th and 13th Armies will liquidate the penetration of the front along the Bogushevsk, Shklov, and Bykhov axes by flank attacks along these axes and cut off the enemy tanks penetrating into the depth.

3) To destroy the enemy grouping penetrating along the Gorki axis by continuous air strikes and the operations of motorized detachments of 57th TD.

So as not to feed the concentrating units of 19th Army into combat in piecemeal fashion, I am designating the concentration regions of 127th, 129th, 38th, and 158th RDs in the Iartsevo and Smolensk region behind the line of the Dnepr and Sot' Rivers.

Timoshenko, Malandin

Source: "Doklad Glavnokomanduiushchego voiskami Zapadnogo Napravleniia ot 13 iiulia 1941 g. Stavke Verkhovnogo Komandovaniia o boevykh deistviiakh voisk Zapadnogo fronta 12 i 13 iiulia 1941 g.," [Report of the Commander-in-Chief of the Western Direction's forces of 13 July 1941 to the *Stavka* of the High

Command about the combat operations of the Western Front's forces on 12 and 13 July 1941], in *SBDVOV*, issue 37, 25-26.

9. Report by the Military Council of the Western Direction of 14 July 1941 to the *Stavka* of the High Command about the Situation in the Western Front on 14 July 1941

To Stalin and Zhukov

The situation in the Western Front on 14 July seems very complicated. The enemy, having profited from his penetration in the Vitebsk, Bogushevsk, Shklov, and Staryi Bykhov region, is energetically committing large mechanized formations into the penetration.

Along the Vitebsk axis, the enemy's forward mechanized units have been penetrating into the Velizh and Demidov regions since the morning of 14 July. Our units are occupying Demidov, where fighting is still going on.

The enemy group, which penetrated at Shklov toward Gorki, was trying to push through to Smolensk this morning.

The forward units of this group are being halted and pushed back toward the southwest by counterattacks by our units from Smolensk and Gusino.

By day's end, the enemy is occupying Krasnyi and Mstislavl', and his main grouping is in the Gorki region.

Enemy aviation displayed great energy on 13 and especially 14 July by subjecting the forces and railroads and dirt roads in the frontal belt to reinforced assault [ground attack] operations and bombing.

Smolensk and objectives adjacent to it became centers of intense raids despite the excellent work of our fighter aviation.

The situation that has taken shape along the front indicates that the enemy is seeking the encirclement of our Vitebsk-Orsha grouping.

Our forces are unstable owing to the protracted withdrawals, the recent sustained fighting, as well as the carelessness in bringing them up to strength and the great losses of weapons.

This is especially the case during attacks. There have been instances of our units running away from enemy air attacks and his forward tank detachments.

The situation has been complicated by the fact that the arrival of new units is being slowed and disorganized by the railroads. Rear service units are arriving in the lead trains, and the combat units are lingering for prolonged periods en route.

Because of this, the *front* does not have reserves and, organizationally, is forced to commit poorly prepared units hurriedly into the forward lines. Many divisions consist of differing units. As far as the tank formations are concerned, they do not have equipment and, in essence, are being turned technically into poorly equipped infantry.

As a result, the enemy is attacking chiefly along the roads with tank units accompanied by aviation in isolation from their infantry, and we decided and assigned our forces the mission to close the penetration that has been formed in the Shklov and Staryi Bykov sector, cut off the penetrating mechanized units, and focus on the destruction of the penetrating groups with all of the forces we have at our disposal.

We will begin these operations in the evening. We will conduct them with all urgency in order to complete them by 16 July.

This evening, our forces succeeded in closing the penetration between Vitebsk and Orsha in the Bogushevskoe region and destroyed 35 enemy tanks and 20 motorcycles.

According to final information, 82 enemy aircraft were shot down and destroyed at their airfields. Our losses were 16 aircraft. On 14 July, 57 enemy aircraft were destroyed, and our losses were 13 aircraft. On 14 July, 3 enemy tank battalions were destroyed by attacks from the skies.

At the same time, we consider the presence of aircraft at the front to be extremely unsatisfactory. On 13 July, we had a total of 130 fighters and 254 bombers and assault aircraft.

We request:

1) Reinforce the *front's* aviation and tank units;

2) Allocate 3,000 vehicles to the *front*; and

3) We ask you to order the HKPS [People's Commissariat of Communications Routes] to restore order in the delivery of ammunition and troop trains.

We are reporting that, because of the continuous bombing and destruction of communications, we are moving to the reserve command point in the Iartsevo region by the morning of 15 July. Simultaneously, we are preparing complete command and control in the Viaz'ma region. We are leaving an operational post in Smolensk.

S. Timoshenko, Ponomarenko

Source: "Doklad voennogo soveta Zapadnogo Napravleniia ot 14 iiulia 1941 g. Stavke Verkhovnogo Komandovaniia ob obstanovke na Zapadnom fronte na 14 iiulia 1941 g." [Report of the Military Council of the Western Direction of 14 July 1941 to the *Stavka* of the Supreme High Command about the situation in the Western Front on 14 July 1941], in *SBDVOV*, issue 37, 30-31.

10. Combat Order No. 065 of the Commander-in-Chief of the Western Direction's Forces of 14 July 1941 on the Destruction of the Penetrating Enemy

Order No. 065 to the Western Direction's Forces

14 July 1941

1. The enemy, having concentrated large forces along the Vitebsk and Mogilev axes, penetrated the front in the Shklov and Bykhov regions, and reached the Velizh and Gorki regions with his mobile groups, while trying to reach Smolensk to encircle our Vitebsk-Orsha grouping. The composition of the enveloping enemy forces has reached four-five motorized corps.

2. In addition to the penetrations along the Vitebsk and Shklov axes, the armies of the Western Direction are firmly defending the remaining front.

3. I am establishing as the mission of the forces of the *front* – to cut off the penetrating enemy from his rear in the sectors: 1) Gorodok and Vitebsk and 2) Orsha and Shklov to strengthen the stability of the *front*.

Throw the enemy's Velizh group back and crush the grouping of enemy mechanized forces which have gone too far in the Gorki, Mstislavl', and Shklov regions.

4. 22nd Army [Ershakov], having smoothed out the front in the center by withdrawing 98th and 112th RDs to the Iukhovichi and Baravukha line and leaning against [relying on] the Polotsk FR, conduct an attack toward Gorodok and Vitebsk with the mission to occupy and stubbornly defend the Sirotino and Zuikovo front. Keep no fewer than one rifle division in army reserve behind the army's left wing.

Boundary on the left – Velizh, Zapadnaia Dvina, Kublichi, and Vitebsk inclusive for 19th Army.

5. 19th Army [Konev], consisting of 162nd, 134th, 129th, and 153rd RDs and 7th MC, will capture the city of Vitebsk by a decisive attack by the end of the day on 16 July and dig in firmly along the Gorodok and Zarech'e line.

Boundary on the left – Iartsevo, Liubovichi, and Zarech'e.

6. 20th Army [Kurochkin], consisting of 229th, 233rd, 73rd, 18th, 100th, 161st, and 110th RDs and 5th MC, will liquidate the penetration along the Orsha and Shklov front by the end of the day on 16 July and dig in firmly in its occupied positions.

57th TD, reinforced by two battalions from 16th Army, will attack from the Krasnyi region toward Gorki on the night of 15 July, while destroying the enemy mechanized columns.

Boundary on the left – Pochinok, Shamovo, Barsuki, and Cherven'.

7. 13th Army [Gerasimenko], consisting of 172nd, 148th, 137th, 132nd, 160th, 151st, 187th, and 53rd RDs, 20th MC, 696th ATR, and a mortar battalion, will liquidate the penetration in the Staryi Bykhov region on 16 July and firmly hold on to its positions along the Dnepr River.

Simultaneously, I am assigning the decisive attack to the units of 13th Army as the most important mission and a matter of honor. 160th and 137th RDs, 20th MC, and 696th ATR will conduct the main attack from the line of the Bosia River toward Gorki and destroy the enemy Gorki grouping.

Boundary on the left – as before.

8. 21st Army [F. I. Kuznetsov], in its previous composition, will fulfill its assigned mission more decisively.

9. 4th Army [Sandalov], consisting of 42nd, 143rd, and 55th RDs, will destroy the enemy penetrating mechanized grouping by operations from the Riasna, Shirki, and Osinovka region toward Gorki from the south in cooperation with 13th Army.

A separate detachment consisting of the airborne corps [4th], 25th MC, and 6th RD, under the overall command of the commander of 4th AbnC [Zhadov], will attack from the Bakhrevka and Krichev region toward Mstislavl' to destroy the enemy Gorki grouping. The detachment is subordinate to 4th Army.

10. 16th Army [Lukin], consisting of -152nd and 46th RDs, while relying on an antitank region, will prevent the enemy Velizh grouping from reaching the Smolensk and Iartscvo road by operations from the Demidov and Dukhovshchina regions. Simultaneously, conduct an attack toward Gorki with the forces of the concentrated divisions and 17th MC to destroy the main enemy mobile grouping in cooperation with other units.

11. The VVS of the *front* have the [following] missions:

1) The forces of *frontal* aviation will cooperate with the ground forces in the liquidation of the penetrations by air strikes against the enemy in the Vitebsk and Shklov regions;

2) Systematically attack enemy ground forces in the Gorki, Mstislavl', and Shklov regions; and

3) The actions of army aviation will be completely subordinated to the interests of the ground forces.

12. We demand all Red Army men, commanders, and political workers display courage, decisiveness, and initiative.

13. The headquarters of the *front* will remain in its previous location.

The Commander-in-Chief of the Western Direction,
    Marshal of the Soviet Union Timoshenko
Member of the Military Council of the Western Direction, [signed]
The Chief of Staff of the Western Front [sic], Malandin

Source: "Boevoi prikaz Glavnokomanduiushchego voiskami Zapadnogo Napravleniia No. 065 ot 14 iiulia 1941 g. na unichtozhenie prorvavshegosia protivnika" [Combat Order No. 065 of the commander-in-chief of the Western Direction's forces of 14 July 1941 on the destruction of the penetrating enemy], in *SBDVOV*, issue 37, 31-33.

11. Order of the Commander-in-Chief of the Western Direction's Forces of 14 July 1942 about Unifying the Command and Control of Forces in the Smolensk Region

Order to the Western Direction's Forces
14 July 1941

For the purpose of unifying command and control and restoring order in the defenses along the approaches to the city of Smolensk, I order:

1. Subordinate all units of the garrison of Smolensk, units arriving by railroad for other armies and unloading in the vicinity of the city of Smolensk, as well as units occupying defensive sectors on the immediate approaches to Smolensk, to the commander of 16th Army, Lieutenant General Comrade Lukin.

2. The commander of 16th Army will unify the command and control of the above units and firmly hold on to the approaches to Smolensk.

3. Encircle, blockade, and destroy the penetrating enemy units with counterattacks by mobile maneuver groups, while extensively exploiting the hours of darkness to achieve those aims.

The Commander-in-Chief of the Western Direction,
    Marshal of the Soviet Union Timoshenko
The Member of the Military Council, [signed]
The Chief of Staff, Malandin

Source: "Prikaz Glavnokomanduiushchego voiskami Zapadnogo Napravleniia ot 14 iiulia 1941 g. ob ob'edinenii upravleniia voiskami v raione gor. Smolensk" [Order of the Commander-in-Chief of the Western

Direction's forces of 14 July 1942 about unifying the command and control of forces in the Smolensk region], in *SBDVOV*, issue 37, 33.

12. Order of the Commander-in-Chief of the Western Direction's Forces of 15 July 1941 about the Creation of a Continuous Front along the Alushkovo, Nevel', Dubrovo, Surazh-Vitebsk, and Zabolotinka Station Line

To General Eremenko
1: 500,000 scale map
15 July 1941

I order:
1. Fulfill the missions assigned by me stubbornly and persistently.
2. For their fulfillment, enlist the services of all of 19th Army's forces, while directing their efforts at the overall aim – the creation of a continuous front, while cutting off the penetrating enemy tanks from their bases and main forces. Organize a new, unified and continuous front along the Alushkovo, Nevel', Dubrovo, Surazh-Vitebsk, and Zabolotinka line, and prepare powerful counterattacks from the Iartsevo region toward Demidov and Smolensk.
3. Inspire all personnel with the knowledge that, in the present situation and operations, the penetrating enemy tanks can themselves fall into encirclement and be destroyed.
4. Demand that every garrison and village resist the tanks so as to scatter their efforts and facilitate their destruction piecemeal on the approaches to Smolensk.
5. Make Smolensk an impenetrable objective for the enemy.
6. Considering the successful operations of 20th Army and the assistance from the east and north, the enemy will be destroyed by the display of initiative, audacity, and energy on the part of [our] command cadre and soldiers.
7. Enlist the services of all personnel in the struggle with tanks and leave minimal forces in the rear.
8. I will maintain communications with you through delegates [liaison officers] in combat aircraft, wire, radio, and armored cars. Undertake measures to organize air signal posts.
9. Report measures taken and [your] plan of action.

> The Commander-in-Chief of the Western Direction,
>   Marshal of the Soviet Union Timoshenko
> The Member of the Military Council of the Western Direction,
>   Ponomarenko
> The Chief of Staff, Lieutenant General Malandin

Source: "Prikaz Glavnokomanduiushchego voiskami Zapadnogo Napravleniia ot 15 iiulia 1941 g. o sozdanii sploshnogo fronta na rubezhe Alushkovo, Nevel', Dubrovo, Surazh-Vitebskii, ct. Zabolotinka" [Order of the Commander-in-Chief of the Western Direction's forces of 15 July 1941 about the creation of a continuous front along the Alushkovo, Nevel', Dubrovo, Surazh-Vitebskii, ct. Zabolotinka line], in *SBDVOV*, issue 37, 34.

13. Order of the Commander-in-Chief of the Western Direction's Forces of 16 July 1941 about a Withdrawal of the Army to the Zaprudy, Ozerishche, and Dubrovo Line

To the Commander of 22nd Army
1: 500,000 scale map
16 July 1941

The situation on 22nd Army's front allows for and requires the defeat and destruction of the enemy by stubborn fighting in successive lines during a withdrawal to the Alushkovo, Zavorui, Lake Ozerishche, and Dubrovo line.

The retention of 174th RD in the Polotsk FR is inadmissible and requires the immediate regrouping of this division to the left wing for active operations.

Special attention must be paid to strengthening and preparing your flanks and energetic actions toward Vitebsk to unite with 19th Army in the Vitebsk region.

I order:

1. While exhausting the enemy with fighting, quietly withdraw the army successively to the Zaprudy, Ozerishche, and Dubrovo line.

2. Close the penetration that has formed between 98th and 112th RDs with all of the army's forces at hand.

3. Organize the destruction of the penetrating enemy tanks and inspire all personnel with the belief that the struggle with penetrating enemy tanks should not trouble anyone, and that tanks cut off from the infantry and their bases cannot threaten encirclement.

To destroy the penetrating enemy tanks, create detachments in each division and, combining their actions on an army-wide scale, encircle and destroy the enemy.

4. Enlist the services of all of the encircled population for the struggle with tanks in order to limit maneuver of the tanks with engineer works and subject them to attack by the detachments.

Everything will depend on how well you succeed in assembling all of the forces scattered in the rear of the divisions and army.

Report your decisions and measures for the fulfillment of this order.

> The Commander-in-Chief of the Western Direction,
>   Marshal of the Soviet Union Timoshenko
> The Member of the Military Council of the Western Direction,
>   Ponomarenko
> The Chief of Staff, Lieutenant General Malandin

Source: "Prıkaz Glavnokomanduiushchego voiskami Zapadnogo Napravleniia ot 16 iiulia 1941 g. komanduiushchemu voiskami 22-i Armii na otvod armii na rubezh Zaprudy, Ozerishche, Dubrovo" [Order of the Commander-in-Chief of the Western Direction's forces of 16 July 1941 about a withdrawal of the army to the Zaprudy, Ozerishche, and Dubrovo line], in *SBDVOV*, issue 37, 34-35.

Appendix D

The Composition and Command Cadre of the *Front* of Reserve Armies, 14 July 1941

FRONT OF RESERVE ARMIES

Commander – Lieutenant General Ivan Aleksandrovich Bogdanov

Commissar – Commissar for State Security 3rd Rank S. N. Kruglov

Chief of Staff – Major General P. I. Liapin

Mission – Formed to control reserve armies in the second defensive belt. Required to occupy positions along the Staraia Russa, Ostashkov, Belyi, Istomino, El'nia, and Briansk line by day's end on 14 July 1941 and prepare for a firm defense, with special attention paid to carefully preparing antitank and antiaircraft defenses.

Headquarters – Mozhaisk from 13 July

First Echelon

- **29th Army** – Lieutenant General Ivan Ivanovich Maslennikov, Deputy Peoples' Commissar for Internal Affairs (NKVD)
  - **Required strength** – five divisions, two corps artillery regiments, three antitank artillery regiments, one fighter aviation regiment, one bomber aviation regiment, and one Il–2 squadron.
  - **Mission** – Firmly defend the Staraia Russa, Demiansk, and Ostashkov line. Pay special attention to organizing defenses along the Staraia Russa–Bologoe, Kholm–Bologoe, and Ostashkov–Vyshnii Volochek axes.
  - **Boundary on the left** – (incl.) Toropets, (incl.) Selizharovo, and Vyshnii Volochek.
  - **Headquarters** – Bologoe
- **30th Army** – Major General Vasilii Afanas'evich Khomenko, former commander of forces in the Ukrainian Border District
  - **Required strength** – five divisions, one corps artillery regiment, and two antitank artillery regiments.
  - **Mission** – Firmly defend the Ostashkov, Selizharovo, Olenino, and Vasilevo line. Pay special attention to organizing defenses along the Toropets–Selizharovo–Kalinin and Velikie Luki–Rzhev–Volokolamsk axes.
  - **Boundary on the left** – Il'ino, (incl.) Nikishino, and Volokolamsk.
  - **Headquarters** – Rzhev
- **24th Army** – Major General Stepan Andrianovich Kalinin, the former commander of the Siberian Military District (replaced in late July by Major General Konstantin Ivanovich Rakutin, former commander of forces in the Baltic Border District)
  - **Required strength** – ten divisions, three gun, one howitzer, and three corps artillery regiments, and four antitank artillery regiments.

- ✦ **Mission** – Firmly defend the Belyi, Izdeshkovo Station, Dorogobuzh, and El'nia line. Pay special attention to organizing defenses along the Iartsevo–Viaz'ma axis.
- ✦ **Boundary on the left** – Pochinok, Barsuki, (incl.), the sawmill, Butyrlino, and (incl.) Medyn'.
- ✦ **Headquarters** – Viaz'ma
- **28th Army** – Major General V. Ia. Kachalov, the former commander of the Arkhangel'sk Military District
  - ✦ **Required strength** – nine divisions, one gun, one howitzer, and four corps artillery regiments, and four antitank artillery regiments.
  - ✦ **Missions** – Firmly defend the Desna River line from Logachevo to Zhukovka, Vysokoe, Sosnovka, and Sinezerki. Pay special attention to organizing defenses along Roslavl'–Medyn' axis and in the Briansk region. Keep the army's reserve, consisting of four divisions, three of them tank, in the Zanoznaia Station and Kirov region.
  - ✦ **Headquarters** – Kirov

Front **Reserve**
- **31st Army** – Major General Vasilii Nikitich Dalmatov, former chief of the Karelian NKVD Border Military District
  - ✦ **Required strength** – six divisions, one corps artillery regiment, and two antitank artillery regiments.
  - ✦ **Mission** – Have five rifle divisions, one tank division, one corps artillery regiment, and two antitank artillery regiments in the Torzhok, Rzhev, Volokolamsk, and Kalinin region.
  - ✦ **Headquarters** – Staritsa
- **32nd Army** – Lieutenant General Nikolai Kuz'mich Klykov, former deputy commander of the Moscow Military District for Training
  - ✦ **Required strength** – seven divisions and one antitank artillery regiment.
  - ✦ **Mission** – Have six rifle divisions, one tank division, and one antitank artillery regiment in the Ruza, Mozhaisk, Maloiaroslavets, Vysokinichi, and Naro–Fominsk region.
  - ✦ **Headquarters** – Naro–Fominsk

Source: "Prikaz Stavki VK No. 00334 o sozdanii fronta rezervnykh armii [Stavka VK order no. 00334 about the creation of the *Front* of Reserve Armies], in V. A. Zolotarev, ed., *Russkii arkhiv: Velikaia Otechestvennaia [voina]: Dokumenty i materialy. 1941 god., T. 16 (5–1)* [The Russian archives: The Great Patriotic [[War]]: Documents and materials. 1941, Vol. 16 (5–1)] (Moscow: "TERRA," 1996], 70–72. Hereafter cited as Zolotarev, "*Stavka* 1941," with appropriate order and page(s).

Appendix E

The Composition and Command Cadre of the *Front* of the Mozhaisk Defense Line, 18 July 1941

FRONT OF THE MOZHAISK DEFENSE LINE

Commander – Lieutenant General of NKVD Troops Pavel Artem'evich Artem'ev, chief of the NKVD's Operations Directorate and commander of the Moscow Military District

Commissar – I. M. Sokolov

Chief of Staff – Major General A. I. Kudriashev

Mission – Occupy the Kushelevo, Iaropolets, Koloch' Station, Il'inskoe, and Detchino line and prepare for a firm defense.

- **32nd Army**
  - **Commander** – Lieutenant General Nikolai Kuz'mich Klykov, former deputy commander of the Moscow Military District for Training
  - **Member of the Military Council** – G. N. Zhilenkov
  - **Chief of Staff** – Colonel I. A. Kuzokov
  - **Composition** – five rifle divisions, including one NKVD and four peoples' militia divisions, one RGK artillery regiment, and three antitank artillery regiments.
  - **Mission** – Firmly defend the Kushelevo, Iaropolets, Chubarovo, and Karacharovo line. Pay special attention to organizing defense of the Rzhev-Volokolamsk and Sychevka-Volokolamsk axes.
  - **Boundary on the left** – (incl.) Savinki, Tarkhanovo, and Pavlovskaia Sloboda.
  - **Headquarters** – Volokolamsk
- **33rd Army**
  - **Commander** – *Kombrig* (Brigade commander) Dmitri Platonovich Onuprienko, former deputy chief of the NKVD's Directorate for Operational Forces and chief of staff of the Moscow Military District
  - **Member of the Military Council** – M. D. Shliakhtin
  - **Chief of Staff** – Lieutenant Colonel I. K. Prostov
  - **Composition** – five rifle divisions, including three NKVD divisions and two peoples' militia divisions, one tank division (109th), one RGK artillery regiment, and three antitank artillery regiments.
  - **Mission** – Firmly defend the Glazovo, Koloch Station, and Sosnovtsy line. Pay special attention to organizing defenses along the Gzhatsk-Mozhaisk-Kubinka axis.
- **34th Army**
  - **Commander** – *Kombrig* Nikolai Nilovich Pronin, former chief of the Command Faculty at the Frunze Academy and commander of 1st Moscow Rifle Division
  - **Member of the Military Council** – I. P. Voinov
  - **Chief of Staff** – *Kombrig* A. G. Galkin

+ **Composition** – five rifle divisions, including one NKVD division and four peoples' militia divisions, one RGK artillery regiment, and three antitank artillery regiments.
+ **Mission** – Firmly defend the Nikitskoe, Red'kino, and Nozdrino line. Pay special attention to organizing defenses along the Iukhnov-Medyn'-Maloiaroslavets axis.
+ **Headquarters** – Maloiaroslavets

Note – Soon after, the *Stavka* also created a new 35th Army under the Front of Reserve Armies. After the *Stavka* renumbered 35th Army as 49th Army, it formed a new 35th Army in the Far East.

Source: "Prikaz Stavki VK No. 00409 o formirovanii fronta Mozhaiskoi linii oborony [Stavka VK order no. 00409 about the formation of the *Front* of the Mozhaisk line of defense], in Zolotarev, "*Stavka* 1941," 77-78.

Appendix F

Army Group Center's Encirclement Battle at Smolensk, 16-23 July 1941

German 6. Führer Directive No. 33, The Further Conduct of the War in the East, 19 July 1941

The Führer and Supreme High Command of the Armed Forces (OKW).
Führer headquarters
OKW, Headquarters of the Operations Directorate.
19 July 1941
Department for the Defense of the Country (1st Dept.).
No. 441230/41. Top Secret

Directive No. 33,
The Further Conduct of the War in the East

1. The second offensive to the East has been completed by the penetration of the "Stalin Line" along the entire front and by a further deep advance by the panzer groups to the east. Army Group Center requires considerable time to liquidate the strong enemy combat groups, which continue to remain between our mobile formations.

The Kiev fortifications and the operations by the Soviets' 5th Army's forces in our rear have inhibited active operations and free maneuver on Army Group South's northern flank.

2. The objective of further operations should be to prevent the escape of large enemy forces into the depth of Russian territory and to annihilate them. To do so, prepare [as follows] along the following axes:

a) **The Southeastern sector of the Eastern Front**. The most important mission is to destroy the enemy's 12th and 6th Armies by a concentrated offensive west of the Dnepr River, while preventing their withdrawal behind the river.

Ensure the protection of this operation from the south with the main Rumanian forces.

The complete destruction of the enemy's 5th Army can be realized most rapidly by means of a closely coordinated offensive by the forces on Army Group Center's southern flank and Army Group "South's" northern flank.

Simultaneously with the turn of Army Group Center's infantry divisions to the south, new forces, first and foremost mobile, will enter the battle after they have fulfilled the missions assigned to them now and after they have been resupplied and also protect themselves from the direction of Moscow. These forces will have the mission to prevent a further withdrawal to the east of Russian units, which have crossed to the eastern bank of the Dnepr River, and to destroy them.

49

b) **The Central sector of the Eastern Front**. After the destruction of the numerous encircled enemy units and resolution of supply problems, the mission of Army Group Center's forces will be, while carrying out a further offensive on Moscow with the forces of infantry formations and mobile formation which are not participating in the offensive toward the southeast beyond the line of the Dnepr, to sever communications on the Moscow – Leningrad line and, at the same time, protect the right flank of Army Group North, which has been attacking toward Leningrad.

c) **The Northern sector of the Eastern Front**. Resume the advance toward Leningrad only after the Eighteenth Army has restored contact with the Fourth Panzer Group and the Sixteenth Army's forces are protecting its eastern flank. When that is accomplished, Army Group North must strive to prevent Soviet forces, which are continuing to operate in Estonia, from withdrawing to Leningrad. It is desirable to capture as rapidly as possible the islands in the Baltic Sea, which can be Soviet fleet strong points.

d) **The Finnish Front**. The missions of the Finns' main forces, strengthened by the German 163rd Infantry Division, as before, remains to attack the enemy and, while delivering the main blow east of Lake Ladoga and later in cooperation with the forces of Army Group North, destroy him. The objectives of the offensive operations, conducted under the direction of the commands of XXXVI Army and the Mountain Infantry Corps, remain unchanged. Since there are no possibilities of realizing strong support by aircraft formations, we must reckon with the possibility of temporary delays in the operations.

3. The mission of the Air Force [*Luftwaffe*] to begin with is, as forces are freed up in the central sector of the front, to support the offensives of the forces on the main axes of the southern sector of the front. The aircraft and antiaircraft artillery enlisted in this ought to be concentrated in appropriate regions by means of rapid deployment forward of additional forces and also by means of regroupings.

It is necessary to begin, as rapidly as possible, with the force of Second Air Fleet, temporarily reinforced by bomber aircraft from the West and air raids on Moscow, which should appear to be "retribution" for the raids by Russian aircraft on Bucharest and Helsinki.

4. The missions of the Navy [*Kriegsmarine*] remain defense of sea communications, especially in the interests of protecting ground operations, so far as conditions at sea and in the air permit. Further, the forces of the fleet must be directed at, while creating a threat to enemy naval bases, in so far as possible preventing the departure of the combat forces of his fleet for internment in Swedish ports.

As the naval forces in the Baltic Sea are freed up (torpedo cutters and mine sweepers – originally grouped in one flotilla), they must be transferred to the Mediterranean Sea. For the support of the German forces in Finland, whose operations are hindered owing to the transport of enemy reinforcements by sea, it is necessary to dispatch some quantity of submarines to the Barents Sea.

5. All three types of armed forces in the West and in the North should anticipate possible English strikes against the islands in the English Channel and the coast of Norway. It is necessary to prepare the Luftwaffe for their rapid transfer from the West to any region in Norway

[Signed] Hitler

Source: *Sbornik voenno-istoricheskikh materialov Velikoi Otechestvennoi voiny, vypusk 18* [Collection of military-historical materials of the Great Patriotic War, issue 18] (Moscow: Voenizdat, 1960), 231-232. Prepared by the Military-Historical Department of the Military-Scientific Directorate of the Red Army General Staff and classified secret.

1. Combat Order No. 066 of the Commander-in-Chief of the Western Direction's Forces of 17 July 1941 on the Defense of the City of Smolensk

Order No. 066 to the Western Direction's Forces
17 July 1941

The State Defense Committee pointed out in its special order that command cadre of the Western Front's units are imbued with an evacuation mood, and they regard the matter of withdrawing their forces from Smolensk and surrendering the city to the enemy too lightly.

If this mood accords with their actions, the State Defense Committee considers such a mood among the command cadre to be criminal, bordering on betrayal of the Motherland.

The State Defense Committee has ordered us to eliminate such a mood, which discredits the name of the Red Army, with an iron hand. Do not surrender the city of Smolensk under any circumstances.

I order:

1. The commander of 16th Army [Lukin] will prevent the surrender of Smolensk by an all-round defense employing all of its forces and weapons in the Smolensk region, including the concentrating 129th, 127th, 38th, and 158th RDs of 19th Army , all of the artillery of the Smolensk garrison and 16th and part of 19th Armies, and 51st BEPO.

2. The commander of 44th RC [Iushkevich], consisting of 25th RC and 23rd MC, and the units withdrawing to the Iartsevo region, and an artillery regiment, and companies of T-26 tanks, will organize an antitank region in the vicinity of Zuevo, Gavrilovo, and Grishino regions and deploy it into the Iartsevo bridgehead and along the Dnepr River in the Iartsevo and Pridneprovskaia [along the Dnepr] sector, with the mission of preventing the enemy from penetrating toward Smolensk from the Dukhovshchina region.

3. The commander of 101st TD [former 52nd TD of 26th MC, under the command of Colonel Grigorii Mikhailovich Mikhailov] will concentrate in the Svishchevo Station region by day's end on 17 July and destroy the enemy motor-mechanized units in the Dukhovshchina region by 0400 hours on 18 July by decisive attacks along the Dukhovshchina and Smolensk axis. Move the forward units of the division to Iartsevo by the end of the day on 17 July.

4. The commander of 69th MD [Colonel Petr Nikolaevich Domracheev] will concentrate in the Dubrovitsa region and attack the enemy's motor-mechanized units operating toward Kiriakino and Syro Lipki at 0400 hours on 18 July.

Both divisions will direct their further actions at the destruction of the enemy's motor-mechanized units in the Smolensk region.

5. Major General Rokossovsky is entrusted with directing the operations of the mechanized units. My deputy, Lieutenant General Comrade Eremenko, will support the fulfillment of this order.

6. The commander of the air forces of the *front* will support the operations of 101st TD and 69th MD with a specially assigned group of fighter, bombers, and assault aircraft:

1) Protect the entry of the tank division and motorized division into their concentration region on the instructions of the commanders of the tank and motorized divisions; and

2) Conduct an air strike against the enemy Dukhovshchina grouping with all of the *front's* aviation at 0330 hours on 18 July.

> The Commander-in-Chief of the Western Direction,
>   Marshal of the USSR Timoshenko
> The Member of the Military Council of the Western Direction, [signed]
> The Chief of Staff of the Western Front, General Malandin

Source: "Boevoi prikaz Glavnokomanduiushchego voiskami Zapadnogo Napravleniia No. 066 ot 17 iiulia 1941 g. na oboronu gor. Smolensk" [Combat Order No. 066 of the commander-in-chief of the Western Direction's forces of 17 July 1941 on the defense of the city of Smolensk], in *SBDVOV*, issue 37, 37-38.

2. Operational Summary No. 1 of the Headquarters of 16th Army of 17 July 1941 about the Positions of the Army's Forces

Operational Summary No. 1 at 2300 hours on 17 July 1941,
Headquarters 16th Army, in the grove west of Zhukovo State Farm
1:100,000 scale map (1939)

First. 16th Army continued to hold onto the Zagor'e, Maloe Vozmishche, Buda, Kuprino, and Katyn' Station line on 17 July 1941. Separate detachments assembled from 46th RD and the withdrawing units of 129th RD conducted attacks to capture Demidov and Smolensk.

Second. 32nd RC. 46th RD attacked the southern outskirts of Demidov with its detachment of two rifle battalions and two artillery battalions. The results of this attack are being confirmed. Its remaining battalions are operating in Major General Gorodniansky's (the commander of 129th RD) detachment for possession of Smolensk.

Third. 152nd RD, consisting of five rifle battalions, continued to conduct reconnaissance before the forward edge. The reconnaissance platoon of 646th RR encountered 4 enemy tanks in Blonnaia. The division is continuing to hold on to the Zagor'e, Maloe Vozmishche, Buda, Kuprino, and Katyn' Station line. There is no enemy to its front. Its remaining four battalions are operating [as follows]: 1st Bn, 626th RR, together with the detachment of 46th RD, for possession of Demidov; 1st Bn, 480th RR, with 17th TD, are defending the Svinaia River and Litivlia line; 3rd Bn, 544th RR, together with 57th TD, went over to the defense in the forest north of Krasnyi; and 3rd Bn, 480th RR, withdrew to Smolensk after fighting at Gorokhovo (its location is unknown).

Fourth. The detachment of Major General Gorodniansky, assembled from units of 46th and 129th RDs, was fighting for possession of Smolensk. Its assembled under-strength battalions occupied [the following] positions: the battalion of 334th RR – Karmachi [Karmanichi] and Sitniki; 1st Bn, 314th RR – the eastern outskirts of Korolevka and northwestern slope of Marker 251; and 3rd Bn, 457th RR, which was attacking on the left wing, lost communications (its location has not been established). The detachment went over to the attack toward Smolensk at first light on 17 July, together with units of 34th RC, which are operating toward the southern outskirts of Smolensk.

Headquarters of 32nd RC – the grove 2 kilometers west of Berezhany. Losses are being calculated.

The Chief of Staff of 16th Army, Colonel Shalin
The Chief of the Operations Department, Colonel Roshchin

Source: "Operativnaia svodka shtaba 16-i Armii No. 1 ot 17 iiulia 1941 g. o polozhenii voisk armii" [Operational summary no. 1 of the headquarters of 16th Army of 17 July 1941 about the positions of the army's forces], in *SBDVOV*, issue 37, 205.

3. *Stavka* VK Order No. 00436 Concerning the Appointment of Higher Command Cadre

19 July 1941

1. Appoint Marshal of the Soviet Union Comrade Shaposhnikov, Boris Mikhailovich, as chief of staff of the Main Command of the Western Direction.

2. Appoint Lieutenant General Comrade Eremenko, A. I., as commander of the Western Front.

3. Appoint Lieutenant General Comrade Sokolovsky, V. D., as chief of staff of the Western Front and Comrade Malandin, G. K., as chief of the Operations Department of the Western Front.

4. Appoint Comrade Bulganin, N. A., as member of the Military Council of the Main Command of the Western Direction.

5. Appoint Comrades Ponomarenko, P. K., and Popov, D. M., as members of the Military Council of the Western Front.

The *Stavka* of the Supreme High Command

Source: "Prikaz Stavki VK No. 00436 o naznachenii vysshego komandnogo sostava" [*Stavka* VK order no. 00436 concerning the appointment of higher command cadre], in Zolotarev, "*Stavka* 1941," 82.

4. Operational Directive No. 19 of the Commander-in-Chief of the Western Direction's Forces of 18 July 1941 on Offensive and Defensive Operations

To the Commanders of 22nd, 20th, 13th, 4th, 16th, and 21st Armies
1:500,000 scale map
Directive No. 19, Headquarters, Western Direction
0130 hours 18 July 1941

16th Army is repelling attacks and holding on to Smolensk. It is attacking toward Demidov with its right wing.

On 18 July, I assigned the *front's* armies the [following] missions:

1. 22nd Army will exhaust the forces of the enemy day and night by the decisive actions of detachments.

The army, while fulfilling previously assigned missions, will prevent a penetration of the enemy group to Velikie Lukin with the forces of local garrisons, reinforcements, the population, and a rifle regiment of 126th RD dispatched on vehicles. Conduct flank attacks toward Vitebsk with left-wing units and paralyze enemy operations in that direction. Under no circumstance surrender the city of Velikie Luki.

I hold the commander of the army and the member of the Military Council personably responsible for fulfillment.

2. 20th Army, while relying on 16th Army's defense along the Kholm and Sipochi Station front, will hold onto its front. Subject the enemy group on the Smolensk axis to threat of encirclement by attacks toward Gorki and Monastyrskie from the southern and western direction.

5th MC will tie down the enemy grouping in the Krasnyi region on 18 July by active operations.

3. 13th Army, while holding onto its front, will liquidate the penetration between the army's Mogilev and Bykhov groupings by decisive operations by 151st RD toward Bykhov.

I am entrusting supervision of 4th and 13th Armies' combat operations to the commander of 13th Army, Lieutenant General Gerasimenko.

4. 16th Army will continue to fulfill its assigned mission in accordance with Order No. 065 and prevent the enemy from seizing Smolensk.

5. The commander of 13th Army will conduct a decisive blow along the Bykhov-Bobruisk axis and decisively force the fulfillment of previously assigned missions.

I am paying particular attention to the completely unwarranted delay in the indicated operation.

The Commander-in-Chief, Marshal of the Soviet Union Timoshenko
The Member of the Military Council, [signed]
The Chief of Staff of the front, Lieutenant General Malandin

Source: "Operativnaia direktiva Glavnokomanduiushchego voiskami Zapadnogo Napravleniia No. 19 ot 18 iiulia 1941 g. na nastupatel'nye i oboronitel'nye deistviia" [Operational directive no. 19 of the commander-in-chief of the Western Direction's forces of 19 July 1941 on offensive and defensive operations], in *SBDVOV*, issue 37, 38-39.

5. Excerpt from Operational Summary No. 45 of the Western Front at 2000 hours on 18 July 1941 about the Combat Operations of the *Front's* Forces

Operational Summary No. 45 at 2000 hours on 18 July 1941,
Headquarters, Western Front
1: 500,000 map

First. During the day on 18 July, the Western Front's forces continued fierce fighting with enemy units penetrating toward Nevel', Demidov, Smolensk, and Propoisk and conducted an offensive toward Bobruisk ... ..

Third. 19th Army. The units of the army, which withdrew in disorder, are assembling in the Viaz'ma and Dorogobuzh region.

The headquarters of 25th RC is assembling in Viaz'ma.

162nd RD, according to information from the Front of Reserve Armies' headquarters, after the battles in the Surazh and Vitebsk regions, withdrew to the Nelidovo region (100 kilometers west of Rzhev), where it was subordinated to 30th Army.

There is no other information about the location of the army's headquarters and the army's other units because of an absence of communications. The communications liaison officers that were sent out have still not returned.

Fourth. 20th Army is conducting intense fighting with enemy tank and motorized units but without sufficient quantities of ammunition, fuel, and foodstuffs.

144th RD is attacking the enemy in the Rudnia region, where, apparently, a motorized regiment of the enemy's 12th Tank Division is defending without fuel.

69th RC (229th and 233rd RDs). In the corps' sector, an assemblage of enemy motorized infantry and up to 2,000 vehicles without fuel has been identified in the vicinity of Dobromysl'. The presence of 17th TD's and 35th ID's units has been noted in the Bogushevskoe region.

73rd RD has successfully repulsed attacks by up to an enemy TD (probably the 18th) and all of its attempts to cross the Dnepr River at Dubrovno and Rossasna. (A report by Kurochkin).

5th MC, which is facing up to two enemy divisions in the Liady and Syrokoren'e region, is conducting a fighting withdrawal to the crossing at Gusino ... ..

Eighth. 16th Army. 158th and 127th RDs occupied a defenses in the sector from the state farm (10 kilometers south of Smolensk) to Grinevo.

7th MC is assembling in the Sosnovka sector (22 kilometers northeast of Viaz'ma).

Other information has not been received. An enciphered telegram has been received about the army's situation. Once it is worked out, additional information will be reported.

> The Chief of Staff of the Western Front, Lieutenant General Malandin
> The Military Commissar of the *front's* headquarters,
>   Regimental Commissar Anshakov
> The Chief of the Operations Department, *Kombrig* Liubarsky

Source: "Operativnaia svodka shtaba Zapadnogo fronta No. 45 k 2000 chasam 18 iiulia 1941 g. o boevykh deistviiakh voisk fronta" [Operational summary no. 45 of the Western Front at 2000 hours on 18 July 1941 about the combat operations of the *front's* forces], in *SBDVOV*, 94-96.

6. Operational Summary No. 2 of the Headquarters of 16th Army of 19 July 1941 about the Combat Operations of the Army's Forces in the Demidov, Kholm, and Smolensk Regions

Operational Summary No. 2 at 2000 hours 19 July 1941,

Headquarters 16th Army,
at the northern edge of the forest west of Zhukovo State Farm
1:100,000 scale map (1939)

First. 16th Army fought for possession of Kholm and Demidov during the day on 18 and 19 July. It conducted a regrouping to the Zagor'e, Agafonovo, Borodenka, Kuprino, and Katyn' Station line. In cooperation with 34th RC, it continued an attack toward Smolensk, having occupied its northern suburbs. Simultaneously, it fought with enemy airborne landings in the Iartsevo and Terekhi region with destroyer detachments.

Second. 32nd RCs. 46th RD continued to hold onto the Donets and Akatovo line with three rifle battalions and three artillery battalions and, simultaneously, conducted an attack toward Demidov.

A rifle battalion of 647th RR held back the enemy attacking from Kholm along the Donets and Akatovo line. Its right flank was enveloped by small enemy mobile groups, which were penetrating from Bichno and Iushino.

3rd Bn, 314th RR, and a rifle battalion of 647th RR continued to attack toward Demidov and captured Senino, where they seized the headquarters of an enemy artillery regiment.

Third. 152nd RD carried out a regrouping to its defensive line, occupying [the following] (100,000 map): 544th RR (less five rifle companies) along the Iavishche, Kasplia, and Bol'shoe Vozmishche line; 646th RR (less six rifle companies) along the Borodenka, Zyki, and Ermaki line; and 480th RR (less 5th Rifle Company), along the Kuprino, Katyn' Station, and to the Dnepr River line, with its reconnaissance groups in contact with the enemy. On its left wing, we noticed preparatory work by the enemy for crossings over the Dnepr River in the Krasnyi Bor and Nizhnaia Iasennaia region.

Fourth. The detachment of Major General Gorodniansky [129th RD] is continuing to conduct sustained fighting for Smolensk with alternating success for either side. The northwestern outskirts of Smolensk were occupied by his detachment for the third time, and it occupied the line (on the 100,000 map) by day's end on 19 July.

1st Bn, 340th RR, with a rifle battalion of 720th RR, is on the western edge of Smolensk and the airfield.

3rd Bn, 457th RR is in the northern outskirts of Smolensk.

343rd RR (less one rifle battalion) – the Marker 251 line.

Headquarters of 32nd RC – the grove 2 kilometers east of Opol'e.

The Chief of Staff of 16th Army, Colonel Shalin
The Chief of the Operations Department, Colonel Roshchin

Source: "Operativnaia svodka shtaba 16-i Armii No. 2 ot19 iiulia 1941 g. o boevykh deistviiakh voisk armii v raionakh Demidov, Kholm, Smolensk" [Operational summary no. 2 of the headquarters of 16th Army of 19 July 1941 about the combat operations of the army's forces in the Demidov, Kholm, and Smolensk regions], in *SBDVOV*, issue 37, 206.

7. Combat Report No. 18/op of the Headquarters of 16th Army of 20 July 1941 to the Headquarters of the Western Front about the Positions of the Army's Forces

To the Chief of Staff of the *Front*

Combat Report No. 18/op at 2000 hours 20 July 1941,

Headquarters, 16th Army,

at the northern edge of the forest west of Zhukovo State Farm

1:500,000 scale map

1. The enemy, reinforced by two battalions of motorized infantry, a battalion of artillery, a battalion of mortars, and no fewer than two companies of tanks, is along the Smolensk, Donets, Kholm, and Demidov line on 20 July. The overall grouping of enemy before the army's front is no fewer than one motorized division and two-three tank battalions, not counting the enemy in front of 127th RD and 158th RD positions south (or southeast) from Smolensk. Aircraft have been dropping cargos in the Sgibino region.

2. The army's units are occupying [the following] positions at 2000 hours on 20 July: the motor-mechanized units of 32nd RC's 46th RD (three battalions), after enemy counterattacks on 19 July with tanks, aircraft, and infantry on vehicles, withdrew its right wing to the Opol'e region [25 kilometers north of Smolensk]. The left flank of the division is at Peresudy Station. Up to two and one half battalions of enemy motorized infantry and four companies of tanks are before the division's front.

3. 152nd RD occupied the previous Alfimovo, Buda, and Katyn' Station line up to 1200 hours on 20 July.

By order of the army's commander, the division shifted to the Muk and Iatsinino region on 20 July for an assault on Smolensk together with 129th RD.

It came in contact with groups of infantry of a small reconnaissance group on the right wing and two battalions of motorized infantry and up to a battalion of artillery brought up anew to the Borovaia region (southern bank of the Dnepr River).

4. 129th RD (4 battalions), while attacking Smolensk from the north, seized the airfield with its left wing and halted along the line of the Chernichka River with its left wing.

There are up to two battalions of enemy motorized infantry and battalions of artillery and tanks before the division's front.

5. The enemy's main means of suppression are: the employment of massed mortar and automatic weapons fire and the constant pressure of aviation, which is operating extraordinarily impudently while flying over the battlefield in hedge-hopping flights.

6. Shortages of food and ammunition, especially for regimental and divisional artillery's antiaircraft guns (107mm), are continuing to be felt by the army's units.

Communications means [radios] are absent in the headquarters of a number of units, which, in turn, extraordinarily complicates the organization of command and control of the fighting. Up to this time, medical assistance is not arranged as it should be.

The filling out of the units at the expense of those who returned from various units that lost contact with the front has been prohibited by order of the commander since it has a negative influence on the combat steadfastness of the subunits.

The Chief of Staff of 16th Army, Shalin

Source: "Boevoe donesenie shtaba 16-i Armii No. 18/op ot 20 iiulia 1941 g. shtaba Zapadnogo fronta o polozhenii voisk armii" [Combat report no. 18/op of the headquarters of 16th Army of 20 July 1941 to the headquarters of the Western Front about the positions of the army's forces], in *SBDVOV*, issue 37, 207.

8. Information from the Headquarters of 16th Army of 21 July 1941 to the Headquarters of 20th and 19th Armies about a Transition to an Attack toward Smolensk from the North

To the Chiefs of Staff of 20th and 19th Armies
0145 hours 21 July 1941

16th Army went over to the attack toward Smolensk from the north at 0100 hours on 21 July. The 19th Army will attack southeastward and southward from the Dresna, Bublevka, and Shabanova line at 0500 hours.

Shalin

Source: "Informatsiia shtaba 16-i Armii ot 21 iiulia 1941 g. stabam 20-i i 19-i Armii o perekhode v nastuplenie na Smolensk s severa" [Information from the headquarters of 16th Army of 21 July 1941 to the headquarters of 20th and 19th Armies about a transition to an offensive toward Smolensk from the north], in *SBDVOV*, issue 37, 208.

9. Operational Summary No. 50 of the Western Front on 21 July 1941 about the Combat Operations of the *Front's* Forces (see Map 3)

Operational Summary No. 50 at 0800 hours on 21 July 1941,
Headquarters, Western Front
1:500,000 scale map

First. The *front's* forces continued to conduct sustained fighting with enemy units that have penetrated toward Nevel', Velikie Luki, Demidov, Smolensk, and Krichev and engaged in combat with enemy tank units that have penetrated into the Iartsevo region.

Second. 22nd Army. The army's units conducted a firm holding action on the right wing and withdrew from encirclement in the center. Our forces cleared Velikie Luki of enemy at 0500 hours.

126th RD, with two rifle regiments, conducted sustained fighting with an enemy force of up to an infantry division and withdrew and dug in along the Usadishche and Gory line.

170th RD is fighting along the Stan'kovo and Lake Udrai line with one group at 0600 hours on 21 July, and a second group of 170th RD is encircled in the forests west of Ust'-Dolyssy and trying to escape encirclement, but without sufficient ammunition.

51st RC (112th and 98th RDs) escaped from encirclement at 2400 hours on 20 July and is penetrating toward the northeast to link up with 170th RD's units. The corps' advanced units cut across the Pustoshka and Nevel' highway in the Begunovo and Barkony sector at 1500 hours on 20 July.

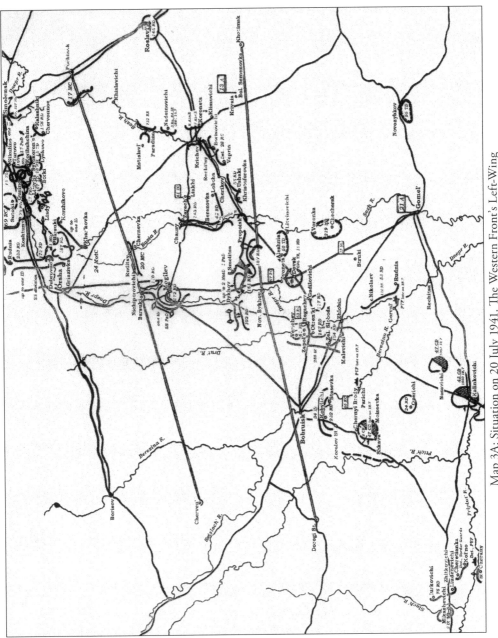

Map 3A: Situation on 20 July 1941. The Western Front's Left-Wing

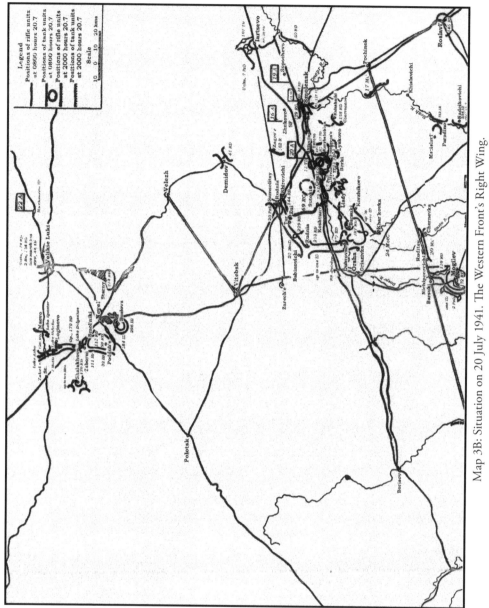

Map 3B: Situation on 20 July 1941. The Western Front's Right Wing.

62nd RC (174th and 186th RDs) was encircled in the Novokholmsk region. The corps could not escape from encirclement by 2400 hours on 20 July, fighting is going on, and the corps will try to escape encirclement in the direction of 51st RC's' operations.

214th RD was fighting with enemy motorized units attacking from Nevel' toward Reka station region at 0600 hours on 21 July.

Velikie Luki was completely occupied by our forces at 0500 hours on 21 July, and the enemy withdrew toward Nevel'.

Units of the Velikie Luki garrison (units of 179th RD, two rifle battalions of 134th RD, two march-battalions, and the remnants of 48th TD's motorized rifle regiment) are attacking the enemy from the east and southeast.

Third. 19th Army. During the day on 20 July and overnight on 20-21 July, separate units of the army continued fighting in the Smolensk region.

127th RD was attacked along the Roslavl' road at 0400 hours on 20 July by enemy motorized infantry with 20 tanks and artillery supported by two batteries of heavy artillery, and the enemy succeeded in penetrating into the division's dispositions and destroyed a forward battery of 391st ArtyR. A further advance by the enemy was repulsed by our artillery and a stubborn defense by the division's units.

The enemy left 9 tanks and many vehicles on the battlefield. The division is restoring its previous positions.

The division was attacked for a second time at 0800 on 20 July by 9 enemy tanks and a battery.

As a result of two days of fighting, the division repelled two enemy attacks and destroyed 15 enemy tanks during the fighting.

127th RD is occupying positions at Dresna and Brilevka at day's end on 20 July, and 159th RD is at Shtalov and to the south.

29th RR, 38th RD, together with 129th RD, are holding firmly to Sortirovochnaia Station, the railroad bridge across the Dnepr River, and Pokrovskaia Gora. Fighting is going on along the northern outskirts of Smolensk.

50th RD, at 0600 on 21 July, continued to prepare a defensive line in the (incl.) Buliany and Pridneprovskaia Station sector along the eastern bank of the Dnepr River.

The positions of the army's remaining units are being verified.

Headquarters, 19th Army – the woods 3 kilometers from Kurdymovo.

Fourth. 20th Army. The army continued to concentrate its units along a new defensive line on 20 July, while conducting brief counterattacks in the direction of Rudnia.

144th RD, under pressure of superior enemy forces (up to an infantry division), supported by artillery and tanks, abandoned Rudnia at 2000 hours on 20 July, and the division's right wing regiments withdrew to the Dvorishche and Bat'kovo line.

153rd RD withdrew to the region of 69th RC. There are a total of 800 men in the division.

The positions of the remaining units of 20th Army are being confirmed as of 0600 hours on 21 July.

Headquarters, 20th Army – Svetitsy.

Fifth paragraph does not exist in this order.

Sixth. 16th Army, while holding off enemy attacks from Donets and Kholm all day on 20 July, is withdrawing its right wing back to Opol'e. The army carried out a regrouping for an attack on Smolensk and was occupying [the following] positions at 2400 hours on 20 July:

46th RD –Opol'e and the forests to the southwest, from which it is organizing a counterattack on an enemy motorized battalion with 30-40 tanks in the Kholm region.

152nd RD has concentrated with its main forces in the Luk region.

129th RD was fighting in the northwestern outskirts of Smolensk.

Headquarters, 16th Army – Zhukovo State Farm.

Group Major General Rokossovsky:

101st TD fought unsuccessfully on 20 July southwest of Iartsevo, where it encountered a strong enemy antitank defense.

69th MD (107th TD on 17 July) concentrated in the Belyi region at day's end on 20 July and is beginning to operate toward Lake Shchuch'e and Dukhovshchina on 21 July.

Seventh. 13th Army. On 20 July the army's units continued to hold out in the Mogilev region and were fighting along the eastern bank of the Sozh River, trying to restore their positions in the Krichev region.

61st RC (110th and 172nd RDs, 20th MC, and 57th RR, 148th RD, less one battalion, and 453rd RR, 132nd RD) organized an all-round defense and firmly held on to [the following] lines:

20th MC – 26th TD, while protecting the eastern axis, occupies the Gladkovo, Sukhari, Bol'shoe Bushkovo, and Kirp (west of Chernevka) line;

210th MRD (less one battalion) occupies the (incl.) Chernevka and north of Domany line; and

38th TD – along the Nichiporovichi and Nikolaevka line.

Headquarters, 20th MC – the forest west of Ekhany.

110th RD (less 394th and 441st RRs), with 514th MRR (less one battalion) is firmly defending the (incl.) Nikolaevka and Par (east of Polykovichi) line.

172nd RD, with one rifle battalion of 514th RR and 394th RR, 110th RD, 307th RR, 148th RD, and one rifle battalion of 543rd RR, 161st RD, is firmly holding on to the bridgehead in the Mogilev region along the Polykovichi, Pashkovo, Tishovka, Buinichi, (incl.) Pechery, and Bol'shaia Borovka line.

411th RR – the reserve of the commander, 61st Rifle Corps – in the Novyi Liubuzh region.

Headquarters, 61st RC – the forest east of Shapochitsy.

20th RC. We have no information about the positions of the units of the corps.

4th AbnC, having begun an attack in the direction of Krichev on the morning of 19 July, 7th AbnB reached Korenets and the forest to the west, where it was halted by enemy fire from the direction of Mikheevichi.

8th AbnB reached the forest east of Polokhovo.

Further news about positions has not arrived.

Headquarters, 4th AbnC – Klimovichi.

Headquarters, 13th Army – Rodnia.

Eighth. 4th Army. Information about the positions of the army's units has not been received as of the time this operational summary is being compiled.

Ninth. 21st Army conducting sustained combat with enemy units approaching the Rzhavka, Kulikovka, Pribor, V'iun, Rekhta, and Rudnia line and along the Stasevka, Borovaia, Gleb, Rudnia, and Chernye Brody line along the approaches to Bobruisk from the south on 20 July.

Units of 53rd AC (255th, 267th, and 52nd IDs) are operating along the Rogachev and Zhlobin front on the army's front.

43rd AC (131st and 134th IDs) is operating along the Stasevka, Gleb, Rudnia, and Chernye Brody front.

Units of 45th and 293rd IDs are apparently operating along the Pinsk axis.

67th RC (187th, 151st, and 102nd RDs) are fighting in their previous positions. Up to a regiment of enemy infantry, attacking at the boundary of 187th and 151st RDs, reached and captured the northeastern outskirts of Obidovichi at 1400 hours on 20 July. Subsequent enemy attempts to penetrate along the highway to Dobsk were repelled by units of 50th TD.

Headquarters, 67th RC – Zvonets.

63rd RC (61st, 167th, and 154th RDs) were fighting in their previous positions by the end of the day on 20 July. Along the corps' front while it was going over to the defense, units of 53rd AC repeatedly tried to counterattack toward Zhlobin, but all of the counterattacks were repulsed.

Headquarters, 63rd RC – the pioneer camp in Rogachev.

66th RC – 232nd RD is occupying its previous line. Units of 131st and 134th IDs are in front of the division.

797th RR is protecting the left flank of the division in the Chernye Brody, Protasy, and Ugly sector. In front of the regiment, 445th and 432nd IRs are counterattacking toward Parichi.

A concentration of infantry has been detected in the Porech'e region at day's end on 19 July.

Headquarters, 66th RC – Drazhnia.

BEPO No. 52 was fighting with the enemy in the vicinity of Rabkor Station, while hindering his concentration in the Karpilovka region.

75th RD is fighting for possession of Zhitkovichi at 1800 hours on 20 July, facing units of 45th and 293rd IDs, which are trying to envelop Zhitkovichi from the north and south. The results of the fighting are being verified.

No reports have been received about 117th RD, 110th RR, and Kurmashev's detachment.

25th MC: 50th TD was fighting for the southern outskirts of Obidovichi;

219th MRD tried to seize Propoisk with a motorized rifle regiment from 1200-1800 hours on 20 July but without results; and

55th TD is concentrated in its previous concentration region.

47th CD – is on the march from the Nasavichi region to the Ozarichi region at the end of the day on 20 July.

43rd CD is concentrating in the Kalinkovichi region.

32nd CD [destined to reinforce Gorodovikov's cavalry group] – its first train began to arrive at Vasilevichi Station on 20 July.

Headquarters, 21st Army – Gomel'.

Tenth. The VVS of the *front*, during the second half of the day on 20 July and overnight on 20-21 July, continued to conduct reconnaissance and destruction of the enemy's Dukhovshchina grouping in cooperation with tanks.

Our losses during the second half of the day were 20 aircraft, with one IL-2 not returning to its airfield. Of those aircraft which did not return in the previous summary, 1 SB aircraft and 1 Iak-2 aircraft landed at their airfield by day's end on 20 July.

Enemy losses – 1 ME-109 and 1 ME-110 were shot down.

> The Chief of Staff of the Western Front, Lieutenant General Malandin
> The Military Commissar of the Western Front,
>   Regimental Commissar Anshakov
> The Chief of the Operations Department, *Kombrig* Liubarsky

Source: Operativnaia svodka shtaba Zapadnogo fronta No. 50 ot 21 iiulia 1941 g. o boevykh deistviiakh voisk fronta" [Operational summary no. 50 of the Western Front on 21 July 1941 about the combat operations of the *front's* forces], in *SBDVOV*, issue 37, 98-100.

10. Operational Summary No. 5 of the Headquarters of 16th Army of 21 July 1941 about the Combat Operations of the Army's Forces for the Capture of the City of Smolensk

Operational Summary No. 5 at 2000 hours on 21 July 1941,
Headquarters, 16th Army,
at the northern edge of the woods west of Zhukovo State Farm
1:500,000 scale map (1939)

First. 16th Army, having begun its attack toward Smolensk at 0100 hours on 21 July, has conducted sustained street fighting for possession of the northern part of the city all day long. Simultaneously, separate detachments struggled with enemy tank strongpoints in the vicinity of Syro-Lipki and held off an enemy attack from Demidov toward the southeast. In light of the tardy attack by 19th Army's 34th RC, the combined attack on Smolensk by 127th and 158th RDs against the southern and southeastern outskirts of the city have not been carried out.

Second. 46th RD is operating with three composite detachments to destroy the enemy in the region south of Demidov and Syro-Lipki. By day's end, the detachments were located [as follows]: two detachments encircled the enemy in the Syro-Lipki region; and the detachment operating against the enemy's Demidov grouping occupied the woods in the Peresudy Station region.

Third. 152nd RD has conducted persistent street fighting all day for possession of the western outskirts of Smolensk. 480th RR (less one battalion) occupied Smolensk Station and advanced 1 kilometer deep into the center of the city by day's end. 544th RR reached the Dnepr River. Losses are being calculated.

Fourth. 129th RD, consisting of four under-strength battalions, went over to the attack toward the northern part of Smolensk at 0100 hours on 21 July. Overcoming fire resistance, it occupied [the following] front (50,000 map):

343rd RR (around 330 men) – the road junction 1 kilometer north of Smolensk.
457th RR (around 470 men) – the northern slope of Hill 251.9.
The losses of personnel during the day has reached 40%.

The Chief of Staff of 16th Army, Colonel Shalin
The Chief of the Operations Department, Colonel Roshchin

Source: "Operativnaia svodka shtaba 16-i Armii No. 5 ot 21 iiulia 1941 g. o boevykh deistviiakh voisk armii po ovladeniiu gor. Smolensk" [Operational summary no. 5 of the headquarters of 16th Army of 21 July 1941 about the combat operations of the army's forces for the capture of the city of Smolensk], in *SBDVOV*, issue 37, 208.

11. Operational Summary No. 55 of the Headquarters of the Western Front on 23 July 1941 about the Combat Operations of the *Front's* Forces

Operational Summary No. 55 of the Headquarters of the Western Front
at 2000 hours on 23 July 1941,
1;500,000 scale map

First. Fierce fighting with superior enemy forces went on with superior enemy forces in the Nevel', Smolensk, and El'nia regions on 23 July.

Second. 22nd Army, while organizing a defense along the Lovat' River and Lake Serutskoe line, is continuing the struggle for the escape of 51st RC's units from encirclement.

29th RC is defending the Pestovo, Velikie Luki, (incl.) and Shchukino sector along the Lovat' River. Part of the corps is helping 51st RC escape from encirclement.

126th RD is in its previous positions.

179th RD, while defending Velikie Luki, is continuing its attack toward Nevel' with part of its force.

214th RD is situated in the Rogatkino and Shchukino regions. No news has been received on 23 July.

62nd RC (174th and 186th RDs) is defending the Shchukino, Poreche, and Lake Serutskoe line since 23 July and taking measures for the escape from encirclement of the discovered remnants of 19th Army's 134th RD in the Prikhaby, Baranovo, and Karpovo region (all points 20-25 kilometers north of Velizh).

Headquarters, 62nd Rifle Corps – Teterkino (7 kilometers southwest of Mulina).

51st RC (112th and 98th RDs) is fighting in encirclement.

Up to 2,000 men in the sanitary [medical] facilities of the corps have not been evacuated.

170th RD was attacking southwestward from the Kozhemiachkino region on the morning of 23 July, with the aim of assisting the escape of 51st RC's units from encirclement. Information about the outcome of the fighting has not been received by 1800 hours on 23 July.

Headquarters, 22nd Army – Nazimovo Station.

Group Maslennikov [29th Army, but should read Group Khomenko from 30th Army] moved forward to the Chikhachi and Lake Zhizhitskoe line on 23 July and reached [the following positions] by 0600 hours of the 23rd: 256th and 252nd Rifle Divisions reached the Belyi line and 242nd RD was en route in their rear.

243rd RD unloaded at Skvortsovo Station at 1000 hours on 23 July to occupy the Dubrovka and Zasenovo line.

Group headquarters – Martiukhova … ..

Third. 20th Army, after regrouping for an attack against the enemy penetrating toward Smolensk overnight on 21-22 July and on the morning of 22 July, on 23 July was defending the Bol'shaia Ploskaia, Berezina River, and northern bank of the Dnepr River line, while repelling persistent enemy attacks from Rudnia and along the Orsha-Smolensk road.

69th RC: 144th RD, as a result of sustained combat and under pressure of enemy infantry and air strikes, withdrew to and occupied the (incl.) Molevo Boloto and Bol'shaia Ploskaia Station line by 1100 hours on 22 July;

233rd RD is fighting along the (incl.) Bol'shaia Ploskaia Station and Shchedritsy line;

229th RD, while repelling attacks by enemy infantry, was fighting along the Orlovka and (incl.) Dubrovno line;

73rd RD is defending the Dubrovna and Mikhailovka sector along the Dnepr River, while repelling persistent attacks by enemy infantry and aircraft from the west along the Orsha-Smolensk road;

57th TD occupied Vydra on the morning of 22 July with its forward units, having cut off enemy forces there; and

There are no changes in 153rd RD's and 5th MC's positions.

Group Kalinin. The group units were concentrated in their jumping off positions for the attack on 23 July [as follows]:

91st RD was concentrated in the Vetlitsa, Pecheninki, and Syrokoren'e region; and

89th RD – in the Retaze and Ivanino region.

There is no information about 166th RD.

Group headquarters – Vadino Station.

Fourth. 16th Army. Units of 16th Army continued to conduct sustained street fighting for possession of Smolensk on 22 July. The enemy, offering stubborn resistance, slowly withdrew to the northern bank of the Dnepr River.

The army's units, having captured the northwestern and northern parts of the city, approached the northern bank of the Dnepr River.

32nd RC: 152nd RD captured the northwestern part of Smolensk and was fighting in the northeastern part of the city, while assisting 129th RD;

129th RD, while attacking the northern outskirts of Smolensk on 22 July, reached the water tower and the cemetery with its right wing and, cooperating with 152nd RD, continued a struggle for possession of the northeastern part of the city;

46th RD, under strong air attacks and pressure from enemy mobile groups, which bypassed it from the flanks and rear, suffered significant losses and withdrew to the Pomogailovo, Dushatino, and Kholm line, where it is putting itself in order with the mission to seize Syro-Lipki and Domanov and protect the rear areas of 16th and 20th Armies.

34th RC – 127th RD (up to 600 men) and 158th RD (about 100 men), trained and armed (almost without machine guns), attacked toward Riabtsevo Station at

1200 hours on 22 July, with up to a regiment of motorized infantry with artillery, small groups of tanks, and several armored vehicles in front of them. After a five-hour battle, the remnants of 127th and 158th RDs abandoned Riabtsevo Station and withdrew toward Lozyn' at 1400 hours on 22 July.

Headquarters, 16th Army – the grove north of Zhukovo State Farm.

Group Khomenko. Information has not been received about the positions of its units.

[The Western Front's Operational Summary No. 54, issued at 0800 hours on 23 July 1941, stated:

Group Khomenko (242nd, 250th, 251st RDs and 50th and 53rd CDs). The forward units of the group are reaching the Maksimovka and Petropol'e line and the main forces, the Panovo, Belyi, Miakishevo line (reported by the General Staff. 53rd CD, having finished unloading at Toropa Station by 1000 hours on 22 July 1941, reached its concentration region by the morning of 23 July 1941. 50th CD was on the march to its concentration region from 0800 hours on 22 July 1941. The Group headquarters – Nikulino. Archival citation, f. 208, op. 10169ss, d. 7, l. 241].

Group Rokossovsky. After fighting along the Vop River, the group's units were concentrating along the eastern bank of the Vop River in jumping-off positions for the attack.

107th TD reached the Korytnia, Pochinok, and Pokikhino region. Information about the positions of 101st TD has not been received.

38th RD, under repeated raids by enemy aircraft and enemy artillery and mortar fire, withdrew and dug in along the eastern bank of the Vop River, destroying the crossings behind it.

Group headquarters – Krasnobaenka … ..

Group Kachalov dislodged the enemy's forward units by 1700 hours on 23 July and, while under constant pressure by enemy aircraft, was fighting for the crossings over the Stomet' River (18 kilometers southeast of Pochinok).

Group headquarters – Stodolishche … .

The Chief of Staff of the Western Front, Lieutenant General Sokolovsky
The Military Commissar of the Western Front's headquarters,
    Regimental Commissar Anshakov
The Chief of the Operations Department, Lieutenant General Malandin

Source: "Operativnaia svodka shtaba Zapadnogo fronta No. 55 k 20 chasam 23 iiulia 1941 g. o boevykh deistviiakh voisk fronta" [Operational summary no. 55 of the headquarters of the Western Front of 2000 hours on 23 July 1941 about the combat operations of the *front's* forces], in *SBDVOV*, issue 37, 101-102.

12. Intelligence Summary No. 53 of the Headquarters of the Western Front at 2000 hours on 23 July 1941 about Enemy Combat Operations

Intelligence Summary No. 53,
Headquarters, Western Front
2000 hours on 23 July 1941
1:500,000 scale map

First. The enemy, while directing his main efforts along the Vitebsk and Smolensk axes, brought significant forces forward on 22 and 23 July with the aim of liquidating our Smolensk grouping.

On the Nevel' axis, the enemy is trying to complete offensive action toward Nevel' and Velikie Luki, while transferring part of his forces from the Nevel' and Gorodok regions toward Il'ino and Toropets.

On the Mogilev axis, the enemy is going over to an active defense along the Sozh River and, simultaneously, continuing to encircle the Mogilev grouping.

On the Rogachev and Pinsk axes, the enemy is continuing to concentrate forces for a transition to a general offensive.

Second. The Nevel' axis.

The enemy, after completing offensive operations against our Nevel' grouping with a force of five-six divisions, is continuing to regroup his forces from the Nevel' and Gorodok regions toward Il'ino and Toropets on 22 and 23 July, with the aim of protecting the Vitebsk axis against a flank attack from the north.

Combat of a local nature is going on in the Novosokol'niki and Velikie Luki region.

The enemy has prepared populated points, forests, ravines, defiles, and roads as antitank regions.

Third. The Vitebsk axis.

The enemy, while conducting an attack toward Iartsevo with the main forces of 39th MC, has had no success along the Vitebsk axis. Simultaneously, he has brought up to two infantry divisions forward to the Velizh, Kresty, and Solov'evo region, with the aim of protecting against a flank attack by our forces from the north.

The enemy is preparing defensive lines in the Karpovka and Lomonosovo Station region.

According to air observations, in the period from 0600 to 1700 hours on 23 July,-we have noted the movement of columns along the Nevel' and Usviaty highway and at Lopatino, Solov'evo, Velizh, Kresty, and Il'ino and the approach of a column of up to a battalion of tanks in the Dukhovshchina region.

Fourth. The Smolensk axis

On the Smolensk axis, the enemy has brought three divisions forward (5th ID, an SS Division, and an unknown division) to the Kasplia, Rudnia, and Komissarovo region [northwest and north of Smolensk] and up to one motorized and one panzer division to the Lenino and Krasnoe region [west of Smolensk].

The enemy went over to the attack in the general direction of Smolensk on the morning of 23 July and pushed our units southeastward from Rudnia.

17th and 18th PzDs' units went over to the defense locally in the El'nia, Kazanka, and Pochinok region [south and southeast of Smolensk] with the aim of protecting the concentration of SS *"Das Reich"* Division for a subsequent attack toward Smolensk and Dorogobuzh.

Fighting of a local nature is taking place in the Korobchino and Riabtsevo region (southeast of Smolensk).

The operations of Group Guderian are being supported by the First Aviation Corps.

Fifth. The Mogilev axis.

On the Mogilev axis, the enemy, while going on the defense along the Sozh River, is holding on to the eastern bank at Krichev on 22 and 23 July, and the forward units of 4th PzD are moving along the highway toward Roslavl'. As a result of fighting along the Petrovichi and Studenets line, 39th PzR withdrew to the Mstislavovochi region, while suffering heavy losses.

In the Mogilev region, the enemy is continuing to fight against the Mogilev grouping with a force of up to five divisions.

Sixth. The Rogachev axis.

On the Rogachev axis, the enemy continued concentrating the units of 43rd AC in the Porech'e region on 23 July, with the aim of delivering a flank attack on 21st Army's units. In the Novyi Bykhov region, the enemy had no success and suffered losses of up to two battalions of infantry after going over to the attack toward Dovsk with a forces of 31st ID and 1st CD.

On the Pinsk axis, the enemy is continuing to press our units toward the east.

Conclusion

The enemy has committed up to three-four fresh divisions along the entire front from 21 to 23 July and, after regrouping his forces to the central axis, directed his main effort to liquidate the Smolensk grouping [16th, 19th, and 20th Army] by attacking with three divisions toward Smolensk from the west and, simultaneously, completing the encirclement in the Iartsevo region, while protecting his main attack in the Kresty, Il'ino, and Solov'evo region against attacks by our units from the north.

On the Nevel' axis, his main efforts are being directed at preventing a withdrawal of our forces to the east.

On the Rogachev axis, the enemy is creating a threat to the left wing of our army.

The Chief of Staff of the Western Front, Lieutenant General Sokolovsky
The Military Commissar of the Western Front's headquarters,
    Regimental Commissar Anshakov
The Chief of the Western Front's Intelligence Department,
    Colonel Korneev
The Military Commissar of the Western Front's Intelligence Department,
    Battalion Commissar Steblovtsev

Source: "Razvedyvatel'naia svodka shtaba Zapadnogo fronta No. 53 k 20 chasam 23 iiulia 1941 g. o boevykh deistviiakh protivnika" [Intelligence summary no. 53 of the headquarters of the Western Front at 2000 hours 23 July 1941 about enemy combat operations], in *SBDVOV*, issue 37, 104-105.

13. Report of the Commander of the Forces of 16th Army on 24 July 1941 to the Commander-in-Chief of the Western Direction's Forces about the Combat Operations of the Army's Forces for the Capture of the City of Smolensk

To the Commander-in-Chief of the Western Direction
To the Commander of the Western Front
Early on 24 July 1941

The enemy is stubbornly defending Smolensk and is concentrating fresh forces the Kasplia and Vydra region. Vydra is occupied by the enemy with up to two battalions.

16th Army did not fulfill its missions of fully cleaning out the northern part of the city by 23 July, and the units of 34th RC and 46th RD are continuing to assemble their personnel and put them in order.

152nd RD is fighting within the city, while cooperating with 129th RD in the seizure of the eastern outskirts of the northern part of the city. Two battalions of 152nd RD have not yet been returned to the division from 20th Army.

129th RD fought along the approaches to the northern part of the city today and attacked on its wings, with the right wing reaching the hanger of the airfield and the left wing – Tantsovka.

46th RD assembled its personnel on 23 July and overnight on 23-24 July and put them in order. It will begin reaching the region for the attack, Shchetkino and Nikeevshchina [4-5 kilometers east of Smolensk], by first light on 24 July and carry out a relief of 129th RD's units.

34th RC is assembling its personnel and putting its units in order in the vicinity of Hill 315 and Lozyn'.

The motorized regiment, attached to me from Rokossovsky, has still not arrived.

I have decided to seize the northern part of the city with the units of 152nd, 129th, and 46th RDs during the day on 24 July and continue assembling and putting in order 9th RC and concentrating the units of 3rd RC.

All of 16th Army's units are being concentrated in jumping-off positions to force the Dnepr River and seize the southern part of Smolensk.

I request orders:

1. To accelerate the arrival of the motorized regiment group of Rokossovsky and fill out 20 companies with commanders and political workers and the 3 battalions of 46th RD, which are unloading and concentrating in the Roslavl' region.

2. Return to 152nd RD the two battalions transferred to 20th Army.

Lukin, Lobachev

Source: "Doklad komanduiushchego voiskami 16-i Armii ot 24 iiulia 1941 g. Glavnokomanduiushchemu voiskami Zapadnogo Napravleniia o boevykh deistviiakh voisk armii po ovladeniiu gor. Smolensk" [Report of the commander of the forces of 16th Army on 24 July 1941 to the commander-in-chief of the Western Direction's forces about the combat operations of the army's forces for the capture of the city of Smolensk], in *SBDVOV*, issue 37, 209.

Appendix G

The First Soviet Counteroffensive, 23-31 July 1941

German 7. Supplement to Führer Directive No. 33, 23 July 1941

The Chief of Staff of the Supreme High Command
of the Armed Forces (OKW).
Führer headquarters
Chief of Staff of the Operations Directorate.
23 July 1941
Department for the Defense of the Country (1st Dept.),
No. 442254/41. Top Secret

Supplement to Directive No. 33,
The Further Conduct of the War in the East

After the report of the High Command of the Ground Forces, as a supplement and broadening of Directive No. 33, on 22 July the Führer has ordered:

1. **The Southern sector of the Eastern Front**. The enemy still located west of the Dnepr must be finally crushed and entirely annihilated. As soon as the operational situation and logistical support permits, First and Second Panzer Groups, subordinate to Fourth Panzer Army's headquarters [a new command to be established under Rundstedt], together with the infantry and mountain infantry divisions following them, after capturing the Khar'kov industrial region, must undertake an offensive across the Don into the Caucasus. The priority mission of the main mass of infantry divisions is the capture of the Ukraine, the Crimea, and the territory of the Russian Federation to the Don. When that is accomplished, Rumanian forces will be entrusted with occupation administration of the regions southwest of the Bug River;

The immediate task is the capturing of the Ukraine, the Crimea, and the territory of the Russian Federation up to the Don by the main mass of infantry divisions. While doing so, Rumanian forces are entrusted with occupation services in the region southwest of the Southern Bug.

2. **The Central sector of the Eastern Front**. After the situation improves in the Smolensk region and on its southern flank, Army Group Center must defeat the enemy located between Smolensk and Moscow with sufficiently powerful infantry formations from both of its armies and advance with its left flank as far as possible to the east and capture Moscow.

Temporarily assign Third Panzer Group to Army Group North to support the latter's right flank and encircle the enemy in the Leningrad region. To fulfill the subsequent missions – the advance to the Volga – my intention is to return Third

Panzer Group's mobile formations to their former subordination [but not Second Panzer Group];

For fulfilling the subsequent missions – the offensive to the Volga – my intention is to return Third Panzer Group's mobile formations to their former subordination.

3. **The Northern sector of the Eastern Front**. Having received control of Third Panzer Group, Army Group North will be capable of allocating large infantry forces for the offensive on Leningrad, thus avoiding the expenditure of mobile formations on frontal attacks in difficult terrain.

Enemy forces still operating in Estonia must be destroyed. While doing so, it is necessary to prevent their transport by ship and penetration through Narva toward Leningrad. Upon fulfilling its missions, Third Panzer Group must once again be transferred to Army Group Center's control;

4. Subsequently, as soon as conditions permit, the High Command of the Ground forces [OKH] will withdraw part of Army Group North's forces, including Fourth Panzer Group, and also part of Army Group South's infantry force, to the Homeland.

While doing so, the combat readiness of Third Panzer Group must be fully restored at the expense of transferring equipment and personnel to it from Fourth Panzer Group. If necessary, First and Second Panzer Groups must accomplish their missions by combining their formations [still under Army Group South].

5. The orders given to the Navy and the Luftwaffe in Directive No. 33 remain in effect.

In addition to these, the Navy and the Luftwaffe ease the position of the Mountain Infantry Corps: first – my means of decisive actions by the Navy in the Barents Sea; and second – by transferring several groups of bomber aircraft to the area of combat operations in Finland, which will be accomplished after completion of the fighting in the Smolensk region. Also conduct these measures to repel English attempts to meddle in the struggle for the coasts of the Arctic Sea.

6. The forces which are being allocated for the execution of security services in occupied regions are sufficient for the fulfillment of missions only in the case if any and all resistance will be liquidated by means of judicial punishment of the guilty and the spreading of such fear and terror on the part of the occupying authorities, which nibbles away any popular desires to resist.

Entrust responsibility for tranquility in the occupied regions to appropriate commands with the forces located at their disposal.

[signed] Keitel

Source: *Sbornik voenno-istoricheskikh materialov Velikoi Otechestvennoi voiny, vypusk 18* [Collection of military-historical materials of the Great Patriotic War, issue 18] (Moscow: Voenizdat, 1960), 233-234. Prepared by the Military-Historical Department of the Military-Scientific Directorate of the Red Army General Staff and classified secret.

1. *Stavka* VK Directive to the Commander of the Forces of the *Front* of Reserve Armies about the Creation of Operational Groups of Forces and their Deployment for an Operations for the Destruction of the Enemy's Smolensk Grouping

Copies: To the Commander-in-Chief of the Western Direction's Forces
To the Commanders of the *Front's* Operational Groups
2125 hours on 20 July 1941

For the conduct of an operation to encircle and destroy the enemy's Smolensk grouping, the *Stavka* orders:

1. Group Maslennikov [29th Army], consisting of 252nd, 256th, and 243rd RDs and BEPO Nos. 53 and 82, will reach the Chikhachi (40 kilometers northwest of Toropets) and Lake Zhizhitskoe at Artemovo Station line by the end of the day on 23 July and prepare a defense protecting the Toropets axis.

Dispatch a detachment no larger than a battalion for the protection of the group's flank in the Knyazhovo region (25 kilometers north of Chikhachi).

Deploy the group's headquarters in Selishche (22 kilometers west of Toropets).

2. Group Khomenko [30th Army], consisting of 242nd, 251st, and 250th RDs, will advance to the Maksimovka (22 kilometers southwest of Belyi) and Petropol'e line by the end of the day on 22 July, having in mind an attack in the general direction of Dukhovshchina on the morning of 23 July.

Establish communications with 50th and 53rd CDs, which have been ordered to concentrate in the Zhaboedovo, Shchuch'e, and Zharkovskii Station region (40-50 kilometers west of Belyi) by the end of the day on 21 July and which are subordinated to a [cavalry] group for a joint attack toward Dukhovshchina.

Deploy the group's headquarters in the Belyi region.

3. Group Kalinin [24th Army] – 53rd RC (89th, 91st, and 166th RDs), will advance to the Vop' River along the Vetlitsy (30 kilometers northeast of Iartsevo) and mouth of the Vop' River line by the end of the day on 22 July and be prepared to exploit the success of the attack by Group Khomenko.

166th RD will concentrate in the Miakishevo (20 kilometers southeast of Belyi), Petropol'e, and Nikitinka Station region by the end of the day on 22 July for operations in second echelon behind Group Khomenko.

4. Group Kachalov [28th Army], consisting of 149th and 145th RDs and 104th TD, will concentrate in the Krapivenskii, Vezhniki, and Roslavl' region by the end of the day on 21 July for an attack in the general direction of Smolensk on the morning of 22 July.

5. The commander of the Red Army's VVS will attach [the following] aviation by the end of the day on 21 July:

a) For Group Maslennikov – 31st AD;

b) For Group Khomenko – 190th AAR and 122nd FAR; and.

c) For Group Kachalov – 209th AAR and 239th FAR.

6. All groups will become subordinate to Comrade Timoshenko, the Commander-in-Chief of the Western Main Direction, from whom they will receive their missions when they reach their jumping-off positions.

Report receipt and fulfillment of this directive.

The Chief of the General Staff Army, General Zhukov

Source: "Direktiva Stavki VK komanduiushchemu voiskami Fronta Rezervnykh Armii o sozdanii operativnykh grupp voisk, ikh razvertyvanii dlia operatsii po razgromu Smolenskoi gruppirovki protivnika" [*Stavka* VK directive to the commander of the forces of the Front of Reserve Armies about the creation of operational groups of forces and their deployment for an operations for the destruction of the enemy Smolensk grouping], in Zolotarev, "*Stavka* 1941," 85

2. Combat Order No. 0076 of the Commander-in-Chief of the Western Direction's Forces of 21 July 1941 on the Destruction of the Enemy in the Vicinity of the City of Smolensk

Order No. 0076 to the Western Direction's Forces
21 July 1941

1. The enemy is striving to encircle our forces in the Smolensk region by the operations of large motor-mechanized units in the direction of Iartsevo and El'nia.

On 21 July the enemy concentrated 7th PzD in the Dukhovshchina region, 20th MotD in the Shchuch'e and Ozera region, and more than a tank division with infantry along the El'nia axis.

The enemy are striving to encircle the *front's* forces in the Mogilev, Smolensk, and Nevel' regions with their main forces.

2. Encircle and destroy the enemy east of Smolensk by concentrated attacks by the groups in the general direction of Smolensk: Khomenko – from the Belyi region; Rokossovsky – from the Iartsevo region; and Kachalov – from the Roslavl' region.

3. Group Maslennikov will reach the Chikhachi and Lake Zhizhitskoe line and protect the Toropets axis.

4. Group Khomenko, consisting of 242nd, 250th, 251st, and 166th RDs, the cavalry group (50th and 53rd CDs), 190th AAR, and 122nd FAR, will occupy its designated jumping-off positions and immediately dispatch strong forward detachments to the Dubovitsa, Zamosh'e; and Baturino line, after itself protecting the exits from the forested-swampy region toward the south.

Go over to the attack toward the Kholm and Dukhovshchina line on the morning of 23 July, with 166th RD echeloned behind the left wing, with the mission to encircle and destroy the enemy in the Dukhovshchina region, together with Group Rokossovsky, by 25 July.

Assign the cavalry group the mission – while operating from the Shchuch'e and Ozero region beginning on 23 July, reach the Demidov and Kholm line by 25 July.

Dispatch a strong flank detachment toward Velizh.

Assign the cavalry group [the following] missions: destruction of the enemy rear, headquarters, communications and groups and prevent an enemy attack against the main forces operating toward the south from Velizh.

Upon fulfillment of its assigned missions, Group Khomenko must have in mind operations toward Smolensk, while protecting itself along the Vitebsk axis.

Boundary on the left – Vetlitsy and Dukhovshchina (incl.).

5. Group Rokossovsky, consisting of 101st and 107th TDs, 91st, 89th, and 38th RDs, and 509th ATR, will occupy jumping-off positions along the Vop' River from

Vetlitsy to the mouth of the Vop'River, with mobile units in the Dukhovshchina and Iartsevo region.

Attack the enemy along the Dukhovshchina axis on the morning of 23 July and, in cooperation with Group Khomenko, destroy the enemy in the Shchuch'e, Ozero, Demidov, Dukhovshchina, and Iartsevo region.

Subsequently, have in view operations toward Smolensk.

6. Group Kachalov, consisting of 145th and 149th RDs, 104th TD, 209th AAR, and 239th FAR, while protecting itself [against attacks] from El'nia, will attack along the highway to Smolensk on 22 July and, while destroying the opposing enemy units, will reach the Engel'gartovskaia Station, Pochinok, and Khislavichi line by 23 July; subsequently, attack toward Smolensk while protecting itself [against attacks] from the west.

7. 20th Army, while stubbornly defending its existing positions, will disorganize the enemy's rear by active operations by groups toward Gorki.

8. 22nd Army will tie down [contain] the enemy with local attacks beginning on the morning of 22 July.

9. 13th Army will captured Propoisk and Krichev.

10. 21st Army will energetically fulfill its previously assigned missions.

11. The VVS of the armies will operate in the interests of the ground forces on the battlefield.

12. *Frontal* aviation:

a) Protect Rokossovsky's mobile group and Group Khomenko from the air throughout the entire operation;

b) Conduct an attack against groups of enemy in the Dukhovshchina region and neutralize his resistance in the course of operations by the mobile groups; and

c) Prevent an enemy attack against Group Kachalov from the west.

13. The operational post of the headquarters of the Western Direction's forces beginning on 22 July – Vadino Station.

14. Report orders given and received.

> The Commander-in-Chief of the Western Direction's forces,
>   Marshal of the Soviet Union S. Timoshenko
> The Member of the Military Council of the Western Direction, [signed]
> The Chief of Staff of the Western Direction,
>   Marshal of the Soviet Union Shaposhnikov

Source: "Boevoi prikaz Glavnokomanduiushchego voiskami Zapadnogo Napravleniia No. 0076 ot 21 iiulia 1941 g. na unichtozhenie protivnika v raione gor. Smolensk" [Combat order no. 0076 of the commander-in-chief of the Western Direction's forces of 21 July 1941 on the destruction of the enemy in the vicinity of the city of Smolensk], in *SBDVOV*, issue 37, 42-43.

3. Report of the Chief of the Operations Department of the Headquarters of the Main Command of the Western Direction of 21 July 1941 to the Chief of Staff about the Creation of Reserves (see Map 4)

To the Chief of Staff of the Western Direction

A Report about the Creation of Reserves

At the present time, the Western Front does not have the necessary reserves to counter penetrations by the enemy and surprises and for developing success.

According to the concentration plan there should have been two reserve armies – the 19th and 4th. However, the former was concentrated southeast of Vitebsk, at a time when the front passed along the Lepel' and Tolochin line, that is, at a distance of 100-150 kilometers, and 4th Army was formed in the Propoisk region, with two divisions in the Novozybkov region, that is, at a distance of 40 kilometers from the front lines. Such a distance of the reserve armies from the front does not protect their concentration and formation, that is, with present offensive tempos (40 kilometers per day), the units have been subjected to chance and uninterrupted actions of enemy aviation.

The course of events in the presence of the enemy's second consecutive operation has confirmed the above.

The units, not being ready, were forced into battle in piecemeal fashion, without command and control means and their rear [services] (19th Army) and poorly organized and armed (4th Army), and the *front* lost its reserves during the course of the first few days.

In order to avoid a similar phenomenon, I request [the following]:

1. Withdraw all units that have suffered great losses of personnel and equipment: 64th, 108th, 10th, and 161st RDs and the headquarters of 2nd and 44th RCs with corps units, to the Gzhatsk and Medyn' region for filling out and material resupply over the next 5-7 days.

2. Together with the headquarters of 44th RC, you include 35th RC from 13th Army in 16th Army, having subordinated to it 158th, 127th, and 50th RDs and, after entrusting 35th RC with assembling and re-forming 158th, 127th, and 50th RDs, take in the units arriving in the Roslavl' region. Re-form 50th RD at the front.

3. Withdraw the headquarters of 19th and 4th Armies into the rear area, with the 19th Army stationed at Medyn' and 4th Army at Sukhinichi.

Subordinate the headquarters of 34th RC and 129th, 158th, 127th, 38th, and 134th RDs to 16th Army.

4. Withdraw the remnants of 7th and 17th MCs and 24th, 137th, 132nd, 148th, and 160th RDs to the Sukhinichi region. Form two [100-series] tank divisions from the mechanized corps.

Entrust the headquarters of 4th Army with the formation of the formations [divisions] indicated above.

5. Include 121st and 155th RDs, which are forming, in 21st Army, having entrusted it with their formation, chiefly their rearmament, and having obliged, in the first instance, the Artillery Directorate of the *front* to supply these divisions with artillery weapons.

6. Form two automobile regiments each in 4th and 19th Armies' locations at the expense of vehicles which can be taken by road from units withdrawing from the front. Employ these automobile regiments exclusively as reserves of the *front* for maneuvering reserves.

7. Complete all measures for the withdrawal of units reorganizing and rearming for 19th Army no later than 27 July and for 4th Army – no later than 3-5 August.

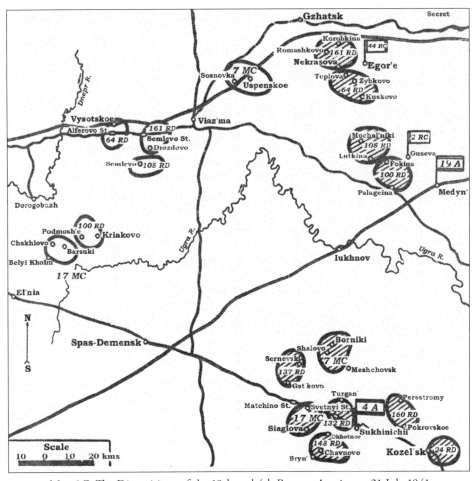

Map 3C: The Dispositions of the 19th and 4th Reserve Armies on 21 July 1941

Attachment: A map of the dispositions of the armies (19th and 4th Armies) (**see Map 4**).

The Chief of the Operations Department of the headquarters of the
Western Direction, *Kombrig* Liubarsky
The Deputy Chief of the Operations Department, Colonel Fomin

Source: "Doklad nachal'nika operativnogo otdela shtaba Glavnogo Komandovaniia Zapadnogo Napravleniia ot 21 iiulia 1941 g. nachal'niku shtaba o sozdanii rezervov" [Report of the chief of the Operations Department of the headquarters of the Main Command of the Western Direction of 21 July 1941 to the chief of staff about the creation of reserves], in *SBDVOV*, issue 37, 44-45.

4. Combat Order No. 035 of the Commander of the Forces of 28th Army of 22 July 1941 on the Attack by the Army's Group of Forces toward Smolensk

Combat Order No. 035, Headquarters, 28th Army,
Perenka State Farm, 2300 hours on 22 July 1941
1:50,000 scale map

1. The enemy, while protecting himself with separate detachments along the Krichev. Mstislavl', Khislovichi, and Pochinok line, is trying to encircle our forces in the Smolensk region.

2. On the right, 24th and 28th Armies are defending and continuing to develop defenses along the Vop' River, Uzha River, El'nia River, Desna River to Zhukovka, Zhagi, Krasnoe, and Sosnovka line.

On the left, 13th Army is tying the enemy down with energetic short duration attacks along the Propoisk and Krichev lines.

Frontal aviation has the mission of preventing an enemy against our group of forces from the west.

3. The Group of Forces [Group Kachalov] (149th and 145th RDs, 104th TD, [31st] MRR,, 643rd CAR, 364th CAR, 209th AAR, and 239th FAR), while protecting themselves from the side of El'nia and destroying the opposing enemy, will attack the rear of the enemy's El'nia grouping in the direction of Smolensk. Reach the Strigino, Pochinok, and Trutnevo line by day's end of 23 July, and, subsequently, attack toward Smolensk. Begin the attack – 0400 hours on 23 July 1941 [penciled entry 2200 hours on 22 July 1941.

4. 149th RD, with 320th RGK GAR and 1st Bn, 488th CAR, will capture the Chernavka, Voroshilovo, and Likhnovo line at first light on 23 July 1941. Subsequently seize crossings in the Khmara and Machuly State Farm sector with strong advanced guards.

Subsequently capture Pochinok.

Boundary on the left – (incl.) the Roslavl' road and Smolensk.

5. 145th RD, with 643rd and 364th CARs, 3rd Bn, 649th CAR, and 3rd Bn, 489th HAR, and 4th Bn, 753rd ATR, will reach the Panacovka, Golubi, and Nov-Derebuzh region by first light on 23 July 1941. Drive the enemy from the line of the Stomet' River and capture the Vas'kovo Station, Zamostitse, and Mikhailovka line with strong advanced guards.

Subsequently have in mind [plan to] seizing crossings over the Khmara River in the sector of the Roslavl' road, Smolensk, Bol'shaia Inochka, and Malye Lipki.

6. Allocate the 3rd Rifle Battalion of the composite regiment, which is subordinate to your army, for securing the Warsaw road toward Krichev.

7. 104th TD will concentrate – Khmara, Nikanorovka, and Gvozdovka by 1500 23 July 1941 and be prepared for combined operations with 149th and 145th RDs for the seizure of the Pochinok region.

8. The motorized regiment – my reserve, will concentrate in the vicinity of the woods at Dubrovka by 1400 hours of 23 July 1941, having in mind developing success along the Roslavl'-Smolensk road.

9. The VVS will support the attacking units and suppress the enemy defending the crossings over the Stomet' River in the period 0600-0800 23 July 1941 and, subsequently, over the Khmara River.

10. The headquarters of the Operational Group from 1200 hours on 23 July 1941 – the woods west of Lysovka.

11. The basing of the group of forces – Roslavl'.

The Commander of 28th Army, Lieutenant General Kachalov
The Member of the Military Council of the Army,
    Brigade Commissar Kolesnikov
The Chief of Staff of the headquarters, Colonel Zuev

Source: "Boevoi prikaz komanduiushchego voiskami 28-i Armii no. 035 ot 22 iiulia 1941 g. na nastuplenie gruppoi voisk armii v napravlenii Smolensk" [Combat order no. 035 of the commander of the forces of 28th Army of 22 July 1941 on the attack of the army's group of forces toward Smolensk], *SBDVOV*, issue 37, 348.

5. Combat Order No. 037 of the Headquarters of 28th Army of 23 July 1941 about the Elimination of Shortcoming in the Combat Operations of the Forces

Combat Order No. 037, Headquarters, 28th Army,
the woods southeast of Stodolishche, 23 July 1941
1: 50,000 scale map

1. As a result of the fighting on 23 July 1941, the defending units of the enemy have been thrown back behind the Stomet' River. The enemy withdrew during the first and decisive onslaught.

2. The units have not fulfilled the missions assigned for 23 July.

a) [The following] has been noted: a) the completely inadequate tempo of advance of both 145th and 149th RDs. 104th TD lagged behind intolerably;

b) There is no audacity of the part of the commanders, beginning with the squad leaders;

c) A desire to attack frontally predominates. Brush and woods are not exploited for local envelopments of the enemy's flanks;

d) Instead of reinforcing the onslaught and accelerating the movement of the retreating enemy, they frequently pursue on all fours [by crawling forward];

e) The power of infantry fire to suppress firing points and advance forward is not fully exploited;

f) The artillery is slow in fulfilling assigned missions because the artillery observers lag behind the infantry; and

g) Observation of the battlefield is poorly organized. This explains the scantiness of information about the strength and actions of the enemy.

3. The commander orders:

1) 145th and 149th RDs will continue to fulfill the missions assigned to them for 23 July. The attack will begin at 0400 hours on 24 July.

2) Eliminate all deficiencies pointed out above.

3) Secure complete cooperation between the infantry and artillery and bring artillery forward in timely fashion, while not permitting it to lag behind the infantry. You are obliged to echelon the artillery. When there is any sort of hold up of the infantry, artillery fire will pave the way and observers and commanders of batteries will work on behalf of the infantry leaders (commanders of platoons and companies). As a rule, regimental artillery will move forward within the combat formations of the infantry.

4. [editor – there was no paragraph 4 in the order]

5. Conduct reconnaissance and night "snatches" in the sector of every regiment on the night of 23-24 July to seize prisoners.

6. The operational group and CPs [command posts] will move forward closer to their units to control the fighting directly.

7. Report about the results of the fighting every four hours by short messages, telegrams, radiograms, and signals about positions achieved and the actions of the enemy.

> The Chief of Staff of 28th Army, Major General Egorov
> The Brigade Commissar of the army's headquarters,
> Senior Political Worker [*Politruk*] Simansky
> The Chief of the Operations Department of the Army's headquarters,
> Colonel Zuev

Source: "Boevoe rasporiazhenie shtaba 28-i Armii no. 037 ot 23 iiulia 1941 g. ob ustranenii nedostatkov v boevykh deistviiakh voisk" [Combat order no. 037 of the headquarters of 28th Army of 23 July 1941 about the elimination of shortcoming in the combat operations of the forces], *SBDVOV*, issue 37, 349.

6. Excerpt from Operational Summary No. 55 of the Headquarters of the Western Front at 2000 hours on 23 July 1941 about the Combat Operations of the *Front's* Forces

Operational Summary No. 55 of the Headquarters of the Western Front
at 2000 hours 23 July 1941,
1: 500,000 scale map

Group Maslennikov moved forward to the Chikhachi and Lake Zhizhitskoe line at 0600 hours on 23 July, 250th and 251st RDs reached the Belyi line, and 242nd RD was echeloned to the rear on the march at 0600 hours on the 23rd [erroneous, because the inked in entry, "250th, 251st, and 242nd RDs were in Group Khomenko rather than Group Maslennikov"].

243ᵈ RD unloaded at Skvortsovo Station at 1000 hours on 23 July to occupy the Dubrovka and Zasenovo line.

Headquarters of the group– Martiukhova … ..

Group Kalinin. The units of the group were concentrated in their jumping off positions for the attack on 23 July:

91st RD was concentrated in the Vetlitsa, Pecheninki, and Syrokoren'e region; and 89th RD – in the Retaze and Ivanino region.

There is no information about 166th RD.

Headquarters of the group – Vadino Station … .

Group Khomenko. Information has not been received about the positions of its units.

Group Rokossovsky. After fighting along the Vop'River, the units of this group were concentrating along the eastern bank of the Vop'River in jumping-off positions for the attack.

107th TD reached the Korytnia, Pochinok, and Pokikhino region [probably referring to Group Khomenko's 104th TD].

Information about the positions of 101st TD has not been received.

38th RD, under repeated raids by enemy aircraft and enemy artillery and mortar fire, withdrew and dug in along the eastern bank of the Vop'River, destroying the crossings behind it.

Headquarters of the group – Krasnobaenka … ..

Group Kachalov dislodged the enemy's forward units by 1700 hours on 23 July and, while under constant pressure by enemy aircraft, was fighting for the crossings over the Stomet' River (18 kilometers southeast of Pochinok).

Headquarters of the group – Stodolishche … .

Source: "Operativnaia svodka shtaba Zapadnogo fronta No. 55 k 20 chasam 23 iiulia 1941 g. o boevykh deistviiakh voisk fronta" [Operational summary no. 55 of the headquarters of the Western Front of 2000 hours on 23 July 1941 about the combat operations of the *front's* forces], in *SBDVOV,* issue 37, 101-102.

7. Report of the Military Council of the Western Direction of 24 July 1941 to the *Stavka* of the High Command about the Situation in the Western Front

To Comrade Stalin

Copies: To the Chief of the General Staff of the Red Army, Comrade Zhukov

1700 hours on 24 July 1941

As a result of sustained fighting in Smolensk, the units of 16th Army are continuing to hold on to the northern, northwestern, and eastern parts of the city, all the while attacking the enemy who occupied the southern and southwestern parts of the city. After two days of enemy counterattacks, 127th and 158th Rifle Divisions of 34th RC, which have been attacking from the south against the southern part of Smolensk, suffering heavy losses, withdrew behind the Dnepr in the Korolevo and Lozheikovo region. At 1600 hours on 23 July, a motorized regiment formed from the withdrawn 17th MC (1,600 bayonets) was thrown in by us from Iartsevo to Comrade Lukin [16th Army].

The 20th Army of Comrade Kurochkin, while holding off attacks by up to 7 enemy divisions, inflicted defeat on two German divisions, especially the newly-arrived 5th Infantry Division, which was attacking toward Rudnia and toward the east. Especially effective and successful action in the smashing of 5th Infantry Division was a battery of "RS" [Rocket artillery], which inflicted such losses on it by three volleys against the enemy concentrated in Rudnia that it rescued wounded and picked up the dead all day long, having halted the offensive for an entire day. Three volleys remain in the battery. We request you send another two-three batteries with shells. The 20th Army is regrouping its 5th MC and protecting the rear of Comrade Lukin, as well as preparing itself, in cooperation with Comrade Khomenko, for an attack in the rear of the enemy's Iartsevo grouping.

A bloody battle has been going on in the Iartsevo region for three days, with heavy losses on both sides, during which the enemy is employing massive air strikes and is destroying our artillery and inflicting heavy losses on our infantry when they counterattack.

Today, on the morning of 24 July, a part of Comrade Rokossovsky's group which has been operating at Iartsevo was forced to withdraw to the eastern bank of the Vop' River, where it has dug in. The offensive by Comrades Khomenko's and Kalinin's Groups and 107th Tank Division, as well, began this morning. Enemy aircraft attacked Comrade Khomenko. Information from air reconnaissance indicates that the enemy is concentrating groups for an attack in the Velizh region, and we have noted movement of his columns from this region both toward the northeast and to the north – toward Toropets.

Today, according to information from air reconnaissance at 1218 hours, motor-mechanized units are moving along the road from Vitebsk toward Smolensk. Thus, the enemy is preparing counterattacks against our attacking Group of Comrade Khomenko and the Group of Comrade Kalinin.

In the El'nia region, according to air reconnaissance, the enemy are withdrawing to the west. We still have no information from the headquarters of Bogdanov's *front* regarding how the fighting is going on at El'nia. We urgently believe it necessary 19th Rifle Division, reinforced by a tank battalion at the expense of 105th Tank Division, continue to pursue the enemy so that it will then be committed to the Group of Comrade Kachalov. Our experience over the past two days indicates that Comrade Bogdanov's *front* and 24th Army's commander [Kalinin] lack communications with their units and, therefore, do not know what they are doing at the forward edge of the defense in timely enough fashion. It is necessary to pay attention to the reliability of communications both in Comrade Bogdanov's *front* and in his armies.

Today, on the second day [of his offensive], the Group of Comrade Kachalov is fighting in the region south of Pochinok.

In 13th Army, the Mogilev corps, which is surrounded by 5 infantry divisions, defeated two enemy divisions as a result of sustained fighting, especially on 22 and 23 July. The Germans organized a ring around Mogilev, and the commander of 13th Army has been ordered to begin an attack to link up with the Mogilev Corps, together with the units of 21st Army and 4th Army, while putting his army in order.

The enemy has very quickly gathered his forces against 21st Army and already disposes of three corps. It is necessary to speed up the concentration of Group Comrade Gorodovikov since it can be too late.

Velikie Luki is in our hands. The enemy, while withdrawing from Velikie Luki to Nevel', is holding on in two groups and trying to encircle the corps of Comrade Markov [51st Rifle Corps commanded by Major General Akim Petrovich Markov], to which units of 22nd Army are moving to assist. The main forces of 22nd Army are occupying positions behind the Lovat' River.

All efforts are being made to destroy the enemy north of Smolensk, straighten out the front to the south, and create routes to resupply the forces whose mission is to advance forward quickly to the Vitebsk, Orsha, and Mogilev line.

> The Commander-in-Chief of the Western Direction's forces,
>   Marshal of the Soviet Union S. Timoshenko
> The Member of the Military Council of the Western Direction, [signed]
> The Chief of Staff of the Western Direction,
>   Marshal of the Soviet Union Shaposhnikov

Source: "Doklad Voennogo Soveta Zapadnogo Napravleniia ot 24 iiulia 1941 g. Stavke Verkhovnogo Komandovaniia ob obstanovke na Zapadnom fronte" [Report of the Military Council of the Western Direction of 24 July 1941 to the *Stavka* of the High Command about the situation in the Western Front], in *SBDVOV*, issue 37, 50-51.

8. Combat Order No. 042 of the Headquarters of 28th Army of 24 July 1941 about a Continuation of the Offensive

To the Commanders of 145th and 149th RDs and 104th TD
To the Chief of the Group's Artillery and the Chief of Auto-Armored Forces (ABT)
Combat Order No. 042, Headquarters, 28th Army,
the forest southeast of Stodolishche,
2300 hours on 24 July 1941
1:50,000 scale map

The combat operations on 24 July achieved success and the units advanced forward only in the sector of 145th RD (along one axis).

The commander of 149th RD, Major General [Fedor Dmitrievich] Zakharov, did not organize for combat.

The artillery within the RGK (*Stavka* Reserve), corps, and force artillery operated at maximum distances without cooperating with the infantry.

As a result, the units, having encountered organized resistance by an insignificant enemy force, not only did not advance forward but also withdrew loosing points they seized the day before.

The Military Council takes notice of and demands that commanders, commissars, and political workers directly control the fighting, be is their companies and battalions, and, in particular, when necessary, compel their units to fulfill their assigned mission by personnel example.

The army commander orders:

1. Continue to fulfill your assigned missions on 25 July, especially the commander of 149th RD, who allowed the withdrawal of his units from the positions they previously occupied.

2. The commander of 104th TD will allocate 5 T-34 tanks under the command of a decisive commander and place them at the disposal of the commander of 149th RD in the Lysovka region by 0500 hours. The remainder of the forces will put themselves in combat readiness during the night for possible operations toward the north and northwest. Strengthen reconnaissance and combat security during the night.

3. The commanders of 145th and 149th RDs will replace the losses in their companies at the expense of those who fled to the rear and truncation of specialized units and rear service organs and allocate all of those combat capable and weaponry to the rifle and machine gun companies.

4. Seize prisoners and capture separate points in the enemy's defense system during the night by decisive reconnaissance raids and reconnaissances-in-force.

5. Deploy "hunters" [okhotniki] and throw separate well-armed groups into the rear of the enemy's defenses.

6. Warn the soldiers, commanders, and political workers that we will take severe measures right up to execution for the loss and abandonment of weapons of the battlefield. Deploy commands from the Supply, Food, and other department forward to the battlefield for the collection of weapons from the dead as well as trophies [captured equipment].

7. The chief of the group's artillery, personally and with his own staff, will be in the combat formations of the divisions' artillery units and will not permit firing without forward observation posts in the infantry subunits and firing on unobserved targets.

> The Chief of Staff of the army, Major General Egorov
> The Brigade Military Commissar,
>   Senior Political Worker [Politruk] Simansky
> The Chief of the Operations Department of the Army's headquarters,
>   Colonel Zuev

Source: "Boevoe rasporiazhenie shtaba 28-i Armii no. 042 ot 24 iiulia 1941 g. o prodolzhenii nastupleniia" [Combat order no. 042 of the headquarters of 28th Army of 24 July 1941 about a continuation of the offensive], *SBDVOV*, issue 37, 350.

9. Combat Order of the Commander-in-Chief of the Western Direction's Forces of 25 July 1941 to the Commander of the Central Front's Forces on an Offensive in the General Direction of Mogilev

Copies: To the Commander of the Central Front
           To the Commander of the Western Front
           To the Chief of the General Staff
           1810 hours on 25 July 1941

1. We are counterattacking against the enemy facing the Western Front to the north and south of Smolensk.

The enemy facing the Central Front, having captured Krichev, are continuing their encirclement of the Mogilev corps, and our cavalry are raiding in the enemy's rear.

2. I am ordering the Central Front immediately to clear its rear area of the Red Army soldiers and commanders scattered throughout and send them to fill out the divisions.

Exploiting the raid by our cavalry {Gorodovikov], 13th Army and the right wing of 21st Army will immediately go over to the attack in the general direction of Mogilev, with the mission to link up with the Mogilev corps, while 13th Army protects the left flank of Group Kachalov, while having in mind a subsequent advance to the Dnepr River.

3. Take decisive measures to organize the *front's* and armies' rears.

4. Report orders given.

> The Commander-in-Chief of the Western Direction, S. Timoshenko
> The Member of the Military Council of the Western Direction [signed]
> The Chief of Staff, B. Shaposhnikov

Source: "Boevoi prikaz Glavnokomanduiushchego voiskami Zapadnogo Napravleniia ot 25 iiulia 1941 g. komanduiushchemu voiskami Tsentral'nogo fronta na nastuplenie v obshchem napravlenii na Mogilev" [Combat order of the commander-in-chief of the Western Direction's forces of 25 July 1941 to the commander of the Central Front's forces on an offensive in the general direction of Mogilev], in *SBDVOV*, issue 37, 51-52.

10. Combat Order No. 046 of the Headquarters of 28th Army of 26 July 1941 to the Army's Operational Group of Forces about Seizing Crossings over the Khmara River

To the Commanders of 145th and 149th RDs and 104th TD
Combat Order No. 046/op, Headquarters, 28th Army,
to Group Headquarters in the forest southeast of Lysovka,
0100 hours on 26 July 1941
1: 100,000 map

The army commander orders that the main mission on 26 July will be the seizure of crossings over the Khmara River, to which end:

1. 145th RD will seize crossings along the Tsyganovka Commune and Kiselevka line [10 kilometers south and south-southwest of Pochinok] with its forward units by the end of the day on 26 July.

2. 149th RD, with 4 T-34 tanks, will destroy the enemy in front of the division and reach the line of the Khmara River in the Ponizovka and railroad line sector [10 kilometers south and south-southeast of Pochinok] with its forward units by the end of the day.

3. 104th TD, while facilitating the rapid advance of the group with a detachment consisting of 5 T-34 tanks, 5 BT-7 tanks, and a battalion of motorized infantry under the command of the commander of the motorized rifle regiment, will capture the Egorovka, Kazatchina, and Kukueva region [14-17 kilometers southeast of Pochinok]. The remaining forces of the division will remain in the positions they occupy and,

without revealing themselves, conduct reconnaissance toward the east and 53rd RD, while establishing communications with it. Conduct reconnaissance northeastward as far as Verbilovo [31 kilometers east of Pochinok] to determine whether or not the enemy occupies this point and toward the north to determine the presence of the enemy in the villages of Poguliaevka, Sviridovka, and Shumaevo [22-27 kilometers east-southeast of Pochinok].

The Chief of Staff, Major General Egorov
The Military Commissar, Senior Political Worker [*Politruk*] Simansky
The Chief of the Operations Department, Colonel Zuev

Source: "Boevoe rasporiazhenie shtaba 28-i Armii no. 046 ot 26 iiulia 1941 g. operativnoi gruppe voisk armii na zakhvat pereprav cherez r. Khmara" [Combat order no. 046 of the headquarters of 28th Army of 26 July 1941 to the army's operational group of forces about seizing crossings over the Khmara River], *SBDVOV*, issue 37, 351.

11. Combat Order No. 077 of the Commander of the Western Front's Forces of 26 July 1941 to Group Khomenko on the Destruction of the Enemy in the Dukhovshchina Region

Order No. 077 to the Western Front's Forces
0240 hours on 26 July 1941

1. Insignificant forces of the enemy's 20th PzD, not more than a single regiment, are operating in front of Group Khomenko.

7th PzD is defending in the Dukhovshchina region.

2. The mission of the *front* remains as before – the destruction of the enemy in the Dukhovshchina region by the combined operations of Groups Khomenko and Kalinin.

3. On the right, units of 22nd Army and Group Maslennikov are defending along the Lovat' River and Lake Zhizhetskoe line.

On the left, units of [Group] Kalinin are defending along the Vop'River.

4. Decision: Press the enemy into the swamp and destroy him; subsequently, by attacking toward the southwest, encircle the enemy's Dukhovshchina grouping.

5. Group Khomenko:

250th RD will destroy the enemy in the Okolitsa region and, subsequently, develop the attack toward Svity. Capture the Sutoki region by the end of the day.

Boundary on the left – (incl.) Lukino, Usty, and (incl.) Morokhovo Station.

242nd RD will develop the offensive in the general direction of Chalishchev, Berezovka, and Boldino. Capture the Boldino, Deviatoe, and Tychinki region by the end of the day.

Boundary on the left – Kholomidina, Baturino, and Shelepy.

251st RD will attack toward Teribki and Baturino and capture the Pozhinki, Sukharevo, and Lelimovo region by the end of the day on 26 July.

6. 166th RD, operating from the Korytnia and Pokikino front toward the west, together with the tank division, will destroy the opposing enemy and reach

the Novo-Vysokoe, Krapivnia, and Pochinok front and all points 8 kilometers south of Baturino.

Headquarters of the division – along the Novo-Pokrovskoe and Bogoliubovo axis.

7. 107th TD will operate toward Baturino, Pozhinki, and Lelimovo and, in cooperation with 251st and 166th RDs, will destroy the enemy in the Baturino region, after which it will concentrate in the Lelemovo and Nifki region.

8. The cavalry group, under the command of *Kombrig* Mel'nik, will operate along the Komarovo and Dukhovshchina axis and, while avoiding frontal combat, will envelop the enemy grouping from the flank.

Disrupt work in the enemy's rear and his command and control by audacious operations and destroy his communications.

Reach the Ovsiannikovo and Muzhitskov line by the end of the day.

9. VVS. 1. Group aviation will cooperate with the ground forces on the battlefield. 2. *Frontal* aviation: a) will conduct air strikes against the enemy in the Demidov and Dukhovshchina region; and b) cooperate with the aviation of Group Khomenko by means of suppressing artillery fire after preliminary reconnaissance in the regions southwest of Baturino. 3. Protect the operations of the forces from enemy aviation.

10. Operational post of Group Khomenko beginning at 0700 hours on 26 July – the Polynets region.

The Commander-in-Chief of the Western Front,
Lieutenant General Eremenko
The Member of the Military Council, Division Commissar Lestev
The Chief of Staff, Lieutenant General Malandin

Source: "Boevoi prikaz komanduiushchego voiskami Zapadnogo fronta No. 077 ot 26 iiulia 1941 g. Gruppe Khomenko na unichtozhenie protivnika v raione Dukhovshchina" [Combat order no. 077 of the commander of the Western Front's forces of 26 July 1941 to Group Khomenko on the destruction of the enemy in the Dukhovshchina region], in *SBDVOV*, issue 37, 108-109.

12. Individual Combat Order of the Commander-in-Chief of the Western Direction's Forces of 26 July 1941 to the Commander of Group Lieutenant General Maslennikov on an Offensive in the Direction of Demidov

To the Commander of Group Comrade Maslennikov
Copies: To the Commander of 22nd Army, Comrade Ershakov
          To the Commander of the Western Front, Comrade Eremenko
0430 hours on 26 July 1941

1. For the purpose of quickly liquidating the enemy's Iartsevo-Dukhovshchina grouping, I am ordering you to deploy to the Olenitsa and Sevast'ianovo sector along Western Dvina River with two rifle divisions on 26 July and, having crossed the Western Dvina River, attack toward Il'ino and further to Demidov, while protecting yourself [against attack] from the Velizh region with strong flank detachments.

2. Leave one rifle division along the Sloboda, Nazimovo Station, and Zolotukhino front, inclusive, for the protection of Toropets from the west, having subordinated

it to the commander of 22nd Army, Comrade Ershakov. Dig the divisions in and take all measures for antiaircraft defense.

3. Report fulfillment.

Timoshenko, Shaposhnikov

Source: "Chastnyi boevoi prikaz Glavnokomanduiushchego voiskami Zapadnogo Napravleniia ot 26 iiulia 1941 g. komanduiushchemu Gruppoi General-Leitenantu Maslennikovu na nastuplenie v napravlenii Demidov" [Individual combat order of the commander-in-chief of the Western Direction's forces of 26 July 1941 to the commander of Group Lieutenant General Maslennikov on an offensive in the direction of Demidov], in SBDVOV, issue 37, 52.

13. Extract from Operational Summary No. 59 of the Headquarters of the Western Front at 0800 hours on 26 July 1941 about the Combat Operations of the *Front's* Forces

Operational Summary No. 59 at 0800 hours on 26 July,
Headquarters, Western Front
1:500,000 scale map

Group Maslennikov completed its concentration on the morning of 25 July and continued preparation of the Chikhachi and Lake Zhizhitskoe defensive line.

256th RD – in the Chikhachi, Nazimovo Station, and Selishche (23 kilometers west of Toropets) region.

252nd RD – in the Dubrovna, Borodkina, and Suslovo region.

243rd RD, in second echelon, occupies defenses in the Sementsevo, Ershevo, and Ladygovo region. On the Western Dvina River, a reinforced rifle regiment from Group Maslennikov was thrown in against Il'ino on the night of 26 July.

Headquarters of the group – Selishche (10 kilometers southwest of Toropets ... ..

Group Kachalov continued its attack toward Pochinok, while encountering stubborn enemy resistance on its right wing and reached [the following] by the end of the day on 25 July:

104th TD – Kovaly and Zabor'e, with its forward units along the Riabtsy, Solovka, and Seminovo line;

149th RD – on the Nikulino and Osinovka line; and

145th RD captured Maslovka Station and Dmitrievka.

Headquarters of the group – west of Kovrigin Kholm.

Group Khomenko was continuing to fight with enemy motorized infantry along a line 2 kilometers north of Chernyi Ruchei on 25 July.

250th RD captured Okolitsa and continued its attack on Chernyi Ruchei, having before it up to a battalion of infantry from 20th Motorized Division, a reinforced artillery battalion, and 25-30 mortars.

242nd RD reached the Sergeevka line, having before it up to a battalion of infantry, a reinforced battery of artillery, and 25-30 mortars.

251st RD (less one rifle regiment) went over to the attack from the Petropol'e line at 2000 hours on 25 July, with the mission of assisting 107th TD.

Information has not been received about the positions of 50th and 53rd CDs.

Headquarters of the group – west of Panovo.

Group Kalinin fought for Lelimovo and Korytnia with one division and for northern Iartsevo with two divisions during the day.

166th RD crossed from Lelimovo toward the south at 1100 hours on 24 July with one rifle regiment. At the same time, 107th TD, after reaching a line 4-8 kilometers southwest of Pochinok, engaged in combat with enemy motorized infantry with tanks.

By this time, having received an order, 166th RD began a withdrawal. The enemy exploited 166th RD's withdrawal and went over to the attack from Erokhov toward Korytnia to envelop 107th TD's right flank, and, because of this, the latter began a withdrawal. By 0900 on 25 July, two [regimental] columns [of 107th TD] occupied a line 4-6 kilometers northwest of Pakikino, and one regiment put itself in order in the region 6 kilometers northeast of Pakikino.

By this time, 166th RD, having withdrawn its regiment from Lelimovo, reached the Korytnia region, having protected 107th TD with its right wing and protected the left flank of 107th TD in the Pakikino region with its other regiment, the third regiment of 166th RD concentrated in the region 6 kilometers east of Korytnia.

According to information [received] at 1420 hours of 25 July, 107th TD was fighting with the enemy (up to one motorized division) in the region 4-8 kilometers northwest of Pochinok. Repeated attacks by an enemy force of up to two battalions of tanks, one regiment of motorized infantry, and two artillery battalions were repulsed at 1830 hours with heavy losses for both sides.

91st and 89th RDs are digging in along the eastern bank of the Vop'River from Sediba to Shamovo.

Group Rokossovsky's 38th RD and 101st TD continued to hold on to the Dubrovo and Iartsevo sector on the eastern bank of the Vop'River all day on 25 July, while repelling all enemy attacks, in readiness to go over to the attack at 1700 hours on 25 July, with the mission of destroying the enemy Iartsevo grouping.

According to information from Kalinin, the enemy is bringing up small groups of infantry on vehicles to Rokossovsky's *front* … ..

For the Chief of Staff of the Western Front,
Marshal of the Soviet Union Shaposhnikov

Source: "Operativnaia svodka shtaba Zapadnogo fronta No. 59 k 8 chasam 26 iiulia 1941 g. o boevykh deistviiakh voisk fronta" [Operational summary no. 59 of the headquarters of the Western Front of 0800 hours on 26 July 1941 about the combat operations of the *front's* forces], in *SBDVOV*, issue 37, 106-107.

14. Combat Order No. 047/op of the Headquarters of 28th Army of 26 July 1941 to the Army's Operational Group of Forces about a Continuation of the Offensive, with the Aim of Seizing Crossings over the Khmara River

Combat Order No. 047/op, Headquarters, 28th Army,
the forest 1 kilometer southeast of Stodolishche,
to the Forces of Operational Group Comrade Kachalov,
2100 hours on 26 July 1941

1. The group's units, while attacking in the general direction of Pochinok on the right wing on 26 July 1941, reached [the following positions]:

104th TD – Pustosh', Fadeeva Buda, Timakhovka, and Kalinovka [27-29 kilometers southeast of Pochinok];

149th RD – Chernavka, Voroshilovo, and (incl.) Lyndovka [24-26 kilometers south-southeast of Pochinok]; and

145th RD – Osinovka, Poluevo, Martynovka, and Barsukovskie Farm [24-28 kilometers south of Pochinok], having not permitted a withdrawal on its left wing.

2. The operational group, while tying the enemy down in the Osinovka and Barsukovskie Farm sector and further along the Khmara River to Novyi Derebuzh [24-38 kilometers south of Pochinok], will destroy the opposing enemy with its main forces on 27 July 1941 and reach the Shumaevo [24 kilometers east-southeast of Pochinok] and Machuly State Farm sector [10 kilometers southeast of Pochinok], while seizing crossings over the Khmara River.

The commander of the army orders:

104th TD, after destroying the enemy's Shumaevo grouping, will capture crossings over the Khmara River in the Poguliaevka and Egorovka sector [24 kilometers east to 28 kilometers east-southeast of Pochinok]. Conduct reinforced reconnaissance against this grouping and, after determining its presence, smash it with short attacks. Report on the commencement of operations by wire or radio.

149th RD will capture crossings over the Khmara River in the Ponizovka [24 kilometers southeast of Pochinok] and railroad line sector [7 kilometers south of Pochinok]. Beforehand, destroy the enemy remaining in the Voroshilovo region. Retain no less than a regiment is second echelon.

145th RD will defend the Osinovka and Stomiatka region [24 kilometers south-southeast to 30 kilometers south of Pochinok] region and further along the Khmara River, while keeping no fewer than two companies in the Novyi Derebuzh region. Have in mind a subsequent advance together with 149th RD's 340th and 729th RRs. Dig trenches during the night.

All of the divisions will send out reconnaissance units and separate reconnaissance groups during the night with the mission to determine the strength and composition of the enemy and to seize controlled prisoners.

The motorized rifle regiment [31st] will remain in the Kubarki region [10 kilometers southeast of Stodolishche], after allocating one company to the disposal of the commander of 145th RD for the purposes of reconnaissance.

The beginning of the attack – 0500 hours on 27 July 1941.

Reporting by 149th RD and 104th TD – will be in accordance with the radio signal table, by telephone, and by special courier.

The Chief of Staff of 28th Army, Major General Egorov

Source: "Boevoe rasporiazhenie shtaba 28-i Armii no. 047/op ot 26 iiulia 1941 g. operativnoi gruppe voisk armii o prodolzhenii nastupleniia s tsel'iu zakhvat pereprav cherez r. Khmara" [Combat order no. 047/op of the headquarters of 28th Army of 26 July 1941 to the army's operational group of forces about a continuation of the offensive with the aim of seizing crossings over the Khmara River], *SBDVOV*, issue 37, 351.

15. Individual Combat Order of the Commander-in-Chief of the Western Direction's Forces of 26 July 1941 to the Commander of Group Comrade Kalinin on an Offensive in the General Direction of Shchelkin

Copies: To the Commander of Group Comrade Kalinin
To the Commander of Group Comrade Rokossovsky
To the Commander of Group Comrade Khomenko
To the Commander of the Western Front, Comrade Eremenko

2330 hours on 26 July 1941

1. The enemy, with a force of 1 motorized division, supported by tanks, is holding back the offensive by Group Khomenko and 166th RD and 107th Tank Division.

The Germans conducted an attack against Group Comrade Rokossovsky all day on 26 July, while trying to cross to the eastern bank of the Dnepr River.

2. Group Comrade Khomenko reached the Okolitsa, Sergeevka, and Petropol'e front by days end on 26 July, while having 166th Division and 107th Tank Division directly in front of it and in front of its left flank, and with the previous mission – attacking toward Dukhovshchina.

3. Group Comrade Rokossovsky is holding on to the eastern bank of the Vop'River.

4. I am ordering 91st Rifle and 89th Rifle Divisions of your group [Kalinin] to go over to the attack in the general direction of Shchelkin on the morning of 27 July, having in mind subsequently reaching the Krivtsy, El'kovo, and Sushcheva front.

Conduct the attack in echeloned formation, with 91st Division on the left wing and 89th Division on the right wing.

5. Report orders given.

S. Timoshenko, B. Shaposhnikov

Source: "Chastnyi boevoi prikaz Glavnokomanduiushchego voiskami Zapadnogo Napravleniia ot 26 iiulia 1941 g. komanduiushchemu gruppoi tov. Kalinina na nastuplenie v obshchem napravlenii na Shchelkina" [Individual Combat order of the Commander-in-Chief of the Western Direction's forces of 26 July 1941 to the commander Group Comrade Kalinin on an offensive in the general direction of Shchelkina], in *SBDVOV*, issue 37, 53.

16. Report of the Military Council of the Western Direction of 27 July 1941 to the *Stavka* of the High Command about the Situation in the Western and Central Fronts

By Bodo immediately
through the operational duty officer
To Comrade Stalin
Copy: To the Chief of the General Staff
0800 hours on 27 July 1941

The operation to destroy the enemy's Iartsevo-Dukhovshchina grouping has developed at a slower than desired tempo during the last two days.

The reasons for this include:

1. The constant reinforcement of the enemy;

2. The concentration by him of strong aviation in the region, and

3. The insufficient readiness of Group Khomenko's units, which became spread out while on the march and entered combat in piecemeal fashion.

As a result, we [the military council] have sent Comrade Eremenko to Comrade Khomenko's group to combine its operations with 166th Rifle and 107th Tank Divisions from Group Kalinin.

The attachment to the *front* of High Command aviation now permits us to throw stronger aviation into the affair.

On 26 July the enemy is tried to cut Group Rokossovsky off from the Vop' River and drive it back to its eastern bank. However, all attempts to do so have been beaten back.

By the end of the day on 26 July, the situation of the Iartsevo-Dukhovshchina grouping was as follows: Group Khomenko reached the Okolitsa, Sergeevka, and Petropol'e front. The cavalry group of Comrade Khomenko occupies the Chernyi Ruchei, Bulatovo, Volgino, Zaikovo, Efremovo and Dubovoe region, where heavy fighting is going on. The 107th Tank and 166th Rifle Divisions are situated along the Esennaia and Korytnitsa front. The 91st and 89th Rifle Divisions of Group Kalinin are located behind the Vop' River along the Sediby and Shamovo front, and the group of Comrade Rokossovsky is behind the Vop' River on both sides of Iartsevo, while holding on to the town of Iartsevo.

Not only the Group of Comrade Khomenko but also the Group of Comrade Kalinin have been ordered to continue their offensive on 27 July in the general direction of Shchelkino and Dukhovshchina. The group of Comrade Rokossovsky must also continue active operations. All of the *front's* and main command's bomber aircraft have been sent by us against the enemy's Iartsevo-Dukhovshchina grouping.

In addition, we have committed the re-established 44th [Rifle] Corps into the Svishchevo Station region and to the south (to the Solov'evo crossing over the Dnepr), which must prevent the enemy's Iartsevo and El'nia groupings from linking up.

The successful struggle of our 16th Army around Smolensk and in the city of Smolensk is continuing. On 26 July [enemy] 131st Infantry Division, which has just arrived in Smolensk, was smashed by the forces of 16th Army. Attempts by the enemy to envelop our 16th and 20th Armies from the north have been repulsed by 20th Army, which, on 25 and 26 July, smashed 5 German infantry divisions and is now battling with approaching German panzer divisions [17th and 18th]. The 16th and 20th Armies are fighting well, but their forces are diminishing, and, therefore, we have accelerated our attack against the Iartsevo-Dukhovshchina grouping.

The next step in the struggle – it is against Group Guderian, which has seized El'nia and has offered stubborn resistance to Group Kachalov from Roslavl' to Smolensk south of Pochinok. The 24th Army's attacks around El'nia have still not provided positive results and have allowed the Germans to throw forces against Kachalov. This group, not yet 20 kilometers from Pochinok, while enveloping the enemy with its left wing has now been forced to halt its offensive and fold its left wing back because a fresh enemy infantry division is reaching this flank from the direction of Monastyrshchina. Therefore, the attack by Group Kachalov will be disrupted by the German seizure and retention of El'nia.

In light of the fact that 61st Rifle Corps' defense of Mogilev attracted to itself up to 5 infantry division and is being conducted so energetically that it has tied down large enemy forces, we have ordered the commander of 13th Army to hold on to Mogilev at all cost and have ordered both him, as well as the commander of the Central Front, Comrade Kuznetsov, to go over to the attack toward Mogilev and, subsequently, protect the left flank of Kachalov and reach the Dnepr. However, the commander of 13th Army not only failed to urge the commander of the encircled corps, Bakunin, forward, but, when the moment appeared to abandon Mogilev, also began a withdrawal to the east and only then reported.

With this movement, the corps created a difficult situation for itself and freed up enemy divisions which could maneuver against 13th and 21st Armies. Immediately after receiving the news about the withdrawal from Mogilev and about the street fighting still continuing there, an order was given to the commander of 13th Army to halt the withdrawal from Mogilev and to hold on to the city at all cost, but corps commander Bakunin, who rudely violated the order of the command, was relieved by Colonel Voevodin, who steadfastly stood for the defense of Mogilev, and Bakunin was turned over to the judgment of the court.

We do not yet have any news about the operations of Group Comrade Gorodovikov, but the Germans have already been forced to convoy supply cargo and personnel by vehicles accompanied by tanks.

On 22nd Army's front, supported by fresh forces, the enemy is trying to seize Velikie Luki by means of partial penetrations of our dispositions. Two rifle divisions are being taken from Group Maslennikov to attack the enemy's Iartsevo-Dukhovshchina grouping and for an attack toward Il'ino and further to the south.

Thus, the enemy is trying to throw us back from Velikie Luki to the east in order to take the majority of forces from there to reinforce his Iartsevo-Dukhovshchina group. On the other hand, the Germans have assigned themselves the mission to link up the Iartsevo-Dukhovshchina group with the El'nia group and, having encircled our 16th and 20th Armies, at the same time, threaten Viaz'ma.

It is necessary:

1. You provide us with an additional two cavalry divisions in order to use them for an attack against the enemy's rear in the forests toward Vitebsk and Lepel'.

2. Since we have an opportunity to restore rapidly the units of 158th, 127th, and 38th Rifle Divisions from the Western Front and many divisions from the Central Front, chiefly for the reinforcement of 13th Army, guns and military equipment are necessary to carry out these measures, which we will ask you for in a separate message.

S. Timoshenko, B. Shaposhnikov

Source: "Doklad Voennogo Soveta Zapadnogo Napravleniia ot 27 iiulia 1941 g. Stavke Verkhovnogo Komandovaniia ob obstanovke na Zapadnom i Tsentral'nom frontakh" [Report of the Military Council of the Western Direction of 27 July 1941 to the *Stavka* of the High Command about the situation in the Western and Central Fronts], in *SBDVOV*, issue 37, 53-54.

17. Combat Order No. 052/op of the Headquarters of 28th Army of 27 July 1941 about a Continuation of the Offensive with the Aim of Seizing a Crossing on the Khmara River

To the Commanders of 104th TD, 145th and 149th RD, and the Motorized Rifle Regiment and Composite Regiment.

Combat Order No. 052/op, Headquarters, 28th Army,

the forest east of Stodolishche, to the Group headquarters,

2030 hours on 27 July 1941

1:100,000 scale map

The commander of the army orders:

Continue the attack on 28 July and fulfill the [following] assigned missions:

1. 104th TD will reach the Egorovka and Starinki region [15-18 kilometers east-southeast of Pochinok] and capture crossings over the Khmara River. Protect yourself from the east and northeast. Reinforce the security in your rear with scouting armored cars and tanks.

2. 149th RD will continue to fulfill its assigned missions by energetic attacks and, while preventing the enemy from digging in long intermediate lines, capture crossings over the Khmara River in the Ponizovka and railroad line sector.

The division's separate reconnaissance battalion will maintain close contact with 104th TD's units.

3. 145th RD, after protecting the Dumanichskie and Novyi Derebuzh line [7 kilometers west to 13 kilometers south-southwest of Stodolishche] with one battalion, will go over to a decisive attack with its remaining forces and capture crossings over the Khmara River in the Tsyganovka Commune and Kiselevka sector [10 kilometers south on Pochinok].

Return the motorized rifle company to the Stodolishche region after reconnoitering and protecting the Khislavichi region with the forces of the reconnaissance battalion and an allocated battalion.

4. The composite regiment, after being relieved by units of 222nd RD, will concentrate in the vicinity of the forest at the village of Krapivinskii No. 1 by a night march.

> The Chief of Staff of 28th Army, Major General Egorov
> The Military Commissar, Senior Political Worker [*Politruk*] Simansky
> The Chief of the Operations Department, Colonel Zuev

Source: "Boevoe rasporiazhenie shtaba 28-i Armii no. 052/op ot 27 iiulia 1941 g. voiskam operativnoi gruppy armii o prodolzhenii nastupleniia s tsel'iu zakhvata pereprav na p. Khmara" [Combat order no. 052/op of the headquarters of 28th Army of 27 July 1941 about a continuation of the offensive with the aim of seizing a crossing on the Khmara River], *SBDVOV*, issue 37, 352.

18. Order of the Headquarters of the Main Command of the Western Direction of 28 July 1941 to the Commanders of the Groups about Increasing Activity [Energy] in the Combat Operations of the Forces

To the Commander of Group Comrade Maslennikov

To the Commander of Group Comrade Khomenko
To the Commander of Group Comrade Kalinin
To the Commander of Group Comrade Rokossovsky
To the Commander of Group Comrade Kachalov
Copies: To the Commander of the Western Front, Comrade Eremenko
               To the Operational Post for a report to the Commander-in-Chief

1. The enemy aims and seeks to disguise his unpreparedness for active operations with small attacks on various sectors of our front.

2. The commander-in-chief is ordering we demand the most decisive active operations on the part of all commanders and soldiers and not a single hour be lost our offensive, and therefore:

1) All of the commanders of groups will conduct the most decisive attacks, while denying enemy [the opportunity] to put his forces in order and collect himself after our attacks.

2) Do not overestimate the strength of the enemy and do not think that he is strong and that he does not suffer losses and, therefore, is steadfast and invincible. On the contrary, the enemy is suffering heavy losses and is holding on under our attacks with great difficulty.

3) The commander-in-chief categorically demands that all of the commanders of groups, corps, divisions, and regiments be closer to the forces on the field of battle, personally observe the course of the fighting, and immediately intervene in the operations of the troops in those instances when they display insufficient energy [*aktivnost'*].

4) The commander-in-chief categorically demands you report about the course of the battle every 4 hours, beginning at 0500 in the morning. I warn you that those guilty of crimes will be punished right up to being handed over to the judgment of a military tribunal.

Report about the receipt of this order immediately.

B. Shaposhnikov

Source: "Prikazanie shtaba Glavnogo Komandovaniia Zapadnogo Napravleniia ot 28 iiulia1941 g. komanduiushchim gruppami o povyshenii aktivnosti v boevykh deistviiakh voisk" [Order of the headquarters of the Main Command of the Western Direction of 28 July 1941 to the commanders of the groups about increasing activity [energy] in the combat operations of the forces, in *SBDVOV*, issue 37, 57.

19. Combat Order No. 058/op of the Commander of the Forces of 28th Army of 28 July 1941 on the Offensive with the Aim of Seizing a Crossing on the Khmara River

Combat Order No. 058/op
to the Forces of 28th Army's Group
8 July 1941   the forest 1 kilometer southeast of Stodolishche

It is intolerable that the forces of the group of 28th Army have been delayed for far too long while trying to overcome individual centers of resistance and firing points of the German 263rd Division.

The units have marked time in place for four days and sometimes have been stopped in front of groups of motorcyclists or separate antitank guns.

I **demand** that all commanders, political workers, and soldiers seize crossings over the Khmara River at all cost tomorrow on 29 July.

The enemy in front of the units of the group has already begun a withdrawal and still one more blow is needed to destroy him in front of the crossings over the Khmara River.

I order:

104th TD to exploit the already begun withdrawal by the German units and, having occupied the crossings at Egorovka and Starinki [15-17 kilometers east-southeast of Pochinok], assist the advance of 149th RD, while conducting an attack on Stupino and Zhary [15-18 kilometers southeast of Pochinok] with no less than a company of tanks and a company of motorized infantry in order to cut off the enemy's routes of withdrawal and destroy him.

149th RD, along with 104th TD, to destroy the opposing enemy and seize the crossings in the Ponizovka and Machuly sector by a decisive advance forward. Keep one regiment in second echelon.

145th RD, while protecting the group's flank with a force of no less than a battalion, attack decisively forward along the road and railroad [to Pochinok]. Have 403rd Regiment (less one battalion) echeloned behind the left wing and 599th Regiment (less one battalion) – in the division's reserve.

The motorized rifle regiment [31st] will continue reconnoitering toward Khislavichi with one company and hold on to Stodolishche with one company for operations toward the west.

The composite regiment will concentrate in the Krapivinskii No. 1 region by 0800 hours on 29 July 1941.

222nd RD will continue to defend the Roslavl' strong point.

The armored train will reach Stodolishche by 0600 hours and be prepared to support the attack by 145th RD.

Continue the attack at first light on 29 July 1941, while maintaining cooperation with the artillery.

All commanders of formations will report about the beginning of the attack.

The commander of the group's forces, Lieutenant General Kachalov
The Member of the Military Council, Brigade Commissar Kolesnikov
The Chief of Staff, Major General Egorov

Source: "Boevoe prikaz komanduiushchego voiskami 28-i Armii no. 058/op ot 28 iiulia 1941 g. na nastuplenie s tsel'iu zakhvata pereprav cherez p. Khmara" [Combat order no. 058/op of the commander of the forces of 28th Army of 28 July 1941 on the offensive with the aim of seizing a crossing on the Khmara River], *SBDVOV*, issue 37, 353.

20. Order No. 059/op of the Military Council of 28th Army of 30 July 1941 to the Forces of the Army's Operational Group about the Elimination of Shortcomings in Combat Operations

Order No. 059/op
to the Forces of the Operational Group
30 July 1941   the forest 1 kilometer southeast of Stodolishche

Combat experience demonstrates that the extremely slow advance and destruction of the weakened enemy is occurring because of the weak leadership of the fighting on the part of all levels of command cadre.

The Military Council of the army demands that command cadre be in the immediate vicinity of their forces, supervise the fighting on the battlefield, and personally intervene and demand an advance is those cases when the advance has been halted and the forces are displaying insufficient activity [energy].

Henceforth, [the following] is necessary:

The commanders of companies and their political workers be in their platoons, the commanders of battalions – in their companies, the commanders and commissars of regiments – in their battalions, the commanders of divisions – in their regiment and be in the combat formations from which they can better observe the sector and more properly direct the fighting.

The headquarters of the divisions and regiments be as close as possible to their forces and have their observation posts on the immediate battlefield. Up to this time, we have observed cases of isolation of the artillery from the infantry. I categorically demand you have the artillery closer to the infantry and you have close contract with them.

For the purposes of liquidating enemy resistance along separate axes and centers of resistance and depriving him of aviation support, conduct night operations by well-trained groups to infiltrate [the enemy's defenses] and for the destruction of individual enemy centers of resistance, headquarters, communications centers, and rear service installations.

Force reconnaissance organs, which have been sent out, have provided neither information about the enemy nor daily information not only about the enemy but also about their own locations, and the headquarters are not taking measures for the timely receipt of on news about the enemy. Up to this time, the commanders of units and formations do not know the grouping of enemy forces in their sectors, and, consequently, the forces are operating blindly and marking time in place.

I demand that unit and formation commanders assign missions to the reconnaissance groups and detachments personally and exercise strict control of their fulfillment of these missions.

The Military Council demands from everyone decisive movement forward and destruction of the Fascists by any means, while denying them rest. Encircle and destroy them!

The Commander of 28th Army, Lieutenant General Kachalov
The Member of the Military Council, Brigade Commissar Kolesnikov
The Chief of Staff, Colonel Zuev.

Source: "Prikaz Voennogo Soveta 28-i Armii no. 059/op ot 30 iiulia 1941 g. voiskam operativnoi gruppy armii ob obstranenii nedostatkov v boevykh deistviiakh" [Order no. 059/op of the Military Council of the forces of the army's operational group of 30 July 1941 about the elimination of shortcomings in combat operations], *SBDVOV*, issue 37, 354.

Appendix H

The Struggle for the Smolensk Pocket, 23-31 July 1941

1. Combat Order No. 36 of the Commander of the Forces of 20th Army of 25 July 1941 on the Repelling of Enemy Attempts to Penetrate to the City of Smolensk

To the Headquarters of the *Front*
Combat Order No. 36, Headquarter, 20th Army,
2100 hours on 25 July 1941
Map: 1: 100,000

1. Up to 1 enemy infantry division is defending the Toporovo, Iushino, and Syro-Lipki sector along the Dukhovshchina axis, and 5th ID, which has suffered heavy losses, is defending the Negodiaevo, Anufrino, Bartikhovo, and Mokrushino region.

Up to 4 battalions with tanks and artillery are trying to develop the attack toward Mirskoe and Tishino. Small groups are operating along the highway.

2. 20th Army is fending off the enemy offensive and preventing his penetration to Smolensk.

3. Group Rokossovsky is conducting an attack from the Iartsevo region along the highway and toward Dukhovshchina.

16th Army is continuing to clear the enemy from Smolensk.

4. 153rd RD, with attached units, will give up the (incl.) Vydra and Hill 213.7 sector by 2400 hours on 25 July and will occupy and firmly hold on to the (incl.) Boloto, west of Kiseli, Bannyi Ostrov, and Verkhov'e line by 0400 hours on 26 July. Have a reserve of up to a regiment in the Bochary region.

Boundary on the left – (incl.) Zhukovo State Farm, Bochary, and Ivlevo.

5. 69th RC (144th and 229th RDs) with attached units, having taken over the Vydra, Debritsy, and Zybki combat sector from 153rd RD and 57th TD at 2400 hours on 25 July, will occupy and firmly defend the Vydra, Hill 213.7, Zybki, Rebiaki, and Kurino line by 0400 hours on 26 July. Have a reserve of up to a regiment in the Kholm region. Boundary on the left – Romanenki, Kurino, and Samodelki.

Headquarters of the corps – in its previous location.

6. 57th TD, after turning over its sector to 69th RC at 2400 hours on 25 July, will concentrate in the Morzhovka, Kovshi, and Korelly region. Route of movement – Kholm and the highway. Division headquarters – Korelly. The attached battalion from 152nd RD will concentrate in the Krasnyi Bor region by the morning of 26 July and become subordinate to the commander of 152nd RD.

7. 73rd RD, 233rd RD, and 5th MC will remain in their occupied positions.

8. CP – as before.

The Commander of 20th Army, Lieutenant General Kurochkin
The Member of the Military Council, Corps Commissar Semenovsky
The Chief of Staff of 20th Army, Major General Korneev

Source: "Boevoi prikaz komanduiushchego voiskami 20-i Armii No. 36 ot 25 iiulia 1941 g. na Otrazhenie popytok proryva protivnika k gor. Smolensk" [Combat order no. 36 of the commander of the forces of 20th Army of 25 July 1941 on the repelling of enemy attempts to penetrate to the city of Smolensk], in *SBDVOV*, issue 37, 264-265.

2. Excerpts from, Operational Summary No. 59 of the Headquarters of the Western Front at 0800 hours on 26 July 1941 about the Combat Operations of the *Front's* Forces

Operational Summary No. 59 at 0800 hours on 26 July 1941,
Headquarters, Western Front
1:500,000 scale map

First. The forces of the Western Front conducted fighting on the entire front on 25 July, which was especially intense along the Velikie Luki, Smolensk, and Mogilev axes, while continuing the slow movement of new forces with the aim of liquidating the penetration in the Smolensk region … .

Third. 20th Army [Kurochkin]. 20th Army's units (153rd RD, 57th TD, and 144th RD) fought prolonged battles night and day on 25 July in the Vydra and Volkovaia region against units of enemy 5th ID, which were in lodged in field type fortifications (dugouts and full-profile trenches) on Hill 213.7 (100,000 scale map) and around the villages of Ershi, Garitsy, Savenki, and Bol'shoe and Maloe Vozmishche. We held on to all of these points except the last two.

A motorized detachment of 5th MC, operating toward Kasplia to attack the rear of enemy 5th ID in the region 4 kilometers southwest of Kholm, routed an enemy motorized company, and, after destroying 5 tankettes, it ran into enemy fortifications.

The enemy brought a great number of tanks forward from the north toward Iushino and Opol'e – probably 15th Bavarian Division. According to tentative estimates, in combat on 25 July, two infantry regiments were smashed, and 15-20 tanks and tankettes (of these, no fewer than 10 heavy and 5 light), 25 antitank guns, many machine guns and submachine guns, up to 100 motorcycles with machine guns and automatic weapons, and 200 velocipedes [bicycles] were destroyed. Multiple rocket launcher rounds played a great role in the destruction of the fortifications and flame field weapons [Molotov cocktails, etc.] sowed panic in the enemy's ranks as they ran for safety.

Fourth. 16th Army [Lukin]. The army's units continued their attack to capture the southeastern part of Smolensk on the morning of 25 July and clean out centers of enemy resistance, while fortifying the positions they seized.

152nd RD, after digging in on the northern bank of the Dnepr River, cleared the northern part of Smolensk of enemy remnants.

129th RD conducted stubborn fighting to capture the northeastern part of Smolensk.

Headquarters, 16th Army – Zhukovo State Farm … .

For the Chief of Staff of the Western Front,
Marshal of the Soviet Union B. Shaposhnikov

Source: "Operativnaia svodka shtaba Zapadnogo fronta No. 59 k 8 chasam 26 iiulia 1941 g. o boevykh deistviiakh voisk fronta" [Operational summary of the headquarters of the Western Front no. 59 at 0800 hours on 26 July 1941 about the combat operations of the *front's* forces], in *SBDVOV*, issue 37, 106-107.

3. Report by the Military Council of 20th Army of 27 July 1941 to the Commander-in-Chief of the Western Direction about the Condition and Possibilities of the Army and the Decision Reached

To the Commander-in-Chief of the Western Direction,
Marshal of the Soviet Union S. K. Timoshenko

I am reporting:

1. 20th Army, while actively defending and inflicting a series of defeats on the enemy by counterattacks, occupies the following positions at 1200 hours on 27 July:

57th TD has been concentrated in the Shokino State Farm (20 kilometers north of Kardymovo Station), Zezerino, Prudishche, Isaevshchina, and Kornilovka region with the mission to prevent the enemy from [advancing to] the south and be prepared to attack toward Dukhovshchina into the flank and rear of the enemy 7th PzD, which occupies a defense along the Iartsevo and Strogova line.

5th MC occupied jumping-off positions along the Zaluzh'e, Pomogailova, Smugulino, and Koshelevo line with the mission to prevent the enemy [from reaching] Smolensk toward the south and the aim of destroying the enemy's Dukhovshchina tank grouping.

233rd RD is being moved up from reserve to a defensive line with the mission of preventing the enemy from moving southward toward Smolensk and in readiness for an attack northward toward Krasnosel'e to protect the army's defenses in the west from the north and a counterattack toward Dukhovshchina. The division has 1 rifle regiment in second echelon in the Dubrovo and Penisnar region.

153rd RD, after protecting the withdrawal of 144th RD from the front into the army's reserve on the night of 26-27 July, is occupying a defense along the Nastas'ino and (incl.) Nizhnaia Dubrovka line by 1200 hours on 27 July, with the mission of preventing an enemy penetration from the west toward the east.

73rd RD, after protecting the withdrawal of 229th RD into the army's reserve on the night of 26-27 July, is occupying a defense along the Nizhnaia Dubrovka, Gnezdovo, and Dnepr River line to Novosel'e by 1200 hours on 27 July, with the mission to prevent an enemy penetration along the Smolensk highway and his forcing of the Dnepr River.

144th RD was concentrating in the Matiushino, Zamosh'c, and Kozarevo region by 1200 hours on 27 July and is in the army's reserve.

229th RD was concentrating in the Riasino, Pechersk, and Korokhotino region by 1200 hours on 27 July and is in the army's reserve.

2. The army is actively repelling an offensive by no fewer than 4 enemy infantry divisions with tanks. The 15th Bavarian Division is conducting an attack with part of its forces from the Iushkino and Opol'e Station front; 5th ID – [from] the Verkhov'e

and Volokovaia; 28th ID – [from] Buda and Kuprino; and 35th ID – [from] Kuprino and Borok. In addition, apparently, units of enemy 18th PzD are operating along the southern bank of the Dnepr River.

3. 20th Army, while occupying s 70 kilometer front in the shape of an ellipse with open flanks, has interrupted communications and is not being supplied with ammunition and fuel.

4. The army, which was not fully concentrated before the operation, has significant shortages in personnel and equipment and is in the following condition by 28 July:

a) During the period from 1 through 25 July, the army conducted 7-8 counterstrokes against the enemy, not counting the counterattacks organized by the commanders of its formations [divisions]. From 1 through 20 July, the army's losses numbered 24,000 men. In addition, from 20 through 26 July, in the most intense period of combat, the losses probably amounted to no fewer than 10,000 men.

The army's formations: 73rd RD, 5th MC, 57th TD, 229th RD, 144th RD, and the tank division, arrived in the army considerably under strength. Because of this and also the losses, at present, the strengths of the army's divisions amount to 30-35% of their required strength. The strength of the army's division range from 4,000 to 6,500 men, and, furthermore, to a significant degree, this quantity of personnel are in rear and rear service units. The number of personnel who can conduct direct combat are considerably smaller.

Throughout this entire period, the army received 1,000 personnel replacements at a time when it required 70,000 men and 9,000 horses. Attempts to fill out the army at the expense of rank-and-file soldiers and junior command cadre, who were stragglers from their units, had no great effect, since the majority of these personnel were unarmed and lacked uniforms, and there are no reserves of weapons and uniforms in the army.

b) The army's and formations' communications units have no more than 25-30% of their communications equipment and transport.

c) There are very few engineer and pontoon units in the army.

The shortage of sapper subunits in combat units amounts to 30-35%. Road and bridge equipment is completely absent.

d) As of 28 July, the [army's] VVS had Il-2 and SB-7 aircraft, and the SB were used only at night or at great altitudes during the day. The VVS are not only incapable of protecting the army's operations from the skies but they are also unable to inflict any sort of notable strikes against the enemy. In those instances when enemy aviation is absent, we strike him wherever he appears – but success often goes to his side.

e) The remaining tanks on 26 July [include]: 17th TD [5th MC] – 29, 13th TD [5th MC] – 29, and 57th TD – 7-8.

f) The army has [the following number] of guns, not counting antitank: 229th RD – 28, 233rd RD – 18, 144th RD – 30, 153rd RD – 20, 73rd RD – 47, 5th MC – 34, and RGK corps artillery regiments – 98 guns, for a total of 177 guns and 120 antitank guns.

In addition, we are short 75 artillery tractors, about 50 kilometers of cable, and 100 vehicles.

g) The foodstuffs in the army are basically adequate, an average of 0.5-1 combat loads of ammunition remain in the forces, and 0.3 combat loads are in forward warehouses. Fuel – 1.5 refills.

There are completely no reserves of 120mm mines, 76mm antiaircraft shells, and 152mm rounds in forward warehouses ... ..

5. Scanty information from above and from neighbors about the positions of the *front's* forces and the opposing enemy does not allow for comprehensive analysis of the situation. I estimate it to be as follows:

The enemy's main mobile groupings are located in the Dukhovshchina and El'nia regions, and they are holding their ground in Smolensk with the forces of two divisions. From the northeast, Group Khomenko is attacking from the Belyi region (according to agent reports on 23 July, it is still in enemy hands) toward the southwest. Supposedly, one tank division is attacking directly toward Dukhovshchina. Group Rokossovsky, while digging in along the Vop'River, is attacking directly toward Dukhovshchina from the east without noticeable success, having before it 7th PzD, with motorized infantry, which are occupying defenses along the Popova, Iartsevo Station, and Stogova front.

Lukin [16th Army] has still not completely cleared the northern part of Smolensk of enemy, who have brought forward [to the city] the fresh 137th ID with heavy tanks.

With the forces and equipment he presently has, he can hardly occupy Smolensk. On 20th Army's front, the 4 approaching enemy infantry divisions and motorized units, whose attack aims to defeat 20th Army and cut it off completely from the [*front's*] remaining forces, are presently being held off and repelled by the army.

Simultaneously, the army, by constantly allocating its reserves, is inflicting partial defeats on the enemy.

6. Based on these conditions and an evaluation of the situation, the following missions can be assigned to the army:

a) While inflicting partial defeats on the enemy, stubbornly defend in its positions and, while avoiding concentrated enemy attacks and not letting itself be destroyed, withdraw to the Dnepr River and, for the time being, occupy a firm defense until reinforced by any means possible from Rokossovsky on the left.

b) While stubbornly defending from the west and north in its occupied positions, help 16th Army seize the southern part of Smolensk by an attack across the Dnepr River with a force of one-two weak divisions.

In spite of the great political importance of holding on to Smolensk, this variant has little chance of success, and, in the case of failure, it places 20th and 16th Armies' units under the threat of complete destruction. The absence of shells, aircraft, pontoon equipment, the under-strength divisions, and the unfavorable operational situation, when the attack must be carried out under threat of an enemy penetration to Smolensk from the west and north, forces us to reject this mission.

c) While stubbornly defending along the front lines to the west, prevent the enemy from [advancing] to Smolensk from the north with a force of three rifle divisions (153rd, 73rd, and 144th RDs). Simultaneously, 5th MC, 57th TD, and

229th RD will attack against the enemy's Dukhovshchina grouping – its 7th PzD from the southwest and south and against its flank and rear to cooperate with its destruction by Groups Rokossovsky and Khomenko.

The attack toward Dukhovshchina will be protected from the north by an advance by 233rd RD to the Zherespeia River.

The success of this attack would permit cutting off one enemy pincer with which he is trying to envelop 20th and 16th Armies and Group Rokossovsky from the north. The destruction of the enemy's Dukhovshchina grouping would give the right wing of the *front* full freedom of maneuver and, while freeing 20th and 16th Armies from their unfavorable operational situation, would allow then to go over to more active operations in the future.

In the event this attack fails, it would nevertheless permit broadening of the armies' maneuver space from south to north, which, at the present time, is exposed throughout by field artillery and, simultaneously, provide the possibility of withdrawing the army to a more favorable situation.

I have decided to conduct the last variant.

The Commander of 20th Army, Lieutenant General Kurochkin
The Member of the Military Council, Corps Commissar Semenovsky
The Chief of Staff, Major General Korneev

Source: "Doklad voennogo soveta 20-i Armii ot 27 iiulia 1941 g. Glavnokomanduiushchemu voiskami Zapadnogo Napravleniia o sostoianii, obespechennosti armii i priniatom reshenii" [Report by the military council of 20th Army of 27 July 1941 to the Commander-in-Chief of the Western Direction about the condition and possibilities of the army and decision reached], in *SBDVOV*, issue 37, 265-268.

4. Combat Report No. 23/op of the Commander of the Forces of 16th Army of 27 July 1941 to the Commander-in-Chief of the Western Direction's Forces about the Combat Operations of the Army's Forces to Capture the City of Smolensk

To the Commander-in-Chief of the Western Direction
To the Commander of the Western Front
Combat Order No. 23/op, Headquarters, 16th Army,
2100 hours on 27 July 1941
1:500,000 and 1:100,000 maps

1. The enemy, with a force of up to a motorized division (probably SS), reinforced by two battalions of tanks and 1-2 battalions of artillery, is continuing to defend Smolensk firmly. While suffering heavy losses in dead, the garrison of the defense of Smolensk was reinforced by 137th ID (447th, 448th, and 449th IRs and 150th AR) on the night of 25-26 July, which was thrown into the battle from the march.

2. The army's units repeatedly went over to the attack daily from 16 through 27 July, in the daytime and at night, to seize Smolensk. Especially fierce fighting began at 0200 hours on 26 July, which continues to this time. As a result of this fighting, the newly arrived 137th ID has suffered exceptionally heavy casualties, which alone left more than 500 men dead. The political-morale state of the soldiers, in light of the

losses suffered, is extremely fatigued and reduced. I consider both regiments (448th and 449th) as destroyed and the reserve regiment, 447th Regiment, defending one third of the city – as not combat ready, especially for a firm defense. The backbone of the defense, as before, continues to remain the remnants of the SS division, which is lodged in individual homes and apartments, which carried away its dead and wounded during its withdrawal and whose soldiers do not surrender. Combat of an especially fierce nature developed around the liquidation of sites within the city (cemeteries, and others).

The army occupied all of the northern part of the city of Smolensk by the morning of 27 July, having cut off the main withdrawal routes of the enemy across the Dnepr River to the southern part. Sustained street fighting is continuing for the liquidation of individual strong regions and centers of defense. I would especially like to mention the organization, energy, and audacity displayed in battle by the personnel of 152nd RD and 129th RDs. The 129th RD, which is composed of detachments formed from those who withdrew from the front and from separate subunits of other divisions and who, at the beginning of the battle for possession of Smolensk, were scattered during the breaching of the lines by the actions of bomber aviation, has now become one of the more steadfast divisions.

During the period of operations at Smolensk, the army's units have lost up to 500 dead and more than 230 men wounded. The losses of the enemy are considerably higher. In the near future, I will turn to forcing the Dnepr River and seizing the southern part of Smolensk

Conclusion

1. As a result of the 10-days of fighting for Smolensk, more than an enemy infantry division has been smashed. The remnants are continuing to defend the city, with the massive support of automatic guns and mortars, constant and almost unpunished bombing by aviation, and the use of obstacles by flamethrower tanks.

2. The army's units, while fulfilling their mission of regaining the city of Smolensk, seized the northern part by the morning of 27 July and are conducting clean-up of urban centers of resistance and also preparing for the final seizure of the entire city.

Lukin, Lobachev, Shalin

Source: "Boevoe donesenie komanduiushchego voiskami 16-i Armii no. 23/op ot 27 iiulia 1941 g. komanduiushchemu voiskami Zapadnogo Napravlenii o boevykh deistviiakh voisk armii po ovladeniiu gor. Smolensk" [Combat report no. 23/op of the commander of the forces of 16th Army of 27 July 1941 to the commander-in-chief of the Western Direction's forces about the combat operations of the army's forces for the capture of Smolensk], in *SBDVOV*, issue 37, 210-211.

5. Combat Order No. 03 of the Commander of the Operational Group of Forces of the Iartsevo Axis of 28 July 1941 on an Attack in the General Direction of Dukhovshchina

Combat Order No. 03, Headquarters,
Operational Group of Forces of the Iartsevo Axis,
the forest 1 kilometer southeast of Fedosovo,

2400 hours on 28 July 1941

1. The enemy, having encountered stubborn resistance by our forces and losing confidence in the development of offensive operations, went over to a defense in the Skachikhino, Iartsevo, Svishchevo, and Solov'evo sector along the western bank of the Vop' River.

2. On the right, 89th RD is attacking from the Kapyrovshchina and Shamovoa line and developing the attack toward Riadyni and Kolkovichi.

On the left, Group Kachalov is attacking from the Roslavl' region in the general direction of Pochinok and Smolensk.

3. The forces of the Group of the Iartsevo Axis will go over to the attack from the line of the Vop' River in the Novosel'e and Solov'evo sector at 1100 hours on 29 July 1941 [*subsequently changed to 0800 hours on 30 July 1941*], with the immediate mission to destroy the Iartsevo-Solov'evo grouping of enemy forces and subsequently develop the attack toward Dukhovshchina by enveloping it from the southwest.

4. 101st TD (without 203rd and 202nd TR), with 700th ATR, will attack the enemy in the Novosel'e and Khatyni sector to capture the Novosel'e (west of Kudinovo) line and reach the Marker 201.6, Samuilov, and Marker 221.3 line by day's end on 29 July 1941.

Boundary on the left – (incl.) Ul'khova, Sloboda, (incl.) Panina, and (incl.) Mal'tsova.

5. 38th RD, with 509th ATR, 3rd Bn, 49th CAR, 471st CAR, and a sapper company of 169th EngBn, will attack the enemy in the sector from Iartsevo to Marker 174.7, with the immediate mission to capture the Hill 234.9, (incl.) Pologi, and Pervomaiskii region and, subsequently, while developing the attack along the road to Dukhovshchina, reach the Mal'tsova and Cheryshina line by day's end on 29 July.

To protect the right flank, leave a detachment consisting of two companies of infantry with 6 AT guns in the occupied Chazhiki and Ozerishche sector, with the mission to prevent the enemy from crossing to the eastern bank of the Vop' River.

Boundary on the left – Shikino, (incl.) Marker 169.9, (incl.) Pologi, Hill 231.0, and (incl.) Sveevka.

6. 44th RC (64th and 108th RDs), with a sapper company from 169th EngBn, will go over to the attack in the Svishchevo and Solov'evo sector and, while stubbornly protecting its left flank against an enemy counterattack from the southwest, will have the immediate mission to reach the Starosel'e, Matrenina, and Popova front; subsequently, while developing the attack toward Lopatkina and Grishino, reach the Dedeshina, Mushkovichi, and Bobry front by the end of the day on 29 July.

7. The composite motorized regiment (two battalions) of 7th MC, 202nd and 203rd TRs, and two batteries of 18th HARegiment – my reserve, will concentrate in the Krasnobaenka, Poluliaevka, Volyntsovo, and Borovlevo region by the morning of 29 July 1941 and, when the infantry reach the Panina and Kuz'mina line, will attack toward Iartsevo behind 108th RD and further along the road to Dukhovshchina.

I am entrusting command of all of the reserve units to the commander of 101st TD and his staff.

8. Artillery. Artillery preparation – 30 minutes. Readiness of the artillery – by 0900 hours on 29 July 1941.

Missions: Suppress mortars, machine guns, and AT guns in [the following] areas: Hill 198.6, the southeastern outskirts of Novosel'e, the southeastern edge of the woods southwest of Novosel'e, the eastern edge of Khatyni, the grove north of Iartsevo, the eastern edge of the woods south of Marker 174.7, and enemy firing points along the forward edge of the enemy's defenses. Prevent enemy counterattacks from the Kholm and Novosel'e (western) region, from Semukhina and Soprykina and Semenova and Stogova, and from the woods south of Matrenina and Porovaeva.

9. The group of forces 'chief of Engineers will start constructing permanent crossings over the Vop' River at Novosel'e and Svishchevo with the forces of 42nd Miner's Battalion and sapper companies of 169th EngBn when the infantry reach the Novosel'e, Panina, and Pologi line, while continuing to create obstacles in accordance with the instructions I have given.

10. Supply stations – Dorogobuzh Station. Transport – in accordance with the instructions of the commanders of divisions and separate units.

11. Command post – the woods 1 kilometer southeast of Fedosovo. Observation post – the woods 1 kilometer southwest of Ol'khovo. The subsequent axis of movement is toward Iartsevo and, further, along the road to Dukhovshchina.

> The Commander of the Operational Group of Forces for the Iartsevo Axis,
>   Major General Rokossovsky
> For the Commissar of the Group of Forces of the Iartsevo Axis,
>   Regimental Commissar Vlaskin
> The Chief of Staff of the Group, Colonel Malinin

Source: "Boevoi prikaz komanduiushchego Operativnoi Gruppoi Voisk Iartsevo Napravleniia No. 03 ot 28 iiulia 1941 g. na nastuplenie v obshchem napravlenii na Dukhovshchina" [Combat order no. 03 of the commander of the Operational Group of Forces of the Iartsevo Axis of 28 July 1941 on an attack in the general direction of Dukhovshchina], in *SBDVOV*, issue 37, 411-412.

6. Operational Summary of the Headquarters of 16th Army of 29 July 1941 to the Headquarters of the Western Front about the Situation and Provisioning of 16th Army's Forces

To the Chiefs of Staff of the Western Front and Western Direction
Operational Summary, 1400 hours on 29 July 1941

16th Army has occupied a defense along the axis of the Stabna River, Izoven'ka, the Dnepr River, and Kolania, with part of its forces attacking with the mission of reaching Smolensk.

129th RD's 457th RR is in defenses in the Muzhilovo and Isakovo State Farm sector along and east of the Stabna River. 393rd RR is moving to the western edge of the Muzhilovo woods [5-7 kilometers northeast and east of Smolensk].

152nd Rifle Division is moving at this time: 580th RR to south of the [map] inscription "Korokhotkino," saddling the Smolensk road; and 544th RR to the south of Korokhotkino [5 kilometers northeast of Smolensk], both facing toward Smolensk.

46th RD – is along the front through Izoven'ka to the Dnepr railroad bridge at Sheinovka [5 kilometers east of Smolensk]; 646th RR – the southern outskirts of Nikeevshchina [5 kilometers northeast of Smolensk]; 518th RR – Izoven'ka and the highway [6 kilometers northeast of Smolensk]; and 29th RR – the highway to the Dnepr River [5 kilometers east of Smolensk].

34th RC is in defenses along the Mokh-Bogdanovka and Oblogino front [6-17 kilometers east and southeast of Smolensk].

The enemy went on the attack at 0800 hours on 29 July, throwing 152nd RD back to the east.

At 1400 hours an [enemy] force of up to a regiment began an attack in the general direction of the Stabna River, and, while throwing the regiments of 152nd RD back to the defenses of 129th RD, the enemy used a great quantity of mortars and artillery, and aircraft bombed 152nd RD's units several times. The division suffered heavy losses from enemy fire and withdrew to the right flank of 129th RD in Tserkovishchi, from where it began concentrating in the Sen'kovo region at 2300 hours to prepare a defensive line.

The commander of the division, Colonel Cheryshev, was wounded twice but remained in action.

129th RD is stubbornly defending the Stabna River line. 343rd RR withdrew to the division's defensive front and, together with 457th RR, is defending along the Stabna River line.

46th RD. Around 1600 hours, up to a battalion of enemy infantry was along the old Smolensk road, and up to two companies penetrated the defense and are exploiting success eastward along the road. 46th RD withdrew to Sosnovka (1:50,000 map) by 2200 hours, where it went over to the defense and was struck on its left wing by the enemy who crossed the Dnepr River and prepared an attack supported by mortars and aviation groups of 10-18 aircraft in several raids.

I am continuing to occupy defenses along the eastern bank of the Dnepr River from Mokh-Bogdanovka to Oblogino, with mobile reserves protecting in the vicinity of the crossings along the Korolevo and Lozyn' front. The boundary established with 20th Army: Zagor'e, Astragach State Farm, Ignatovshchina, and the airfield hangers. All of 16th Army's units operating north of the designated boundary should be relieved on the night of 29-30 July. No information about the relief has been received as of 0530 hours.

Supplies of ammunition (shells):

50mm mines: 34th RC – 1,000; 46th RD – 1,580; and 129th RD – unknown;

82mm mines: 34th RC – 60, but none in the other units;

122 [should read 120] mm mines: 46th RD – 20, but none in the other units;

45mm shells: 46th RD – 940; 129th RD – 400; 34th RC – 594; and 152nd RD – 2,748;

76mm shells (1927 model): 34th RC – 525; 132nd RD – 300, but none in the other units;

76mm shells (1902/30 models): 46th RD – 120; 152nd RD – 150, but none in other units;

antiaircraft shells (1931 model): 34th RC – 88; and separate AA battalions – 1,054;

122mm shells: 152nd RD – 100; 46th RD – 200, but none in other units;

152mm shells (1934/37 model): 34th RC – 133; and 126th CAR – 636; and

152mm shells (1909/37 models): 152nd RD – 450, but none in 34th RC and the other units.

Shalin, Sedenkov, and Bulanov

Source: "Operativnaia svodka shtaba 16-i Armii ot 29 iiulia 1941 g. shtaba Zapadnogo fronta o polozhenii i obespechennosti voisk armii" [Operational summary of the headquarters of 16th Army of 29 July 1941 about the situation and provisioning of 16th Army's forces], in *SBDVOV*, issue 37, 211-212.

7. Combat Order No. 00277 of the Commander-in-Chief of the Western Direction's Forces of 29 July 1941 to the Commanders of the Forces of 20th and 16th Armies on the Capture of Smolensk

To the Commander of 20th Army, Kurochkin
To the Commander of 16th Army, Lukin
Copies: To the Chief of the General Staff of the Red Army, Zhukov
               To Comrade Shaposhnikov for immediate transmission to Comrade
               Kurochkin
Combat Order No. 00297, 29 July 1941

From your morning summary of 29 July, I ascertained, first, that you are carrying out a risky withdrawal despite orders to hold on to your positions, which is all the more intolerable in light of the operations being conducted by Groups Khomenko, Kalinin, and Rokossovsky, whose orders you are aware of. None of your reports and messages indicates that it is necessary to withdraw; to the contrary, your armies are fighting successfully. Your withdrawal helps the enemy create strong groupings to disrupt the operations we are conducting.

I order:

Immediately halt the withdrawal of 16th and 20th Armies' from positions west of Smolensk. Clear the enemy from Smolensk and keep it [the city] in your hands. Do not abandon any position for any reason without my orders. You and Lukin will answer for this.

Source: ""Boevoe rasporiazhenie Glavnokomanduiushchego voiskami Zapadnogo Napravleniia ot 29 iiulia 1941 g. komanduiushchemu voiskami 20-i i 16-i Armii na ovladenie gor. Smolensk" [Combat order of the commander-in-chief of the Western Direction's Forces of 29 July 1941 to the commanders of the forces of 20th and 16th Armies on the capture of Smolensk], in *SBDVOV*, issue 37, 60.

8. Combat Order No. 020/op of the Commander of the Forces of 16th Army on 30 July about the Capture of the Northeastern Part of the City of Smolensk

Combat Order No. 020/op, Headquarters, 16th Army,
the grove south of Mordvino,
1430 hours 30 July 1941
Map 1: 100,000

1. The enemy went over to the attack from the Pechersk, Piskarikha, and Oblogino line with up to two infantry divisions on 29 July, pushed the right wing

of the army back considerably to the east, and reached the line of the Stabna River and the western bank of the Dnepr River on 30 July.

2. On the right, 20th Army will go over to the attack on the morning of 31 July, with the mission of capturing the northern outskirts of Smolensk with its left wing units.

The boundary with it – (incl.) Kuchepovo, (incl.) Dubrovo, (incl.) Peresvetovo, (incl.) Zevakino, Astragan State Farm, (incl.) Ignatovshchina, and Smolensk.

3. I have decided to defend the entire front of the army firmly along the Kolodnia River, Kolodnia, and northeast bank of the Dnepr River line and, in the event of an enemy attack, to take not a single step back – die but do not withdraw. 46th RD, with reinforcing units, 152nd RD, with reinforcing units, and 129th RD, with reinforcing units, will go over to a decisive attack at 0400 hours on 31 July and, together with the left wing units of 20th Army, will capture the northeastern part of Smolensk on 31 July. The army's remaining units will firmly hold onto the Dnepr River from Kolodnia and to the south.

The beginning of the attack – 0400 hours on 31 July.

4. 46th RD, with previously attached reinforcing units, will firmly defend the Sen'kovo (northern) and Sen'kovo (southern) line and, in case of an enemy attack, take not a single step back – die but do not withdraw. Go over to the attack from jumping-off positions along the Kolodnia River at 0400 hours on 31 July, with the immediate mission to capture the western bank of the Izoven'ka River and, subsequently, attack toward Smolensk Station.

The boundary on the left – Sen'kovo (southern), Magalenshchina, and the churches in the northeastern outskirts of Smolensk.

5. 152nd RD, with previously reinforcing units, will immediately move a forward detachment forward to the Verkhniaia Kolodnia and Nizhnaia Kolodnia line, with the mission of preventing an enemy penetration to the east. After occupying jumping-off positions for the attack along the line of the forward detachment, attack at 0300 hours on 31 July, with the immediate mission to capture the northeastern outskirts of Smolensk. Subsequently, attack along the railroad toward Smolensk Station, while continuing to concentrate the division's main forces in the Grechishino, Tokari, and Koniuski region on 30 July.

The boundary on the left – the railroad and the northern bank of the Dnepr River.

6. 129th RD, with previously attached reinforcing units, will firmly defend along the Kolodnia River, Rogachevo, and Nemyt'ka Cooperative line and, in the case of an enemy attack, take not a single step back – die but do not withdraw. After the relief of 129th RD by 73rd RD's units on the night of 30-31 July, concentrate in the vicinity of Astragan State Farm (incl.) and Koshaevo, attack in second echelon behind 46th RD, and be prepared to exploit success for the capturing of the northeastern outskirts of Smolensk.

7. Create no fewer than two destroyer detachments of 5-15 men each in all of the divisions, for which you will select the best persons most attached to our Motherland, with the mission of [conducting] diversionary actions in the enemy's rear.

8. The country is conducting an unyielding struggle with a deadly enemy – Fascism – and will inflict a mortal blow on it. The country and the *Stavka* demand

that we return Smolensk into our hands at any and all costs, all the more so to prevent the disruption and protect the conduct of the already begun large-scale operation to liquidate and destroy the overextended enemy.

Retreat means death, and we have nowhere to withdraw – the crossings and bridges in the rear are being blown up by the enemy.

Comrade commanders, political workers, and soldiers of 16th Army! Understand that our responsibility before our country is great. Without regard for our lives, we are obliged to fulfill our mission, and we will fulfill it.

We will employ the severest measures on the spot to panic-mongers, cowards, and traitors according to wartime laws.

Command Post – the grove south of Mordnino.

> The Commander of 16th Army, Lieutenant General Lukin
> The Member of the Military Council, Division Commissar Lobachev
> The Chief of Staff, Colonel Shalin

Source: "Boevoi prikaz komanduiushchego voiskami 16-i Armii No. 020/op ot 30 iiulia 1941 g. na ovladenie severo-vostochnoi chast'iu gor. Smolensk" [Combat order no. 020/op of the commander of the forces of 16th Army on 30 July about the capture of the northeastern part of the city of Smolensk], in *SBDVOV*, issue 37, 212-213.

9. Report of the Commander of the Forces of 16th Army of 31 July 1941 to the Commander-in-Chief of the Western Direction's Forces about the Combat Operations of the Army's Forces

To Timoshenko

Up to this time, the attack 16th Army's units began on 29 July of this year has been experiencing very tense conditions complicated by the absence of the real assistance of tanks.

On 16th Army's right wing – 129th RD has been under constant pressure of the enemy since 1400 hours on 29 July, and its neighbor on the right – 73rd RD, is either completely out of contact or is withdrawing to the east without advanced warning. As, for example, at 0100 hours Sliusarev [commander or chief of staff of 73rd RD] was with the commander of 20th Army. He assured me that his units would be located in the Sukhodol, Korelli, and Stupino region [15-17 kilometers east-northeast of Smolensk] when, actually, according to his words in a personal telephone conversation at 1005 hours, his units were located in the Sobol'ki, Pashkino, and Krasovo region [20 kilometers east-northeast of Smolensk].

At the time, beginning at 0400 hours, when 16th Army's units were fighting in the sector where the boundary lines with 20th Army's units were mutually agreed upon, their absence became apparent, and this forced 129th RD, in particular, to extend its flank to the north, while subjecting it to an attack. The enemy penetrated along the railroad from the Korelli and Kolodnia front with a force of no less than a division and reached Siniavinskii State Farm, having torn our 16th Army's units into two parts.

I had no forces with which to parry the attack. And, since I feared separation from 20th Army in the center and all of the forces concentrated to the north (46th and 169th RDs); and, while believing the Smolensk axis to be the main axis and possibly Comrade Kurochkin was also in difficulty and [sic] … . northern direction, but to my requests about coordination of operations and about a transition of his units to a counterattack with the aim of liquidating the attacking enemy along a broad front so as not to lead to suffering losses to either his or 16th Army's units thanks to isolated operations by the units … . [sic, but possibly, "we were pressed] all the more to the east.

My request to the commander of 20th Army about a transition of 17th TD to the attack (the division was 4 kilometers in my rear at Zevakino and Pomelniki) was turned down by the army commander, justified by the fact that the situation was still not clear and that 73rd RD, which had fled and could not provide genuine help, was at Zevakino. Your order, which obliged the commander of 20th Army to render me assistance, was not fulfilled.

All of this was aggravated by the complete destruction of the heavy machine guns of 46th and 129th RDs in the battle and the presence of numerous artillery pieces which were inoperable because of an absence of shells. Thus, for example, 129th RD, while twice preparing to fire, conducted not a single firing.

I am reporting expressly to force 20th Army's units to occupy the northern and southern front and an assigned boundary line that provides an opportunity to coordinate operations with 34th RC's units south of the railroad and thus infinitely stretched out to the south.

It seems to me that, in the existing situation at the front, the central axis must be the Smolensk [axis], and this must be taken into consideration by 20th Army.

I am reporting as stated.

Lukin, Lobachev

Source: "Doklad komanduiushchego voiskami 16-i Armii ot 31 iiulia 1941 g. Glavnokomanduiushchemu voiskami Zapadnogo Napravleniia o boevykh deistviiakh voisk armii" [Report of the commander of the forces of 16th Army of 31 July 1941 to the commander-in-chief of the Western Direction's forces about the combat operations of the army's forces], in *SBDVOV*, issue 37, 214-215.

10. Report of the Military Council of the Western Direction of 31 July 1941 to the *Stavka* of the High Command about the Reasons for the Withdrawal of our Forces from the City of Smolensk

To Comrade Stalin
Copy: To Comrade Shaposhnikov
31 July 1941

1. 20th Army, together with 16th Army and without sanction of the command, withdrew eastward from Smolensk and abandoned Smolensk in the following circumstances.

20th Army, from the beginning of its half encirclement, has been continuously attacked by large enemy forces of up to 6 infantry divisions and 1 panzer division, with a large quantity of aircraft. The enemy was reinforced by two fresh divisions beginning on 27 July. During this period of fighting, 20th and 16th Armies have suffered immense losses.

As a result, 20th Army, while fighting intense battles, withdrew toward the east north of Smolensk under heavy enemy pressure.

While withdrawing its left wing 73rd RD on 28 July, 20th Army uncovered the right flank and rear of 16th Army's 152nd RD, which was fighting in the northern part of Smolensk. The 152nd RD, observing the withdrawal of 73rd Rifle Division, and, according to the reports of Lukin, under strong enemy fire and attacks against its flanks and rear, in accordance with orders of the commander of 152nd RD, began to withdraw eastward from Smolensk. Behind 152nd RD, 129th RD withdrew from the northeastern part of Smolensk.

2. The command and headquarters of the Western Direction and *front* became aware of the situation in Smolensk from the reports of Kurochkin on the night of 27-28 and on 29 July. Immediately, an order was given to Kurochkin to halt the withdrawal of 152nd and 129th RDs and restore the situation. Upon clarification of the situation, an order was given to Kurochkin on 29 July to combine the leadership of 20th and 16th Armies and, while using 20th Army's reserves, to restore the situation in Smolensk.

3. The counterattacks undertaken by the forces of 152nd, 73rd, and 46th RDs on 29 July were unsuccessful, and the units withdrew eastward from Smolensk to the Sukhodol and Tokari line with heavy losses.

4. Kurochkin gave the [following] order – The remnants of 152nd, 129th, and 46th RD will go over to the attack from the Sukhodol and Tokari line toward Smolensk once again at 0300 hours on 31 July.

5. The situation on the front of 16th and 20th Armies is [as follows] at this time:

The enemy – 129th ID, 15th Bavarian Division, the remnants of 5th ID and 35th ID, and 137th ID with tanks – have been conducting attacks in the direction of Veina, Perfilova, Korelly, and Sen'kovo since first light on 31 July.

The divisions of 20th and 16th Armies, which have been melting away in prolonged and continuous intense fighting (only 1-2,000 fighters remain in the ranks of the divisions), are repelling attacks by the enemy along the Shokino State Farm, Berezhniany, Perfilova, Psardy, Tokari, Mokhraia Bogdanovka, and Oblogino front. Ammunition and fuel is running out in the armies. Resupply is going on only on a limited scale by air (10 TB-3 aircraft per night).

6. The decision reached by the Command of the Western Direction and the [Western] Front:

Hold on to the positions we occupy in the west and northwest. Conduct an attack with part of our forces (57th TD, 229th RD, and 5th MC) in the general direction of Iartsevo in order to defeat the enemy's Iartsevo grouping in cooperation with Group Rokossovsky and free up the supply routes to 16th and 20th Armies.

Timoshenko
Chief of Staff of the Western Front, Sokolovsky

Source: "Doklad Voennogo Soveta Zapadnogo Napravleniia ot 31 iiulia 1941 g. Stavke Verkhovnogo Komandovaniia o prichinakh otkhoda nashikh voisk iz gor. Smolensk" [Report of the Military Council of the Western Direction of 31 July 1941 to the *Stavka* of the High Command about the reasons for the withdrawal of our forces from the city of Smolensk], in *SBDVOV*, issue 37, 60-61.

11. Combat Order of the Headquarters of the Main Command of the Western Direction of 28 July 1941 to the Commander of Group of Forces, Major General Rokossovsky, on the Destruction of the Enemy in the Vicinity of Iartsevo and the Solov'evo Crossing

To the Commander of the Group of Forces, Major General Rokossovsky
To the Commander of 44th Rifle Corps, Iushkevich
Copy: To the Chief of the General Staff

On 27 July, the enemy, with a force of up to 20 tankettes, a group of motorcycles, and a group of tanks operating from northwest of Iartsevo, pushed our covering battalion to the eastern bank of the Vop'River and seized the Solov'evo crossing. By the end of the day, we noted his hurried entrenchment work along the western bank of the Vop' [River] in the sector south of Iartsevo and Zadnia.

The main command orders:

Beginning on the morning of 28 July, the group of forces consisting of 101st TD and 38th, 64th, and 108th RD of 44th RC will destroy the enemy in the Iartsevo region and the Solov'evo crossing and subsequently develop the attack toward Dukhovshchina, while enveloping it from the southwest.

B. Shaposhnikov

Source: "Boevoe rasporiazhenie shtaba Glavnogo Komandovaniia Zapadnogo Napravleniia ot 28 iiulia 1941 g. komanduiushchim gruppoi voisk General-Maior Rokossovskomu na unichtozhenie protivnika v raione Iartsevo, Solov'evskaia pereprava" [Combat order of the headquarters of the Main Command of the Western Direction of 28 July 1941 to the commander of Group of Forces, Major General Rokossovsky, on the destruction of the enemy in the vicinity of Iartsevo and the Solov'evo crossing], in *SBDVOV*, issue 37, 57-58.

12. Extract from, Operational Summary No. 66 of the Headquarters of the Western Front at 2000 hours on 29 July 1941 about the Combat Operations of the *Front's* Forces

Operational Summary No. 66 at 2000 hours 29 July 1941,
Headquarters, Western Front
1: 500,000 and 1: 100,000 scale map

Sixth. Group Rokossovsky. The group's units are firmly holding on to their previous positions along the eastern bank of the Vop' River and concentrating at crossings over the Vop' River south of Iartsevo, while going over to the attack toward the west with part of its forces.

101st TD – in its previous positions.

38th RD is fighting in the Khatyni and Iartsevo sector and the forest to the southwest.

At 1200 hours on 28 July, a composite detachment consisting of 2 battalions of motorized infantry from 7th MC attacked across the Vop' River toward Svishchevo, which it occupied. No enemy was found in the Svishchevo region.

152nd ATBn, 108th RD, is defending the crossing over the Vop' River in the Pishino region with a half-company.

44th RC (64th and 108th RDs) are continuing concentrating along the line of the Vop' River in the vicinity of the crossings at Svishchevo and Solov'evo.

At 1300 hours on 29 July, the corps' units occupied the following positions:

64th RD had concentrated in jumping-off positions for an attack in the Marker 169.9 and Skrushevskoe sector on the eastern bank of the Vop' River

108th RD, after forcing the Vop' River at 0900 on 29 July, captured the western edge of the woods east of Bol'shie and Malye Gorki and Zadnia.

539th RR, 108th RD, forced the Vop' River in the Skrushevskoe and Osinovskoe sector … .

17th MR capture Pnevo.

Units of 7th Panzer and 20th Motorized Divisions are operating against 44th RC.

Group headquarters – the woods 1 kilometer southeast of Fedosova … ..

Eighth. 20th Army conducted sustained fighting all day on 27 July, repelling fierce enemy attacks from the west. The group's mobile units attacked northward and northeastward along the highways.

57th TD, in fighting, occupied Shokino State Farm and Hill 189.3, after driving up to 2 battalions of the enemy 129th ID toward the northeast. The division's units are protecting the Martianoe and Hill 231.6 line.

The positions of the army's remaining units are unchanged.

Army headquarters – the woods north of Kovaleva.

Chief of Staff of the Western Front, Lieutenant General B. Sokolovsky
Member of the Military Council, Regimental Commissar Anshakov
Deputy Chief of the Operations Department of the Western Front's
Headquarters, Western Front, Major General Rubtsov

Source: "Operativnaia svodka shtaba Zapadnogo fronta No. 66 k 20 chasam 29 iiulia 1941 g. o boevykh deistviiakh voisk fronta" [Operational summary of the headquarters of the Western Front no. 66 at 2000 hours on 29 July 1941 about the combat operations of the *front's* forces], in *SBDVOV*, issue 37, 113-115.

13. Report of the Military Council of 20th Army of 30 July 1941 to the Military Council of the Western Direction about the Situation of the Army's Forces and the Decision on the Capture of the City of Smolensk

To the Military Council of the Western Direction
0200 hours 30 July 1941

1. We received your order on restoring the situation in Smolensk at 1900 hours on 29 July. Before receiving your order we organized a counterattack with 152nd RD, part of 73rd RD, and 46th RD. The attack had no success, and the units withdrew with heavy losses.

2. At this time, the following conditions exist in the front: 57th TD and 5th MC slowly advanced toward the north in intense fighting and occupied the Shokino State Farm, Veina, Zaitseva, and Terekhia front, with the defenses of 129th ID in front of them.

The enemy penetrated our front in the Lavrovo and Riazanovo sector at the boundary of 1st MRD and 233rd RD with a force of up to one division (presumably, 15th Bavarian) and developed an attack toward Staroe Koriavino. A counterattack by the units of 1st MRD and 233rd and 144th RD succeeded in halting the enemy penetration, but the units got mixed up and dug in along the Smugulino and Perfilovo line. 153rd RD also slowly withdrew under pressure from 5-6 separate detachments, which bypassed the flanks of its subunits, and occupied the Perfilova and Bukova line by day's end.

73rd RD, while conducting stubborn fighting toward Smolensk, tried to restore the situation but was thrown back to the Stabna River.

229th RD fought stubborn battles to clear the *front's* communications to the east and north along the Morevo, Mashkino, Pokryshkino, and Kuz'mishkino line. The enemy occupied a defense with full-profile trenches with a force of no less than a regiment. The composition of the division, in fact, is comparable to a reinforced battalion.

Thus, by 1900 hours on 29 July, there were no reserves at my disposal.

On the morning of 30 July, I will withdraw 17th TD into reserve in the Voroshnia region and 73rd RD to Kotiki and Puzanovo (replenished from supply carts). 17th TD has 15 tanks and ¼ refill of fuel and can fire only in place.

The artillery units in the army each have 10-15 rounds per gun remaining and from one tenth to one refill of fuel. Without resupply of fuel and ammunition on 30 and 31 July, all transport and artillery will be paralyzed.

3. At 2340 hours Lukin reported that the enemy penetrated 46th RD's front in the vicinity of Sheinovka and is developing an attack along the Smolensk and Moscow road. There are no shells for the heavy machine guns in 46th RD, its artillery has been withdrawn into the rear of 152nd RD after the unsuccessful attack to restore the situation, and while suffering heavy losses, it withdrew in small groups to the Sukhodol and Sen'kova line, where they are assembling.

4. I decided to fulfill your order [in this fashion]:

a) Straining all of the army's efforts, gather up the remaining shells and fuel from the units and transfer them to the units designated for the attack on Smolensk.

b) Defend along the Shokin State Farm, Veina, Petrovskoe, and Bukova front with the remnants of 1st MRD and 233rd and 144th RDs and hold on to that line at any human cost.

c) Deploy 153rd and 73rd RD, with reinforcements, along the narrow Bukova and Sukhodol front and capture the northwestern part of Smolensk by an attack toward Korokhotkino and Korolevka. The remnants of 16th Army's 152nd, 129th, and 46th RDs will deploy along the Sukhodol and Tokari front and, attacking along the railroad, will capture the northeastern part of Smolensk. The beginning of the attack – 0300 hours on 31 July 1941.

d) 229th RD will continue to destroy the enemy along the communications [routes] and seize crossings.

In spite of the heavy losses and the absence of shells and fuel, the armies will nonetheless fight and strike a blow against the enemy. There is no sort of confusion. The troops will operate steadfastly. But those that are called divisions, although some of them have concentrated 50%, themselves represent in the best case 2-3 battalions with small caliber artillery, which are being provided with shells but are without the support of regimental, division, and heavy artillery. The tanks are standing in place.

I request instructions for 108th RD to free up the crossings, together with 229th RD.

The army, without supply of shells and fuel, has fought with the enemy not less than ten days. The absence of supply can lead the army to catastrophe.

> The Commander of 20th Army, Lieutenant General Kurochkin
> The Member of the Military Council, Corps Commissar Semenovsky
> The Chief of Staff, Major General Korneev

Source: "Doklad voennogo soveta 20-i Armii ot 30 iiulia 1941 g. Glavnokomanduiushchemu voiskami Zapadnogo Napravleniia o polozhenii voisk armii I reshenii na ovladenie gor. Smolensk" [Report of the military council of 20th Army of 30 July 1941 to the Commander-in-Chief of the Western Direction about the situation of the forces of the army and the decision on the capture of the city of Smolensk], in SBDVOV, issue 37, 268-269.

14. Combat Order No. 12 of the Commander of Operational Group of Forces of the Iartsevo Axis of 31 July 1941 on the Destruction of the Enemy in the Solov'evo and Kamenka Regions

To the Commander of 44th Rifle Corps
Combat Order No. 12, Headquarters,
Operational Group of Forces of the Iartsevo Axis,
the forest 1 kilometer southeast of Fedosovo,
1900 hours on 31 July 1941

1. The enemy is trying to cut the routes of withdrawal of the units of Kurochkin's army, which is moving from the Kamenka region toward the Solov'evo crossing, with a force of up to one infantry regiment with artillery and mortars.

2. The commander-in-chief has ordered we clear the Solov'evo and Kamenka road of enemy for the movement of our transports with supplies and subsequently, for the passage of the units of Kurochkin's army.

I order:

1) Cease the attack by two regiments of 64th RD and dig in [as follows]:

   a) 30th RR – along occupied lines with the mission to protect 38th RD's left flank;

   b) 159th RR – reliably protect the crossings over the Vop' River at Svishchevo; and

   c) Subordinate 288th RR to the commander of 108th RD.

2. Go over to the attack with the forces of 108th RD, with 288th RR, 64th Rifle Division, and a company of T-26 tanks from 101st TD, having subordinated 17th MR, which is defending the crossing at Solov'evo, to the commander of 108th

RD, and conduct an attack in the general direction of Zadnia and Usinino with the mission to destroy the enemy along that axis and free up the road for the passage of transport with GSM [fuel and lubricants] and ammunition to 20th Army.

3) Turn your personal attention and the attention of the corps' staff to the direct command and control and leadership of 108th RD's combat actions.

4) Report fulfillment.

> The Commander of the Operational Group of Forces of the Iartsevo Axis,
>   Major General Rokossovsky
> The Chief of Staff of the Group of Forces of the Iartsevo Axis,
>   Colonel Malinin

Source: "Boevoi rasporiazhenie komanduiushchego Operativnoi Gruppoi Voisk Iartsevo Napravleniia No. 12 ot 31 iiulia 1941 g. komandiru 44-go Strelkovogo Korpusa na unichtozhenie protivnika v raione Solov'evo, Kamenka" [Combat order no. 12 of the commander of Operational Group of Forces of the Iartsevo Axis of 31 July 1941 on the destruction of the enemy in the Solov'evo and Kamenka regions], in *SBDVOV*, issue 37, 412-413.

15. Combat Order of the Commander of Operational Group of Forces of the Iartsevo Axis of 31 July 1941 to the Commander of 44th Rifle Corps on an Attack in Cooperation with Group Kurochkin

To the Commander of 44th Rifle Corps
Headquarters, Operational Group of Forces of the Iartsevo Axis,
the forest 1 kilometer southeast of Fedosovo,
2245 hours 31 July 1941
Map 1: 100,000 scale

1. The enemy has been trying to conduct an attack against the weakened units of 20th Army from the northwest and west since the morning of 31 July 1941 and, simultaneously, is striving to seize the crossings over the Vop' River in the Iartsevo, Svishchevo, and Solov'evo sector.

2. Comrade Kurochkin's group, having protected itself from the northwest and west, is attacking with a shock group (no fewer than one rifle division and tank units) along the Matrenina and Mushkovichi front (9-10 kilometers southwest and west of Iartsevo).

3. 108th RD, with attached units, while fulfilling the missions assigned to it by Order No. 12 of 31 July 1941, after capturing the Berezuevo and Usinino line and establishing communications with Comrade Kurochkin, will have in mind [plan] an attack toward the north along the Aleksandrovka, Podvoshch'e, and Korolevo front in cooperation with his [Kurochkin's] shock group.

> The Commander of the Operational Group of Forces of the Iartsevo Axis,
>   Major General Rokossovsky
> The Chief of Staff of the Group of Forces of the Iartsevo Axis,
>   Colonel Malinin

Source: "Boevoi rasporiazhenie komanduiushchego Operativnoi Gruppoi Voisk Iartsevskogo Napravleniia ot 31 iiulia 1941 g. komandiru 44-go Strelkovogo Korpusa na nastuplenie vo vzaimodeistvii s gruppoi Kurochkina" [Combat order of the commander of Operational Group of Forces on the Iartsevo Axis of 31 July 1941 to the commander of 44th Rifle Corps on an attack in cooperation with Group Kurochkin], in *SBDVOV*, issue 37, 413-414.

16. Combat Order No. 13 of the Commander of Operational Group of Forces of the Iartsevo Axis No. 13 of 31 July 1941 to the Commanders of 101st Tank and 38th Rifle Divisions about Digging in along the Lines you have Reached

Combat Order No. 13, Headquarters,
Operational Group of Forces of the Iartsevo Axis,
the forest 1 kilometer southeast of Fedosovo,
31 July 1941

To the Commanders of 101st Tank Division and 38th Rifle Division
Copy: To the Commander of 44th Rifle Corps

Halt any further attack.

Dig in along your occupied positions and prepare to defend them firmly.

Conduct combat reconnaissance along the division's front.

The commander of 101st TD will reliably protect his right flank.

The commander of 38th RD will establish communications with the commander of 30th RR, 64th RD, which occupies the woods south of Marker 174.7. 30th Regiment has the mission to protect reliably the left flank of 38th RD.

The Commander of the Operational Group of Forces of the Iartsevo Axis,
Major General Rokossovsky
The Chief of Staff, Colonel Malinin

Source: "Boevoi rasporiazhenie komanduiushchego Operativnoi Gruppoi Voisk Iartsevo Napravleniia No. 13 ot 31 iiulia 1941 g. komandiram 101-i Tankovoi i 38-i Strelkovoi Divizii o zakreplenii na dostignutykh rubezhakh" [Combat order of the commander of Operational Group of Forces of the Iartsevo Axis No. 13 of 31 July 1941 to the commanders of 101st Tank and 38th Rifle Divisions about digging in along the lines you have reached], in *SBDVOV*, issue 37, 414.

Appendix I

The Northern Flank: Nevel' and Velikie Luki, 16-31 July 1941

German 8. The High Command of the Ground Forces (OKH) to Army Group Center, 0510 hours on 24 July 1941

The High Command of the Ground Forces [OKH]
General Staff. Operations Department.
24 July 1941
No. 1390/41. Secret   0510 hours

To: Army Group Center

In accordance with a decision of the Führer with regard to the further conduct of operations, Army Group Center has the [following] mission: immediately after completing the fighting for Smolensk, the remaining infantry formations of Second and Ninth Armies will destroy the enemy located between Smolensk and Moscow and move the forces on the left flank forward as far as possible and then occupy the industrial regions north and south of Moscow. The commitment of the mobile formations into actions against enemy positions on the Dorogobuzh, Kholm, Rzhev, and Ostashkov line should be avoided.

Third Panzer Group, after the completion of fighting in the sector of Army Group Center will be re-subordinated to Army Group North, with the mission of disrupting communications between Moscow and Leningrad, beginning with the seizure of the Valdai Hills. After fulfilling missions in Army Group North's the area of operations, Third and Fourth Panzer Groups will be employed by Army Group Center.

The subordination of Third Panzer Group to Army Group North must be coordinated between the commands of the two army groups. Inform the High Command of the Ground Forces about the results.

Second Panzer Group and the infantry divisions of Army Group Center, which have advanced across the Dnepr from the region south of Mogilev, will form groupings under the overall command of Field Marshal von Kluge to begin offensive operations toward Gomel and Briansk, together with Army Group South.

Submit reports about the groupings of forces and the period of readiness to a conference to take place at the chief of the OKH's General Staff no later than 25 July. The boundary line between the army groups remains as before. The Velikie Luki, Toropets, and Ostashkov road is located in the dispositions of Army Group North.

The command of Army Group Center will submit a report about the further conduct of operations to the east and the periods of its forces readiness by 25 July 1941.

The time for conducting the conference at the Chief of the General Staff will be announced additionally.

The High Command of the Ground Forces

Source: *Sbornik voenno-istoricheskikh materialov Velikoi Otechestvennoi voiny, vypusk 18* [Collection of military-historical materials of the Great Patriotic War, issue 18] (Moscow: Voenizdat, 1960), 235. Prepared by the Military-Historical Department of the Military-Scientific Directorate of the Red Army General Staff and classified secret.

1. Combat Order of the Commander of the Forces of 22nd Army of 21 July 1941 on the Concentration and Combat Protection of 62nd Rifle Corps

To the Commander of 62nd RC

1. We are occupying Velikie Luki.

2. 29th RC (179th and 214th RDs) are attacking toward Nevel' with to aim of destroying the enemy and assisting your withdrawal. 179th RD, in regard to time, should be in the Stupino region (7 kilometers north of Porech'e, and 214th RD – in the Lake Odgast region 8-10 kilometers northeast of Zui.

3. An automobile column (50 vehicles) with ammunition, fuel, and food is being sent to you in the Zui region

4. Your region will be protected by fighter aircraft.

5. 29th RC (northwest of you) will remain in place and assemble the corps before the automobile column arrives from Toropets and reaches your positions.

Ershakov, Leonov, Zakharov

Source: "Boevoe rasporiazhenie komanduiushchego voiskami 22-i Armii ot 21 iiulia 1941 g. na sosredotochenie i boevoe obespechenie 62-go Strelkovogo korpusa] [Combat order of the commander of the forces of 22nd Army of 21 July 1941 on the concentration and combat protection of 62nd Rifle Corps], in *SBDVOV*, issue 37, 299.

2. Combat Order No. 07 of the Commander of the Forces of 22nd Army of 21 July 1941 on the Destruction of the Enemy South of Velikie Luki

To the Commanders of 179th, 126th, and 214th RDs
To the Commanders of 366th RR, 48th TD, and the Chief of the Velikie Luki Garrison, Major General Silkin
Combat Order No. 07/op,
Headquarters, 22nd Army Nazimovo,
21 July 1941
1:50,000 and 100,000 scale maps

1. We are occupying Velikie Luki. The enemy is withdrawing toward the south and fighting in the Porech'e and Staraia Reka regions with our 214th RD, which is attacking toward the north.

2. The commander of 179th RD will subordinate 366th RR to itself and, together with the commander of 48th TD, will liquidate the remnants of the enemy south of Velikie Luki by no later than 1000 hours on 21 July, after which you will turn the division (without 234th RR and 48th TD) toward the south with the aim of destroying the enemy fighting with 214th RD.

Fill out 234th RR by day's end on 21 July.

3. The commander of 48th TD, upon liquidation of the enemy south of Velikie Luki together with the commander of 179th RD, will occupy defenses along the western, southwestern, and southern outskirts of Velikie Luki.

4. Appoint Major General Silkin as the chief of the garrison at Velikie Luki.

The Commander of 22nd Army, Lieutenant General Ershakov
The Member of the Military Council, Corps Commissar Leonov
The Chief of Staff of 22nd Army, Major General Zakharov

Source: "Boevoi prikaz komanduiushchego voiskami 22-i Armii No. 07 ot 21 iiulia 1941 g. na unichtozhenie protivnika iuzhnee Velikie Luki" [Combat order no. 07 of the commander of the forces of 22nd Army on the destruction of the enemy south of Velikie Luki], in *SBDVOV*, issue 37, 300.

3. Combat Order of the Commander of the Forces of 22nd Army of 26 July 1941 to the Commanders of 29th and 62nd Rifle Corps on Holding onto Velikie Luki

To the Commander of 29th Rifle Corps
To the Commander of 62nd Rifle Corps
Copy: to Major General Silkin (through the commander of 29th RC)

The commander-in-chief, under the signatures of Timoshenko and Shaposhnikov, once again confirms, "Hold on to Velikie Luki come what may. Liquidate the penetration by the enemy on the flank."

I demand greater steadfastness in the defense of their positions from the commanders of corps and divisions.

Do not permit withdrawals without orders.

I am entrusting personal responsibility for the defense of Velikie Luki to General Samokhin [Major General Aleksandr Georgievich Samokhin, commander of 29th RC] and Commissar Danilov.

Karmanov [Major General Ivan Petrovich Karmanov, commander of 62nd RC] will firmly protect the junction [boundary line] with Samokhin and support him in so far as possible in the successful struggle for the Velikie Luki region and also prevent such a penetration or envelopment of Biriukov's [Major General Nikolai Ivanovich Biriukov, commander of 186th RD] left flank. Form mobile groups once again.

Ershakov, Leonov, Zakharov

Source: "Boevoe rasporiazhenie komanduiushchego voiskami 22-i Armii ot 26 iiulia 1941 g. komandiram 29-go i 62-go strelkovykh korpusov na uderzhanie Velikie Luki" [Combat order of the commander of the forces of 22nd Army of 26 July 1941 to the commanders of 29th and 62nd Rifle Corps on holding onto Velikie Luki], in *SBDVOV*, issue 37, 303.

Appendix J

The Southern Flank, the Fall of Mogilev and the Problem of 21st Army (Guderian's Advance to the Sozh River), 16-31 July 1941

1. Operational Summary No. 41 of the Headquarters of the Western Front of 2000 hours on 16 July 1941 about the Combat Operations of the *Front's* Forces

Operational Summary No. 41 at 2000 hours on 16 July 1941,
Headquarters, Western Front
1: 50,000 scale map

First. During the day on 16 July, the forces of the Western Front fought fiercely to liquidate the enemy forces penetrating along the Nevel', Vitebsk, Smolensk, Gorki, and Propoisk axes and conducted an attack toward Bobruisk.

Second. 22nd Army fought sustained battles with enemy units, especially along the Idritsa and Nevel' and Dretun' and Nevel' axes.

51st RC – 179th RD's units fought in the Zabel'e region. During this fighting, its headquarters was encircled. The majority of its headquarters commanders perished.

170th RD – attacked toward Nevel' with part of its forces. There is no information about the results of the fighting.

112th and 98th RDs fought along the Lake Liva Gorbachevo and Dvorishche line.

The detachment, which was defending Nevel' (part of the Nevel' garrison and a MRR of 48th TD), being pursued by enemy motorized units, withdrew to Velikie Luki.

The headquarters of 22nd Army moved to the Nazimovo Station region at 2100 hours.

Third. 19th Army carried out a regrouping during the day with the aim of preparing an offensive for the capture of the Vitebsk region and, simultaneously, prepared an antitank line along the Shalatoni and Lelekvinskaia Station line.

7th MC (14th and 18th TDs) set about preparing antitank positions along the Shalatoni and Bolotinka line and, simultaneously, prepared for an offensive together with 34th RC.

158th RD (720th RR and one rifle battalion) is assembling in the Novoselki region at day's end. There is no news about the remainder of the division.

162nd RD assembled in the Baksheevo region for the preparation of antitank positions at Motyki.

129th RD was on the march to its jumping-off positions for the offensive by 2200 hours. The head of the column – at the junction of the Moscow and Leningrad highway.

38th RD is completing its concentration in the Iartsevo region.

158th RD [sic] is concentrating from the Riabtsevo Station, Grinevo, Moksheevo, Sloboda, and Pan'skoe region to the Nikulino, Korovino, and Turovo region.

There is no news about the location of the remaining units and the corps' headquarters. No information has been received about the positions of the army's remaining units as of 16 July.

Headquarters of 19th Army – Bol'shaia Ploskaia, and the woods at Kapustino (10 kilometers southeast of Rudnia) beginning at 2400 hours on 16 July.

Fourth. 20th Army was conducting sustained fighting along the line of the Orshitsa and Dnepr Rivers up to 1630 hours on 15 July.

69th RC. 73rd RD is fighting stubbornly with enemy units in the Seletka and Orsha sector along the Orshitsa River.

Information has not been received from 69th RC's remaining units.

18th RD occupies the Dnepr River line in the (incl.) Orsha, Oktiabr' State Farm, and Prontsevka sector. The left wing regiment of the division attacked the enemy in Kopys' on the morning of 14 July, but was soon forced to abandon Oktiabr' State Farm by enemy artillery fire.

144th RD. A battalion of the division, faced by up to two companies of enemy infantry with 5-7 tanks, fought its way into and occupied Liady.

1st MRD destroyed up to a battalion of motorized infantry of the enemy 18th PzD and its rear area at 1800 hours on 15 July by an attack on Chirino, capturing 150 prisoners, including 6 officers, 40 vehicles, a cash box, staff documents, and submachine guns.

The enemy strengthened their attacks in the Orsha region on the morning of 16 July. At the same time, it was determined that up to 50 tanks and up to 180 vehicles with infantry were moving from Orsha to Dubrovno.

5th MC – is in the region north of Krasnoe, where it was subjected to repeated fierce enemy bombing raids.

Fifth. 13th Army. The army's units continued operations against penetrating enemy tanks and motorized infantry. As a consequence of the enemy having penetrated into the depth of the army's dispositions and disrupted the army's command and control of forces, communications, and supply routes, during the second half of the day on 16 July, the army commander decided to withdraw the army's units to an intermediate defense line along the Pronia River.

The army's units withdrew to [the following] positions by 1600-1800 hours on 16 July:

20th MC – the Orsha and Domany front, facing small groups of enemy;

110th RD – the Nichiporovichi and Nizhnyi Prudki front;

172nd RD – Trebukhi and Vil'chitsy, while slowly withdrawing toward Kureni;

507th RR (148th RD) – the Dashkovka and Makhovo front;

137th RD – Smol and Kopani; and

132nd RD – (incl.) Kopani and Usushek.

All of the army's units are withdrawing toward the east. No information has been received about the army's other units.

Headquarters of 13th Army – the forest 5-7 kilometers east of Krichev.

Sixth. 21st Army. The army's forces are continuing their attack in the general direction of Bobruisk. Small groups of tanks are withdrawing westward opposite the army's front.

67th RC (102nd and 151st RDs), having completed forcing the Dnepr River, reached the Rogachev and Bykhov Station railroad. Exact information about the positions of the corps' units has not been received.

Headquarters of 67th RC – in the forest 5 kilometers east of Guta.

Small subunits of tanks and motorized infantry are operating in front of the corps. A concentration of infantry has been noted in the Falevichi region. The movement of columns of infantry along the road from Bobruisk to Rogachev, with its head at Bykhov, was detected at 0645 hours on 15 July.

63rd RC (167th and 154th RDs) continued its attack toward the west. Other information about the position of the corps has not been received.

66th RC: 232nd RD There is no news about the position of the division's units.

Colonel Kurmashev's detachment reached the Drazhnia and Zapol'e front at 1500 hours on 15 July and is facing toward the northeast.

The remnants of 24th RD, which have been combined into detachments, have been concentrated in the Kosarichi region and to the south.

75th RD withdrew to the Gulevichi and Vilcha front, along the Sluch' River, where it is fighting with units of enemy 40th ID.

25th MC arrived forward in the Krichev region at 0015 hours on 16 July 1941 in order to fulfill its mission in accordance with *front* Order No. 065.

Headquarters of 50th Army – Gomel'

Seventh. 4th Army conducted defensive work in the Zarech'e and Malyi Propoisk sector along the Pronia River line and started liquidating enemy tanks and motorized units that penetrated into the Propoisk region on the morning of 16 July.

28th RC: 143rd RD is occupying defenses along the Zarech'e and Berezovka line; 42nd RD is defending the Zakrupets and mouth of the Pronia River line. At 0300 hours on 15 July, 100 enemy tanks and motorized infantry penetrated the front at the boundary between 42nd and 55th RDs, seized Malyi Propoisk, and advanced along the highway to Krichev. The division is continuing to defend along the Pronia River in its previous positions.

55th RD, while defending in the (incl.) Propoisk and Kamenka Station sector along the Sozh River line, began liquidating enemy tanks and motorized infantry that have penetrated, in cooperation with 6th RD and part of 4th AbnC's forces.

6th RD, having halted the penetrating tanks and motorized infantry along the Ozery and Aleksandrovka (Second) line, set about liquidating the penetration on the morning of 16 July.

No news has been received about the remaining units.

Headquarters of 4th Army – the forest 6-7 kilometers east of Krichev.

Eighth. 16th Army. No news received.

[From Operational Summary No. 42 of the Headquarters of the Western Front at 0800 hours on 17 July 1941, the entry for 16th Army read: "Sixth. 16th Army. the

army prepared to attack the northern outskirts of Smolensk on 16 July 1941. 46th RD attacked from the Kholm and Motyka region toward Demidov at 1330 hours on 16 July 1941. The results of the fighting are being clarified. It is quiet on the division's front . . . ."]

Ninth. The VVS of the *front* and armies destroyed enemy aircraft at their airfields, bombed the crossings over the Dnepr River, destroyed enemy tanks and motorized infantry, protected our most important objectives in the rear, and conducted reconnaissance of the enemy on the night of 14-15 July, during the day on 15 July and overnight of 15-16 July.

One enemy ME-109 aircraft was shot down. Our losses – one MIG did not return to its airfield.

> The Chief of Staff of the Western Front, Lieutenant General Malandin
> The Chief of the Operations Department, *Kombrig* Liubarsky

Source: "Operativnaia svodka shtaba Zapadnogo fronta No. 41 k 20 chasam 16 iiulia 1941 g. o boevykh deistviiakh voisk fronta," [Operational summary No. 41 of the headquarters of the Western Front of 2000 hours on 16 July 1941 about the combat operations of the *front's* forces], in *SBDVOV*, issue 37, 91.

2. Report of the Headquarters of 13th Army about the Positions and Condition of its Forces on 21 July 1941

Report about the Positions and Condition of the Units on 21 July 1941

20th MC, consisting of 26th and 38th TDs and 210th MRD occupied [the following] defense lines by the morning of 21 July:

a) 26th TD – Gladkovo, Sukhari, Bol'shoe Bushkovo, and Zhdanovichi, with its front toward the east;

b) 210th MRD occupies a defense along the Ugly, Gromaki, and Ladyzhino line: and

c) 38th TD occupies a defense along the (incl.) Ladyzhino, Cherepy, Nichiporovichi line.

There is no information about the dispositions of 20th MC's regiments and their condition on 21 July.

Headquarters of 20th MC – the forest 2 kilometers east of Rusenka.

53rd RD, with 3rd Bn, 438th CAR, and 301st HA Regiment, while defending the Shklov and Pleshchitsy sector along the eastern bank of the Dnepr River, was smashed as a result of an enemy penetration in the Shklov region, and its remnants withdrew to the Pochinok region; the composite detachment (about a company) of 223rd RR is operating as part of 110th RD.

61st RC is defending the Mogilev region and the fortifications of the Mogilev bridgehead:

110th RD, with 1st Bn, 438th CAR, and without 411th R, but with 514th RR (without one battalion), is firmly defending the (incl.) Nikolaevka, Nizhnyi Prudki, and Pavlovka defensive line.

425th RR is defending the (incl.) Nikolaevka, Nizhnyi Prudki, and Ozer'e sector.

411th RR – in the commander of 61st RC's reserve – is concentrated in the woods 2 kilometer north of Novyi Liubuzh.

The composite company of 223rd RR, 457th Sep. AABn (without equipment), and a chemical company – the commander of 110th RD's reserve – is in the woods northwest of Telegi.

850 men from march battalions arrived at the disposal of the commander of 110th RD on 18 July and were concentrated in the forest southwest of Evdokimovichi.

Headquarters of 110th RD – the woods southwest of Telegi.

172nd RD, consisting of 394th RR, 388th RR, 747th RR, 148th RD's 507th Regiment (without one battalion), one battalion of 161st RD's 543rd RR, and a battalion of 514th RR, are defending the Polykovichi, Pashkovo, Tishovka, Buinichi Station, Grebenovo, Poletniki, Bol'shaia Borovka, and Liubuzh line. Units reinforcing 172nd RD – 601st HAR and 200th and 209th ATBns.

394th RR is defending the Polykovichi and (incl.) Zatish'e sector;

388th RR – Zatish'e and Buinichi Station; and

747th RR, with 507th RR (without one battalion) and the battalion of 543rd RR, are defending the Brody, Grebenovo, Poletniki, Bol'shaia Borovka, and Liubuzh sector, with their fronts to the south;

2nd Bn, 514th RR – the commander of 172nd RD's reserve – is in the Kholmy region and the forest to the southeast.

Headquarters of 172nd RD – the southwestern outskirts of Mogilev.

20th RC:

137th RD concentrated in the forest north of Ostrovy. There is no information about the dispositions and the numerical strengths of 137th RD's units.

132nd RD followed after 137th RD's units on the morning of 20 July. The exact locations and numerical strengths of its units are unknown. Information about 137th and 132nd RDs' units requires clarification.

160th RD's remnants were formed into a composite detachment in the Poniatovka region.

There is no information about the locations and combat and numerical strengths of 143rd RD.

187th RD – 236th RR is operating in the Rogi region as part of 21st Army. There is no information about the division's remaining regiments.

4th AbnC is putting itself in order after days of fighting along the Krichev axis.

8th [Abn] Brigade attacked toward Studenets on 20 July, but was driven back by subunits of enemy 39th TR and, while preparing for a new attack toward Krichev, occupied a line in the Pogumenskii and Bradzany sector along the eastern bank of the Sazhenka River by day's end on 20 July.

7th [Abn] Brigade was putting itself in order after withdrawing to the P. Velikan, Griazivets, Koronets, the grove north of Koronets, and Zamost'e line, while preparing a new attack toward Krichev.

The Composite Battalion concentrated in the Klimovichi region by 2000 hours on 20 July.

Headquarters of 4th AbnC – Klimovichi.

Colonel Grishin's detachment is moving along the highway between Aleksandrovka No. 1 and Aleksandrovka No. 2 on the morning of 20 July. There is no information about the detachment's combat composition.

The Chief of Staff of 13th Army, *Kombrig* Petrushevsky
The Chief of the Operations Department, Lieutenant Colonel Ivanov

Source: "Svedeniia shtaba 13-i Armii o polozhenii i sostoianii voisk na 21 iiulia 1941 g" [Report of the headquarters of 13th Army about the positions and condition of its forces on 21 July 1941], in *SBDVOV*, issue 37, 196-197.

3. Excerpt from Operational Summary No. 45 of the Headquarters of the Western Front at 2000 hours on 18 July 1941 about the Combat Operations of the *Front's* Forces

Operational Summary No. 45 at 2000 hours 18 July 1941,
Headquarters, Western Front
1:500,000 scale map

Fifth. 13th Army. No information received. Liaison delegates [officers] sent by aircraft have still not returned.

Sixth. 21st Army. The army's units continued attacks in the general direction of Bobruisk during the day. The enemy, offering stubborn resistance, often counterattacked, supported by strong mortar and artillery fire. More than four infantry divisions with tanks are operating against 63rd RC's units.

67th RC is continuing to protect the army's right flank.

187th RD, situated in its previous positions, is protecting the corps from the right.

15th RD is continuing its attack, which began at 0300 hours on 18 July, toward Bykhov Station. The results of the attack are being clarified.

102nd RD is continuing its attack from the Novyi Bykhov region toward the northwest, which began at 0700 hours on 18 July. Information has not been received about the results of the fighting.

Headquarters of 67th RC – the forest east of Zvonets.

63rd RC (61st, 167th, and 154th RDs) is fighting in its previous positions, while repelling local enemy counterattacks. The positions of the corps' units are being verified.

The corps' losses – killed – 15, wounded – 300, and 6 tankettes destroyed.

Headquarters of the corps – the Pioneer Camp (east of Rogachev).

66th RC. 232nd RD was fighting along the Borovaia, Korolev Station, and Slobodka line.

117th RD and 110th RR, 53rd RD, occupied a defense in its previous sector along the eastern bank of the Dnepr River.

News has not been received about the positions of the units of Kurmashev's Group.

A detachment of the Pinsk Military Flotilla was fighting with the enemy in the vicinity of Novaia Belitsa (5 kilometers north of Parichi) along the Berezina River.

The remnants of 24th RD were being concentrated in the Ozarichi region.

75th RD repelled an enemy attack along the Lenino and Mlynok line along the Sluch' River. Up to an infantry division (probably the 40th) with cavalry are operating in front of the division.

Headquarters of 66th RC – Peschanaia Rudnia.

25th MC: 50th TD is in the Voshchanka and Aleshnia region. A detachment of 10 tanks and a motorized company have been fighting in the Mashevskaia Sloboda region since 1300 hours on 17 July. The detachment destroyed 70-80 wheeled vehicles, 10 tanks, and up to 500 soldiers and officers during the fighting.

219th MRD is being concentrated in the Chechersk and Voronovka region.

55th TD – is in its previous positions at Novozybkov.

Headquarters of 25th MC – Koromna.

Headquarters of 21st Army – Gomel'

Seventh. 4th Army is continuing to fight stubbornly with enemy penetrating along the Cherikov axis.

28th RC: 42nd RD, as a result of the enemy's penetration, withdrew its left wing and occupies the Zakrupets, Gizhenka, and Novinka front, with its front facing west and south.

6th RD is defending the (incl.) Dolgoe, Sokolovka, and Polepenskii line with two RRs (less one battalion).

55th RD, while conducting a regrouping, occupies a defense along the eastern bank of the Sozh River, with 107th RR in the Kremianka and Kamenka Station sector and one rifle battalion along the eastern bank of the Udocha River in Cherikov. The division's remaining units were concentrated in the forested region south of Cherikov.

4th AbnC is protecting the crossings over the Sozh River at Khislavichi, Mstislavl', and Krichev with two brigades and four battalions.

The enemy concentrated 28 tanks, including 4 heavy, 42 armored personnel carriers, 115 motorcycles, 17 guns (including 5 heavy), and up to 150 vehicles in the Krichev region, under the protection of 10 fighters and 10 bombers.

The front is wide open from Krichev to Roslavl'.

Headquarters of 4th Army – Kostiukevichi … .

> The Chief of Staff of the Western Front, Lieutenant General Malandin
> The Military Commissar of the Headquarters of the *Front*,
> > Regimental Commissar Anshakov
> The Chief of the Operations Department, *Kombrig* Liubarsky

Source: "Operativnaia svodka shtaba Zapadnogo fronta No. 45 ot 20 chasam 18 iiulia 1941 g. o boevykh deistviiakh voisk fronta" [Operational summary no. 45 of the Headquarters of the Western Front on 2000 hours on 18 July 1941 about the combat operations of the *front's* forces], in *SBDVOV*, issue 37, 95-96.

4. Combat Order No. 05 of the Commander of the Forces of 21st Army of 22 July 1941 on the Destruction of the Enemy's Bobruisk-Bykhov Grouping

Combat Order No. 05,
Headquarters, 21st Army, Gomel',
1730 hours on 22 July 1941
1:100,000 and 1:500,000 scale maps

1. The army's mission – as before – destroy the enemy's Bobruisk-Bykhov grouping

2. 25th MC (50th TD and 219th MRD) and 696th ATR will capture Propoisk, destroy the enemy's Propoisk grouping, and cut the enemy's Krichev-Propoisk supply route. Be prepared to destroy the enemy's Bykhov grouping in cooperation with 67th RC and prepare an attack toward Shelomy, Krasnitsa, and Slobodka.

3. 67th RC (102nd, 151st, and 187th RDs MMP [sic], 387th HAR, and 16th MtrBtry) will firmly hold onto its occupied positions from Prudok to Dobryi Dub, Stalin State Farm, and Dubrovskii village.

Conduct a regrouping on the night of 22-23 July and be prepared to go over to the attack on the morning of 23 July, with the mission of destroying the enemy's Bykhov grouping.

4. 63rd RC (61st, 167th, and 154th RDs, 110th RR, and 36th LAR, with previous reinforcements) will continue to fulfill its assigned missions.

5. 117th RD and 387th HAR will reach the Dovsk region on the morning of 23 July and become subordinate to the commander of 67th RC.

155th RD will concentrate in the Dovsk region as my reserve at day's end on 23 July.

6. 66th RC (232nd RD, one RR of the FR, and 32nd CD's tank regiment) will destroy the enemy along the Moshna Station and Ratmirovichi axis by a surprise attack at 1200 hours on 23 July. Support 66th RC with one flight of the aviation-regiment on order of 66th RC's commander.

75th RD will firmly defend the Beleva, Naida, and Liaskovichi line and prevent an enemy penetration toward the east.

7. 24th RD will send out strong groups of partisans along the Glussk, Selets, BVO Collective Farm, and Novoselki line on the evening of 23 July, with the mission of operating in close coordination with 66th RC and protecting the operations of our cavalry.

8. The Chief of Artillery of 21st Army will combine command and control of 67th and 63rd RCs' artillery on 23 July, with the aim of strict direction of the use of all the power of the artillery in support of the offensive.

Prepare fire obstacles at the boundary between 67th and 63rd RCs.

AA artillery will reliably protect the Dovsk region.

CP [Command Post] – in the Dovsk region.

9. The commander of the army's VVS will direct the main efforts of the air forces on 22, 23, and 24 July at the destruction of the enemy groupings in the Propoisk and Bykhov regions. Support the offensive by 66th RC with one regimental flight. Protect the transport of 115th RD.

Prepare a strike against the enemy in the event he goes over to the attack against 66th RC.

In addition, employ small groups to support 75th RD's defense, and also protect the attack by 25th MC and 67th RC with fighter aircraft.

10. Corps and division commanders will firmly hold the command and control of their units in their hands. Suppress panic and cowardice by any means.

> The Commander of the Army, Colonel General Kuznetsov
> The Member of the Military Council, Division Commissar Kolonin
> The Chief of Staff of the Army, Major General Gordov

Source: "Boevoi prikaz komanduiushchego voiskami 21-i Armii No. 05 ot 22 iiulia 1941 g. na unichtozhenie Bobruisko-Bykhovskoi gruppirovki protivnika" [Combat order no. 05 of the commander of the forces of 21st Army of 22 July 1941 on the destruction of the enemy's Bobruisk-Bykhov grouping], in *SBDVOV*, issue 37, 287-288.

5. Excerpt from Operational Summary No. 55 of the Headquarters of the Western Front at 2000 hours on 23 July 1941 about the Combat Operations of the *Front's* Forces

Operational Summary No. 55 at 2000 hours on 23 July 1941,

Headquarters, Western Front

1:500,000 scale map

First. On 23 July fierce battle is raging along the front with superior enemy forces in the Nevel', Smolensk, and El'nia regions … ..

Fifth. 13th Army is continuing to conduct the struggle in the Mogilev, Propoisk, and Krichev regions.

61st RC has been subjected to bitter attacks by up to 5 enemy infantry divisions from the Pleshchitsy, Kniazhitsy, Selets, Vil'chitsy, and Dary regions since the morning of 22 July. As a result, at 1330 hours on 22 July, the enemy succeeded in seizing Lupolovo. The battle is continuing. The enemy is covering the Mogilev region with aerostatic obstacles.

4th AbnC's units conducted an attack toward Krichev from the east on 22 and 23 July. The attacks had no success.

Headquarters of 13th Army – the forest east of Rodnia.

Sixth. 4th Army, having attacked toward Propoisk from the west with the units of 28th and 20th RCs, in cooperation with 219th MRD, captured the northeastern outskirts of Propoisk; the attack is continuing.

According to information from 13th Army, the remaining units of 20th RC reached the crossings over the Sozh River at Aleksandrovka 1 and 2 from the Pronia River line. The commander of 20th RC [Major General Stepan Illarionovich Eremin] is wounded.

Headquarters, 4th Army – the forest 6 kilometers west of Krasnopol'e.

Group Kachalov dislodged the enemy's forward units by 1700 hours on 23 July and is fighting for crossings over the Stomet' River (18 kilometers southeast of Pochinok), while under constant pressure of enemy aircraft.

Headquarters of the Group – Stodolishche.

Seventh. 21st Army's units were fighting in their previous positions at 1400 hours on 23 July. As before, units of enemy 53rd, 43rd, and 35th ACs, 3rd and 4th PzDs, 1st CD, and 117th IR are operating opposite the army's front.

67th RC: 187th RD firmly defending the Peregon and Bakhan' front;

151st RD is defending the Zatish'e and Iskany line; and

102nd RD captured the southwestern outskirts of Lazarovichi and Koromka line by 1400 hours on 22 July.

Headquarters of the corps – Zvonets.

63rd RC – is in its previous positions.

117th RD received the mission to concentrate in the Dovsk region by the morning of 23 July.

155th RD is concentrating in the Dovsk region by the end of 23 July.

66th RC – 232nd RD is continuing to fulfill its assigned mission for the capture of the Novaia Belitsa and Slobodka line.

Kurmashev's detachment was fighting in the vicinity of Rabkor Station at day's end on 22 July.

BEPO [Armored Train] No. 52 was fighting encircled in the Zales'e region at day's end on 22 July.

BEPO No. 50 is at Kontsevichi Station.

Headquarters of 66th Rifle Corps – Kobyl'shchiki.

25th MC (50th TD and 219th MRD) – fighting for possession of Propoisk.

55th TD passed through Zimnitsa with part of its forces.

Information about the positions of the remaining units has not been received by 1800 hours on 23 July.

Eighth. The VVS of the *front* fulfilled their missions for the destruction of enemy motor-mechanized units along the El'nia and Iartsevo axes. Cargo was dropped on the Mogilev airfield for our forces.

Enemy losses for 23 July: two DO-17, one HE-112, two ME-110, and one APADO shot down, for a total of 6 aircraft.

Our losses: 3 MIG-3, two I-16, and 2 SB shot down, 3 TB-3, two IL-2, and two I-16 did not return to their airfields; and one SB was lost in an accident.

> The Chief of Staff of the Western Front, Lieutenant General Sokolovsky
> The Military Commissar of the Headquarters,
>   Regimental Commissar Anshakov
> The Chief of the Operations Department, Lieutenant General Malandin

Source: "Operativnaia svodka shtaba Zapadnogo fronta No. 55 k 20 chasam 23 iiulia 1941 g. o boevykh deistviiakh voisk fronta" [Operational summary no. 55 of the headquarters of the Western Front of 2000 hours on 23 July 1941 about the combat operations of the *front's* forces], in *SBDVOV*, issue 37, 103-104.

6. *Stavka* VK Order No. 00493 about the Division of the Western Front

23 July 1941

With the aim of facilitating command and control of forces, the *Stavka* of the High Command orders:

1. Divide the Western Front into the Western and Central [Fronts].

2. Place 22nd, 16th, 20th, and 19th Armies in the composition of the Western Front.

3. Include 13th and 21st Armies in the composition of the newly-formed Central Front. Disband 4th Army, including its formations in 13th Army.

4. Establish the boundary between the Western and Central Front [as]: Briansk, Roslavl', Shklov, and Minsk, all points inclusive for the Western Front.

5. Consider the Gomel', Bobruisk, and Volkovysk axes as the Central Front's main operational axes.

6. Appoint the commander of 21st Army, Colonel General Kuznetsov as the commander of the Central Front. Deploy the *front's* headquarters from the headquarters of 4th Army.

7. Carry out the division of the *fronts* beginning at 2400 hours on 24 July.

8. The commander of the Central Front will establish the order of battle of 13th and 21st Armies and submit it to the *Stavka* for approval.

9. Report receipt and fulfillment.

For the *Stavka* of the High Command

Zhukov

Source: "Prikaz Stavki VK No. 00493 o razdelenii Zapadnogo fronta" [*Stavka* order no. 00493 about the division of the Western Front], in Zolotarev, "*Stavka* VK 1941," 88-89.

7. Excerpt from Operational Summary No. 59 of the Headquarters of the Western Front at 0800 hours on 26 July 1941 about the Combat Operations of the *Front's* Forces

Operational Summary No. 59 at 0800 hours on 26 July 1941,
Headquarters, Western Front
1:500,000 scale map

First. The forces of the Western Front fought along the entire front on 25 July, especially fiercely along the Velikie Luki, Smolensk, and Mogilev axes, while continuing the slow advance of new forces with the aim of liquidating the penetration in the Smolensk region … ..

Fifth. 13th Army. The army's units were fighting sustained battles in the Mogilev and Propoisk regions all day on 25 July.

61st RC (according to a report by Lieutenant Colonel Ivanov and the Chief of the Staff of the army, *Kombrig* Petrushevsky) abandoned Mogilev under pressure from up to five enemy infantry divisions reinforced by tanks and withdrew to the Bol'shoe Bushkovo and Vas'kovichi line by the end of the day. However, units are still holding on to Mogilev and have been ordered to hold out in Mogilev at all costs.

20th RC continued to cross to the southeastern bank of the Sozh River in the vicinity of Aleksandrovka 2 with its units and, simultaneously, was attacking toward Propoisk from the east. The attempts to capture Propoisk have failed, and Propoisk is in enemy's hands.

4th AbnC put itself in order [reorganized] in the Krichev Station No. 2, Mikheevichi, and Kamenka region all day on 25 July.

Headquarters of 13th Army – Rudnia

Sixth. 4th Army. 28th RC continues to defend the southeastern bank of the Sozh River along the Borisovichi and Kliny line. An attack on Propoisk during the day on 25 July by part of the corps' forces had no success.

Headquarters of 4th Army – the forest 6 kilometers west of Krasnopol'e … …

Seventh. 21st Army. No changes in the army's positions at the time this summary was prepared.

Information has not been received about Group Gorodovikov … .

Eighth. The VVS of the *front* continued to deliver concentrated strikes against enemy forces, while assisting the ground forces.

Enemy losses: 1 Iu-88 and 1 "AIST" shot down and, according to additional information, 2 ME-109 and one aerostatic balloon shot down. Total: 4 aircraft and one aerostatic balloon.

Our losses: for 25 July 1 SB shot down, 2 TB-3 destroyed on the ground, and 3 PE-2 did not return to their airfileds.

The Commander of the Western Front, Lieutenant General Eremenko
The Member of the Military Council, Division Commissar Lestev
The Chief of Staff, Lieutenant General Malandin

Source: "Operativnaia svodka shtaba Zapadnogo fronta No. 59 k 8 chasam 26 iiulia 1941 g. o boevykh deistviiakh voisk fronta" [Operational summary no. 59 of the headquarters of the Western Front of 0800 hours on 26 July 1941 about the combat operations of the *front*], in *SBDVOV*, issue 37, 106-108.

8. *Stavka* VK Directive to the Commander of the Forces of the Central Front about Forbidding the Withdrawal of 63rd Rifle Corps, and Activation of Combat Operations for the Defense of the Right Bank of the Dnepr River
28 July 1941

Your proposal about a withdrawal of the main forces of 63rd Rifle Corps from the western bank of the Dnepr to the eastern bank and leaving it for the defense of the approaches to Zhlobin, Rogachev, and the Dnepr River cannot be accepted for the following reasons:

1. A defense of the western bank of the Dnepr with small forces will be quickly overcome by the enemy, and the enemy will seize Zhlobin and Rogachev.

2. The enemy, having seized the right bank of the Dnepr River, will quickly organize a defense with small forces and throw in the freed up forces to the southeast or throw them in to reinforce its Smolensk grouping.

We believe it is extremely necessary to operate as actively as possible on the Central Front so as to tie down as many enemy forces as possible by active operations.

The *Stavka* forbids you to withdraw 63rd Rifle Corps to the eastern bank of the Dnepr and demands you destroy the enemy by active operations. We especially need to expand extensive destroyer operations during the night and to destroy the enemy by small detachments, the fires of howitzer artillery and mortars and air strikes.

Stalin, Zhukov

Source: "Direktiva Stavki VK komanduiushchemu voiskami Tsentral'nogo fronta o zapreshchenii otvoda 63-go Strelkovogo korpusa i aktivizatsii boevykh deistvii po oborone pravoberezh'ia Dnepra" [*Stavka* VK directive to the commander of the forces of the Central Front about forbidding the withdrawal of 63rd Rifle Corps and activation of combat operations for the defense of the right bank of the Dnepr River], in Zolotarev, "*Stavka* VK, 1941," 97.

Appendix K

Armeegruppe Guderian's Destruction of Group Kachalov, 31 July-6 August 1941

German 9. Führer Directive No. 34, 30 July 1941

The Führer and Supreme High Command of
the Armed Forces (OKW).
Führer headquarters
OKW, Headquarters of the Operations Directorate.
30 July 1941
Department for the Defense of the Country (1st Dept.).
No. 441298/41. Top Secret
Directive No. 34

The course of events in recent days, the appearance of large enemy forces before the front and flanks of Army Group Center, the supply situation, and the necessity of giving the Second and Third Panzer Groups 10 days to restore and refill their formations has forced a temporary postponement of the fulfillment of aims and missions set forth on Directive No. 33 of 19 July and the supplement to it of 23 July.

Accordingly, I order:

I. 1. In the northern sector of the Eastern Front, continue the offensive toward Leningrad, while making the main attack between Lake Il'men' and the Narva River with the objective to encircle Leningrad and establish contact with the Finnish Army.

This offensive must be limited to the Volkhov sector north of Lake Il'men' and south of this lake – continue as deeply to the northeast as required to protect the right flank of forces attacking north of Lake Il'men'. Restore the situation in the Velikie Luki region beforehand. All forces that are not being employed in the offensive south of Lake Il'men' must be transferred to the forces which are attacking on the northern flank.

Do not begin the anticipated offensive by the Third Panzer Group to the Valdai Hills until its combat readiness and the operational readiness of its panzer formations have been fully restored. Instead, the forces on Army Group Center's left flank must advance northeastward to such a depth as will be sufficient to protect Army Group North's right flank.

The priority missions of all of the Eighteenth Army's forces are the clearing of all enemy forces from Estonia. After this, its divisions can begin to advance toward Leningrad.

2. Army Group Center will go on the defense, while employing for it the most favorable terrain in its sector.

Occupy favorable jumping-off positions in the interest of conducting subsequent offensive operations against the Soviet 21st Army and conduct limited objective offensive operations to this end.

As soon as the situation permits, withdraw Second and Third Panzer Groups from combat and quickly refill and refit them.

3. For the time being, Army Group South will continue operations in the southern sector of the front with only its own forces to destroy the large enemy forces west of the Dnepr and create conditions for the subsequent crossing of First Panzer Group to the eastern bank of the Dnepr by seizing bridgeheads at and south of Kiev.

Draw the Soviet 5th Army, which is operating in the swampy region northwest of Kiev, into combat west of the Dnepr River and destroy it. Prevent this army from penetrating northward across the Pripiat River

4. The Finnish Front. Halt the offensive toward Kandalaska. In the Mountain Infantry Corps' sector, eliminate the threat to the flank from the direction of Motov Bay. Leave at the disposal of the XXXVI Corps' command the quantity of forces necessary for conducting a defense and for carrying out false measures for the preparation of an offensive.

Simultaneously, undertake attempts to sever the Murmansk railroad in the sector of III (Finnish) Army Corps, first and foremost, along the Loukhi axis, having thrown in there forces sufficient for fulfilling that mission. Transfer all of the remaining forces to the Army of Karelia. In the event the offensive in III (Finnish) Army Corps' sector misfires because of the difficult terrain conditions, bring up German units and transfer them to the Army of Karelia. This concerns, first and foremost, motorized units, tanks, and heavy artillery.

Provide 6th Mountain Infantry Division with all types of transport available to the Mountain Infantry Corps.

The possibility of using the Narvik and Luleo railroad on Swedish territory will be clarified by the Ministry of Foreign Affairs.

II. The Air Force [*Luftwaffe*]:

1. The northern sector of the front.

Aviation will shift the main efforts of the air offensive to the northern sector of the front, for which the main forces of VIII Air Corps will be transferred to the First Air Fleet. These forces must be transferred rapidly enough so that they can support Army Group North's offensive along the main attack axis from the very beginning (the morning of 6 August).

2. The central sector of the front.

The mission of the air forces which remain in Army Group Center is to provide antiaircraft defense on the fronts of Second and Ninth Armies and support their offensive. Continue the air offensive against Moscow.

3. The southern sector of the front.

The mission is as before. A lessening of the air forces operating with Army Group South is not envisioned.

4. Finland.

The chief mission of the Fifth Air Fleet is to ensure support of the Mountain Infantry Corps' offensive. In addition, it is necessary to support the offensive of III (Finnish) Army Corps along the axes promising the most success. It is necessary to conduct appropriate preparatory measures for rendering support to the Army of Karelia.

[signed] Hitler

Source: *Sbornik voenno-istoricheskikh materialov Velikoi Otechestvennoi voiny, vypusk 18* [Collection of military-historical materials of the Great Patriotic War, issue 18] (Moscow: Voenizdat, 1960), 236-237. Prepared by the Military-Historical Department of the Military-Scientific Directorate of the Red Army General Staff and classified secret.

1. Individual Combat Order of the Commander-in-Chief of the Western Direction's Forces of 1 August 1941 to the Group of Comrade Kachalov on the Offensive toward Pochinok

To Comrade Kachalov

2200 hours on 1 August 1941. 1:100,000 scale map

1. In spite of the clear superiority of your group in tanks and artillery during the initial period of the operation, you have not achieved decisive success because you have incorrectly appreciated the tactics of the enemy, who are operating before you with separate detachments, while skillfully maneuvering equipment and raids by tanks and aircraft.

2. You need to destroy centers of enemy resistance with strong groupings of infantry in cooperation with tanks and artillery. Your tanks are operating in isolated fashion, and the majority of the artillery is operating from great depths [ranges]. The infantry are fighting without adequate support by artillery and tanks.

I order:

1. Decisively continue the offensive with the immediate mission to capture the Pochinok region. Assign the cavalry the mission of reaching the enemy's rear from behind your flank.

2. Employ the tank division in close cooperation with the infantry with obligatory strong artillery support.

3. Use the artillery as antitank guns and infantry support groups in the division's systems of combat formations.

4. Destroy the enemy with destroyer detachments of infantry in skillful and decisive night operations.

S. Timoshenko

Source: "Chastnyi boevoi prikaz Glavnokomanduiushchego voiskami Zapadnogo Napravleniia ot 1 avgusta 1941 g. gruppe tov. Kachalova na nastuplenie v napravlenii Pochinok" [Particular combat order of the commander-in-chief of the Western Direction of 1 August 1941 to the Group of Comrade Kachalov on the offensive toward Pochinok], SBDVOV, issue 37, 62.

2. Combat Order No. 9 of the Commander of the Forces of 28th Army of 1 August 1941 on Preparations to Repel an Offensive by Enemy Motor-Mechanized Units

Combat Order No. 9,
Headquarters, Operational Group Lieutenant General Kachalov,
the woods 1 kilometer southeast of Stodolishche, 1 August 1941
1:100,000 and 50,000 scale maps

1. After an artillery preparation, enemy mobile motor-mechanized units, with forces of more than a regiment, began an offensive along the Rudnia Novaia, Zharkovka, Shipenko, Pechersk, Burianka, Pecherskaia Buda, and Vydritsa front beginning at 0500 hours on 1 August.

An enemy reconnaissance group (motorcyclists) – are at Ryzhovka. About 100 tanks and motorized infantry penetrated to Zvenchatka on the highway to Roslavl' at 1710 hours on 1 August 1941.

Simultaneously, the enemy actively resisted the offensive by the units of the *front's* group.

2. I order:

a) 104th TD will restore order in its tanks and equipment and report on its readiness. Continue reconnaissance and observation of the enemy.

b) 149th RD will continue to conduct reconnaissance along the division's front and withdraw one regiment into second echelon.

c) 145th RD, while continuing to conduct reconnaissance along the division's front, will hold onto its occupied positions. Withdraw 599th RR, including its 3rd Battalion, to the Efremovka, Torchilovka, and Kuz'minichi region [10 kilometers west of Stodolishche], while conducting reconnaissance toward the west.

The separate reconnaissance battalion will concentrate in – Ivanovka, Volkarezino, and Zakharovka [5 kilometers east of Stodolishche].

d) 31st Motorized Rifle Regiment will occupy a defense in the Hill 173.5, Novyi Derebuzh, and Zabegaevka sector [10-12 kilometers south of Stodolishche], while conducting foot reconnaissance toward Timokhovka and Krutilovka and toward Pervomaiskii, Steklian, and Bolotov, and in the general direction of Zakhar'ino [northwest to southwest].

Maintain contract with 599th RR at Rogotinskaia and, on the left – with the Composite Regiment in the Krapivinskaia region.

I am attaching 12 AT guns to you, which you must keep in readiness to repel enemy tanks.

The guns will arrive from Stodolishche and Novyi Derebuzh.

e) The commander of the Composite Regiment, while remaining in the Krapivinskaia region, will be prepared to attack toward Novyi Derebuzh. Maintain contact with 31st MRR – in Novyi Derebuzh and Zabegaevka, and with 222nd RD's units along the road to the northern side of Roslavl'.

Dangerous tank axes: Bytenka and Kagarinskaia, the Roslavl' highway south of Krapivinskaia No. 1, and Bykovka.

I am attaching 3rd Bn, 758th ATR, which will reach you from the Bykovka region [14 kilometers north-northwest of Roslavl'].

[Pay] special attention to – the organization of an antitank defense toward the highway to Roslavl'.

Conduct reconnaissance: along the road to Kartsevo, Dubrovka, Novoe Zasel'e, Bolokhonovka, and Petrovichi, and along the Warsaw highway.

Second dangerous tank axis – Petrovo, Osinovka, and Zakhar'ino.

I am attaching for your disposal 24 antitank guns from the Kozlovka region, with which to protect the dangerous tank axes. The Warsaw highway is an especially dangerous tank axis.

Echelon the antitank guns in depth; however, have groups of tank destroyers with bottles of flammable mixtures around each of the guns. Also use field artillery for the purposes of AT defense. Protect the AT guns against enemy air and ground attacks with machine guns and carefully conceal them.

f) All unit and subunit commanders will organize and deploy antitank observation and notification posts forward, after supplying them with signal means (rockets), from the combat security line to the line of the second echelons, inclusively, and along the flanks, which will conduct careful observation and, in the event of a threat of a tank attack, will give the signal, and, subsequently, employ signal posts along the entire front. Upon receipt of a signal, all of the artillery will be ready to repel tank attacks.

All of the AT artillery, field artillery, and long-range artillery, except the main positions, will prepare open firing positions along two-three axes for repelling tanks. Upon receiving a warning signal of tank danger along a threatening axis, long-range artillery will move forward into the open positions and conduct direct fire against the tanks.

Send this order down to battalion commanders, inclusively, and in the final point, to company commanders.

> The Commander of 28th Army, Lieutenant General Kachalov
> The Member of the Military Council, Brigade Commissar Kolesnikov
> The Chief of Staff, Major General Egorov

Source: "Boevoi prikaz komanduiushchego voiskami 28-i Armii no. 9 ot 1 avgusta 1941 g. na podgotovku k otrazheniiu nastupleniia motomekhanizirovannykh chastei protivnika" [Combat order no. 9 of the commander of the forces of 28th Army of 1 August 1941 on preparations to repel an offensive by enemy motor-mechanized units], *SBDVOV*, issue 37, 355-356.

3. Combat Order No. 10 of the Commander of the Forces of 28th Army of 2 August 1941 on the Conduct of an Attack against the Rear of the Enemy's El'nia Grouping

Order to the Forces of 28th Army No. 10
2 August 1941   the woods 1 kilometer southeast of Stodolishche

The forces of the army are holding back an offensive by the enemy along the Ivanovka, Zimnitsy, Osinovka, Efremovka, Novyi Derebuzh, Pechkury, and Roslavl' front. The enemy is trying to wedge in between the fortified lines along the Desna River and the army's right flank. Especially tense fighting is under way along the

Novyi Derebuzh, Pechkury, and Roslavl' axis from the direction of Khislavichi, Mstislavl', and Krichev [from the west and southwest].

I consider the chief mission of the army to be holding on to the Stomet' River line [running from east to west 6 kilometers north of Stodolishche] and the Roslavl' region and conducting an attack in the general direction of Egorovka, Khmara [18 kilometers north of Stodolishche], and Pochinok [28 kilometers north-northwest of Stodolishche], into the rear of the enemy's El'nia grouping.

I order:

104th TD, protected by the motorized rifle regiment, which is holding onto the Novosel'e and Borisovka line, will concentrate in Selibka, Chernavka, and Nedobraia [12-15 kilometers northeast of Stodolishche] on the night of 2-3 August 1941. Be prepared to attack northward as part of 149th RD after being subordinated to the commander of the latter.

149th RD, having turned its sector over to 145th RD, with 104th TD, 1st Bn, 488th CAR, and 3rd Bn, 320th GAR, will concentrate in the Postarok, Nikulino, and Voroshilovo region [7-10 kilometers north-northeast of Stodolishche] and attack northward at 0500 hours on 3 August 1941. Mission – capture the crossings at Egorovka and, subsequently, attack toward Pochinok, while protecting the army's right flank.

145th RD, with 3rd Bn, 649th CAR and 4th Bn, 320th GAR, after occupying the Hill 212.6, Hill 192.1, Osinovka, Moshek, Shantilovo, and Dumanichskie line [north to south, 6-7 kilometers west of Stodolishche] with two regiments, will concentrate two regiments in the Stodolishche, Barsukovskie, and Borshchevka region [southward 10 kilometers from Stodolishche] and hold them in readiness for operations toward the west and south.

31st Motorized Regiment, with 1st Bn, 18th ATR and 1st Bn, 320th GAR, will hold on to the Novyi Derebuzh region [13 kilometers south-southwest of Stodolishche].

The Composite Regiment, with 3rd Bn, 578th ATR, will hold onto the Pechkury, Bytenka, Krapivinskii, and No. 1 region [12 kilometers south of Stodolishche].

222nd RD, with 2nd and 3rd Bns, 18th ATR, will hold onto the Chepishchevo, Astakovskaia, and Slobodishche line with the main center of resistance – Roslavl.

21st and 52nd CDs will concentrate [as follows]: 21st CD – the Stodolishche, Kruglikovskaia Dacha, and Tereshok region [7 kilometers south from Stodolishche]; and 52nd CD – Krapivinskii, Kubarki, and Morgunovka in readiness to attack from behind 145th RD's left wing in the general northwestward direction..

My CP – 1 kilometer southeast of Stodolishche.

The Commander of 28th Army, Lieutenant General Kachalov
The Member of the Military Council, Brigade Commissar Kolesnikov
The Chief of Staff, Major General Egorov

Source: "Boevoi prikaz komanduiushchego voiskami 28-i Armii no. 10 ot 2 avgusta 1941 g. na nanesenii udara po tylam El'ninskoi gruppirovki protivnika" [Combat order no. 10 of the commander of the forces of 28th Army of 2 August 1941 on the conduct of an attack against the rear of the enemy's El'nia grouping], *SBDVOV*, issue 37, 356-357.

4. Report No. 0039 by the Reserve Front's Chief of Staff of 3 August 1941 to the Commander of the Forces of the Reserve Front about the Situation of the Forces at Roslavl'

To General of the Army Comrade Zhukov

Transmitted to Colonel Novikov at 1730 hours on 3 August 1941

No. 0039

This report has been delayed as a consequence of the absence of communications.

1. I am reporting about the situation at Roslavl'.

According to a report by Lieutenant General Zakharkhin, the enemy went over to the attack against 222nd [Rifle] Division's entire front beginning at 1100 hours on 2 August. As the chief of 43rd Army's Operations Department has determined, the enemy forces consist of no less than one infantry division, reinforced by tanks, armored vehicles, and motorcycles. The enemy attacked from the direction of Chernatka toward Polshino and strongly from the west toward Hill 234.0 (5 kilometers west of Roslavl'). The 3rd axis – Osinovka and also Hill 234.0. 10-15 tanks attacked along the highway to Roslavl'.

Small groups are attacking along the remainder of the front. The absence of the enemy's artillery has been noted.

Along all of the main axes, 1-2 infantry battalions attacked behind the tanks, reinforced by a large quantity of mortars.

While employing its shock groups, 222nd Division repelled the enemy attacks until 1900 hours. By 2000 hours the enemy succeeded in penetrating along separate axes and approached Polshino and Hill 234.0. However, it was never threatening, and our infantry held on firmly. At 2300 hours on 2 August, the division's commander and commissar reached the units to organize the defenses.

Today at 0400 hours, Comrade Zakharkin spoke with the division's headquarters, which considers the situation stable. The enemy have been operating mainly with aircraft. Beginning at 1100 hours on 2 August and up to the fall of darkness, aircraft bombed constantly. The Moscow-Roslavl' road was also kept under uninterrupted bombing and strafing. Yesterday, 4 bombers were shot down by the division's light weapons.

On the right flank, 53rd [Rifle] Division is conducting reconnaissance in both directions. The enemy's 197th Infantry Division has been noted against 222nd RD.

According to a report by 43rd Army's headquarters received at 1400 hours on 3 August, 222nd RD turned out to be half-encircled on the morning of 3 August as a result of the fighting and began a fighting withdrawal to the line of the Oster River at 0800, with the aim to straddle the Moscow and Briansk highway.

The division suffered considerable losses in the fighting on 1 and 2 August, the quantity of which is being clarified, but, simultaneously, also inflicted .heavy losses on the enemy in personnel and tanks.

During the fighting, 774th Regiment of that division was cut off and remained in the Laskovo and Zhabinskoe region. The division commander believes that this regiment will reach Group Kachalov's left wing.

The 222nd RD seized operational documents of the enemy tank corps, which indicate that the corps must capture the city of Roslavl' by 1 August. According to a report by regimental commander Meshcherekov, an enemy column of up to 1,000 men with vehicles was destroyed on the night of 2-3 August. At present, they are calculating the sum of trophies.

The General Staff will receive a report about them.

2. The 43rd Army's commander requests permission for the occupation of a defense by 258th RD along the previously fortified Zhukovka and Stolby line (50 kilometers northwest and west of Briansk), and, at the same time, a defense line for that division along the Gorodets, Opakhan', and Hill 178 line (500,000 map) was indicated by the General Staff

Lieutenant General Bogdanov sanctioned the decision of General Zakharkin on the movement of 258th Division into the previously prepared line, which is being reported to the General Staff. The 258th RD unloaded from 11 trains in the Sel'tso and Briansk region; and one regiment is already occupying defenses.

3. Lieutenant General Bogdanov ordered me to present to the General Staff the question of reserve subordination of 222nd RD to the headquarters of the *Front* of Reserve Armies. Major General Vasilevsky promised to ask a question about transferring of the entire Roslavl' axis to us, and, for that purpose, 109th TD is arriving in the Spas-Demensk region today.

4. On the extreme right flank of 38th Army, 254th RD is fighting with enemy in the composition of 11th Army and has subordinated itself to the commander of 11th Army on the spur of the moment. A question was put to the General Staff about the orderly cooperation along that axis by means of a transfer of 254th RD to 11th Army and the establishment of a boundary with 11th Army.

An answer has not yet been received.

5. The General Staff has asked for your personal opinion on the question of a defense along the Briansk axis and on the matter of subordinating the Roslavl' group to the Reserve Front.

6. The Chief of the General Staff, in spite of all of the information received from you about the operations at El'nia that we transmitted regularly, expressed the wish to receive a generalized report for a report to the *Stavka* under your signature.

Chief of Staff of the *Front* of Reserve Armies, Major General Liapin

Source: "Doklad nachal'nika shtaba Rezervnogo fronta ot 3 avgusta 1941 g komanduiushchemu voiskami Rezervnogo fronta o polozhenii voisk u Roslavl'" [Report by the Reserve Front's chief of staff of 3 August 1941 to the commander of the forces of the Reserve Front about the situation of the forces at Roslavl'], *SBDVOV*, issue 37, 165-166.

5. *Stavka* VK Directive No. 00679 to the Commanders of the Forces of the Western, Reserve, and Central Fronts about the Re-subordination of Forces
2030 hours on 3 August 1941

In light of the development of an enemy offensive at Roslavl', the *Stavka* orders, effective 0600 hours on 4 August:

1. Transfer Group Kachalov, consisting of 145th and 149th Rifle Divisions, 104th Tank Division, and all of the group's reinforcing units, as well as 222nd Rifle

Division, with its attached units, and the approaching 109th Tank Division from the Western Front to the Reserve Front.

2. Transfer 21st and 52nd Cavalry Division of Comrade Gorodovikov to the Central Front at the same time.

3. Report fulfillment.

> On behalf of the *Stavka* of the High Command
> B. Shaposhnikov

Source: "Direktiva Stavki VK no. 00679 komanduiushchim voiskami Zapadnogo, Rezervnogo, i Tsental'nogo frontov o perepodchinenii voisk" [Stavka VK directive no. 00679 to the commanders of the Western, Reserve, and Central Fronts about the re-subordination of forces], Zolotarev, "*Stavka* 1941," 101.

6. Individual Combat Order of the Deputy Commander of the Forces of the Reserve Front No. 0017/op of 4 August 1941 to the Commander of the Group of Forces of Lieutenant General Kachalov on a Withdrawal of the Group's Left Wing and Center to the Faddeeva Buda and Ostrik River Line

To General Kachalov
Order No. 0017/op,
0510 hours on 4 August 1941

I order you to withdraw the group's left wing and center to the Faddeeva Buda and Ostrik River line, where you will establish contact with 222nd RD.

Immediately withdraw the rear [services] and artillery units behind the defensive front of 53rd RD behind the Shat'kova, Borovka, and Krutogorka line.

The main routes of withdrawing the rear [services]:

a) Dudarevka, Borok, Mokhai, and Shat'kovo;

b) Voroshilovo, Gerasimovka, Riabtsy, Postush'e, and Vetrovka; and

c) Berezovka (4 kilometers northwest of Stodolishche), Lysovka, Kovali, Starosel'e, Bogdanovo, and Novosloveni.

To secure the rear routes, immediately throw detachments, reinforced by artillery, to the Krasniki, Barsuki, Khateevka, Moshchanka, Rakovka, Vorovka, and Mikhailovka line and along the highway to the south.

> The Commander of the Reserve Front, Army General Zhukov
> The Member of the Military Council, Kruglov
> The Chief of Staff, Major General Liapin

Source: "Chastnyi boevoi prikaz komanduiushchego voiskami Rezervnogo fronta no. 0017/op ot 4 avgusta 1941 g. komanduiushchemu gruppoi voisk General-Leitenantu Kachalovu na otvod levogo flange i tsentra gruppy na rubezh Faddeeva Buda, r. Ostrik" [Individual combat order of the deputy commander of the forces of the Reserve Front no. 0017/op of 4 August 1941 to the commander of the Group of Forces of Lieutenant General Kachalov on a withdrawal of the group's left wing and center to the Faddeeva Buda and Ostrik River line], *SBDVOV*, issue 37, 167-168.

7. Combat Order of the Headquarters of the Reserve Front of 4 August 1941 about the Subordination of Group Kachalov's Units to the Commander of 43rd Army's Forces

Immediately transmit to General Zakharkin
1240 hours on 4 August 1941

Apparently, the headquarters of Kachalov is encircled.

The *front* commander orders you to take the units of his group under your command and carry out Order No. 0017/op.

Liapin

Source: "Boevoe rasporiazhenie shtaba Rezervnogo fronta ot 4 avgusta 1941 g. o podchinenii komanduiushchemu voiskami 43-i Armii chastei gruppy Kachalova" [Combat order of the headquarters of the Reserve Front of 4 August 1941 about the subordination of Group Kachalov's units to the commander of 43rd Army's forces], *SBDVOV*, issue 37, 169.

8. Combat Order No. 1 of the Commander of the Group of Forces of 28th Army of 4 August 1941 on a Regrouping

Combat Order No. 1, Group Headquarter,
the woods 1 kilometer south of Bykovka,
1830 hours on 4 August 1941
1:100,000 scale map

1. The group will cease attacks toward Roslavl' and regroup for an attack along a new axis, for the purposes of:

1) While protecting the Khoski and Glinki front [from 15 kilometers northwest of Roslavl' northward to southeast of Stodolishche] with reinforced battalions, attack [eastward] toward Riabinki [16 kilometers south-southeast of Stodolishche and 14 kilometers north of Roslavl'], Borovka, Malakhovka, Novaia Danilovka, Novyi Usokhi, and Staroe Kurgan'e [15 kilometers east-northeast of Roslavl']. Conduct the attack in two columns.

2) The right column, consisting of 340th RR, 516th HAR, and 2 tanks – will attack toward Riabinki [13 kilometers north of Roslavl'], Krucha, Peshchiki [12 kilometers northeast of Roslavl'], Trisel'e, Novyi Usokhi, and Staroe Kurgan'e [15 kilometers east-northeast of Roslavl']. Mission: while destroying the opposing enemy units and holding onto the Peshchiki and Krucha line, protect the main force's attack toward Usokhi and Staroe Kurgan'e. Begin the attack at 2000 hours on 4 August 1941.

3) The left column – consisting of the Composite Regiment with one tank, 320th GAR, and 18th ATR, will attack toward the Roslavl' highway, the southern outskirts of Bykovka [15 kilometers south-southeast of Stodolishche and 15 kilometers north of Roslavl'], Hill 179.1, Pavlovka, Borovka, Malakhovka, Prisel'e, Novyi Usokhi, and Staroe Kurgan'e axis. Mission: having protected the group's combat formation on the northern outskirts of Bykovka and Hill 186.5 front up to 0200 hours on 5 August 1941 and while destroying the opposing enemy in cooperation with 145th

RD, reach the vicinity of the woods northeast of Staroe Kurgan'e by the morning of 5 August 1941. Begin the attack by the main forces at 2200 hours on 4 August 1941.

4) 774th RR, with 3rd Bn, 649th CAR and 3rd Bn, 364th CAR, will protect the regrouping of the group's units along the Khoski and Glinki front up to 0200 hours on 5 August 1941 and, subsequently, protect the group's rear with rear guards, attack along the march route of the right column, and reach the region of the woods south and southeast of Staroe Kurgan'e by day's end on 5 August 1941. Begin the attack at 0200 hours on 5 August 1941.

5) The group's transports and rear service organs will follow at the rear of the column under the protection of read guard units.

6) I will follow along the right column's march route. My deputy is – the commander of 340th RR.

The Commander of the Group, Colonel Zuev

Source: "Boevoi prikaz komanduiushchego gruppoi voisk 28-i Armii no. 1 ot 4 avgusta 1941 g. na peregruppirovku" [Combat order no. 1 of the commander of the group of forces of 28th Army of 4 August 1941 on a regrouping], *SBDVOV*, issue 37, 357-358.

9. Directive No. 22 of the Commander of the Forces of the Reserve Front of 5 August about the Elimination of Shortcomings in the Organization and Conduct of Combat Operations

To the Commander of 24th Army
To the Commanders of 100th, 103rd, 19th, 120th, 105th, and 106th [Rifle] Divisions
No. 22

As a result of combat experience received in the El'nia region, the following main shortcomings have appeared in the operations of our forces:

1. Poor reconnoitering of the enemy and very poor detection of his firing points. The absence of skill on the part of commanders and soldiers prevents us from taking prisoners daily.

2. Weak reconnoitering of targets, the distance of forward and main observation posts for artillery of all types from the first foxholes of our infantry, the infrequent use of artillery for direct fire, and the entire lack of use of ricochet firing by howitzer batteries causes the low efficacy of our artillery fire.

3. The artillery expends many shells on its fault and at the fault of combined-arms (infantry) commanders who have ordered shelling for the sake of noise [sensation] and the satisfaction of farfetched "requests" from below.

The commanders and commissars of units [regiments] and formations [divisions] display unjustified indulgence to the huge expenditure of shells and mines without any real benefit.

4. The required densities of artillery and mortar fire against objectives subject to seizure by the infantry are not always created. At the same time, the targets being processed for artillery and mortar fire are being attacked by infantry late, and enemy firing points, which remain intact, manage to wait and inflict strikes against and

even halt the attackers. Frequently, the infantry employ their own firing weapons poorly during preparations for the attack and the attack itself.

5. The personal linkage and contact between infantry and artillery commanders is weak, battery commanders are situated far behind the infantry's forward trenches, missions are seldom assigned on the ground, and there is a general desire to remain seated [concealed] in slit trenches and dug outs.

6. The very poor behavior by company and battery personnel provide cowards and traitors with complete opportunities to escape into the rear at any time.

Losses in personnel and horses, combat equipment, and the expenditure of combat shots are also poorly accounted for.

I order:

Eliminate all of the deficiencies pointed out above, employ all types of fire efficiently, and exploit the results of fire actions against the enemy to a maximum for successful attacks and the exploitation of success.

The Commander of the *Front* of Reserve Armies, Army General Zhukov

Source: "Direktiva komanduiushchego voiskami Reservnogo fronta no. 22 ot 5 avgusta ob ustranenii nedostatkov v organizatsii i vvedenii boevykh deistvii" [Directive no. 22 of the commander of the forces of the Reserve Front of 5 August about the elimination of shortcomings in the organization and conduct of combat operations], *SBDVOV*, issue 37, 169-170.

10. Instruction of the Military Council of the Reserve Front of 5 August 1941 to the Commander of the Forces of 28th Army on the Organization of a Defense

To Comrade Zakharkin
0312 hours on 5 August 1941

I am transmitting instructions from the *front's* Military Council

1. The actions of 222nd RD are clearly criminal in nature. The division commander and units commanders and commissars have not restored order in the division and are continuing to conduct disorganized combat, while retreating to the east without any sort of orders. This panicky retreat places Group Kachalov in a very difficult situation.

Warn the division commander and units commanders and commissars that, if they do not correct the situation and continue to retreat further without orders, the division and unit commanders will be arrested and turned over for trial as traitors to the Motherland.

2. Withdraw Group Kachalov's left wing and center, as was pointed out in my order, after turning the left flank back toward Krasnaia Sloboda.

3. Destroy the enemy company that has penetrated into the Bogdanovo region [41 kilometers northeast of Roslavl'], while preventing it from exploiting to the Desna River's western bank.

4. I am subordinating 109th TD to you; keep the tank division in your reserve with the mission to prevent an enemy penetration across the defensive front.

Dig unserviceable tanks and small numbers of motorized resources into the ground, straddling the Moscow highway and especially dangerous axes.

5. Employ all of 222nd RD's retreating subunits as reinforcements for 53rd RD. Immediately restore order in Group Kachalov's subunits and place them in the defense as a second echelon behind 53rd RD. Assemble 104th TD's tank subunits and position them in the Shat'kovo, Svetilovo, and Peredel'niki region.

6. Immediately dispatch reconnaissance from 217th RD to the Pustosel, Sviridovka, Asel'e, Dolgoe, and Novyi Krupets line and connect them up with 258th RD's units along the Zhukovka and Belogolovki line.

Liapin

Source: Ukazaniia voennogo soveta Rezervnogo fronta ot 5 avgusta 1941 g. komanduiushchemu voiskami 28-i armii po organizatsii oborony" [Instruction of the Military Council of the Reserve Front of 5 August 1941 to the commander of the forces of 28th Army on the organization of a defense], *SBDVOV*, issue 37, 170.

11. Combat Order of the Headquarters of the Reserve Front of 5 August 1941 to the Commander of the Forces of 24th Army about Changes in the System of Artillery Defenses in 107th Rifle Division's Sector

To the Commander of 24th Army
5 August 1941

The commander of the Reserve Front has ordered:

Construct a system of artillery defenses in the 107th RD's operational sector in order to be ready to repel possible attacks by enemy motor-mechanized units from the south and southwest toward Dorogobuzh.

To fulfill that mission, deploy no fewer than twenty guns of 533rd ATR along the Hills 232.5, 256.9, 240.6, 246.9, and 206.0 line, thus closing off the main routes of possible enemy movement. The remaining artillery of 107th RD must be ready to operate against enemy motor-mechanized units toward the south and southwest. The artillery group, which is operating on the front of 100th and 103rd [Rifle] Divisions, must be ready for action against enemy motor-mechanized forces from the west and southwest. 880th ATR is assigned the mission of repelling possible attacks by enemy motor-mechanized units from the east and southeast from its occupied regions. All of the artillery attached to 120th and 106th RDs must be ready to repel possible attacks by enemy motor-mechanized units from the south and southwest. Prepare a mobile reserve of 12 guns at the expense of 879th and 880th [AT] Regiments, while not removing guns from strong points before receipt of missions to the mobile reserve.

Period of readiness – by day's end on 6 August 1941; and send a combat report with the scheme of fire by special messenger by 2400 hours on 6 August.

The Chief of Staff of the Reserve Front, Major General Liapin
The Commissar of the Reserve Front's Headquarters,
Brigade Commissar Priakhin

Source: "Boevoe rasporiazhenie shtaba Rezervnogo fronta ot 5 avgusta 1941 g. komanduiushchemu voiskami 24-i Armii ob izmenenii sistemy artilleriiskoi oborony v polose 107-i strelkovoi divizii" [Combat order of the headquarters of the Reserve Front of 5 August 1941 to the commander of the forces of 24th Army about changes in the system of artillery defenses in 107th Rifle Division's sector], SBDVOV, issue 37, 171.

12. *Stavka* VK Directive No. 00731 to the Commanders of the Forces of the Reserve and Western Fronts on the Defeat of the Enemy's El'nia Grouping
0216 hours on 6 August 1941

For the purposes of the final defeat of the enemy's El'nia grouping, the responsibility of the Reserve Front's commander, Army General Zhukov, the *Stavka* orders:

1. Comrade Zhukov, having reinforced the units operating at El'nia with 107th Rifle Division and two regiments of 100th Rifle Division, with its artillery, will continue an energetic and decisive offensive at El'nia, with the mission of encircling and destroying the enemy's El'nia grouping.

2. The commander of the Western Front, Marshal Timoshenko, upon receipt of this directive, will transfer two regiments of 100th Rifle Division, with its artillery, to the disposition of the commander of the Reserve Front.

Relieve 107th Rifle Division with units from the Western Front by 2000 hours on 6 August, having occupied its positions along the Dorogobuzh, Usviat'e, Kas'kovo, and Kalita front.

3. The commander of the Western Front will lengthen his left wing from the Solov'evo crossing along the Dnepr River south of Pridneprovskaia Station and further to the southeast along the railroad to Dobromino Station.

4. For the conduct of the El'nia operation, on order of the Chief of the VVS [Air Forces], on 6 August rebase two light bomber and two fighter regiments from Reserve of the High Command to the disposal of the commander of the Reserve Front.

To strengthen the aviation of the Reserve Front, on 6 August rebase two light bomber and one fighter regiment from the Reserve of the High Command to the Roslavl' axis.

5. Confirm receipt and immediately submit a plan of the operation at El'nia.

The *Stavka* of the High Command
I. Stalin
B. Shaposhnikov

Source: "Direktiva Stavki VK no. 00731 komanduiushchim voiskami Rezervnogo i Zapadnogo frontov o merakh po razgromu El'ninskoi gruppirovki protivnika" [*Stavka* VK directive no. 00731 to the commanders of the Reserve and Western Fronts on the defeat of the enemy's El'nia grouping], in Zolotarev, "*Stavka* 1941," 106.

13. Report by the Headquarters of the Reserve Front of 7 August 1941 to the General Staff about the Withdrawal of Group Kachalov's Forces
By Bodo [Baudot teletype]
To Moscow and the Chief of the General Staff, Comrade Shaposhnikov

A Report

about Group Kachalov, prepared on the basis of conversations by direct line on 6 August 1941 of Army General Zhukov with the Member of the Military Council of Group Kachalov, Kolesnikov [Brigade Commissar Vasilii Timofeevich Kolesnikov], and the chief of Group Kachalov's VVS, Major General Butorin [Major General of Aviation Tikhon Ivanovich Butorin], commander of 63rd and 80th Rifle Corps in 1943 and 1944], who escaped from encirclement.

Before the encirclement, Group Kachalov occupied the following positions: the motor-mechanized division – Guta Bogovka; 149th RD – Rudnia, Berezhok, and Panasovka [27 kilometers southeast of Pochino]; and 145th RD – Poluevo, (incl.) Kupreevka, Stodolishche, and Maloe Stodolishche [25-30 kilometers south-southeast of Pochinok]. The army's headquarters was located in Stodolishche and Zasizh'e forest.

The enemy conducted an attack with one motor-mechanized division from the El'nia axis and occupied Starinka and Dubovka [30 kilometers southeast of Pochinok]. The enemy attacking from the Pochinok region, occupied positions along the Stomet' River [25-30 kilometers south-southeast of Pochinok] and crossed the Stomet' River at several places. A group of enemy of undetermined strength conducted an attack from Krichev toward Maloe Stodolishche against 145th RD's left flank. At the same time, large enemy motor-mechanized columns advanced from the Krichev region toward Roslavl'.

By the evening of 2 August, the enemy pushed back 104th TD's right wing and strengthened activity on 149th RD's front. The enemy, attacking from the direction of Krichev, occupied Roslavl', advanced along the Roslavl'-Smolensk road, and captured the village of Krapivinskii Vtoroi [40 kilometers south-southeast of Pochinok], while spreading out [northward] toward Osinovka and Golaevka. The group of enemy attacking from the direction of Khislavichi [32 kilometers southwest of Pochinok] actively operated against 145th RD's left flank.

According to an order of the German corps commander, found on the body of a German officer, the division operating from El'nia had the mission to capture Starinka and Ermolino and, when the southern group achieved success, encircle the "Reds" operating along the Roslavl' axis.

At the end of the day on 2 August, the commander made a decision on a withdrawal, which required 149th RD to withdraw [southeastward] through Bogovka, Piataia, Eliseevskie, and Samodidino and further to the east. 145th RD had to withdraw [southeastward] through Misovka, Dubrovka, Starinka, Dorotovka, and Rakovka and further to the east.

Colonel Zuev's [Major General Fedor Andreevich Zuev, future chief of staff, 43rd Army] group was to withdraw [southeastward] through Shkuratovka, Pavlovka, and Budka and further to the east. The 28th Army's headquarters was supposed to move behind 145th RD.

The units began to fulfill the order to withdraw at 2000 hours on 2 August. During the withdrawal, the first encounter with the enemy took place at 0300-0400 hours on 3 August in the vicinity of the village of Starinka [40 kilometers southeast of Pochinok and 23 kilometers north of Roslavl'], where fierce fighting continued up to 1700-1800 hours on 3 August.

The enemy, bringing motorized units forward, exerted great pressure on 149th RD, pushing it back to Kovrigin Kholm and occupying the line of the hill west of Starinka to the forest 1 kilometer southeast of Dubovka, while creating a threat in the direction of Dubovka.

Kachalov remained in the village of Starinka to restore order, from which 145th and 149th RD's units moved, while trying to punch through toward Ermolino [3 kilometers southeast of Starinka].

Groups Egorov [Major General Pavel Grigor'evich Egorov, chief of staff, 28th Army, who was later killed in action] and Kolesnikov [Commissar, Group Kachalov] began moving toward the northeast at around 0600 hours on 4 August but were met by organized enemy fire from the woods west of Budka and the village of Moshchanka [15 kilometers north-northeast of Roslavl'].

With the help of tanks and artillery fire, the groups managed to occupy the village of Budka and advance toward Prisel'e and Novaia Lipovka [3 kilometers southeast of Budka]. Continuing its movement, Group Egorov reached the village of Murinka on the western bank of the Oster River [5 kilometers east of Prisel'e]. Around 200 vehicles and a considerable number of artillery and cargo assembled in this village by 1800 hours.

At this time, the enemy opened artillery fire from the direction of Utekhovo Vtoroe and Safronovo [2-4 kilometers north of Murinka], from the heights west of the village of Murinka, and from the village of Koski [2 kilometers south of Murinka].

After the artillery and machine gun firing on the village of Murinka, enemy tankettes and motorcycles appeared from the points indicated, and, simultaneously, the enemy opened heavy mortar and machine gun fire on our units from the eastern bank of the river and from the villages of Lipovka, Maksimovka, and Nadvornoe [north, west and east of Murinka]. Lacking crossing equipment, the units began to throw everything away and swam or forded their way across.

The impossibility of the wheeled vehicles to get down to and cross the river led to the fact that all of the army's equipment and vehicular transport was abandoned in the village of Murinka.

The personnel threw themselves into the river in panic and began crossing under enemy artillery and machine gun fire, with the ammunition vehicles burning from exploding shells in the village of Murinka to their rear.

With a great deal of difficulty, the command cadre assembled some quantity of soldiers in the forest east of Murinka by about 2000 hours.

Major General Egorov, who also turned up in this forest, decided to create three detachments and continue the withdrawal toward the east or northeast. While giving instructions about the order of the subsequent withdrawal, enemy mobile groups opened fire from all sides. After throwing a group of tanks forward, the column began to punch through toward the east. Whether or not the entire group of Egorov punched through is unknown. Only Major General Butorin, the chief of Kachalov's VVS, penetrated in a tank. The Member of the Military Council, Kolesnikov, also escaped from encirclement with a group of 500 men. Other groups penetrated along the highway and assembled in Ekimovichi [on the Desna River 35 kilometers northeast of Roslavl'].

On 5 August, in the fighting at Starinka, where they intended to penetrate, Kachalov participated in the attack with a tank. After the attack, he went in a southern direction from Starinka. A group headed by Battalion Commissar Krylov reached the Koski region, but was halted there by the enemy.

Group Kachalov escaped in broken up separate groups.

Measures are being taken to search for Group Kachalov's remaining units.

Detachments reinforced with tanks and antitank guns are being sent to meet Kachalov.

We are continuing the searches with aircraft escorted by fighters.

[**Annotation**] – "Fulfilled. Sent by BODO [Baudot secure teletype] through Lieutenant Colonel Andreevo of the Operations Department of the General Staff. 0028 hours on 7 August 1941 [signed] Lieutenant Colonel Kuznetsov."

Source: "Donesenie shtaba Rezervnogo fronta ot 7 avgusta 1941 g. General'nomu Shtabu o otkhode voisk Gruppy Kachalova" [Report by the headquarters of the Reserve Front of 7 August 1941 to the General Staff about the withdrawal of Group Kachalov's forces], in *SBDVOV*, issue 37, 175-176.

Appendix L

The Reduction of the Smolensk Pocket, 1-6 August 1941

1. Intelligence Summary No. 69 of the Headquarters of the Western Front at 0800 hours on 1 August 1941 about the Combat Operations of the Enemy

Intelligence Summary No. 69,
Headquarters, Western Front at 0800 hours on 1 August 1941
1:100,000 and 500,000 scale maps

First. The enemy did not conduct active offensive operations during the day on 31 July 1941. He carried out unsuccessful counterattacks in separate sectors and, simultaneously, he brought up reserves along Velikie Luki, Iartsevo, and El'nia axes.

Second. The Nevel' axis

The enemy continued counterattacks during the day on 31 July, but had no success. Simultaneously, he brought reserves forward in the Shcherginikha and Bandina regions [30-40 kilometers southeast of Velikie Luki], where he concentrated up to two-three infantry divisions with artillery.

According to troop reconnaissance, during the second half of the day on 31 July, up to a battalion of infantry and 50 cavalrymen with mortars and artillery occupied defenses 1.5 kilometers west of Ploskish'.

According to agent information, documents, and prisoner-of-war interrogations, it was established that, in the fighting to encircle our units, 110th ID was operating northwest of Nevel', – 206th ID, from Nevel' to Kocherzhino, – 253rd ID, from the south toward Pogrebishche and Vorkovo, – 14th MotD from the northwest in the Dubinska, Gorodishche, and Pogrebishche sector and from the direction of the Leningrad highway, and separate subunits of 471st and 451st IRs [Security] were operating with ambushes at Begunovo and Dubenskoe.

According to a German reconnaissance agent [*Abwehr*] captured on 30 July, about 200 aircraft, which are conducting raids on Moscow, are located at the airfield in Borisov. (This information must be verified.)

The collective farms in regions the enemy has occupied have not been disbanded, but they suggest the collective farmers harvest the grain. They are seizing the produce from the population by force.

Third. The Iartsevo axis.

The enemy is continuing to conduct defensive fighting along the Chernyi Ruchei, Iakovtsevo, Shelepy, Karpovo, Vetlitsy, and Riadyni line with units from 19th and 20th PzDs, 106th ID, 20th MotD, and 7th and 12th PzDs.

News has not been received about the operations and positions of enemy units northeast and south of Iartsevo.

Combat has determined that up to two battalions of 20th PzD, reinforced by artillery and three batteries of mortars, are operating in the Ostrov region.

Units of 106th ID (240th IR) are operating south of Markovo. A concentration of of up to two battalions of infantry has been detected in the vicinity of Krasnitsa.

According to the testimony of a captured corporal from 74th IR, who was captured on 30 July in the Chamintsevo region, 19th PzD is located in Chernyi Ruchei region. The division is severely worn down and under strength. According to the prisoner, the arrival of three divisions from the Smolensk region to relieve 19th and 20th PzDs is expected on 2-3 August.

According to information from prisoners, 240th IR [106th ID] is being transferred to the combat region from Smolensk in trucks and was sent to Smolensk by foot march. Simultaneously, the remaining regiment of 106th ID (241st IR) is arriving in the region of combat operations.

20th PzD suffered heavy losses in killed and wounded (up to 600 men) on 29 and 30 July, and 10 tanks, 3 guns, automatic weapons, and other trophies were seized by our units.

Units of 12th PzD arrived to relieve units of 19th PzD's units, which must go into reserve, and 12th PzD must have gone into reserve for rest and reinforcement after 10 days of fighting, since it suffered heavy losses in men and equipment. The personnel losses amounted to 75% in separate companies; a significant part of the tanks attached to companies have been lost, and the remaining tanks are severely run down.

The political-morale condition of the soldiers is characterized by an ignorance of the aims of the war, fear of Soviet weapons, and an unwillingness to fight and weariness.

Fourth. The Smolensk axis

The enemy is continuing to press our units toward the east and reached the line from northwest of Shakino [30 kilometers northeast of Smolensk and 20 kilometers southwest of Iartsevo], with its front toward the south, and, according to information that requires verification, Pnevo, Pnevskaia Sloboda, and Zabor'e (west of the Vop'River) [6-10 kilometers southwest of Solov'evo].

Fifth. The El'nia axis

News about the enemy situation along the El'nia axis will be provided later because the information is being received at 0800 hours.

A ME-109 aircraft was shot down on 28 July in the Gorokhovyi Bor region. ... .

Conclusion

The enemy along the Velikie Luki axis, having concentrated up to two-three divisions in the Plaksino [20 kilometers south-southeast of Velikie Luki] and Bandina [30 kilometers south-southeast of Velikie Luki] region, apparently will go over the offensive operations toward the north in the direction of Velikopol'e Station [15 kilometers east of Velikie Luki], with the aim to cut the communications of the Velikie Luki grouping.

The Chief of Staff of the Western Front, Lieutenant General Sokolovsky
The Military Commissar of the Headquarters of the Western Front, Regimental Commissar Anshakov

The Chief of the Intelligence Department of the Headquarters of the
    Western Fronts, Colonel Korneev
The Military Commissar of the Headquarters of the Western Front,
    Senior Battalion Commissar, Steblovtsev

Source: "Razvedyvatel'naia svodka shtaba Zapadnogo fronta No. 69 k 8 chasam 1 avgusta 1941 g. o boevykh deistviiakh protivnika" [Intelligence summary no. 69 of the headquarters of the Western Front at 0800 hours on 1 August 1941 about the combat operations of the enemy], in *SBDVOV*, issue 37, 118-119.

2. Combat Report of the Commander of the Forces of 16th Army of 1 August 1941 to the Commander-in-Chief of the Western Direction's Forces about the Situation of the Army's Forces

To the Commander-in-Chief
Combat Report, Headquarters, 16th Army,
Parshchina, at 1900 hours

   1. The enemy went over to the attack at 0600 hours on 1 August with a force of up to an infantry division, reinforced by artillery and mortars and supported by large aircraft formations, and, having thrown 20th Army's left wing back and bypassed the flank and rear of 229th RD, concentrated his main attack against 16th Army, with a force of [sic] … regiments, continued to exploit success at the boundary between 152nd RD and 34th RC, and is conducting reconnaissance toward Dukhovskaia [15 kilometers east of Smolensk].

   2. In connection with the withdrawal of the left wing units, which immediately uncovered the flank and rear of the division to a depth of 2-3 kilometers while concentrating the attackers' main attack against it, the division is conducting fierce fighting and repeatedly launching counterattacks but, while suffering heavy losses and without artillery and machine guns, is conducting a fighting withdrawal to the east under pressure of superior enemy forces. All the while, the division is holding on to the Mordvino meridian.

   There are no neighbors on the right.

   129th RD, while under pressure from flank attacks, is suffering heavy losses. The situation is difficult.

   3. 152nd RD is withdrawing to the east under attacks from the front and envelopment from the flanks by an enemy forces of up to two regiments.

   At 1900 hours, 152nd RD occupies the Dukhovshchina [should read Dukhovskaia] and Staroe Shishlovo line [15 kilometers east of Smolensk].

   4. 34th Rifle Corps. In 158th RD's sector, the enemy is continuing to press the division's right flank, and up to two enemy battalions are penetrating toward Dukhovskaia and Siniavino.

   At 1700 hours, the division occupies the Siniavino Station, Hill 215.2, and Mitino front strong point [15-16 kilometers east-southeast of Smolensk].

   127th RD occupies a defense along the Mitino and Oblogino front [15 kilometers southeast of Smolensk], inclusive.

The enemy in the division's sector is trying to penetrate at the boundary between 158th and 127th RDs. Enemy movement to envelop the divisions has been noted along the Dnepr River and to the south.

5. 46th RD concentrated in the Zalesovo and Hill 228.5 region by the morning of 1 August, with 646th RR in the Dukhovskaia region, with the mission to avoid giving the enemy an opportunity to develop success along the railroad and prevent it from cutting 34th RC off from the army.

6. The situation is tense. The losses in the force are heavy. There are no shells. There are only a few heavy machine guns in the divisions and, in some of them, none whatsoever. There has been no assistance from our neighbors, and, on the contrary, the unrestrained withdrawal of 20th Army's left wing places us under constant threat of envelopment and attacks in our rear. I am undertaking every measure to hold onto the Mordvino, Dukhovskaia, Rogachev, and Kuznetsovo line [15-20 kilometers east to southeast of Smolensk].

During the night, I am moving 46th RD to the Laptevo, Popovo, and Tiushino line [24-27 kilometers east-southeast of Smolensk], with small groups along the Dnepr River front to the south.

The enemy occupies the railroad crossing over the Dnepr River at Sobshino [30 kilometers east-southeast of Smolensk] – with up to a company of infantry with a battery and 10 tanks.

According to information from reconnaissance and the local population, there is an enemy concentration at Elmino.

Lukin, Shalin, Lobachev
[Annotation] "Sent at 0145 hours on 2 August"

Source: "Boevoe donesenie komanduiushchego voiskami 16-i Armii ot 1 avgusta 1941 g. Glavnokomanduiushchemu voiskami Zapadnogo Napravleniia o polozhenii voisk armii" [Combat report of the commander of the forces of 16th Army of 1 August 1941 to the commander-in-chief of the Western Direction's forces about the situation of the army's forces], *SBDVOV*, issue 37, 215-216.

3. Combat Order No. 14 of the Commander of the Operational Group of Forces of the Iartsevo Axis of 1 August 1941 on an Attack

Combat Order No. 14, Headquarters,
Operational Group of Forces of the Iartsevo Axis,
the woods 1 kilometer southeast of Fedosovo,
1900 hours on 1 August 1941
1:100,000 and 50,000 scale maps

38th RD was forced to withdraw because of its insecure flanks. The restoration of the lost positions, once again with unsecured flanks, can also lead to failure and groundless losses in personnel.

I order:

Go over to the attack at 2300 hours on 1 August 1941 and reliably fortify the [following] lines:

a) The commander of 101st TD, with 101st MRR's forces – Novosel'e (west) and Hill 217.9 [3-5 kilometers north of Iartsevo];

b) 38th RD – Hill 209.2, the unnamed hill 1 kilometer north of Pervomaiskii; and the crest of the hill 1 kilometer west of Pervomaiskii; and

c) The commander of 64th RD, with 159th RR, having occupied the Svishchevo region [6 kilometers south of Iartsevo] and reliably secured for itself the crossing across the Vop' River, will capture the Pologi and unnamed hill line 1 kilometer west of Pologi [5-6 kilometers west of Iartsevo] with 30th RR.

> The Commander of Group of Forces of the Iartsevo Axis,
> Major General Rokossovsky
> The Chief of Staff, Colonel Malanin

Source: "Boevoe rasporiazhenie komanduiushchego Operativnoi Gruppoi Voisk Iartsevskogo Napravleniia no. 14 ot 1 avgusta 1941 g. na nastuplenie" [Combat order no. 14 of the commander of the Operational Group of Forces of the Iartsevo Axis of 1 August 1941 on an attack], *SBDVOV*, issue 37, 415.

4. Combat Order No. 024/op of the Commander of the Forces of 16th Army of 2 August 1941 on the Defense of a Line along the Bol'shoi Vopets River, Tiushino, and Vernebisovo, and along the Dnepr River

Combat Order No. 024/op, Headquarters, 16th Army,
the edge of the woods 1 kilometer south of Morivo State Farm,
0900 hours on 2 August 1941
1:100,000 scale map (1923-26)

1. The enemy is continuing to develop an attack in the general direction of the east, while threatening the army's right flank army and the boundary between 152nd RD and 34th RC and pushing our units toward the east.

2. On the right, 20th Army is defending positions along the general line of the railroad.

Boundaries are as before.

3. I decided on a stubborn defense of the Bol'shoi Vopets River, Tiushino, Vernebisovo, and Dnepr River line [25-30 kilometers east and southeast of Smolensk] to prevent an enemy penetration toward the east and southeast.

4. 129th RD will occupy the Peresvetovo and (inc.) Puzovo sector [25 kilometers east of Smolensk] along the eastern bank of the Bol'shoi Vopets River for defense, with the mission of preventing an enemy penetration toward Shchiurikovo and Liubkovo by a stubborn defense.

Boundary on the left – (incl.) Novo-Shishlovo, Puzino, (incl.) Kulikovo, and the barn.

5. 152nd RD will occupy the Puzovo and (incl.) Tiushino sector [15 kilometers east-southeast of Smolensk] for defense, with the forward edge along the heights on the eastern bank of the Bol'shoi Vopets River.

Mission: prevent an enemy penetration to Liubkovo and Zavrazh'e.

Boundary on the left – Pavlikhina, Bulavkina, and Nadva, 2 kilometers southeast of Kolpino.

6. 34th RC will occupy the Tiushino, Popova, Zaluzh'e, and Vernebisovo sector for defense, with strong security detachments in the Sobshino and Malinovka sector [30-35 kilometers east-southeast of Smolensk] on the western bank of the Dnepr River.

Mission: Prevent an enemy penetration toward the east and northeast. Reliably protect the regions of crossings over the Dnepr River in order to prevent an enemy penetration from Sobshino toward the army's flank and rear.

7. 46th Rifle Division will concentrate in the vicinity of the barn, 2 kilometers south of Golovino.

Mission: force the Dnepr River and reach the Bereznia and Sel'tso region [18 kilometers south of Solov'evo and 40-45 kilometers east of Smolensk], after protecting the region of the crossings over the Dnepr River from the east and southeast. Subsequently, while protecting yourself from the northeast, move forward to Suborovka [6 kilometers south-southwest of Bereznia] and Vishniaki [5 kilometers south-southeast of Bereznia], while preventing the enemy from reaching the routes of the army's withdrawal from Dobromino and Vasil'evo [4 kilometers south of Suborovka and Vishniaki].

8. The army's Chief of Artillery will reliably protect the (incl.) Golovino and Malinovka front along the Dnepr River with antiaircraft artillery weapons.

9. The army's Chief of Engineer Services will immediately begin laying three crossings on the Dnepr River and prepare 5 fords along the Malinovka and (incl.) Golovino front.

10. CP – the edge of the forest 1 kilometer south of Morivo State Farm

The Commander of 16th Army, Lieutenant General Lukin
The Member of the Military Council, Division Commissar Lobachev
The Chief of Staff of the army, Colonel Shalin

Source: "Boevoi prikaz komanduiushchego voiskami 16-i Armii no. 024/op ot 2 avgusta 1941 g. na oboronu rubezha po r. Bol'shoi Vopets, Tiushino, and Vernebisovo, i po r. Dnepr" [Combat order no. 024/op of the commander of the forces of 16th Army of 2 August 1941 on the defense of a line along the Bol'shoi Vopets River, Vernebisovo, and along the Dnepr River], *SBDVOV*, issue 37, 216-217.

5. Combat Order No. 49 of the Commander of the Forces of 20th Army of 2 August 1941 about the Withdrawal of 20th and 16th Armies behind the Dnepr River

Combat Order No. 49, Headquarters, 20th Army,
1930 hours on 2 August 1941
1:100,000 scale maps

1. The enemy continues to press 16th and 20th Armies toward the Dnepr River, having cut off their communications and while trying to break up their front and defeat them in detail.

2. 20th and 16th Armies are holding on to the Il'ia Pustoi, Tveritsy, Kurdimova, Khmost' River, and Bol'shoi Vopets line with part of their forces and withdrawing behind the Dnepr River with their remaining forces.

3. 57th TD and 1st MRD, while holding on to the Il'ia Pustoi, Trisviat'e [30 kilometers northeast of Smolensk], and Kurdimova [19 kilometers east-northeast of Smolensk] line, and while conducting a mobile defense on the Orleia and Los'mena line, will penetrate to the crossings across the Vop' River by an attack toward Mikhailovka and Pishchino [12 kilometers south of Iartsevo] and occupy a defense along the Vop' River in the sector from the forest to the mouth of the Vop' River by 0500 hours on 4 August.

Rear service units will concentrate in the vicinity of the forest west of Prost'.

CP – the grove north of Porovaeva.

Boundary on the left – the Dnepr River, Buianova, (incl.) Zadnia, Fal'kovichi, and Trisviat'e.

4. 5th MC, with 229th and 233rd RDs, will concentrate all of its efforts along the Usinino, Zadnia, Pnevo, and Makeevka axis beginning at 0400 hours on 3 August, penetrate across the Dnepr River at Solov'evo and Makeevka, and, while covering itself along the positions of 233rd RD, beginning from the Khmost' River, Orleia, and the Vodva Rivers, occupy a defense behind the Dnepr River in the sector from the mouth of the Vop' River to the mouth of the Ustrom River by 0500 hours on 4 August.

Rear service organs will concentrate in the vicinity of the forest south of Podkholmitsa. 229th RD's rear will concentrate in the Terenino region.

CP – the forest of Karpovo and Dvoriansk.

Boundary on the left – Mikhailovka, Kopovniki, Dkrushevo, and (incl.) Ryblovo.

5. 69th RC (144th and 153rd RDs) will firmly hold the Khmost' River with part of its forces beginning at 0400 3 August and, while employing a mobile defense along the Nadva and Orleia River lines, punch through to the crossings on the Dnepr River in the sector from (incl.) Zabor'e to the mouth of the Ustrom River, and occupy a defense along the Dnepr River in the sector indicated by 0500 hours on 4 August.

Rear service organs will concentrate in the Novoselki, Borovka, Balakireva, and Zaprud'e sector.

CP – Vachkovo State Farm.

Boundary on the left – the boundary with 16th Army.

6. 73rd RD will leave from its occupied region at 2200 hours on 2 August and seize crossing over the Dnepr River in the Zabor'e and Sarai sector (4 kilometers south of Zabor'e) [13 kilometers south of Solov'evo] by 0400 hours on 3 August, having dispatched strong forward detachments to seize the Kolodezi and Mileevo region in order to protect the crossings by the army's units along the roads to the east.

Rear service organs will concentrate in the Pleshcheevo, Smorodinka, and Krasnyi Kholm region.

CP – the grove south of Liakhovo.

7. 16th Army will firmly hold onto the Bol'shoi Vopets River with part of its forces and concentrate its main efforts on seizing and holding onto the Golovino and Voronitsy crossings and occupying and defending the Dnepr River in the indicated sector by 0500 hours on 4 August.

The boundary between 20th and 16th Armies – Krasnyi Kholm, Balakireva, Novyi Platovets, Kalinovka, Golovino, Babaeva, Slotov, and Koptev (all for 20th Army).

8. During the withdrawal behind the Dnepr River, unit commanders and commissars are personally responsible before their Motherland and government for taking all of their equipment beyond the Dnepr River.

9. For constructing and organizing the crossings, use all of the crossing means at hand in the troop formations, engineer units, and the local population, paying particular attention:

a) To construct crossings concealed from the enemy from the air, using crossings with pontoon equipment only at night, while dismantling them by morning. Construct pontoon bridges with their surfaces 15-20 centimeters under the water, and also use rafts, boats, ferries, and other crossing means; and

b) To finding fords. Horse transports, cavalry units, and horse-drawn artillery will cross at fords, while protecting their approach routes in advance.

10. All formation commanders will concentrate all of their antiaircraft weapons in the vicinity of the crossings.

11. Hold on to the lines of the Khmost' and Bol'shoi Vopets Rivers at all costs up to the end of the day on 3 August.

Hold on to the lines of the Orleia and Nadva Rivers until the end of the day on 4 August.

12. Send, in the first place, the wounded and the artillery and tanks that have no ammunition and fuel, and then, the rear services of the army and troop formations, and troops units and formations across the crossings to the eastern bank of the Dnepr River.

> The Commander of the Forces of 20th Army,
> Lieutenant General Kurochkin
> The Member of the Military Council, Semenovsky
> The Chief of Staff of 20th Army, Major General Korneev

Source: "Boevoi prikaz komanduiushchego voiskami 20 i Armii no. 49 ot 2 avgusta 1941 g. na otvod voisk 20-i i 16-i Armii za r. Dnepr" [Combat order no. 49 of the commander of the forces of 20th Army of 2 August 1941 about the withdrawal of 20th and 16th Armies behind the Dnepr River], *SBDVOV*, issue 37, 270-271.

6. Individual Combat Order of the Commander-in-Chief of the Western Direction's Forces of 3 August 1941 to the Commander of the Forces of 20th Army on a Withdrawal of the Army's Forces to the Eastern Bank of the Dnepr River

To Comrade Kurochkin
Copies: To: Lukin and Rokossovsky
1025 hours on 3 August

The immediate mission is to destroy the enemy battalion, which is disrupting the supply of ammunition and fuel to the Hill 165.9, Pnevo, and Mit'kov region [5-9 kilometers southwest of Solov'evo] and help 108th RD crush the enemy southwest of Zadnia [1 kilometer west of Solov'evo], after protecting the arrival of all supply units to the eastern bank of the Dnepr in the Solov'evo sector and the Ratchino crossing [12 kilometers south-southwest of Solov'evo].

Create a zone of obstacles between the Khmost' [running from north to south 18 kilometers west of Solov'evo] and Dnepr Rivers on the front: to the right – the Zadnia-Smolensk road, and to the left – the El'nia-Smolensk railroad.

After protecting yourself with obstacle detachments, withdraw your main forces to the eastern bank of the Dnepr River, where they will firmly dig in, while protecting themselves from the El'nia axis [the left].

Timoshenko, Sokolovsky

Source: "Chastnyi boevoi prikaz Glavnokomanduiushchego voiskami Zapadnogo Napravleniia ot 3 avgusta 1941 g. komanduiushchemu voiskami 20-i Armii na otvod voisk armii na vostochnyi bereg p. Dnepr" [Individual combat order of the commander-in-chief of the Western Direction's forces of 3 August 1941 to the commander of the forces of 20th Army on a withdrawal of the army's forces to the eastern bank of the Dnepr River], *SBDVOV*, issue 37, 64-65.

7. Individual Combat Order of the Deputy Commander of the Forces of the Reserve Front of 3 August 1941 to the Commander of the Forces of 24th Army on Preparations to Repel the Attacking Enemy

To the Commander of 24th Army
Headquarters, Reserve Front,
Gzhatsk, 1800 hours on 3 August 1941

The 20th and 16th Armies are hurriedly withdrawing toward the east from the Smolensk region. The enemy is taking measures to penetrate into our defensive belt on the shoulders of the withdrawing soldiers.

I order:

Prevent an enemy penetration into the defensive system of 24th Army's divisions, for which it is necessary to:

1) After letting the main mass of our forces withdrawing along every separate axis to pass through, halt the enemy movement with artillery obstacle fire. In the event the enemy approaches before our withdrawing units, when the enemy appears, immediately destroy them with all types of fire.

2) Bring all sectors of mining for the destruction of bridges and roads by explosives to a state of readiness for immediate action and, when the enemy appears, immediately carry out the destruction along specific axes.

3) Mine all sectors envisioned in the mining plan at the last moment and in the immediate threat of an enemy attack.

4) Conduct reconnaissance with small parties on foot (from a squad to a platoon) 6-8 kilometers from the forward edge,

The Deputy Commander of the Forces of the Reserve Front,
    Lieutenant General Bogdanov
The Member of the Military Council, Kruglov
The Chief of Staff of the Reserve Front, Major General Liapin

Source: "Chastnyi boevoi prikaz zamestitelia komanduiushchego voiskami Rezervnogo fronta ot 3 avgusta 1941 g. komanduiushchemu voiskami 24-i Armii na podgotovku k otrazheniiu nastupaiushchego protivnika" [Individual combat order of the deputy commander of the forces of the Reserve Front of 3 August 1941 to the commander of the forces of 24th Army on preparations to repel the attacking enemy], *SBDVOV*, issue 37, 166-167.

8. Individual Combat Order of the Commander of the Forces of the Reserve Front of 3 August 1941 to the Commander of the Forces of 24th Army on the Encirclement of the Enemy in the El'nia Region

To the Commander of 24th Army, Major General Comrade Rakutin
To the Commanders of 19th, 103rd, 105th, 106th, and 120th [Rifle] Divisions
1850 hours on 3 August

The results of the one and one half day-long offensive against the enemy, which are occupying the El'nia region, do not respond to the requirements of my order.

I demanded that you advance no fewer than 8-10 kilometers toward El'nia in the initial days. The majority of units advanced 2-3 kilometers, and some did not even advance a single meter.

19th RD, having occupied Klematina in a daylight battle, abandoned the occupied point during the night and withdrew to their jumping-off positions. Such paltry results of the attack are consequences of the failure of division and regimental commanders to fulfill my orders concerning personal example and punishment of all of those who, instead of attacking and decisively moving forward, sit in the brush and trenches, and all of those who conduct themselves in a cowardly manner and do not serve as a personal example of bravery and courage.

103rd [Rifle] Division, which had especially reinforced artillery support – a battery of multiple rocket launchers ["*Katiushas*"], and aircraft support, has disgracefully marked time almost in place up to this time. 19th Rifle Division's commander and commissar will be arrested by us and will be immediately judged for cowardice and failure to fulfill orders, the unit commanders who abandoned the Klematina region without orders will be immediately arrested, and all of those who will not fulfill combat orders precisely and who conceal themselves out of cowardice in combat situations will be mercilessly brought to trial.

Our operating units are many times superior to the enemy in artillery. The enemy does not even have a full load of ammunition and is conducting very limited fires. The enemy, in essence, is half encircled. With a sufficiently strong blow, the enemy will be immediately smashed.

I order:

1. Completely encircle and take captive the enemy's entire El'nia grouping on 4 August. Begin the attacks at 0700 hours on 4 August. Conduct a two-hour artillery preparation before the attack, while destroying enemy firing points.

2. In light of the apparent weakness of company and battalion commanders, the commanders and commissars of divisions, regiments, and persons especially selected by the senior and higher command cadre and commissars will personally lead the shock groups and battalions in the attacks. In the shock platoons, select commanders

and political workers who have shown themselves to be especially brave in combat and who wish to distinguish themselves before the Motherland.

3. Once again, warn 103rd RD's command cadre about criminal behavior toward the fulfillment of orders, and I especially give notice that, if the enemy is not smashed and the divisions do not reach their designated regions on 4 August, the commanders will be arrested and sent for judgment to a Military Tribunal. Reinforce 103rd RD with another battery of multiple rocket launchers ["*Katiushas*"].

4. Report fulfillment at 2400 hours on 4 August 1941.

> The Commander of the *front*, Hero of the Soviet Union,
> Army General Zhukov

Source: "Chastnyi boevoi prikaz komanduiushchego voiskami Rezervnogo fronta ot 3 avgusta 1941 g. komanduiushchemu voiskami 24-i Armii na okruzhenie protivnika v raione El'nia" [Individual combat order of the deputy commander of the forces of the Reserve Front of 3 August 1941 to the commander of the forces of 24th Army on the encirclement of the enemy in the El'nia region], *SBDVOV*, issue 37, 167-168.

9. Operational Summary No. 76 of the Headquarters of the Western Front at 2000 hours 3 August 1941 about the Combat Operations of the *Front's* Forces

Operational Summary No. 76 at 2000 hours on 3 August 1941,
Headquarters of the Western Front
1:500,000 and 100,000 scale maps

First. Fierce combat continued along the entire front during the day.

Second. 22nd Army. The army's forces continued to repel enemy attacks along the entire front during the day and are holding onto their positions by the end of the day on 3 August.

29th RC – 48th TD. The enemy went over to the attack along the [following] axes: with the forces of up to a battalion – toward Eremeevo and with two battalions – toward Malakhovo [18 kilometers west-southwest of Velikie Luki]. The enemy attacks have been repelled, and 48th TD is holding on to its positions.

A concentration of enemy infantry has been noted in the Shiripina and Batalikha region in front of the division.

214th RD. Up to regiment of enemy infantry attacked against the division toward Lazava and Zadezha. The results of the fighting are being clarified.

62nd RC: 170th RD, after repelling an attack by up to a regiment of enemy infantry, is holding onto its previous positions;

174th RD, having repelled an attack by up to battalion of enemy infantry and going over to the attack, captured Hill 127.4. The enemy withdrew toward Krasnopol'e.

186th RD is holding onto its previous positions. A concentration of up to half an enemy infantry regiment has been noted in the forest west of Krasnopol'e in the Veshnia region.

A concentration of infantry and armored vehicles has been established in the Kurilovo, D'iakova, and Sharapova region.

A concentration of infantry has been identified in the Bor Glamazdy region.

256th RD is fighting with one regiment in the Ploskosh' region, with up to one infantry division opposite its front in the Volok region. Yet another rifle regiment of the division is moving there. The third rifle regiment – is in its previous positions.

Headquarters of 22nd Army – Nazimovo Station.

Third. Group Maslennikov. 252nd RD – is in its previous positions preparing to force the Western Dvina River and, simultaneously, organizing antitank regions in Garabuchikha, Nikulino, Khlebanikha, Pozharishche, Olenitsa No. 1, and Krasnyi Sosny [50 kilometers south-southwest to 50 kilometers south of Toropets].

243rd RD crossed to the southern bank of the Western Dvina River with two regiments and reached the Baevo, Voskresenskoe, and Poiarkovo line [55 kilometers south of Toropets].

Small groups from the enemy 14th MotD are operating opposite the division's front.

Headquarters of the group – Bentsy [36 kilometers south of Toropets].

Fourth. Group Khomenko was continuing its attacks with its main forces on the morning of 3 August, while overcoming strong enemy resistance.

250th RD is conducting defensive fighting along the Los'mino, Dvorishche, and Okolitsa line [19-25 kilometers southwest of Belyi] at 1515 hours on 3 August. It is facing units of 19th PzD (73rd and 74th PzGrenRs).

242nd RD continued its attack toward Zhidki beginning at 1515 hours on 3 August. The division blew up an enemy ammunition dump in the Zhidki region with its artillery fire. The results are being verified.

251st RD had been attacking toward Zhidki and Pochinok No. 2 since the morning of 3 August. Small groups of enemy are withdrawing toward Sechenki opposite the division's front.

107th TD continued its attack toward Gorodno. Their is no information about the results.

Headquarters of the group – the forest 2 kilometers northeast of Podzaitsevo.

Fifth. 19th Army [former Group Kalinin] continued its attack on the morning of 3 August.

166th RD exploited the success of its left wing from the Brakudeno and Sechenki line [35 kilometers east-northeast of Iartsevo], captured Gutarovo at 1700 hours on 3 August, and is fighting for Mamonovo [30 kilometers east-northeast of Iartsevo].

91st and 89th RDs are fighting in their previous positions.

162nd RD concentrated in the Vadino region by 1100 hours.

50th RD is resting and replenishing in its previous positions.

Headquarters of 19th Army – Vadino

Sixth. Group Rokossovsky. The group's units continued to fight along the western bank of the Vop' River on the morning of 3 August. The enemy is continuing to defend stubbornly the Novosel'e, Pologi, Bol'shie Gorki, Zadnia, and Pnevo line [from 5 kilometers north of Iartsevo to 5 kilometers west of Iartsevo to 5 kilometers southwest of Solov'evo]. Essentially, there were no changes in the group's positions on 3 August.

Seventh. 16th and 20th Armies were conducting rear guard fighting along the Pnevskaia Sloboda and the State Farm west of Morevo line [from 9-18 kilometers west-southwest of Solov'evo] and further along the Khmost' River to the Dnepr River at Malinovka [20 kilometers southwest of Solov'evo] by 1200 hours on 3 August.

229th RD of 20th Army crossed to the eastern bank of the Dnepr River at Ratchino (5 kilometers east of Morevo).

34th RC was moving from the Morevo region to the crossing at Ratchino and to the south.

The transport of fuel and ammunition for 16th and 20th Armies to the western bank of the Dnepr River at Ratchino is continuing.

Headquarters of 20th Army – Dubrova (4 kilometers east of Morevo).

Eighth. Group Kachalov. On 2 August the group's forces continued to conduct sustained fighting with the enemy, which were enveloping the group's flanks and developing a penetration toward Roslavl'.

104th TD began an echeloned withdrawal to the Nikitina, Borisovochka, and Egorovka region at 1300 hours on 2 August under an onslaught by the enemy from the Ivanino region.

149th RD was fighting along the Zimnitsy, Storino, and Smychkovo line at 1330 hours on 2 August.

145th RD was defending the (incl.) Smychkovo and Zhigalovo line [20 kilometers south-southeast of Pochinok] with two regiments at 1330 hours on 2 August and protecting the Dundukovka, Efremovka, Gorchilovka, and Dumanichskie front [20-30 kilometers south of Pochinok] from the west with its third regiment

31st MRR withdrew to Novyi Derebuzh, with up to a reinforced battalion with 15 tanks and 30 motorcycles to its front.

The Composite Regiment developed an attack from the Markers 175.3 and 185.9 line toward Andreevskie and Pechkury. Up to a battalion of infantry with armored personnel carriers and motorcycles are in front of the regiment.

The units enumerated above, while holding off the enemy offensive, remained in the positions indicated at day's end on 2 August.

According to information from the Central Front, after fighting in the Poniatovka, and Novaia Dubovichka region, 52nd and 21st CDs withdrew to the south – one to the Krasnopol'e region, and the second – to Pozhyr and Fedorovka.

Headquarters of the group – Stodolishche [30 kilometers south of Pochinok].

222nd RD, unable to withstand the onslaught of the enemy penetrating along the Roslavl' axis, began to withdraw from the Oster River line (15 kilometers west of Roslavl') at 1300 hours on 2 August, with two regiments toward Roslavl' and one regiment (774th) toward the northeast.

The division's units withdrew to Roslavl' in disorder by day's end on 2 August. Units of enemy 189th ID are operating opposite the division's front. Communications have been lost with the division's 774th RR.

Beginning at 1100 hours on 3 August, two regiments of the division are withdrawing to the Oster River (13 kilometers northeast of Roslavl') to organize a defense.

The division's units are putting themselves in order.

Headquarters of 222nd RD – Lugi [20 kilometers east-northeast of Roslavl'].

Ninth. Since the morning of 3 August, the VVS of the *front* conducted reconnaissance of the enemy in the Iartsevo, Zadnia, Kurdymovo, and Roslavl'

regions, bombed tank columns in the same regions, and protected the crossings for 20th Army's forces.

Enemy losses: according to preliminary information, 5 bombers shot down. Our losses: 3 PE-2 aircraft did not return to their airfields.

The Chief of Staff of the Western Front, Lieutenant General Sokolovsky
The Military Commissar of the Headquarters of the Western Front,
    Regimental Commissar Anshakov
The Chief of the Operations Department of the Headquarters of the
    Western Front, Major General Rubtsov

Source: "Operativnaia svodka shtaba Zapadnogo fronta No. 76 k 20 chasam 3 avgusta 1941 g. o boevykh deistviiakh voisk fronta" [Operational summary no. 76 of the headquarters of the Western Front at 2000 hours 3 August 1941 about the combat operations of the *front's* forces], *SBDVOV*, issue 37, 120-121.

10. Report No. 011 of the Military Council of 20th Army of 4 August 1941 to the Commander-in-Chief of the Western Direction's Forces about the Condition of 20th and 16th Armies' Forces

To the Commander-in-Chief of the Western Direction, Marshal Timoshenko

1. 20th and 16th Armies, under strong pressure from 129th, 15th, 5th, 28th, 35th, and 137th Infantry Divisions and an SS Division, will be forcing their way through to the Dnepr River on 3 and 4 August, protected by strong cover from the north and west, to occupy a defense.

57th TD, with 1st MRD, will break through to the crossing at Pishchino. On the morning of 3 August, it was fighting in the Likhovskoe region [9-10 kilometers west-northwest of Solov'evo].

5th MC, with 229th RD, protected by 233rd RD along the Khmost' River, is breaking through toward the Solov'evo and Makeevka crossings. They were fighting in Usinino [8 kilometers west of Solov'evo].

69th RC (144th and 153rd RD), protected by 73rd RD along the line of the Khmost' River, is withdrawing behind the Dnepr River in the sector from the mouth of the Ustrom River to Zabor'e [5-9 kilometers south and south-southwest of Solov'evo].

16th Army is withdrawing to the Zabor'e and Voronitsy front [9-19 kilometers south-southwest of Solov'evo].

2. The army's units are completely exhausted after a period of almost 35 days of fighting. 229th RD on 2 August had [the following]: 783rd RR – 125 men, 1 heavy machine gun, and 8 sub-machine guns; and 804th RR – 160 men, 3 heavy machine guns, 5 sub-machine guns, and 1 – 45mm gun.

73rd RD's combat composition is 100 men, with 4-5 machine guns, in each regiment.

The combat composition is no greater in the other divisions, and, moreover, this composition has been formed at the expense of detaching personnel from the rear services.

After the fighting to reach beyond the Dnepr River, the army's composition will decrease even more.

The army's units began to cross the Dnepr River on the morning of 2 August. Two crossings were bombed 4-5 times by the enemy and were destroyed. Crossings were once again laid in another place on the night of 2-3 August, but were also subjected to destruction; however, the crossing of infantry, tanks, and horse-drawn artillery was carried out on ferries.

With the *front's* help, crossings will once again be laid on the night of 3-4 August, and, in the first place, the heavy artillery, tanks, and other heavy cargo will cross.

There are apprehensions that some portion of the remaining heavy equipment cannot be evacuated.

3. The army has inflicted huge losses on the enemy over the period of 35 days of combat, but itself needs filling out [replacements].

> The Commander of the Forces of 20th Army,
>   Lieutenant General Kurochkin
> The Member of the Military Council, Corps Commissar Semenovsky
> The Chief of Staff of 20th Army, Major General Korneev
> Prepared late on 3 August 1941

Source: "Donesenie voennogo soveta 20-i Armii ot 4 avgusta 1941 g. Glavnokomanduiushchemu voiskami Zapadnogo Napravleniia o sostoianii voisk 20-i i 16-i Armii" [Report by the Military Council of 20th Army of 4 August 1941 to the commander-in-chief of the Western Direction's forces about the condition of 20th and 16th Armies' forces], *SBDVOV*, issue 37, 271-272.

11. Combat Order No. 046 of the Commander of the Forces of the Western Front of 4 August 1941 on the Destruction of the Enemy's Dukhovshchina Grouping

Combat Order No. 046, Headquarters, Western Front,
Kasnia Station,
2255 hours on 4 August 1941
1: 500,000 scale map

1. The enemy, while offering stubborn resistance along the entire front, is trying to encircle 16th and 20th Armies' withdrawing units. Simultaneously, the enemy is developing active operations at the boundaries with neighboring *fronts*. The main enemy grouping of up to 16 infantry divisions is operating along the Smolensk-Viaz'ma axis.

2. On the right, the units on 27th Army's left wing are withdrawing to the Peno region. The boundary on the right – Bologoe and Navsa Station.

On the left, the Reserve Front's units, including Group Kachalov, are fighting in the El'nia and Stodolishche region. The boundary with them – Utriumovo Station, Rozhdestvo Station, and Monastyrshchina.

3. The Western Front will withdraw 20th and 16th Armies' units behind the Dnepr River and has the mission: while firmly holding onto the *front's* left wing

along the Dnepr River line and repelling enemy attacks against its right wing, will smash and destroy the enemy Dukhovshchina grouping in its center.

4. 22nd Army, while continuing an active defense of its occupied positions, will simultaneously destroy the enemy grouping penetrating toward Volok in cooperation with 27th Army's units.

Boundary on the left –Vysokoe, (incl.) Staraia Toropa, Lake Velinskoe, and Gorodok.

5. 29th Army [former Group Maslennikov] will destroy the opposing enemy units by a concentrated strike with 243rd and 252nd RDs toward Il'ino and, having seized crossings over the Western Dvina River at Kresty and Korelevshchina [60-80 kilometers north-northeast of Demidov] and having advanced strong protection [covering forces] toward Velizh, will reach the Olenitsa and Zamoshchitsa front by day's end on 6 August and develop a subsequent attack toward Demidov.

Boundary on the left – Rzhev, Zharkovskii Station, and Manikhi.

The Cavalry Group, while enveloping the enemy defenses, will reach the Zakhody and Safonovo line on 6 August for decisive operations against the enemy's rear toward Dukhovshchina.

6. 30th Army [former Group Khomenko], with the main grouping on your left wing, reach the Dubovitsa. Lomonosovo, and Krivtsy line on 6 August by a decisive attack in the general direction of Krasigovo.

Boundary on the left – Sereda, Novoduginskaia Station, Igor'evskaia Station, Karpova, Krivtsy, and Sheviaki.

7. 19th Army, consisting of 166th, 91st, 89th, 50th, and 152nd RD, with reinforcing units, will attack toward Dukhovshchina with its right wing and reach the Ploshchevo and Sushchevo line on 6 August.

Boundary on the left – Komiagino Station, (incl.) Novosel'e, and Barsuki.

8. Group Rokossovsky will attack with its left wing toward Zadnia and Grishino, while protecting the arrival of 20th Army's units at the Solov'evo and Pishchino crossings over the Dnepr River [10-15 kilometers south of Iartsevo]. Subsequently, after 20th Army's units arrive beyond the Dnepr River, develop an attack with your right wing and reach the Vorotyshino, Stogovo, and Zadnia line by 7 August.

Boundary on the left – Viaz'ma, (incl.) Dorogobuzh, Zadnia, and Kasplia (35 kilometers northwest of Smolensk).

9. 20th Army, while continuing to withdraw behind the Dnepr River, will occupy positions along the Dnepr River on the (incl.) Solov'evo, Zabor'e, Sel'tso, Ustrom River, and Brykino front by day's end on 5 August

Withdraw the army's main forces into army reserve in the Dorogobuzh region and restore their combat readiness.

Boundary on the left – the boundary with the armies of the Reserve Front.

10. 16th Army, upon its arrival on the eastern bank of the Dnepr River, will withdraw the army's units into *front* reserve and concentrate them in the Ostashkovo, Prudishche, and Stogovo Station region.

Headquarters of 16th Army – the Semlevo Station region.

The Commander of the Forces of the Western Front,
Marshal of the Soviet Union S. Timoshenko

The Member of the Military Council of the Western Front, [signed]
The Chief of Staff of the Western Front, Lieutenant General Sokolovsky

Source: "Boevoi prikaz komanduiushchego voiskami Zapadnogo fronta no. 046 ot 4 avgusta 1941 g. na unichtozhenie Dukhovshchinskoi gruppirovki protivnika" [Combat order no. 046 of the commander of the forces of the Western Front of 4 August 1941 on the destruction of the enemy's Dukhovshchina grouping], *SBDVOV,* issue 36, 124-125.

12. Report No. 010 of the Commander of the Forces of 20th Army of 5 August 1941 to the Commander-in-Chief of the Western Direction about the Course of Crossings of the Army's Forces behind the Dnepr River

To the Commander-in-Chief Marshal Timoshenko
1:100,000 scale map
0130 hours on 5 August 1941

1. On 4 August the army's units continued crossing through the Ratchino crossing. The aircraft of the direction brought huge benefit. The enemy did not manage to bomb the crossings.

2. 5th MC began the crossing, while beforehand inflicting defeat on the enemy's Pnevo grouping and passing through Pnevo to freedom.

The overwhelming part of the personnel and equipment, mainly the light artillery of 144th, 153rd, 73rd, and 229th RD, which was not destroyed in combat, crossed over the Dnepr River, as well as a portion of the heavy artillery and rocket launcher batteries. Some part of the auto-transport remained behind because of insufficient fuel.

144th RD (about 440 men) occupied defenses at the mouth of the Ustrom River and 3 kilometers to the south by day's end on 4 August. 153rd RD (about 750 men) occupied defenses southward to Pashkovo [4-10 kilometers south-southwest of Solov'evo], inclusively.

The units of 5th MCs, 57th TD, and 1st MRD are assembling in the woods south of Podkholmitsa, 229th RD – in Terenino, 73rd RD – in Shegaki, and 233rd RD – crossed in several groups.

Liziukov's detachment [from Group Iartsevo] is holding onto the crossing at Ratchino, together with army units, and drove the enemy from the Kucherovo and Mileevo region [15-17 kilometers south-southeast of Solov'evo] toward Hill 224.8 with part of its forces.

16th Army's units are assembling in the Kucherovo, Balakirevo, and Tiushino region, and a detachment of 100 men is being sent to the crossing over the Dnepr River south of Zabor'e. The units are continuing to cross the equipment.

The Commander of the Forces of 20th Army,
    Lieutenant General Kurochkin
The Member of the Military Council, Corps Commissar Semenovsky
The Chief of Staff of 20th Army, Major General Korneev

Source: "Donesenie komanduiushchego voiskami 20-i Armii no. 010 ot 5 avgusta 1941 g. Glavnokomanduiushchemu voiskami Zapadnogo Napravleniia o khode perepravy voisk armii za r. Dnepr"

[Report of the commander of the forces of 20th Army no. 010 of 5 August 1941 to the commander-in-chief of the Western Direction about the course of crossings of the army's forces behind the Dnepr River], *SBDVOV*, issue 37, 272-273.

13. Combat Order No. 4 of the Commander of the Operational Group of Forces of the Iartsevo Axis of 5 August 1941 on a Withdrawal of the Group's Forces behind the Vop' River and the Organization of a Defense on its Eastern Bank

Combat Order No. 4,
Headquarters, Group of Forces of the Iartsevo Axis,
the woods 1 kilometer southeast of Fedosovo, 1800 hours on 5 August 1941
1:100,000 and 50,000 scale maps

1. Units of the enemy 18th and 107th IDs are operating in the Novosel'e, Iartsevo, Svishchevo, and Zadnia sector opposite our group's front.

An influx of fresh forces began beginning at 1200 hours on 5 August. The unloading of an enemy artillery train occurred at Stogovo Station [10 kilometers west of Iartsevo].

2. On the right, 19th Army's 89th RD is fighting along the Borodulino and Dubrovka front [12-17 kilometers north of Iartsevo].

The boundary with it – Komiagino Station, (incl.) Novosel'e, and Barsuki.

On the left, 20th Army's 144th RD has the mission to occupy and hold onto a [defensive] belt with its forward edge in the Korovniki and Osova sector [17-25 kilometers south of Iartsevo] along the eastern bank of the Dnepr River. The boundary with it – Viaz'ma, (incl.) Dorogobuzh, Zadnia, and Kasplia (35 kilometers northwest of Smolensk).

3. The group's forces, at the onset of darkness on 5 August 1941, will withdraw behind the Vop' River, with the mission to defend firmly the Dubrovo, Iartsevo, Rabochii Poselok, Skrushevskoe, and Pereles'e sector along the eastern bank of the Vop'River' and prevent an enemy penetration east of the Vop' River. [Deploy] combat security along the Novosel'e (east), Hill 247.9, Hill 209.2, road junction 2 kilometers east of Zubovo, Svishchevo, the western outskirts of Brianka, and the western outskirts of Pishchino line. After the withdrawal of your forces, mine all of the crossings and fords. Use obstacles extensively within the belt.

4. 101st TD, with 700th ATR (without one battalion), will occupy and defend a [defensive] belt with its forward edge in the Lesnoe Ozerishche and (incl.) Gorodok sector along the eastern bank of the Vop' River.

Position 202nd and 203rd TRs in the woods west of Vyshegor, and employ them only on my orders.

Boundary on the left – Staroe Seutovo, (incl.) Gorodok, and Semukhino.

5. 38th RD (without two companies), with 3rd Bn, 49th CAR and 1st Bn, 700th ATR, will occupy a defensive belt with its forward in the Gorodok, Iartsevo, and Marker 169.9 sector edge along the eastern bank of the Vop' River.

Boundary on the left – Der'ino, Shikino, Marker 169.9, Starosel'e, and Semenova.

6. 44th RC, with 872nd ATR, will occupy and firmly defend a belt, with its forward edge in the (incl.) Marker 169.9, Skrushevskoe Farm, and Pereles'e sector along the eastern bank of the Vop' River, while anchoring its left flank on the Dnepr River.

7. The commander of 38th RD will secure the group's right flank and ensure communications with 89th RD by moving a detachment consisting of two rifle companies and six antitank guns forward to the Padelishche and Chizhiki line [5 kilometers north of Iartsevo].

8. My reserve – 18th MRR and a special designation battery. Deploy in the woods 1.5 kilometers southeast of Ozerishche and prepare to counterattack toward: a) Vyshegor and Chizhiki; and b) Vyshegor and Gorodok.

9. Supply station – Dorogobuzh Station. Transport – on the instructions of division and separate units commanders.

10. CP – the woods 1 kilometer southeast of Fedosovo.

> The Commander of the Group of Forces of the Iartsevo Axis,
>   Major General Rokossovsky
> The Military Commissar of the Group of Forces of the Iartsevo Axis,
>   Battalion Commissar Shapiro
> The Chief of Staff of the group, Colonel Malinin

Source: "Boevoe prikaz komanduiushchego Operativnoi Gruppoi Voisk Iartsevskogo Napravleniia no. 4 ot 5 avgusta 1941 g. na otvod voisk gruppy za r. Vop' i organizatsiiu oborony na ee vostochnom beregu" [Combat order no. 4 of the commander of the Operational Group of Forces of the Iartsevo Axis of 5 August 1941 on a withdrawal of the group's forces behind the Vop' River and the organization of a defense on its eastern bank], *SBDVOV*, issue 37, 415-416.

14. Report of the Military Council of 16th Army of 5 August 1941 to the Military Council of the Western Front about the Condition of the Army's Forces

Top secret

To the Military Council of the Western Front

Tens of personnel without commanders and no headquarters remain in the divisions, and the rear services are being assembled in the Gorodok, Simonovo, Bogatkino, and Papovka region [25-45 kilometers southeast of Solov'evo].

46th, 129th, 127th, 158th, and 152nd RDs are located in the Kolodezi and Sel'tso, Slizovo, and Mileevo region [8-15 kilometers east of the Dnepr River and 15-18 kilometers south of Solov'evo].

Inasmuch as the units crossed at various crossings, therefore, they are going in various directions.

I believe that the divisions are still fighting, and, therefore, I can neither assemble them nor fill them out.

It is not possible to assemble them in the regions indicated to me since, although in small groups, the enemy is located in the places indicated.

I request you indicate the regions and provide several days to restore order in the army's units.

Details by post.

Lukin   Lobachev

Source: "Doklad voennogo soveta 16-i Armii ot 5 avgusta 1941 g. voennomu sovetu Zapadnogo fronta o sostoianii voisk armii" [Report of the Military Council of 16th Army of 5 August 1941 to the Military Council of the Western Front about the condition of the army's forces, *SBDVOV*, issue 37, 217.

15. Combat Order No. 50 of the Commander of the Forces of 20th Army of 5 August 1941 on Defensive Positions along the Dnepr River

Combat Order No. 50, Headquarters, 20th Army
2240 hours on 5 August 1941
1:100,000 scale map

1. The enemy reached the western bank of the Dnepr River in the sector from Solov'evo to the forest south of Golovino with forward units of approaching fresh 20th MotD and 8th ID and units of 7th PzD.

17th MotD's [PzD] units are operating in the Kolodez, Monchino, Iazveno, and Mileevo region [east of the Dnepr River and 15-18 kilometers south of Solov'evo]. Small units from it are trying to penetrate toward Mileevo and Balakirevo [12 kilometers southeast of Solov'evo].

2. On the right – Group Rokossovsky is attacking toward Zadnia and Grishino, while protecting the arrival of 20th Army's units behind the Dnepr River.

The boundary with it – (incl.) Viaz'ma, Dorogobuzh, (incl.) Zadnia, and (incl.) Kasplia.

On the left – Group Kachalov is fighting in the Pochinok and El'nia regions.

The boundary with it – Ugriumovo Station, Rozhdestvo Station, and Monastyrshchina.

3. 20th Army, while completing its withdrawal to the eastern bank of the Dnepr River, has the mission to defend the front along the Dnepr and Ustrom Rivers from Solov'evo to Brykino [30 kilometers south-southeast of Solov'evo] with the forces of 3 divisions.

The army's remaining units will reach the Podkholmitsa, Zaprud'e, and Gorodok region in army reserve, where they will be situated in full combat readiness.

4. 144th RD, with Sakhno's and Shepeliuk's detachments, will occupy and defend positions along the eastern bank of the Dnepr River in the sector (incl.) from the crossing at Solov'evo up to the bend in the Dnepr River 1 kilometer north of Zabor'e.

Boundary on the left – Novoselki, (incl.) the woods northwest of Zabor'e, and Fedurno.

CP – the woods in the Kushkovo region.

5. 153rd RD, with Golovin's, Tarasov's, and Kashchenko's detachments, will occupy and defend positions along the Dnepr River from the bend in the Dnepr River 1 kilometer north of Zabor'e to the mouth of the Mertvaia River [12 kilometers south-southwest of Solov'evo], and further to Kolodezi.

Kashchenko's detachment, which will be employed only with my approval, will remain in the Klimovo region in my reseve.

CP – the woods east of Osovo.

Boundary on the left – (incl.) Zubovo, Kolodezi, and (incl.) Sobshino.

6. 73rd RD, having relieved 16th Army's units along the (incl.) Kolodezi, Sel'tso, Hill 236.5 (1 kilometer south of Slizovo), Hill 224.8, and Klemiatino line, will occupy and defend the line indicated. Simultaneously, conduct reinforced reconnaissance from the line of the Ustrom River in the (incl.) Klemiatino and Brykino sector until 161st RD reaches it.

Conduct reconnaissance toward the El'nia-Smolensk railroad.

Boundary on the left – the boundary of the army.

CP – the woods north of Vasiuki.

7. The army will concentrate its main forces in my reserve and be combat ready in the [following] regions by 1600 hours on 6 August:

5th MC – the woods south of Podkholmitsa, 57th TD – from the woods 1 km northwest of Terenino to the woods north of Gorodok, 229th RD – Terenino and the woods south of Terenino, and 233rd RD – the Zaprud'e region.

> The Commander of the Forces of 20th Army,
>   Lieutenant General Kurochkin
> The Member of the Military Council, Corps Commissar Semenovsky
> The Chief of Staff of 20th Army, Major General Korneev

Source: "Boevoi prikaz komanduiushchego voiskami 20 i Armii no. 50 ot 5 avgusta 1941 g. na oboronu rubezha po r. Dnepr" [Combat order no. 50 of the commander of the forces of 20th Army of 5 August 1941 on defensive positions along the Dnepr River], *SBDVOV*, issue 37, 273-274.

16. Combat Order No. 027/op of the Commander of the Forces of 16th Army of 6 August 1941 to the Army's Forces about the Relief of 107th Rifle Division's Units

Combat Order No. 027/op, Headquarters, 16th Army,
the forest northeast of Krasnyi Kholm,
1525 hours on 6 August 1941
1: 100,000 scale map

1. On the basis of an order from the Western Direction's commander-in-chief, 16th Army will relieve 107th RD's units in the Dorogobuzh, Usviat'e, and Kalita region by 2000 hours on 6 August.

I order:

a) 34th RC, with previous reinforcing units, will relieve the units of 765th and 474th Rifle Regiments along the Nedniki and (incl.) Iakovskoe front before 2000 hours on 6 August.

Boundary on to the left – Sergeevka, Aleshkino, (incl.) Iakovskoe, and Samoilovo.

Place reinforced combat security along the southern bank of the Dnepr River to Dorogobuzh

b) 152nd RD, with previous reinforcing units, will relieve the defending units of 1st Bn, 586th RR along the Iakovskoe and Kalita front [30-32 kilometers southeast of Solov'evo].

Boundary on the left – Chamovo, Pleshivtsevo, Filaty, Kalita, and Leonovo. Send reinforced combat security forward to the Usovo and Erilovo front.

2. Division commanders will personally go to their defensive sectors and look over and take over engineer defensive works, obstacles, and maps.

3. Command Post – the forest northeast of Krasnyi Kholm

> The Commander of 16th Army, Lieutenant General Lukin
> The Member of the Military Council, Division Commissar Lobachev
> The Chief of Staff of the army, Colonel Shalin

Source: "Boevoi prikaz komanduiushchego voiskami 16-i Armii no. 027/op ot 6 avgusta 1941 g. voiskam armii o smene chastei 107-i Strelkovoi Divizii" [Combat order no. 027/op of the commander of the forces of 16th Army of 6 August 1941 to the army's forces about the relief of 107th Rifle Division's units], *SBDVOV*, issue 37, 217-218.

17. Combat Order No. 52 of the Commander of the Forces of 20th Army of 7 August 1941 on the Defense of the Dnepr River Line by 20th and 16th Armies' Forces

Combat Order No. 52, Headquarters, 20th Army,
0120 hours on 7 August 1941
1:100,000 scale map

1. The enemy reached the front of the crossings at Solov'evo, Ratchino, Sel'tso, and Klemiatino with units of 7th PzD, 20th MotD, 8th ID, and 17th MotID, while trying to force the Dnepr River at Pnevo and to the south at Ratchino.

2. On the right, the units on Group Rokossovsky's left wing are fighting for Zadnia. The boundary with it – (incl.) Viaz'ma, Dorogobuzh, and the crossing at Solov'evo.

On the left, 24th Army's units are fighting for the Ushakovo and Lavrovo line. The boundary with it – Podmosh'e, Rozhdestvo, and Rykachevo.

3. 20th and 16th Armies, united under my overall command, will firmly defend the front along the Dnepr River from the crossing at Solov'evo to the barn (5 kilometers south of Zabor'e), Slizovo, Vaskiuki, Mikhailovka, and Kazanka, while concentrating the main forces on its left wing.

4. 144th RD, with Comrades Shepeliuk's and Sakhno's detchments, will continue to defend firmly the sector of the crossing at Solov'evo to the bend in the Dnepr River 1 kilometer north of Zabor'e.

Boundary on the left – Novoselki and Mit'kovo.

CP – Kushkovo.

5. 153rd RD, with Tarasov's and Kashchenko's detachments and a company of border guards troops, will defend the Dnepr River line from the bend in the Dnepr River (1 kilometer north of Zabor'e) to Marker 179.1, and the woods 1 kilometer north of Kolodezi, while sending detachments to the Dnepr River's eastern bank, with the aim of preventing the enemy from forcing the Dnepr River.

Boundary on the left – (incl.) Balakirevo, (incl.) Kolodezi, and Sobshino.

CP – Osovo.

6. 73rd RD, having relieved 46th and 129th RDs' units, will occupy and firmly defend the Kolodezi, Slizovo, and Mileevo line by 0600 hours on 7 August, having sent a detachment to Korsun'ia, with the aim of preventing the enemy from forcing the Dnepr River.

Boundary on the left –Berezkino, Mileevo, and Vasil'evo.

CP – the woods south of Novyi Platovets.

7. 161st RD, with 129th RD's artillery, will occupy and firmly defend the Ustrom River line in the sector from Vasiuki to Mikhailovka

Boundary on the left – Basmanovo, Mikhailovka, and Liabovo.

CP – the woods in the Iurkino region.

8. 46th RD, having turned its combat sector over to 73rd RD, will occupy and defend the (incl.) Mikhailovka, Goravitsy, and Kazanka line by 0700 hours on 7 August 1941.

The army's cavalry squadron will conduct reconnaissance toward the south;

CP – the woods in the Ivashenki region.

9. 16th Army, upon relief of 107th RD by 127th, 152nd, and 158th RDs' units along the Dorogobuzh and Usviat'e line and further along the Uzha River to Staroe Rozhdestvo, will continue to fortify their occupied positions, paying special attention to the defense of the El'nia and Dorogobuzh road.

Headquarters of the army – Blagoveshchenskoe (8 kilometers east of Dorogobuzh).

10. 233rd RD will leave the region it occupies at 0300 hours on 7 August 1941 and concentrate in the Balakirevo, Naidenovo, and Samoilovo region by 0600 hours on 7 August 1941, and, while situated in my reserve, will prepare to be employed along the western and southern axes.

11. 129th RD, having given its combat sector to 46th and 161st RDs' units and having transferred its artillery to 161st RD for temporary use, will concentrate in the Bobrovo (First) region by 0800 hours on 7 August, where, situated in my reserve, it will prepare to be employed toward the southeast or south. Headquarters – the woods south of Bobrovo.

12. 229th RD, while remaining in the Terenino region in my reserve and putting itself into order, will prepare to be employed toward Chelnovaia.

13. 1st MRD, while remaining in the Gorodok region in my reserve, will put itself into order.

14. 5th MC, with 57th TD, while following along the Dorogobuzh march route and the auto-highway, will concentrate in the Korobkino, Romashkovo, and Nekrasovo region (20 kilometers southeast of Gzhatsk), where it will be at the disposal of the *front*.

15. CP – Novoselki

The Commander of the Group of Armies, Lieutenant General Lukin
The Member of the Military Council, Corps Commissar Semenovsky
The Chief of Staff of the Group, Major General Korneev

Source: "Boevoi prikaz komanduiushchego voiskami 20 i Armii no. 52 ot 7 avgusta 1941 g. na oboronu voiskami 20-i i 16-i Armii rubezha po r. Dnepr" [Combat order no. 52 of the commander of the forces

of 20th Army of 7 August 1941 on the defense of the Dnepr River line by 20th and 16th Armies' forces],
SBDVOV, issue 37, 274-275.

18. Report by the Headquarters of 16th Army of 7 August 1941 to the Western Front's Headquarters about the Transfer of all of 16th Army's Units to the Composition of 20th Army

To the Chief of Staff of the Western Front

All of 16th Army's units have been transferred to 20th Army and moved to their concentration regions.

The hauling out of equipment and material from the western bank of the Dnepr River by 16th Army has ceased.

The blowing up of the crossing has been carried out by local means, and the enemy offered weak fire resistance to the crossings.

It is incorrect that 20th Army is assigning a guard battalion to the crossing and is undertaking energetic measures for the hauling out of equipment and materials, consisting of the greater proportion of vehicles and artillery.

Colonel Ponomarev
Accepted at 1415 hours on 7 August 1941

Source: "Donesenie shtaba 16-i Armii ot 7 avgusta 1941 g. shtabu Zapadnogo fronta o peredache vsekh chastei 16-i Armii v sostav 20-i Armii" [Report by the headquarters of 16th Army of 7 August 1941 to the Western Front's headquarters about the transfer of all of 16th Army's units to the composition of 20th Army], *SBDVOV*, issue 37, 218.

19. Operational Summary No. 84 of the Headquarters of the Western Front at 2000 hours 7 August 1941 about the Combat Operations of the *Front's* Forces

Operational Summary No. 84 at 2000 hours on 7 August 1941,
Headquarters, Western Front
1:500,000 and 100,000 scale maps

First. Sparse artillery firing and reconnaissance raids occurred across the entire front.

Second. 22nd Army. The positions of the army's units are unchanged. Sparse artillery exchanges and reconnoitering by both sides occurred during the day on 7 August.

In the Grishino region, a group of enemy was destroyed by our reconnaissance scouts, and 34 bicycles and standards were seized.

Reconnaissance detected up to a battalion of infantry with artillery in the Liakhnovo region. The enemy is carrying out entrenching work in the Lake Sorito and Kuznetsovo region [15-20 kilometers south of Velikie Luki].

256th RD continued to attack toward Volok.

Headquarters, of 22nd Army – Nazimovo Station [30 kilometers east of Velikie Luki].

Third. Group Maslennikov.

252nd RD – 924th RR – position unchanged.

928th and 932nd RRs, under pressure of superior enemy forces, withdrew to the northern bank of the Western Dvina River and went over to the defense [as follows]: 928th RR – along the Vypolzovo and Petrovo line [40-45 kilometers south-southeast of Toropets] and 932nd RR – Liubovitsy, Olenitsa, and Ust'e line [50-65 kilometers south of Toropets].

243rd RD, while continuing its attack toward Il'ino [58 kilometers south of Toropets], was fighting for the Tolkachi, Hill 193.8, Zakhody, Bodnevka, and Liubimovo line [45 kilometers south of Toropets] at 1630 hours on 7 August.

50th and 53rd CDs – no news received.

[*Operational summary no.' 86 at 2000 hours on 8 August stated, "The Cavalry Group (50th and 53rd CDs), according to verified data, withdrew [as follows], 50th CD to the Emlen' region [70 kilometers west of Belyi] and 53rd CD – to the Ordynka region [55 kilometers west of Belyi] at 2200 hours on 6 August.*]

Headquarters of the group – Bentsy [37 kilometers south of Toropets].

Fourth. 30th Army. The positions of the army's units are unchanged. [*Operational summary no. 85 at 0800 hours on 8 August stated, "30th Army halted its offensive at nightfall on 7 August. The enemy displayed no activity. By 0600 hours on 8 August, the units of the army occupied [the following positions]: 250th RD – Los'mino, Demiakhi (southern), and Buraia [-15-19 kilometers southwest of Belyi]; 242nd RD – Morokhovo Station, Novoe Morokhovo, and Dolgoe, with one battalion of 900th Regiment in the Klintsy region; 251st Rifle Division – (incl.) Guliaevo, eastern outskirts of Zhukova, and Sloboda; and 107th TD – Nazemenki and Hill 236.6".*]

Fifth. 19th Army, while carrying out a local regrouping, continued its attack beginning at 0700 hours on 7 August. The attack by the army's units developed extremely slowly, and the enemy offered stubborn resistance.

The units (166th, 162nd and 91st RDs).achieved insignificant success by 1800 hours only in individual sectors of the front

166th RD captured Demeshonki with its right wing, and the positions were unchanged in remaining sectors of the front.

162nd RD reached the eastern edge of the woods (1 kilometer west of Ust'e) [28 kilometers north-northeast of Iartsevo] with its right wing and is fighting in the forests west of Zaovrazh'e with its left wing.

91st RD advanced to within ¾ of a kilometer west of Gorbatovskaia [25 kilometers north of Iartsevo] and Dura with its right wing and in its center.

89th RD is fighting in its previous positions.

303rd, 321st, and 11th EngBns conducted defensive work along the Neelovo and Gorodok line.

Sixth. Group Rokossovsky. The group's units occupied defenses in their previous positions in the (incl.) Kurganovo and Iartsevo sector along the eastern bank of the Vop' River and the northern bank of the Dnepr River at Solov'evo.

There were no changes in the positions of the group's units.

Seventh. 20th Army, while carrying out a partial regrouping on the night of 6-7 August, occupied an echeloned defense line on the Solov'evo, Zabor'e, Mileevo, Brykino, and Kazanka [18 kilometers south-southeast to 31 kilometers southeast of Solov'evo and 18 kilometers northwest of El'nia] front along the eastern bank of the Dnepr River.

144th RD is defending the line of the crossings at Solov'evo and (incl.) Zabor'e. The enemy occupied the western bank of the Dnepr River with small groups. The enemy has mined several sectors of the road along the western bank.

153rd RD is defending the Zabor'e and Marker 179.1 line. The division's units liquidated a platoon of enemy which had penetrated to the eastern bank at Ratchino.

73rd RD, after relieving 129th RD's units, occupied the Kolodezi, Slizovo, Mileevo, and Vasiuki defense line [16 kilometers south to 19 kilometers southeast of Solov'evo] at 0230 hours on 7 August.

161st RD approached the Vasiuki and Mikhailovka line [19-25 kilometers southeast of Solov'evo] at 0400 hours on 7 August and set about organizing a defense.

46th RD is being relieved by 73rd RD's units along the Kolodezi and Mileevo line at 0230 hours and will come forward to occupy the (incl.) Mikhailovka and Kazanka defense line [25-31 kilometers southeast of Solov'evo] at 0700 hours.

233rd RD, having crossed to the eastern bank of the Dnepr River, will shift from the Zaprud'e region [15 kilometers east-southeast of Solov'evo] to the Balakirevo, Naidenovo, and Samoilovo region [15-20 kilometers southeast of Solov'evo] by 0800 hours on 7 August.

129th RD will turn its combat sector over to 73rd RD and move forward into the Bobrovo region.

229th RD and 1st MRD – are in their previous positions.

34th RC reached its defense line and relieved 107th RD's units in [the following] sectors:

127th RD – Usviat'e and Vygor' [25 kilometers east to 26 kilometers east-southeast of Solov'evo];

158th RD – Vygor' and Kas'kovo [26 kilometers east-southeast to 28 kilometers southeast of Solov'evo]; and

152nd RD – Kas'kovo and Kalita [28-33 kilometers southeast of Solov'evo].

5th MC and 57th TD – are in their previous regions but will shift to the region southeast of Gzhatsk in *front* reserve on the night of 7-8 August.

In order to continue crossing the army's remaining logistical units and material from the Dnepr River's western to eastern bank, 153rd and 73rd RDs' units will attack the enemy and capture Ratchino and Liakhovo [9-12 kilometers southwest of Solov'evo], with the aim of throwing the enemy back from the crossing regions.

Headquarters of 20th Army – Novoselki [11 kilometers south-southeast of Solov'evo].

Headquarters of 16th Army – was withdrawn into *front* reserve in the region north of Dorogobuzh.

Headquarters of 2nd RC, with the corps' units, will be transferred to Briansk. Two trains will be sent out by 1700 hours on 7 August, and the remaining three will load and complete their departure by 2400 hours on 7 August.

Eighth. The VVS of the *front* conducted reconnaissance in the sector of the front beginning on the morning of 7 August, and, while cooperating with the ground forces, destroyed enemy motor-mechanized units and enemy artillery and infantry.

Information about enemy losses and our losses for the first half of the day has not been received.

The Chief of Staff of the Western Front, Lieutenant General Sokolovsky
The Military Commissar of the Western Front, Regimental Commissar Anshakov
The Chief of the Operations Department, Lieutenant General Malandin

Source: "Operativnaia svodka shtaba Zapadnogo fronta No. 84 k 20 chasam 7 avgusta 1941 g. o boevykh deistviiakh voisk fronta" [Operational summary no. 84 of the headquarters of the Western Front at 2000 hours 7 August 1941 about the combat operations of the *front's* forces], *SBDVOV*, issue 37, 128-129.

Appendix M

The *Stavka* Regroups its Forces, 30 July-11 August 1941

1. *Stavka* VK Order No. 00583 Concerning the Formation of the Reserve Front

30 July 1941

1. Form the headquarters of the Reserve Front to unite the operations of reserve armies along the Rzhev-Viaz'ma line.

Appoint the Deputy People's Commissar of Defense, Army General Zhukov, as the *front's* commander.

[Appoint] Comrades Kruglov and Popov as members of the *front's* Military Council [commissars].

Use the headquarters of the First and Second Reserve Groups to form the *front's* headquarters.

The headquarters of the Reserve Front beginning on 30 July 1941 – Gzhatsk

2. Include in the Reserve Front's composition:

a) 34th Army, consisting of 254th, 245th, 259th, 262nd, and 257th RD, 25th and 54th CDs, 264th and 644th CARs, 171st and 759th ATRs, and 16th and 95th Armored Trains.

The boundary line on the left – Zarech'e (20 kilometers northwest of Vyshnii Volochek), Firovo, Naumovo (25 kilometers west of Ostashkov), and Lake Luchanskoe.

Headquarters of the army – Liubnitsa Station.

b) 31st Army, consisting of 249th, 247th, 119th, 246th, and 244th RDs, 110th TD, 43rd CAR, and 766th and 533rd ATRs.

The boundary line on the left – the Moscow Sea, Kniazh'i Gory, Pomel'nitsa Station, Shiparevo, and Shchuch'e.

Headquarters of the army – Rzhev

c) 24th Army, consisting of 248th, 194th, 133rd, 178th, 107th, 19th, and 120th RDs, 102nd TD, 103rd MD, 542nd, 392nd, and 685th CARs, 305th and 573rd GARs, 18th, 509th, 871st, 872nd, 874th, 876th, 879th, and 880th ATRs, and 43rd AAA Btry on railroad cars.

The boundary line on the left – Ugriumovo Station, Luzhki (60 kilometers south of Viaz'ma), Popovka (10 kilometers south of El'nia), and Pochinok.

Headquarters of the army – Semlevo.

d) 43rd Army, consisting of 53rd, 217th, and 222nd RDs, 105th TD, 106th MD, 448th, 364th, 643rd, and 207th CARs, 320th GAR, 760th, 753rd, and 761st ATRs, and 41st AA Btry on railroad cars.

Deploy 43rd Army on the base of 33rd RC.

Appoint Lieutenant General Comrade Zakharkin, Deputy Commander of the Moscow Military District, as the army's commander.

Headquarters of the army – Kirov

e) 32nd Army, consisting of 2nd, 7th, 18th, 13th, and 8th Peoples' Militia Divisions [DNO] and 873rd and 875th ATRs.

The army will concentrate by marching on foot in the Viaz'ma region by the morning of 4 August 1941 and occupy the Bogoroditskoe, Lysovo, Podrezovo, Panfilovo, and Godunovka line.

Headquarters of the army – Viaz'ma.

3. Include 4th and 6th Peoples' Militia Divisions and 761st and 765th ATRs in the Reserve Front's composition once they complete their formation.

The *Stavka* of the High Command
Stalin
Zhukov

Source: "Prikaz Stavki VK no. 00583 o formirovanii Rezervnogo fronta" [*Stavka* VK order no. 00583 concerning the formation of the Reserve Front], in Zolotarev, "*Stavka* 1941," 98-99.

2. *Stavka* VK Directive No. 00732 to the Commanders of the Reserve and Western Fronts about the Reserve Front's Composition (see Map 5)

0220 hours on 6 August 1941

For the purpose of improving command and control in the Reserve Front, include in its composition:

a) 31st Army, consisting of 249th, 247th, 119th, 246th, and 244th RDs, 43rd CAR, and 766th and 533rd ATRs.

Boundary line on the left – the Moscow Sea, Kniazh'i Gory, Pomel'nitsa Station, Shiparevo, and Shchuch'e.

Headquarters of the army – Rzhev.

Commander of the army – Major General Dolmatov

b) 35th Army, having allocated to it from 24th Army 248th, 194th, 260th, 220th, and 298th RDs, 4th People's Militia Division, and reinforcing artillery units by order of the Reserve Front's commander.

Boundary line on the left – Vadino Station and Kasnia Station – for 35th Army [inclusively].

Form 35th Army's headquarters from 35th RC's headquarters and place it in Novo-Dugino.

Commander of the army – Lieutenant General Zakharkin.

c) 24th Army, consisting of 133rd, 178th, 107th, 19th, 120th, and 100th RDs, 106th MD, and 6th People's Militia Division. Artillery means of reinforcements – in accordance with orders of the Reserve Front's commander.

Keep 278th, 269th, 280th, and 309th RDs in the army's reserve.

Boundary line on the left – Ugriumovo Station, Luzhki, Popovka, and Pochinok, all for 24th Army [inclusively].

Headquarters of the army – Semlevo.

Commander of the army – Major General Rakutin.

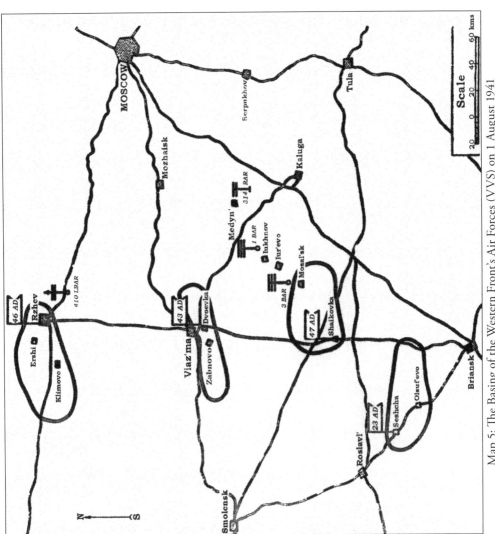

Map 5: The Basing of the Western Front's Air Forces (VVS) on 1 August 1941

d) 43rd Army, consisting of 53rd, 217th, 222nd, 145th, and 149th RDs, 104th and 109th TDs, 448th, 364th, 643rd, and 207th CARs, 320th GAR, and 760th ATR.

Keep 211th, 279th, and 303rd RDs in the army's reserve.

Boundary line on the left – (incl.) Brovka, Zhukovka, and Shumiachi.

Headquarters of the army – Kirov.

Commander of the army – Lieutenant General Kurochkin.

e) 2nd Separate Rifle Corps, consisting of 258th, 260th, and 290th RDs, the 2nd RC's corps artillery regiments, and 753rd and 761st ATRs.

Headquarters of the corps – Briansk.

Commander of the corps – Major General Ermakov.

The Western Front's commander will immediately send 2nd RC's headquarters and corps' units to Briansk.

f) In the *front's* reserve:

32nd Army, consisting of 2nd, 7th, 8th, 13th, and 18th People's Militia Divisions and 873rd and 875th Antitank Artillery Regiments.

Headquarters of the army – Viaz'ma.

Commander of the army – Lieutenant General Klykov.

33rd Army, consisting of 9th, 5th, 1st, 17th, and 21st People's Militia Divisions and 877th and 878th ATRs.

Headquarters of the army – Spas-Demensk.

Commander of the army – *Kombrig* Onuprienko.

45th and 55th Cavalry Divisions and 765th ATR.

The *Stavka* of the High Command
I. Stalin
B. Shaposhnikov

Source: "Direktiva Stavki VK no. 00732 komanduiushchim voiskami Rezervnogo i Zapadnogo frontov o sostav Rezervnogo fronta" [*Stavka* VK directive no. 00732 to the commanders of the Reserve and Western Fronts about the Reserve Front's composition], in Zolotarev, "*Stavka* 1941," 106-107.

3. *Stavka* VK Directive No. 00731 to the Commanders of the Forces of the Reserve and Western Fronts about Measures for the Destruction of the Enemy's El'nia Grouping (see Map 6)

0216 hours on 6 August 1941

For the purposes of the final destruction of the enemy's El'nia grouping, the *Stavka* orders, under the personal responsibility of the Reserve Front's commander, Army General Comrade Zhukov:

1. Comrade Zhukov, having reinforced his units operating at El'nia, will continue an energetic and decisive attack on El'nia with 107th Rifle Division and two regiments of 100th Rifle Division, with their artillery, with the mission of encircling and destroying the enemy's El'nia grouping.

2. Upon receipt of this directive, the commander of the Western Front, Marshal Timoshenko, will transfer two regiments of 100th Rifle Division, with their artillery, to the disposition of the commander of the Reserve Front.

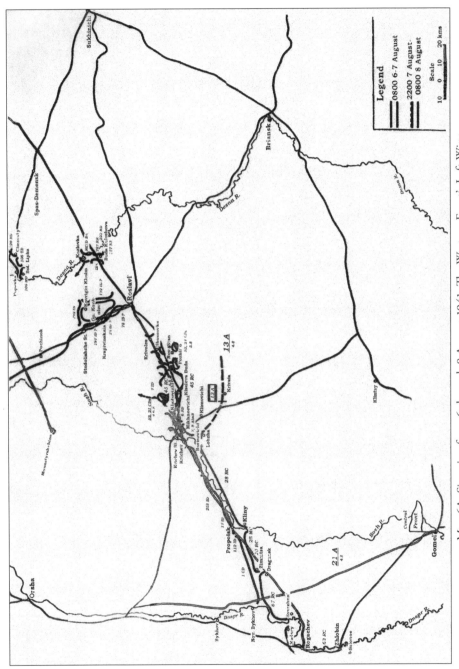

Map 6A: Situation from 6 through 8 August 1941. The Western Front's Left Wing

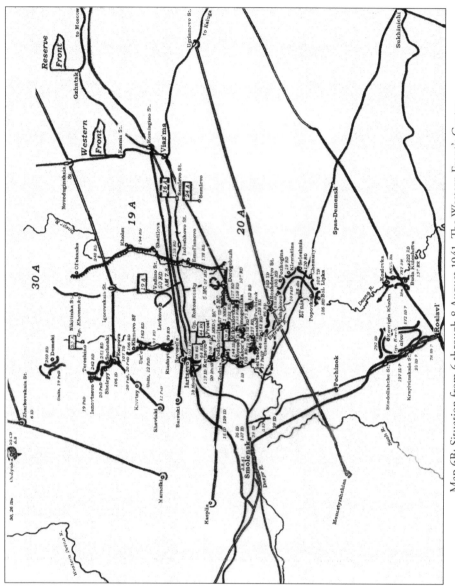

Map 6B: Situation from 6 through 8 August 1941. The Western Front's Center.

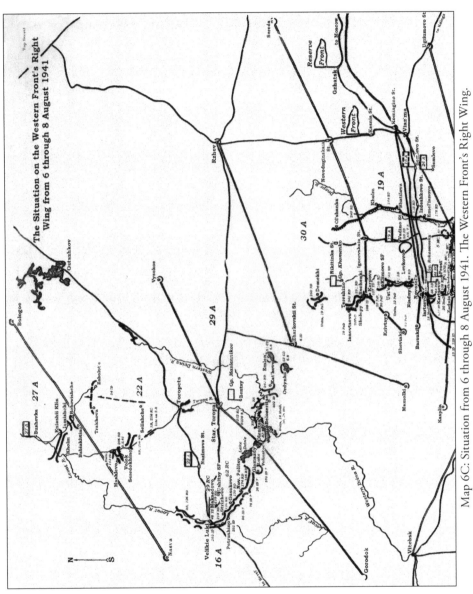

Map 6C: Situation from 6 through 8 August 1941. The Western Front's Right Wing.

Relieve 107th Rifle Division with units of the Western Front by 2000 hours on 6 August, having occupied its positions along the Dorogobuzh, Usviat'e, Kas'kovo, and Kalita front [north of El'nia].

3. The commander of the Western Front will extend his left wing [flank] from the Solov'evo crossings southward along the Dnepr River to Pridneprovskaia Station and farther southeast along the railroad to Dobromino Station [platform] [25 kilometers south of Solov'evo and 35 kilometers northwest of El'nia].

4. For conducting the operation at El'nia, on 6 August rebase two light bomber [regiments] and one fighter regiment at the disposal of the chief of the Air Forces (VVS) from the Reserve of the High Command to the disposal of the commander of the Reserve Front.

To reinforce the Reserve Front's aviation, on 6 August rebase two light bomber and one fighter regiment from the Reserve of the High Command to the Roslavl' axis.

5. Confirm receipt and immediately submit a plan for the operation at El'nia.

The *Stavka* of the High Command
I. Stalin
B. Shaposhnikov

Source: "Direktiva Stavki VK no. 00731 komanduiushchim voiskami Rezervnogo i Zapadnogo frontov o merakh po razgromu El'ninskoi gruppirovki protivnika" [*Stavka* VK directive no. 00731 to the commanders of the forces of the Reserve and Western Fronts about measures for the destruction of the enemy's El'nia grouping], in Zolotarev, "*Stavka* 1941," 106.

4. Individual Combat Order No 19/op of the Commander of the Forces of the Reserve Front of 6 August 1941 to the Commander of the Forces of 24th Army on the Destruction of the Enemy's El'nia Grouping

To the Commander of 24th Army, Major General Rakutin
Copy: To the Commander of 43rd Army
Combat Order No. 19/op, Headquarters, Reserve Front,
2000 hours on 6 August 1941
1:100,000 scale map

1. In the El'nia region, enemy units occupy a defense along the Bykovo, Semeshino, Klematina, Maloe Pronino, and Bol'shaia Lipnia front with small groups. Reconnaissance has established that units of 16th ID, 248th ID, 20th PzD's 49th MotR, 29th MotD's 86th MotR, and 31st and 41st EngBns are operating in this region. According to information from prisoners, an SS Division and 10th PzD are being withdrawn from the El'nia region. According to the same information, the enemy's El'nia grouping has a considerable quantity of artillery.

2. The *Stavka* of the High Command, attaching exceptional importance to the El'nia region, has ordered you to destroy the enemy's El'nia grouping and reach the Dobromino Station, Berniki, Babarykin, Kholm, Staroe Shcherbino, and Svetilovo line. Link up with the Western Front's left flank in the vicinity of Dobromino Station.

3. The operation to destroy the enemy's El'nia grouping is entrusted personally to Major General Comrade Rakutin.

The composition of the operational group: 107th, 100th, 103rd, 19th, and 120th RDs, 106th MD, 105th and 102nd TDs, a company of T-34 tanks, 184 combat aircraft, 275th and 488th CARs, and 573rd and 305th GARs.

4. Organize the operational group's main attack from the Dubrovezh'e and Ushakovo region.

107th RD, with 102nd TD and two reinforcing artillery regiments, will attack from the Dubrovezh'e and Ivanovskie Farm region and deliver a powerful blow toward Viazovka, Gur'evo, Lysovka, and Leonidovo.

100th RD, with 10 T-34 tanks, will attack from the Bykovo and Ustinovo line toward Chantsovo and the northwestern outskirts of El'nia.

103rd RD will attack from the Ushakovo and Lavrovo line through Petrianino and Sofievka toward the northern outskirts of El'nia.

19th and 120th RDs and 105th TD, with attached reinforcements, will attack in the general direction of the southeastern part of El'nia.

106th MD will attack from the Mal'tsevo and Bol'shaia Lipnia line in the general direction of Bitiakovka and Leonidovo.

With the shock group's advance from the Dubovezh'e region toward the south, seize the Bezzabot State Farm, Novoselovka, Tishovo, Kharnia, and Leonovo line and organize a firm defense along that line, with the objective to prevent an enemy penetration enemy toward El'nia.

Upon completion of the liquidation of the enemy in El'nia, part of the group will move forward to the Dobromino Station, Berniki, and Staroe Shcherbino defense line.

Move reinforced detachments forward into the Svetilovo and Shat'kova region by day's end on 7 August to protect your left flank. The detachments moving forward will link up with the units on 53rd RD's left wing. Render the Svetilovo and Shat'kovo region impassible and lay mines.

5. Conduct the operation according to the following plan:

a) On 6-7 August, conduct careful reconnaissance of enemy targets and dispositions;

b) Carefully organize cooperation of the infantry with tanks, artillery, and the batteries of rocket launchers and the ground forces with aviation.

c) Work out tactics and techniques for destroying enemy firing points in cooperation with all types of forces and with neighbors with the commanders of platoons, companies, battalions, batteries, and artillery battalions. Pay special attention to working out target designation and the identification of their own ground forces by aircraft.

d) Complete transporting shells, bombs, and fuel and organize airfield services for aviation and the organization of communications and messenger services by day's end on 7 August,

6. Deploy 879th ATR and 6th DNO [People's Militia Division] to secure the depths along the Borisovka, Gorodok, and Ugra River line, having occupied defenses in prepared lines.

Leave 533rd and 880th ATRs in antitank lines according to the previously issued instructions. Leave a company of KV tanks (7 vehicles) at the disposal of 880th ATR's commander as an antitank reserve.

7. Conduct concealed ranging [adjustment] fires with 107th and 100th RDs' artillery. Destroy enemy fortified points by methodical artillery fire over the course of time.

8. Present a plan of operations by courier by 1200 hours on 7 August, and be prepared to report on the terrain.

> The Commander of the Reserve Front, Army General Zhukov
> The Member of the Military Council, Kruglov
> The Chief of Staff, Major General Liapin

Source: "Chastnyi boevoi prikaz komanduiushchego voiskami Rezervnogo fronta No. 19/op ot 6 avgusta 1941 g. komanduiushchemu voiskami 24-i Armii na unichtozhenie El'ninskoi gruppirovki protivnika" [Individual combat order no 19/op of the commander of the forces of the Reserve Front of 6 August 1941 to the commander of the forces of 24th Army on the destruction of the enemy's El'nia grouping], *SBDVOV*, issue 37, 171-172.

5. Combat Order No 0021/op of the Commander of the Forces of the Reserve Front of 6 August 1941 to the Commanders of the Forces of 24th and 43rd Armies on the Destruction of the Enemy's El'nia and Roslavl' Groupings

Combat Order No. 0021/op, Headquarters, Reserve Front,
Gzhatsk, 2130 hours on 6 August 1941
1:500,000 scale map

1. The Reserve Front is defending the Ostashkov, Selizharovo, El'tsy, Olenino, Shentrapalovka, Aksiunina, Mal'tsevo, Nishnevo, Mitino Station, Blagoveshchenskoe, Dorogobuzh, Usviat'e, Rozhdestvo Station, Peredel'niki, Mikhailovka, Zhukovka, and Sosnovka front; and, simultaneously, 24th and 43rd Armies will conduct an operation for the destruction of the enemy's El'nia and Roslavl' groupings.

2. 31st Army, consisting of 249th, 247th, 119th, 246th, and 244th RD, 43rd CAR, 10 naval artillery guns, and 533rd and 766th ATRs, will defend its previous positions in accordance with the Reserve Front Order No. 2/op.

Conduct reconnaissance along the Lake Luchane, Moshnitsa River, Andreapol', and Belyi line.

Boundary on the right – as before.

Keep reserve divisions in their present positions.

Boundary on the left – Moscow Sea, Kniazh'i Gory, Pomelnitsa Station, Shiparevo, and Shchuch'e.

Headquarters of the army – Rzhev.

3. 35th Army, consisting of 248th, 194th, and 220th RDs, 3rd Bn, 392nd CAR, and 765th ATR, will defend the (incl.) Aksiunina, Ivashkov, and Bonakova line and further along the eastern bank of the Dnepr River to Sumarokovo.

Hold in reserve: 298th RD – [in] Sychevka; 4th DNO – Novo-Duginskaia; and 269th RD – Tumanovo.

Conduct reconnaissance along the Vop' River line.

Boundary on the left – Kasnia Station and Badino Station.

Deploy the army's headquarters from 35th RC's headquarters and position it in Novo-Duginskaia.

4. 24th Army, consisting of 133rd, 178th, 107th, 19th, 120th, and 100th RDs, units of 102nd and 105th TDs, 106th MD, 6th DNO, 423rd LAR, 685th and 275th CARs, 305th and 573rd GARs, 20 naval artillery guns, 76th Sep. MRL ["*Katiusha*"] Btry, 533rd,872nd, 877th, 879th, and 880th ATRs, and 43rd AABtry on railroad cars, will defend the Serkova, Blagoveshchenskoe, Dorogobuzh, Usviat'e, and Kalita line, while conducting an operation in the Mitino, Popovka, and El'nia region to destroy the enemy's El'nia grouping.

Keep 280th RD in the army's reserve in the Sloboda region (15 kilometers southwest of Viaz'ma), 278th RD in the Put'kova region, and 309th RD in the Voronovo region.

Conduct reconnaissance along the Iartsevo and Gorodok line.

Boundary on the left – Ugriumovo Station, Luzhki, Popovka, and Pochinok.

Headquarters of the army – Semlevo.

5. 43rd Army, consisting of 53rd, 217th, 222nd, 145th, and 149th RDs, 104th and 109th TDs, 364th, 646th, and 207th CARs, 320th GAR, and 760th ATR, will defend the (incl.) Popovka, Kholmets, Snopot, and (incl.) Zhukovka line; and, simultaneously, organize an operation to destroy the enemy's Roslavl' grouping.

Keep in army reserve: 303rd RD in the Mamonovo region; 211th RD in the Baretka region, and 279th RD in the Liudinovo region.

Boundary on the left – Borovka, Zhukovka, and Shumiachi.

Headquarters of the army – Kirov

6. 2nd Separate Rifle Corps, consisting of 258th, 260th, and 290th RDs, 151st CAR, and 753rd and 761st ATRs, will defend the Zhukovka, Vysokoe, and Makarovo line, with the chief mission of protecting the Briansk axis.

Keep one rifle division in reserve in the Sel'tso region. Prepare a cut-off position along the Makarovo, Krupets, and Sosnovka line. Conduct reconnaissance along the Sukromlia, Mglin, and Pochep line.

Headquarters of the corps – Briansk

7. *Front* reserve:

a) 32nd Army, consisting of 2nd, 7th, 8th, 13th, and 18th DNOs and 873rd and 875th ATRs, while continuing to prepare the Selo Station, Sapegino, Semlevo, and Bol'shoe Starosel'e defensive line, will organize and systematically conduct combat training its units in accordance with the Reserve Front's Order No. 016.

Headquarters of the army – Viaz'ma

b) 33rd Army, consisting of 9th, 5th, 1st, 17th, and 21st DNOs and 878th and 876th ATRs, while continuing to prepare the Selishche, Ratki, and Podlesnaia defensive line, will organize and systematically conduct combat training of its units in accordance with the Reserve Front's Order No. 016.

Headquarters of the army – Spas-Demensk.

c) 45th Cavalry Division will concentrate in the Gzhatsk region.

8. Aviation:

a) While cooperating with 24th and 43rd Armies on the battlefield, support the ground forces as they fulfill their missions to destroy the enemy's El'nia and Roslavl' groupings.

b) Protect the regrouping of 24th and 43rd Armies' forces.

The Commander of the Reserve Front, Army General Zhukov
The Member of the Military Council, Kruglov
The Chief of Staff, Major General Liapin

Source: "Boevoi prikaz komanduiushchego voiskami Rezervnogo fronta no. 0021/op ot 6 avgusta 1941 g. komanduiushchim voiskami 24-i i 43-i Armii na unichtozhenie El'ninskoi i Roslavl'skoi gruppirovok protivnika" [Combat order no 0021/op of the commander of the forces of the Reserve Front of 6 August 1941 to the commanders of the forces of 24th and 43rd Armies on the destruction of the enemy's El'nia and Roslavl' groupings], *SBDVOV*, issue 37, 173-174.

6. Combat Report No. 17 of the Headquarters of the Reserve Front of 7 August 1941 about the Combat Operations of the Reserve Front's Forces

To the Chief of the General Staff
Copy: To the Chief of Staff of the Western Front
Combat Report No. 17,
Headquarters, Reserve Front,
Gzhatsk, 2130 hours on 7 August 1941
1:100,000 scale map

1) Along the El'nia axis, 24th Army's operational group did not conduct active operations. Artillery and machine guns exchanged fire along the front. Enemy aircraft conducted raids against 106th MD's artillery OPs on 7 August. The positions of the El'nia operational group's units are unchanged.

2) Along the Roslavl' axis, 222nd RD conducted sustained fighting with the enemy along the Antonovka, Blagoveshchenka, and Monakhi line. Under an onslaught by an enemy force of no less than one infantry regiment, with tanks and aircraft, the division withdrew slowly to the east.

At 1630 hours an enciphered message was sent to the army's headquarters on order of the *front* commander about withdrawing the division to the forward edge of the [army's] main defensive belt.

Information about the fulfillment of that order has not been received as of 2000 hours,

3) 53rd Rifle Division is occupying its previous positions. During the day, an enemy division opposite the division's front gradually concentrated its forces in populated points along the Desna River's western bank.

An especially strong enemy grouping (no less than an infantry division) has concentrated opposite the division's right wing west of Shat'kova [20 kilometers south of El'nia].

4) Along the remainder of the *front*, the Reserve Front's armies are continuing to fulfill the *front* commander's Order No. 0021/op of 6 August 1941.

The Chief of Staff of the *front*, Major General Liapin
The Commissar of the army's headquarters,
   Brigade Commissar Priakhin

Source: "Boevoe donesenie shtaba Rezervnogo fronta no. 17 ot 7 avgusta 1941 g. General'nomu Shtabu o boevykh deistviiakh voisk Rezervnogo fronta" [Combat report no. 17 of the headquarters of the Reserve Front of 7 August 1941 about the combat operations of the Reserve Front's forces], *SBDVOV*, issue 37, 175.

7. *Stavka* VGK Directive No. 00815 to the Commander of the Forces of the Western Front about a Threat to Disrupt the Operation to Destroy the Enemy's El'nia Grouping

1550 hours on 9 August 1941

In accordance with *Stavka* directive No. 00731 dated 6 August 1941, the Western Front was obliged to move its flank units to the left and occupy the Pridneprovskaia Station and Dobromino Station front.

However, this has not been fulfilled as of today.

Rakutin's 102nd TD is fighting at Leikino, Goravitsy, and Sel'tso, which are occupied by the enemy.

The failure to fulfill this directive not only creates a threat to the right flank of Rakutin's group but also threatens to disrupt the operation to destroy the enemy's El'nia grouping.

For a report to the *Stavka*, I request you report immediately why the directive has not been fulfilled and what measures you are undertaking to protect Rakutin's right flank reliably.

   B. Shaposhnikov

Source: "Direktiva Stavki VGK no. 00815 komanduiushchim voiskami Zapadnogo fronta ob ugroze sryva operatsii po unichtozheniiu El'ninskoi gruppirovki protivnika" [*Stavka* VGK directive no. 00815 to the commander of the forces of the Western Front about a threat to disrupt the operation to destroy the enemy's El'nia grouping], in Zolotarev, "*Stavka* 1941," 109.

8. *Stavka* VGK Directive No. 00825 to the Commander of the Forces of the Reserve Front about the Re-subordination of a Cavalry Division

9 August 1941

From among the two cavalry divisions at your disposal, the Supreme High Command finds it necessary to transfer one of these to the Mglin and Unecha region to protect the junction between the Central Front and the 2nd Rifle Corps.

   B. Shaposhnikov

Source: "Direktiva Stavki VGK no. 00825 komanduiushchim voiskami Rezervnogo fronta o perepodchinenii kavaleriiskoi divizii" [*Stavka* VGK directive no. 00825 to the commander of the forces of the Reserve Front about the re-subordination of a cavalry division], Zolotarev, "*Stavka* VGK 1941," 110.

9. *Stavka* VGK Directive No. 00857 to the Commander of the Forces of the Reserve Front about Erecting a Defense Line along the Snopot River

2100 hours on 11 August 1941

A report has been received from Comrade Voronov [the chief of Red Army artillery and representative of the *Stavka*], in the *Stavka's* name, which points out that the dispositions on the left flank of 33rd Army's defensive line barely encompasses the Roslavl'-Moscow highway and, therefore, does not protect that axis sufficiently reliably.

The forward edge of 33rd Army's defense has many open approaches from the enemy's side and is difficult to defend. Comrade Voronov proposes you construct a defensive line along the Snopot River and deploy 43rd and 33rd Armies' forces along it.

I request you report your opinion of the above for a report to the *Stavka*.

B. Shaposhnikov

Source: "Direktiva Stavki VGK no. 00857 komanduiushchim voiskami Rezervnogo fronta o postroenii rubezha oborony po r. Snopot" [*Stavka* VGK directive no. 00857 to the commander of the forces of the Reserve Front about erecting a defense line along the Snopot River], in Zolotarev, "*Stavka* 1941," 112-113.

10. *Stavka* VGK Directive No. 00850 to the Commander of the Forces of the Reserve Front about the Renaming of 35th Army

2100 hours on 11 August 1941

Copies to: The commander-in-chief of the forces of the Western Front

In a change to *Stavka* directive No. 00732, dated 6 August 1941, 35th Army is renamed 49th Army, effective 0000 hours on 12 August.

Source: "Direktiva Stavki VGK no. 00850 komanduiushchim voiskami Rezervnogo fronta o pereimenovanii 35-i armii" [*Stavka* VGK directive no. 00850 to the commander of the forces of the Reserve Front about the renaming of 35th Army], in Zolotarev, "*Stavka* 1941," 113.

Appendix N

Armeegruppe Guderian's and Second Army's Southward March and the Fall of Gomel', 8-21 August 1941

1. *Stavka* VGK Directive No. 00880 to the Commander of the Forces of the Western Front Concerning the Inadmissibility of 3rd Army's Unjustified Withdrawal

Copy to: The Commander-in-Chief of the Forces of the Southwestern Direction
0515 hours on 12 August 1941

Despite the absence of overwhelming enemy superiority, Kuznetsov is continuing to withdraw without resisting properly, by doing so creating a serious situation for Potapov [5th Army, on 3rd Army's left flank]. The *front's* Military Council must compel Kuznetsov to fight as he should and not abandon his positions to the enemy without a fight. This situation cannot continue any longer.

B. Shaposhnikov

Source: "Direktiva Stavki VGK No. 00880 komanduiushchemu voiskami Zapadnogo Fronta o nedopushchenii neopravdannogo otkhoda 3-i Armii" [*Stavka* directive no. 00880 to the commander of the forces of the Western Front concerning the inadmissibility of 3rd Army's unjustified withdrawal], Zolotarev, "*Stavka* VGK 1941," 113.

2. *Stavka* VGK Directive No. 00926 to the Commanders of the Forces of the Central and Reserve Fronts about the Organization of the Briansk Front

2245 hours on 14 August 1941

1. For the sake of improving command and control, organize the Briansk Front directly subordinate to the Supreme High Command.

Appoint Lieutenant General Eremenko as commander of the Briansk Front, Major General Ermakov as the deputy *front* commander, and Major General Zakharov as the *front's* chief of staff.

Use the headquarters of 20th Rifle and 25th Mechanized Corps to form the *front's* headquarters.

Place the *front's* headquarters in the Briansk region.

The boundary lines of the Briansk Front are:

– With the Reserve Front – Mtsensk, (incl.) Zhizdra, Pochinok, and (incl.) Smolensk; and

– With the Central Front – Novgorod-Severskii, (incl.) Gaishin, and Mogilev.

2. The composition of the Briansk Front is:

a) 50th Army, consisting of 217th, 279th, 258th, 260th, 290th, 278th, 269th, and 280th Rifle Divisions, 55th Cavalry Division, 2nd and 20th Rifle Corps' corps artillery regiments, and 761st and 753rd Antitank Artillery Regiments.

Form the army's headquarters on the base of 2nd RC's headquarters.

Appoint Major General Petrov as the army's commander.

Headquarters of the army – in the Vygonichi region.

Boundary line on the left – Trubchevsk, Severnaia Rassukha, Klimovichi, and (incl.) and Moliatichi.

b) 13th Army, consisting of 137th, 121st, 148th, 132nd, 6th, 155th, 307th, and 285th RDs, 50th TD, 52nd and 21st CD, and the airborne corps.

c) Hold 229th, 287th, and 283rd RDs and 4th CD in the *front's* reserve.

3. Confirm fulfillment.

The Supreme High Commander, I. Stalin
The Chief of the General Staff, B. Shaposhnikov

Source: "Direktiva Stavki VGK No. 00926 komanduiushchim voiskami Tsentral'nogo i Rezervnogo frontov ob organizatsii Brianskogo fronta" [*Stavka* VGK directive no. 00926 to the commanders of the forces of the Central and Reserve Fronts about the organization of the Briansk Front], in Zolotarev, "*Stavka* 1941," 116.

3. Report by the Commander of the Forces of the Reserve Front No. 2402 to the Supreme High Commander about the Situation and Measures for Opposing the Enemy Entering into the Southwestern Front's Rear

19 August 1941

1. The enemy, having confirmed that we have concentrated large forces along the routes to Moscow, and with the Central Front and the Velikie Luki grouping of our forces on his flanks, has temporarily abandoned an advance on Moscow and, while transitioning to an active defense against the Western and Reserve Fronts, has thrown all of his mobile and panzer shock units against the Central, Southwestern, and Southern Fronts.

The enemy's possible concept is to crush the Central Front and, by reaching the Chernigov, Konotop, and Priluki regions, to smash the Southwestern Front's armies by a blow into their rear, after which to conduct his main attack on Moscow by enveloping the Briansk forest, and [launch] a strike into the Donbas.

I believe that the enemy well knows our defensive system and the entire operational-strategic grouping of our forces well and understands our future capabilities.

Apparently, we have among our very senior workers [leaders] those who are closely associated with the overall situation, and the enemy has his own people. Apparently, Kachalov and Ponedelin are playing a criminal role in this matter.

According to accounts of participants in Group Kachalov's fighting, as soon as small groups of enemy tanks appeared, he [Kachalov] sat in aT-34 tank and departed in an unknown direction. All say that Kachalov purposely went over to the German side. In the T-34 tank in which Kachalov left, he forbade even his personal adjutant to sit.

2. To oppose the enemy and prevent the destruction of the Central Front and the enemy from reaching the Southwestern Front's rear, I believe it is my duty to report my thoughts about the necessity for assembling a large grouping in the Glukhov, Chernigov, and Konotop region as soon as possible. Deploy a covering echelon concentration along the Desna River right now.

It is necessary to include in this grouping:

1. Up to 1,000 tanks, which can be assembled at the expense of the mechanized corps from the Trans-Baikal Military District, tanks of the RGK [Reserve of the High Command], and an additional 300 tanks taken from the Far Eastern Front.

2. Up to 10 rifle divisions.

3. 3-4 cavalry divisions.

4. 400-500 aircraft, assembled at the expense of the Trans-Baikal military District, the Air Forces of the Navy, and the Air Forces of the Moscow PVO [Air Defense] Zone.

If we ourselves establish more active means for opposing this very dangerous enemy action, we need to assemble the entire proposed grouping in the Briansk region immediately, from which we can strike the enemy in the flank. Now, without waiting for the final concentration of the Briansk grouping, it would be expedient to reinforce the Western Front's right wing with another 4-5 rifle divisions and 8-10 heavy RGK regiments and immediately conduct an attack, with the objective of reaching the Polotsk, Vitebsk, and Smolensk front.

A blow by the Western Front's right wing, with the objective of reaching the Polotsk, Vitebsk, and Smolensk front, will be very beneficial to our forces' operations along the Desna River.

Zhukov

Source: "Doklad komanduiushchego voiskami Rezervnogo fronta No. 2402 Verkhovnomu Glavnokomanduiushchemu ob obstanovke i merakh po protivodeistviiu protivniku v vykhode na tyly Iugo-zapadnogo fronta" [Report of the commander of the forces of the Reserve Front no.2402 to the Supreme High Commander about the situation and measures for opposing the enemy entering into the Southwestern Front's rear], in Zolotarev, "*Stavka* 1941," 361.

4. *Stavka* VGK Directive No. 001082 to the Commander of the Forces of the Reserve Front about Forestalling an Enemy Envelopment of the Kiev Grouping of Forces and the Encirclement of 3rd and 21st Armies

1730 hours on 19 August 1941

I consider your report concerning the likely movement of the Germans toward Chernigov, Konotop, and Priluki to be correct. The German advance in that direction will mean the envelopment of our Kiev grouping from the eastern bank of the Dnepr

River and the encirclement of our 3rd and 21st Armies. As is well known, one column of enemy has already crossed the Unecha River and reached Starodub. In anticipation of such an undesirable case and to forestall them [the enemy], the Briansk Front has been created with Eremenko at its head. Other measures are being taken, about which I will report to you in person. We are hoping to stop the Germans.

Stalin
Shaposhnikov

Source: "Direktiva Stavki VGK No. 001082 komanduiushchemu voiskami Rezervnogo frontov ob predotvrashchenii obkhoda protivnikom Kievskoi gruppirovki voisk i okruzhenie 3-i i 21-i Armii" [*Stavka* VGK directive no. 001082 to the commander of the forces of the Reserve Front about forestalling an enemy envelopment of the Kiev grouping of forces and the encirclement of 3rd and 21st Armies], in Zolotarev, "*Stavka* 1941," 119-120.

5. *Stavka* VGK Directive No. 001092 to the Commanders of the Forces of the Central and Southwestern Fronts about a Withdrawal of the Forces of 3rd Army behind the Dnepr River
2010 hours on 19 August 1941

In connection with the situation that has taken shape, the Supreme High Commander orders: while holding on to the Klintsy, Gomel', and Gorval' front, begin the successive withdrawal of 3rd Army's forces to the Gorval' and Loev sector behind the Dnepr River.

Carry out the withdrawal from line to line, in organized fashion. Without fail, before the withdrawal, all of the weapons of the Mozyr' Fortified Region must be evacuated, and, as the withdrawal begins, the installations of the Mozyr' Fortified Region [must be] destroyed.

For the *Stavka* of the Supreme High Command
Chief of the General Staff, B. Shaposhnikov

Source: "Direktiva Stavki VGK No. 001092 komanduiushchim voiskami Tsentral'nogo i Iugo-Zapadnogo frontov, Glavnokomanduiushchemu voiskami Iugo-Zapadnogo Napravleniia ob otvode voisk 3-i Armii za Dnepr" [*Stavka* VGK directive no. 001092 to the commanders of the forces of the Central and Southwestern Fronts about a withdrawal of 3rd Army's forces behind the Dnepr River], in Zolotarev, "*Stavka* 1941," 121.

6. *Stavka* VGK Directive No. 001139 to the Commander of the Forces of the Briansk Front about Protecting the Boundary with the Central Front
2200 hours on 20 August 1941

1. According to a report by Colonel Argunov, 13th Army is withdrawing to occupy a defensive line along the Sudost' River.

In connection with the threat created from the direction of Starodub, I draw your special attention to protecting the boundary with the Central Front.

The right wing of the Central Front's 21st Army is withdrawing to the Luzhki, Lobanovka, and Zamyshevo line. In connection with this, 13th Army will withdraw to the Solovo, Borshchevo, and Pogar line and further along the Sudost' River. Keep the *front's* reserve behind the boundary.

2. Report fulfillment.

B. Shaposhnikov

Source: "Direktiva Stavki VGK No. 001139 komanduiushchemu voiskami Brianskogo fronta ob obespechenie styka s Tsentral'nym frontom" [*Stavka* VGK directive no. 001139 to the commander of the forces of the Briansk Front about protecting the boundary with the Central Front], in Zolotarev, "*Stavka* 1941," 122.

7. *Stavka* VGK Directive No. 001140 to the Commander of the Forces of the Central Front about Protecting the Boundary with the Briansk Front
2200 hours 20 August 1941

1. In connection with the situation at Starodub and the gap that has formed with the Briansk Front's left wing, 21st Army will withdraw to the Luzhki, Lobanovka, Zamyshevo, and Novoe Mesto front and further along the Iput' River and Sozh River to Babovichi.

The Briansk Front's 13th Army will withdraw to the Solovo, Borshchevo, and Pogar front and further along the Sudost' River.

2. Pay attention to protecting the boundary between 21st and 3rd Armies, for which you will have 3rd Army's right flank on the western bank of the Uza River from (incl.) Babovichi to Teleshi and further to Chernoe. In addition, keep your reserve behind this boundary.

3. Report fulfillment.

B. Shaposhnikov

Source: "Direktiva Stavki VGK No. 001140 komanduiushchemu voiskami Tsentral'nogo fronta ob obespechenie styka s Brianskim frontom" [*Stavka* VGK directive no. 001140 to the commander of the forces of the Central Front about protecting the boundary with the Briansk Front], in Zolotarev, "*Stavka* 1941," 122-123.

Appendix O

The Second Soviet Counteroffensive: The Western Front's Dukhovshchina Offensive, 6-24 August 1941

German 10. Supplement to Führer Directive No. 34, 12 August 1941

The Supreme High Command of
the Armed Forces (OKW).
Führer headquarters
Headquarters of the Operations Directorate.
12 August 1941
Department for the Defense of the Country (1st Dept.).
No. 441376/41. Top Secret

Supplement to Directive No. 34

The Führer has ordered the following on the further conduct of operations as an addition to Directive No. 34:

1. **The Southern sector of the Eastern Front**. As a result of the decisive battle in the Uman' region, Army Group South has achieved complete superiority over the enemy and has secured freedom of maneuver for the conduct of further operations on that side of the Dnepr. As soon as its forces firmly dig in on the eastern bank of that river and ensure rear area communications, they will be able to achieve the large-scale operational aims assigned to them with their own forces, with appropriate use of Allied forces and in cooperation with Rumanian ground forces.

Its missions are as follows:

a) Prevent the planned creation of a defensive front along the Dnepr by the enemy. To do so, it is necessary to destroy the largest enemy units located west of the Dnepr and capture bridgeheads on the eastern bank of that river as rapidly as possible;

b) Capture the Crimea, which, being an enemy air base, poses an especially great threat to the Rumanian oil fields; and

c) Seize the Donets Basin and the Khar'kov industrial region.

The fighting to capture the Crimea may require mountain infantry forces. It is necessary to verify the possibility of their crossing the Kerch Straits for employment in a subsequent offensive toward Batumi.

Halt the offensive on Kiev. As soon as ammunition resupply permits, bombing from the air must destroy the city.

The entire range of missions depends on these actions being carried out sequentially rather than simultaneously by means of maximum massing of forces.

In the first instance, achieve the greatest concentration of forces by committing additional groups of bomber aircraft to support combat operations in the region between Kanev and Boguslav and then to assist the creation of a bridgehead on the eastern bank of the Dnepr River.

3. **The Central sector of the Eastern Front**. The priority mission in this sector is to eliminate the enemy flank positions wedging to the west, which are tying down large forces of Army Group Center's infantry. In the southern portion of the central sector of the front, pay particular attention to the organization of the mixed flanks of Army Groups' Center and South according to time and axis.

Deprive the Russian 5th Army of any operational capabilities by seizing the communications leading to Ovrich and Mozyr' and, finally, destroy its forces.

In the northern part of the central sector of the front, defeat the enemy west of Toropets as rapidly as possible by committing mobile forces into combat. Advance Army Group Center's left flank far enough to the north that Army Group North will not fear for its right flank and will be capable of reinforcing its forces advancing on Leningrad with infantry divisions.

Regardless, undertake measures to transfer this or that division (for example, the 102nd Infantry Division) to Army Group north as a reserve.

Only after the threatening situation on the flanks has been completely eliminated and the panzer groups have been refitted will conditions be conducive for an offensive by deeply echeloned flank groupings across a broad front against the large enemy forces concentrated for the defense of Moscow.

The aim of this offensive is to capture the enemy's entire complex of state economic and communications centers in the Moscow region before the onset of winter, by doing so depriving him of the capability for restoring his destroyed armed forces and smashing the functioning of state control apparatus.

Complete the operation against Leningrad before the offensive along the Moscow axis begins and return the aircraft units transferred earlier by the Second Air Fleet to the First Air Fleet to their former subordination.

4. **The Northern sector of the Front**. The offensive being conducted here must lead to the encirclement of Leningrad and a link up with Finnish forces.

Insofar as the situation with airfields permits, in the interest of the effective employment of aviation, it is important that it be employed as far as possible massed along distinct axes.

As soon as the situation permits, you should liquidate enemy naval and air bases on Dago [Hiiumaa] and Ezel [Saaremaa] Islands by the joint efforts of ground, naval, and air forces. While doing so it is particularly important to destroy enemy airfields from which air raids on Berlin are carried out.

The High Command of the Ground Forces (OKH) is entrusted with coordinating the conducted measures.

> The Chief of Staff of the Supreme High Command
> of the Armed Forces [OKW],
> [signed] Keitel

Source: *Sbornik voenno-istoricheskikh materialov Velikoi Otechestvennoi voiny, vypusk 18* [Collection of military-historical materials of the Great Patriotic War, issue 18] (Moscow: Voenizdat, 1960), 238-240. Prepared by the Military-Historical Department of the Military-Scientific Directorate of the Red Army General Staff and classified secret.

1. Report by the Headquarters of the Western Front of 12 August 1941 to the General Staff about Intended Offensive Operations along the Dukhovshchina-Smolensk and El'nia-Roslavl' Axes

1800 hours on 12 August 1941
Moscow
To Comrade Stavrovsky

At the present time, we have the following situation in the *front*.

The enemy opposite our Western Front has gone over to the defense, while opposing our offensives in Khomenko's [30th Army], Konev's [19th Army], and Lukin's [20th Army] sectors with his small reserves.

Konev's offensive, in cooperation with Khomenko's and Rokossovsky's [16th Army], which continued on the morning of 11 August, with the missions – to penetrate the enemy's front and link up with 1,500-man group of General Boldin, was crowned with success by the evening of 11 August. Group Boldin escaped with 1,500 armed men and with a large number of carts and three guns. According to Konev's report, up to 2,000 men of the enemy's 5th ID were destroyed in this offensive. Kurochkin began this division's rout, and Konev finished off its remnants yesterday.

On 11 August, the enemy opposed Lukin's offensive three times with counterattacks, supported by strong artillery and small groups of aircraft. Lukin's divisions, while inflicting heavy losses on the enemy, are advancing slowly to the line designated by the *Stavka* and protecting the flank of the Reserve Front's El'nia grouping.

Recent operations demonstrate that the enemy is severely exhausted, and, in some sectors of the defense, the enemy lacks any reserves. The great losses in men and weapons, which our units are suffering, have extremely weakened our units. This circumstance does not permit our forces at hand to overcome the resistance and conduct operations with decisive aims.

This situation may lead to the fact that, the enemy, while continuing to protect himself with comparatively small forces opposite our Western Front, will assemble additional forces along the Roslavl' axis, and, after completing the Roslavl' operation (if the enemy is successful), he, having untied his hands on the Western Front's southern wing, will have an opportunity to assemble forces for simultaneous attacks against the Western and Reserve Fronts.

As a result, it seems to us that the following aims are expedient:

a) Distracting enemy forces from the Roslavl' axis;

b) Defeating and destroying enemy forces on the Smolensk axis – we are presenting to you the following two variants of actions of the Western Front for examination:

First variant. Having reinforced the Western Front with three rifle and two tank divisions and one cavalry divisions and while employing them in Konev's and

Khomenko's sectors, to attack with the [following] missions – Konev and Khomenko, in cooperation with Maslennikov [29th Army], toward Dukhovshchina and Smolensk, and Lukin and Rokossovsky, in cooperation with the Reserve Front's El'nia Group [24th Army], toward Smolensk and Pochinok.

In the event Rokossovsky's and Lukin's operations develop successfully, the Reserve Front's El'nia Group, after destroying the enemy at El'nia, must develop the attack toward Roslavl' to strike the rear of the main enemy grouping [Guderian's Second Panzer Group], which has been operating southward and southeastward from Roslavl'

All the while, the Central Front should conduct an offensive on its right wing with the mission – to tie down the enemy's forces moving southward and southeastward from Roslavl' [Guderian's Second Panzer Group].

The indicated variant of a reinforced Western Front, in favorable circumstances, could take the form of an operation with limited objectives, that is, to exhaust the enemy's Smolensk grouping and distract the enemy's forces for a prolonged period from the Central Front and the Roslavl' axis.

Second variant. For a decisive operation aimed at the final destruction of the enemy opposite the Western Front and his grouping operating along the Roslavl' axis, it is necessary to reinforce the Western Front with at least eight rifle, three tank, and two cavalry divisions, with the mission to reach west of Smolensk and, in cooperation with the Central Front and the Reserve Front's El'nia Group, to defeat the main enemy forces operating along the Smolensk and Roslavl' axes.

In this and the other variant, further preparations and filling out by the main forces of the Reserve Front's armies seems possible.

If they prove successful, these operations will certainly compel the enemy to conduct passive operations along the Velikie Luki and Gomel' front for a prolonged period.

Zapadovsky, Iartsev

Source: "Doklad shtaba Zapadnogo fronta ot 12 avgusta 1941 g. General'nomu Shtabu o namechaemykh nastupatel'nykh operatsiiakh na Dukhovshchinsko-Smolenskom i El'ninsko-Roslavl'skom napravleniiakh" [Report by the headquarters of the Western Front of 12 August 1941 to the General Staff about intended offensive operations along the Dukhovshchina-Smolensk and El'nia-Roslavl' axes], *SBDVOV*, issue 41 (Moscow: Voenizdat, 1960), 11-12.

2. Combat Order No. 01 of the Commander of the Forces of 16th Army of 15 August 1941 about Preparations for an Offensive

Combat Order No. 01, Headquarters, 16th Army,
the forest 1 kilometer southeast of Khotenovo,
1100 hours on 15 August 1941
1:50,000 and 100,000 scale maps

1. The enemy is defending along the western bank of the Vop' River with a force of four infantry divisions. The forward edge of the defense is in the form of separate centers of resistance, with full-profile foxholes, manned by reinforced rifle companies

along the Chistaia, Novosel'e, Khatyni, Pologi, Alferova, Bol'shie and Malye Gorki, and Zadnia line. Enemy reserves are in [the following] regions:

    a) Kokhanovo, Makeevo, and Krovopuskovo;

    b) Samuilovo, Semukhino, and Soprykino; and

    c) Luk'ianovo, Chadovishchi, and Mamonovo.

    2. On the right – 89th RD (19th Army) on the Dubrovka, Kuz'mino, and Kharina line.

    The boundary with it: Ianovo, (incl.) Rybki, Prisel'e, and (incl.) Rafenina.

    On the left – 144th RD (20th Army) on the Korovniki and Osova line.

    The boundary with it: (incl.) Dorogobuzh, Zadnia, and Kasplia.

    3. 16th Army will conduct a regrouping on the night of 15-16 August 1941 to concentrate forces for an offensive on its right wing.

    4. 64th RD, after transferring its defensive sector to 108th RD, will concentrate in the Podylishche, Chizhiki, and Liada region on the night of 15-16 August 1941.

    March-route of the division – Petrova, Bolychevo, Sivtsova, Bessuetnaia, Krapivka 2, and Liada. Conduct a reconnaissance of the march-route before nightfall.

    From the concentration region, having protected the crossing over the Vop' River in the Prisel'e region by occupying it with a force of a reinforced rifle battalion, be prepared to attack toward Miagchenki and Skachkovo with all of your forces.

    Boundary on the left: Gridina, Chizhiki, (incl.) Novosel'e (eastern), and Samulova.

    5. 101st TD (with 18th MRR) will be prepared to attack from the positions you occupy toward Novosel'e (eastern) and Kholm with all of your forces.

    Boundary on the left: Svishchevo, (incl.) Hill 207.2, and Semukhina.

    6. 44th RC (38th and 108th RDs) will occupy and firmly defend a belt in the Hill 207.2, Iartsevo, Skrushevskie, and Buianovo sector. 38th RD will remain in the sector it occupies, but 64th RD's sector will be occupied by 108th RD's forces.

    7. Supply station – Dorogobuzh Station.

    8. All units will be prepared for the regrouping by 2000 hours on 15 August 1941. Carry out the regrouping according to additional instructions.

    9. Headquarters of the army – the woods 1 kilometer southeast of Khotenova.

    The Commander of 16th Army, Major General Rokossovsky
    The Member of the Military Council of the army,
        Division Commissar Lobachev
    The Chief of Staff of the army, Colonel Malinin

Source: "Boevoi prikaz komanduiushchego voiskami 16-i Armii No. 01 ot 15 avgusta 1941 g. o podgotovke voisk armii k nastupleniiu" [Combat order no. 01 of the commander of the forces of 16th Army of 15 August 1941 about preparations for an offensive], *SBDVOV*, issue 41, 137-138.

3. Order No. 0109 of the Commander of the Forces of the Western Front of 15 August 1941 about the Characteristics of Enemy Tactics and the Employment of the *Front's* Forces in Night Operations

Order No. 0109 of the forces of the Western Front

15 August 1941

The experiences of the 52-day struggle with the German Fascists, who have encroached on our holy land, vividly reveal the characteristics of German Army tactics.

The basis of these, which have genuine importance for the Western Front's forces at the present time, are:

1. **The strongest side** of the enemy still remains mortars and antitank guns, the actions of motorcyclists, and the deep penetration of small groups of tanks in cooperation with aviation, which create the outward appearance of encirclements, [and] the well-organized system of fires (the interaction of fire and maneuver).

2. **The weakest side**: During attacks by our infantry and cavalry, German infantry display cowardice; they do not employ bayonet attacks but [instead] they withdraw, they lie low, and they repel by fire. Combat actions against enemy tank and motorized units has established the inability of the Germans to repel surprise night attacks against tanks, armored vehicles, and motor transport that have halted for the night in villages and along the roads. As a rule, the Germans, while situated in night laager [camps] in populated points, post weak security at short distances, which can be destroyed relatively easily by energetic operations by the attackers. The panzer and motorized divisions are severely exhausted and suffer great losses. During surprise night assaults, the Germans abandon their tanks, guns, vehicles, and machine guns.

3. The enemy opposite the Western Direction's forces generally defend along a broad front by means of creating company centers of resistance with large intervals between them. In individual [separate] sectors, independent mortar batteries are being established without infantry protection.

4. The enemy is operating in considerable isolation from his bases. His communications are subjected to the actions of our partisans in regions of the rear largely unfamiliar to him.

Taken together, all of this creates favorable conditions for night raids and operations by separate small detachments under the cover of night.

I order:

Immediately employ extensive night operations by night shock detachments in accordance with the brief instructions attached [see "Short Instructions on the Organization of Night Shock Detachments, dated 15 August 1941].

The overall aim of these actions: exhaustion of the enemy and destruction of his forces and weapons, which, in the final analysis, must create intolerable conditions for the enemy and prepare the ground for our decisive offensive operations.

> The Commander of the Western Front's forces,
> Marshal of the Soviet Union S. Timoshenko
> The Member of the Military Council of the Western Front, [signed]
> The Chief of Staff of the Western Front, Lieutenant General Sokolovsky

Source: "Prikaz komanduiushchego voiskami Zapadnogo fronta no. 0109 ot 15 avgusta 1941 g. ob osobennostiakh taktiki protivnika i razvertyvanii voiskami fronta nochnykh deistvii" [Order no. 0109 of the commander of the forces of the Western Front of 15 August 1941 about the characteristics of enemy tactics and the employment of the *front's* forces in night operations], *SBDVOV*, issue 41, 13-14.

4. Report by the Commander of the Forces of the Western Front of 15 August 1941 to the Supreme High Commander about an Offensive Operation along the Dukhovshchina Axis

Special importance

Moscow

To the Supreme High Commander, Comrade Stalin

100,000 scale map

In order to prevent the enemy from restoring order in his units, and also with the aim of destroying the enemy grouping in the Dukhovshchina region, I intend to conduct the following operation:

First. To encircle and destroy the enemy's 106th ID, 5th ID, 28th ID, and 900th MotR [brigade] with concentric attacks by two groups from [the following] fronts: 1) Staroe Morokhovo and Markovo; and 2) Potelitsa and Prisel'e.

Second. To create [the following] groupings:

Northern – consisting of 242nd, 251st, and 166th RDs, 107th TD, and 45th CD, under the overall command of Khomenko;

Southern – consisting of 89th, 50th, and 64th RDs, and 101st TD, under the command of Konev; and

Covering Group – consisting of 91st and 162nd RDs along the Markovo and Potelitsa front.

Third. To begin the offensive on 17 August having used 15 and 16 August to regroup the forces and organize the offensive.

Fourth. For the fulfillment of this plan, withdraw 101st and 64th RDs from 16th Army's front at the expense of widening 38th and 108th RDs' defensive front. 45th CD will moved forward from the Gzhatsk region along the Andreevskaia and Kaniutino march-route and concentrate in the forest in the Kaniutino region by day's end on 17 August, while operating in second echelon during the first stage of the operation.

Fifth. For the development [exploitation] of success, after moving a covering force of two rifle divisions toward Vorontsovo, Starina, and Teterino, send the cavalry division and 107th TD from behind the Northern Group's right flank into the enemy's rear to envelop Dukhovshchina from the west.

Sixth. For the purpose of concealing the intended operation, 30th Army's and 19th Army's units will continue to conduct local attacks on 15 and 16 August, with the missions of destroying individual enemy centers of resistance and occupying the most favorable jumping-off positions for the offensive.

Seventh. For the strengthening of the shock groups, I ask you to allocate: 1) two rifle divisions, one for Maslennikov, in order to exclude the possibility of an enemy penetration toward the north, and a second for Khomenko to reinforce his grouping; and 2) 100 tanks to provide the capability for rapidly committing a prepared motorized rife division, consisting of one tank and two motorized regiments, into combat along Group Konev's axis.

The Commander of the Western Front's forces,
Marshal of the Soviet Union S. Timoshenko
The Member of the Military Council of the Western Front, [signed]

Source: "Doklad komanduiushchego voiskami Zapadnogo fronta ot 15 avgusta 1941 g. Verkhovnomu Glavnokomanduiushchemu o nastupatel'noi operatsii na Dukhovshchinskom napravlenii" [Report of the commander of the forces of the Western Front of 15 August 1941 to the Supreme High Commander about an offensive operation along the Dukhovshchina axis], *SBDVOV*, issue 41, 14-15.

5. Combat Order No. 01/op of the Commander of the Forces of the Western Front of 15 August 1941 on the Destruction of the Enemy's Dukhovshchina Grouping

Combat Order No. 01, Headquarters, Western Front,
15 August 1941
(see Map 7)

1) The enemy, having shifted his main forces against the Central Front, has gone over to the defense along the entire Western Front. Up to three enemy infantry divisions and one panzer division are defending opposite 30th and 19th Armies' fronts.

Presumably, an enemy reserve of up to one motorized division is in the Zviakino region.

2) On the right – 27th Army is successfully deploying to liquidate the enemy in the Kholm region with its left wing. The boundary with it is as before. On the left – the Reserve Front is conducting an offensive with the mission of liquidating the enemy's El'nia grouping.

3) The Western Front will encircle and destroy the enemy's Dukhovshchina grouping by concentric attacks with 30th and 19th Armies in the general direction of Dukhovshchina and reach the Starina, Dukhovshchina, and Iartsevo line with its center.

4) 22nd Army will continue to fulfill its assigned missions, while holding firmly to its occupied positions. The boundary on the left is as before.

5) 29th Army will attack toward Il'ino and reach the Velizh and Il'ino line on 19 August. Cavalry Group Dovator will penetrate into the enemy's rear at first light on 16 August, while destroying his [the enemy's] rear area objectives and supply bases in the Velizh, Demidov, and Dukhovshchina regions. The boundary on the left is as before.

6) 30th Army, consisting of 250th, 242nd, 259th, and 162nd RDs, 107th TD, and 45th CD, reinforced by 46th MAD, 392nd and 542nd CARs, 30 batteries of M-13s [*Katiushas*], 871st ATR, 253rd and 291st Sapper Bns, and 51st Pontoon-Bridge Bn, while protecting its right flank toward Belyi, will attack toward Dukhovshchina on the morning of 17 August and destroy the enemy by decisive operations. By the end of the day, commit 45th CD and 107th TD into the enemy's rear to exploit the attack by enveloping Dukhovshchina from the west. Reach the line of the Velitsa River with your main forces by 19 August 1941.

Subsequently, while protecting yourself from the west along the Dubovitsa, Starina, and Verdino line with two divisions, prepare to develop the strike northwestward of Dukhovshchina. The boundary on the left: Novoduginskaia, Markovo (incl.), and Dukhovshchina.

7) 19th Army, consisting of 166th, 91st, 50th, 64th, and 89th RDs and 101st TD, reinforced 43rd MAD, 120th HAR, one battalion of 302nd HAR, 596th HAR, 311th GAR, 6th and 19th Batteries of M-13s, 874th ATR, 321st Sep. Sapper Bn, and

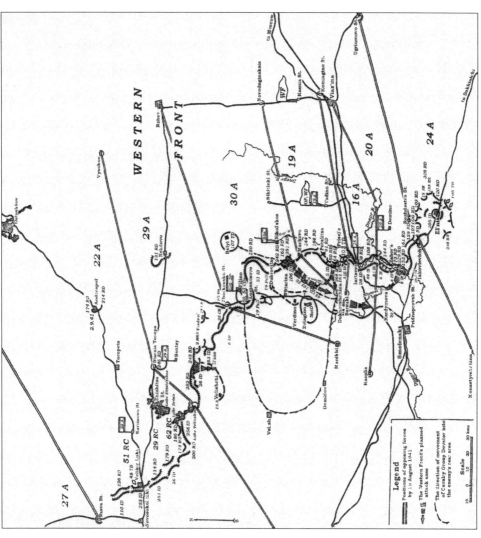

Map 7: The Western Front's Situation and Force Missions according to Combat Order No. 01/op of 15 August 1941

42nd EngBn, having left reinforced 166th RD on the Markovo and Potelitsa front, will attack from the Potelitsa and Prisel'e front toward Dukhovshchina with five divisions on the morning of 17 August, with the mission, in cooperation with 30th Army, to encircle and destroy the enemy in the region to the east of Dukhovshchina, with your forward units along the Khmost' River. Subsequently, while protecting your operations from the west, prepare an attack with your main forces toward the south.

8) 16th Army, consisting of 38th and 108th RDs, will firmly defend the positions it occupies, having paid special attention to defense of the Iartsevo and Dorogobuzh axes.

As 19th Army advances, allocate strong forward detachments to protect 19th Army's flank.

The boundary on the left is as before.

9) 20th Army will continue to fulfill its previously assigned missions, while preparing, when 19th Army develops its blow south of Dukhovshchina, to attack from the Zabor'e and Pridneprovskaia Station front toward Kardymova Station with the forces of three divisions on the morning of 19 August.

10) VVS:

a) Work over 30th and 19th Armies' main attack sectors with air strikes on the nights of 15-16 August and 16-17 August.

b) Conduct strikes with all the forces of bomber aviation against the forward edge of the enemy's defenses along the axes of 30th and 19th Armies' main attacks from 0700 to 0715 hours on 17 August.

c) Prevent enemy forces from approaching the Dukhovshchina region from the southwest and west.

d) Protect the groupings of 30th and 19th Armies' forces in accordance with the requests of the commanders of 30th and 19th Armies.

11) Operational post of the *front's* headquarters – Vadino

Timoshenko
Sokolovsky

Source: "Boevoi prikaz komanduiushchego voiskami Zapadnogo fronta no. 01/op ot 15 avgusta 1941 g. na unichtozhenie Dukhovshchinskoi gruppirovki protivnika" [Combat order no. 01 of the commander of the forces of the Western Front of 15 August 1941 on the destruction of the enemy's Dukhovshchina grouping], *SBDVOV*, issue 41, 17-18.

6. Extract from a Report by the Senior Assistant Chief of the Operations Department of the Western Front's Headquarters to the Chief of the Operations Department of the Western Front's Headquarters Concerning 20th Army's Combat Operations during the Period from 9 through 15 August 1941 (see Map 8)

To the Chief of the Operations Department, Headquarters, Western Front
16 August 1941

Report about the Course of Military Operations on 20th Army's Front during the Period from 9-15 August 1941

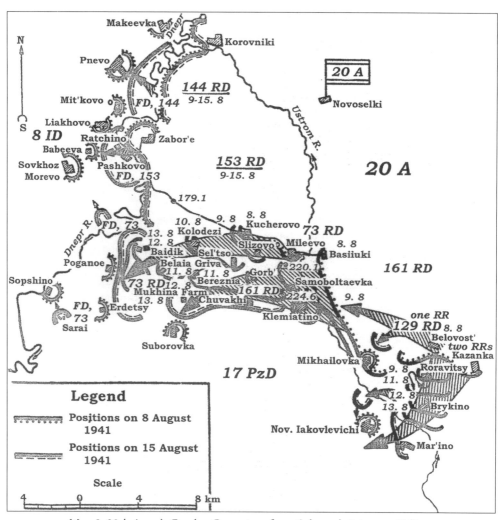

Map 8: 20th Army's Combat Operations from 6 through 8 August 1941

The overall nature of operations on 20th Army's front during the period from 9-15 August 1941 was an offensive by the army's main forces toward the southwest, with the objective of reaching the Pridneprovskaia Station and Dobromino Station line along the railroad, while simultaneously tying down enemy forces on the western bank of the Dnepr River.

The Tempo of the Offensive

20th Army's units were deployed for the offensive in positions along the western bank of the Dnepr River – from (incl.) Makeevo to Hills 165.9 (incl.). Liakhovo, Ratchino, Pashkovo, and Golovino, and further along the eastern bank of the Dnepr River – from Hill 179.1 to Kucherovo, Mileevo, Vasiuki, Mikhailovka, Belovost', and Kazanka in the following composition: 144th RD, 153rd RD, 73rd RD, 161st RD, and 129th RD, with 229th RD in reserve in the Terenino and Mikhailovka region and 127th and 152nd RDs in the second defensive belt in the Usviat'e, Kas'kovo, and Kamenka sector along the eastern bank of the Uzha River.

Headquarters of the army – Novoselki.

144th and 153rd RD, with 3-4 forward detachments in the strength of a reinforced battalion each along the western bank of the Dnepr River, firmly captured [the following] positions from 9 through 12 August: 144th RD – (incl.) Makeevo, Hill 165.9, and the woods to the south. Subsequently, the detachments approached Makeevo, Pnevo, and Mit'kovo and, after encountering heavy enemy resistance, dug in along that line. Attempts to capture the positions indicated were unsuccessful. During the period from 9 through 15 August, the forward detachments advanced 1.5-2 kilometers, thus, at a tempo of advance of 300-400 meters per day.

153rd RD. Its forward detachments were halted by enemy fire in positions from the heights east of Liakhovo to Dubrova and the southwestern edge of the woods south of Golovino. Repeated enemy counterattacks from the vicinity of Morevo State Farm toward Pashkovo denied the forward detachments the opportunity to exploit success toward the west.

From 9-15 August, the forward detachments advanced 1.5-2 kilometers, at an average tempo of advance of 300-400 meters per day.

73rd RD, while attacking toward Kucherovo, Kolodezi, Belaia Griva, and Erdetsy, reached positions from Baidik to Poganoe and Erdetsy with its forward detachments by day's end on 15 August, meaning, therefore, an advance of 8 kilometers on the right wing at an average tempo of 1-1.4 kilometers per day and on its left wing – 13 kilometers at an average tempo of 1.5-1.75 kilometers per day.

161st RD attacked toward Vasiuki, Hill 236.5, and Motovo. By day's end on 15 August, the division reached the Mukhino State Farm, Motovo, Chuvakhi, and northern outskirts of Klemiatino line, where it was halted by enemy fire.

From 9-15 August, the division advanced 10 kilometers on its right wing, at an average tempo of 1.3-1.5 kilometers per day and 3 kilometers on its left wing, at an average tempo of 400-500 meters per day.

129th RD attacked with one rifle regiment from the vicinity of the woods south of Chentsovo toward Klemiatino. The regiment penetrated into Klemiatino by day's end on 15 August and fought street battles. The regiment's advance during this period was 2 kilometers, for an average tempo of 250-300 meters per day.

Two of the division's regiments captured positions from the crossing over the Ustrom River, 1.5 kilometers northeast of Novyi Iakovlevichi, to Mar'ino. The advance was 7 kilometers, for an average tempo of 1 kilometer per day.

In general, the army's units recorded an extremely insignificant advance forward, and, in places, the units have been limited to marking time in a single place. This is explained, first and foremost, by the disorganization of the offensive itself, the purposelessness of the commanders of the attacking units, and their unwillingness to search for the enemy's flanks (457th RR in the Klemiatino region).

The absence of sufficiently thoughtful and organized cooperation of the infantry with the artillery and with neighbors is leading to frontal attacks with extremely limited success and subsequent unnecessary losses in personnel.

Units and subunits are coming to a halt under the pressure of the fire of one-two machine guns and two-three mortars. As an order by 20th Army's commander reads, "These insignificant weapons are halting the attacks of entire units" [Order No. 0016 of the commander of 20th Army, dated 13 August 1941]. When two-three enemy tanks or aircraft appear, the units become flustered and withdraw without the influence of enemy infantry and their fire weapons. Infantry on the battlefield neither dig in to the ground nor find cover in foxholes and, therefore, are easily vulnerable to artillery fire and air strikes.

According to 20th Army's Order No. 0014, dated 8 August 1941, the 20th Army's composition includes: the headquarters of 34th RC, 144th, 153rd, 73rd, 161st, 129th, 229th, 127th, and 152nd RD, and 7th and 126th CARs.

Thereafter, the headquarters of 34th RC and 158th RD were disbanded and incorporated into 127th RD. 46th RD has been used to fill out 129th RD and 233rd RD – [to fill out] 73rd RD. The entire army's combat composition is expressed in the following figures:

The 20th Army's Composition as of 6 August

Category	Former 16th Army	Former 20th Army	Total as of 6 August
Officers	–	3,446	–
NCOs and enlisted men	13,956	23,149	40,560
Horses	1,801	2,042	3,843
Vehicles	105	123	228
BT tanks	–	3	3
T-26 tanks	–	3	6
T-37 tanks	–	16	16
Armored cars	–	20	20
Rifles	7,971	19,998	21,969
Automatic weapons	–	128	128

Category	Former 16th Army	Former 20th Army	Total as of 6 August
Heavy machine guns	16	84	100
Sub-machine guns	41	195	236
122mm guns	14	27	41
107mm guns	–	1	1
76mm guns	19	18	37
45mm guns	–	10	10
152mm howitzers	2	18	20
120mm mortars	6	3	9
82mm mortars	2	–	2
50mm mortars	6	10	10

These figures do not include 5th MC, 1st MRD, and a few other units dispatched to the rear after 16th and 20th Armies' escape from encirclement. Exact information about 20th Army's composition by 15 August 1941 has not been received. [**Author's note**: These figures substantiate the assertion above that roughly 50,000 men escaped the Smolensk encirclement]

The operational density by 9 August 1941 was approximately [as follows]: The army occupied a 40 kilometer front, as follows [per kilometer]: RD – one per 8 kilometers (considering 46th RD in 129th RD and 233rd RD in 73rd RD), guns – 2.5, tanks – 0.5, armored vehicles – 0.5, machine guns – 2.5, mortars – 0.5, and rifles – 550.

The correlation of forces according to the day of combat.

According to the Intelligence Department of the Western Front's headquarters, 20th Army operated against:

9 August – 3 IRs (40th MotR, 17th PzD, 90th MotR, 20th PzD, and 28th IR, 8th ID. Combat composition unknown.

10 August – + (2 PzBns: 10 dug-in tanks); and 3-4 ArtyBns – all in action.

11 August – same as above

12 August – +2 SS IRs (11th SS IR, SS ID); and (1 PzBn)

13 August – + (up to 1 PzCo)

14 August – 28th IR, 8th ID left. One destroyed (2nd Bn, 4th SS IR)

15 August – + (up to 1 Arty Bn)

(Approximate total from 9-15 August – up to 3 IDs, 2-3 SS IRs, up to 4-5 Arty Bns, up to 3 Pz Bns, 1 Pz Co, with 10 dug-in tanks).

Based on these figures, the daily correlation of forces on the army's front was [as follows]:

Daily Correlation of Forces on 20th Army's Front

Date	Our Forces			Enemy Forces		
	RDs	Arty Bns*	Pz Bns	IDs	Arty Bns	Pz Bns
9	6	13	1	1	3-4	–
10	6	13	1	1	3-4	2
11	6	13	1	1	3-4	2
12	6	13	1	about2	3-4	1
13	6	13	1	about2	3-4	1
14	6	13	1	2	3-4	1
15	6	13	1	2	4-5	1

Note: * The quantity of battalions is based on the presence of 109 guns in the army on 9 August divided by 12 guns per battalion.

Expressed numerically, the approximate correlation of forces is [as follows]:

In infantry – 6 to 1 in our favor
In artillery – 13 to 4 in our favor
In tanks – 2 to 1 in the enemy's favor

Since two-thirds of 20th Army's forces were in forward positions and one-third were in the depths, the correlation at the front is [as follows]:

In infantry – 5 to 1 in our favor
In artillery – 8 to 1 in our favor
In tanks – 2 to 1 in the enemy's favor

The great superiority of our forces in infantry and artillery on the offensive, however, is not being exploited by our formation commanders, who usually distribute [their forces] more or less uniformly across the front. As a result, as pointed out above, the density [of forces] along the entire front was not high (even for defensive operations).

The Nature of Enemy Operations on 20th Army's Front from 9-15 August 1941

The infantry were characterized by great maneuverability and shifting of forces at night and along country roads. The units did not occupy populated points, and they frequently went through the forests. The presence of Finns, Czechs, and Poles was noticed in the units (replacements from reserve battalions).

The artillery demonstrated great activity [*aktivnost'*] in cooperation with mortars and machine gun fires.

Tanks did not take an active part in the fighting at the front.

In recent days, aircraft [aviation] decreased their activity. The majority were occupied by reconnaissance and seldom bombed.

The Nature of Fortifications

During the period from 9-15 August 1941, the enemy defended actively, based chiefly on a system of mortar and machine gun fires.

The units' losses of personnel and equipment and their replacement.

According to reports by the army's headquarters, during the period from 9-15 August, the army's units suffered the following losses:

Killed – 105 men
Wounded – 441 men
Died of wounds – 89 men
Total – 635 men

According to incomplete information from the Medical Department, from 10-11 August alone, there were 879 men in the *front's* hospitals and 1,265 men in the army's hospital.

The divergence in this information occurs as a result of the inexact reports from the units about their losses.

The Medical Department, where information about the actual loses of the units is more realistic, does not have a clear picture of this matter at present.

The Manning Department reported that, from 9-15 August, 20th Army received 9 march-battalions, with a total of 9,000 men [replacements]. In addition, 9 march-battalions with 640 men each, 5,760 men in all, were detailed for and sent to 152nd RD and 2,100 horses for all of the army's units.

During the period up to 15 August, [the following] were withdrawn from the western bank to the eastern bank of the Dnepr River:

Equipment withdrawn from the Western Bank to the Eastern Bank of the Dnepr River by 20th Army

Trucks	280	Mortars	3
Light trucks	14	Heavy machine guns	9
Tractors	43	Sub-machine guns	22
Tanks	5	Telephones	22
Guns	93	Field kitchens	29
Radios	2	Arty periscopes	1
Carts, sledges, etc.	402	Horses	588
Watertrucks	2	Boxes of explosives	1
Motorcycles	4		

Artillery, aviation, and tank support.

a) Artillery, lacking sufficiently close communications with the infantry, sometimes failed to support infantry operations.

Thus, for example, instances are being noted when the artillery of 161st RD was situated in firing positions at a distance of 12 kilometers from the forward regiment, lacking not only its forward observers but also any sort of communications with its supported infantry and, on the other hand, with the commanders and commissars of the formations and units (see Order No. 0016 of the commander of 20th Army, dated 13 August 1941). This inculcated incorrect notions in the soldiers that an offensive can be begun only after the artillery destroy all of the firing points. Hence – the "hope' of the infantry for artillery and a fixation on looking back.

b) Tank units did not operate on 20th Army's front.

c) During the period from 9-15 August 1941, aviation carried out sorties in front of the army's front to suppress and destroy the following targets:

a) Populated points;

b) Centers of resistance; and

c) Against vehicular columns, concentration areas, and against reserves approaching the front.

According to information from VVS headquarters, cooperation with aircraft was organized satisfactorily.

However, the forces did not always fulfill the requirements for communications with aircraft (did not always emplace position markings).

Instances were noted when our aircraft arrived at their targets late.

Attachment: Map of 20th Army's area of operations [see Map 41, 25]

The Chief of 20th Army's Sector, Colonel Vasil'ev

Source: "Doklad starshego pomoshchnika nachal'nika operativnogo otdela shtaba Zapadnogo fronta nachal'niku operativnogo otdela shtaba fronta o boevykh deistviiakh voisk 20-i Armii v period s 9 po 15 avgusta 1941 g. [Report of the senior assistant chief of the Operations Department of the Western Front's headquarters to the chief of the Operations Department of the Western Front's headquarters concerning the combat operations of 20th Army's forces during the period from 9 through 15 August 1941], SBDVOV, issue 41, 20-25.

7. Excerpt from Information of the Headquarters of the Western Front Concerning the Combat and Numerical Composition of 20th Army's Forces on 15 August 1941

20th Army's Combat Composition on 15 August 1941

Unit	Personnel	Rifles	Machine guns	Guns	Mortars
229th RD	2,968	1,848	43	9	–
129th RD	5,322	3,763	45	56	7
144th RD	5,537	3,353	84	24	29
73rd RD	6,947	4,062	57	14	8
161st RD	7,188	5,464	95	13	–
153rd RD	5,497	2,444	39	21	13
152nd RD	No data available – left the army				
Hqs					
TOTAL	**29,309**	**20,944**	**363**	**123**	**47**

Notes: Does not include the army's headquarters and 152nd RD.

Approaching replacements without weapons – 4,150 men

Information received from Colonel Alekseev

Colonel Vasil'ev

Source: "Svedeniia shtaba Zapadnogo fronta o boevom i chislennom sostave voisk 20-i Armii na 15 avgusta 1941 g. [Information of the headquarters of the Western Front about the combat and numerical composition of 20th Army's forces on 15 August 1941], *SBDVOV*, issue 41, 211.

8. Report by the Commander of 19th Army of 16 August 1941 to the Commander of the Western Front's Forces about the Decision for an Offensive Operation

To the Commander-in-Chief of the Western Direction

0200 hours on 16 August 1941

Your order No. 01/op was received at 1845 hours, deciphered by 1130 hours, and has been fully studied. All is understood.

I am reporting my principal decision [plan]:

1. I will deliver my main attack with five divisions (91st, 50th, 89th, 64th, and 101st) from the Gorbatovskaia and Prisel'e front in the general direction of Dukhovshchina, with the mission to reach the Semenovo, Sirotinka, Popova, and (incl.) Novosel'e line by day's end on 17 August. All of the divisions will be in one echelon, and the divisions' sectors will be 2-3 kilometers. 101st TD will be in the Borodulino and Prisel'e region on the left wing. The tanks in my reserve are for developing the penetration.

2. 166th RD, while defending along the Zaria, Priglovo, Zanino 1, and Kaniutino front, will deliver a supporting attack toward Losevo from the (incl.) Kaniutino and Gorbatovskaia 2 front.

3. The artillery preparation will be one half hour by means of fire raids.

4. I request you send 100th RD to the Drozdovo (22 kilometers northwest of Dorogobuzh), Aleshino, and Vasil'eva region.

I also ask you to report the time it reaches its designated region.

5. The day of 16 August is for the organization of cooperation on the ground.

6. I will submit the order and operational plan to you additionally.

Konev, Shelakov

Source: "Doklad komanduiushchego voiskami 19-i Armii ot 16 avgusta 1941. komanduiushchemu voiskami Zapadnogo fronta o reshenii na nastupatel'nuiu operatsiiu" [Report by the commander of 19th Army of 16 August 1941 to the commander of the Western Front's forces about the decision for an offensive operation], *SBDVOV*, issue 41, 157.

9. Combat Order No. 027 of the Commander of the Forces of 19th Army on the Occupation of Jumping-off Positions for the Offensive

Combat Order No. 027, CP, Commander, 19th Army,
the woods 1 kilometer east of Vasilisino,
0200 hours on 16 August 1941
1:50,000 scale map

1. Units of 900th Armored [Motorized] Brigade and 5th and newly-arrived 35th IDs continue to defend in the army's sector.

2. On the right, 30th Army and, on the left, 16th Army, are fulfilling their previous missions.

3. 19th Army will conduct a regrouping and occupy jumping-off positions by 0200 hours on 17 August 1941.

4. 166th RD will firmly hold onto the Pogorel'tsy, Shestaki 2, Zaria, Priglovo, Zanino 1, Lopatchinka, and (incl.) Gorbatovskaia 2 line.

CP – in its previous position.

Boundary on the left: (incl.) Briukhachi, (incl.) Pechenichino, Gorbatovskaia 2, and (incl.) Balashova.

5. 91st RD will occupy jumping-off positions along the Gorbatovskaia 2, Dura, and Shuklino line by 0200 hours on 17 August 1941 … ..

CP – in its previous position.

Boundary on the left: (incl.) Novaia Guta, Shuklion, and (incl.) Kazakova.

6. 50th RD will occupy jumping-off positions along the Turova and Dubrovka line by 0200 hours on 17 August 1941.

CP by 2000 hours on 16 August 1941 – the woods 0.5 kilometers northeast of Bobrovtsy.

Boundary of the left: Novaia Aleksandrovskaia, Dubrovka, and Ivanova.

7. 89th RD will occupy jumping-off positions along the (incl.) Dubrovka, Kuz'mino, and Novyi Riadyni line by 0200 hours on 17 August 1941.

CP by 2000 hours on 16 August 1941 – the "Sapogom" grove (1 kilometer northwest of Neelovo).

Boundary on the left: Avdiukovo, Novaia Riadyni, and Nefedovshchina.

8. 64th RD will occupy jumping-off positions along the Tserkov' and Novyi Riadyni, eastern slope of Hill 203.4, and Borodulino line by 0200 hours on 17 August 1941.

CP by 2000 hours – the road crossing 1 kilometer east of Shamova.

Boundary on the left: (incl.) Hill 220.8, Borodulino, and Osopova.

9. 101st TD will occupy jumping-off positions along the Prisel'e and Skachikhina line by 0200 hours on 17 August 1941.

The tank regiment – is my reserve – in the region of the woods 0.5 kilometers northwest of Liada.

CP by 2000 hours on 16 August 1941 – the Kovaleva region.

10. I require all commanders carry out commanders' reconnaissance and organize cooperation between infantry and artillery on the ground. Pay special attention to cooperation at the infantry and artillery battalion and company and battery level.

Give instructions in the battalions for the arrival of the companies in their jumping-off positions for the offensive.

Carry out the movement of forces exclusively at night and strictly observe *maskirovka* [camouflage].

Organize active reconnaissance on the night of 16-17 August, with the mission of determining the enemy's grouping and to seize controlled prisoners in 166th, 91st, and 89th RDs' sectors.

11. CP and headquarters of the army – in previous positions.

12. Submit operational and reconnaissance summaries by 0100, 1300, and 2000 hours daily.

> The Commander of 19th Army, Lieutenant General Konev
> The Member of the Military Council, Division Commissar Sheklanov
> The Chief of Staff of 19th Army, [signed]

Source: "Boevoi prikaz komanduiushchego voiskami 19-i Armii No. 027 ot 16 avgusta 1941 na zaniatie iskhodnogo polozheniia dlia nastupleniia" [Combat order no. 027 of the commander of the forces of 19th Army on the occupation of jumping-off positions for the offensive], *SBDVOV*, issue 41, 159-160.

10. Combat Order No. 036 of the Commander of the Forces of 30th Army of 16 August 1941 on an Offensive toward Shanino, Dorofeevo, and Ponomari

Combat Order No. 036, Headquarters, 30th Army,
the woods 2 kilometers northeast of Podzaitsevo,
0550 hours on 16 August 1941
1:100,000 and 50,000 scale maps

1. The enemy is defending the Los'mino, Chernyi Ruchei, Staroe Morokhovo, Erkhovo, Staroe Selo, Sechenki, Ol'khovka village, and Torchilovo line opposite the army's front with units of 19th and 20th PzDs and 106th ID. His tactical reserves are at Chichata, Gorodno, and Pavlovshchina. Operational reserves: at Zviakino and a motorized division in Dukhovshchina.

2. On the right, [a Cavalry Group] (50th and 53rd CDs) is penetrating into the enemy's rear at first light on 16 August, while operating along the Evlen' axis into the Velizh, Demidov, and Dukhovshchina regions. The boundary on the right is as before.

On the left, 19th Army is attacking toward Dukhovshchina; the boundary with it is: Novoduginskaia, Markovo, and (incl.) Dukhovshchina.

3. 30th Army, consisting of 250th RD, 242nd RD, 151st RD, 162nd RD, 107th TD, and 45th CD, reinforced 46th MAD, 399th and 542nd CAR, 30th Btry of M-13 [*Katiushas*], 871st ATR, 263rd and 291st Sapper Bns, and 51st Pontoon-Bridge Bn, while protecting the right flank toward Belyi with 250th RD's forces, will attack with its main force in the general direction of Shanino, Dorofeevo, and Ponomari on the morning of 17 August 1941 and destroy the opposing enemy by decisive operations, while developing success with 45th CD and 107th TD, which are being thrown into the enemy's rear to envelop Dukhovshchina from the west.

The main forces will reach the line of the Velitsa River by 19 August 1941.

Subsequently, after protecting [against enemy attacks] from the west along the Dubovitsa, Starina, and Verdino line with 242nd and 251st RDs, exploit the attack toward [the region] northwest of Dukhovshchina. Begin the attack at 0800 hours on 17 August.

4. 250th RD, with 2nd Bn, 542nd CAR, 12th Mortar Battalion (without one company), and a battery from 871st ATR, will protect the previously occupied line and prevent an enemy penetration toward Belyi.

Subsequently, prepare an attack in the general direction of Dubovitsa.

The boundary on the left: Prokshina, Priboltiisk, and (incl.) Dentialovo.

5. 242nd RD, with 1st Bn, 392nd CAR, having protected the Orlovo, (incl.) Staroe Morokhovo, and (incl.) Novoe Morokhovo line with one regiment, attack toward Erkhovo and Churkino with two regiments to destroy the opposing enemy, with the immediate mission to reach the Ta River [should read Rekta River] at Staroe Sochnevo.

Subsequently, develop the attack in the general direction of Starina [35 kilometers north of Dukhovshchina].

The boundary on the left: (incl.) Volkovo, (incl.) Nikol'skoe, Storozhok, (incl.) Shelepy, Staroe Sochnevo, and Starina.

6. 251st RD, with two battalions from 392nd CAR, one company from 12th Mortar Battalion, two batteries of 871st ATR, and one company of 51st Pontoon-Bridge Bn, having blockaded the enemy's center of resistance in the Staroe Selo region with two battalions, will attack toward Shelepy and Pominki with the division's main forces, with the immediate mission to reach the (incl.) Staroe Sochnevo and Khadobuzha line.

Subsequently, be prepared to develop the attack in the general direction of Verdino.

The boundary on the left: Parosinov, Lukina, (incl.) Korytnia, (incl.) Smerdishche, Staroe Selo, Khadobuzha, and Verdino.

7. 162nd RD, with 542nd CAR (without one battalion), a battery of 871st ATR, and one company of 263rd Sep. Sapper Bn, will destroy the opposing enemy by an attack with the main forces toward Gordienki, Sechenki, and Maloe Repino, with the immediate mission to reach the (incl.) Khadobuzha and Staroe Selo (coordinates 4474) line.

Subsequently, be prepared to develop the attack in the general direction of Ponomari.

The boundary on the left: Bykovo, Krapivnia, Beskhvostovo, Krechets, Dorofeevo, and Kuz'mishchino.

8. 107th TD will deliver a secondary attack toward Bol'shoe Repino, Novoselki, and Petrovo Selo with one RR, concentrate its main forces in the vicinity of Novovysokoe Farm by 0400 hours on 17 August, while following after 251st RD's main forces from the Nekliudovo and Staroe Selo line, 2 kilometers northeast of Dorofeevo, and, together with 45th CD, penetrate for operations against the enemy's rear to envelop Dukhovshchina from the west.

Subsequently, be prepared to develop the attack toward [the region] northwest of Dukhovshchina.

9. 45th CD will concentrate in the Kvoktushino, Pod'ezzhalovo, and Lakashevo region and be prepared for a penetration from the Nekliudovo and Staroe Selo line with 107th TD for operations against the enemy's rear in an envelopment of Dukhovshchina from the west.

45th CD's commander is entrusted with overall command of the penetration group.

10. Reserve – one battalion of 134th RD and the tank battalions of 250th, 242nd, and 251st RDs – will concentrate in the forested region 0.5 kilometers south of Podzaitsevo by 0400 hours on 17 August. The direction of movement – Lelimovo, Sopino, and Mikhailovshchina.

11. Artillery: Be ready at 0400 hours on 17 August. Artillery preparation – 45 minutes. **To the commanders of the [artillery] units**:

a) During the period of the artillery preparation, destroy enemy firing means along the forward edge.

b) Suppress enemy fortified centers of resistance, mortar batteries, and artillery.

c) Protect the attack by infantry and tanks on 162nd RD's and 251st RD's main axes and [conduct] a fire barrage to a depth of one kilometer.

d) Prevent counterattacks by enemy tanks and infantry from the direction of Iakovtsevo and Gorodno.

e) Prevent the movement of enemy reserves from the Grivets and Pavlovshchina region.

f) Protect the successful advance of infantry and tanks into the depths, while offering constant support by fire and wheels [movement].

12. VVS. Missions:

1) Beginning at first light, repeat raids against the Zviagino Farm, Shilovichi, and Pavlovshchina regions and operations against the enemy in the Iakovtsevo, Novosechnevo, Shelepy, Shanino, Maloe Repino, Gorodno, and Punino regions to destroy enemy reserves.

2) Operations against [the following] march-routes:

a) Vorontsovo, Bor, and Prechistoe; and

b) Bol'shoe Repino, Voropaevo, Shilovichi, and Dukhovshchina – to paralyze the enemy's movement and the approach of his reserves from the west by smoke charges.

3) Conduct reconnaissance:

a) Prechistoe and Dukhovshchina; and

b) Budnitsa, Shchuch'e, and Prechistoe;

4) Protect the grouping of the army's main forces from the skies.

13. CP – the woods 2 kilometers northeast of Podzaitsevo.

Axis of movement – Mikhailovshchina and Khodobuzha.

The Commander of 30th Army, Khomenko
The Member of the Military Council, Abramov
The Chief of Staff, Baderko

Source: "Boevoi prikaz komanduiushchego voiskami 30-i Armii No. 036 ot 16 avgusta 1941 na nastuplenie v napravlenii Shanino, Dorofeevo, Ponomari" [Combat order no. 036 of the commander of the forces of 30th Army of 16 August 1941 on an offensive toward Shanino, Dorofeevo, and Ponomari], *SBDVOV*, issue 41, 281-282.

11. Extract from Combat Order No. 55 of the Commander of the Forces of 20th Army on the Capture of the Sopshino, Dobromino, Klokovo, and Glinka Line

Combat Order No. 55, Headquarters, 20th Army,
1430 hours on 16 August 1941
1:50,000 scale map

1. The enemy has gone over to the defense with up to five regiments along the Makeevo, Mit'kovo, Dubrova, the woods south of Golovino, Malinovka, Suborovka, Klemiatino, and Novyi Iakovlevskii line, while trying to contain our units' offensive in separate sectors with unsuccessful counterattacks.

2. 20th Army, while firmly holding on to the Dnepr River line and the heights west of Ratchino and Pashkovo, is continuing its offensive with its left wing, with the mission to capture Sopshino, Dobromino, Klokovo, and Glinka.

3. On the right, 16th Army is defending the Dnepr River.

The boundary with it is as before.

On the left, 107th RD [24th Army] is attacking toward Bezzabot State Farm.

4. 144th RD will firmly defend the Dnepr River in the sector from the crossing at Solov'evo [southward] to the woods 2 kilometers east of Lagunovo, with forward detachments at Makeevo, Pnevo, and Mit'kovo. Conduct a relief of 153rd RD's units from the bend in the Dnepr River to the woods east of Lagunovo on the night of 17 August.

The boundary on the left: (incl.) Novoselki, (incl.) Osovo, and (incl.) Mashkino.

5. 153rd RD, while firmly holding onto the Dnepr River in the sector from Lagunovo to the inscription "barn" (4 kilometers south of Golovino), will secure the heights west of Ratchino, Golovino, and the eastern part of the woods south of Golovino at all cost. Having given up the (incl.) Golovino and barn sector to 229th RD on the night of 17-18 August, occupy jumping-off positions at (incl.) Liakhovo, Dubrova, and Golovino for an attack toward Fedurno.

The boundary on the left: Zubovo, Kolodezi, the inscription "barn" on the western bank of the Dnepr River, and Morevo State Farm.

6. 73rd RD, while continuing its attack, will occupy Sopshino and the railroad bridge by day's end, and, while holding on to the meadow west of the barn, seize the southern edge of the woods east of Kolpino and Malinovka with forward detachments.

Subsequently, while reliably protecting the region you occupy, prepare to attack toward Malinovka, Kolpino, and Goncharovo.

The boundary on the left: Slizovo, Bereznia, Erdetsy, and Sopshino.

7. 161st RD, while continuing the attack on the morning of 16 August, will occupy Dobromino and Klokovo Station by day's end.

Subsequently, while firmly holding that line, occupy Sopshino and the railroad bridge east of Pridneprovskaia Station with one regiment, while protecting 73rd RD's left flank.

The boundary on the left is as before.

8. 129th RD, while continuing the attack on the morning of 16 August, will capture the Klokovo and Glinka line by day's end.

9. 229th RD, while continuing to fortify the Kovali and Borovka line, will concentrate in the woods 2 kilometers northwest of Kolodezi by 2400 hours on 17 August and, after crossing the Dnepr River, will relieve 153rd and 73rd RDs' units by 0400 hours on 18 August and occupy jumping-off positions for an attack in the sector from (incl.) Golovino to the inscription "barn" sector on the western bank of the Dnepr River, in readiness to attack toward Morevo State Farm. Have no fewer than one and one half RRs on the eastern bank of the Dnepr River.

10. The Chief of Artillery will put the artillery weapons in order by 18 August, having prepared to employ the artillery reinforcements in the Ratchino and Malinovka sector.

11. The Chief of Engineers will construct roads in the Belaia Griva and Baidik and Dnepr River and Baidik sectors and a separate shed 1 kilometer north of Paganoe on 16 and 17 August.

Carry out a personal reconnaissance of the possibilities for placing bridges on the Dnepr River in two sectors, Golovino and the barn and two – in the Malinovka region, one of them for heavy cargo.

12. The division commanders will undertake organized measures for filling out the units with personnel and weapons.

13. The Chief of the Rear Directorate, Major Genera Andreev, will procure material means for fulfilling the assigned missions.

14. The chief of the army's Chemical Services and the division commanders will provide the units with bottles filled with flammable liquids "KS" [kerosene] on the basis of 1,500 pieces per division.

> The Commander of 20th Army, Lieutenant General Kurochkin
> The Member of the Military Council, Corps Commissar Semenovsky
> The Chief of staff of the army, Major General Korneev

Source: "Boevoi prikaz komanduiushchego voiskami 20-i Armii No. 55 ot 16 avgusta 1941 na ovladenie rubezhom Sopshino, Dobromino, Klokovo, Glinka" [Combat order no. 55 of the commander of the forces of 20th Army on the capture of the Sopshino, Dobromino, Klokovo, and Glinka line], *SBDVOV*, issue 41, 212-213.

12. Combat Report No. 06 of the Headquarters of 19th Army of 16 August 1941 to the *Front's* Chief of Staff about the Concentration of 50th and 64th Rifle and 101st Tank Divisions

Combat Report No. 06, CP, Commander, 19th Army,
the woods 1 kilometer east of Vasilisino,
1500 hours on 16 August 1941
1:50,000 and 100,000 scale maps

The formations assigned to 19th Army reached their appointed regions on the morning of 16 August 1941 and are situated in the following positions:

1) 50th RD concentrated by 0430 hours: 2nd RR (without 1st Bn) – in the woods 1 kilometer east of Zavod; 49th RR, with 202nd AR – in the woods northwest of Gavrilovo; 359th RR – in the woods 1.5 kilometer east of Vasilisino; separate RBn, 68th and 81st Sep. Sapper Bns – in the woods 2 kilometers southeast of Zavod; 10th MRBn – in the woods west of Novaia Guta; and 41st AutoBn – in the woods 1.5 kilometer southeast of Baran'i Gorki. CP – the woods north of marker 232.7.

2) 101st Separate Tank Division concentrated by 0700 hours: 101st Pontoon-Bridge Bn – in the woods north of Subor; 202nd TR – in the grove southwest of Radiukino; 101st Sep. AABn– in the grove east of Novo-Aleksandrovskoe; 101st AR – in the grove west of Novo-Aleksandrovskoe; and 101st MRR (without the two battalions relieving 38th RD) – in the woods west of Kozhykhovo. CP – the woods north of Lanino.

3) 64th RD reached the Rybki and Starosel'e region and the woods to the southeast by 0730 hours.

The Chief of Staff of 19th Army, [Colonel V. F. Malyshkin]
The Military Commissar of the headquarters,
Brigade Commissar Kazbintsev

Source: "Boevoe donesenie shtaba 19-i Armii No. 06 ot 16 avgusta 1941 g. nachal'niku shtaba fronta o sosredotochenie 50-i i64-i Strelkovykh i 101-i Tankovoi Divizii" [Combat report no. 06 of the headquarters of 19th Army of 16 August 1941 to the *front's* chief of staff about the concentration of 50th and 64th Rifle and 101st Tank Divisions], *SBDVOV*, issue 41, 160.

13. Combat Order No. 028 of the Commander of the Forces of 19th Army on the Destruction of the Enemy's Dukhovshchina Grouping

Combat Order No. 028, CP, Commander 19th Army,
the woods 1 kilometer east of Vasilisino,
1520 hours on 16 August 1941
1: 50,000 scale map

1. The units of 900th Armored [Motorized] Brigade and 5th ID, which have been exhausted in previous fighting, and newly-arrived 35th ID are defending in the army's offensive sector. The enemy is trying to halt the offensive by the army's forces by separate centers of resistance and counterattacks by small groups of forces of no more than company size. His reserve is presumably up to one motorized division in the Zviakino region.

2. On the right – 30th Army will go over to the offensive in the general direction of Dukhovshchina on the morning of 17 August 1941.

The boundary with it: Novoduginskaia, Markovo, (incl.) Dukhovshchina.

On the left – 16th Army is defending along the eastern bank of the Vop' River. The boundary with it is as before.

3. 19th Army will tie down the enemy by an active defense on the right wing and will go over to the offensive in its center and with its left wing on the morning of 17

August 1941, with the mission to encircle and destroy the enemy's Dukhovshchina Grouping, in cooperation with 30th Army.

The army will capture the Novo-Losevo 1, Barsuki, Zamiatina, Hill 218.5 (2 kilometers west of Muzhilovo), Osinovki, and (incl.) Novosel'e line by day's end on 17 August 1941. Subsequently, it will attack toward Dukhovshchina. Begin the attack on my special orders.

4. 166th RD, with 3rd Bn, 874th ATR, is defending positions from Shupeki to Shestaki 2, Zaria, Priglovo, Zanino 1, and Zaovrazh'e. It will attack toward Motevo with its left wing. Protect the junction with the units on 30th Army's left flank and prevent an enemy penetration toward Lopatchinka and Sediba at the junction with [the army].

The boundary on the left: (incl.) Briukhachi, (incl.) Pechenichino, (incl.) Gorbatovskaia 2, (incl.) Balashova, and Myshkova.

5. 91st RD, with 120th HAR, 1st Co., 111th Mortar Bn, and 5th and 874th ATRs, will penetrate the enemy's defenses in the Potelitsa and Zadnia sector. The main attack will be toward Potelitsa, Balashova, and Shchelkina. Capture the Semenkova and Sirotinka line by the end of the day on 17 August 1941 and subsequently attack toward Shchelkina and Pavlovo.

The boundary on the left: (incl.) Novaia Guta, Staroe Shuklino, (incl.) Kazakova, Mashutino, and Hill 232.9 (5 kilometers northeast of Dukhovshchina).

6. 50th RD, with 4th Bn, 302nd HAR, 2nd and 3rd Cos., 111th Mortar Bn, and 4th Bn, 874th ATR, will penetrate the enemy's defense in the Staraia Korov'ia and Hill 202.2 (north of Dubrovka) sector. The main attack will be toward Dubrovka and Novaia Korov'ia, capture the Zamiatino and Shishkino line by day's end on 17 August 1941, and subsequently attack toward Kulagino and Mishino.

The boundary on the left: Novoe Aleksandrovskoe, Dubrovka, Ivanova, Sushchevo, and the southwestern corner of the grove in the Lupshevo region.

7. 89th RD will penetrate the enemy's defense in the Hill 205.1 (1 kilometer northwest of Kuz'mino) and Novyi Riadyni sector. Deliver the main attack toward Bulanina and Batyeva and capture the Hill 218.5 (2 kilometers west of Muzhilova) and western edge of the groves (west of Zaitsev State Farm) line.

The boundary on the left: Avdiukovo, Novyi Riadyni, Zaitsev State Farm, and Kulagino.

8. 64th RD, with 596th HAR, and 1st and 2nd Bns, 874th ATR, will penetrate the enemy's defenses in the (incl.) Staryi Riadyni and Hill 203.4 (1.5 kilometers west of Kharino) sector. The main attack will be toward Hill 203.4 and the northern outskirts of Kolkovichi. Seize crossings over the Tsarevich River in the Siniakova and Petrova sector by day's end on 17 August 1941. Subsequently attack toward Sel'tso, Stepanovka, and Hill 228.2 (in the Labrevo region). The boundary on the left: (incl.) 220.8 (north of Vlaskovo), Borodulino, Osipova, (incl.) Potapova, and (incl.) Hill 236.7 (north of Uzval'e).

9. 101st TD (without the tank regiment), while launching an attack by its right wing, will attack toward Miagchenki, Kokhanovo, and Makeeva in cooperation with 64th RD. Capture the Kokhanovo and (incl.) Novosel'e line by day's end on 17 August 1941. Subsequently attack toward Krovopuskovo and Borki. Protect the junction with the units on 16th Army's right flank

10. Reserve: The tank regiment of 101st TD in the vicinity of the woods north of Shk. Mostishche. Be prepared to develop the attack in 64th RD's sector, together with the second echelon, toward Leskovki, Kolkovichi, and Petrova and toward Miagchenki, Skachkova, and Borniki, with the mission to destroy the enemy in the Osipova and Skachkova region and seize the crossings at Siniakova and Petrova.

11. Artillery. Readiness – 0300 hours on 17 August 1941. The artillery preparation – 45 minutes.

Missions:

1) Suppress firing points along the Potelitsa and Miagchenki front on the forward edge;

2) Suppress enemy artillery in the Potelitsa and Kriukova region and prepare DON against the Losevo, Balashova, Makov'e, and Nefedovshchina regions; and

3) Support the commitment of the tank reserve in 64th RD's and 101st TD's sector with the fires of 3-4 battalions;

12. The VVS of 19th Army. Missions:

1) Suppress personnel and firing points in the Staraia Korov'ia and Hill 200.2 (north of Dubrovka) sector;

2) Suppress enemy artillery in strong points in the Kriukova and Stepankina region;

3) Prevent the approach of enemy reserves from the Loinia River line and suppress enemy infantry concentrations in the Balashova, Makov'e, Nefedovshchina, and Stepankina region;

4) Protect the regrouping of the army in the Potelitsa, Vasilisino, and Prisel'e region and the main grouping in the same region; and

5) Be prepared to support the tank reserve.

The VVS of the *front* will strike enemy personnel, artillery, and mortars with bomber operations in the [following] regions: Hill 205.1 (2 kilometers southwest of Dubrovka), Hill 208.0 (2 kilometers southwest of Miaksheva), Sel'kovo, Leskovki, Potelitsa, and Zadnia.

13. Signals for cooperation:

1) From the Air Forces; "I am your aircraft."

On 17 August 1941 – the main signal during the day – a red rocket Duplicated: in time of light – a shown undercarriage, and in time of darkness – fire all of the side weapons for 30 seconds.

On 18 August 1941 – the main signal during the day – a green rocket.

Duplicated: in time of light – several continuous right and left banks, and in time of darkness – the same as on 17 August 1941.

2) From the infantry to the VVS on 17 and 18 August 1941 – In the daytime – a square from white material with its corner toward the enemy, and at night – a yellow rocket toward the enemy.

3) From tanks and motor-mechanized forces. During the day – a white circle on the turret and cockpit with a radius of 25 centimeters.

Signals between infantry, artillery, and tanks will be established by order of the commanders of divisions.

1) The shifting of artillery fire – a series of red rockets or by radio – 222;

2) The cessation of fire – a series of white rockets or by radio – 555;

3) The designation of targets – tracer bullets.

14. CP – the woods 1 kilometer east of Vasilisino, the headquarters of the army – Vadino.

15. Submit operational and reconnaissance summaries at 0100, 1300, and 2000 hours daily.

The Commander of 19th Army, Lieutenant General Konev
The Member of the Military Council of 19th Army,
    Division Commissar Sheklanov
The Chief of Staff of 19th Army, [Colonel Malyshkin]

Source: "Boevoi prikaz komanduiushchego voiskami 19-i Armii No. 028 ot 16 avgusta 1941 na unichtozhenie Dukhovshchinskoi gruppirovki protivnika" [Combat order no. 028 of the commander of the forces of 19th Army on the destruction of the enemy's Dukhovshchina grouping], *SBDVOV*, issue 41, 160-162.

14. Operational Summary No. 102 of the Headquarters of the Western Front at 2000 hours on 16 August 1941 about the Combat Operations of the *Front's* Forces (see Map 7)

Operational Summary No. 102 at 2000 hours on 16 August 1941,
Headquarters. Western Front
1:500,000 and 100,000 scale maps

First. The situation on the right wing of the *front* is unchanged. In the *front's* center, the forces are conducting fighting of a local nature to improve jumping-off positions. A regrouping of forces is under way.

The offensive of the forces on the left wing is developing slowly, while encountering stubborn enemy resistance.

Second. 22nd Army. The positions of the army's units are unchanged. The forces continue to strengthen the positions they occupy.

Headquarters of 22nd Army – Nazimovo Station

Third. 29th Army. The army's units are continuing to strengthen their defensive positions and are carrying out partial regroupings to strengthen the army's left wing.

1st MRR transferred from the Pichevakha region to the Elaga region by 0300 hours on 16 August.

29th RR, at the same time, transferred from the Bol. Gorovakha region to the Elmen' and Rovnyi Bor grove region, with the mission to protect the army's left wing from the south along the Mezha River.

50th and 53rd Cavalry Divisions are moving from the Lake Plovnoe and Emlen' region to fulfill missions in accordance with Order No. 01/op.

There were no changes in the positions of the army's remaining units.

Headquarters of 29th Army – Bentsy.

Fourth. 30th Army is fighting to improve its jumping-off positions and carrying out preparations in accordance with the Western Front's Order No. 01/op.

162nd RD entered into the Shurkino, Zamosh'e, and Kurganovo region (all points 18-20 kilometers southeast of Staroe Morokhovo).

45th CD is on the march to the Lukashovo, Klokutino, and Pod'ezzhalovo region (all points 15 kilometers southeast of Staroe Morokhovo). During the day on 16 August, it is resting in the forest west of Tupishino (40 kilometers southeast of Sychevka). The division will arrive on the night of 16-17 August and complete its concentration by the morning on 17 August.

Fifth. 19th Army, while fighting to improve its jumping-off positions, is carrying out preparations in accordance with Order No. 01/op. It concentrated in [the following] regions by 0930 hours on 16 August:

50th RD – Zavod (20 kilometers west of Vadino Station);

64th RD – Sergeikovo and Rybki (25 kilometers southwest of Vadino Station); and

101st TD –Liada and Kozhukhova (12-15 kilometers northeast of Iartsevo.

Sixth. 16th Army. The army's units, while conducting a regrouping, dug in along their previous lines, while repelling local enemy attacks.

38th RD repelled an attack by up to an enemy battalion toward Dubrovo from the Ust'e and Tsarevich River with artillery fire at 0600 hours on 16 August.

The enemy suffered heavy losses.

108th RD drove off and dispersed up to two enemy companies, which were trying to attack toward Solov'evo from the Zadnia region, with artillery and machine gun fire at 0600 hours on 16 August.

Headquarters of 16th Army – the woods 1.5 kilometers northeast of Khotenova.

Seventh. 20th Army, while continuing to attack with its left wing, fought stubbornly with the enemy, which exchanged ground in counterattacks.

144th and 153rd RDs' units fortified their previous positions.

73rd RD is attacking toward Zlydnia with its right wing and fighting to capture Erdetsy on its left wing.

161st RD, in its previous positions, repelled enemy counterattacks from the direction of Suborovka and Samodurovka.

129th RD's 475th RR captured Klemiatino. The division's remaining units are continuing their attack toward Iakovlevichi from the Shiparevy and Mar'ino line.

Headquarters of the army – Dezhino.

Eighth. The VVS of the *front* cooperated with the army's units and conducted reconnaissance in the first half of the day.

1st Heavy Aviation Regiment bombed enemy airfield at Smolensk and troops concentrations and warehouses in the Gorodok, Nevel' Station, and Novosokol'niki regions on the night of 16 August. It conducted 13 aircraft sorties and dropped [the following] bombs: 95 FAB-100, 49 FAB-82, 9 FAB-70, 16 AO-25, 10 AO-8, 20 AO-2.5, 10 ZAB-50, and 32 KS ampoules. It also dropped 350,000 leaflets.

43rd MAD conducted 32 aircraft sorties on 20th Army's front.

47th MAD conducted 24 aircraft sorties on 19th Army's front.

46th MAD conducted 11 aircraft sorties on 30th Army's front.

31st MAD cooperated with 22nd Army's units and conducted 17 aircraft sorties.

38th RAS photographed the enemy's defensive belt in the Karpovo and Zamosh'e sector along the Vop' River.

The divisions conducted a total of 88 aircraft sorties, including 51 fighter, 31 bomber, and 6 assault [ground attack].

They dropped [the following] bombs: 10 FAB-100, 34 FAB-50, 8 ZAB-50, 30 AO-25, 40 AO-15, 140 ZAB-1, 39 RS, 650 BS, 7,210 ShKAS, and 2,430 ShBAK.

There is no information about enemy losses.

Our losses: 2 TB-3 aircraft, of which 1 was destroyed during landing, and the other did not return from fulfilling its mission.

> The Chief of Staff of the Western Front, Lieutenant General Sokolovsky
> The Military Commissar of the Western Front's headquarters,
>   Regimental Commissar Anshakov
> The Chief of the Operations Department, Lieutenant General Malandin

Source: "Operativnaia svodka shtaba Zapadnogo fronta No. 102 k 20 chasam 16 avgusta 1941 g. o boevykh deistviiakh voisk fronta" [Operational summary no. 102 of the headquarters of the Western Front at 2000 hours on 16 August 1941 about the combat operations of the *front's* forces], SBDVOV, issue 41, 25-27.

15. Combat Order of the Commander of the Forces of the Western Front of 16 August 1941 to the Commander of the Forces of 30th Army about Corrections in the Attack Plan of the Army's Forces

To the Commander of 30th Army
1: 100,000 map
16 August 1941

I approve your basic decision with the following corrections.

1. Have the direction for developing 251st RD's success [changed] toward Zviagino.

2. Do not withdraw the tanks into reserve but leave them in the divisions, while planning for 244th RD to reach the Simonovo region by the morning of 18 August. Keep this division, as a reserve, echeloned behind 251st RD's right wing.

3. 161st and 251st RDs and 107th TD, having seizing the crossings over the Vop'River', should reach the Nekliudovo and Selo station line by day's end on 17 August, with the mission – to push through 45th CD and 107th TD along that axis on the morning of 18 August for operations in accordance with the assigned mission.

4. Begin the artillery preparation at 0900 hours on 17 August.

> The Commander of the Western Front's Forces,
>   Marshal of the Soviet Union Timoshenko
> The Member of the Military Council of the Western Front, [signed]

Source: "Boevoe rasporiazhenie komanduiushchego voiskami Zapadnogo fronta ot 16 avgusta 1941 g. komanduiushchemu voiskami 30-i Armii o vnesenii popravok v reshenic na nastuplenie voisk armii" [Combat order of the commander of the forces of the Western Front of 16 August 1941 to the commander of the forces of 30th Army about corrections in the attack plan of the army's forces], SBDVOV, issue 41, 32.

16. Operational Summary No. 145 of the Headquarters of 19th Army at 0500 hours on 17 August 1941 about the Occupation of Jumping-off Positions and Preparations for the Offensive

Operational Summary No. 145, CP, Commander, 19th Army,
the woods 1 kilometer east of Vasilisino,
0500 hours on 17 August 1941
1: 50,000 and 100,000 scale maps

1. During the night of 16-17 August 1941, the army's forces occupied jumping-off positions, while preparing to fulfill the army commander's Order No. 028.

2. 166th RD continued to dig into its previously occupied positions and was prepared to fulfill its assigned missions by 2000 hours. The enemy displayed no activity. The divisions' losses for 15 August 1941: enlisted dead – 15 and enlisted wounded – 33. Horses killed – 2. Trophies (during the seizure of the grove west of Bitiagovo): shells 37mm – 72, mines 37mm – 30, mines 81mm – 18, shells 75mm – 6, hand grenades – 15, rifle ammunition – 2,000 rounds, and greatcoats – 6.

CP – the grove 1.5 kilometers northeast of Shushlovo.

3. 91st RD prepared to fulfill its assigned missions. 613th and 561st RRs are occupying their previous combat formation. 503rd RR arrived in the Dura region and entered the southern edge of the grove at Dura at 2400 hours on 16 August 1941.

CP – the brush 500 meters northeast of Bukhvalova.

4. 50th RD began arriving in its jumping-off positions for the offensive. The division's units were still moving at 2400 hours.

CP – the woods 1 kilometer northeast of Bobrovitsa.

5. 89th RD began its regrouping after nightfall, while giving up the sector on the right to 49th RR and on the left to 288th RR. Losses for 16 August 1941: enlisted men killed – 2 and wounded – 19.

CP – the ravine 500 meters west of Novoselki.

6. 64th RD is moving into jumping-off positions for the offensive.

7. 101st TD is reaching positions designated by its order.

8. Communications are working with interruptions because of breaks in the wire by passing forces.

9. The condition of the roads is satisfactory.

The Chief of Staff of 19th Army, [Colonel Malyshkin]
The Military Commissar of 19th Army's headquarters,
    Brigade Commissar Kazbintsev
The Chief of the Operations Department, Colonel Maslov

Source: "Operativnaia svodka shtaba 19-i Armii No. 145 k 5 chasam 17 avgusta 1941 g. o zaniatii voiskami iskhodnogo polozheniia i podgotovke k nastupleniiu" [Operational summary no. 145 of the headquarters of 19th Army at 0500 hours on 17 August 1941 about the occupation of jumping-off positions and preparations for the offensive] *SBDVOV*, issue 41, 163.

17. Combat Order of the Headquarters of 19th Army of 17 August 1941 to the Commanders of 91st and 50th Rifle Divisions about the Commitment of the Divisions' Second Echelons into Combat

To the Commanders of 91st and 50th RDs

Large-scale tactical success has been noted along the Kriukova axis. Makov'e, where an enemy antiaircraft battery has been destroyed, has been captured by 50th RD's units.

The commander of 19th Army orders:

1) 91st RD will commit its second echelon from behind its left wing and develop success toward Pochepova.

2) 50th RD will commit its second echelon toward Kriukova and Makov'e.

The Deputy Chief of Staff of 19th Army, Colonel Maslov

Source: "Boevoe rasporiazhenie shtaba 19-i Armii ot 17 avgusta 1941 g. komandiram 91-i i 50- i Strelkovykh Divizii o vvode v boi vtorykh eshelonov divizii" [Combat order of the headquarters of 19th Army of 17 August 1941 to the commanders of 91st and 50th Rifle Divisions about the commitment of the divisions' second echelons into combat], *SBDVOV*, issue 41, 164.

18. Operational Summary No. 103 of the Headquarters of the Western Front at 0800 hours on 17 August 1941 about the Occupation of Jumping-off Positions for the Offensive by the *Front's* Forces

Operational Summary No. 103 at 0800 hours on 17 August 1941,
Headquarters, Western Front
1:500,000 and 100,000 scale maps

First. The situation is unchanged on the *front's* right wing. There is occasional rifle-machine gun, artillery firing, and raids by reconnaissance scouts along the front. In the center, the forces are entering their jumping-off positions by the morning of 17 August, while carrying out a regrouping.

The offensive of the forces on the left wing is developing slowly, while encountering stubborn enemy resistance.

Second. 22nd Army. The positions of the army's units are unchanged … ..

Third. 29th Army. The army's units, while continuing to defend their previous positions, are conducting preparations for an attack … ..

Fourth. 30th Army occupied jumping-off positions for the attack. News has not arrived about 45th CD.

Fifth. 19th Army occupied jumping-off positions for the attack in accordance with Order No. 01/op on the night of 17 August.

166th RD is on the Shupenki, Shestaki 2, Zaria, Priglovo, Zanino 1, and Zaovrazh'e front and is ready to fulfill its mission – with an attack with its left wing.

91st RD is on the Gorbatovskaia and Shuklino front.

50th RD is on the (incl.) Shuklino and Dubrovka front.

89th RD is on the (incl.) Dubrovka and Novyi Riadyni front.

64th RD is on the (incl.) Novyi Riadyni front.

101st TD is on the Kurganovo and Manchina front.

Losses in the army's units for 16 August: killed – 17 men and wounded – 52 men.

Sixth. 16th Army. The enemy is not active on the army's front. The units, having finished their regrouping, are digging in along the eastern bank of the Vop' River [as follows].

38th RD – in the sector from Lake Ozerishche to (incl.) Marker 169.9.

108th RD – in the sector from Marker 169.9 to Buianovo.

Headquarters of the army – the woods 1 kilometer northeast of Khotenova.

Seventh. 20th Army is fighting in the positions it occupies, while repelling enemy counterattacks from the Chuvakhi region.

On the night of 16-17 August, [the following] were withdrawn from the western bank of the Dnepr River: guns – 5, trucks – 13, boxes of explosives – 2, field kitchens – 2, transports [carts] – 1, and 2 carts with equipment.

Eighth. The VVS of the *front* continued to cooperate with the army's units and conducted reconnaissance in the second half of the day on 16 August. They conducted 108 aircraft sorties, including fighter – 78, bomber – 31, and assault – 9.

Bombs dropped include: 44 FAB-100, 104 FAB-50, 2 ZAB-50, 25 AO-25, 64 AO-15, 440 ZAB-1, and 94 KS ampoules, and 25800 ShKAS and 5,030 ShVAK were pushed out.

43rd MAD bombed enemy troop concentrations in the Vasil'evo, Mit'kovo, and Pnevo regions and enemy troop columns along the Pochinok-El'nia road, protected the marches of our motor-mechanized columns in the Pan'tiukhi concentration area, and conducted reconnaissance for 20th Army. It conducted 31 aircraft sorties.

47th MAD destroyed enemy motor-mechanized units and artillery in the Dukhovshchina region and along the road to Iartsevo and conducted reconnaissance in the Dukhovshchina and Smolensk region. It conducted 38 aircraft sorties.

46th MAD carried out repeated raids against enemy infantry and artillery in the Shelepy and Shanino region. It conducted 4 aircraft sorties.

31st MAD attacked enemy forces in the Tserkovishche region, bombed fuel warehouses in Danchenko, and conducted reconnaissance in 22nd Army's sector. It conducted 35 aircraft sorties.

Enemy losses: shot down 1 KhE-111 and 1 Iu-88.

Our losses: The enemy shot down 1 I-16 aircraft with antiaircraft fire (it landed on our territory). One LAGG-3 aircraft and 4 IL-2 aircraft did not return to their airfields, of which 3 were forced to land in their own territory, but the degree of damage is being clarified, and 1 IL-2 has not been found.

The Chief of Staff of the Western Front, Lieutenant General Sokolovsky
The Military Commissar of the Western Front's headquarters,
    Regimental Commissar Anshakov
The Chief of the Operations Department, Lieutenant General Malandin

Source: "Operativnaia svodka shtaba Zapadnogo fronta No. 103 k 8 chasam 17 avgusta 1941 g. o zaniatii voiskami fronta iskhodnogo polozheniia dlia nastupleniia" [Operational summary no. 103 of the headquarters of the Western Front at 0800 hours on 17 August 1941 about the occupation of jumping-off positions for the offensive by the *front's* forces], *SBDVOV*, issue 41, 33-34.

19. Combat Report by the Headquarters of the Western Front of 17 August 1941 to the Chief of the General Staff about the Beginning of the Offensive Operation

Moscow

To the Chief of the General Staff, Marshal Shaposhnikov

1:100,000 scale map

After 1030 hours on 17 August 1941

I am reporting fulfillment of Western Front's Order No. 01/op.

1) The units occupied their jumping-off positions in timely fashion.

2) The artillery preparation began at 0900 hours on 17 August.

3) The attack was at 1000 hours, and the attack was preceded by an air strike by all of the forces of the *front's* VVS except 31st FAD.

4) 246th RD was dispatched by 1000 hours on 17 August on 11 trains, 5 were unloading and 3 are loading.

5) 244th RD is on the march. 907th RR was dispatched by vehicles at 1900 hours on 16 August, the horse-drawn echelon began moving at 0130 hours on 17 August, and the 1st vehicular echelon of the main force was dispatched at 0800 hours, with an estimate that 244th RD will concentrate in the Simonovo region by the morning of 18 August. In addition to the cavalry, they will follow by foot march.

6) The tank battalion from Kubinka was unloading at Vadino at 0500 hours on 17 August.

Malandin, Anshakov

Source: "Boevoe donesenie shtaba Zapadnogo fronta ot 17 avgusta 1941 g. nachal'niku General'nogo Shtaba o nachale nastupatel'noi operatsii" [Combat report of the headquarters of the Western Front of 17 August 1941 to the Chief of the General Staff about the beginning of the offensive operation], *SBDVOV*, issue 41, 35.

20. Operational Summary No. 0146 of the Headquarters of 19th Army at 1700 hours on 17 August 1941 about the Combat Operations of the Army's Forces

Operational Summary No. 0146, CP, Commander, 19th Army,

the woods 1 kilometer east of Vasilisino,

1700 hours on 17 August 1941

1; 50,000 and 100,000 scale maps

1. The army's forces launched an attack from 1000-1030 hours on 17 August 1941 after an hour-long preparation and air strikes against the forward edge of the enemy's defense and are conducting sustained fighting with the defending enemy along the Pogorel'tsy, Shestaki 2, Zaria, Priglovo, Zanino 1, Lopatchinki, Gorbatovskaia, Shuklino, Dubrovka, Kuz'mino, Riadyni, Prisel'e, and Skachikhino line, while encountering strong enemy fire and being subjected to intense machine gun and mortar fire.

2. 166th RD, while protecting the army's right flank with part of its forces, attacked at 1000 hours and was fighting for the Pogorel'tsy, Shestaki 2, Priglovo, Zanino 1, and Lopatchinki line at 1300 hours.

Losses for the night: killed – 12 and wounded – 44 men.

3. 91st RD attacked at 1000 hours and reached the grove 300 meters south of Zubova, the eastern edge of the grove at Dura, the western edge of the long grove east of Tserkov', and Shuklino line by 1400 hours.

Headquarters of the division – the brush 500 meters northeast of Bukhvalova.

4. 50th RD, having begun its attack at 1000 hours, occupied Turova, the northern edge of the grove south of Turova, the western edge of the grove south of Turova, Marker 200.2, and the western edge of the grove 500 meters to the west by 1200 hours.

Headquarters of the division – the woods 1 kilometer northeast of Bobrovtsy.

5. 89th RD began its attack at 1020 hours and was fighting along the Marker 212.4 and Novyi Riadyni line by 1200 hours.

6. 64th RD began its attack at 1030 hours and occupied Tserkov', Staryi Riadyni, and Marker 208.4 by 1200 hours.

7. 101st TD began its attack at 1000 hours, and 101st MRR occupied Prisel'e and the northwestern slopes of Marker 216.5, 18th MRR was fighting for Hill 216.4 and Skachikhino, and 202nd TR concentrated in the woods 1 kilometer east of Padylishche by 1200 hours.

CP – the woods north of Korovenka.

7. The condition of the roads in satisfactory, and communications are working in good order.

The Chief of Staff of 19th Army, [Colonel Malyshkin]
The Military Commissar of 19th Army's headquarters,
    Brigade Commissar Kazbintsev
The Chief of the Operations Department, Colonel Maslov

Source: "Operativnaia svodka shtaba 19-i Armii No. 0146 k 17 chasam 17 avgusta 1941 g. o boevykh deistviiakh voisk armii" [Operational summary no. 0146 of the headquarters of 19th Army at 1700 hours on 17 August 1941 about the combat operations of the army's forces], *SBDVOV*, issue 41, 164-165.

21. Combat Order of the Commander of the Forces of the Western Front of 17 August 1941 to the Commander of the Forces of 20th Army about Corrections in the Attack Plan of the Army's Forces

To Comrade Lukin
1:100,000 scale map
1800 hours on 17 August 1941

In general, I agree with your decision.

I am introducing the following corrections:

1) Commit 161st RD in the sector from Sopshino to the railroad bridge across the Dnepr River and Dobromino.

2) Commit 129th RD in the (incl.) Dobromino and (incl.) Klokova sector, having left one regiment at the junction [boundary] with 24th Reserve Army to protect the Novyi Iakovlevichi and Glinka axis.

3) Have 153rd, 229th, and 33rd RDs conduct an attack west of the Dnepr River. Begin the attack when 161st and 129th RDs reach the El'nia-Smolensk railroad.

The Commander of the Forces of the Western Front,
Marshal of the Soviet Union Timoshenko
The Member of the Military Council of the Western Front, [signed]

Source: "Boevoe rasporiazhenie komanduiushchego voiskami Zapadnogo fronta ot 17 avgusta 1941 g. komanduiushchemu voiskami 20-i Armii o vnesenii popravok v reshenie na nastuplenie voisk armii" [Combat order of the commander of the forces of the Western Front of 17 August 1941 to the commander of the forces of 20th Army about corrections in the attack plan of the army's forces], *SBDVOV*, issue 41, 36.

22. Operational Summary No. 104 of the Headquarters of the Western Front at 2000 hours on 17 August 1941 about the Transition of the *Front's* Forces to the Offensive and the Results of the Fighting

Operational Summary No. 104 at 2000 hours on 17 August 1941,
Headquarters, Western Front
1:500,000 and 100,000 scale maps

First. The situation on the *front's* right wing is unchanged. In the *front's* center and on the left wing, the offensive we have begun is developing slowly, while encountering stubborn enemy resistance.

Second. 22nd Army. The positions of the units are unchanged. There is occasional artillery and mortar fire on the front. The forces are continuing to fortify their previous positions and conduct reconnaissance.

Headquarters of 22nd Army – Nazimovo Station.

Third. 29th Army. The situation on the front is unchanged. The units are preparing to fulfill Order No. 01/op. The enemy opposite the army's front is continuing defensive work, while periodically conducting fire raids of the dispositions of the army's forces.

The Cavalry Group (50th and 53rd CDs), having advanced southeastward from the Lake Plovnoe and Emlen' region on the night of 16 August and having dislodged small enemy mounted patrols in the Borki, Nizhi, and Karakovo sector along the Mezha River, reached Kotovo, Filino, Budnitsa, and Frolovo with forward detachments on 16 August.

Frolovo was occupied by up to two squadrons of enemy cavalry. News has not been received about the cavalry group's subsequent operations.

Headquarters of 29th Army – Bentsy.

Fourth. 30th Army, while continuing to defend on its right wing, attacked with the forces of 4 divisions in the Staroe Morokhovo, Novoe Morokhovo, and Gordeenki sector in its center and on its left wing, after an hour-long artillery preparation.

250th RD and the right-flank regiment of 242nd RD are defending along the previous Los'mino, Sel'tso, Chalishevo, and (incl.) Staroe Morokhovo line as of 1700 hours.

242nd RD attacked in the Staroe Morokhovo and Erkhovo sector with two regiments, advanced 150-200 meters, and was halted in front of the barbed wire by strong enemy fire and could advance no further.

251st RD attacked in the Pochinoi 2 and Guliaevo sector and is fighting to capture Gordeenki from the north with its left wing.

162nd RD attacked in the Mikhailovshchina and Beskhvostovo sector, advanced 400 meters, and encountered organized enemy fire and could advance no further.

107th TD was counterattacked by an enemy force of up to a battalion from the grove west of Karpovo at 1030 hours. The enemy counterattack was repulsed. The enemy left 200 bodies on the battlefield. The division is fighting along the Il'ino, Solov'evo, Zhukova, Nazemenki, (incl.) Sekachi, and Torchilovo line [subsequent reports indicated Il'ino and Solov'evo were erroneous place names].

Fifth. 19th Army. The army's units launched an offensive between 1000 and 1030 hours after an artillery preparation and air strikes against the enemy's forward edge.

The army appeared to have achieved success in its center and on its left wing by 1400 hours. The enemy in these sectors of the front withdrew westward in small groups, leaving personal weapons and other equipment on the battlefield.

166th RD, while protecting the Shupeki, Zanino 1, and Kaniutino front, attacked in the (incl.) Kaniutino and Zaovrazh'e sector on its left wing with one regiment. It had no success.

91st RD attacked the enemy on the Gorbatovskaia and Staroe front at 1000 hours. It occupied the eastern outskirts of Zadnia with its left wing by 1400 hours and is fighting in its previous positions on the remainder of its front.

50th RD attacked the enemy along the Gurova and Dubrovka front at 1000 hours. It advanced 1.5 to 2 kilometers on its right wing by 1400 hours and occupied Kriukova and Staroe. It captured the eastern outskirts of Makov'e with its forward units. Along the remaining sector of its front, it is fighting for possession of the eastern edge of the grove southeast of Kriukova.

89th RD attacked the enemy along the (incl.) Dubrovka and Novyi Riadyni front at 1020 hours. It had no success in advancing and is fighting in its previous positions.

64th RD attacked the enemy in the (incl.) Riadyni and Borodulino sector and reached the sector from the church in Staryi Riadyni to the heights at Marker 203.4 by 1200 hours. The attack is continuing.

101st TD attacked the enemy in the Kurganovo and Chizhiki sector at 1000 hours and captured Prisel'e, the north-western slope of Hill 216.4, and Skachikhino at 1200 hours. The division's attack is continuing. The enemy is withdrawing in small groups toward Miachenki.

Sixth. 16th Army. There have been no changes in the positions of the units of the army.

The enemy is conducting occasional artillery fire on the army's front.

Seventh. 20th Army. The army continued its offensive toward Pridneprovskaia Station and Dobromino Station on the morning of 17 August, while overcoming stubborn enemy resistance.

144th RD, having relieved 153rd RD's units in the sector from the bend in the Dnepr River east of Pnevo to the woods 1 kilometer northwest of Marker 195.6, occupied the (incl.) Solov'evo and (incl.) Marker 195.6 linc. Its forward units fortified their previous positions along the western bank of the Dnepr River.

153rd RD, having given up its defensive sector [see above], occupied the Marker 195.6 and (incl.) Baidik line. Its forward units fortified their previous positions along the western bank of the Dnepr River.

The enemy is continuing defensive work on the division's front.

73rd RD conducted reinforced reconnaissance toward Titkovo and Zlydnia. Its forward detachment engaged in fierce fighting for possession of Marker 169.7 with enemy infantry in foxholes, reinforced by two mortar batteries, 4 heavy caliber machine guns, and several tanks dug into the ground on the eastern outskirts of Sopshino after first light on 17 August.

The division captured Zlydnia at 1345 hours.

161st RD continued its attack on the morning of 17 August and, while overcoming stubborn enemy resistance, captured [the following] at 1300 hours: 603rd RR – the line of the stream west of Suborovka to Marker 249.9; 242nd RR – the cemetery west of Chuvakhi; and 477th RR – the northern slope of marker 228.0 and enemy foxholes on the northwestern outskirts of Klemiatino.

129th RD's 457th RR, after repelling a night counterattack by an enemy company, supported by mortar and machine gun fire and two tanks from the direction of Marker 228.0, continued its attack toward this hill at 0500 hours.

343rd and 348th RRs attacked toward Novyi Iakovlevichi while encountering stubborn enemy resistance.

229th RD is in its previous positions preparing for an attack in the Kolodezi region.

Overnight on 17 August [the following] were withdrawn from the western bank of the Dnepr River: trucks – 6, guns – 4, rifles – 48, tractors – 1, carts – 7, and field kitchens – 1.

Eighth. The VVS of the *front* cooperated with the armies' units and conducted reconnaissance. It brought pressure to bear on enemy reserves approaching the front and protected auto-transport of cargo along the Rzhev and Belyi axes.

It carried out a total of 151 aircraft sorties overnight and during the first half of the day on 17 August, including 69 fighter, 73 bomber, and 9 assault.

Bombs dropped included: 262 FAB-100, 74 FAB-82, 92 FAB-70, 70 FAB-50, 10 ZAB-50, 34 FAB-32, 213 AO-25, 223 AO-15, 204 AO-10, 48 AO-8, 2 SAB-3, 54 ZAB-3, 556 AO-2.5, and 99 KZ ampoules, it launched 66 RS, 2,700 ShBAK, and 8,500 ShKAS, and dropped 553,000 leaflets.

23rd AD and 1st and 3rd Heavy Aviation Regiments bombed enemy force concentrations and airfields in the Lake Shchuch'e and Dukhovshchina regions, transporters in Usviat'e and El'nia, the rail centers at Vitebsk and Orsha, the airfield at Smolensk, and the enemy supply station at Gorodok on the night of 17 August. They carried out a total of 23 aircraft sorties.

43rd MAD operated with 19th Army's forces, conducted reconnaissance, and protected our units in the Ust'e and Prisel'e region and carried out 31 aircraft sorties.

46th MAD operated with 30th Army's units. It carried out 33 aircraft sorties.

47th MAD cooperated with 19th and 30th Armies' units, destroyed enemy reserves approaching the front, and protected auto-transport along the Rzhev and Belyi march-routes. It carried out 43 aircraft sorties.

31st MAD operated with 22nd Army's units. It carried out 16 aircraft sorties.

38th RAS conducted reconnaissance along the Iartsevo, Arkhipovka, and Ploskoe and Zadnia, Smolensk, Gusino Station, Pochinok, and El'nia axes. It carried out 5 aircraft sorties.

There is no news about enemy losses.

Our losses: one SB aircraft shot down.

The Chief of Staff of the Western Front, Lieutenant General Sokolovsky
The Military Commissar of the Western Front's headquarters,
    Regimental Commissar Anshakov
The Deputy Chief of the Operations Department,
    Major General Rubtsov

Source: "Operativnaia svodka shtaba Zapadnogo fronta No. 104 k 2000 chasam 17 avgusta 1941 g. o perekhod voisk fronta v nastuplenie i rezul'tatakh boia" [Operational summary no. 104 of the headquarters of the Western Front at 2000 hours on 17 August 1941 about the transition of the *front's* forces to the offensive and the results of the fighting], *SBDVOV*, issue 41, 36-39.

23. Combat Order No. 029 of the Commander of the Forces of 19th Army of 18 August 1941 on a Continuation of the Offensive with the Aim of Exploiting 50th Rifle Division's Success

Combat Order No. 029, CP, commander, 19th Army,
The woods 1 kilometer east of Vasilisino,
0200 hours on 18 August 1941
1: 50,000 scale map

1. During the course of 17 August 1941, the army's forces penetrated the enemy's defenses in the Potelitsa and Miaksheva sector by successful operations. Units of the enemy's 900th Armored [Motorized] Brigade, 5th ID, and 312th and 336th IR, while suffering heavy losses, withdrew in small groups toward the west and northwest. The appearance of enemy reserves of up to one infantry division with 15-20 tanks from Dukhovshchina is possible.

2. Neighbors are continuing to fulfill their previous missions. The boundary with them is as before.

3. 19th Army will develop the success achieved in 50th RD's sector during the night, while striking a blow with 91st RD's left wing and 50th RD's right wing and continue the offensive on the morning of 18 August 1941, with the mission to encircle and destroy the enemy's Dukhovshchina grouping in cooperation with 30th Army. Reach the Tsarevich River line by day's end on 18 August 1941, and subsequently attack toward Dukhovshchina.

4. 166th RD will fulfill the mission assigned by Order No. 028. The boundary on the left is as before.

5. 91st RD, with its previous reinforcing units, will develop success on its left wing during the night and fulfill the mission assigned by Order No. 028 by day's end on 18 August 1941. Reach the Myshkovo and Sel'tso line with your forward units. The boundary on the left is as before.

6. 50th RD, with its previous reinforcing units, will develop success toward Makov'e and capture the Tsesnevo and Sushchevo line by day's end on 18 August 1941.

I am subordinating 159th RR and 202nd TR to you, which you will use for the attack toward Makov'e and Sushchevo, with the mission to capture the crossings at

Sushchevo and Siniakovo. Destroy and cut off the enemy's withdrawal. The boundary is as before.

7. 89th RD will develop an offensive from Stepankina toward Bolotina and fulfill the mission assigned by Order No. 028 by day's end on 18 August 1941. The boundary is as before.

8. 64th RD will capture Sel'kovo and Leskovki on the night of 17-18 August and fulfill the mission assigned by Order No. 028 by day's end on 18 August 1941.

9. 101st TD (without 202nd TR) will fulfill the mission assigned by combat Order No. 028 on 18 August 1941, while protecting the army's left flank.

10. Artillery. Missions:

a) Assist in the development of success in 91st, 50th, and 89th RD's sectors. Support 89th RD's attack with one battalion from 596th GAR;

b) Protect 202nd TR's and 159th RR's commitment into the penetration and operations in the depths; and

c) Prevent enemy counterattacks against the penetrating units' flanks and the approach of reserves from the depths.

11. The VVS of 19th Army:

a) In cooperation with 91st and 50th RDs ' units, suppress enemy personnel in the [following] regions: Balashova, Pochetsova, Hill 217.0 (2 kilometers east of Balashova), Bolotino, Nefedovshchina, and Batyeva;.

b) Assist 202nd TR's commitment into the penetration in the Kriukovo and Stepankina sector and into the depths up to the line of the Loinia River and, subsequently, up to the Tsarevich River toward Sushchevo;

c) Prevent the approach of enemy reserves from the lines of the Loinia and Tsarevich Rivers; and

d) Protect the army's groupings in the Potelitsa, Balashova, Leskovki, and Vasilisino region.

12. Signals for cooperation on 18 August 1941 will be in accordance with Order No. 028.

13. CP and headquarters of the army are as before.

14. Submit operational and reconnaissance summaries at 0100, 1300, and 2000 hours.

The Commander of 19th Army, Lieutenant General Konev
The Member of the Military Council of 19th Army,
    Division Commissar Sheklanov
The Chief of Staff of 19th Army, [Colonel Malyshkin]

Source: "Boevoi prikaz komanduiushchego voiskami 19-i Armii No. 029 ot 18 avgusta 1941 g. na prodolzhenii nastupleniia s tsel'iu razvitiia uspekha 50-i Strelkovoi Divizii" [Combat order no. 029 of the commander of the forces of 19th Army of 18 August 1941 on a continuation of the offensive with the aim of exploiting 50th Rifle Division's Success], *SBDVOV*, issue 41, 165-166.

24. Combat Order No. 56 of the Commander of the Forces of 20th Army about Preparations of the Army's Forces for an Offensive

Combat Order No. 56, Headquarters, 20th Army,

0250 hours on 18 August 1941
1:50,000 scale map

1. The enemy is defending the Suborovka, Hill 249.9, Hill 221.3, Hill 228.0, Kolzaki, and Novyi Iakovlevskii line with two regiments.

2. 20th Army, while preparing an offensive toward the west, will conduct an operation with part of its forces to protect its left flank and reach the railroad at Pridneprovskaia Station and Glinka Station.

3. 144th RD, while continuing to fortify its defensive positions on the eastern bank of the Dnepr River, will hold onto the bridgehead you occupy on the western bank of the Dnepr River and prepare to seize Mit'kovo.

The boundary on the left: (incl.) Klimovo, (incl.) Zabor'e, Liakhovo, and (incl.) Mashkino (southern).

CP – Kushkovo.

4. 153rd RD, while continuing to fortify its defensive positions on the eastern bank of the Dnepr River, will hold onto the bridgehead its occupies on the western bank of the Dnepr River at all cost and prepare an attack toward Mashkino.

The boundary on the left: Iaroshenki, (incl.) the barn (south of Zabor'e), Ratchino, the grove 2 kilometers west of Ratchino, and (incl.) Fedurno.

CP – the grove 1 kilometer southwest of Zabor'e.

5. 229th RD will relieve 153rd and 73rd RDs' units on the night of 18 August, defend positions along the Dnepr River's eastern bank, and, while holding onto the bridgehead you occupy on the western bank, prepare for an attack toward Morevo State Farm.

The boundary on the left: Kucherovo, the farm (4 kilometers northwest of Kolodezi), and Morevo State Farm.

CP – the woods on the western bank of the Mertvaia River.

6. 73rd RD, while continuing its attack, will reach the Dnepr River in the sector from the farm (3 kilometers south of Zabor'e) to the mouth of the Nerupeno River and Sopshino by day's end on 18 August and seize the grove northeast of Kolpino and Malinovka with forward detachments. Hold onto Bereznia with one regiment, while protecting the division's rear and 161st RD's flank.

7. 161st RD, with 302nd HAR, 467th CAR, and three batteries of 872nd ATR, having left one battalion against Suborovka, will attack from the Chuvakhi and Hill 224.8 line toward Samodurovka, Orly Farm, Vasilevo, and Dobromino with its remaining forces at 1000 hours on 19 August and capture Dobromino and Dobromino Station by day's end.

Group DD [long-range artillery group] – 126th CAR and 592nd GAR. Group commander – the commander of 126th CAR.

The mission of the group – strike enemy batteries in the Suborovka region, the woods east of Dobromino and Vasilevo. and Alekseevo and the woods to the southwest and southeast.

8. 129th RD, while digging on with one regiment, with an artillery battalion, in the sector from the mouth of the Trubel'nia River to Nov. Brykina State Farm on the Ustrom River and while attacking Iakovlevo with four battalions and the remaining

artillery, will attack from Klemiatino toward Obzhorovka and Alekseevo at 1000 hours on 19 August and capture Vasilevo by day's end.

One RR, without one battalion but with two batteries of 872nd ATR, will withdraw to the Krutenki, Goravtsy, and Belovost' region in reserve, to be employed only on my orders.

9. 152nd RD will fulfill the mission assigned to it.

10. CP is in its previous location

Lukin, Semenovsky, and Korneev

Source: "Boevoi prikaz komanduiushchego voiskami 20-i Armii No. 56 ot 18 avgusta 1941 o podgotovke voisk armii k nastupleniiu " [Combat order no. 56 of the commander of the forces of 20th Army about preparations of the army's forces for an offensive], *SBDVOV*, issue 41, 213-214.

25. Operational Summary No. 105 of the Headquarters of the Western Front at 0800 hours on 18 August 1941 about the Combat Operations of the *Front's* Forces

Operational Summary No. 105 at 0800 hours on 18 August 1941,

Headquarters, Western Front

1:500,000 and 100,000 scale maps

First. The situation on the *front's* right wing is unchanged. In the center of the *front,* the offensive is developing slowly while encountering stubborn enemy resistance. On the left wing, the forces are fighting in the positions they have reached.

Second. 22nd Army. The positions of the army's units are unchanged.

The army's units, while digging into their defensive positions, are repelling local enemy attacks and conducting reconnaissance.

The enemy conducted heavy mortar and artillery fire against the Velikie Luki region.

The army's losses for 16 August: killed – 33, wounded – 70 men.

Headquarters of 22nd Army – Nazimovo Station.

Third. 29th Army. The army's units went over to a concentric offensive in the general direction of Il'ino at 2130 hours on 17 August. The units are moving slowly forward, while meeting strong enemy machine gun, mortar, and artillery fire and the stubborn resistance of his defense.

252nd RD, having forced the Western Dvina River at Klinok, is developing an attack toward Marker 169.8 with its right wing and was fighting 2 kilometers southwest of Agryzkovo with its left wing at 0300 hours on 18 August.

243rd RD, at the same time, was fighting in positions from 1 kilometer northeast of Andreevskaia to Malyi Borok.

1st MRR was fighting at crossings over the Mezha River at Kanat and Krivaia Luka.

29th CR is protecting the army's left flank in the Lake Plovnoe and Emlen' region.

Armored Train No. 53 is protecting the Zharkovskii Station and Borki axis.

246th RD – One rifle regiment arrived on 17 August, which is concentrating in the Turlachikha, Pichevakha, and Mikhalevo region (as the army commander's reserve).

The division's remaining trains of the division are arriving.

Headquarters of 29th Army – Bentsy.

Fourth. 30th Army continued to fight in its previous positions during the second half of the day on 17 August.

The army's units conducted preparations all night long for the offensive on the morning of 18 August.

The army will continue its offensive at 0900 hours on 18 August.

45th CD is concentrating in the Kvoktushino, Pod'ezzhalovo, and Lukashevo region.

Losses for 17 August: 185 men killed or wounded.

Fifth. 19th Army continued to conduct an offensive along its entire front on the second half of the day.

50th RD's forward units captured Makov'e, and one rifle company reached the Loinia River at Kazakova by 2100 hours on 17 August.

At the same time, 89th RD's units occupied Novaia Korov'ia and Stepankina.

64th RD captured Hill 203.4.

50th RD, after an enemy counterattack, withdrew to the eastern outskirts of Kriukovo and the woods to the south by 2300 hours. The positions of 50th RD's units are being verified.

The army's units in remaining sectors of the front occupy their previous positions at 0500 hours on 18 August.

The army will continue its offensive since 0700 hours on 18 August while developing success in 50th RD's.

In the fighting in the Zadnia, Makov'e, and Kriukova region on 17 August, according to preliminary count [the following] were seized: 12 guns of various calibers, 5 sub-machine guns, 10 bicycles, 1 radio station, and 1 prisoner. In addition, one enemy battery and one tank were destroyed in Makov'e.

The losses of the army for 17 August: 37 killed and 43 wounded.

Sixth. 16th Army. There have been no changes in the positions of the army's units. The enemy is displaying no activity.

Seventh. 20th Army was fighting along previous lines and conducting a partial regrouping at day's end on 17 August and on the morning of 18 August.

73rd RD captured Novaia Malinovka with one rifle regiment and was fighting along the Novaia Malinovka, Zlydnia, the stream southeast of Zlydnia, Marker 169.7, and the western edge of the woods at Erdetsy line by 1600 hours on 17 August. Repeated attacks by the division's units toward Marker 169.7 were repelled by strong enemy mortar and machine gun fire, with the support of tanks.

161st RD continued stubborn fighting to capture the centers of resistance at Suborovka, Chuvakhi, and Hill 228.0.

Up to two enemy battalions in foxholes, two-three mortar batteries, and two tanks dug into the ground are opposite the division's front.

Losses: 29 men killed and 93 wounded, including the commander of 477th RR, Major Minshikov.

129th RD – 453rd RR, under the pressure of strong mortar and machine gun fire from Marker 228.0 and Gorodok, abandoned the western outskirts of Klemiatino.

343rd and 438th RRs' attacks toward Novyi Iakovlevichi failed, and the units withdrew to the Ustrom River in the sector from the farm south of Mikhailovka to Brykino after leaving covering forces along the Podenkovo, Ustrom River, and Mar'ino line.

229th RD completed concentrating in the vicinity of Marker 179.1 and the woods to the northwest for the subsequent relief of 153rd and 73rd RDs' units in the sector from Zabor'e to the farm 2 kilometers west of Marker 179.1.

The remaining units were fighting in their previous positions.

On 17 August [the following] were withdrawn to the eastern bank of the Dnepr River: trucks – 2, light vehicles – 1, carts – 1, and field kitchens – 1.

Eighth. The VVS of the *front* continued to cooperate with the army's units, conducted reconnaissance, blocked the approach of enemy reserves, and protected auto-transport on the Rzhev and Belyi march-routes during the second half of the day on 17 August.

They carried out 108 aircraft sorties during the second half of the day, including 34 bomber, 68 fighter, and 8 assault. Overall, they dropped [the following] bombs: 26 FAB-100, 81 FAB-50, 4 AO-25, and 126 AO-8, launched 47 RS, 550 BS, 2,150 ShBAK, and 19,900 ShKAS, and scattered 68,200 leaflets.

43rd MAD bombed enemy troop concentrations and artillery positions in the Losevo, Azerinki, Batyeva, Nefedovshchina, and Gorodno regions, accompanied [escorted] bombers, and protected the railroad center and airfield at Viaz'ma.

47th MAD continued to cooperate with 19th and 30th Armies' forces, operated against automobile columns on the road 15 kilometers northwest of Dukhovshchina, bombed separate groups of tanks and vehicles in the Sushchevo, Medvedevo, and Pliushchevo regions, and protected auto-transport on the Rzhev and Belyi march-routes. It carried out 29 aircraft sorties.

46th MAD continued to cooperate with 30th Army's units, attacked concentrations of infantry, artillery, and tanks in the Shelepy region, and bombed automobile columns on the road in the vicinity of Dukhovshchina. It carried out 41 aircraft sorties.

31st MAD attacked enemy forces on the southern bank of Lake Dvin'e and conducted reconnaissance in the Velikie Luki and Lake Dvin'e regions. It carried out 33 aircraft sorties.

38th RAS continued reconnaissance along the Iartsevo, Arkhipovka, and Bol'shoe Ploskoe and Zadnia, Smolensk, and Gusino Station axes.

Enemy losses in the second half of the day: 1 ME-109 shot down.

Our losses: 1 SB shot down, 1 I-16 was lost in an accident, and 4 LAGG-3 did not return to their airfields.

News has not yet been received about 23rd and 46th MADs' night operations.

The Chief of Staff of the Western Front, Lieutenant General Sokolovsky
The Military Commissar of the Western Front's headquarters,
    Regimental Commissar Anshakov
The Chief of the Operations Department, Lieutenant General Malandin

Source: "Operativnaia svodka shtaba Zapadnogo fronta No. 105 k 8 chasam 18 avgusta 1941 g. o boevykh deistviiakh voisk fronta" [Operational summary no. 105 of the headquarters of the Western Front at 0800 hours on 18 August 1941 about the combat operations of the *front's* forces], *SBDVOV*, issue 41, 40-42.

26. Combat Order of the Commander of the Forces of 19th Army of 18 August 1941 about the Development of Success in 64th Rifle Division's Sector

To the Commanders of 50th and 91st RDs, 89th, 64th, and 166th RD, and 101st TD
0915 hours on 18 August 1941

1. The enemy has begun to withdraw, and many trophies are being seized in 64th RD's sector.
2. The commander of 50th RD will immediately commit 202nd TR toward Makov'e.
3. The commander of 91st RD will decisively assist 50th RD's attack.
4. The commander of 64th RD will decisively attack on his front.

Konev, Sheklanov

Source: "Boevoe rasporiazhenie komanduiushchego voiskami 19-i Armii ot 18 avgusta 1941 g. o razvitii uspekha v polose 64-i Strelkovoi Divizii" [Combat order of the commander of the forces of 19th Army of 18 August 1941 about the development of success in 64th Rifle Division's sector], *SBDVOV*, issue 41, 166.

27. Combat Order of the Headquarters of 30th Army of 18 August 1941 to the Commander of 244th Rifle Division about the Preparation of the Division for an Attack along the Dukhovshchina Axis

To the Commander of 244th RD
Copy: To the Commander of 107th TD
Combat Order No. 017, Headquarters, 30th Army,
the woods 2 kilometers northeast of Podzaitsevo,
1400 hours on 18 August 1941
1;100,000 scale map

1. An appreciation of the enemy and the operations of our forces has been reported [to me] orally.
2. 244th RD, while remaining in its concentration area at Simonovo, Kholopovo, Tarasovo, and Novo-Aleksandrovskoe, will be prepared for operations toward Mikhailovshchina, Fomenki, Nekliudova, and Dukhovshchina.
Relieve 107th TD's 120th MRR along the Zhukovo, Sloboda, Nazemenki, and Karpovo line with one RR and attack with it, while delivering an attack with the right wing toward Bol'shoe Repino, Novoselki, and Petrovo Selo, having simultaneously protected on the left wing with small observation groups.
Complete the relief by 0400 hours on 19 August.
The boundaries for it [244th RD] are: on the right, with 251st RD – (incl.) Krapivnia, (incl.) Beskhvostovo, (incl.) Krechets, and (incl.) Dorofeevo; and
On the left, with 166th RD – (incl.) Shurkino, (incl.) Markovo, and Berdino.

3. The division will conduct reconnaissance at the junction of our army and 166th RD.

>The Chief of Staff of 30th Army, Lieutenant Colonel Baderko
>The Military Commissar of 30th Army's headquarters,
>>Regimental Commissar Sukharev
>The Chief of the Operations Department, Colonel Busarov

Source: "Boevoi rasporiazhenie shtaba 30-i Armii ot 18 avgusta 1941 komandiru 244-i Strelkovoi Divizii o podgotovke divizii k nastupleniiu na Dukhovshchinskom napravlenii" [Combat order of the headquarters of 30th Army of 18 August 1941 to the commander of 244th Rifle Division about the preparation of the division for an attack along the Dukhovshchina axis], *SBDVOV*, issue 41, 283-284.

28. Combat Order of the Chief of Staff of 19th Army of 18 August 1941 about Division Commanders Moving their Command Posts Closer to the Combat Formations of their Attacking Forces

To the Commanders of 91st, 50th, 89th, and 64th RDs and 101st TD
1404 hours on 18 August 1941

The dispositions of your CPs do not provide for reliable command and control of your forces in the conditions of modern battle.

Immediately move them forward, while establishing reliable communications with your units [as follows].

91st RD – the grove at Dura, 50th RD – the grove south of Turova, 89th RD – the Kuz'mino region, 64th RD – Novyi Riadyni, and 101st TD – Prisel'e.

>The Chief of Staff of 19th Army, [Colonel Malyshkin]

Source: "Boevoe rasporiazhenie nachal'nika shtaba 19-i Armii ot 18 avgusta 1941 g. o priblizhenii komandnykh punktov komandirov divizii k boevym poriadkam nastupaiushchikh voisk" [Combat order of the chief of staff of 19th Army of 18 August 1941 about division commanders moving their command posts closer to the combat formations of their attacking forces], *SBDVOV*, issue 41, 167.

29. Combat Order No. 2 of the Headquarters of 20th Army of 18 August to the Commanders of 144th, 153rd, 229th, and 73rd Rifle Divisions about Holding on to the Bridgeheads on the Right Bank of the Dnepr River

To Pronin, Gagen, Kozlov, and Akimov
1530 hours on 18 August 1941

The army commander reminds you once more about the necessity for holding onto the bridgeheads on the western bank of the Dnepr River at all cost and in spite of possible enemy counterattacks.

Korneev

Source: "Boevoe rasporiazhenie shtaba 20-i Armii No. 2 ot 18 avgusta 1941 komandiram 144, 153, 229-i i 73-i Strelkovykh Divizii ob uderzhanie platsdarma na pravom beregu r. Dnepr" [Combat order no. 2 of the headquarters of 20th Army of 18 August to the commanders of 144th, 153rd, 229th, and 73rd Rifle Divisions about holding on to the bridgeheads on the right bank of the Dnepr River], *SBDVOV*, issue 41, 214.

30. Combat Report of the Headquarters of 19th Army of 18 August 1941 to the Chief of Staff of the Western Front about the Course of the Army's Offensive

To the Chief of Staff of the Western Front
Copies: To the Chiefs of Staff of 30th and 16th Armies
Combat Report No. 09, CP, Commander 19th Army,
1640 hours on 18 August 1941
1: 50,000 scale map

    The army's forces are continuing the offensive, while having success in the Potelitsa, Kriukovo, Bulanina, and Leskovki sectors. 64th RD's and 101st TD's forward subunits are approaching the Loinia River in the Gorodno, Miagchenki, and Skachikhino sector at 1300 hours, having before them enemy who are withdrawing behind the Loinia River in small groups. 202nd TR is being committed in the Kriukovo and Korov'ia Novaia sector to develop 50th RD's success. There are losses and trophies, and the offensive is continuing.

        The Chief of Staff of 19th Army, [Colonel Malyshkin]
        The Military Commissar of 19th Army's headquarters,
            Brigade Commissar Kazbintsev
        The Chief of the Operations Department, Colonel Maslov

Source: Boevoe donesenie shtaba 19-i Armii No. 09 ot 18 avgusta 1941 g. nachal'niku shtaba Zapadnogo fronta o khode nastupleniia voisk armii" [Combat report of the headquarters of 19th Army of 18 August 1941 to the chief of staff of the Western Front about the course of the army's offensive], *SBDVOV*, issue 41, 168.

31. Operational Summary No. 64 of the Headquarters of 30th Army of 18 August 1941 about the Operations of the Army's Forces

Operational Summary No. 64, Headquarters, 30th Army,
the woods 2 kilometers northeast of Podzaitsevo
the evening on 18 August 1941
1:100,000 scale map

    1. The enemy, while offering resistance, is periodically launching counterattacks.
    2. The army's units, after an artillery preparation, which began at 0800 hours, and bombing, which began at 0820 hours, went over to the offensive. The offensive has not yet had success.
    250th RD. 926th RR, in accordance with the order, entered its concentration region of Baturino (5886), Pozhimki (5886), and the forest northeast of Pozhimki at 1200 hours on 18 August 1941, from which it will be used for an attack toward

Dolgoe and Koreshelepy (5080), and the remaining units did not conduct combat operations and are occupying their previous sectors.

Headquarters of the division – Lukin near Toropino.

242nd RD. 900th RR occupied Hill 212.2 at 0945 hours on 18 August 1941.

At 1045 hours, the regiment was pushed out of its jumping-off positions by an enemy force of up to a reinforced battalion, supported by artillery and mortar fire.

Headquarters of the division – the grove west of Sukharevo.

162nd RD. 720th RR is fighting for Hill 218.7, and the enemy is offering stubborn resistance from a well-organized defense and system of fire; and 627th RR is fighting for Hill 220.9.

The regiment moved into open gun positions and is continuing direct fire to destroy the enemy firing points. The battle is continuing.

Headquarters of the division – Hill 216.3.

251st RD – the division's units are fighting for Staroe Selo and Gordeenki.

107th TD – the units' positions are unchanged. At 1520 hours on 18 August 1941, two enemy aircraft bombed the dispositions of the division's units southeast of Lukashevo.

Headquarters of the division – the grove west of Barinovo.

45th CD was fully concentrated in jumping-off positions in the Vinokurovo region.

244nd RD. The division's units reached the [following] regions at 0930 hours on 18 August 1941: Turinka (7296), Samonikha (7094), and Tsvetushino [20-25 kilometers south of Belyi]. At 1530 hours an order was given to 244th RD's commander to relieve 107th TD's 120th RR in the Sloboda, Karpova, and Hill 230.3 region with one regiment on the night of 19 August 1941 and for the division to be ready to develop army's offensive along the main attack axis.

3. Losses – 327 men killed and wounded.

4. Trophies – 5 enemy prisoners seized. The enemy lost a large number of killed and wounded.

5. It rained in the sector of the army at 1540 hours. Movement along the roads became difficult, and telephone communications with the division worked with interruptions.

> The Chief of Staff of 30th Army, Baderko
> The Military Commissar, Sukharev

Source: "Operativnaia svodka shtaba 30-i Armii No. 64 ot 18 avgusta 1941 g. o boevykh deistviiakh voisk armii" [Operational summary no. 64 of the headquarters of 30th Army of 18 August 1941 about the operations of the army's forces], *SBDVOV*, issue 41, 284-285.

32. Operational Summary No. 106 of the Headquarters of the Western Front at 2000 hours on 18 August 1941 about the Combat Operations of the *Front's* Forces

Operational Summary No. 106 at 2000 hours on 18 August 1941,
Headquarters, Western Front
1:500,000 and 100,000 scale maps

First. The situation on the Velikie Luki axis is unchanged. In the *front's* center and on its left wing, the forces are continuing the offensive, while overcoming stubborn enemy resistance.

Second. 22nd Army. The army's units are continuing to fortify their positions and conduct reconnaissance.

There is artillery and mortar fire along the front.

A detachment of 126th RD's 365th RR, which conducted night "snatches" in the Bobrovo region on the night of 17 August, destroyed up to an enemy company (253th ID), a tankette, and a light vehicle and seized a map of the situation, two AT guns with shells, and one motorcycle. Having fulfilled its mission, the detachment returned to the regiment with the trophies.

Third. 29th Army. The army's units, while developing the attack toward Il'ino, are conducting sustained fighting with the enemy.

252nd RD's 924th RR, after driving the enemy from the Sumari region, reached Bobrovo. The enemy is slowly withdrawing toward the south.

932nd RR, after forcing the Western Dvina River in the vicinity of Ust'e, reached the Rudnia region, where it encountered strong enemy resistance.

927th RR captured Glazovo and is fighting for the strong point of Pishchulino. The enemy is offering stubborn resistance.

243rd RD, while conducting night operations, encountered stubborn enemy resistance and heavy artillery and mortar fire. The division reached the front from 1 kilometer east of Trubniki to the unnamed heights north of Pesochek with two regiments, while enveloping the strong point at Pesochek from the north and fighting for the unnamed heights south of Andreevskaia.

The left wing regiment fought for the Bodievka and Vias'kovo line, meeting stubborn enemy resistance. Fire from the strong point at Katkovo is hindering the advance.

Our attacks were greeted by fire from dugouts and bunkers.

The division's units destroyed up to 4 enemy companies.

1st MRR is fighting to capture the strong points at Katkovo, Kanat, and Krivaia Luka. The enemy left more than 250 bodies on the battlefield in the Krivaia Luka and Zabornitsa region.

29th CR is protecting the army's flank in the Zekeevo sector and the sector from Borki and Zekeevo along the Mezha River.

BEPO [Armored Train] No. 53, while protecting the army's left flank, is exchanging fire with the enemy in the direction of Zharkovskii Station.

246th RD, after unloading, has the mission to concentrate in the Ust'e, Petugovo, and Anashchiki region.

Headquarters of 29th Army – Bentsy

Fourth. 30th Army, while continuing to defend the Los'mino, Demekhi, Sel'tso, Chalishchevo, Staroe Morokhovo, and Novoe Morokhovo front, resumed the offensive at 0830 hours on 18 August. The enemy, defending individual centers of resistance, offered stubborn resistance.

At 1030 hours the army was fighting [as follows]:

250th RD – in its previous positions.

242nd RD captured Hill 215.2 but, as a result of enemy counterattacks from the Shelepy region, withdrew to its jumping-off positions, while continuing to fight the enemy.

251st RD is fighting to capture the crests of Hills 218.7 and 220.9 (see 1:50,000 map).

162nd RD is continuing to fight in its previous positions.

107th TD advanced 400 meters by 1030 hours. A further advance by the division was halted by strong enemy mortar and machine gun fire.

45th CD concentrated in the Kvoktushino, Pod'ezzhalovo, and Lukashevo region at 1000 hours.

244th RD's 907th RR concentrated in the Simonovo region (20 kilometers south of Belyi) by vehicle [auto-echelon]. The horse-drawn echelon will complete its concentration by day's end on 19 August.

Fifth. 19th Army, while overcoming stubborn enemy resistance, is developing its attack successfully at 1800 hours.

91st RD, while throwing the enemy back, reached the eastern outskirts of Zubovo, the grove south of Zubovo, and individual houses west of Zadnia. The division's attack is continuing.

50th RD, by means of a decisive dash toward Makov'e, drove back the enemy who had seized Makov'e with a counterattack on the night of 18 August and recaptured Makov'e and Hill 219.4, inflicting heavy losses on the enemy, and are continuing their advance.

202nd TR, which is advancing toward Sushchevo, is being thrown forward to exploit 50th RD's success.

89th RD threw the enemy back toward the west with an attack toward Gorodno, while developing the attack toward the west.

64th RD, having forced the Tsarevich River and captured Zaitsevo State Farm and the villages of Popovo and Osipovo, is continuing its attack.

101st TD, without its TR, forced the Tsarevich River and, having dug in on the heights along the western bank of the Tsarevich River, is continuing its attack toward the west.

Sixth. 16th Army. There were no changes in the positions of the army's units. There is occasional artillery and mortar fire on the division's front.

Seventh. 20th Army is continuing to develop its offensive toward Pridneprovskaia and Dobromino Stations, while carrying out a regrouping for a subsequent offensive toward the northwest.

144th RD is fighting in the sector from the farm south of Makeevo to the farm west of Marker 165.9 and the ravine south of Mit'kovo on the western bank of the Dnepr River with its forward units, with its main forces in the sector from the farm 1 kilometer west of Korovniki to Marker 195.6 along the eastern bank of the Dnepr River. The enemy is offering strong fire resistance from Makeevo, Pnevo, and Liakhovo.

153rd RD, while occupying the Logunovo and Pashkovo sector along the western bank of the Dnepr River with its main forces, is preparing to attack toward Mashkino.

505th RR concentrated in the woods south of Osovo at 0600 hours on 18 August.

229th RD occupied the sector from (incl.) Pashkovo to the barn 3 kilometers south of Golovino by 0400 hours on 18 August.

73rd RD is fighting for possession of the eastern outskirts of Sopshino, Hill 169.7, and Erdetsy.

413th RR occupies Bereznia, protecting 161st RD's flank.

161st RD fought in its previous positions overnight and on the morning of 18 August, while carrying out a regrouping for an attack toward Obzhorovka.

The attacks by the division's units on the night of 17-18 August were unsuccessful.

Enemy counterattacks in the vicinity of Mogilitsy Farm and Samoboltaevka were repelled by the division's units

One enemy mortar and one machine gun were destroyed by our artillery.

129th RD is digging into positions from the farm south of Mikhailovka to Novaia Brykino, with covering units in the grove 2 kilometers southeast of Podenkovo and east of Mar'ino, while carrying out a regrouping for an attack toward Alekseevo and Vasil'evo.

457th RR repelled an enemy attack, supported by mortar fire and accompanied by provocative shouts in the Russian language in the Klemiatino region on the night of 18 August. There were exchanges of mortar and machine gun fire in the rest of the division's front.

[The following] were withdrawn from the western to the eastern bank [of the Dnepr River] on the night of 17-18 August: trucks – 3, light vehicles –1, 150mm guns – 2, and carts – 5.

Eighth. The VVS of the *front* cooperated with the ground forces on the battlefield, conducted reconnaissance, and protected the concentration of our reserves on the first half of the day on 18 August.

They carried out a total of 129 aircraft sorties, including 46 bomber and 83 fighter. They dropped [the following] bombs: 43 FAB-100, 1 FAB-82, 4 FAB-70, 38 FAB-50, 5 FAB-32, 96 AO-25, 162 AO-8, 910 AO-2.5, 206 of various caliber, and 177 KS ampoules and scattered 145,000 leaflets.

23rd AD bombed the airfield at Kamenka on the night of 17-18 August, and, as a result of the bombing, three seats of fire and one explosion were observed.

43rd MAD operated on 19th Army's front and destroyed an assembly of enemy forces in the Rakhmanino and Zamiatino region.

47th MAD cooperated with 19th and 30th Armies' units and conducted reconnaissance. It carried out a total of 20 aircraft sorties.

46th MAD operated on 20th Army's front and protected the Rzhev and Belyi auto-transport march-routes. It carried out 46 aircraft sorties.

31st MAD operated with 22nd Army's units, protected the unloading of our forces at Toropa Station, and conducted reconnaissance. It carried out 31 aircraft sorties.

38th RAS conducted reconnaissance in the Iartsevo, Gusino Station, Monastyrshchina, Pochinok, and El'nia region. It carried out 5 aircraft sorties.

Losses of the enemy: one ME-109 aircraft was shot down.

Our losses: 2 SB aircraft were shot down by enemy antiaircraft fire. One SB aircraft tipped over while landing. The aircraft burned. One TB-3 aircraft did not return from fulfilling its mission.

The LAGG-3 aircraft, which did not return from its mission on 17 August has been discovered on its own territory, and the aircraft is intact.

The Chief of Staff of the Western Front, Lieutenant General Sokolovsky
The Military Commissar of the Western Front's headquarters,
    Regimental Commissar Anshakov
The Chief of the Operations Department,
    Major General Rubtsov for Lieutenant General Malandin

Source: "Operativnaia svodka shtaba Zapadnogo fronta No. 106 k 2000 chasam 18 avgusta 1941 g. o boevykh deistviiakh voisk fronta" [Operational summary no. 106 of the headquarters of the Western Front at 2000 hours on 18 August 1941 about the combat operations of *front's* forces], *SBDVOV*, issue 41, 45-47.

33. Extracts from Combat Orders of the Headquarters of 19th Army of 18 August 1941 to the Commanders of the Army's Divisions

2120 hours – to 89th RD
    Energetically continue the attack to reach the Loinia River, where you will dig in with one rifle regiment. Continue the cleanup of your attack sector up to the Loinia River with your main forces.
    50th RD reached the Loinia River and is linking up with 64th RD, whose right wing regiment has occupied the Zaitseva State Farm region and is conducting an attack toward Muzhilova and Batyeva.
2125 hours – to 50th RD
    Capture and dig in along the Zamiatina and Hill 218.1 line.
    Send detachments to pursue and reconnoiter the enemy in your sector.
    Establish communications with 64th RD's units in the Muzhilova region on your left.
2130 hours – to 91st RD
    Energetically attack to reach the Loinia River, where you will dig in.
    Send detachments to pursue and reconnoiter the enemy.
    50th RD reached the Loinia River.
2140 hours – to 101st TD
    Capture the Hill 222.8 and Chistaia line, where you will dig in.
    Send detachments to pursue and reconnoiter the enemy in your sector.
    64th RD captured Kolkovichi and is fulfilling analogous missions.
2150 hours – to 166th RD:
    Energetically attack with you left flank to seize the Moteva and Hill 220.5 line, where you will dig in.
    Send detachments toward Losevo and Azarinki to pursue and reconnoiter the enemy.
    91st RD's units have the mission to reach the Loinia River in the Balashova and Kazakova sector.

The Chief of Staff of 19th Army, [Colonel Malyshkin]
The Military Commissar of 19th Army's headquarters,
    Brigade Commissar Kazbintsev
The Chief of the Operations Department, Colonel Maslov

Source: "Boevye rasporiazheniia shtaba 19-i Armii ot 18 avgusta 1941" [Combat orders of the headquarters of 19th Army of 18 August 1941], *SBDVOV*, issue 41, 168-170.

34. Combat Order No. 030 of the Commander of the Forces of 19th Army of 19 August 1941 on the Development of the Offensive toward Dukhovshchina

Combat Order No. 030, CP, Commander 19th Army,
the woods 1 kilometer east of Vasilisino,
0200 hours on 19 August 1941
1: 50,000 scale map

    1. The enemy, while committing 900th MotR and 5th and 161st IDs into battle unit by unit, has been beaten and is withdrawing toward the west, while trying to dig into intermediate lines along the Loinia and Tsarevich Rivers. The approach of some enemy reserves of motorized infantry, with tanks and artillery, from the Dukhovshchina region is possible.

    2. Neighbors are continuing to fulfill their assigned missions. The boundaries are as before.

    3. 19th Army, beginning at 0800 on 19 August 1941, will develop the success it has achieved in the general direction of Dukhovshchina, while pursuing and destroying the withdrawing and defeated units of 161st ID, and encircle and destroy the enemy in the Balashova and Pochepova region and the forests east of these points with part of its forces.

    4. 166th RD will continue to conduct a defense on its right wing and will attack toward Zubova and Losevo with its left wing, with the mission to destroy the enemy in the Motevo, Hill 220.5 (1 kilometer northwest of Potelitsa), and Losevo region in cooperation with 91st and 50th RDs, and capture the Losevo and Azarinki line by day's end. The boundary on the left is as before.

    5. 91st RD, with its previous reinforcements, will continue to develop success, while delivering the main attack with its right wing in the general direction of Balashova, Pochepova, and the woods east of Balashova. Reach the Myshkovo and Mashutino front by day's end on 19 August 1941. Seize and hold the crossings across the Tsarevich River at Maleevka and Pavlovo. The boundaries are as before.

    6. 50th RD, with its previous reinforcements and a composite tank battalion, will continue to develop success toward Kolugino with its main forces and toward Pochepova and Balashova by a short strike with one rifle regiment, with the tank battalion, to encircle and destroy the enemy in the Balashova and Pochepova regions and the forest east of those points, together with 91st and 166th RDs. Reach the (incl.) Mashutino and Sushchevo front by day's end on 19 August 1941 and seize and hold the crossings across the Tsarevich River in the vicinity of the House of Invalids with forward units.

    The boundary on the left: Dubrovka, Batyevo, Sushchevo, and Hill 229.4.

    7. 64th RD, with its previous reinforcements, will destroy the enemy in the Muzhilova, Turishchevo, and Zaitseva State Farm region, dig into positions from Turishchevo to the separate groves west and south of Zaitseva State Farm line. Seize and hold crossings across the Tsarevich River at Navol'nia and Sloboda with forward units. The boundary on the left is as before.

8. 101st TD, with its previous reinforcements, will capture and dig in along the Popova and Novosel'e (eastern) line, after sending detachments to pursue and reconnoiter the enemy to the Potapova and Samuilova line.

9. The Reserve:

a) 89th RD will clear enemy remnants from the Sel'kovo, Batyevo, and Trukhanova region and concentrate in the Sel'kovo, 1 kilometer southwest of Batyevo, Trukhanova, and Miaksheva region by 1000 hours on 19 August 1941.

b) Transfer 202nd TR and the composite army [tank] battalion to subordination to the commander of 50th RD by 0400 hours on 19 August 1941, having concentrated it in the woods east of Makov'e, and occupy an all-round defense in the vicinity of the woods south of Bolotino with the remaining forces. Be prepared for operations against enemy reserves approaching from the Dukhovshchina region and enemy columns withdrawing from the Myshkovo, Pesnevo, Sushchevo, and Rakhmanino region.

c) 159th RR – in its previous region.

10. Artillery. Missions:

a) Suppress enemy artillery batteries in the Borniki, Kastalanova, Losevo, Barsuki, Ivaniki, and Balashova regions.

b) Prevent enemy units from withdrawing to the crossings in the Balashova, Kazakova, Bolotino, Zaitseva State Farm, and Kal'kovichi region.

c). Prevent enemy reserves from approaching from Losevo, Rakhmanina, and Sushchevo.

Expenditure of ammunition during the day's fighting – 0.5 combat loads.

10. The VVS of 19th Army:

a) Conduct reconnaissance with the mission to determine the nature of the enemy in the Markovo, Voskresensk, Shatuny, and Vrakulino region and the approach of enemy reserves from the Dukhovshchina axes, and determine the grouping and character of enemy operations in the Berdino, Kepeshnia Station, and Ponizov'e region;

b) Prevent the approach of enemy reserves from the line of the Tsarevich River;

c) Be ready for combined operations with 202nd TR to destroy the enemy at the crossings over the Tsarevich River; and

d) Protect army's grouping in the Ust'e, Balashova, Bolotino, Trukhanova, and Vasilisino region. Pay special attention to providing cover for 89th RD and 202nd TR.

12. CP and headquarters of the army – at previous locations.

13. Submit operational and reconnaissance summaries at 0100, 1300, and 2000 hours.

> The Commander of 19th Army, Lieutenant General Konev
> The Member of the Military Council, Division Commissar Sheklanov
> The Chief of Staff of 19th Army, [Colonel Malyshkin]

Source: "Boevoi prikaz komanduiushchego voiskami 19-i Armii No. 030 ot 19 avgusta 1941 g. na razvitie nastupleniia s v napravlenii Dukhovshchina " [Combat order no. 030 of the commander of the forces of

19th Army of 19 August 1941 on the development of the offensive toward Dukhovshchina], *SBDVOV*, issue 41, 171-173.

35. Combat Order No. 9 of the Commander of the Forces of 29th Army of 19 August 1941 on the Destruction of the Enemy's Il'inskoe Grouping

Combat Order No. 9, Headquarters, 29th Army,
Bentsy,
1900 hours on 19 August 1941
1:50,000 scale map

1. The enemy, while going over to the defense opposite the army's front, is continuing to strengthen the field fortified region at Il'ino and centers of resistance in the Katkovo and Hills 195.0 and 209.6 regions and assembling his forces in the Liubovitsy and Khlebanikha region.

Two new enemy groups of up to two infantry regiments have been detected in the Bol'shaia Zheleznitsa, Podzhogi Farm, Krivaia Luka Farm, and Prudok regions opposite the army' left wing, and there is a concentration of enemy infantry in the Borok region.

The enemy has increased his air activity, especially bomber aircraft operating together with ground troops on the battlefield.

2. 29th Army, while delivering the main attack on its left wing with two divisions from the Baevo and Ias'kovo Farm line and a secondary attack with two regiments from the Ust'e and Vypolzovo line toward Il'ino, will destroy the enemy's Il'ino grouping by a decisive offensive, while subsequently developing success toward Demidov.

On the right, 924th RR (252nd RD) is protecting 29th Army with defensive AT regions in Krivets, Samodumova, Osinovka, Olenitsa 1, and Krasnye Sosny.

On the left, a cavalry screen of the Composite Brigade's 29th CR along the Mezha River is protecting the army's left wing.

3. Further on the right, 22nd Army is continuing to defend firmly the positions it occupies.

The boundary with it: (incl.) Vysokaia, Star. Toropa, (incl.) Lake Velinskoe, and (incl.) Gorodok.

Further on the left, 30th Army, while protecting its right flank toward Belyi, is attacking toward Dukhovshchina.

The boundary with it: (incl.) Rzhev, Zharkovskaia Station, and Manikhi..

4. 252nd RD, with two batteries of 309th ATBn and one battery of 644th CAR, while defending the Krivets, Samodumova, Osinovka, Olenitsa 1, and Krasnye Sosny sector with 924th RR, will attack toward Sinichino and develop the attack with two regiments toward Belyi Lug Farm, Ivan Trud Farm, Vas'kovo, Starosel'e, and Velizh, while capturing the Marker 171.6 (1 kilometer southwest of Velizh) and protecting the fulfillment of the missions of the army's main forces.

The division's regiments, while forcing the Western Dvina River in the Ust'e and Vypolzovo region, will unite their flanks along the Marker 197.6 and Sinichino line, while exploiting the attack toward the southwest.

The boundary on the left: Neretto, Bol. Griada State Farm, and Kozly.

5. 246th RD, with one battery of 309th ATBn and two batteries of 644th CAR, will concentrate in jumping-off regions at Baevo (middle), Baevo (south), and Poiarkovo on the night of 19-20 August, attack in two echelons toward Shelygany, Andreevskoe, Andreevskie Farm, Iur'evo, and Klin, and capture Il'ino, and destroy the enemy's Il'ino grouping together with 243rd RD.

One regiment of the division will protect the main forces's attack from the right with an attack toward Trubniki, Sokovichino, Belozeritsa, Pushniki, and Grablino 3, while protecting further from the north with one company in the Belozeritsa region, one company in the ground between the lakes 1 kilometer south of Timofeevo Farm, and a battalion in the Grablino 3, Hill 202.0, and Kochegarovo region.

The boundary on the left: Velesa, Nov. Borovye, (incl.) Marker 193.8, (incl.) Pesochek State Farm, Marker 186.8, (incl.) Marker 195.5, Masiagino, Marker 187.9, (incl.) Romanovo, and (incl.) Zaitsy.

6. 243rd RD, with one battery of 303rd ATBn and one battery of 644th CAR, will attack along the main attack axis toward Novinka Farm, Tselpino Farm, Porosiatnikovo Farm, and Parakhino, with the mission to reach the (incl.) Marker 194.3, Tselpino Farm, and Tiul'ki line and, together with 246th RD, capture the eastern outskirts of Il'ino and destroy the enemy's Il'ino grouping, while reaching the (incl.) Reshetki, (incl.) Markovo, Berezino, and Il'ino region.

The boundary on the left: Puzhonki, Ias'kovo Farm, Sheinovo Farm, Tiul'ki, (incl.) Korechevka Farm, and (incl.) Podol.

7. The Composite Brigade (without 2nd MRR), after capturing the center of resistance at Katkovo, together with 243rd RD, will attack toward Vysochert, Khaltomino Farm, and Gavril'tsevo, while protecting the main attack force from the left and covering the Vysochert, Erzovo Farm, and Khaltomino Farm axes.

29th CR will protect the line of the Mezha River with separate mounted patrols and pickets along the [following] axes: Zabornitsa, Krivaia Luka, Glinskoe, Zekeevo, Viazovnia, and Borki, while preventing enemy reconnaissance from penetration northward and northeastward.

8. BEPO [Armored Train] No. 53 is being transferred to the operational subordination of the Composite Brigade's commander, with the mission of illuminating and protecting the Zharkovskii Station and Borki axis.

9. The Army Reserves: 2nd MRR (of the Composite Brigade) will be concentrated in the Demidovo, Korotyshi, and Pikalikha region.

10. Artillery. Readiness at 1300 hours on 20 August 1941.

Missions:

1) Work over the enemy's firing system and strong points with 252nd and 243rd RDs' artillery.

2) Protect the infantry's transition to the attack with a 20-minute fire raid in accordance with the operational plan.

3) Prevent counterattacks from the direction of the forest mass east of Belozeritsa and the approach of [enemy] reserves from Il'ino, Kanat, and Bol'shaia Zheleznitsa.

4) Antitank reserve – two batteries of 303rd ATBn – in the Bentsy region. Mission – prevent the approach of tanks from the north and occupy a strong point in the Sevast'ianovo and Brod region with one armored company.

11. The VVS – 31st MAD.

Missions:

1) Protect and secure 246th and 243rd RDs' concentration and attacks in the Baevo, Putnoe Farm, and Zabor'e region beginning at first light on 20 August.

2) Conduct reconnaissance (by plan) and, when discovered, destroy columns of enemy along [the following] roads: a) Velizh and Il'ino; b) Nikolaevskoe and Kanat; and c) Il'ino and Prudok.

3) Destroy enemy airfields and divisional headquarters in the region southeast of the Lake Kolodno district.

4) Set fire to the Katkovo Fortified Region at 1400 hours on 20 August.

5) Suppress enemy artillery and mortar batteries in the Rudnia, Sutrmino, and Porosiatnikovo regions.

12. The Deputy Commander for the Rear [Rear Services] will support the conduct of the operation with ammunition and forage after determining the routes of transport and evacuation for 246th and 243rd RDs and while considering the road junctions and various supply stations with the extremely limited quantity of roads in the immediate rear of the units and formations.

13. The Chief of Engineer Troops will support the conduct of the operation by repairing roads from divisions operating along the main attack axis up to the regions of the crossings on the Western Dvina River and support the crossings by laying bridges across the Western Dvina River in the vicinity of Ust'e, Vekishkino, Sevast'ianovo, and Brod.

14. Begin the offensive – according to the operational plan.

15. CP – 1st echelon of the army's headquarters – Bentsy and further along the axis of movement to Il'ino.

16. Submit reports:

1) About readiness for the offensive and the occupation of jumping-off positions for the offensive;

2) Upon reaching the Sokovichno, Novinki Farm, Borat'kovo Farm, Volokhovo Farm, Belozeritsa, Tselpino Farm, and Tiul'ki line; and

3) Upon the capture of Il'ino.

The Commander of 29th Army, Lieutenant General Maslennikov
The Member of the Military Council of 29th Army,
    Divisional Commissar Gurov
The Chief of Staff of 29th Army, Major General Sharapov

Source: "Boevoi prikaz komanduiushchego voiskami 29-i Armii No. 9 ot 19 avgusta 1941 g. na unichtozhenie Il'inskoi gruppirovki protivnika" [Combat order no. 9 of the commander of the forces of 29th Army of 19 August 1941 on the destruction of the enemy Il'ino grouping], *SBDVOV*, issue 41, 262-263.

36. Combat Report No. 010 of the Commander of 19th Army of 19 August 1941 to the Commander of the Western Front's Forces about the Combat Operations of the Army's Forces and Decisions [Orders] on 19 August 1941

To Timoshenko

Copies: To the Commanders of 30th and 16th Armies

Combat Report No. 010, CP, Commander of 19th Army,
the woods 1 kilometer east of Vasilisino
early on 19 August 1941
1:50,000 scale map

1. Under attack by the army's units, the defeated units of enemy 161st ID withdrew to the western bank of the Loinia and Tsarevich Rivers. In the center and on the left wing, the enemy withdrew is disorder. The enemy abandoned a large number of bodies on the battlefield and threw away personal weapons and equipment.

2. The army smashed enemy resistance by a decisive offensive and, while developing success, seized the western bank of the Loinia and Tsarevich Rivers in the Zamiatina, Muzhilova, and Zaitseva State Farm regions and in the vicinity of Hill 209.9, 3 kilometers northeast of Novosel'e.

I should mention the special impetuosity and bravery of 50th and 64th RD and 101st TD, to which the army is indebted for today's success. On the right wing, while conducting active reconnaissance, 166th RD is occupying its previous positions. 91st RD captured Potelitsa and Hill 216.5, 1.5 kilometers southwest of Zadnia.

3. I have decided to develop the successes we have achieved in the general direction of Dukhovshchina on 19 August 1941, while destroying and pursuing the defeated units of enemy 161st ID, and reach the [following] positions: 166th RD – from Borniki to (incl.) Balashova; 91st RD – from Myshkovo to Mashutino; 64th RD – from (incl.) Sushchevo to (incl.) Popova; and 101st TD – from Popova to Novosel'e.

My reserve – 89th RD – in the Sel'kovo (northern), Trukhanova, and Stepankina region and 202nd TR – in the woods southeast of Bolotino.

4. I request reinforcement by fighters, since, today, during the first half of the day, enemy aviation has already carried out raids with groups of 9-12 aircraft against the army's units on the main attack axis and against the crossings over the Vop' River in the Kopyrovshchina region.

Konev, Sheklanov

Source: "Boevoe donesenie komanduiushchego voiskami 19-i Armii No. 010 ot 19 avgusta 1941 g. komanduiushchemu voiskami Zapadnogo fronta o boevykh deistviiakh voisk armii 18 avgusta i o svoem reshenii na 19 avgusta 1941 g." [Combat report no. 010 of the commander of 19th Army of 19 August 1941 to the commander of the Western Front's forces about the combat operations of the army's forces and decisions [orders] for 19 August 1941], *SBDVOV*, issue 41, 172-173.

37. Combat Report No. 011 of the Headquarters of 19th Army of 19 August 1941 to the Chief of Staff of the Western Front about a Transition of the Army's Forces to an Offensive

To the Chief of Staff of the Western Front
Copies: To the Chiefs of Staff of 30th and 16th Armies
Combat Report No. 011, CP, Commander of 19th Army,
the woods 1 kilometer east of Vasilisino,
1200 hours on 19 August 1941
1:50,000 scale map

At 0800 hours on 19 August, the army's forces army went over to an offensive, fulfilling the mission set forth by Order No. 030, except for 50th RD, whose units did not succeed in regrouping and occupying their jumping-of positions during the night. The offensive began at 1100 hours.

> The Chief of Staff of 19th Army, [Colonel Malyshkin]
> The Military Commissar of 19th Army's headquarters,
>   Brigade Commissar Kazbintsev

Source: "Boevoe donesenie shtaba 19-i Armii No. 011 ot 19 avgusta 1941 g. nachal'niku shtaba Zapadnogo fronta o perekhod voisk armii v nastuplenie" [Combat report no. 011 of the headquarters of 19th Army of 19 August 1941 to the chief of staff of the Western Front about a transition of the army's forces to an offensive], *SBDVOV*, issue 41, 173.

38. Operational Summary No. 108 of the Headquarters of the Western Front at 2000 hours on 19 August 1941 about the Combat Operations of the *Front's* Forces

Operational Summary No. 108 at 2000 hours on 19 August 1941,
Headquarters, Western Front
1:500,000 and 100,000 scale maps

First. The situation is unchanged on the Velikie Luki axis. In the *front's* center and on its left wing, the forces are continuing the offensive, while overcoming stubborn enemy resistance.

Second. 22nd Army. The army's units are continuing to fortify their positions and conduct reconnaissance ... .. The situation in the army is unchanged ... .

Third. 29th Army.

252nd RD – 924th and 932nd RRs, under pressure of the enemy supported by aircraft, withdrew to their jumping-off positions on the northern bank of the Western Dvina River.

928th RR, under heavy enemy pressure, abandoned Agryzkovo and withdrew to Glazkovo, where it is conducting sustained fighting with attacking enemy units.

243rd RD continued fighting along the Trubniki and Andreevskaia line and captured Pesochek at 1500 hours on 19 August. The division is conducting sustained fighting and being subjected to strong air strikes and counterattacks by the enemy.

1st MRR blockaded the strong point at Katkovo.

29th CR and BEPO 53 are fulfilling their previous missions.

During the fighting on 18 August in the Shelygany region, the commander of a squad in 912th RR, Sergeant Musenko, held off an enemy company attacking from the Sokovichino region for 18 hours. As a result, the enemy attack was repelled.

According to verified data, on 18 August 252nd RD's 924th RR destroyed the headquarters of the enemy's 3rd Battalion, 78th IR, and seized one gun, ammunition, and documents. A colonel and senior lieutenant were killed.

From the captured documents, it was clear that the enemy had to begin an attack on the army on 17 August.

Headquarters of 29th Army – Bentsy.

Fourth. The Cavalry Group reached the [following] regions on 19 August:

50th CD – Filino, Trusilovo, Ivashkina, and Pristan'; and

53rd CD – Boiarshchino, Lomonosovo Station, and Zaikova and have the mission of operating toward Lake Velisto.

The enemy was thrown back from the northern bank of the Mezha River to his main defensive line from Tukolovo to Vasil'evo, Ust'e, and Frolovo by the cavalry group's operations. Units of 2nd ID, which arrived from Germany, are operating on the cavalry group's front. the cavalry group's reconnaissance units destroyed 200 infantrymen and dispersed 4th IR's headquarters (in Ust'e) by night raids. As a result, the enemy retreated in panic, while burning the village and driving away the cattle. Solov'evo, Ivashkino, Murav'evo, and a number of others [villages] were burned down. The cavalry group's losses: 10 killed and 71 men wounded.

Headquarters of the group – the woods 1 kilometer north of Filino.

Fifth. 30th Army went over to the attack at 1330 hours on 19 August. The enemy offered stubborn resistance. At 1600 hours, the army's units were fighting at:

250th RD – in its previous positions.

242nd RD, having captured Hill 200.0 (southwest of Zhidki), is advancing forward slowly.

162nd RD, cooperating with 107th TD's tanks, destroyed opposing enemy units and reached the eastern outskirts of Shelepy, and fighting is underway for possession of that village. 45th CD was committed to combat to develop the success achieved in 162nd RD's sector while operating toward Shelepy.

244th RD – its main forces are in the Novo-Vysokoe region and one RR in the Sloboda and Torchilovo sector. The division's horse-drawn echelon is expected to arrive at 1800 hours on 19 August, although confirmation has not been received about its arrival.

Losses in the army' units: 45 men killed and 451 wounded.

Sixth. 19th Army continued its offensive at 0800 hours on 19 August, while developing the success it achieved in the center and on the right wing.

The defeated units of enemy 161st ID withdrew westward while offering resistance.

According to information as of 1200 hours, 50th and 64th RDs are successfully developing their attack from the Kazakov and Muzhilovo line.

101st TD's 101st Regiment fought for the Skachkova and Chistaia front on the western bank of the Tsarevich River with two battalions.

166th RDn is fighting in its previous positions.

89th RD – is in second echelon in the Sel'kovo, Gorodno, and Miakishevo region. The enemy abandoned up to 200 bodies in the Kolkovichi region.

Trophies. According to preliminary data, [the following] were seized: 4 105mm guns with 1,000 shells, 45 boxes of mines, 3 light vehicles, 21 rifles, 1 mortar, and 1 headquarters vehicle.

Three batteries of 45mm guns, 4 antitank guns, and up to a battalion of infantry were destroyed. [A subsequent report claimed that 9 105mm guns, 3 150mm guns, 2 75mm guns, 1,500 shells, and topographic maps and orders of the 161st Infantry Division's 336th Regiment were seized.]

Losses: 8 tanks burned and 4 destroyed.

The commander of 3rd Bn, 202nd TR, Senior Lieutenant Korshunov, died a hero's death when he, together with its crew, perished in a burning tank.

Seventh. 16th Army, while assisting 19th Army's offensive, and protecting its left wing, began an attack with its left-flank 38th RD in the general direction of Novosel'e and Samuilova at 1500 hours on 19 August, with the immediate mission to capture the Samuilova and Kudinova line.

38th RD's main grouping reached the western bank of the Vop' River in the sector from the southern slope of the heights with the Marker 200 near Skachikhino to Hill 196.6 by 1800 hours.

108th RD – positions unchanged.

Eighth. 20th Army. The army's units, having completed a regrouping, continued their offensive southward at 1000 hours on 19 August after an artillery preparation, while simultaneously preparing an attack toward the northwest in its center.

144th RD is digging into its previous positions. Attacks toward Mit'kovo were unsuccessful.

153rd RD is digging into its previous positions. Its 505th RR concentrated in the region west of Zabor'e by 2400 hours on 18 August.

The enemy conducted methodical artillery fire against the Zabor'e and Osova region and the crossings over the Dnepr River on the night of 18-19 and the morning of 19 August.

229th RD is digging into its previous lines.

73rd RD has continued its attack toward Kolpino since 0940 hours, while encountering stiff enemy resistance.

161st RD attacked along the Chukhachi and Hill 224.8 front at 1000 hours on 19 August after an artillery preparation and, overcoming strong enemy resistance, occupied the northwestern slopes of Hill 224.8 by 1300 hours. It seized 30-40 boxes with 37mm shells. The division is continuing the attack.

129th RD attacked at 1000 hours on 19 August after an hour-long artillery preparation and was fighting fierce street battles in Klemiatino at 1600 hours. Its 343rd RR approached the eastern outskirts of Gorodok.

Ninth. The *Front's* Reserves – 1st TD in the woods south of Vadino.

Tenth. The VVS of the *front* cooperated with the ground forces on the battlefield, operated against approaching enemy reserves, and protected the concentration of our forces.

They carried out a total of 107 aircraft sorties, including 51 bomber and 56 fighter. They carried out 36 aircraft sorties at night.

They dropped [the following] bombs: 24 FAB-100, 6 FAB-82, 6 AO-82, 99 FAB-70, 40 FAB-50, 2 SAB-25, 44 AO-32, 34 AO-10, 146 AO-2.5, and 5,172 KS ampoules. They dropped 427,000 leaflets.

23rd MAD operated against the enemy and burned the forests in the Boldino, Skaliaevka, Lomonosovo, Ushchapovo, Ivoshino, Sushchevo, Khudkova, Butsevo, Bykhovo, Krivtsy, and Ponkratova region. Many large seats of fire were created. Powerful explosions were observed.

46th MAD bombed and burned the forest in the vicinity of Lake Shchuch'e, setting many fires, with explosions in places. The division cooperated with 30th Army's units beginning on the morning of 19 August.

47th MAD bombed enemy forces on the night of 18-19 August and created fires in the Dukhovshchina region (to a radius of 5-6 kilometers). It protected 19th Army's units beginning on the morning of 19 August.

43rd MAD cooperated with 19th Army's forces, and 31st MAD, with 29th Army's forces.

The Chief of Staff of the Western Front, Lieutenant General Sokolovsky

The Military Commissar of the Western Front's headquarters,
 Regimental Commissar Anshakov

The Chief of the Operations Department, Lieutenant General Malandin

Source: "Operativnaia svodka shtaba Zapadnogo fronta No. 108 k 2000 chasam 19 avgusta 1941 g. o boevykh deistviiakh voisk fronta" [Operational summary no. 108 of the headquarters of the Western Front at 2000 hours on 19 August 1941 about the combat operations of the *front's* forces], *SBDVOV*, issue 41, 48-50.

39. Excerpts from Combat Orders Nos. 031, 032, and 033 of the Commander of the Forces of 19th Army of 20-21 August 1941
Combat Order No. 031 at 0215 hours on 20 August

1. The enemy, having thrown in insignificant reserves from the Dukhovshchina region and neighboring sectors of the front, is trying to resist the army's offensive along the western bank of the Loinia and Tsarevich Rivers.

2. Neighbors are fulfilling their previous missions.

3. 19th Army, while protecting itself with an active defense on its right flank, will continue the attack at 0900 hours on 20 August 1941, with the mission to destroy the remnants of 5th and 161st IDs and newly approaching enemy reserves in the Myshkovo, Sushchevo, and Muzhilova regions. Reach the Myshkovo, Sushchevo, Rafenina, and Novosel'e front with the main forces and seize crossings over the Tsarevich River in the Zhukovo, Pavlovo, and Novo-Nikol'skoe State Farm (House of Invalids) region with forward units by day's end.

4. 166th RD will actively defend the Shupeki, Krasnitsa, Zaria, and Zanino 1 line. On the left wing, continue the attack with the mission to destroy the enemy in Moteva and Zubova.

The boundary on the left is as before.

5. 91st RD's 613th RR, cooperating with 166th RD's units, will continue destroying the enemy in the vicinity of the groves south of Zubova. Attack toward Shchelkina with your main forces, while protecting yourselves from the Ivaniki and Krotovo axes, and capture the Myshkovo and Mashutino line and seize crossings over the Tsarevich River at Zhukovo and Pavlovo with your forward units by day's end.

The boundary of the left is as before.

6. 50th RD, with 202nd TR, will attack toward Kalugino and capture the (incl.) Mashutino and Sushchevo line by day's end. Seize crossings over the Tsarevich River in the vicinity of Novo-Nikol'skoe State Farm (House of Invalids) with forward units.

The boundary of the left is as before.

7. 64th RD will attack, while delivering your main attack toward Petrovo, Sel'tso, and Kulagino and reach the (incl.) Sushchevo and Rafenino front by day's end

The boundary on the left is as before.

8. 101st TD will attack toward Krovopuskovo and reach the (incl.) Rafenino and Novosel'e front by day's end, while protecting the army's left flank.

9. Reserve: 89th RD will concentrate in the Staraia Korov'ia, Kriukovo, Hill 217.0, and Stepankina front by 0600 hours on 20 August 1941. Have AT artillery along the Zadnia and Kriukovo line and be prepared to attack from behind 91st RD's right flank and at the boundary between 91st and 50th RDs.

10. Artillery: Be ready by 0500 hours on 20 August 1941. Artillery preparation – 30 minutes.

Missions:

1) Suppress enemy mortar batteries and personnel in the Hill 190.3, Kazakova, Hills 212.6, 216.1, and 211.6, Muzhilova, Popova, Petrova, and Hill 222.8 sector. Provide massed fire raids along 50th and 64th RDs' main attack axes.

2) Suppress enemy artillery in the Moseevka and Borniki, Ivaniki and Barsuki, and Rakhmanino and Kalugino regions.

3) Prevent enemy counterattacks from the Losevo, Semenovo, and Bykova regions.

4) Prepare DON [acronym unknown] at the crossings over the Tsarevich River in the Zhukova, Novo-Nikol'skoe State Farm, and Sushchevo region.

11. The VVS of 19th Army. Missions:

1) Destroy enemy personnel, tanks, and artillery in the offensive sector of 91st and 50th RDs in cooperation with the ground forces. At 0855 hours on 20 August 1941, destroy the tanks and mortar batteries in the Zamiatino, Hill 216.1 (2 kilometers west of Bolotino), Shishkino, Hill 211.6, and Kulagino sector.

2) Destroy the enemy at the crossings over the Tsarevich River, in the Zhukovo and Sushchevo sector.

3). Destroy the enemy reserves approaching from the Dukhovshchina axis

... .

Combat Order No. 032 at 0240 hours on 21 August

1. The enemy is trying to dig into positions along the Loinia and Tsarevich Rivers with 5th and 161st IDs' and 900th Panzer [Motorized] Brigade's units, which have suffered partial defeats in previous fighting, and with reserves approaching from the depths.

2. Neighbors are continuing to fulfill their previous missions.

3. 19th Army will continue an attack in the general direction of Dukhovshchina at 0800 hours on 21 August 1941.

4. 166th RD, while firmly defending on its right wing, will organize an antitank defense in the Lopatchinki and Gorbatovskaia sector and prevent enemy tanks from penetrating in that sector. Liquidate the enemy's center of defense in the Zubova region.

The boundary on the left is as before.

5. 91st RD, having firmly organized an antitank defense in the Gorbatovskaia, Potelitsa, and Hill 217.0 (2 kilometer west of Zadnia) sector, will attack toward Pochepova and Shchelkina with its left wing.

The boundary on the left is as before.

6. 50th RD, with 202nd TR, will attack toward Kalugino and capture the Mashutino and Sushchevo sector by day's end. Seize crossings over the Tsarevich River in the Novo-Nikol'skoe (House of Invalids) sector with forward units. Deploy the division's CP in the woods 1 kilometer west of Stepankina.

The boundary on the left is as before.

7. 64th RD will attack, while delivering the main attack toward Petrovo, Sel'tso, and Kulagino, and reach the (incl.) Sushchevo and Rafenino front by day's end.

The boundary on the left is as before.

8. 101st TD will attack toward Krovopuskovo and reach the (incl.) Rafenino and Novosel'e front by day's end, while protecting the army's left flank.

9. 89th RD will organize an AT defense with its front toward the north, northwest, and west in the region it occupies. Be prepared to develop an attack toward Makov'e, Kalugino, and Sushchevo.

10. Artillery. Readiness at 0500 hours.

1) Artillery preparation from 0730 to 0800 hours.

2) Prevent enemy tanks from penetrating into the Losevo and Balashova region.

3) Suppress enemy artillery in the Moteva, Kastalanova, Balashova, and Hill 220.5 regions.

4) Prepare one battalion of 311th AR to fight with enemy tanks along the Gorbatovskaia and Potelitsa axis.

11. The VVS of 19th Army, in cooperation with the ground forces, will destroy the enemy in the Lozevo, Ivaniki, Bykovo, Sushchevo, and Makov'e regions.

1) First strike – against the enemy tank group in the Moteva, Losevo, Semenkovo, and Balashova region.

2) Second – Strike the enemy in the Sirotinka, Afanas'evo, Shishkina, Muzhilova, and Sushchevo region at 0750 hours, in coordination with 50th and 64th RDs.

3) Destroy enemy motor-mechanized units approaching from the depths in the Losevo and Semenkovo region and the crossings over the Tsarevich River at Novo-Nikol'skoe and Sushchevo by successive strikes.

4) Protect the army's groupings in the Potelitsa, Makov'e, Miagchenki, and Vasilisino regions and movement of forces along the march-route: Neelovo, Gavrilovo, and Kapyrovshchina.

Combat Order No. 033 at 2340 hours on 21 August

1. The enemy, who is once again bringing reserves forward, has been trying to halt the army's offensive since the morning of 21 August 1941 with counterattacks by motor-mechanized units in the Potelitsa, Pochepova, and Zaitseva State Farm region and by extensive use of aircraft on the battlefield. The army's forces are repelling the counterattacks. The impudent enemy is being thrown back to their jumping-off positions, with heavy losses in personnel and equipment. According to the testimony of prisoners, 161st ID has been routed.

2. Neighbors are continuing to fulfill their previous missions.

3. 19th Army will continue its offensive from 0930 hours on 22 August 1941 in the general direction of Dukhovshchina, with the mission to destroy the enemy between the Loinia and Tsarevich Rivers. Reach the Krotovo, Mashutino, Sushchevo,

Potapova, and Samuilova front by day's end, while seizing the Kislova, Rytvino, Ponizov'e, Lupshevo, and Griaznoki front with forward units.

4. 244th RD will protect the army's right flank by a defense in the Shupeki, Shestaki 2, Krasnitsa, Zaria, and Priglova Farm line. Attack toward Zanino 2 and Isakovka with your main forces. Capture the Moseevka and Borniki line by day's end. Seize Novolosevo 1 and Novoselishche with forward units.

The boundary on the left: L'vovo, (incl.) Zhukovo, Mamonovo, Borniki, and (incl.) Krotovo..

5. 166th RD, with 36th and 874th ATRs, will attack toward Moteva and Losevo. Capture the Krotovo and the western edge of the grove southwest of Krotovo line by day's end.

The boundary on the left: Briukhachi, (incl.) Pechenichino, (incl.) 2nd Gorbatovskaia, Barsuki, and (incl.) Pankratova.

6. 91st RD, with 120th GAR, and 1st, 2nd, and 5th Bns, 874th ATR, will attack toward Balashova and Myshkovo. Capture the Hill 230.0 (0.5 kilometers north of Myshkovo) and Hill 226.2 (0.5 south of Myshkovo) and seize Rytvino and Ponizov'e line by day's end.

The boundary on the left: (incl.) Hill 245.6 (0.5 kilometers north of Novoa Guta), (incl.) Shuklino, (incl.) Rytvino, Shchelkina, and Ponizov'e.

7. 89th RD (without 390th RR but with a howitzer battalion of 311th AR) will attack toward Hill 220.3 and Sel'tso. Capture the Hill 224.9 (0.5 kilometer north of Sel'tso) and Mashutino line by day's end.

The boundary on the left: the brick factory 1 kilometer southwest of Novaia Guta, Hill 221.5 (southeast of Sorokaren'e), Makov'e, Mashutino, Hill 232.9 (1 kilometer east of Afanas'evo).

8. 50th RD, with 4th Bn, 302nd HAR, 1st Bn, 596th AR, and 874th ATR, will attack toward Afanas'evo and Kalugino. Capture the (incl.) Mashutino and Sushchevo line by day's end. Seize the grove 1 kilometer east of Butsevo, with forward units.

The boundary on the left: Nov. Komarovo, (incl.) Neelovo, Batyevo, (incl.) Muzhilova, Mel'nitsa, (incl.) the mouth of the Kostinka River, and (incl. Hill 229.4, 4 kilometers north of Lupshevo.

9. 64th RD, with 596th AR (without 1st Bn), will attack, while delivering the main attack toward Sel'tso and Kulagino. Reach the Sushchevo and Khudkova front by day's end. Seize the Lupshevo and Griaznoki line with forward units.

The boundary on the left: Ianova, Novoselok, (incl.) the church at Skachkovo, Potapova, and (incl.) Hill 236.7 (south of Griaznoki).

10. 101st TD, while delivering its main attack toward Krovopuskovo, will capture the Potapova and (incl.) Novosel'e line by day's end and protect the army's left flank. Capture the Uzval'e and Borotyshino line with forward units.

11. Reserve: My 390th RR in the Potelitsa and Zadnia region.

12. Artillery. Readiness by 0500 hours on 22 August 1941. Artillery preparation – from 0900 to 0930 hours.

Missions:

1) Suppress enemy artillery in the Rakhmanino, Shchelkina, and Kalugino region.

2) Suppress mortar enemy batteries and personnel along the forward edge.

3) Prevent enemy counterattacks from the Moseevka, Borniki, Losevo, and Krotovo region by fire from three battalions.

13. The VVS. Missions:

1) Suppress enemy personnel and mortars along the forward edge in the [following] regions: Losevo, Balashova, Sirotinki, Zamiatina, Hill 216.1 (1.5 kilometers south of Zamiatina), Shishkino, Siniakova, and Sloboda. The first strike will be against personnel along the forward edge.

2) Suppress artillery in the Shchelkina and Rakhmanino region.

3) Destroy enemy tanks in the Losevo, Shchelkina, Sushchevo, and Balashova region.

4) Prevent the approach of enemy reserves along the Dukhovshchina axis.

5) Protect the operations of the army's forces in the Lopatchinki, Makov'e, Miagchenki, and Vasilisino sector.

6) Reconnoiter the regions: 1) Zanino, Moseevka, Novo-Losevo 1, and Kastalanova; and 2) Krotovo, Ponizov'e, and Sushchevo.

14. CP – the woods 1 kilometer east of Vasilisino. Headquarters of the army – Vadino.

15. Submit operational and intelligence reports at: 0100, 1300, and 2000 hours.

16. Glorious soldiers of 19th Army! You have already dealt the Fascist dogs a shattering blow. Forward to new victories! For the Homeland and for the great Stalin!

Konev, Sheklanov, Malyshkin

Source: "Boevoi prikazy komanduiushchego voiskami 19-i Armii Nos. 031, 032, i 033 ot 20-21 avgusta 1941 g.[Combat orders nos. 031, 032, and 033 of the commander of the forces of 19th Army of 20-21 August 1941], *SBDVOV*, issue 41, 173-178.

40. Extracts from Combat Orders of the Commander of the Forces of 20th Army from 21-23 August 1941

Combat Order No. 57 at 2230 hours on 21 August

1. The SS Division "Great Germany" [*Grossdeutschland*], while operating in prepared centers of resistance in Pnevo, Mit'kovo, and Titkovo, is defending: Pnevo, Mit'kovo, Liakhovo, Dubrova, the woods south of Golovino, and Malinovka, with reserves in Fedurno and Vachkovo State Farm region.

263rd ID, which was relieved by the SS division, is along the Suborovka, Klemiatino, and Iakovlevichi line.

2. On the right, 108th RD is defending the Vop' River.

The boundary with it is as before.

On the left, 107th RD is attacking toward Bezzabot State Farm.

The boundary with it is as before.

3. 20th Army, while defending against the enemy's southern grouping, will go on the offensive at 0900 hours on 22 August in the general direction of Kardymova, with the mission to smash the SS division and reach the Khmost' River.

4. 144th RD, while firmly defending the Dnepr River line from the crossing at Solov'evo [southward] to the woods 1 kilometer north of Zabor'e, will attack Mit'kovo

at 0900 hours on 22 August and capture it by day's end, while protecting the flank of the army's shock group.

The boundary on the left: (all points incl.) Klimova, Zabor'e, Liakhovo, and Mashkino.

5. 153rd RD, with 302nd HAR and 3 batteries of 872nd ATR, will attack from the line it occupies west of Logunovo and Ratchino toward Liakhovo and the hill west of Ratchino at 0900 hours on 22 August and, after destroying the opposing enemy, capture the Mashkino and (incl.) Fedurno line by day's end.

The boundary on the left; Iaroshenki, (incl.) the barn (1 kilometer south of Zabor'e), the southern outskirts of Ratchino, the woods 0.5 kilometers north of Babeeva, and (incl.) Fedurno..

6. 229th RD, with 592nd GAR and two batteries of 872nd ATR, will attack from the jumping-off positions it occupies on the southwestern outskirts of Pashkovo, Golovino and 300 meters east of the edge of the grove south of Golovino toward Pashkovo and Babeeva at 0900 hours on 22 August and, after smashing the opposing enemy, capture Fedurno and Starinovo by day's end.

The boundary on the left: Kucherovo, the farm 3.5 kilometers south of Zabor'e, and Morevo State Farm.

CP from 0400 hours – the woods 1.5 kilometers south of Zabor'e.

7. 73rd RD, while firmly defending the sector from the barn 1 kilometer north of Baidik to Sopshino and protecting itself from the left, will attack with the remainder of its forces at 0900 hours on 22 August from jumping-of positions ts subunits occupy on the western bank of the Dnepr River toward Ryzhkovo and Remenishche.

CP from 0400 hours on 22 August – the woods 0.5 kilometers north of Baidik.

The boundary on the left; Slizovo, Bereznia, Erdetsy, and Sopshino.

8. 161st RD, with 129th EngBn, will firmly defend the positions it occupies and, at all cost, prevent the enemy [from advancing] north of the Motovo, Hill 205.9, Chuvakhi, Hill 224.8, and (incl.) Klemiatino line, while keeping no less than a rifle regiment in reserve in the Hill 221.7 (0.5 kilometers west of Sel'tso), Gorby, and Slizovo region and having prepared a defensive line from Sel'tso to Hills 236.5 and 221.1.

Organize an attack to seize Suborovka, Hill 221.3, and Hill 228.0 with separate detachments with artillery support.

The boundary on the left: Lunevo, (incl.) Vasiuki, (incl.) Kelmiatino, Voloboevo, and Gorbovo.

CP – the woods north of Gorby.

9. 129th RD will firmly defend the Klemiatino and Novoe Brykino Farm sector along the eastern bank of the Ustrom River and prevent, at all cost, a penetration by the enemy toward Goravitsy, Krasnosel'e, Mikhailovka, Safonovo, and especially Klemiatino and Chentsovo … ..

Combat Order No. 58 at 0820 hours on 22 August

1. The enemy on the army's right wing is defending west of the Dnepr River with an SS division and, opposite the left wing, brought up 263rd ID to take the place of the "Great Germany" Division.

2. 20th Army, while defending along the Dnepr River with two divisions [73rd and 144th] and, while holding on to bridgeheads on the western bank, will go over to an offensive with four rifle divisions [229th, 153rd, 161st, and 129th], reinforced

by heavy artillery, on the morning of 23 August, with the mission of defeating the enemy 263rd ID and reaching the railroad at Dobromino and Glinka Station ... ..

Combat Order late on 23 August

1. The enemy 263rd ID, numbering no more than 3,000 men, is defending the Suborovka, Vishniaki, Pogubilka, Klemiatino, and Iakovlevichi front with all three regiments in a single line.

2. 229th, 153rd, 161st, and 129th RD will continue their attack at 1030 hours on 24 August and fulfill the missions assigned to them by Order No. 58 by day's end ... .

Lukin, Semenovsky, Korneev

Sources: "Boevye prikazy i rasporiazhenie komanduiushchego voiskami 20-i Armii ot 20-23 avgusta 1941 g." [Combat orders of the commander of the forces of 20th Army from 20-23 August 1941], *SBDVOV*, issue 41, 216-220.

41. Combat Order of the Headquarters of the Western Front of 20 August 1941 to the Commander of 1st Tank Division about Preparing the Division to Exploit 19th Army's Success

To the Commanders of 1st TD and 509th ATR

Copy: To the Commander of 19th Army, Vadino, and to Naidenov and Vorob'ev

The Commander-in-Chief today ordered the commitment of 1st TD, with 509th ATR, in the Kapyrovshchina, Manchino, and Avdiukovo region on the night of 20-21 August.

Upon arrival in the region indicated, remain at the disposal of the Main Command, but immediately communicate with the commander of 19th Army and have a responsible representative at his CP. Constantly be aware of the situation on 19th Army's front and be prepared for operations to exploit 19th Army's success.

Sokolovsky, Anshakov

Source: "Boevoe rasporiazhenie shtaba Zapadnogo fronta ot 20 avgusta 1941 g. komandiru 1-i Tankovoi Divizii o podgotovke divizii k razvitiiu uspekha 19-i Armii" [Combat order of the headquarters of the Western Front of 20 August 1941 to the commander of 1st Tank Division about preparing the division to exploit 19th Army's success], *SBDVOV*, issue 41, 50.

42. Combat Report of the Commander of the Forces of 19th Army of 21 August 1941 to the Commander of the Western Front's Forces about the Combat Operations of the Army's Forces on 21 August and Decisions [Orders] for 22 August 1941

To the Commander-in-Chief of the Western Front

Copies: To the Commander of 30th Army

To the Commander of 16th Army

To the Headquarters of 19th Army

Late on 21 August 1941

1. During the course of the day on 21 August, the army fought with approaching enemy reserves who were trying to halt our offensive by counterattacks along the Gorbatovskaia, Potelitsa, and Pochepova line and further along the Loinia River to Muzhilova, the woods 2 kilometers west of Muzhilova, Popova, Skachkovo, and Chistaia.

2. The fighting in the Potelitsa and Pochepova sectors, where the enemy apparently delivered his counterstroke by committing up to 70-80 tanks and up to a regiment of motorized infantry into combat, was distinguished by its exceptional bitterness, and the enemy counterattacked with a force of up to 50 tanks and up to a battalion of motorized infantry in the Pochepova and Kazakova sector.

The enemy counterattacks were repelled with heavy losses to him. According to preliminary information, more than 70 enemy tanks and many vehicles were destroyed by us in these sectors. By evening, the enemy managed to wedge into 91st RD's dispositions in the region south and southeast of Hill 220.5 (1 kilometer northwest of Potelitsa). All the while, 91st RD's units held onto Potelitsa, Zadnia, Hill 217.9, the woods to the east of Balashova, and Pochepova.

In the Popova and Petrova region, the enemy abandoned more than 300 bodies on the battlefield, and in the Pochepova region – 250 bodies. We seized 54 prisoners (among them 2 officers) of 7th and 364th IRs.

Enemy aircraft appeared all day long by employing dive bombers on the battlefield and in the immediate rear along the crossings over the Vop' River and there was especially significant activity before evening. The crossings at Kapyrovshchina and Podylishche were destroyed. In some periods of the air battle, more than 30 enemy aircraft were in the skies simultaneously, especially along 50th RD's axis.

According to incomplete information, we seized 1 75mm gun, about 10 heavy and light machine guns, one radio, and one antitank gun. Our losses – 12 tanks, and the remaining are being verified.

3. I have decided:

To liquidate the enemy group which has wedged into 91st RD's dispositions during the night;

To continue the offensive at 0930 hours on 22 August, with the mission to destroy the enemy between the Loinia and Tsarevich Rivers by delivering attacks with 166th, 91st, 89th, 50th, 64th, and 101st Divisions in single echelon; and

To reach the Krotovo, Mashutino, Sushchevo, Potapova, and Samuilova front by day's end, while seizing the Kislova, Rytvino, Ponizov'e, Lupshevo, and Griaznoki line with forward units.

244th RD will conduct a secondary attack toward Zanino 2 and Isakovka with its left wing.

Konev, Sheklanov

Source: "Boevoe donesenie komanduiushchego voiskami 19-i Armii ot 21 avgusta 1941 g. komanduiushchemu voiskami Zapadnogo fronta o boevykh deistviiakh voisk armii 21 avgusta i reshenii na 22 avgusta 1941 g." [Combat report of the commander of the forces of 19th Army of 21 August 1941 to the commander of the Western Front's forces about the combat operations of the army's forces and decisions [orders] for 22 August 1941], *SBDVOV*, issue 41, 178-179.

43. Operational Summary No. 110 of the Headquarters of the Western Front at 2000 hours on 20 August 1941 about the Combat Operations of the *Front's* Forces during the Day on 20 August 1941

Operational Summary No. 110 at 2000 hours on 20 August 1941,
Headquarters, Western Front
1:500,000 and 100,000 scale maps

First. The situation on the Velikie Luki axis is unchanged. In the *front's* center and on its left wing, the forces are continuing the offensive while overcoming stubborn enemy resistance.

Second. 22nd Army. The forces are continuing to fortify their occupied positions
... .

Third. 29th Army. The army's units occupy their previous positions.

1st MRR is fighting in the Katkovo region, and Katkovo is burning.

There are artillery and mortar exchanges along the remainder of the front.

246th RD is completing its concentration in the Baevo, Shelygany, and Poiarkovo region.

The enemy lost about 300 men killed or wounded in fighting in the Andreevskaia and Katkovo region (in 243rd RD's sector) on 19 August, and 2 mortar batteries were destroyed there.

Headquarters of 29th Army – Bentsy.

Fourth. The Cavalry Group (50th and 53rd CDs). No news has been received.

Fifth. 30th Army went over to the offensive on the Novoe Morokhovo, Guliaevo, Beskhvostovo, and Sloboda front at 1300 hours after an hour-long artillery preparation and air strikes by bomber aircraft, while concentrating its main efforts along the Shelepy axis. In the main attack sector, the army's units penetrated to Pochinoi 2 and Shelepy.

251st and 162nd RDs were conducting fierce fighting to widen the penetration in this sector at 1700 hours.

244th RD and 45th CD are in their previous regions preparing to exploit success along the main axis.

Sixth. 19th Army continued its offensive toward Dukhovshchina at 0900 hours on 20 August. The enemy, after bringing forward reserves of up to one panzer division, supported by tanks and aircraft, counterattacked fiercely against our attacking units throughout the day. Our forces successfully repelled all of the enemy's counterattacks.

By 1700 hours, the army's units were fighting at:

166th RD is fighting in its previous positions.

The attack toward Motevo by the division's left wing had no success.

91st RD. Repeated attempts by the division to capture the center of resistance in the woods northeast of Potelitsa were unsuccessful.

50th RD, having repelled enemy counterattacks along the Loinia River, is fighting in positions from the Loinia River to the western edge of the grove west of Makov'e and Bolotino to the woods south of Bolotino.

64th RD, having repelling enemy counterattacks from the vicinity of Zaitsevo State Farm and Popova, forced the Loinia River and is fighting along the eastern outskirts of Muzhilovo, Zaitsevo State Farm, Popova, and Osipova front.

101st TD is fighting along the brush (1 kilometer east of Osipova), the church at Skachkova, and the southern outskirts of Chistaia front.

89th RD – the army's reserve – is concentrated in the Staroe Korov'e, Kriukova, and Bulanina region.

Seventh. 16th Army is continuing its offensive with its right wing, with the aim of reaching the Samuilova and Kudinova line.

38th RDis fighting along the Novosel'e and Khatyni line.

The positions of the remaining units are unchanged.

Eighth. 20th Army is continuing to fulfill its previous missions.

144th RD is fighting to capture Makeevo with part of its forces. The division's remaining units are in their previous positions.

From the dead, the SS "Empire" [*Das Reich*] Division has been identified opposite 144th RD.

153rd RD is fighting in its previous positions.

The enemy is conducting artillery, mortar, and machine gun fire against the division's dispositions.

229th RD is fighting along the Golovino and Sarai [barn] line

73rd RD's positions are unchanged; the enemy is offering stubborn resistance to the division's attack. In the vicinity of the bend in the Dnepr River 2 kilometers southwest of the barn, an attack by the enemy in close order from the forest east of Remenishche was repelled by the division.

392nd RR is fighting to capture Sopshino.

161st RD is continuing its attack. Its 542nd RR captured the grove northwest of Vishniaki and is continuing to press the enemy. Attacks by the division's units toward Pogubilka were unsuccessful.

129th RD continued its attack toward Obzhorovka on the morning of 20 August.

457th RR, as a result of a counterattack by an enemy battalion, abandoned Klemiatino at 0700 hours. Fighting is underway for possession of the remaining part of Klemiatino.

Trophies seized: 2 mortars, 1 antitank gun, 1 sub-machine gun, 3 automatic weapons, 30 mines, and boxes with a great quantity of ammunition.

Ninth. The *front's* reserve: 1st TD is in the woods south of Vadino and 152nd RD is in the Kakushkino region.

Tenth. The VVS of the *front* cooperated with the forces on the battlefield, conducted reconnaissance, and operated against approaching enemy reserves on the night of 19-20 and the morning of 20 August

They conducted a total of 139 aircraft sorties. They dropped [the following] bombs: 58 FAB-100, 17 FAB-82, 142 FAB-50, 2 ZAB-50, 13 FAB-32, 110 AO-25, 347 AO-15 and AO-10, 498 AO-2.5, and 6,509 KS ampoules. They dropped 118,000 leaflets.

23rd MAD operated against concentrations of enemy forces and set fire to the forests in the region east, southeast, and southwest of Dukhovshchina and in the El'nia region on the night of 19-20 August. It carried out 22 aircraft sorties. As a result of the bombing in the regions, a large number of fires appeared, and a great number of explosions were noted.

43rd MAD operated on 19th Army's front, destroyed concentrations of enemy forces in the Klemiatino and Shishkino region, and conducted deep reconnaissance in the Iartsevo, Smolensk, Pochinok, and El'nia sector. It carried out 17 aircraft sorties.

47th MAD conducted a raid on enemy troop concentration in the region 20 kilometers north of Dukhovshchina on the night of 19-20 August. It carried out 4 aircraft sorties. Fires appeared as a result of the bombing in the region. On the morning of 20 August, it conducted reconnaissance, operated against approaching enemy reserves, and protected 19th Army's forces.

46th MAD bombed enemy troop concentrations in the Krivets and Gorodno region on the night of 19-20 August. It carried out 9 aircraft sorties. A large number of fires appeared. During the first half of the day on 20 August, it cooperated with 20th Army's units, bombed the forward edge of the enemy in the region northwest of Gorodno, Churkino, Mashutkino, Fomenko, and Ploskoe, and protected the army's units. The bombs fell on enemy foxholes and artillery positions. It carried out 40 aircraft sorties.

31st MAD cooperated with 29th Army's units, protected the unloading of forces at Velikopol'e Station, conducted reconnaissance in the Nevel' and Usviat'e region, and attacked columns of tanks and artillery on the morning of 20 August. The columns were set ablaze by direct hits. It carried out 26 aircraft sorties.

38th RAS conducted photographic reconnaissance in the Iartsevo, Dukhovshchina, Arkhipovka, Smolensk, and Zadnia regions. It carried out 7 aircraft sorties.

During the first half of the day on 20 August, five enemy aircraft, including two ME-109, 1 ME-110, and 2 Iu-88 aircraft, were shot down.

Our losses: 1 TB-3 was lost in a crash and one IL-2 aircraft did not return to its airfield.

The Chief of Staff of the Western Front, Lieutenant General Sokolovsky
The Military Commissar of the Western Front's headquarters,
    Regimental Commissar Anshakov,
The Chief of the Operations Department, Lieutenant General Malandin

Source: "Operativnaia svodka shtaba Zapadnogo fronta No. 110 k 2000 chasam 20 avgusta 1941 g. o boevykh deistviiakh voisk fronta v techenie dnia 20 avgusta 1941 g." [Operational summary no. 110 of the headquarters of the Western Front at 2000 hours on 20 August 1941 about the combat operations of the *front's* forces during the day on 20 August], *SBDVOV*, issue 41, 51-53.

44. Combat Order of the Commander of the Forces of the Western Front of 21 August 1941 to the Commander of 29th Army's Forces about Refining the Army's Operational Plan for Destroying the Enemy's Il'ino Grouping

To Comrade Maslennikov
1745 hours on 21 August 1941

First. I agree with the overall concept of your plan for destroying the enemy's Il'inskoe Grouping.

Second. Clarity is absent in your order for fulfilling the plan for destroying the enemy. The enumeration of the missions to the companies and battalions slur the missions of the divisions.

Third. I demand 252nd RD, having protection on the right, launch its attack from the Ust'e and Vypolzovo line toward Kozino and Il'ino, and 246th [RD], together with 243rd RD, [attack] from the Baevo and Ias'kovo line in the general direction of Il'ino, and, in no circumstances, allocate subunits or units from these divisions to fulfill secondary missions. You can entrust protection on the left to the Composite Brigade.

Timoshenko

Source: "Boevoe rasporiazhenie komanduiushchego voiskami Zapadnogo fronta ot 21 avgusta 1941 g. komanduiushchemu voiskami 29-i Armii o utochnenii plan operatsii voisk armii po razgromu Il'inskoi gruppirovki protivnika" [Combat order of the commander of the forces of the Western Front of 21 August 1941 to the commander of 29th Army's forces about refining the army's operational plan for destroying the enemy's Il'ino grouping], *SBDVOV*, issue 41, 54.

45. Order of the Commander of the Forces of the Western Front of 21 August 1941 to the Commanders of 19th and 30th Armies about a Partial Regrouping

To the Commanders of 19th and 30th Armies

I order:

1) 45th CD, while remaining at my disposal, will move to the Klinets, Starosel'e, and Kobelevo region on the night of 21-22 August. Place the division's AT assets in the region indicated during the day on 21 August and prepare an AT defense along the Kislaevo and Shershiki and Konishchevo and Pechenicheno axes.

Prepare the cavalry division for commitment into 19th Army's penetration sector on the morning of 22 August, while having direct communications and a responsible representative at the CP of 19th Army's commander.

2) Transfer 244th RD to the subordination of the 19th Army's commander to relieve 166th RD's units in the Markovo, Zanino, and (incl.) Hill 213.9 sector.

Send the division to relieve 166th RD's units during the day on 21 August and complete the relief with the units, rifle and artillery, battalion by battalion, by the morning of 22 August.

166th RD, upon its relief by 244th RD, will occupy the (incl.) Hill 213.9 and (incl.) Gorbatovskaia sector by first light on 22 August and be prepared to attack on 22 August.

I entrust 30th Army's chief of staff, Lieutenant Colonel Baderko, with responsibility for the timely dispatch of 244th RD to relieve 166th RD and for the timely occupation by 244th and 166th RDs of their designated sectors and 19th Army's chief of staff for their readiness to attack on 22 August.

3) 152nd RD will move and concentrate in the Afanas'kovo, Neslovo State Farm, Logunovo, and Rozhnovo State Farm region by first light on 23 August.

The division is for defending the sector from Neslovo State Farm to Nikola Kremianyi State Farm with its forward units and for AT defense along the Obukhovo, Egor'evskoe, and Nikola Kremianyi axes. The division will remain in the *front's* reserve.

4) The Assistant Commander for forces of the ABTU [Auto-Armored Directorate] will concentrate 18th TD in the forest south of Vadino for further reorganization.

Report receipt of this order and the course of its fulfillment.

Timoshenko, V. Sokolovsky

Source: "Prikazanie komanduiushchego voiskami Zapadnogo fronta ot 21 avgusta 1941 g. komanduiushchim voiskami 19-i i 30-i Armii o chastichnoi peregruppirovke voisk" [Order of the commander of the forces of the Western Front of 21 August 1941 to the commanders of 19th and 30th Armies about a partial regrouping], *SBDVOV*, issue 41, 55.

46. Operational Summary No. 112 of the Headquarters of the Western Front at 2000 hours on 21 August 1941 about the Combat Operations of the *Front's* Forces

Operational Summary No. 112 at 2000 hours on 21 August 1941,
Headquarters, Western Front
1:500,000 and 100,000 scale maps

First. The Western Front, while fulfilling its assigned mission, is continuing an offensive by its center toward Dukhovshchina. Simultaneously, its right wing went over to an offensive toward the south, with the aim of destroying the opposing enemy at the junction [boundary] between 22nd and 29th Armies.

Second. 22nd Army, while defending on its right wing, went over to the attack with its center and its left wing at 1300 hours on 21 August, with the aim of destroying the opposing enemy.

51st RC, while protecting the army's right wing with an active defense, attacked southward with part of its forces.

366th RR (126th RD) is defending the Sidorovshchina, Veret'e 1, and Kudelino region.

The separate cavalry division is operating toward Novosokol'niki in the enemy's rear.

48th TD is defending positions from Sergievskaia Sloboda to Eremeevo, Kikino, Mordovishche, and (incl.) Kon'.

214th RD attacked from the Pronino and (incl.) Strizhevo line toward Kuznetsovo with two regiments at 1300 hours on 21 August. It wedged 2-3 kilometers into the enemy's defensive belt. It is defending the (incl.) Kon' and (incl.) Pronino line with one regiment.

Headquarters of 51st RC – Vlaskovo.

29th RC attacked from the Strizhevo, Gusakovo, and Sopki line at 1300 hours on 21 August [as follows]:

126th RD toward Leonovo;

179th RD toward Plaksino and Pirogovo;

170th RD toward Mulina and Pronino; and

98th RD (without one rifle regiment) is in the RC commander's reserve in the Taraskino, Rudnitsa, and Leskovo region. Its one RR is in the army commander's reserve in the Ushitsa State Farm region.

Headquarters of 29th RC – Vatolino.

All of the corps' units advanced 2-3 kilometers by 1500 hours. The units' positions are being verified.

62nd RC. 174th RD is defending the (incl.) Shcherganikha and Berezniki line with part of its forces and attacked from the Bakutino and Matskova line toward Nesterova with its main forces. The division's attack is developing successfully, and the division advanced 3 kilometers by 1500 hours.

186th RD, while defending the Kurilovo, Veliushina, and Karpova line with part of its forces, attacked from the (incl.) Matskova and Merino line toward Luzhki with its main forces, together with 174th RD. The division's attack was held up by very stubborn enemy resistance.

Headquarters of 62nd RC – Annino.

The boundary with 27th Army is being protected by an FD [forward detachment] from 98th RD in the Kniazhovo region (on the Kun'ia River, 35 kilometers southwest of Kholm).

The boundary with 29th Army is being protected by a detachment in the Iamishche, Krasnoe, and Sosny region.

Headquarters of 22nd Army – Nazimovo Station.

Third. 29th Army is continuing preparations for an offensive, and part of the army occupied jumping-off positions in accordance with Order No. 9.

There is artillery and mortar fire on the army's front.

The commander of the Composite Brigade, Colonel Nikolin, was missing-in-action on combat on 19 August in the Katkovo region.

Headquarters of 29th Army – Bentsy.

Fourth. 30th Army was putting itself in order and conducting preparations for an offensive, while occupying its previous positions on the morning of 21 August. The enemy on the army's front conducted artillery and mortar fire against 250th and 162nd RDs' units.

Trophies: 2 heavy machine guns, 5 rifles, and 1 bicycle seized.

Losses of the army for 20 August – 1,312 men killed and wounded.

244th RD, in accordance with the order, began moving to relieve 19th Army's 166th RD in the Markovo, Zanino, and Hill 213.9 sector.

45th CD is preparing to leave on a night march to the Klinets, Starosel'e, and Kobelevo region (all points 22-25 kilometers northwest of Vadino Station), while constituting the *front's* reserve.

Fifth. 19th Army continued its offensive in the general direction of Dukhovshchina at 0800 hours on 21 August.

Up to 50 enemy tanks with infantry counterattacked against 19th Army's right wing at 1400 hours from the Hill 220.5 region towards Potelitsa. Simultaneously, up to two battalions of infantry counterattacked toward Pochelovo. The enemy, who attacked 91st RD on the night of 20-21 August, withdrew his remaining forces after losing two tanks, leaving dead which belonged to 42nd PzBn on the battlefield (requires verification). The enemy attack toward Pochelovo encountered decisive resistance. The fight is continuing with successful results for us.

64th RD is advancing forward, having seized 80 prisoners, two of them officers from the enemy's 28th ID. The [64th] division was subjected to attack by 30 bombers.

101st TD is fighting, while occupying Skachkovo and Chistaia.

Sixth. The Cavalry Group (50th and 53rd CD) – No news received.

Seventh. 16th Army. 38th RD is continuing its attack, while assisting 19th Army's offensive, and captured Novosel'e (eastern) at 1600 hours on 21 August.

108th RD – position unchanged.

Eighth. 20th Army is fulfilling its assigned mission and fighting along the Makeevo, Pnevo, Pashkova, Golovino, Sarai, Sopshino, Motevo, Vishniaki, Pogibilka, Chuvakhi, Samodurovka, Klemiatino, Novo-Aleksandrovka, and Brykino line.

Ninth. The *Front's* reserve:

a) 1st TD, together with 509th ATR, moved from the Vadino region to the Kapyrovshchina, Chizhiki, and Avdiukova region on the night of 20-21 August;

b) 152nd RD is preparing to move from the Kakushkino region to the Afanas'kovo, Neslovo, Lagunovo, and Razhnovo State Farm region; and c) 134th RD is continuing to fill out in the Vladimirovskaia region (30 kilometers southeast of Belyi).

Tenth. The VVS of the *front*. As a result of poor meteorological conditions , the VVS's activities were limited during the first half of the day.

Overall, 46 aircraft sorties were carried out during the first half of the day.

43rd MAD cooperated with 19th Army's units.

46th MAD, while having the mission of cooperating with 30th Army's units, conducted 5 aircraft sorties to disrupt the enemy and protect our forces.

47th MAD cooperated with 19th Army's forces.

A group of 9 IL-2 aircraft with protection from 9 MIG-3 fighters assaulted a column of enemy tanks on the Zamiatino and Balasheva road at 1200 hours. A second strike on that same column was carried out at 1355 hours. The results are unknown.

According to additional information, 4 enemy aircraft were shot down on 20 August.

Our losses: 2 I-16 did not return to their airfields. The MIG-3 aircraft indicated in previous reports as not returning to its airfield was shot down by by enemy fighters.

> The Chief of Staff of the Western Front, Lieutenant General Sokolovsky
> The Military Commissar of the Western Front's headquarters,
>   Regimental Commissar Anshakov
> The Chief of the Operations Department, Lieutenant General Malandin

Source: "Operativnaia svodka shtaba Zapadnogo fronta No. 112 k 2000 chasam 21 avgusta 1941 g. o boevykh deistviiakh voisk fronta" [Operational summary no. 112 of the headquarters of the Western Front at 2000 hours on 21 August 1941 about the combat operations of the *front's* forces], *SBDVOV*, issue 41, 55-57.

47. Report of the Chief of Staff of 19th Army of 22 August 1941 to the Commander of the Western Front's Forces about a Plan for a Further Offensive by the Army's Forces

To the Commander-in-Chief of the Western Front

CP, Commander, 19th Army,

the woods 1 kilometer east of Vasilisino,

1: 50,000 scale map

I am reporting on a plan of operations for developing the army's operations in the immediate future.

1. On 20 and 21 August, the enemy assembled reserves from neighboring sectors of our 30th and 16th Armies' fronts to oppose 19th Army's offensive along the Dukhovshchina axis. During this period, the enemy succeeded in assembling and employing against 19th Army during the second half of 21 August no fewer than two regiments of motorized infantry and up to 150 tanks, apparently, from the odd units of 42nd Panzer Division, 15th Motorized Regiment, and 900th Armored [Motorized] Brigade along the Potelitsa and Losevo axis and 28th ID's 7th IR along the Osipova and Bortniki axis (south of the Tsarevich River). Up to this time, enemy motor-mechanized units have not been identified along these axes from the beginning of the army's offensive, and, therefore, the primary means of resisting our offensive was an active defense by infantry and the actions of enemy dive-bombers. Evidently, the Tsarevich River was an obstacle to regrouping for enemy motor-mechanized units operating north of it.

Significant losses were inflicted on the approaching enemy reserves during the fighting on 21 August.

2. Based on this assessment of the enemy, [in particular], the weakness of his forces south of the Tsarevich River and the suitability of the terrain for the employment of cavalry, I consider it expedient:

A. To maintain the present army grouping and, without weakening the attack in the center toward Makov'e and Pavlovo, to also develop an attack toward Miagchenki, Stepanova, and Dukhovshchina.

B. To employ 45th Sep. CD along the Miagchenki, Stepanova, and Dukhovshchina axis during the second half of 23 August.

To concentrate it in the Maslikhi, Matveenki, and Malinovka region by 0400 hours on 23 August, from which, depending on the conditions, it can be directed to develop success, if required, also in the center.

To commit the cavalry division into combat after the capture of Navol'nia, Sel'tso, Makeeva, and Novosel'e line by 64th RD and 101st TD to capture the region of forest west of Dukhovshchina by day's end on 23 August, from which it can be directed along the northern or southwestern axes.

3. I request fighter cover [protection] for the cavalry division's concentration region on the morning of 23 August, for its advance from this region to the Loinia River, and for its commitment into the penetration during the second half of the day on 23 August.

I request you place one artillery regiment at my disposal, which is especially necessary because of the inclusion of 244th RD and 45th CD in the army's composition.

The Chief of Staff of 19th Army, [Colonel Malyshkin]

Source: "Doklad nachal'nika shtaba 19-i Armii ot 22 avgusta 1941 g. komanduiushchemu voiskami Zapadnogo fronta o plane dal'neishego nastupleniia voisk armii" [Report of the chief of staff of 19th Army of 22 August 1941 to the commander of the Western Front's forces about a plan for a further offensive by the army's forces], *SBDVOV*, issue 41, 179-180.

48. Operational Summary No. 114 of the Headquarters of the Western Front at 2000 hours on 22 August 1941 about the Combat Operations of the *Front's* Forces during the Day on 22 August 1941

Operational Summary No. 114 at 2000 hours on 22 August 1941,
Headquarters, Western Front
1:500,000 and 100,000 scale maps

First. The forces of the *front*, while overcoming stubborn enemy resistance, are developing an offensive toward Usviat'e on the right wing and toward Dukhovshchina in the center.

The *front's* left wing, while fortifying the positions reached, is conducting a regrouping of forces.

Second. 22nd Army, while defending on its right wing, is continuing the offensive in its center and on its left wing on the morning of 22 August.

The enemy, relying on a developed system of obstacles, is offering stubborn resistance, especially in the forested regions, and extensively employing organized artillery and mortar fires and counterattacks.

At 0600 hours on 22 August, the enemy's 110th ID, supported by artillery and mortars, launched a counterattack on 186th RD's front and seized Bardino, Sopki, and Dreki. A group of enemy sub-machine gunners penetrated into Slonovo. Measures are being taken to liquidate the enemy penetration.

In the fighting with 174th RD for Viazoviki on 21 August, the enemy suffered great losses. The division seized 4 heavy machine guns.

Headquarters of 22nd Army – Nazimovo Station

Third. 29th Army went over to the offensive at 1400 hours on 22 August, with the aim of destroying the opposing enemy. The enemy offered stubborn resistance along the entire front, conducted strong artillery and mortar fire, and carried out air raids.

252nd RD, while defending the Krivets, Samodumova, Olenitsa 1, and Krasnyi Sosny sector with one regiment and having forced the Western Dvina River in the Ust'e and Vypozovo region, developed an attack toward Sinichino with two regiments.

246th RD is attacking from the Baevo region toward Andreevskie and Iur'evo.

243rd RD attacked from the Zakhody and Ias'kovo line toward Porosiatnikovo and Parakhino.

1st MRR is continuing its operations toward Katkovo.

29th CR is protecting the army's left flank along the Mezha River.

BEPO [Armored Train] No. 53 is protecting the Zharkovskii Station and Borki axis.

2nd MRR – the army's reserve – is concentrated in the Demidovo, Korotyshi, and Pikalikha region.

Headquarters of 29th Army – 0.5 kilometers south of Poiarkovo.

Fourth. The Cavalry Group (50th and 53rd CDs) was concentrated in the forest north of Ust'e and Podviaz'e. All of its attempts to punch through either with separate detachments or regiments have been unsuccessful. The enemy is stubbornly defending the Shikhtovo, Podviaz'e, and Brekhalovo line.

At 2000 hours on 22 August, the group began reaching the Marker 194.9, the woods north of Nikulino, and the woods southeast of Podviaz'e line.

Local partisans are operating together with the group.

Losses are insignificant – but the number is being clarified.

Fifth. 30th Army is conducting a regrouping, and the units are putting themselves in order and conducting preparations for an attack.

Artillery and mortar exchanges are taking place across the army's front. The enemy is displaying no activity.

250th RD is continuing to occupy [the following]: 918th RR – defenses in the Los'mino and Bulatovo sector, and the remaining units are concentrating in the Pozhinki region.

The army's remaining units are occupying [the following] positions:

242nd RD – Staroe Morokhovo, Novoe Morokhovo, and Zhidki;

162nd RD – Dolgoe and (incl.) Staroe Selo; and

251st RD – Individual huts west of Mikhailovshchina and the edge of the woods 1 kilometer southeast of Sechenki.

107th TD, without 120th MRR, concentrated in the Dolgoe region.

120th MRR, in connection with the arrival of 244th RD's 911th RR from 30th Army, has the mission to defend the Zhukovo, Sloboda, Nazemenki, Karpovo, and Torchilovo line.

244th RD and 45th CD were transferred to the subordination of 19th Army.

134th RD is continuing to fill out in the Vladimirskoe region. One of its rifle regiments, on order of the army commander, will concentrate in the forest 2 kilometers northeast of Podzaitsevo by day's end on 22 August as the army commander's reserve.

Losses: According to verified information for 20 August, 11 tanks were destroyed and burned. 107th TD suffered heavy losses in personnel in the recent fighting. On 22 August, 180 active riflemen remain in the ranks of 237th MRR.

143rd TR – has 115 men lost, and in 143rd TR, the commander was killed, and two battalion commanders and almost all of the company commanders were put out of action.

The military commissar of 251st RD's headquarters, Battalion Commissar Zaitsev, and 927th RR's acting commander, Captain Shamko, were killed.

Trophies: according to verified data, included one 30mm gun with 28 shells, 8 rifles, and one mortar seized.

Destroyed: 8 heavy machine guns, 9 sub-machine guns, 7 mortars, 5 antitank guns, and one artillery battery, and 800 German soldiers and officers were killed.

One enemy transport aircraft was shot down by antiaircraft fire on 22 August.

Sixth. 19th Army, during the day, relieved the units on its right wing and conducted a regrouping of forces. Simultaneously, it continued its attack in the center and on the right wing at 0930 hours, while concentrating its efforts on the destruction of the enemy between the Loinia and Tsarevich Rivers.

The enemy, after bringing reserves forward from the depths, offered stubborn resistance, while trying to halt the advance of our attacking units with local counterattacks by infantry, supported by tanks. The enemy offered the most stubborn resistance in the Potelitsa, Pochepova and Popova, and Skachkova sectors. The enemy suffered heavy losses in the sectors indicated: according to preliminary information, up to 2,000 German soldiers have been destroyed since 17 August, and more than 70 tanks and many vehicles were destroyed on 21 August alone.

On 22 August the enemy is using a new mortar battery [the *Werfer*], which launches eight shells simultaneously, on the battlefield,

By 1700 hours, the army's units were fighting [as follows]:

244th RD – relieved 166th RD's units in the Shupeki and Hill 213.9 sector by 1500 hours; and

166th RD – is regrouping its forces in the Hill 213.9 and Gorbatovskaia sector for an attack toward Motevo and Losevo;

91st RD is conducting an attack on a center of resistance in the Hill 220.8 region with its right wing. After repelling a counterattack by up to two companies of infantry, supported by 15-20 tanks, toward Pochepova at 1100 hours on 22 August, it is continuing to advance toward the western edge of the grove east of Pochepova.

89th RD is assisting 91st RD's attack toward Hill 220.8 with one of its RR and moving two RRs forward into jumping-off positions for an attack in the sector from the unnamed heights (1 kilometer east of Pochepova) to the grove 0.5 kilometers east of Makov'e.

50th RD is fighting fierce battles with the enemy along the line of the Loinia River.

64th RD repelled a counterattack by up to two companies of enemy infantry from the groves south of Petrovo at 1230 hours, while continuing its fighting.

101st TD, while attacking from the Skachkova and Chistaia line, is encountering stubborn enemy resistance. The fighting is continuing.

45th CD concentrated in the vicinity of the forests east of Golobachevo, Zhukova, and Fedoseeva at 0500 hours on 22 August.

Trophies: one 75mm gun, 10 heavy and sub-machine guns, one radio, and an antitank gun.

Losses on 22 August during the repelling of the enemy tank counterattack – 12 tanks.

Seventh. 16th Army. The attack by 38th RD on 22 August was unsuccessful. While being forced to abandon Novosel'e under the pressure of artillery and mortar fire, the division is fighting in positions from the southeastern slopes of Hill 108.6 to the eastern outskirts of Khatyni at 1700 hours on 22 August. As before, 7th IR is operating opposite the division's front.

108th RD – positions unchanged.

According to documents from prisoners seized in the Novosel'e region (eastern), it has been established that 49th IR [28th ID] is along the line from the grove (1 kilometer south of Hill 174.7) to Sel'tso, and up to a regiment of infantry are south of Sel'tso. Up to a regiment of unknown designation is in 108th RD's sector. The enemy on the division's front is displaying no special activity.

Eighth. 20th Army is preparing to fulfill its assigned missions.

144th, 73rd, 161st, and 129th RDs are fortifying their existing positions.

229th and 153rd RDs are on the march to their new concentration areas.

Ninth. The VVS of the *front* cooperated with the ground forces on the battlefield, conducted reconnaissance, and operated against enemy reserves approaching the front overnight on 21-22 August and during the first half of the day on 22 August. They conducted a total of 160 aircraft sorties.

23rd BAD bombed the enemy in the Pesnevo, Leonovo, Rafenina, Osinovka, Losevo, and Zamiatino regions on the night of 21-22 August. It conducted 21 aircraft sorties. Many fires, with individual explosions were created.

43rd MAD cooperated with 19th Army's units.

46th MAD bombed the enemy's forward edge in the Novoselki, Karpovo, and Shelepy region in three consecutive raids on the night of 21-22 August. According to observation of the crews, several fires were set, and explosions were observed. The division has been cooperating with 30th Army's units, protecting the transfers of our forces, and attacking enemy tanks, infantry, and auto transport in the Pokhovichitsy and Shalovichi region since the morning of 22 August. Direct hits were noticed on enemy auto transports and personnel.

31st MAD cooperated with 22nd Army's units.

47th MAD operated against enemy motor-mechanized units, artillery, and infantry in the Loseva and Balasheva region (in 19th Army's sector).

As a result of two repeated attacks on motor-mechanized units, artillery, and infantry, 10-15 tanks and about 22 vehicles were destroyed, one water truck was burned, an ammunition warehouse was destroyed, the fire of two batteries were suppressed, and up to two companies of infantry were destroyed.

Losses of the enemy: one Iu-88 aircraft during the first half of the day.

Our losses: according to additional information on 21 August, one I-16 aircraft was shot down.

The Chief of Staff of the Western Front, Lieutenant General Sokolovsky
The Military Commissar of the Western Front's headquarters,
 Regimental Commissar Anshakov
The Chief of the Operations Department, Lieutenant General Malandin

Source: "Operativnaia svodka shtaba Zapadnogo fronta No. 114 k 2000 chasam 22 avgusta 1941 g. o boevykh deistviiakh voisk fronta v techenie dnia 22 avgusta 1941 g." [Operational summary no. 114 of the headquarters of the Western Front at 2000 hours on 22 August 1941 about the combat operations of the *front's* forces during the day on 22 August 1941], *SBDVOV*, issue 41, 58-61.

49. Combat Order No. 043 of the Commander of the Forces of 30th Army of 22 August 1941 about Consolidation of the Army's Forces in the Positions They Reached and Development of Success during the Night

Combat Order No. 043, Headquarters of 30th Army,
the woods 2 kilometers northeast of Podzaitsevo,
2130 hours on 22 August 1941
1:50,000 scale map

(Given orally and through a liaison representative)

1. The enemy, throwing in his last reserves, is straining all of his efforts trying to hold onto the positions he occupies.

250th RD captured Hill 220.0, 162nd RD – Hill 218.7 and Pochinok [29 kilometers north-northeast of Dukhovshchina]; and 120th RR is fighting on the approaches to Bol'shoe Repino [38 kilometers northeast of Dukhovshchina] with its right wing. The attacks by the remaining units had no success.

2. I order:

242nd RD will dig into the positions is has occupied. Put your units in order, [conduct] night "snatches," and also, being in full combat readiness, prevent the enemy from conducting a counterattack.

250th RD will continue its efforts to develop success during the night by operating with reconnaissance and specialized detachments in separate sectors.

162nd RD will dig into positions it occupies and exploit the night to develop success by operations with reconnaissance and small specialized detachments.

107th TD's 237th RR, together with 162nd RD's right wing, will develop success by small group operations; and the tank regiment will concentrate in the forested region west of Dolgoe and put itself into order. Be prepared to develop 250th and 162nd RDs' success on the morning of 24 August; 120th MRR will dig into the positions it occupies, while actively operating toward Bol'shoe Repino with reconnaissance.

251st RD will locate boundaries in the enemy's combat formations by night operations and, by penetrating into them, achieve a sudden turning point in the offensive, while being prepared to develop it on the morning of 24 August.

> The Commander of 30th Army, Lieutenant General Khomenko
> The Member of the Military Council of the army,
>   Brigade Commissar Abramov
> The Chief of Staff of 30th Army, Lieutenant Colonel Baderko

Source: "Boevoi prikaz komanduiushchego voiskami 30-i Armii No. 043 ot 22 avgusta 1941 g. o zakreplenii voisk armii na dostignutom rubezhe i razvitii uspekha noch'iu" [Combat order no. 043 of the commander of the forces of 30th Army of 22 August 1941 about consolidation of the army's forces in the positions they reached and development of success during the night], *SBDVOV*, issue 41, 288-289.

50. Extracts from Combat Orders and Reports of the Commander of the Forces of 19th Army of 22-23 August 1941

Combat Order No. 035 at 2240 hours on 22 August

1. The enemy, during an attempt to go over to the counteroffensive on 21 August, while suffering heavy losses in personnel and equipment, is trying to organize a defense along the line of the Loinia and Tsarevich Rivers. About 80 enemy tanks were destroyed as a result of the fighting on 21 and 22 August 1941.

2. Neighbors are continuing to fulfill their previous missions.

3. 19th Army will continue its offensive in the general direction of Dukhovshchina at 0830 hours on 23 August 1941, with the mission to destroy the enemy between

the Loinia and Tsarevich Rivers, while cutting off his withdrawal to the crossings across the Tsarevich River.

4. 244th, 166th, 91st, 89th, 50th, and 64th RDs and 101st TD, with their previous reinforcements, will fulfill the missions assigned by my Combat Order No. 033 of 21 August 1941.

5. 50th, 64th, and 101st Divisions will plan for the commitment of 45th CD into the penetration in their divisional sectors.

6. 45th CD will develop the penetration toward Sel'tso, Meikovo, and Dukhovshchina, with the aim to prevent the enemy from withdrawing behind the Tsarevich River and seize the crossings over it in the Navol'nia and Zhukovo sector. Capture the forested region west of Dukhovshchina by day's end.

Plan for the possibility of committing the division into the penetration in 50th RD's sector, that is, toward Sushchevo, Mishina, and Dukhovshchina.

7. To the Chief of Artillery – the artillery will be ready by 0500 hours on 23 August 1941. The artillery preparation will be 30 minutes, from 0800 to 0830 hours. Missions:

1) Protect 45th CD's commitment into the penetration with five battalions and protect it against machine gun and artillery fire from the flanks

2) During the artillery preparation and subsequently, fulfill the missions in my order No. 033.

8. VVS. Missions:

1) On the morning of 23 August 1941, strike enemy firing means and personnel on the forward edge in the [following] regions: Hill 212.6 (at Zamatina), Hill 218.5 (south of Shishkina), Navol'nia, Siniakova, and Bortniki.

2) Suppress enemy artillery and reserves in [the following] regions:

a) Kalugino, Stepanovka, Khudkova, Rafenna, and Navol'nia; and

b) Kalugino, Mashutino, and Sushchevo.

3) Suppress enemy reserves approaching from Dukhovshchina.

4) Protect 45th CD's jumping-off region, its movement into the penetration, and its fulfillment of missions in the depths.

5) Protect the army's groupings in the Mamonov, Losevo, Muzhilova, Osipova, Artamonova, and Vasilisino regions. Special attention to protecting the Kapyrovshcina, Zubovshchina, and Repishche regions.

6) Missions for reconnaissance are as before.

9. CP and headquarters of the army – as before.

10. Operational and intelligence summaries – at previous periods.

Division commanders will receive missions by radio. Liaison officers will present combat orders on the fighting to me by 0600 hours on 23 August 1941.

The Commander of 19th Army, Lieutenant General Konev
The Member of the Military Council of 19th Army,
       Division Commissar Sheklanov
The Chief of Staff of 19th Army, [Colonel Malyshkin]

Combat Report on the Results of the Fighting in the Potelitsa and Balashova Regions and the Plan for the Offensive on 23 August 1941 (late on 22 August)

First. During the day on 22 August, the army completed regrouping on its right wing and continued destroying approaching enemy reserves along the remainder of the front. As a result of the obstinate fighting along the Potelitsa and Balashova axis, 91st and 89th RDs' units inflicted heavy losses on the enemy and, while throwing him back toward the northwest and west, reached the western edge of the woods east of Balashova and occupied Pochepova. According to verified information, 22 German tanks and 3 armored vehicles were destroyed and remained in our dispositions in the region west of Potelitsa. In addition, the enemy succeeded in towing 15 tanks, which were knocked out by our artillery, from this region. No fewer losses were suffered by the enemy in the Pochepova region, where artillery fire knocked out 25 German tanks, and another 15 enemy tanks were destroyed by the attack by our 202nd TR.

Second. As a result of the army's successful fighting on 21 August, the enemy significantly decreased his activity but, nevertheless, held on to the western bank of the Loinia River in the Losevo and Kazakova sector. To the south, our units occupied Kazakova, Muzhilova, and the woods 1 kilometer southeast of Muzhilova.

On the army's left wing, 64th RD and 101st TD continued destroying the remnants of the enemy 364th IR by a combined attack in the Skachkovo and Kakhanovo region.

Third. On 23 August, we decided to continue the offensive in the general direction of Dukhovshchina at 0830 hours, with the mission to destroy the enemy between the Loinia and Tsarevich Rivers. 45th Sep. CD will be committed in 64th RD's sector o exploit success toward Miagchenki, Sel'tso, and Dukhovshchina, with the aim to cut off the enemy's routes of withdrawal across the Tsarevich River and capture the woods west of Dukhovshchina by day's end on 23 August.

Konev, Sheklanov

Combat Report No. 014 on the Resumption of the Offensive on 23 August

1. The army's forces went over to the offensive at 0830 hours on 23 August after a one hour and 30-minute artillery preparation.

2. 45th Sep. CD was concentrated [as follows] by 0500 hours on 23 August: 52nd CR – in the woods southeast of Maslikhi and 0.5 kilometer southwest of Matveenki. 55th CR in the woods in the Hill 224.6 region. 58th CR in the woods northeast of the lumber mill at Raifa.

Headquarters of the division – 1 kilometer east of the lumber mill at Raifa.

The Chief of Staff of 19th Army, [Colonel Malyshkin]
The Military Commissar, Brigade Commissar Kazbintsev

Sources: "Boevye prikazy i doneseniia komanduiushchego voiskami 19 i Armii ot 22 24 avgusta 1941 g [Combat orders and reports of the commander of the forces of 19th Army of 22-23 August 1941], *SBDVOV*, issue 37, 180-183.

51. Order No. 03/op to the Forces of the Western Front of 23 August 1941 about 19th Army's Successful Offensive in the Period from 20-23 August 1941

Order No. 03/op to the Forces of the Western Front
23 August 1941   The Operating Army

Comrade Red Army men, commanders, and political workers!

It has been four days since our 19th Army went over to the offensive against the German-Fascist forces. As should be expected, the initial blow has inflicted a serious defeat on the overextended enemy. The 19th Army's forces, and especially the Red Army men, commanders, and political workers of 64th and 50th Rifle Divisions and 101st Tank Division's 202nd Tank Regiment, showed themselves to be valorous soldiers of our Red Army. Over the three days of battle, they crushingly defeated the Fascist 161st Infantry Division, seized its artillery, crushed its headquarters, seized maps and combat orders, and slaughtered no fewer than three thousand soldiers and officers.

The enemy tried to halt the advance by our forces on 21 and 22 August. He committed large forces of tanks and motorized infantry and attacked our units with great independence. But the days of easy enemy victories have already passed. The German-Fascist forces already know this. The glorious 64th and 50th Rifle Divisions – the leaders of our *front*, and the valiant 47th Aviation Division and its 61st and 215th Assault and 129th Fighter Regiments destroyed the Fascists' tanks and forced the Fascists to retreat in disorder. The enemy lost up to 130 tanks, more than 100 trucks, many guns, ammunition, and thousands of killed and wounded.

I order:

The commander of 19th Army and the commander of the VVS to give governmental awards to all Red Army men, pilots, commanders, and political workers who distinguished themselves in combat and also to units and formations that distinguished themselves.

Comrade Red Army men, commanders, and political workers! Comrade infantrymen, artillery men, *tankists*, cavalrymen, and pilots of the Western Front!

If 19th Army and the pilots of 47th Aviation Division alone inflicted a serious defeat on the enemy, then we will increase this success tenfold with the efforts of all of the forces of the *front* and strike an even more shattering blow on the enemy.

Comrades! The strength of the Fascists has been sapped. They cannot withstand our general decisive pressure. More decisively forward. Deny the enemy either a break or a minute's rest and do not let him collect himself. Be stoic to the end. Forward to victory!

Read this order in all of the companies, batteries, aviation and cavalry squadrons, commands, and headquarters.

The Commander of the Forces of the Western Front, Timoshenko
The Member of the Military Council of the Western Front

Source: "Prikaz No. 03/op voiskam Zapadnogo fronta ot 23 avgusta 1941 g. ob uspeshnom nastuplenii 19-i Armii v period s 20 po 23 avgusta 1941 g." [Order no. 03/op to the forces of the Western Front of 23 August 1941 about 19th Army's successful offensive in the period from 20-23 August 1941], *SBDVOV*, issue 41, 61-62.

52. Combat Order No. 26 of the Commander of the Forces of 29th Army of 23 August 1941 to the Commander of 252nd Rifle Division on the Defense of the Krasnye Sosny, Osinovka, Petrovo, and Averkovo Line

Combat Order No. 26, Headquarters, 29th Army,

Bentsy,

1430 hours on 23 August 1941

1. According to information about 22nd Army's fighting, up to an enemy panzer division penetrated toward Velikie Luki from the west, and forward reconnaissance subunits (up to 10 tankettes and infantry) have been detected in the vicinity of Kun'ia Station, Artemovo Platform, and Gruzdovo [27-35 kilometers east of Velikie Luki] on the morning of 23 August 1941. A threat is being created to 22nd Army's rear and 29th Army's flank.

A grouping of enemy with active offensive actions continue to remain in the Khlebanikha and Borok region [37 kilometers southwest of Staraia Toropa] and in the Liubovitsy and Selishche sector [35 kilometers south-southwest of Staraia Toropa] along the southern bank of the Dvinka River on 29th Army's right flank.

2. On the right, a composite battalion consisting of those selected from a junior officers course and seminar of junior political workers is protecting the isthmus between Lake Kodosno and Lake Zhizhitskoe in the Zasenovo and Pashivkino sector [20 kilometers west of Staraia Toropa].

On the left, the army's shock group (246th and 243rd RDs) is continuing a decisive offensive in the general direction of Il'ino [8 kilometers south of the Western Dvina River and 40 kilometers south of Staraia Toropa]. The sectors of Belianka Farm and Sevast'ianovo [25-27 kilometers south-southeast of Staraia Toropa] are being protected by a sniper company.

3. 252nd RD will go over to a firm all-round defense at nightfall on 23 August 1941, with separate company and platoon strongpoints and AT regions formed into battalion defensive regions in [the following] sectors: 1) Cheremukha Farm, 2) Olenitsa 1, 3) Krasnye Sosny, 4) Ust'e, 5) Averkovo, and 6) Petrovo [on the northern bank of the Western Dvina River 20-25 kilometers south of Staraia Toropa], with the mission to protect firmly positions in the Krasnye Sosny, Krivets, Osinovka, Olenitsa 1, Ust'e, Petrovo, Bukharikha, and Averkovo sectors along the Western Dvina River and prevent an enemy penetration from the south and west.

The boundary on the left: Lake Neretto, Bol'shaia Griada, and Sutrmino.

Be prepared for work, in the first instance, by 0700 hours on 24 August 1941. Be prepared for defense by 0400 hours on 24 August 1941. Carry out work for improving the engineer and defensive structures into a fully equipped and occupied defensive belt. The CP of the commander of 252nd RD, when it goes over to the defense, will be in the forest west of Goluby [3 kilometers north of the Western Dvina River and 20 kilometers south of Staraia Toropa].

4. The army's Chief of Engineer Troops will create reliable engineer obstacles and mine fields along the approaches to 252nd RD's defensive positions, present a plan for the work immediately, and complete the work in as short a period as possible, having employed all obstacle means and reserves of mines.

5. Submit reports: 1) about the beginning of the transition to the defense; 2) upon the concentration of units in their defensive sectors; and 3) about the readiness of the defenses no later than 0500 hours on 24 August 1941.

The Commander of 29th Army, Lieutenant General Maslennikov
The Member of the Military Council, Divisional Commissar Gurov
The Chief of Staff of 29th Army, Colonel Massal'sky [signed by
    Captain N. A. Gorbin, Assistant Chief of the Operations Department]

Source: "Boevoe rasporiazhenie komanduiushchego voiskami 29-i Armii No. 26 ot 23 avgusta 1941 g. komandiru 252-i Strelkovoi Divizii na oboronu rubezha Krasnye Sosny, Osinovka, Petrovo, Averkovo" [Combat order No. 26 of the commander of the forces of 29th Army of 23 August 1941 to the commander of 252nd Rifle Division on the defense of the Krasnye Sosny, Osinovka, Petrovo, and Averkovo line], *SBDVOV*, issue 41, 268.

53. Operational Summary No. 116 of the Headquarters of the Western Front at 2000 hours on 23 August 1941 about the Combat Operations of the *Front's* Forces

Operational Summary No. 116 at 2000 hours on 23 August 1941,
Headquarters, Western Front
1:500,000 and 100,000 scale maps

First. The Western Front, while going over to an offensive with all of its armies on the morning of 23 August, was met with strong enemy counterattacks along its right wing. Along the remainder of the front, the attacking forces are encountering stubborn enemy resistance.

Second. 22nd Army. In connection with the enemy penetration on the army's left wing, while protecting itself from the west, [the army] is organizing a counterstroke, with the aim of destroying the penetrating enemy grouping.

On 22 August the enemy penetrated 186th RD's sector with a force of up to a motorized division with tanks and an infantry division and rushed toward the north and northwest. By the morning of 23 August, the enemy seized Velikopol'e Station and Ushitsy State Farm, and, by 1200 hours on 23 August, he reached Kun'ia and Ushitsy Stations with the advanced elements of two motorized columns, numbering 150 vehicles each.

In addition to sending two detachments on vehicles to the Kun'ia region, a regiment from 98th RD has been dispatched by vehicle to the Palashkovo, Zemlianichino, and Piskunovo region to destroy the penetrating enemy, on the instructions of the 22nd Army's commander, 179th RD is moving into the Lukino region.

A detachment of signalmen dispatched by order of 22nd Army's headquarters, engaged in fighting with small groups of enemy (infantry, motorcyclists, and 4-5 armored vehicles) in the region due north of Begunovo and Kun'ia.

22nd and 29th Armies' aircraft and the *front's* aircraft are attacking the enemy columns.

A detachment of students with up to 250 men has been sent to the vicinity of Zhizhitsa Station in accordance with orders of 29th Army's commander, with the mission to hold onto the ground between the lakes and prevent the enemy from spreading out toward the east.

The positions of 48th TD are unchanged.

News has not been received about the positions of the army's remaining units.

22nd Army's CP displaced to the region of 29th RC's CP.

The rear service units of the army's headquarters have been subjected to air strikes and artillery fire and are relocating from Nazimovo Station to Toropets under the threat of enemy motorized units.

Third. 29th Army. The army's units are continuing their offensive along the entire front.

The attack by two regiments of 252nd RD has been halted by repeated enemy counterattacks in the Shinkino and Marker 160.2 sector (1 kilometer northeast of Vypolzovo) along the southern bank of the Western Dvina River. The enemy is trying to penetrate toward the north and northeast. All of the counterattacks were successfully repelled by the division's units.

246th and 243rd RD are developing a successful attack, while throwing the enemy back toward the west.

1st and 2nd MRRs are fighting to capture Katkovo.

29th CR and BEPO No. 53 are fulfilling their previous missions [flank protection].

246th and 243rd RDs destroyed more than two enemy battalions in the fighting on 22 August.

Obstacles and mines have been emplaced north of Lake Kodosno.

Headquarters of 29th Army – Bentsy and the forest one half kilometer south of Poiarkovo.

Fourth. The Cavalry Group (50th and 53rd CDs) – no news received.

Fifth. 30th Army. The army's units went over to an offensive at 1300 hours on 23 August after an hour-long artillery preparation.

The enemy, while defending along a previously prepared [defensive] line with a force of up to three infantry divisions, offered stubborn fire resistance.

242nd RD, while protecting itself along the Ust'e 1, Moshki, Orlovo, and Staroe Morokhovo line, is attacking toward Erkhovo and Marker 215.2, in cooperation with 250th RD and 107th TD's 143rd TR.

250th RD, without 918th RR, is fighting for Pochinok 2.

162nd RD is fighting for Staroe Selo.

251st RD, while forced to abandon Sechenki, once again approached the eastern outskirts of Sechenki at 1700 hours and is fighting to capture that village.

107th TD's 120th MRR is defending its previous positions.

237th MRR is attacking in second echelon behind 250th RD's right wing.

Sixth. 19th Army went over to the offensive at 0830 hours after a 30-minute artillery preparation. The enemy is offering fire resistance. During the first half of the day, the operations of the army's units were limited chiefly to exchanging fire, and, only in the second half of the day did the division began a slow advance along separate axes.

The army's units were fighting [as follows] at 1700 hours:

244th RD, while defending in the Shupeki, Zaria, and Priglovo sector on the right wing, attacked on the remainder of the front but was unsuccessful; it is now conducting fire exchanges with enemy centers of resistance in the Kuchino, Shcherdina, and Priglovo sector.

Losses: 4 men killed and 21 men wounded and 3 horses killed and 2 wounded.

166th RD is advancing forward slowly in its center and, having enveloped Kaniutino from the north and south, is fighting for possession of that point.

The division's left wing captured the heights south of Zaovrazh'e.

91st RD, while overcoming stubborn enemy resistance, reached the Loinia River in the sector from Azerinki to (incl.) the northern outskirts of Pochepova (seized, although the settlement was abandoned to our forces as a result of previous battles) by 1700 hours.

The losses of the division for 22 August: 28 men killed and 45 wounded. One 76mm gun, one 45mm gun, and one heavy machine gun were destroyed.

89th RD, while attacking toward Sel'tso with two regiments, is fighting to capture Pochepova with its right wing and to reach the Loinia River with its left wing.

Losses: 29 soldiers and 2 junior command cadre killed, 6 soldiers and 1 junior command cadre wounded, and 6 horses killed and 1 wounded.

50th RD, while encountering strong fire resistance from the heights south of Afanas'evo and after repelling a counterattack, captured the eastern outskirts of Kazakova and Ivanova by 1700 hours. The division's attack is continuing.

64th RD, while attacking with its right wing, forced the Tsarevich River and is continuing its attack toward Siniakovo. It reached the grove 1 kilometer southwest of Osipova with its left wing.

101st TD is fighting in its previous positions, with an insignificant advance.

45th CD did not conduct combat operations and is located in its previous assembly area.

Seventh. 16th Army. The positions of the army's units are unchanged.

38th RD attacked toward Novosel'e (eastern) but was unsuccessful.

The enemy offered strong fire resistance.

108th RD – positions unchanged.

Eighth. 20th Army went over to an offensive in the general direction of Dobromino Station with its left wing at 1100 hours on 23 August. The offensive by the army's units is developing successfully.

144th RD, while defending positions along the Dnepr River in the sector from (incl.) the crossing at Solov'evo [southward] to Ratchino, successfully repelled an enemy attack from the Solov'evo region. The division's forward detachments are in Makeevo and Pnevo.

73rd RD is continuing to defend along the eastern bank of the Dnepr River from Zabor'e to Sopshino, while holding onto the Ratchino, Pashkovo, and Golovino region on the western bank.

229th RD attacked from positions from Motovo to the southern edge of the grove 1 kilometer east of Motovo toward Suborovka and Dobromino at 1110 hours on 23 August and, while bypassing Suborovka from the west, reached positions from the stream on the northern outskirts of Suborovka to (incl.) Hill 249.9 by 1200 hours.

It seized 23 men from the enemy's 263rd ID as prisoners.

The enemy withdrew southward in small groups.

153rd RD attacked from the Mogilitsy and Vishniaki line toward Vasilevo, and, while overcoming stubborn enemy resistance, the division reached positions from the northern slopes of the hill 0.5 kilometers southeast of Suborovka to the northern edge of the woods 0.5 kilometers southwest of Vishniaki by 1430 hours.

The enemy withdrew in disorderly groups toward Vasilevo. Two men were taken captive.

161st RD, while attacking from the Hill 205.9, (incl.) northern outskirts of Chuvakhi, and Samodurovka line toward Alekseevo, reached Pogibilka, which it had abandoned earlier, and is fighting to capture it.

The division's advance was held up by strong enemy flanking fire from Hill 228.0.

129th RD is firmly holding onto positions along the Ustrom River, and 457th RR has been attacking toward Prokhlopovka since 1100 hours.

457th RR, while overcoming strong enemy fire resistance, approached the eastern outskirts of Klemiatino once again by 1300 hours.

Ninth. The VVS of the *front* cooperated with the ground forces on the battlefield, conducted reconnaissance, and destroyed enemy reserves approaching the front during the first half of the day on 23 August. They conducted 116 aircraft sorties. Bombs dropped: 12 FAB-100, 144 FAB-50, 11 AO-8, and 1,440 AZh-2 KS.

23rd MAD. Eleven TB-3 aircraft fulfilled special missions on the night of 22-23 August. Two aircraft dropped leaflets in the Mogilev region

43rd MAD cooperated with 19th Army's units and operated against enemy troop concentrations in the Novo-Nikol'skoe, Pesnevo, and Kulagino region. According to crew observations, fires appeared as a result of the bombing.

46th MAD bombed the enemy in the Shikhtovo and Komarova region with 6 aircraft on the night of 22-23 August. Fires appeared in the region of operations.

During the first half of the day, the division cooperated with 29th Army and bombed up to 50 vehicles and tanks in the vicinity of Kun'ia Station.

47th MAD operated against enemy motor-mechanized units, artillery, and infantry in the Sirotinka, Sushchevo, Turishchevo, Afanas'eva, and Siniakova region and protected the unloading of forces at Sychevka Station.

As a result of the bombing of enemy forces, up to 500 infantrymen, up to 15 horses, and one gun were destroyed, fire from two batteries of antiaircraft artillery and two batteries of field artillery were suppressed; although the blows inflicted on tanks were not established, since the latter were located in the forest.

31st MAD cooperated with 22nd Army's forces. Combat flights were not carried out before 1130 hours because of poor meteorological conditions.

The Chief of Staff of the Western Front, Lieutenant General Sokolovsky
The Military Commissar of the Western Front's headquarters,
     Regimental Commissar Anshakov
The Chief of the Operations Department, Lieutenant General Malandin

Source: "Operativnaia svodka shtaba Zapadnogo fronta No. 116 k 2000 chasam 23 avgusta 1941 g. o boevykh deistviiakh voisk fronta" [Operational summary no. 116 of the headquarters of the Western Front at 2000 hours on 23 August 1941 about the combat operations of the *front's* forces], *SBDVOV*, issue 41, 63-66.

54. Operational Summary No. 118 of the Headquarters of the Western Front at 2000 hours on 24 August 1941 about the Combat Operations of the *Front's* Forces

Operational Summary No. 118 at 2000 hours on 24 August 1941,
Headquarters, Western Front
1:500,000 and 100,000 scale maps

First. The Western Front, while continuing its offensive in its center and on its left wing, is organizing on its right wing to liquidate the penetration and destroy enemy units that have penetrated into our rear.

Second. 22nd Army. According to verified data, the enemy forces operating in the army's rear have been determined to be two infantry divisions and two panzer divisions (110th and 206th IDs and 19th and 20th PzDs) and an armored brigade. Judging from a captured order, the enemy is striving to encircle 22nd Army's units.

According to information from 22nd Army's commander, at 1200 hours on 24 August, the enemy has reached the Lake Artemovo, Borok, and Velikopol'e line with his forward units. The main forces of penetrating enemy motor-mechanized units have reached the Peski, Ushitsy Station, and Kun'ia line.

22nd Army's units are occupying their previous positions along the Velikie Luki and Lake Savinskoe front. The situation in the sector of 62nd RC's left wing is unclear. Additionally, the enemy penetrated 174th RD's front in the Podol, Kotin Bor, and Zabolot'e sector on the morning of 24 August.

Ershakov, having concentrated part of 126th and 179th RDs' forces, will launch an attack toward Ushitsy Station, with the aim of inflicting a defeat on the penetrating enemy group. According to unverified information, Ushitsy was taken by Ershakov at 1115 hours on 24 August.

Third. 29th Army. The army's units, while defending on the right wing, are continuing an offensive toward Il'ino on the left wing.

The enemy, while occupying separate centers of resistance with tanks dug into the ground, is conducting strong mortar and artillery fire.

252nd RD organized an all around defense with a system of strong points on the northern bank of the Western Dvina River, while protecting the army's right flank. The enemy along the division's front is displaying no activity.

246th RD went on the offense at 0800 hours on 24 August after a half-hour artillery preparation and attacked enemy strong points on the immediate outskirts of Trubniki and the forest south of Trubniki.

The division's left wing, while cooperating with 243rd RD, is fighting for Hill 209.6, while enveloping it from the south.

In summary of the fighting, the division's units advanced 0.5 kilometer.

243rd RD, while attacking, captured the northeaster outskirts of Malyi Borok and is fighting for Hill 209.6, while enveloping it from the south.

1st and 2nd MRR are continuing the fight for Katkovo.

29th CR is fulfilling its previous mission [flank protection].

The Composite Battalion of students is holding onto the neck of land between the lakes (Lake Kodosno and Lake Zhizhitskoe) in positions from Zasekovo to Pashivkino.

The enemy is conducting artillery and mortar fire against Zhizhitsa Station.

Losses for 22 and 23 August: 227 men killed, 653 wounded, and 38 missing in action.

Headquarters of 29th Army – Bentsy. CP 0.5 kilometer south of Poiarkovo.

Fourth. 30th Army went over to an offensive toward Shelepy and Zarech'e with 162nd RD's units, reinforced by two rifle regiments and 30 tanks.

At first, 162nd RD's attack was unsuccessful, but 251st RD was committed to combat at 1600 hours, and at 1640 hours 251st RD's units, in cooperation with 162nd RD penetrated into Sechenki. The fight in the village is still underway.

Observation established that the enemy in the Gorodno and Krechets region began to withdraw, while driving the cattle with them and carrying off the local population.

162nd and 251st RDs' attacks are continuing.

In the remaining sectors of the front, fire fights are going on in existing positions.

Fifth. 19th Army, while protecting the Shupeki and Priglovo line with part of 244th RD's forces, attacked with its remaining forces at 1230 hours on 24 August.

The enemy, while bringing reserves up from the depths, is striving to halt the attacks by 19th Army's units.

As a result of fierce fighting, 166th RD captured Kaniutino and is fighting in the woods 300-400 meters west of the village, and the division's left wing captured Zubovo.

On the army's left wing, the enemy counterattacked from the Kokhanovo region at 0930 hours against our units at the boundary between 64th RD and 101st TD with a detachment of up to a battalion of infantry in close order formation, but the enemy counterattack was beaten back with heavy losses [to the enemy].

According to preliminary information, [the following were] seized: a four-gun battery (the caliber is being determined), two antitank guns, 5 bicycles, and 2 motorcycles. In addition, five burned out tanks and two trucks were discovered on the battlefield.

In the remaining sectors of the army's front, fierce fighting is underway with counterattacking enemy tanks.

Sixth. 16th Army. The positions of the army's units are unchanged ... ..

Seventh. 20th Army was continuing its offensive in the general direction of Dobromino, while holding firmly to the Dnepr River along a line from the crossing at Solov'evo [southward] to (incl.) Sopshino.

144th and 73rd RDs are occupying their previous positions.

144th RD's reconnaissance units discovered a mine field on the eastern edge of the woods south of Pashkovo.

73rd RD's artillery in the Erdetsy region dispersed a company of enemy infantry, destroying several mortars and forcing enemy infantry at the mouth of the Nadva River to run away.

229th RD is slowly advancing toward Suborovka, while encountering stubborn enemy resistance.

153rd RD was forced to abandon the woods northeast of Vishniaki by an enemy counterattack with tanks and withdrew to the vicinity of Hill 249.9, but, after resuming its attack at 1130 hours, the division once again drove the enemy southward and assaulted and captured the grove northwest of Vishniaki.

161st RD is fighting in its previous positions.

129th RD's positions are unchanged.

CP of 20th Army – the woods southwest of Novoselki.

Eighth. The VVS of the *front* had the missions on 24 August to cooperate with 19th Army's units on the battlefield and destroy penetrating enemy units on 22nd Army's front. Because of poor meteorological conditions, VVS activities were limited. A total of 35 aircraft sorties were flown.

46th MAD bombed penetrating enemy motor-mechanized units and tanks in the vicinity of Kun'ia Station and Nazimova and enemy troop concentrations in the Il'ino region on 24 August. Observation established direct hits on tanks and vehicles in the Kun'ia station and Nazimova region. A large number of fires appeared in the Il'ino region after the bombing.

31st MAD attacked the enemy in the vicinity of Kun'ia Station on the night of 23-24 August and bombed an enemy column in the Peski and Zhigalovo region on the morning of 24 August.

23rd BAD, 43rd MAD, 47th MAD, and 38th RAS did not carry out combat flights due to the poor meteorological conditions.

Enemy losses: According to additional information, one ME-109 aircraft was shot down on 23 August.

Our losses: One MIG-3 aircraft did not return to its airfield.

The 3 IL-2 aircraft that did not return on 21 and 22 August landed in their own territory.

> The Chief of Staff of the Western Front, Lieutenant General Sokolovsky
> The Military Commissar of the Western Front's headquarters,
>   Regimental Commissar Anshakov
> The Chief of the Operations Department, Lieutenant General Malandin

Source: "Operativnaia svodka shtaba Zapadnogo fronta No. 118 k 2000 chasam 24 avgusta 1941 g. o boevykh deistviiakh voisk fronta" [Operational summary no. 118 of the headquarters of the Western Front at 2000 hours on 24 August 1941 about the combat operations of the *front's* forces], *SBDVOV*, issue 41, 70-.72.

55. Report by the Military Council of 19th Army to the Military Council of the Western Front about the Grouping and Combat Operations of the Enemy Opposite the Army's Front during the Period from 17 through 31 August 1941

1 September 1941

After prolonged fighting along the Vop' River, the enemy began a withdrawal toward the west, after which the grouping of German forces was as follows:

First. 35th ID operated to the north of the Krasnitsa, Brakulevo, and Morozova line. South of this line, 5th ID (14th, 56th, and 75th IRs and 44th AR) withdrew and then went over to the defense in the Shatuny and Balashova sector. This division transitioned to the defense, with the forward edge of its main defensive belt along the Panova, Shakhlovo, Novoselishche, Ivaniki, and Balashova line. In front of this defensive belt, the Germans conducted a delaying action, at first along the Mamonovo and Gorbatovskaia line, and then along the Zanino and Zubova line. 5th ID occupied a defense, having three regiments in a single echelon. The defensive front extended 11-12 kilometers. Evidently, as a result of this comparatively broad front, 5th ID did not have large reserves. During the period of the fighting, two reserve groups were determined [as follows]:

a) In the woods northwest of Shakhlovo – up to an infantry battalion; and

b) In the Staraia Kazarina region – up to an infantry battalion.

Overall, 5-6 artillery batteries operated in 5th ID's sector, of which one battery was heavy.

Second. 161st ID (336th, 364th, and 371st IR) operated in the Kapyrovshchina, Kazakova, Chistaia, and Krovopuskovo sector. This division, while conducting a fighting withdrawal, went over to the defense in positions in the Kazakova and Chistaia sector along the Loinia and Tsarevich Rivers.

161st ID occupied a defense with all of its regiments in a single echelon, and the width of the defensive sector reached 12-13 kilometers.

Third. [The following] units were operating in the interval between 5th and 161st IDs: 312th IR, 900th Armored [Motorized] Brigade, and even 1st Bn, of 35th ID's 34th IR was noticed.

Fourth. At the beginning of 19th Army's offensive operation, the densest combat formation of the Germans was north of the Potelitsa and Balashova line. The main mass of enemy artillery was situated in the forest in the Zanino, Losevo, and Moteva regions. This circumstance could be explained only by the fact that, before the beginning of this offensive operation and especially during the period of Group Boldin's escape from encirclement, the main effort of 19th Army's forces were directed on the right wing. In addition, *maskirovka* [camouflage] measures and deceiving the enemy in regard to the actual direction of the main attack played a large role in preparations for the operation.

Thus, 19th Army's offensive, whose main attack was delivered in the Balashova and Nefedovshchina sector, found the German forces in an unfavorable grouping. The main attack, which 91st 89th, 50th, and 64th RDs conducted, focused primarily on the enemy's 161st ID, and, therefore, during the period from 17 through 21 August, this division lost no fewer than two-thirds of its personnel and more than half of its weapons. The German command had to withdraw the remnants of 161st ID from the front and, in order to prevent a penetration of the front, it began to throw units in from the depths and remove units from passive sectors of the front (16th Army). 8th ID's 84th IR and 28th ID's 83rd IR were thrown into the sector from Pochepova to Zaitseva State Farm. The remaining regiments of 28th ID (7th and 49th IRs) occupied positions from Popova to Chistaia, having relieved the remnants of two battalions of 336th and 364th IRs.

During the period from 18 through 23 August, the enemy threw his tanks into the Losevo and Muzhilova sector, and, on the evening of 20 August, his tank subunits made an attempt to penetrate to the crossing over the Vop' River from the direction of Losevo toward Potelitsa and Zadniaia. Besides this, in the period from

20 through 22 August, he tried to deliver attacks with separate groups of tanks (10-30) in the [following] regions: Pochepova, Bolotino, and Muzhilova. However, all of these attempts ended as enemy failures. The enemy, having lost more than 130 tanks, was forced to cease his counterattacks. According to those found dead, it was determined that 7th PzD's units participated in these counterattacks.

Fifth. The fighting in the period from 17 through 22 August compelled the German command to thicken the combat formations of German forces south of the Borniki and Novoselishche line. By day's end on 26 August, by virtue of the heavy losses suffered by 8th ID's 84th IR and 28th ID's 7th IR, units of the enemy's 44th and 87th IDs and 14th MotD, began to approach 19th Army's front. On the basis of interrogations of prisoners on 28 and 29 August, it was determined that 44th ID's units were moving toward Balashova and 87th ID's units – southward toward Stepanidino. At the same time, 14th MotD's 53rd IR relieved 28th ID's 7th IR in the Siniakovo and Osipova sector. Thus, in 18 days of battle, [the following] were smashed along 19th Army's front: 161st ID, 8th ID's 84th IR, and 28th ID's 7th IR. By 1 September, the enemy brought up units of three new divisions, the grouping of which has still not been revealed. Units of 35th ID, 5th ID, 8th ID, 28th ID, 44th ID, 87th ID, 14th MotD, and 7th PzD have been identified along the front. Overall, 30 enemy batteries are operating along the army's front.

Sixth. During the period from 28 through 31 August, the army's units, while conducting offensive fighting, reconnoitered the enemy's defenses. This is shown on the attached scheme [unavailable].

> The Commander of 19th Army, Lieutenant General Konev
> The Member of the Military Council of 19th Army, Divisional
>   Commissar Sheklanov
> The Chief of Staff of 19th Army, [Colonel Malyshkin]

Source: "Doklad voennogo soveta 19-i Armii voennomu sovetu Zapadnogo fronta o gruppirovke i boevykh deistviiakh protivnika pered frontom armii v period s 17 po 31 avgusta 1941 g." [Report by the Military Council of 19th Army to the Military Council of the Western Front about the grouping and combat operations of the enemy opposite the army's front during the period from 17 through 31 August 1941], *SBDVOV*, issue 41, 195-196.

Appendix P

The Second Soviet Counteroffensive: The Reserve Front's El'nia Offensive, 8-24 August 1941

1. Combat Order of the Commander of the Forces of 24th Army of 8 August 1941

To the Commanders of 107th, 100th, 102nd, 19th, 120th, 105th, and 106th Divisions

1. Combat during the first half of 8 August 1942 demonstrated that, in spite of our clear superiority, especially in 107th and 100th RDs' sectors, the advance by our units is very slow. In two hours of fighting, 107th RD advanced 2 kilometers, and 100th RD approximately 1.5-2 kilometers in three hours. The remaining divisions are marking time in place and, while not moving forward, with uncountable complaints about enemy fire.

2. The infantry are not exploiting artillery fire in order to move forward rapidly, and the artillery, while firing many rounds, are having little effect.

3. The infantry artillerymen are firing at blank spaces. Eliminate all of the shortcomings noted above.

Rakutin

Source: Mikhail Lubiagov, *Pod El'nei v sorok pervom* [At El'nia in forty-one] (Smolensk: "Rusich," 2005), 229, citing *TsAMO* [Central Archives of the [Soviet Union's] Ministry of Defense), f. [fond]. 1087, o. [opus] 1, d. [file], l. [page] 70.

2. Order of the Commander of the Forces of the Reserve Front of 9 August 1941 to the Commander of the Forces of 24th Army

To the Commanders of 19th, 100th, 102nd, 103rd, 106th, 107th, and 120th Divisions

The practice of combat in the El'nia region demonstrates that, besides heroic commanders and commissars, we have commanders and commissar who, during the three days of the offensive, did not advance a single kilometer. Such commanders usually use strong mortar, automatic weapons fire, and aircraft bombing to excuse their inactivity and failure to fulfill combat orders, and naïve senior commanders and commissars relate liberally to such commanders and, up to this time, however strange it is, consider marking time in place and the failure to fulfill orders about advance to a designated region usual matter, and the guilty commanders and commissars bear no kind of responsibility.

Unfortunately, there are such commanders who, having reached a line, withdraw to their jumping-off positions without any sort of permission and, in the morning, once again begin to attack a point which was abandoned by them in the evening without any basis.

I DEMAND:

1. Instill in all commanders of platoons, company, battalions, and units [regiments] that any marking time in place and failure to fulfill orders about advancing forward will be looked upon as a display of cowardice and non-fulfillment of orders, with all the resulting consequences.

2. Conduct the most decisive struggle – do not stop at extreme measures – with all commanders and commissars who relate liberally with subunits commanders who mark time in place or fail to fulfill orders about advancing forward to their designated line because of selfish motives or fear of losses.

3. Instill in commanders and commissars who mark time in place with their units for several days that it is far better in fierce combat to achieve your mission and suffer losses than not to achieve any sort of aims and suffer losses every day by marking time in place under enemy fire from day to day.

4. Report to me what you have done to fulfill these instructions personally to me through the commander of 24th Army, Comrade Rakutin.

The Commander of the Reserve Front, Army General Zhukov

Source: Mikhail Lubiagov, *Pod El'nei v sorok pervom* [At El'nia in forty-one] (Smolensk: "Rusich," 2005), 249-250, citing *TsAMO* [Central Archives of the [Soviet Union's] Ministry of Defense), f. 1087, o. 1, d. 5. l. 75.

3. Extracts from Orders and Summary Reports by the Commander of the Forces of 24th Army and the Reserve Front on 10-11 August 1941

11 August 1941 – Rakutin, Commander of 24th Army

100th RD had no success over the course of 8, 9, and 10 August. The division marked time in place, and, as a result, the Group of Forces' fulfillment of the overall operational mission was frustrated. The division commander did not succeed in organizing forward movement, failed to organize the struggle with deserters and panic mongers, and obscenely treated this phenomena in 331st RR and 85th RR liberally.

10 August – Zhukov, Commander of the Reserve Front

Colonel Gruzdev, 100th RD's former chief of staff, having displayed confusion and inactivity, is transferred to command a regiment … . [Gruzdev was demoted to command 85th Rifle Regiment on 11 August]

I am announcing a reprimand to the commander of 100th RD, Major General Russianov, and the commissar of 100th RD, Senior Battalion Commissar, Comrade Filiashkin, for not fulfilling my orders, and am warning that, if the division does not fulfill its assigned mission on 11 and 12 August, I will consider the matter of relieving them of their duties and turning them over for judgment.

Source: Mikhail Lubiagov, *Pod El'nei v sorok pervom* [At El'nia in forty-one] (Smolensk: "Rusich," 2005), 252.

4. Extracts from Combat Orders and Reports of the Commander of the Forces of 24th Army, 10-16 August 1941 [additional to the narrative volume]

10 August – Combat Order No. 013

The army's operational group will fulfill its previously assigned mission for the liberation of El'nia ... . Begin the attack at 0800 hours on 11 August 1941.

11 August – Combat Order No. 015

107th RD and 102nd TD, supported by 275th CAR, 573rd GAR (without 3rd Battalion), 1st and 3rd Batteries, 42nd Rocket Artillery Battalion (M-13), a composite battalion of tanks (KV, T-34, BT, and T-26), two bomber aircraft, and six fighters, must reach the railroad bed 1.25 kilometers south of Voloskovo Farm by day's end on 11 August and attack and destroy the enemy in the vicinity of Lysovka and Podmosh'e Farm with special detachments of up to a battalion each on the night of 11-12 August.

13 August – Combat Order No. 016

The enemy is continuing to resist stubbornly in prepared defenses with units of 14th, 15th, and 268th IDs, 17th MotD, 10th PzD, and newly-arrived regiments belonging to an SS division, while going over to local counterattacks with small groups of tanks in separate sectors ... .

24th Army's forces will continue to fulfill the mission assigned to them in Order No. 015 of 11 August 1941 for the encirclement and destruction of the enemy's El'nia grouping. The 30-minute artillery preparation will be at 0730 hours and the beginning of the attack at 0800 hours on 13 August 1941.

Rakutin, Ivanov, Kondrat'ev

13 August – Combat Report

On the left wing, 105th RD captured Pogarnoe, and 106th MD seized Mal'tsevo and Lipnia. The encirclement ring narrowed with great difficulty and, in the center of the bulge, fierce fighting occurred without any advance ... .

100th RD fought all day for the Bykovo-Ustinovo line, while attacking with one regiment from Perganovo to envelop Bykovo. The commander of 331st RR, Major Nikolai Iakovlevich Soloshenko, was killed in combat.

103rd MD, with two regiments, fought in its previous positions.

19th RD was fighting along the Zhilino-Klemiatino Farm line, east of Podmosh'e, against heavy enemy artillery and mortar fire, counterattacks, and enemy bombing but stood its ground, destroying 400 German soldiers and officers.

14 August – Combat Order No. 017

Continue to attack toward El'nia, skillfully and successfully smashing the enemy ... . The 30-minute artillery preparation will be at 0630 hours and the beginning of the attack at 0700 hours on 14 August 1941

15 August – Fragmentary Order of 24th Army

On the right wing, exploiting the success achieved on 14 August, 102nd TD and 107th RD will continue to encircle the enemy by reaching the El'nia-Boltutino road.

100th RD will continue its attack from the Perganovo region toward Hill 234.0 in the Ageevka region.

The remaining units – 103rd, 19th, `20th, 105th, and 106th Divisions – will dig in along their present line and work out on the ground all questions of cooperation between infantry, artillery, tanks, and aviation.

16 August – Combat Order No. 018

The defeated units of enemy 17th and 15th IDs, SS "*Reich*," 268th ID, and 10th Sep. PzD are continuing to defend the El'nia axis, while going over to local counterattacks … .

24th Army's units will attack along the entire front at 2100 hours on 16 August 1941 for the final encirclement and destruction of the enemy's El'nia grouping … .

107th RD and 102nd TD, with previously assigned reinforcements, after bringing forward a motorized regiment and a tank group, will conduct the main attack on the right wing toward Sadki and Lysovka … .

Source: Mikhail Lubiagov, *Pod El'nei v sorok pervom* [At El'nia in forty-one] (Smolensk: "Rusich," 2005), 248, 261, 276-277, 284-285, 304, 311-313, 322, citing *TsAMO* [Central Archives of the (Soviet Union's) Ministry of Defense], f. 1087, o. 1, d. 5. l. 75-98, 124..

5. Extract from Combat Orders of the Commander of the Forces of 24th Army on 18 and 20 August 1941

18 August – Combat Order No. 019 (paraphrased)

24th Army's main forces will conduct the main attack on the army's right wing, a decisive blow to slam the encirclement ring shut … .

107th RD and the rested and refitted 102nd RD, the latter with the remnants of 105th TD, will conduct the army's main attack in the general direction of Gur'evo, Lysovka, and Leonidovo to close the encirclement ring in the Leonidovo region. Capture the Vypolzovo and Lysovka line at day's end on 18 August … .

In the center, 103rd RD will attack toward Semeshino and Sofievka and reach the Hill 242.3 and Shilovo line by day's end … .

19th RD will capture the Prilepy and Iur'evo line by day's end on 18 August.

18 August – Memorandum of Zhukov, the *front* commander, accompanying Order No. 019:

105th TD, despite my categorical warning about moving forward, has marked time in one place for 10 days and, without achieving any kind of results, has suffered losses.

In light of its inability to resolve independent combat missions, 105th TD is disbanded and will turn its personnel and equipment over to 102nd TD.

Demote the commander of the division, Regimental Commissar Biriukov, in rank because he could not cope with his duties.

2. Relieve the commander of 106th MD, Colonel Alekseev, who has been repeatedly warned about his unsatisfactory fulfillment of combat mission, from his assigned duties and appoint him, at reduced rank, to command 309th RD's 955th RR.

3. Appoint Colonel Brynzov, the former commander of 158th RD, as commander of 106th MD.

4. Relieve Major Mita, the commander of 955th RR, from his duties for the panicky conduct of the regiment and appoint him to the post of battalion commander in the regiment.

5. I am announcing a reprimand of Major General Petrov, the commander of 120th RD, for unsatisfactory and passive fulfillment of his combat missions and am warning him that, if he continues to fulfill assigned missions as poorly, he will be relieved from command and reduced in rank.

Zhukov

20 August at 1020 hours – Combat Order No. 020 (paraphrased)
Continue the offensive and completely fulfill the missions assigned on Order No. 019 by day's end on 21 August … .

Only 120th RD fulfilled its assigned mission on 19 August by repelling an enemy counterattacks and going over to the attack … . but 107th RD operated poorly because the regiments conducting the attack were disorganized … . The 765th RR marked time in place all day long in front of the village of Sadki, and 630th RR captured only the southwestern outskirts of Mitino. Such an offensive tempo did not secure 102nd TD's success …

Source: Mikhail Lubiagov, *Pod El'nei v sorok pervom* [At El'nia in forty-one] (Smolensk: "Rusich," 2005), 248, 261, 276-277, 284-285, 304, 311-313, 322, citing *TsAMO* [Central Archives of the (Soviet Union's) Ministry of Defense], f. 1087, o. 1, d. 5. l. 75-98, 124.

6. *Stavka* VGK Directive No. 001043 to the Commander of the Forces of the Reserve Front about Changes in the Plan of Operations at El'nia
Copy to: The Commander-in-Chief of the Forces of the Western Direction
1600 hours on 18 August 1941

The operation at El'nia has become dragged out, and the enemy is improving his positions and replacing the units exhausted in the fighting each day.

We have found that you have not reinforced your right flank as is necessary by conducting the attack with 102nd TD and 107th and 100th RDs from the Sadki and Gur'evo front in the general direction of Leonidovo.

Assign 103rd MD instead of 100th RD and move 19th RD into the sector of the former for an attack on Sofievka.

Occupy the Vydrina and Klemiatino line with two regiments of 309th RD for the attack on Prilepy.

Reinforce 105th TD at the expense of 120th RD.

Thus, you can achieve success only by a strong right wing.

Report your conclusions.

B. Shaposhnikov

Source: "Direktiva Stavki VGK No. 001043 komanduiushchemu voiskami Rezervnogo fronta ob izmeneniakh v plane operatsii pod El'nei [*Stavka* VGK directive no. 001043 to the commander of the forces of the Reserve Front about changes in the plan of operations at El'nia], in Zolotarev, "*Stavka* VGK 1941," 118.

7. Combat Report of the Commander of the Forces of the Reserve Front to the Supreme High Commander about the Course of Operations in the El'nia Region
0445 hours on 21 August 1941

24th Army's units of the Reserve Front have completely failed to encircle and destroy the German units in the El'nia region by 20 August 1941.

In addition, the enemy committed 137th ID, which was previously stretched out along 43rd Army's front, in the Gur'evo and Sadki region on 19 August.

The enemy has committed a new unit, whose number we have yet to determine, in the Klemiatino and Grichano region.

During the 10 days of operations, I was in all of the divisions and personally familiarized myself with the combat conditions and how the units were conducting themselves.

The majority of the soldiers and commanders are conducting themselves well. They do not fear losses and are already learning the techniques and tactics for destroying the enemy, but all of the units are very under-strength and run down from offensive operations and enemy fire, which has not ceased even in the night over the last few days.

Given the essential numerical weakness of our units, it is not possible to encircle and destroy 4-5 German infantry divisions once and for all.

Further conduct of the battle in our present state will lead to the final loss of the combat effectiveness of the operating units.

It is now necessary to replenish the units to at least 60% in personnel, to bring up more ammunition, to allow the soldiers to rest, and to find weak places in the enemy carefully, and, after that, to attack impetuously.

I request your permission:

1) To cease the general offensive until 24 August;

2) To refill the units with replacements from 14 march-battalions arriving during that period;

3) To familiarize the replacements with the nature of conducting battle and prepare them for action; and

4) To begin the attack with the new forces on the morning of 25 August.

If the situation does not become more difficult along other axes, to employ 303rd RD, which is situated in my reserve at Khoteevka, in the attack.

Before 25 August, the enemy will be destroyed by systematic artillery and mortar fire and air strikes, and prisoners will be seized.

Zhukov

Source: "Boevoe donesenie komanduiushchego voiskami Rezervnogo fronta Verkhovnomu Glavnokomanduiushchemu o khode operatsii v raione El'ni" [Combat report of the commander of the forces of the Reserve Front to the Supreme High Commander about the course of operations in the El'nia region], in Zolotarev, *Stavka* 1941," 363-364.

Appendix Q

The Northern Flank: Group Stumme's Advance to Velikie Luki and Toropets, 21-28 August 1941

German 11. Führer Order, 15 August 1941

The Supreme High Command of
the Armed Forces (OKW).
Führer headquarters
Headquarters of the Operations Directorate.
15 August 1941
Department for the Defense of the Country (1st Dept.).
No. 441386/41. Top Secret

Order

After a report by the High Command of the Ground Forces (OKH), the Führer orders:

1. Army Group Center will halt its further advance on Moscow. Organize a defense in sectors whose nature will prevent any possibility of the enemy conducting enveloping operations and will not require air support to repel his offensive operations.

2. The offensive of Army Group North must produce success in the immediate future. Only after this can we think about resuming the offensive on Moscow. Danger has arisen because of the appearance of enemy cavalry in the Sixteenth Army's rear and the absence of mobile units in the I Army Corps' reserve, which, in spite of strong air support, has halted the promising offensive north of Lake Il'men'.

Without delay, allocate and transfer as great a quantity of mobile formations as possible from General Hoth's panzer group (for example, one panzer and two motorized divisions) to Army Group North.

> Chief of Staff of the Supreme High Command
> of the Armed Forces (OKW)
> [signed] Jodl

Source: *Sbornik voenno-istoricheskikh materialov Velikoi Otechestvennoi voiny, vypusk 18* [Collection of military-historical materials of the Great Patriotic War, issue 18] (Moscow: Voenizdat, 1960), 240-241. Prepared by the Military-Historical Department of the Military-Scientific Directorate of the Red Army General Staff and classified secret.

1. Combat Order of the Commander of the Forces of the Western Front of 18 August 1941 to the Commander of the Forces of 22nd Army about Corrections in the Attack Plan of the Army's Forces

To the Commander of 22nd Army, Comrade Ershakov

I generally approve the offensive plan you submitted, with the following corrections:

1) Begin the offensive on 21 August 1941.

2) When the army's shock group reaches the Lake Siverskoe region, develop a subsequent offensive toward Usviat'e.

3) Protect the main grouping's blow from the west with an attack by 214th and 126th RDs along the Pozhary, Lake Perech'e, Lake Odgast, and Lake Sorito line.

Bear in mind that, at the present time, the *front* cannot reinforce the army with artillery and aircraft; count only on your own forces and weapons. 5,000 107mm shells were sent to 22nd Army on 14 August.

> The Commander of the Forces of the Western Front,
> Marshal of the Soviet Union Timoshenko
> The Member of the Military Council of the Western Front, [signed]

Source: "Boevoe rasporiazhenie komanduiushchego voiskami Zapadnogo fronta ot 18 avgusta 1941 g. komanduiushchemu voiskami 22-i Armii o vnesenii popravok v plan nastupleniia voisk armii" [Combat order of the commander of the forces of the Western Front of 18 August 1941 to the commander of the forces of 22nd Army about corrections in the attack plan of the army's forces], *SBDVOV*, issue 41, 40.

2. Combat Orders of the Commander of the Forces of 22nd Army of 19 August 1941

Combat Order No. 16 at 0345 hours on 19 August

1. Units of the enemy's 253rd, 110th, 206th, and 86th IDs, with an overall strength of up to seven infantry regiments occupying a non-continuous front, have been determined to be active on 22nd Army's front.

2. 22nd Army's units are completing a regrouping, with the aim of a subsequent transition to an offensive.

3. 50th RC (48th TD and 214th RDs) will create a shock group of no fewer than two regiments in the Pronino and B. Im. Bor sector at the expense of the units on 214th RD's right wing, in readiness to go over to the attack from that line.

The boundary on the left: Grechukhina, Karasets, B. Im. Bor, Konnovo, Melkhovo, and Chertezh.

Headquarters of the corps from 2400 hours on 20 August—Vas'kovo.

4. 29th RC (179th, 170th, 98th, and 126th RD):

   a) 179th RD will concentrate in the Vorovo, Taraskino, Shalkovka, and Fedorikha region by daybreak on 20 August;

   b) 98th RD, by two night marches, will concentrate in the Vas'kovo, Kondrashovka Farm, Bykovo Farm, and Diatlino sector by first light on 21 August;

c) 170th RD will continue preparations to go over to the attack according to my previous instructions.

d) 126th RD – is in the positions it occupies; and

e) Headquarters of the corps from 2400 hours on 28 August – the forest east of Vatolino Stafe Farm (southeast).

Complete the regrouping and movement of forces only during the night and in no more than regimental and battalion columns.

The boundary on the left: (incl.) Kun'ia, (incl.) Kozhino, (incl.) Podol, Losevo, Shelupnevka, and Siverst (on Lake Siverskoe).

5. 62nd RC will create a shock group of no fewer than four regiments at the expense of 174th and 186th RDs for going a transition to the attack from the Gorki and Kurilovo 1 line on the nights of 19-20 and 20-21 August … ..

The Commander of 22nd Army, Lieutenant General Ershakov
The Member of the Military Council, Corps Commissar Leonov
The Chief of Staff of 22nd Army, Major General Pigarevich

Combat Order No. 17 at 2145 hours on 19 August

1. On 22nd Army's front, units of the enemy's 253rd, 110th, 86th, and 206th ID, with an overall strength of seven infantry regiments, have gone over to the defense.

2. On the right, 27th Army's units have the mission to capture the Kholm region; on the left, 29th Army's units are developing an offensive, with the aim of destroying the enemy in the Il'ino region … .

3. 22nd Army will go over to an offensive on 21 August.

Immediate mission – destroy the opposing enemy units and reach the Pozhari (on the Lovat' River, 16 kilometers south of Velikie Luki), Lake Porech'e, Lake Odgast, Lake Siroto, Lake and Lake Ordosno line; and subsequently, while protecting its right flank, develop the attack toward Usviaty … ..

4. 51st RC (366th RR, 48th TD, and 214th RD), with 709th HAR, 2nd Bn, 697th ATR, 1st Bn, 102nd AT Bn, and 3rd Bn, 11th Mtr Bn, while protecting the army's left flank, pin down opposing enemy units, while defeating them with an active defense by 366th RR and 48th TD, and prevent the infiltration of separate enemy detachments to the east, north of Velikie Luki.

Attack with the forces of no fewer than two regiments from 214th RD and, by attacking with the left wing, reach the Rozhakovo, Lake Kupuiskoe, and Lake Sekui line, with a FD [forward detachment] in the sector along the Lovat' River … ..

5. 29th RC – 126th RD (without 366th RR), 179th, 170th, and 98th RDs (without one RR), with 545th HAR, 2nd Bn, 56th CAR, 2nd and 4th Bns, 360th HAR, 1st Bn, 730th HAR, and 1st Co., 11th Mtr Bn, while conducting the main attack with 179th, 170th, and 98th RDs' forces from the Vas'kovo and Mokhoniki Farm and a secondary attack with 126th RD's forces from the positions they occupy, will destroy the opposing enemy units and reach [the following]: 126th RD – the (incl.) Lake Sekui and Lake Psovo line and, subsequently, the (incl.) Lake Sekui, Lake Porech'e, and Lake Odgast front; and the main grouping – the Orekhovo and Vinogradovo line and, subsequently, while developing the attack toward the

southeast, reach the (incl.) Lake Odgast, Lake Orel'e, and Lake Siverskoe front, while preventing an enemy withdrawal south of the indicated lakes ... .

6. 62nd RC (174th and 186th RDs), with 390th HAR and 2nd Co., 11th Mtr Bn, while firmly defending 174th RD's right flank 186th RD's left flank, will conduct an offensive with the forces of no fewer than four regiments from the Gorki and Kurilovo line toward Savino (2 kilometers west of Lake Ordosno), having prevented an enemy counterattack against the army's shock group (29th RCs) and its left flank to the southeast. Immediate mission – destroy the opposing enemy units in the Viazoviki, Slepnevo, and Luzhki region and capture Nesterovo and Stolbtsy, while having strong FDs in the Pasika and Bol'shoi and Malyi Potemki region. Subsequently, while developing the attack by the main grouping, reach the (incl.) Lake Siverskoe, Lake Ordosno, and Alekseenki (7 kilometers east of Lake Ordosno) front ... .

7. Senior Lieutenant Pervushin's detachment, with a cavalry squadron from the cavalry division, while continuing to conduct active operations in the lake region, will prevent an enemy penetration between Lake Dvin'e and Lake Zhizhitskoe and on the isthmus between Lake Dvin'e and Lake Velinskoe.

8. 4th RR, 98th RD – the army's reserve, will concentrate it in the Ushitsy State Farm region in readiness to advance along the [following] axes: a) Ushitsy State Farm, Mokriki, Chudino, and Mulina; b) Ushitsy State Farm, Annino, Bukatino, and Bolychi; and c) Annino, Akhromtseva, and Redkino.

9. Separate Cavalry Division (without one squadron), having concentrated in 366th RR's sector, will move to the line of contact of our forces with the enemy's units and, while advancing toward Novo-Sokol'niki, destroy separate enemy units, headquarters, and rear service installations, having disrupted command, control, and communications it his rear ... .

> The Commander of 22nd Army, Lieutenant General Ershakov
> The Member of the Military Council, Corps Commissar Leonov
> The Chief of Staff of 22nd Army, Major General Pigarevich

Sources: "Boevye prikazy komanduiushchego voiskami 22-i Armii ot 19 avgusta 1941 g." [Combat orders of the commander of the forces of 22nd Army of 19 August 1941], *SBDVOV*, issue 41, 235-237.

3. Information from the Reconnaissance Department of the Headquarters of 22nd Army about the Grouping and Actions of the Opposing Enemy from 20 through 23 August 1941

5 September 1941

On the basis of information from all types of reconnaissance, the enemy situation before the army's front seems to be as follows:

1. At the time of army's front was penetrated on the night of 22 August 1941, the enemy opposite the army's front included:

253rd ID – consisting of 453rd, 463rd, and 464th IRs and 253rd AR, which were operating on the army's right wing. According to the testimony of prisoners, the division had 50-60% of its personnel.

86th ID – consisting of 184th, 216th, and 176th IRs and 86th AR, was operating on 253rd ID's left. The division was worn down.

206th ID – consisting of 301st, 312th, and 413th IRs and 206th AR. The division participated continuously in the battles at Polotsk, Nevel', and Velikie Luki. In view of the heavy losses the division suffered, supposedly, it was relieved by 256th ID. The division was in reserve, where it probably received replacements, thus, it will soon reappear at the front.

110th ID – consisting of 262nd, 254th, and 255th IRs occupying a defensive sector in the Viazoviki region.

256th ID – concentrated in the vicinity of Lake Dvin'e.

Thus, up to 4 infantry divisions are located opposite the army's front, and a new enemy grouping was appearing in the Lake Dvin'e region.

2. Beginning on the morning of 22 August, the enemy penetrated the army's front with mobile detachments and, during the second half of the day, captured Kun'ia Station, Velikopol'e, and Ushitsy State Farm. From documents seized – maps and orders for an attack by 19th Panzer Division, it has been determined that 57th Panzer Corps – 19th and 20th Panzer Divisions, reinforced by units from 110th and 206th IDs, and 40th AC, operated in the penetration of 22nd Army's front.

The Assistant Chief of the Intelligence Department, Major Shabunin

Source: "Spravka razvedyvatel'nogo otdela shtaba 22-i Armii o gruppirovke i deistviiakh protivostoiashchego protivnika s 20 po 23 avgusta 1941 g." [Information from the Reconnaissance Department of 22nd Army's headquarters about the grouping and actions of the opposing enemy from 20 through 23 August 1941], *SBDVOV*, issue 41, 239.

4. Combat Report of the Headquarters of the Western Front of 23 August 1941 to the Chief of the General Staff about Measures Taken for Liquidating the Enemy Penetration in 186th Rifle Division's Defensive Sector

To Marshal Shaposhnikov
1:100,000 scale map
23 August 1941

Combat Report

1. The enemy has penetrated 186th RD's front along the Klemiatino axis with forces of up to a motorized division with tanks and up to an infantry division and is developing success toward the north and northwest.

At 1200 hours two enemy motorized columns, each with 150 vehicles, were approaching [the following] with their advanced elements – one at Ushitsy State Farm (18 kilometers southeast of Velikie Luki), and the second – at Kun'ia Station. The enemy's forward units reached Artemovo Platform and Velikopol'e Station, having occupied the latter.

Up to one cavalry regiment is moving along the western shore of Lake Zhiditskoe, and at 1200 hours the cavalry regiment was entering the Pershkovo region.

2. 29th Army's commander decided to employ 98th Rifle Division and the second echelon 170th [Rifle Division] for liquidating the enemy penetration, having

simultaneously protected the northern axis by moving two battalions toward the movement of the enemy motorized columns.

In the event of failure to liquidate the penetration, he intends to withdraw eastward.

3. The *front's* commander has decided to destroy the penetrating enemy units with 22nd Army's forces, about which orders have been given to 22nd Army's commander.

Simultaneously, the *front* commander is dispatching a detachment consisting of two motorcycle regiments, reinforced by two batteries, a tank battalion (19 T-26 tanks), and a sapper battalion, to the vicinity of Staraia Toropa, with the mission to occupy prepared positions from Toropets to Staraia Toropa and with the mission to prevent an enemy penetration toward Andriapol' and Western Dvina.

4. I will report about fulfillment of the liquidation of the enemy.

5. 22nd Army's forces are insufficient for the complete liquidation and encirclement of the penetrating enemy (Group Blumeng). The *front* has possesses no reserves on that axis. It is desirable to allocate two divisions, with the active missions of attacking from the Toropets and Staraia Toropa regions to encircle the enemy in cooperation with 22nd Army's units.

Sokolovsky, Malandin

Source: "Boevoe donesenie shtaba Zapadnogo fronta ot 23 avgusta 1941 g. nachal'niku General'nogo Shtaba o priniatykh merakh po likvidatsii proryva protivnika v polose oborony 186-i Strelkovoi Divizii" [Combat report of the headquarters of the Western Front of 23 August 1941 to the Chief of the General Staff about measures taken for liquidating the enemy penetration in 186th Rifle Division's defensive sector], *SBDVOV*, issue 41, 62-63.

5. Combat Order of the Commander of the Forces of the Western Front of 23 August 1941 to the Commander of 22nd Army's Forces about Holding on to the Positions We Occupy

1200 hours on 23 August 1941
To Comrade Ershakov
Copy: To Maslennikov

The chief missions on 23 and 24 August – is to hold on to the front you occupy.

The commander of 62nd RC [Major General I. P. Karmanov] and the commander of 186th Rifle Division are personally responsible for closing the penetration that has formed.

Allocate all of your forces and all of your attached aircraft to destroy the penetrating enemy units on 23 and 24 August,

The Commander of the Forces of the Western Front, Timoshenko
The Member of the Military Council of the Western Front, [signed]

Source: "Boevoe rasporiazhenie komanduiushchego voiskami Zapadnogo fronta ot 23 avgusta 1941 g. komanduiushchemu voiskami 22-i Armii o uderzhanie zanimaemogo rubezha" [Combat order of the commander of the forces of the Western Front of 23 August 1941 to the commander of 22nd Army's forces about holding on to the positions we occupy], *SBDVOV*, issue 41, 63.

6. Individual Combat Order No. 6 of the Commander of the Forces of 29th Army of 23 August 1941 to the Commander of the Composite Detachment on the Defense of the Toropets, Toropa River, Staraia Toropa, and (incl.) Luk'ianovo Line

To the Commander of the Composite Detachment, Colonel Antosenko
Individual Combat Order No. 6,
Headquarters, 29th Army, Bentsy,
2350 hours on 23 August 1941
1:100,000 scale map

1. The enemy has penetrated 186th RD's front with a force of up to two divisions, one of them a motorized division with a tank regiment, and two motorized columns are exploiting success toward Velikie Luki and from the Kun'ia region toward Toropets. Opposite 29th Army's front, the enemy is stubbornly defending along previously prepared and fortified positions, while trying to conduct an offensive from the Medveditsa, Rumishche, and Dubrovka region.

2. 29th Army is successfully attacking toward Il'ino from the line of the Western Dvina River, while protecting its right flank with one division, which has been transferred to defend the Krivets, Ust'e, Petrovo Farm, and Krasnye Sosny front.

3. On the right, 22nd Army is fighting along the Velikie Luki and Plaksino front and simultaneously organizing the liquidation of the enemy, which has penetrated into the Kun'ia region.

4. The Composite Detachment, consisting of 8th and 9th Motorcycle Regiments, with 45mm and76mm batteries, a tank battalion, and a sapper battalion, after unloading at Toropa Station, will occupy and firmly defend the Toropets, Toropa River, Staraia Toropa, and (incl.) Luk'ianovo line, with the mission to prevent an enemy penetration toward Andreapol' and Western Dvina.

Organize a defense line along the eastern bank of the Toropa River by creating regimental defensive sectors with combat security along the Terebekhovo, Selishche, Babkino, Zadem'ian'e, Iakovlevo, and Ostashkovo line, with its forward edge along the eastern bank of the Toropa River and with all-round defense of each sector and the detachments as a whole.

22nd and 29th Armies' forward detachments will operate forward of the Skvortsovo Station and Zhizhitsa Station meridian, with the mission of holding on to the principal road junctions and the protecting the Composite Detachment's defensive belt. Upon the arrival of the detachment's units in the defensive regions, 22nd and 29th Armies' forward detachments will be subordinate to Colonel Antosenko.

5. BEPO No. 53, which is being transferred to the subordination of the Composite Detachment's commander, will operate along the Zhizhitsa Station and Staraia Toropa Station railroad line.

6. The readiness of the defenses, the tank battalion's concentration area, and [measures for] cooperation with aircraft – [will be sent] additionally.

7. CP – the operational group of the army's headquarters – Bentsy; and the [army headquarter's] 2nd echelon – Staraia Toropa.

8. Send reports: 1) Upon completion of the unloading at Staraia Toropa; 2) Upon the arrival of the detachment's units in the defensive regions; and 3) About the readiness of defenses in the indicated sectors.

The Commander of 29th Army, Lieutenant General Maslennikov
The Member of the Military Council of 29th Army,
    Division Commissar Gurov
The Chief of Staff of 29th Army, Major General Sharapov
The Chief of the Operations Department,
    Colonel Massal'sky [signed by Captain Gorbin]

Sources: "Chastnyi boevoi prikaz komanduiushchego voiskami 29-i Armii No. 6 ot 23 avgusta 1941 g. komandiru svodnogo otriada na oboronu rubezha Toropets, r. Toropa, Staraia Toropa, (incl.) Luk'ianovo" [Individual combat order of the commander of the forces of 29th Army no. 6 of 23 August 1941 to the commander of the composite detachment on the defense of the Toropets, Toropa River, Staraia Toropa, and (incl.) Luk'ianovo line], *SBDVOV,* issue 41, 269.

7. Combat Order of the Commander of the Forces of 29th Army of 24 August 1941 to the Chiefs of the Garrisons at Toropets and Staraia Toropa about Organizing Defenses at these Points

To Lieutenant Colonel Comrade Orlov and Colonel Comrade Devi
Copy: To the Chief of Staff of 22nd Army
0115 hours on 24 August 1941

Before the forces allocated for defending the Toropa River defense line in the Toropets and Staraia Toropa sector arrive, I order:

1. Organize force and agent reconnaissance along the Nazimovka Station and Kun'ia Station axis, with the mission to determine at all cost enemy concentration regions and also establish the axes along which the enemy is spreading out.

2. Occupy prepared defensive regions with the forces of the Toropets and Staraia Toropa garrisons and, under no circumstance, withdraw, while conducting a struggle until the units allocated to you arrive.

3. Employ subunits and units of soldiers who willfully withdrew from forward positions and send them to the previously prepared defensive regions.

4. Prepare and improve the defensive works along the eastern bank of the Toropa River in the Toropets and Staraia Toropa sector by using force sappers and the local population. Mine the sector north of Toropets, inclusively, up to the unnamed lake. Also mine the Komlovo and Romanovo sector, having left a passage along the railroad bed.

5. Detain all soldiers who willfully abandon their forward position, organize them into companies, and send them to the eastern bank of the Toropa River south of Staraia Toropa to occupy the prepared defensive works.

The Commander of 29th Army, Lieutenant General Maslennikov

The Member of the Military Council of 29th Army,
Division Commissar Gurov

Source: "Boevoe rasporiazhenie komanduiushchego voiskami 29-i Armii ot 24 avgusta 1941 g. nachal'nikam garnizonov Toropets i Staraia Toropa ob organizatsii oborony etikh punktov" [Combat order of the commander of the forces of 29th Army of 24 August 1941 to the chiefs of the garrisons at Toropets and Staraia Toropa about organizing defenses at these points], *SBDVOV*, issue 41, 270.

8. Notes of a Conversation between the Chief of Staff of the Western Front and the Chief of the Operations Department of 22nd Army's Headquarters on 24 August 1941 about the Positions of the Army's Forces

Conversation of Lieutenant General Sokolovsky with the Chief of 22nd Army's Operations Department, Nyprianin [Nyrianin],
0400 to 0500 hours on 24 August 1941

Nyrianin – Ershakov left at 1800 hours for the commander of 29th RC, [Major General A. G.] Samokhin.

Sokolovsky – When did you speak with him for the last time?

Nyrianin – The last radiogram was at around 0800 hours on 23 August.

Sokolovsky – Up to what hour did you have communications with 29th RC?

Nyrianin – Communications with 29th RCs lasted up to 1900 hours on 23 August.

Sokolovsky – Did you receive a telegram?

Nyrianin – A telegram was sent to Ershakov by radio at about 1500 hours on 23 August. A receipt was not received.

Sokolovsky – Have you tried to transmit it for a second time?

Nyrianin – I tried, and a copy was transmitted to the commander of 62nd RC, [Major General I. P.] Karmanov.

Sokolovsky – And did Karmanov confirm receipt?

Nyrianin – It was sent from 18 to 1900 hours, but I have no confidence in its receipt. There would be more confidence that an order was received.

Sokolovsky – Repair your communications with Ershakov and with the formation commanders directly by radio and aircraft.

Nyrianin –Today, at 1800 hours on 23 August, a second detachment numbering 200 men was sent out. Orders have been given to the commander of VVS forces. Apparently, I will receive news by morning.

Sokolovsky – What is known about the enemy and your own forces?

Nyrianin – Ershakov was going to bring 179th RD out at 0800 on 23 August and requested aircraft. 179th RD is being thrown against the enemy's flank and rear, and [the positions] of 48th TD were unchanged at 1200 hours. They received a radiogram from Sazanov asking, "What should we do?"

The answer is – remain in place, maintain communications with Samokhin, and protect Samokhin's right flank.

Sokolovsky – What is the enemy doing?

Nyrianin – Infantry, having penetrated to the depth of Kun'ia in the north with forward units by 2100-2200 hours – and with 7 tanks each at three points and the remainder to the west and northwest – an enemy panzer [division] and 110th ID.

110th ID, after entering the penetration, spread out across a wide front. At 16-1700 hours on 23 August, this division's battalions were moving from Kun'ia toward Nazimovo, Ushitsy, and Peski, and the panzer division was concentrating in the Ushitsy, Peski, and Kun'ia regions. The situation at day's end on 22 August along the remaining front is [as follows: Zygin (174th RD) withdrew in association with the defeat in Biriukov's (186th RD) sector. It is stable in the sector of 126th RD and 48th TD, and our units are advancing forward, but slowly. Ershakov, Leonov, and Pigarevich are all right. He is situated in the sector on Sazonov's right.

An order of the Germans has been seized, according to which 110th ID, 206th ID, SS IB, 59th ID, 112th ID , an armored group, and 19th and 20th PzDs, combined under a corps headquarters, have the mission of striking toward Ushitsy and seizing Velikie Luki. The second mission – the infantry are to create centers of resistance, along with the construction of pillboxes y sappers, in the Kun'ia, Zabolot'e, and Shubkovo regions – to not let our units [withdraw] toward the east. We request aviation support.

Sokolovsky –Was an order received?

Nyrianin – An order was received. Communications are occasional [by chance], in a round-about way, along the northern axis.

Sokolovsky – Check up on your communications. What does Ershakov intend to do?

Nyrianin – 179th and 126th RDs' units conducted reconnaissance raids toward Ushitsy but without any results. Enemy aviation is strong.

Sokolovsky – Employ aviation and beat the enemy. Have they liquidated [our] penetration toward the south?

Nyrianin – We are protecting it with detached composite detachments.

Sokolovsky – The primary mission is to defeat the enemy who is trying to encircle us – pass this on to Ershakov.

Source: "Zapis' peregovora nachal'nika shtaba Zapadnogo fronta s nachal'nikom operativnogo otdela shtaba 22-i Armii 24 avgusta 1941 g. o polozhenii voisk armii" [Notes of a conversation between the chief of staff of the Western Front and the chief of the Operations Department of 22nd Army's Headquarters on 24 August 1941 about the positions of the army's forces], *SBDVOV*, issue 41, 68-69.

9. Combat Order No. 18 of the Commander of the Forces of 22nd Army of 24 August 1941 on a Withdrawal of the Army's Forces to the Zadorozh'e, Mishovo, Pleshkovo, and Begunovo Line

Combat Order No. 18,
CP, headquarters of 22nd Army,
Mikhal'ki [12 kilometers east-southeast of Velikie Luki],
1015 hours on 24 August 1941
1:50,000 scale map

1. The enemy, having penetrated the defenses on the army's left wing with a force of up to two panzer divisions, reinforced by one infantry division, has been moving into the Kun'ia and Ushitsy State Farm region, and, while having the missions of encircling and destroying our Velikie Luki grouping, is operating from the east and southeast, while protecting the Kun'ia meridian with an active defense.

2. Firmly hold onto 22nd Army's defensive front in the sectors of 48th TD, 214th RD, and 170th RD until the evening of 24 August 1941, while simultaneously destroying the enemy's units in the Ushitsy State Farm region and the penetration formed by him toward the east.

Beginning at 1600 hours on 24 August 1941, 22nd Army's forces will begin a withdrawal to a defensive positions from Zadorozh'e to Mishovo, Pleshkovo, Begunovo, and (incl.) Lake Zhizhitskoe, which they will occupy on 26 August 1941.

Protect the withdrawal with strong groups saturated with automatic weapons and mortars (a company from each battalion).

3. 51st RC (48th TD and 214th RD.

a) 48th TD, while preventing the enemy from entering Velikie Luki on 24 August 1941 and having a barrier force there, beginning at 1600 hours on 24 August, will withdraw its main forces eastward in the [following] belts: on the right – (incl.) Velikie Luki, Novosel'e, Dubrovka, (incl.) Tret'iakov'y Farm, and Iablonitsy; and on the left – (incl.) Kon', (incl.) Malkina, Grechukhina, Ivanovo, (incl.) Mishovo, and Filiptsevo.

Upon withdrawing, occupy a defensive sector along the Zadorozh'e, Mishovo line.

b) 214th RD will begin withdrawing in close cooperation with 48th TD. Withdraw in the [following] belt: on the right – the boundary with 48th TD and on the left – B. Im. Bor, (incl.) Zadezha north, Taraskino, Fedorikha, (incl.) Gorovastitsa Farm, Grishino, Kun'ia, and Kuznetsovo, while planning going into reserve in the Morozova, Novo-Ivantsova, and Zagoskina region.

4. 29th RC (126, 170th, and 179th RDs):

a) 126th RD, while penetrating to the Ushitsy State Farm region, withdraw to defensive positions from (incl.) Mishovo to Pleshkovo.

The boundary on the left: Lake Ploskoe, Koziulino, Rudneva, (incl.) Monastyrek, Krasnaia Veshnia, Bukhalovo, Kresty, and Pleshkovo.

b) 170th RD , at 1900 hours on 24 August, will withdraw to the Vskuia, Zhukovo, Ushani, (incl.) and Kun'ia River line, which it will firmly hold onto until 48th TD and 214th and 126th RDs arrive behind the Vskupitsa River, after which it will begin a withdrawal in the general direction of Vtorikovo and Zakhartsevo, in 179th RD's wake, with the mission to occupy the (incl.) Pleshkovo and (incl.) Begunovo line for defense.

Hold on to the crossing at Zelenova until the beginning of the withdrawal.

c) 179th RD will organize a penetration and destruction of enemy units in along the Vtorikovo and Zakhartsevo axis, while operating from the Krasnaia Gorka and Monastyrek front. Protect the withdrawal of the army's units from the north and southeast with your own detachments. When you reach the army's defensive line, concentrate in reserve in the Ovechkina, Belodetkovo, Ivantseva, and Fedosovo region.

5. 62nd RC, while operating south of 179th RD, will withdraw in the general direction of Begunovo. When you reach the defensive line, occupy defenses in the Begumovo and (incl.) Lake Zhizhitskoe sector.

6. Complete the withdrawal of detachments left behind to protect the withdrawal only after an order from a senior chief, but no lower than a regimental commander.

7. Division commanders and commissars are personally responsible for the complete evacuation of equipment, rear services, and the wounded.

8. The CP of the army and 29th RC is with 126th RD's 550th RR in its withdrawal sector.

The Commander of 22nd Army, Lieutenant General Ershakov
The Member of the Military Council, Corps Commissar Leonov
The Chief of Staff of the army, Major General Pigarevich

Sources: "Boevoi prikaz komanduiushchego voiskami 22-i Armii No. 18 ot 24 avgusta 1941 g. na otvod voisk armii na rubezh Zadorozh'e, Mishovo, Pleshkovo, Begunovo" [Combat order no. 18 of the commander of the forces of 22nd Army of 24 August 1941 on a withdrawal of the army's forces to the Zadorozh'e, Mishnovo, Pleshkovo, and Begunovo line], *SBDVOV*, issue 41, 240-241.

10. Combat Report of the Headquarters of the Western Front of 24 August 1941 to the Chief of the General Staff about the Situation and a Plan for a Future Offensive by 22nd Army's Forces

Moscow, to Marshal Shaposhnikov
1:100,000 scale map
24 August 1941

1. According to Ershakov's more precise definition of enemy forces, which have penetrated into the Kun'ia region, they have been determined to include 2 IDs and 2 PzDs (110th and 206th IDs and 19th and 20th PzDs). The enemy, as a captured order made apparent, have the objective of encircling Ershakov's group.

On 24 August, the penetrating enemy forces are grouped [as follows]:

a) Forward mobile units seized Artemovo Platform, Borok, and Velikopol'e Station, while protecting the operations of their main forces;

b) The main forces – 19th and 20th PzDs – are concentrated in the Peski, Ushitsy Station, and Kun'ia region; and

c) Infantry with sappers are advancing to organize a screen along the Kun'ia River.

During the course of 23 and 24 August, our aircraft from up to two mixed aviation divisions bombed troop columns and groups of enemy extensively, and inflicted heavy losses on him.

2. As before, Ershakov's situation along the Velikie Luki and Lake Savinskoe front is stable. The situation on 62nd RC's left wing is unclear.

Ershakov, having concentrated part of 126th and 179th RDs' forces, will attack toward Ushitsy State Farm to inflict a defeat on the enemy.

According to unverified information, Ushitsa has been taken by Ershakov at 1115 hours on 24 August, but how subsequent operations are developing is unknown.

Ershakov's intentions:

1) To continue the operations begun toward Ushitsy; and

2) In the event the offensive along that axis is unsuccessful, to concentrate maximum forces on the night of 25 August in order to operate toward the northeast (Ershakov did not report the exact direction of the intended attack variant), while protecting ourselves from the front.

While evaluating the situation with the consideration that Ershakov has no tanks whatsoever, it is unlikely to expect that Ershakov will succeed in defeating so strong an enemy group so saturated with tanks. At the same time, the enemy does not have sufficient forces for simultaneous operations toward the west and east.

On our side, an opportunity exists to encircle the overextended enemy if we strike from Toropets and Staraia Toropa with two-three rifle divisions, with a simultaneous attack by Ershakov from the west.

The reserves the *front* needs along this axis are absent at this time; therefore, for a second time, I am requesting you transfer, if only temporarily, at least two rifle division from the Reserve Front to the disposal of the Western Front and move them to the Toropets region.

I request you report your decision.

Sokolovsky, Malandin

Source: "Boevoe donesenie shtaba Zapadnogo fronta ot 24 avgusta 1941 g nachal'niku General'nogo shtaba ob obstanovke i plane dal'neishego nastupleniia voisk 22-i armii" [Combat report of the headquarters of the Western Front of 24 August 1941 to the Chief of the General Staff about the situation and a plan for a future offensive by 22nd Army's forces], *SBDVOV,* issue 41, 69-70.

11. Notes of a Conversation between the Chief of Staff of the Western Front and the Chief of the Operations Department of 22nd Army's Headquarters on 24 August 1941 about the Army Commander's Decision on an Offensive and the Grouping of Enemy Forces

Late on 24 August

Sokolovsky – Nyrianin

We have received a report from Ershakov, and it is being retransmitted to you by radio.

The contents are:

The two commands of [Colonel E. V.] Bedin [126th RD] and Dvorkin [unknown command] are to attack Ushitsy. Ushitsy may have already been taken at 1115 hours but this information has not yet been verified.

In the event of failure, I will strike from Ushitsy toward the northeast and assemble a fist [shock force] for that purpose during the night.

I have additional information.

1) A group of 50 tanks and motorized infantry are in Rudnia, Poprishche, and Dedkovo. Our aircraft bombed the group at 0900 hours.

There are 8-10 enemy tanks in Maksimovo.

Today, at 1200 hours, our forces were fighting to capture Maksimovo.

The movement of [the following] vehicular columns were noted at 0830 hours:

The 1st from Annino toward the north – 150 vehicles [and the 2nd] from Khvost – to Kharitonov, with its head at Rozhkovo. Judging by the time, it is one and the same column. There are 300 horsemen moving from the south toward Kun'ia, with its head at Kun'ia.

150 vehicles [moving] from Evstigneevo, Pynki, and the region west of Lake Zhizhitskoe. Today, at 1300 hours, up to 20 tanks at Morozova and Zagriaz'e [moved] south into that region.

Reports from Aircraft

Peski to south of Velikopol'e – infantry and 10 tanks are in place. Gorelovo, Pershino State Farm, and east of Velikie Luki – a gathering of infantry (exactly who is unknown).

According to Ershakov's assessment, on the basis of an order seized from the enemy, 19th and 20th PzDs, 110th and 206th IDs, regiments of 59th and 112th IDs, a sapper battalion, and 92nd AR are operating against us.

Sokolovsky – Where is Ershakov now?

Nyrianin – With Samokhin (he was at 51st RC from 0400-0500 hours, from which he conducted the telephone conversation).

The rear services of [Major General N. I.] Biriukov (186th RD), Gvozdev (179th RD), and [Colonel D. I.] Iakovlev (48th TD) are approaching Toropets in disorder. They are now being put in order. We have assembled 5,000 men, of which half are armed; including men from penal battalions, and these are being formed into a detachment with transports (ammunition, food, etc.) and are being sent along the northern road to Velikie Luki.

Orders are being given to protect the northern route from the enemy. It has been confirmed to Ershakov that Ershakov's main mission is to defeat the enemy located in his rear.

The attack axis – will depend on the situation which exists on the spot.

The enemy is now no displaying any special activity opposite the western sector of the front.

Source: "Zapis' peregovora nachal'nika shtaba Zapadnogo fronta s nachal'nikom operativnogo otdela shtaba 22-i Armii 24 avgusta 1941 g. o reshenii komanduiushchego armiei na nastuplenie i gruppirovke voisk protivnika" [Notes of a conversation between the chief of staff of the Western Front and the chief of the Operations Department of 22nd Army's headquarters on 24 August 1941 about the army commander's decision on an offensive and the grouping of enemy forces], *SBDVOV*, issue 41, 73-74.

12. Combat Order of the Commander of the Forces of 29th Army No. 11 of 25 August 1941 about Strengthening Defenses along the Rzhev Axis

Combat Order No. 11, Headquarters, 29th Army,
Bentsy,
0700 hours on 25 August 1941
1:100,000 and 500,000 scale maps

1. The enemy has penetrated 186th Rifle Division's (22nd Army) front with a force of up to two divisions, one of them a motorized division with a tank regiment, and two motorized columns are exploiting success toward Velikie Luki and from the Kun'ia region toward Toropets. The enemy opposite 29th Army's front is stubbornly defending in previously prepared and fortified positions, while trying to conduct an offensive from the Medvitsa [should read Medveditsa], Rumishche, and Dubrova [should read Dubrovka] region.

2. 29th Army is successfully attacking from the Tolkachi, Trubniki, and Pesochek line, while protecting its right flank with one division, which has been transferred for a stubborn defense of the Krivets, Ust'e, Petrovo Farm, and Krasnye Sosny front. It is setting about strengthening its forward and main positions and improving positions along the Western Dvina River.

3. 22nd Army is fighting along the Velikie Luki and Plaksino front and, simultaneously, organizing the liquidation of the enemy which has penetrated into the Kun'ia region.

4. 252nd RD will continue to strengthen and improve the defensive positions it occupies along the Western Dvina River in the Krivets, Olenitsa 1, Ust'e, Petrovo, and Bukharikha sector [55 kilometers south of Toropets] and outfit and fortify the ground in the Arestovo, Poliany, Kokovkino, and Zabor'e up to Lake Deviato sector on the isthmus between Lake Zhatko and Lake Dvin'e [50 kilometers southwest of Toropets], having protected road junctions, defiles, and principal heights.

5. 246th RD will continue the destruction and liquidation of the enemy's Il'ino grouping in accordance with army Order No. 10 and, simultaneously, emplace obstacles and mines on the roads leading from Lake Plovnoe to Mikhailovskoe, from Emlen' across the Rovnyi Bor River, and the junction of the Mel'nitsa, Ozery, and Zabor'e roads [45 kilometers southwest of Staraia Toropa], having left free passages for the conduct of reconnaissance to the line of the Mezha River by 29th CR. Coordinate the emplacement of obstacles and mining with the commander of the Composite Brigade.

6. 243rd RD, together with the Composite Brigade, will block [with obstacles] and mine road junctions and roads toward Katkovo and Kanat [35-42 kilometers south-southeast of Staraia Toropa] and Khalotomino and Prudok [35-40 kilometers south of Staraia Toropa], while blowing up the bridges, crossings, and roads. Closely coordinate the combined actions and distribution of forces and weapons with the Composite Brigade.

7. The Composite Brigade will improve its positions on the heights and defiles and dig in on 25 August 1941, having employed all necessary obstacles along the front and in the depth, with the mission of subsequently strengthening and reinforcing the fortification on which you will rely, while continuing to fulfill the missions assigned to you by the army commander's Order No. 10.

8. Colonel Antosenko's Composite Detachment will fulfill the missions assigned by Individual Order No. 6.

9. In accordance with the Western Front's Order No. 04/op for liquidating any possibility of an enemy penetration along the Rzhev axis, 29th Army will prepare two defensive lines in timely fashion [as follows]: main – along the Podolina, Toropets, Staraia Toropa, and Elovikovo line; and forward – along the Chernost' River,

Dubrovka, Ivantsevo, Barsuki, Levkovo, and the Lakes Kodosno, Zhizhitskoe, and Velinskoe line, with their fronts facing toward the west, while exploiting the labors of the local garrisons and local population.

a) The chief of the garrison at Toropets, Colonel Devi, will outfit and improve the defensive belts of the main and forward line within the [following] boundaries: on the right – the junction of the Kun'ia and Chernost' Rivers and Podolino; and on the left – Sharapovo and Lake Sel'skoe, with all of the forces and equipment at his disposal and by exploiting the local population.

b) Lieutenant Colonel Orlov will outfit and improve the defensive belts of main and forward line within the [following] boundaries: on the right – (incl.) Sharapov and (incl.) Lake Sel'skoe, and on the left – Ravon' and (incl.) Zarech'e with the garrison's forces and the local population.

c) The army's Chief of Engineer Forces will outfit and improve the defensive belts of main and forward lines within the [following] boundaries: on the right – (incl.) Ravon' and Zarech'e, and on the left – Malashaty and Elovikovo, with all of the forces and equipment at his disposal and by exploiting the local population.

Anticipate preparing a defensive line on the Lake Velinskoe, Elovikovo, Sevost'ianovo, and Pikrevo front along the northern bank of the Western Dvina River

10. I am appointing an operational group consisting of operational units from 22nd Army's headquarters and headed by 29th Army's deputy chief of staff, Lieutenant Colonel Fedorov, for supervising the outfitting and strengthening of the defensive lines.

11. Complete work on the first and second stages by 27 August 1941 and on the third stage and final improvement of the lines by 29 August 1941.

Report on the work plans, along with calculations of the [required] forces, weapons, and time, to me at 1600 hours on 25 August 1941. Begin the work for outfitting the lines immediately.

12. My deputy for Rear Services, Colonel Vishnevsky, will rebase the army's rear at Zapadnaia Dvina Station, having completed the rebasing on 26 August 1941.

13. The army's Chief of Engineer Forces will provide the army's formations with necessary technical means, having fully supplied the divisions with mines in accordance with the calculation of obstacles.

> The Commander of 29th Army, Lieutenant General Maslennikov
> The Member of the Military Council of 29th Army,
>   Division Commissar Gurov
> The Chief of Staff of 29th Army, Major General Sharapov

Source: "Boevoi prikaz komanduiushchego voiskami 29-i Armii No. 11 ot 25 avgusta 1941 g. ob usilenii oborony na Rzhevskom napravlenii" [Combat order of the commander of the forces of 29th Army no. 11 of 25 August 1941 about strengthening defenses along the Rzhev axis], *SBDVOV*, issue 41, 270-271.

13. Notes of a Conversation between the Chief of Staff of the Western Front and 22nd Army's Chief of Staff on 25 August 1941 about the Positions of the Army's Forces

Conversation of Lieutenant General Sokolovsky

with 22nd Army's Chief of Staff, Colonel Nyprianin,
1015-1040 hours on 25 August 1941

Sokolovsky –
1. What information do you have today about Ershakov?
2. When did you last have contact with him by radio, where is he located now, and what is he doing?

Nyprianin –
1. There was no radio contact with Ershakov from 1930 hours on 24 August to 0920 hours on 25 August. We have just now received a radiogram from him which is being worked up [de-coded]. I will report soon by enciphered radiogram. The last radio conversation was at around 1600 hours on 24 August, in which he ordered us to provide him information from aerial reconnaissance, chiefly in the Ushitsy region.
2. I do not know his intentions about operations on 25 August.
3. We received a dispatch this evening from the detachment sent to Ershakov. The detachment was in the forests southeast of Velikopol'e Station on the night of 23-24 August, and there was no enemy in that region. Our artillery warehouse was not discovered by the enemy, and the warehouse was intact. I wrote about this in a telegram to Ershakov. A group of soldiers numbering 500-600 men, part armed and part unarmed, under the command of one of the assistant department chiefs in the army's headquarters, turned up in the forest. According to a report by one of these commanders, the road north of the Velikie Luki-Toropets railroad is only weakly controlled by the enemy, that is, there are sometimes individual groups there.

Sokolovsky – Do you now have radio contact with Ershakov?

Nyprianin – We have just received a radiogram from Samokhin, in the region where Ershakov should be located, and, judging by its contents, it may be his location. The radiogram has yet to be deciphered; therefore, I cannot report exactly whether it is from Ershakov or Samokhin.

Sokolovsky – Immediately ask Ershakov by enciphered radiogram where is he, what is he doing, and, briefly, what is the situation? Decipher the radiogram quickly, and send it to me immediately. What army units have you succeeded in assembling in the Toropets and Staraia Toropa region?

Nyprianin – Of those units which participated in the fighting and which are now still located in combat sectors, we have assembled around 600 men in addition to about 400 armed soldiers that were sent to the sectors yesterday, and, in addition, another roughly 300 men were halted directly along intermediate lines and are now located in combat sectors. The exact number – and how many have weapons – has still not been received. All of the unarmed are being assembled primarily in the vicinity of Skvortsovo Station.

Sokolovsky – Have you organized reconnaissance toward Nazimovo and from Zhizhitsa toward the west?

Nyprianin – Chiefly commandant's patrols on vehicles have been organized.

Sokolovsky – Report specifically along which axes, which detachments, when were they sent out to reconnoiter, and what information have you received from them about the enemy? What is aviation doing today, who is supporting Ershakov, do you have communications with them, and what missions have you assigned to them at Ershakov's request or independently based on the intelligence you have about the enemy?

Nyprianin – I repeat – there are no communications with Ershakov, he has not given and cannot give any orders, and I do not know what the situation is there. Reconnaissance has been organized along 12 axes. I will provide you with a detailed report about all of the measures we have taken by enciphered radiogram.

Sokolovsky – Send me the most recent telegram from Ershakov quickly.

Nyprianin – But understand, it is still doubtful whether or not it is from Ershakov.

Sokolovsky – Take measures to establish radio communications with Ershakov.

> Authenticated by Andrieko [Major S. S. Andrieko,
> Assistant Chief of the Operations Department, Headquarters,
> Western Front]

Source: "Zapis peregovora nachal'nika shtaba Zapadnogo fronta s nachal'nikom shtaba 22-i Armii 24 avgusta 1941 g. o polozhenii voisk armii" [Notes of a conversation between the chief of staff of the Western Front and 22nd Army's chief of staff on 25 August 1941 about the positions of the army's forces], *SBDVOV*, issue 41, 79-80.

14. Combat Order No. 18 of 22nd Army's Operational Group of 25 August 1941 on Defense of the Chernost' River, Dubrovka, Pochinok, Barsuki, Piatnitskoe, and Tarasovka Line

Combat Order No. 18, Headquarters of the Operational Group,
Toropets,
25 August 1941
1:100,000 scale map

1. Large enemy tank and motorized units penetrated the defensive front on 22nd Army's left wing and, while developing the attack toward the north and northwest, captured the Velikopol'e Station and Ushitsy State Farm region and occupied the Piatnitskoe (10 kilometers northeast of Kodosno Station) and Nazimova region with forward units.

2. 29th Army (with the OG [operational group] created from those who remained outside of 22nd Army's encircled units), while continuing an offensive on its left wing, with the mission of destroying the enemy's Il'ino grouping, is going on the defense with its remaining forces, with the aim of liquidating the enemy penetration along the Rzhev axis.

3. The OG will go on the defense along the Podolina (24 kilometers northwest of Toropets), Toropets, and Lake Sel'skoe [12 kilometers south of Toropets] front, having forward positions on the Chernost' River, Dubrovka, Pochinok, Barsuki, Piatnitskoe, and Tarasovka line.

4. 709th HAR will defend the sector from Podolina to Khadausova, Hill 179.1, and Ganevo and prevent separate groups of enemy from infiltrating toward Sheino, Moroshkino, and Ganevo.

The boundary on the left: Ivan'kovo, Strel'tsy, Kolotilovo, and Bezova Gora.

5. 196th Automatic Weapons Bn will defend the sector from Karpasy to Hill 191.9, Marker 208.3, and Kamestaia.

The boundary on the left: Kazarino, Hill 19.5, Pershino, and Belorubovo.

6. 137th Sep.AABn, with 13th Sep. ATBn, will occupy the Hill 199.5, Hill 239.5, and Zhelny region for defense and prevent an enemy penetration toward Toropets from the northwest.

The boundary on the left: Hill 255.9, (incl.) Gorka, Nov. Derevnia, Berdovo, and Peschakha.

7. 38th MRBn will defend the Gorka, Iashkino, Hill 199.2, and Martiukhova sector.

The boundary on the left: Beliaevo, Hill 192.2, Dashkovo, and Novo-Troitskoe.

8. 390th HAR, with 179th Sep. ATBn, will occupy the (incl.) Hill 192.2, Lake Zelikovskoe, Kharino, and (incl.) Zarech'e sector for defense, having prevented an enemy penetration to Toropets.

The boundary on the left: Lake Dbshinskoe, Dedino, Toropets, and Tsikorevo.

9. 360th HAR, with 615th HAR, will defend the Shatry, Artiukhovo, and (incl.) Losochi region and create cut-off positions in the Novoe Bridino and (incl.) Mikhali sector.

The boundary on the left: Kruttsy, (incl.) Losochi, and Lake Maslovo.

10. 56th CAR will defend the Losochi, Hill 191.9, Riaslo, and Gal'ianovo sector.

The boundary on the left: Tarasovka (5 kilometers northeast of Kodosno), Novinskoe, Perevoz, and Kurbaty.

11. The Major Kadyshin's composite detachment will occupy separate sectors intersecting the [following] road junctions: at Ekimino and Hill 100.9; and in the vicinity of Hill 153.7, Peski, and Kabanikha, with a reserve group in Ozerets [35 kilometers west of Toropets].

12. The commander of Captain Latkin's composite detachment, will defend the Pochinok region and the Barsuki region [25 kilometers west-southwest of Toropets], with a reserve group in the vicinity of Skvortsovo Station [17 kilometers west-southwest of Toropets].

13. The commander of 697th ATR will occupy the Hill 230.6 region, the Raina region, and Tarasovka [25 kilometers southwest of Toropets] for defense, with a reserve group in the Rusanovo and Hill 225.3 region [15 kilometers southwest of Toropets].

14. Prepared the main defensive belt for firing by 1800 hours on 25 August. Complete defensive work in the main belt by no later than 28 August 1941.

15. CP – the woods 2 kilometers east of Podsoson'e.

The Commander of the OG, Colonel Fedorov
The Member of the Military Council, Brigade Commissar Shevchenko
The Chief of Staff, Colonel Nerianin [Nyrianin]

Source: "Boevoi prikaz komandira operativnoi gruppy 22-i Armii No. 18 ot 25 avgusta 1941 g. na oboronu rubezha r. Chernost', Dubrovka, Pochinok, Barsuki, Piatnitskoe, Tarasovka" [Combat order no. 18 of 22nd Army's operational group of 25 August 1941 on defense of the Chernost' River, Dubrovka, Pochinok, Barsuki, Piatnitskoe, and Tarasovka line], *SBDVOV*, issue 41, 245-246.

15. Combat Order No. 2/op of 22nd Army's Operational Group of 26 August 1941 on the Destruction of the Opposing Enemy

Combat Order No. 2/op, Headquarters of the Operational Group,
in the woods east of Stepanovskoe Farm,
0130 hours on 26 August 1941
1:100,000 scale, 1939 g. edition

1. In fulfillment of the order of the Commander-in-Chief of the Western Front to the units of 22nd Army's Operational Group, **I order**:

a) Antosenko's Composite Detachment, with 697th AR in the Kostino region subordinate to it, will destroy the enemy in the Piatnitskoe region and reach the Hill 228.6, Markovo, Sharapova, and Levkovo Farm line for subsequent operations toward the west to destroy the opposing enemy and capture Hills 240.8, 222.6, 226.0, and 230.5, Staritsy, and Efremkovo.

Colonel Antosenko will destroy the enemy in the vicinity of Zhizhitsa Station [30 kilometers southwest of Toropets] with part of his forces (no fewer than 2 battalions) by an attack from Grishino, Tsarevo, and Buraia, together with the detachment of Major Iurlov, and prevent a penetration by him [the enemy] to the east, while firmly holding onto the ground between the lakes in the Zasenovo, Pashivkovo [should read Pashivkino], and Naumovo State Farm sector. Iurlov's detachment is also subordinated to you.

b) Colonel Nerianin will throw a detachment composed of a force of no fewer than 2,000 bayonets taken from the withdrawing units, into the Lake Sel'skoe, Staraia Toropa, and Semenovskoe defensive region on foot, with the mission to defend this line firmly, having paid special attention to defending the Zhizhitsa Station and Staraia Toropa railroad; (the detachment should not be taken from several units; it would be better if it will represent an entire unit). Deploy the remaining units from the Ozerets, Skvortsovo Station, and Malye Usviaty concentration areas [25-35 kilometers west of Toropets] along the Chernost' River, Baranenki, Ivantsevo, Barsuki, Kolenidovo, and (incl.) Hill 228.6 line [20-25 kilometers southwest of Toropets], with the mission of firmly defending the indicated line with separate units, while having in mind, subsequently, reaching the Akulino, Chmutovo, Pleshkovo, Maloe Koshkino, and Hill 230.5 line [35 kilometers southwest of Toropets]. Determine the order [sequence] for occupation of the line with these units in accordance with an on-the-spot judgment [inspection] and while fulfilling the order of 29th Army's commander, which assigned sectors for 48th TD and 126th RD on the line's right wing.

From the units, which have been holding the forward line, send covering forces: No. 1 – to Gorki and Trostkino Station (5 kilometers west of Nazimovo Station); and No. 2 – to Nazimovo Station and Nazimovo.

Colonel Nerianin is categorically forbidden from moving the approaching units toward Toropets, even if they are unarmed, while bringing them into their own or neighboring units and while pursuing the single goal of accelerating the strengthening of the indicated forward line – in fulfillment of the commander-in-chief of the Western Front's order.

Colonel Nerianin will assign missions to the units that are situated in the forward line personally and on the spot, based on the order of the Western Front's commander-in-chief, that is, to hold onto the indicated line, while restoring order in the units and strengthening the forward defensive line with all of the weapons at his disposal for a subsequent advance to the Akulino, Maseevo Farm, and Sevast'ianovo line.

Colonel Antosenko and Colonel Nerianin will confirm receipt and report fulfillment.

The Commander of the OG, Colonel Fedorov
The Member of the Military Council, Brigade Commissar Shevchenko
The Chief of Staff, Colonel Nerianin

Source: "Boevoi rasporiazhenie komandira operativnoi gruppy 22-i Armii No. 2/op ot 26 avgusta 1941 g. na unichtozhenie protivostoiashchego protivnika " [Combat order no. 2/op of 22nd Army's operational group of 26 August 1941 on the destruction of the opposing enemy], *SBDVOV*, issue 41, 246-247.

16. Individual Combat Order No. 17 of 22nd Army's Operational Group of 26 August 1941 on the Destruction of the Opposing Enemy

Combat Order No. 17, Headquarters of the OG,
in the woods 1 kilometer south of Mikhali,
0200 hours on 26 August 1941
1:100,000 scale, 1939 g. edition

1. The Operational Group, fulfilling the order of the Western Front's commander-in-chief, is defending the Ekimino, Sementsevo, Pochinok, Barsuki, Kostino, and Raina line, with the main defensive positions along the Podolino, Toropets, and Staraia Toropa line.

2. The enemy opposite the OG's front is striving to spread out farther to the northeast in the general direction of Toropets and Ostashkov with small reconnaissance groups.

The enemy is not displaying special activity in front of the OG's forward line. Separate enemy reconnaissance groups, while bursting forward, are seeking to reach the Toropets and Staraia Toropa road, up to a company of enemy threw themselves forward from the Terekhov Lug and Piatnitskoe line at 0300 hours on 25 August 1941, and a company of infantry with four tanks captured Kostino after pressing back 697th AR's subunits.

3. Colonel Antosenko's Composite Detachment (8th and 9th Motorcycle Regiments, a tank battalion, an engineer battalion, and a sapper battalion) will defend positions from (incl.) Novaia Derevnia, along the eastern bank of the Toropa River, to Staraia Toropa and Semenovskoe with the main part of its forces on the morning of 26 August, while attacking toward Chikhachi, Nikulino, Grudtsy, and Pokrovskoe with one rifle and one tank battalion, together with Polukhin's detachment (697th AR) to encircle and destroy the enemy in the Kostino region by attacking him on the flank and rear, while developing success toward the west and reaching the Grudino, Lykovo, Hill 218.5, Sharapov, and Levkovo Farm line.

The boundary on the left: (incl.) Lake Griadetskoe, (incl.) Lake Sel'skoe, (incl.) Chikhachi, Peska River, (incl.) Kudenets Farm, and Hill 216.9.

4. For concerted successful operations, subordinate Polukhin's detachment to Colonel Antosenko, having assigned him initial mission of tying down the enemy in the Kostino region, while subsequently planning to send Polukhin's detachment to occupy the Grudino, Lykovo, Hill 218.5, Sharapov, and Levkovo farm line and concentrate the composite detachment's shock group for destroying the enemy in the Kostino region in the woods near Platichino in readiness for active operations toward the west, with the aim of capturing Hills 226.0, 240.9, and 218.4 with the group.

5. CP of the OG – the woods 1 kilometer south of Mikhali.

6. Send reports: 1st – upon occupation and preparation of the defensive sector; 2nd – upon the shock group's arrival to destroy the enemy in Kostino; 3rd – upon the fulfillment of immediate missions; and 4th – upon the arrival of Polukhin's detachment at the line indicated.

> The Commander of the OG, Colonel Fedorov
> The Member of the Military Council, Brigade Commissar Shevchenko
> The Chief of Staff, Colonel Nerianin

Source: "Chastnyi boevoi prikaz komandira operativnoi gruppy 22-i Armii No. 17 ot 26 avgusta 1941 g. na unichtozhenie protivnika v raione Kostino" [Individual combat order no. 17 of 22nd Army's operational group of 26 August 1941 on the destruction of the opposing enemy], *SBDVOV*, issue 41, 247-248.

17. Notes of a Conversation of the Deputy Chief of Staff of the Western Front on 26 August with the Western Front's Chief of Staff about the Positions of 22nd Army's Forces

2350 hours on 26 August

Lieutenant General Malandin [at 22nd Army's headquarters] and Lieutenant General Sokolovsky

Malandin – I am reporting: I arrived and began to investigate – the situation is thus:

1. Ershakov's units are beginning to withdraw, while using the northern route. Biriukov's division (186th) reached the line of the former forward line – 30-40% [strength], and with three 45mm guns, 3 76mm guns, and 2 155mm guns. It has little organization and requires putting in order. 174th [Rifle] Division just now began withdrawing in broken up groups, but with no equipment. 214th [Rifle] Division, which is also assembling by small groups, is now only the size of a regiment, and there is no news about its equipment.

Major General [A. N.] Rozanov (214th) himself has still not arrived, but his chief of staff is located at Ozertsy.

48th TD withdrew in the best order, with almost up to 70% of its personnel. 179th RD withdrew with no more than 20%, but its personnel are moving, however, nothing is known about its equipment.

170th [RD] appeared in separate disorganized groups and, similarly, 126th and 98th RD. Thus, all have withdrawn, but they do not represent combat capable entities.

Major General [B. A.] Pigarevich [22nd Army's chief of staff] reached and is located in Ozertsy.

Ershakov is not yet there, but a vehicle has been sent for him.

The situation indicates that the encirclement was not complete, and the northern part is open and permits a planned withdrawal. Almost all of the formation commanders have lost command and control. Given these conditions, I note the following:

1. This evening the former forward line will finally be occupied in an organized fashion. Orders have been given to occupy [the following]: on the right – 48th TD will occupy the sector to Kabanikha, to the south – 179th [Rifle Division], on its left – Kadyshev, together with the remnants of 214th RD's units, to the south, Biriukov [186th RD], with Latkin's detachment, and these commands have already occupied the sectors given to them and are reforming organizationally. Given the almost total absence of artillery, orders have been given by me to create mobile batteries from on-hand artillery on the basis of two-three in each division sector along main axes.

Antosenko's detachment is just now moving from the Staraia Toropa region to Lake Zhizhitskoe; it had been given the mission to reach the entire former forward line in order to close off the main Toropa axis, but is apparently late in fulfilling the order. To fulfill these instructions, the commands designated for each chief of sector will send out strong forward detachments no later than 0100 hours during the night, with the missions, while destroying enemy groups, to move forward to the forward line and dig in there. At first light tomorrow, we will organize the main forces' movement into the forward line. They have been categorically ordered not to occupy it in linear fashion, but instead to construct it with deeply echeloned strong points and with the presence of reserves. Tomorrow, at first light, I will go down to the sectors in order to check the course of movement personally.

I forgot to say that Kuznetsov – in the right sector, is, in fact, directing the organization of the defense on the right wing.

I request you report to the commander-in-chief [Timoshenko] that, by tomorrow morning I will, apparently, have the combat composition of those who withdrew, and no-one will leave for the rear.

Question [Sokolovsky] – What information do you have about the enemy?

Answer [Malandin] – According to information from ground reconnaissance, the enemy – includes separate groups along the axis of the routes in front of our unit's front, totals up to one and one half regiments in all. Air reconnaissance has established the movement of columns from the Nazimova region northward and northeastward, apparently, with the aim of cutting off our withdrawal routes.

The report by the *front's* Intelligence Department that the column reached Ozerets was incorrect. Ozerets is ours, but we must expect that the enemy will turn his forces toward the east in so far as he is tied in with no-one to the west.

Question [Sokolovsky] – Have heavy losses been inflicted on the enemy?

Answer [Malandin] – According to the reports of those who withdrew, the enemy has suffered heavy losses, but I cannot answer in more detail until I verify things tomorrow.

Sokolovsky – Good, verify and report, especially in regard to the withdrawal of equipment. I say we need to track it down in order to occupy a seriously prepared defense and organize a rebuff, and we need to supply the forces with individual antitank means such as flammable bottles and grenades and do this as soon as required.

Tomorrow we need to protect our operations with 47th MAD and, second, order mines and antitank mines to be sent, and there are also insufficient shovels.

Source: "Zapis' peregovora zamestitelia nachal'nika shtaba Zapadnogo fronta ot 26 avgusta 1941 g. s nachal'nikom shtaba Zapadnogo fronta o polozhenii voisk 22-i Armii" [Notes of a conversation of the deputy chief of staff of the Western Front on 26 August with the Western Front's chief of staff about the positions of 22nd Army's forces], *SBDVOV*, issue 41, 83-85.

18. Notes of a Conversation of the Chief of Staff of the Western Front of 28 August with the Chief of the Operations Department of the Western Front's Headquarters about the Situation on the *Front's* Right Wing

Conversations of Lieutenants General Malandin and Sokolovsky
Time: 0340 hours on 28 August 1941

Malandin – First. According to our information, the enemy is conducting an offensive with his main forces along the Toropets axis. Two of his columns were noted operating toward the northeast: one was approaching Skvortsovo Station by evening, and the other – Kostino. The northern axis – up to two infantry divisions are operating toward Ozerets. The enemy is trying to cut off the Toropets-Velikie Luki route and, apparently, toward Staraia Toropa, with the enemy's forward units. Along the Skvortsovo and Kostino axes, our units, which were protecting these axes, have withdrawn to the Ozerets, Skvortsovo, and Kostino line. A counterattack was repelled at Ozerets, but, to the west, the enemy succeeded in cutting the route to Velikie Luki.

Sokolovsky – I do not understand where our detachments protecting the Skvortsovo axis divide, and also toward Ozerets. Are not Ershakov's units there?

Malandin – Second. 170th RD withdrew with up to 300 men on 28 August. It has no commander and headquarters and also no equipment. [Other strength reports include]: 174th RD – up to 400 men but no headquarters, and its equipment includes one 122mm gun. 186th RD – up to 2,000 men, three 76mm guns, two 45mm guns, two 122mm guns, and nothing else. 214th RD – up to 2,500 men, but no equipment. 48th TD – up to 2,500 men and two 76mm guns, and 98th RD – up to 300 men, but no equipment and headquarters. 126th RD – up to 3,100 men. It appears better than the others. Equipment, two 76mm guns and 17 machine guns. 179th RD – up to 300 men but no equipment. RGK [Reserve of the High Command] equipment – only two guns of 360th HAR. There are personal weapons. The information is being verified.

Today, of the commanders, [the following] arrived: the commander of 186th RD, Biriukov; the temporary commander of 112th RD, Gavrilov; the commander of 29th RC, Samokhin; the commander of 214th RD, Rozanov; 22nd Army's chief of staff, Pigarevich; and the chief of artillery, Nichkov.

The [following] have not yet arrived: the commander of 174th RD, Zygin; the commander of 62nd RC, Karmanov; the commander of 170th RD, Colonel Laskin;

and Colonel Bunin. Of the commissars, [the following have arrived]: Udolov, Evseev, and Osadchev. Up to this time, Ershakov and Leonov [have not arrived].

Third. The withdrawn commands do not represent full value because of losses in personnel and equipment, and also in light of the considerable disorder in their command organs.

Fourth. We cannot fulfill the orders in regard to occupying the army's forward line due to the difficult situation. The forward detachments sent out on 26 August were pushed back to their jumping-off positions by the enemy, and the units dug in along the main line with adjustments made as a consequence of the fighting on 27 August.

Fifth. The missions of the commands supplied by Maslennikov [29th Army] are being sent to me by enciphered telegram.

Sixth: Measures are being taken for strengthening protection along the Rzhev axis. The Toropets axis is being reinforced at the expense of 126th RD's units. The rear line is being brought to readiness.

Seventh: It is necessary to strengthen the army with equipment and replacements, and communications means are absent. It would be expedient to restore order in 22nd Army's command and control and entrust Pigarevich with command until Ershakov's arrival. At this time, simultaneously with the operations to repel the enemy offensive, work is being conducted on the organization and restoration of order in the command. It would not be bad if, while this work is being done, we could have one command in reserve in the vicinity of Zapadnaia Dvina.

Authenticated by Major Andrieko

Source: "Zapis' peregovora nachal'nika shtaba Zapadnogo fronta s nachal'nikom operativnogo otdela shtaba Zapadnogo fronta ot 28 avgusta 1941 g. o polozhenii na pravom kryle fronta" [Notes of a conversation of the chief of staff of the Western Front of 26 August with the chief of the Operations Department of the Western Front's headquarters about the situation on the *front*'s right wing], *SBDVOV*, issue 41, 88-89.

19. Combat Order No. 12 of the Commander of the Forces of 29th Army on 28 August 1941 on Defending our Occupied Positions

Combat Order No. 12, Headquarters, 29th Army,
Bentsy,
Late morning on 28 August 1941
1:100,000 scale map

1. The enemy opposite 29th Army's front are continuing to strengthen their defense, while created pillboxes and bunkers, and are simultaneously concentrating significant forces in the Il'ino region. Groupings of units are continuing to concentrate against the army' right wing in the Khlebanikha region and against the army's left wing in the Bol'shaia Zheleznitsa and Kanat regions. Small groups of enemy with tanks are occupying the Fatievo, Ivantsevo, and Trubnino line, and we have noted the approach of new enemy columns from Nazimovo Station toward Ozerets.

2. 29th Army will go over to a firm defense along the lines it has reached on 28 August 1941, with the mission to prevent an enemy penetration along the northeastern and northern axes toward Staraia Toropa, Toropets, and Rzhev.

3. On the right, 22nd Army in going over to the defense along the Chernost' River, Pal'tsevo, Barsuki, Lake Kodosno, Naumovo State Farm, and Lake Zhizhitskoe line.

On the left, 30th Army is attacking toward Shelepy and Zarech'e. The boundaries are as before.

4. 252nd RD, with 309th Sep. ATBn and 4th Btry, 644th CAR, will continue to strengthen and improve the defensive line it occupies in the Krivets, Olenitsa 1, Ust'e, Petrovo, and Bukharikha sector along the Western Dvina River and the ground in the Arestovo, Poliany, Kokovkino, Zabor'e sector on the isthmus between Lake Zhatko and Lake Dvin'e up to Lake Deviato, having closed down the isthmus and the roads in the Uzmen' region, with the mission to prevent an enemy penetration toward the north.

The boundary on the left: Lake Neretto, Bol'shaia Griada Farm, and Sinichino.

5. 246th RD, with 6th Btry, 644th CAR, will immediately go over to a firm defense in the Beliankin Farm, Pavlova Luka, Trubniki sector and further along your occupied line, with the mission to prevent an enemy penetration toward the north.

The boundary on the left: Sharapovo, Malaia Gorovakha, (incl.) Salovo, and (incl.) Masiagino.

Long-range artillery group 246 – 1st Bn, 644th CAR.

6. 243rd RD, with 5th Btry, 644th CAR, will immediately go over to a firm defense of the sector from the positions you occupy to the positions of the Composite Brigade's 1st and 2nd MRRs and to Borovye and Novye Borovye, with the mission to prevent an enemy penetration toward the north and southeast.

The boundary on the left: Marker 184.9, (2044), Pashkovo, Borovye, Hill 175.3, Lake Putnoe, and Prudok.

7. The Composite Brigade, with one battalion of 1st MRR and an artillery battalion, will occupy and defend the Hills 175.5 and 174.6 region along the Borsovka, Hill 184.6, and Lake Borovny line with company and platoon strong points and centers of resistance in close fire coordination between them, with the mission to prevent an enemy penetration toward the north and protect the army's left flank.

29th CR will fulfill its assigned mission for providing reconnaissance along the Mezha River.

8. The army's reserve – the Composite Brigade, without one battalion but with 29th CR's artillery battalion – concentrated in the Malaia Gorovakha, Svetlyi Ruchei, and the woods southeast of Osinovka region, will prepare a defense along the Bol'shaia Gorovakha and Safronovka line and counterattacks toward: 1) Khvatkovo and Bentsy; 2) Korotyshi, Mikhalevo, and Dedovo; and 3) Romanovo, Salovo, and Andreevskaia.

9. Artillery. Be ready – 1900 hours on 28 August 1941.

Missions:

1) Prevent enemy attacks from the [following] directions: Khlebanikha, Rudnia, the woods west of Sokovichino, Andreevskaia, Katkovo, and Kanat.

2) Prevent the approach of enemy reserves from the Il'ino and Kanat axes.

3) Suppress enemy artillery in the Sokovichino, Andreevskie Farm, and Vysochert.

10. Proceed immediately to strengthen the positions you occupy. In the first instance, complete the work on protecting the forward edge with antitank and anti-infantry obstacles and entrenching work by day's end on 29 August 1941.

Protect the forward edge and flanks of the main axes with antitank and anti-infantry obstacles and create antitank regions in the depth, while using for that purpose, in the first instance, local and on-hand means. Within their boundaries, the rifle divisions will exploit already created antitank and anti-infantry obstacles along the southern and northern banks of the Western Dvina River.

The army's Chief of Engineer Forces will continue strengthen [the following] rear defensive lines in an antitank respect:

a) Facing west along the Toropa River; and

b) Facing south – Lake Zadnee, Lake Neretto, Lake Bentsy, Lake Kotovo, Lake Benetto, and Lake Verezhuni.

The army's formations will outfit all of their trenches with head defensive covers and overhead covers with constructed embrasures and carefully camouflage all defensive structures. Organize defensive regions, strong points, and centers of resistance with consideration for all-round defense of regimental and battalions regions. Create antitank and anti-infantry obstacles in close coordination with firing systems.

The army's Chief of Engineer Forces will support the equipping of the sectors and lines with necessary materials for anti-infantry obstacles.

11. The defense will be ready at first light on 28 August 1941. Be ready for the first stage of work by 1800 hours on 28 August 1941.

12. CPs of the divisions: 252nd RD – in the Averkovo region; 246th RD – the woods west of Poiarkovo; 243rd RD – in the vicinity of Hill 201.5; and the Composite Brigade – in the vicinity of the woods east of Svetlyi Ruchei.

13. The first echelon of the army's headquarters – Bentsy

14. Present reports: 1) on the readiness of the defense; and 2) upon completion of work on outfitting the antitank and anti-infantry obstacles.

The Commander of 29th Army, Lieutenant General Maslennikov
The Member of the Military Council of 29th Army,
    Divisional Commissar Gurov
The Chief of Staff of 29th Army, Major General Shaparov

Source: "Boevoi prikaz komanduiushchego voiskami 29-i Armii No. 12 ot 28 avgusta 1941 g. na oboronu zanimaemogo rubezha" [Combat order No. 12 of the commander of the forces of 29th Army of 28 August 1941 on the defense of our occupied positions], *SBDVOV*, issue 41, 272-273.

20. Combat Order No. 19 of the Commander of the Forces of 22nd Army on 28 August 1941 on the Defense of the Chernost' River, Pal'tsevo, Barsuki, Lake Kodosno, and Naumovo State Farm Line

Combat Order No. 19, Headquarters of 22nd Army,
the woods 1 kilometer east of Stepanovskie Farm,

2300 hours on 28 August 1941
1:100,000 scale map, 1939 edition

Before the withdrawal from encirclement of all of 22nd Army's units and formations led by 22nd Army's Military Council, the commander-in-chief, Marshal Timoshenko, entrusted 29th Army's Military Council with restoring order in the withdrawing units and defending with these units, with the mission of holding onto forward positions at Akulino and Pleshkovo.

Small groups of enemy with tanks are occupying the Fatieva, Ivantsevo, Trubino, and Zhizhitsa Station line [35 kilometers southwest of Toropets]. At 1600 hours on 26 August, air reconnaissance noticed the movement of a column of up to 200 vehicles from Nazimovo Station toward Ozerets.

Enemy operations toward Toropets and Staraia Toropa are likely in the immediate future.

I order:

1. 22nd Army's units, upon their withdrawal from encirclement, will occupy and firmly defend the Chernost' River, Pal'tsevo, Barsuki, Lake Kodosno, and Naumovo State Farm line by the night of 27 August, while bringing yourself to combat readiness, with the mission to occupy the Trubitsy, Maloe Koshkino, and Artemovo Platform forward defensive line.

2. 48th TD will secure and defend the Akulino and Hill 201.1 (south of Koptevo) sector.

The boundary on the left: Zarech'e, Vesnitsy, (incl.) Ivantsevo, and Borok.

CP – Ogorodtsy.

3. The DD [Destroyer Division] of the commander of 51st RC, Colonel Comrade Sazonov, having combined units (from 179th, 126th, and 214th RDs and Kadyshev's detachment), will withdraw, having occupied the Kudinovo and Shamarino sector for defense.

The boundary on the left: Mikhali, Ol'khovatka, Hill 216.9, and Mishino-Shamarino, Mishovo.

CP – Plinty.

4. The commander of 186th RD, Major General Biriukov, with Captain Latkin's detachment, will seize and defend the Tarasy and Fedotkovo sector.

The boundary on the left: Kurbaty, Novaia Derevnia, Grishino, Mishkovo, Peshchanka, and Fedotkovo.

CP – Kornilova.

5. Colonel Antosenko's Composite Detachment, with Major Polukhin's detachment, having seized the Fedotkovo and (incl.) Lake Zhizhitskoe line and organized a defense while paying special attention to the Staraia Toropa Station axis, will destroy the opposing enemy by a decisive attack on the morning of 27 August.

CP – Glubokovo.

6. Divisional sectors will construct all-round defenses, with battalion centers of resistance echeloned in depth.

7. For struggling with tanks, have mobile batteries and destroyer detachments in each divisional sector, with large reserves of explosive bottles ["Molotov cocktails"].

8. The army's reserve: 170th RD – concentrate in the Ivantsevo, Korpeiki, and Martynov region. Be prepared for operations toward Nazimovo.

174th RD –concentrate in the Ogorody, Sokolikhino, and Plotavki region, prepared for operations toward Ivantsevo and Lake Kodosno.

98th RD – concentrate in the woods 1 kilometer east of Zhizhitsa Station, prepared for operations along the railroad to Artemovo Platform.

9. Main Defense Line – Chernost' River, Ivantsevo, Levkovo Farm, and Karevo; and continue to strengthen and improve this line.

10. Rear Defense Line – the Toropets and Staraia Toropa line.

11. 126th RD will defend the (incl.) Novaia Derevnia, Staraia Toropa, and Semenovskoe line.

12. Formations and units in the main defensive line, within their boundaries, will send out forward detachments 1-2 companies strong and with machine pistols on the night of 6-27 August, with the mission to seize the Akulino, Tarasy State Farm, and Fediunino line.

13. 22nd Army's Chief of Engineers will continue to fulfill work according to the earlier established plan with two engineer battalions. With the two battalions:

a) Flood the Bol'shie Usviaty, Barsuch'i Gory, and Shepelevka region, mine and create obstacles on the main roads between the forward and main defensive lines, and employ craters, blockages, and road landmines extensively.

b) Direct work on the creation of antitank obstacles along the forward edge of the forward defensive line.

14. CP of the army – the woods 1 kilometer east of Stepanovskie Farm, and subsequently – Skvortsovo Station.

15. Send reports: 1st – upon preparation of the defensive sectors, and 2nd – upon taking possession of the lines with forward detachments and divisional sectors by forward units.

The army's Military Council obliges the commanders and commissars of formations and units to remind all personnel about the demands of the People's Commissar of Defense, Comrade Stalin, regarding the conduct of all soldiers in battle.

Our aviation and 22nd Army's units will inflict serious casualties on the enemy and decisively resist along the defensive lines indicated above to spoil the enemy's plan.

The Commander of 22nd Army, Lieutenant General Maslennikov
The Member of the Military Council, Divisional Commissar Gurov
The Deputy Chief of Staff, Colonel Fedorov

Source: "Boevoi prikaz komanduiushchego voiskami 22-i Armii No. 19 ot 26 avgusta 1941 g. na oboronu rubezha r. Chernost', Pal'tsevo, Barsuki, oz. Kodosno, svkh. Naumovo" [Combat order No. 19 of the commander of the forces of 22nd Army on 28 August 1941 on the defense of the Chernost' River, Pal'tsevo, Barsuki, Lake Kodosno, and Naumovo State Farm line], *SBDVOV*, issue 41, 248-249.

Appendix R

The Northern Flank: Group Stumme's Advance to Zapadnaia Dvina, 29 August-9 September

1. Individual Combat Order No. 21 of the Commander of the Forces of 22nd Army of 28 August 1941 on the Defense of the Podolina, Gorka, and Staraia Toropa Line

Individual Combat Order No. 21, Headquarters, 22nd Army,

Martisovo,

1700 hours on 28 August 1941

1. The enemy is continuing an offensive along the army's entire front with the forces of 19th and 20th PzDs and 30th MotD.

2. On the right – 27th Army. The boundary with it is as before. On the left – 29th Army, and the boundary with it is as before.

3. The army's units are conducting stubborn defensive fighting to the west of the previously prepared rear defense line along the Podolina, Hill 191.9, Gorka, Lake Zalikovskoe, Rechane, and Staraia Toropa front.

4. 709th HAR will continue to defend the Podolina, (incl.) Hill 179.1, and Ganevo sector.

5. 196th Auto Bn will continue defending the Hill 179.1, Hill191.9, and Kamestaia sector.

6. 137th Sep.AABn and 13th Sep.ATBn will defend Hill 199.5, Gorka, and Zhelny.

7. 186th RD, with 36th MRBn, will defend the (incl.) Gorka, Hill 199.2 and Martiukhovo sector.

8. 126th RD, with 390th HAR and 179th Sep.ATBn, will defend (incl.) Hill 199.2, Lake Zalikovskoe, and Zarech'e.

9. 360th HAR, with 615th HAR, will continue to defend the Lake Zalikovskoe, Rechane, and Novoe Bridino sector.

10. Antosenko's detachment will withdraw to the Lepekhnino and Mit'kovo front.

11. The boundaries – as before (see Combat Order No. 18).

12. Entrust the commander of 29th RC, Major General Samokhin, with the grouping north of Lake Zalikovskoe and Toropets, inclusively. Entrust Colonel Sazonov (51st RC) with the grouping south of Toropets. They will personally answer for the strengthening of the regions and defensive sectors.

13. Construct a defense, while echeloning it in depth and relying on centers of resistance. Destroy the enemy groups, which have penetrated into the depths with counterattacks.

14. I am subordinating the Commandant of the town of Toropets, Colonel Devi, to the commander of 29th RC.

15. CP – Martisovo Station.

> The Commander of 22nd Army, Major General Iushkevich*
> The Member of the Military Council, Brigade Commissar Shevchenko
> The Chief of Staff of the army, Major General Pigarevich
> Sent by telephone in the clear to 29th RC's chief of staff at 0400-0430
> hours on 29 August about subordinating Devi to Samokhin.

* General Iushkevich was appointed commander of the army on 28 August.

Source: "Chastnyi boevoi prikaz komanduiushchego voiskami 22-i Armii No. 21 ot 28 avgusta 1941 g. na oboronu rubezha Podolina, Gorka, Staraia Toropa" [Individual combat order of the commander of the forces of 22nd Army no. 12 of 28 August 1941 on the defense of the Podolina, Gorka, and Staraia Toropa line], *SBDVOV*, issue 41, 250.

2. Report by the Chief of Staff of the Western Front to the Chief of the General Staff about the Positions of 22nd Army's Forces by Day's End on 28 August

To the Chief of the General Staff of the Red Army
1:100,000 scale maps

I am briefly reporting about the situation on 22nd Army's front at day's end on 28 August 1941.

First. The army's units basically withdrew to the rear line by 2000 hours on 28 August under enemy pressure.

Second. 186th RD is assembled and occupied the Nishevitsy (11 kilometers northwest of Toropets) and Iakshino line for defense.

126th RD is on the Iakshino and Zalikov'e line. A small enemy tank group enemy penetrated at the boundary between these divisions. An order is being given to destroy it.

To the north, 98th and 214th RDs are supposed to withdraw, but we have no information about them. Antosenko's detachment began withdrawing from the Kostino region to positions south of Toropets at about 2200 hours.

The composite student battalion is defending the Zhizhitsa Station region.

Third. Up to four battalions of enemy infantry, reinforced by tanks, are directly in front of the units occupying our rear positions. His main forces are some distance west and southwest of Toropets. This information required verification.

Fourth. The commander-in-chief ordered Maslennikov to move one RD and the motorized brigade to the Staraia Toropa region by the morning of 29 August.

Sokolovsky

Source: "Doklad nachal'nika shtaba Zapadnogo fronta ot 28 avgusta 1941 g. nachal'niku General'nogo Shtaba o polozhenii voisk 22-i Armii k iskhodu 28 avgusta 1941 g." [Report of the chief of staff of the Western Front to the chief of the General Staff about the positions of 22nd Army's forces by day's end on 28 August], *SBDVOV*, issue 41, 93.

3. Combat Order No. 23 of the Commander of the Forces of 22nd Army of 30 August 1941 to the Commander of the Central Sector on an Advance to the Line of the Isthmus between Lakes Iassy, Solomennoe, and Kudinskoe, with the Aim of Preparing an Offensive to Capture the City of Toropets

To Major General Comrade Samokhin
Individual Combat Order No. 23, Headquarters, 22nd Army,
Martisovo,
0130 hours on 30 August 1941
1:100,000 scale map

I order you to move units into the isthmus between Lake Iassy, Lake Kudinskoe, and Lake Solomennoe, while planning to organize an immediate offensive to seize Toropets upon reaching the line indicated. Take every measure possible to prevent an enemy penetration toward the east.

Report all of your units' actions to this headquarters immediately, while preventing any lapse in communications. Use radio, delegates [liaison officers], and mobile means to the utmost.

The Commander of 22nd Army, Major General Iushkevich
The Member of the Military Council, Brigade Commissar Shevchenko
The Chief of Staff of 22nd Army, Colonel Shalin
[Note: Major General Boris Alekseevich Pigarevich was chief of staff
   until 29 August]

Source: "Chastnyi boevoi prikaz komanduiushchego voiskami 22-i Armii No. 23 ot 30 avgusta 1941 g. komandiru tsentral'nogo uchastka na vydvizhenie voisk na rubezh peresheika mezhdu Ozerami Iassy, Solomennoe, Kudinskoe s tsel'iu podgotovki nastupleniia dlia ovladeniia gor. Toropets" [Individual combat order no. 23 of the commander of the forces of 22nd Army of 30 August 1941 to the commander of the central sector on an advance to the line of the isthmus between Lakes Iassy, Solomennoe, and Kudinskoe, with the aim of preparing an offensive to capture the city of Toropets], *SBDVOV*, issue 41, 251.

4. Report by the Military Council of the Western Front to the Supreme High Commander about the Situation on 22nd Army's Front

Moscow, to Comrade Stalin
0300 hours on 30 August 1941

We are reporting about the positions 22nd Army's front.
22nd Army suffered heavy losses in the fighting in encirclement in the Velikie Luki region, especially in equipment. All of the army's divisions escaped from the encirclement with strengths of from 400 to 4,000 men, with insignificant quantities

of guns and heavy machine guns, which numbered in the single figures in a number of divisions.

Broken up groups and detachments, which are still fighting, remain in the enemy's rear in the Velikie Luki region. Ershakov [22nd Army's commander] and Leonov, the Member of 22nd Army's Military Council, are with one of these groups. There are no communications with them.

22nd Army's units which escaped from encirclement, separate detachments from rear service units, and the composite detachment of Colonel Antosenko, which was formed by the *front*, were broken up in sustained fighting with enemy motor-mechanized units in several places on 27 and 28 August, and withdrew under great pressure to the vicinity of the town of Toropets on the night of 29 August.

As of 2200 hours on 29 August, the situation is as follows. Since 1200 hours, 186th and 126th RDs' units are fighting on the western and northeastern outskirts of Toropets, 48th and 214th RDs' units are fighting north of Toropets, and Antosenko's composite detachment is fighting south of Toropets. The separate groups of tanks and sub-machine gunners that penetrated into Toropets during the day are being destroyed. At 1200 hours two motorized infantry divisions and one panzer division were identified in the Toropets region.

The enemy's Velikie Luki grouping, consisting of up to 10 divisions, including two panzer, despite heavy losses suffered as a result of the fighting, are continuing to develop the offensive toward Toropets.

We have undertaken the following measures:

Formed a composite detachment under the command of Colonel Antosenko consisting of two motorized regiments, a battalion of tanks, and an artillery battalion, which, at the present time, is operating south of Toropets;

Transferred one antitank regiment and one artillery regiment, which have arrived in the place;

Transferred 246th RD and 2 motorized regiments from Maslennikov, with the [following] missions – 246th RD to protect the Staraia Toropa region and the two motorized regiments to occupy the crossings over the Western Dvina southeast of Toropets;

Before Ershakov's arrival, entrusted command of 22nd Army's units to Major General Iushkevich, the former commander of 44th [Rifle] Corps. Comrade Boldin, with a group of operations workers, has been sent there; and

Taken severe measures to restore order and discipline in 22nd Army's units. The commanders of 186th RD and 48th RD are being sent for judgment to a military tribunal for willfully abandoning their positions.

The situation, however, remains critical.

The enemy's occupation of the Toropets line has created the threat of his spreading out from Toropets along the Toropets, Nelidovo, and Rzhev axis and also the Toropets, Nelidovo, and Belyi axis into the rear of Maslennikov and Khomenko.

In this regard, we urgently request the *front's* help by the immediate allocation of two rifle divisions with tank battalions, one tank brigade, and three aviation regiments, including one regiment of fighters, one of assault aircraft, and one of bombers. We also request help with weapons and equipment for two regiments of divisional artillery.

The Military Council of the Western Front

Source: "Doklad voennogo soveta Zapadnogo fronta ot 30 avgusta 1941 g. Verkhovnomu Glavnokomanduiushchemu o polozhenii na fronte 22-i Armii" [Report by the Military Council of the Western Front of 30 August 1941 to the Supreme High Commander about the situation on 22nd Army's front], *SBDVOV*, issue 41, 99-100.

5. Individual Combat Order No. 29 of the Commander of the Forces of 22nd Army of 30 August 1941 to the Commander of 48th Rifle Division on Defense of the Toropa River Line

To the Commander of 48th RD, Colonel Iushchuk
Copies: To Major General Samokhin and Colonel Solenov
Individual Combat Order No. 29, Headquarters, 22nd Army,
Martisovo,
1030 hours on 30 August 1941
1:100,000 scale map

1. 48th RD will occupy and defend the line of the Toropa River in the Zaprud'e, Gavrilovskoe, (incl.) Pereles'e; and Borovskoe region in readiness to attack toward Gorodok and the northern outskirts of Toropets, together with Major General Samokhin's units.

The division commander will restore order in his subordinate units and prepare the indicated sector for a firm defense by exploiting all of the engineer obstacles and barriers available along the line of the Toropa River.

2. For protection of the army's right wing, establish a covering force, with the mission to close off all of the roads into the Kresty and Borok region from the northwest, while firmly holding onto connections with the neighbor on the left, as well as Colonel Solenov's units, which are defending the main positions along the Podolino, Karpasy, Bol'shoe Semich'e, and Petrovskoe line.

3. Conduct constant reconnaissance from the defended line's right flank northwestward to Petrikievo and Nekrashchevo and also toward Gorodok and Toropets.

4. Maintain uninterrupted communications with the army's headquarters by using radio and mobile means extensively, and send a liaison delegate to the army's headquarters immediately.

5. CP of 48th RD – Belogubovo.

6. Send reports: 1st – upon the readiness and occupation of the defensive sector; 2nd – upon receipt of new information from reconnaissance sent out to the northwest and toward Toropets; and 3rd – upon the establishment of full cooperation for a combined attack with Major General Samokhin's units.

7. CP of the army's headquarters – Martisovo, and, subsequently, Markovskii Mokh (6 kilometers south of Andreapol').

The Commander of 22nd Army, Major General Iushkevich
The Member of the Military Council, Brigade Commissar Shevchenko
The Chief of Staff of 22nd Army, Colonel Shalin

Source: "Chastnyi boevoi prikaz komanduiushchego voiskami 22-i Armii No. 29 ot 30 avgusta 1941 g. komandiru 48-i Strelkovoi Divizii na oboronu rubezh po r. Toropa" [Individual combat order no. 29 of the commander of the forces of 22nd Army of 30 August 1941 to the commander of 48th Rifle Division on defense of the Toropa River line], *SBDVOV*, issue 41, 252.

6. Combat Order No. 14 of the Commander of the Forces of 29th Army of 30 August 1941 about Strengthening Defenses along the Rzhev Axis

Combat Order No. 14, Headquarters, 29th Army,
the woods 0.5 kilometers east of Konovo,
2100 hours on 31 August 1941
1:100,000 scale map

1. The enemy is conducting offensives along the 1) Toropets and Lake Griadetskoe, and 2) Zhizhitsa Station and Staraia Toropa axes with large forces and with tanks and artillery, while displaying activity in the Palkhova and Sokhi regions and while operating together with bomber and fighter aircraft.

2. 29th Army, while protecting itself from the north along the Lake Bol'shoe Moshno and Lake Griadetskoe line, from the west – Lake Griadetskoe and Lake Pesno, and from the south – along the northern bank of the Western Dvina River from Olenitsa to Zui, will reach the eastern bank of the Western Dvina River, Iamishche, and Barlovo line with its main forces by day's end on 31 August 1941, with the mission to prevent the enemy from spreading out toward the east and southeast.

3. 22nd Army's units are operating to the right. The boundary with it: Lake Kodosno, Iamishche, and Vysokoe.

4. 246th RD, with Colonel Antosenko's detachment subordinate to it, will reach the area south of Lake Griadetskoe by forced march along the Seliane, Koriakino, and Griadtsy march-route, with the mission to halt the enemy offensive along the Toropets and Nelidovo highway and, in the event of strong pressure, to hold onto it along the Lake Bol'shoe Moshno, Lake Griadetskoe, and Lake Pesno line, while protecting the arrival of the army's main forces on the eastern bank of the Western Dvina River.

The division's CP will be in the woods northeast of Klin.

5. The Composite Division, before the main forces arrive, will hold onto the region of the bridge across the Western Dvina River along the Toropets and Nelidovo highway. When 243rd RD is concentrated, give up your defensive sector and revert to reserve in the Spiridovo, Rykovo, and Novo-Polutino region in readiness to operate toward: 1) Spiridovo and Iamishche; 2) Spiridovo and Zheleznovo; and 3) Spiridovo and Khotino; and prepare a rear line from Zuevo to Ostrozhko.

CP of the division – Hill 203.7 southwest of Borok.

6. 252nd RD, with 309th Sep.ATBn, having left the division's 932nd RR, reinforced by an artillery battalion and sapper company, to cover the division's entire line, will set out along the Anashchinki, Reshetnino, Sharapovo, Mikheeva, Litvinovo, Korovnitsa, Mel'nitsa, and Zapadnaia Dvina march-route, with the mission to occupy and firmly hold onto the Khotino, Barlovo, Shibareva, and Avakonovo defense sector along the Western Dvina River and prevent the enemy from spreading out to the east. Prepare a rear line along the eastern bank of the Velesa River.

Readiness of the defense – by day's end on 31 August 1941.

CP of the division – the woods west of Malyi Ozerki.

7. 243rd RD, while covering along the western bank of the Western Dvina from the south with one regiment, will set out with the remaining forces along the Korotyshi, Romanovo, Konovo, Moseevka, Larioshkovo, Barlovo, Tsibarervo, Svishchevo, Shemetovo, and Borok march-route by forced march, with the mission to occupy the Iamishche, Zaozerki, and Borok defense sector and prevent the enemy from spreading out toward the east.

The boundary on the left: Kurbat, Semichino, (incl.) Khotino, and Khoromy.

CP – Hill 203.7.

8. 29th CR will fulfill its previously assigned mission. In the event of an enemy offensive with large forces, withdraw and concentrate in the Obukhovo region, with the mission to conduct active reconnaissance along the [following] axes: 1) Obukhovo and Belki; 2) Obukhovo and Koshchenki Station, and 3) Obukhovo and Cherneia.

CP – Obukhovo.

9. The covering units, while conducting holding actions along their divisions' march-routes, will begin the withdrawal on the night of 1 September 1941 and concentrate in the regions in accordance with the division commanders' orders.

10. Artillery. 644th CAR will reach the Korovki region by a forced march along the Bol'shaia Gorovakha, Romanovo, Konovo, Larioshkovo, Papotkina, and Korovki march-route and occupy firing positions.

Missions:

a) Prevent the enemy from approaching toward Andronovo, Moshnitsa, Semichino, and Trofimovo.

b) Suppress enemy artillery.

c) Prevent the enemy from crossing the Western Dvina River at Zheleznovo, Kudinovo, and Zapadnaia Dvina Station.

Readiness to open fire – by 0400 hours on 1 September 1941.

11. The Chief of Engineer Forces will prepare obstacle belts in the sector on the right – from Iamishche to Lake Kodosno, and on the left – from Lake Zharki to Lake Velinskoe and, during a withdrawal of the forces, will destroy all railroad bridges and bridges over the Toropa and Western Dvina Rivers, while exploiting all of the forces and equipment of both the engineer forces and the formations.

12. 46th MAD, at first light on 31 August 1941, [will]:

a) Protect the withdrawal of the units to their new defensive line in the Zapadnaia Dvina, Staraia Toropa, Zhizhitsa Station, Olenitsa, Anashchinki, Sharapovo, Romanovo, and Petrilovo region by patrolling in the skies;

b) Conduct constant reconnaissance of the enemy along the [following] roads: Toropets and Zhelezovo; Toropets and Staraia Toropa; Priluki and Averkovo; and Il'ino and Sevost'ianovo; and

c) Immediately destroy discovered columns of the enemy, while blocking their approach to the Western Dvina River from the northwest, west, and southwest, and report about them immediately.

13. CP of 29th Army up to 1200 hours on 31 August 1941 – the woods east of Konovo, and, subsequently, Hill 183.1, 3.5 kilometers west of Zaborenko.

14. Present reports: 1) about the beginning of the offensive by [the enemy's] main force; 2) about the withdrawal to your regions; 3) the readiness of the defenses; 4) the withdrawal of the covering units; and 5) upon the arrival of the covering units in their regions.

> The Commander of 29th Army, Lieutenant General Maslennikov
> The Member of the Military Council of 29th Army,
>   Divisional Commissar Gurov
> The Chief of Staff of 29th Army, Major General Sharapov

Source: "Boevoi prikaz komanduiushchego voiskami 29-i Armii No. 14 ot 30 avgusta 1941 g. ob usilenii oborony na Rzhevskom napravlenii" [Combat order no. 14 of the commander of the forces of 29th Army of 31 August 1941 about strengthening defenses along the Rzhev axis], *SBDVOV*, issue 41, 274-275.

7. Report by the Military Council of the Western Front of 30 August 1941 to the Supreme High Commander about the Abandoning of Toropets by 22nd Army's Forces and about the Decision to Withdraw 29th Army's Right Wing Formations behind the Western Dvina River

Moscow, To Comrade Stalin
2350 hours on 30 August 1941

We are reporting:

Toropets has been abandoned by our units on the night of 30 August 1941 after fierce street fighting. During the day on 30 August, the enemy continued to develop his offensive with large motor-mechanized units (57th PzC) from Toropets toward the southeast. His forward units – tanks and motorized infantry, reached the Lake Iassy, Lake Kudinskoe, Lake Griadetskoe, and Lake Bol'shoe Moshno region by 1930 hours.

We have not succeeded in stopping the enemy, and he is continuing to spread out toward the Western Dvina River.

Therefore, during the first half of the day on 30 August, an immediate threat has been created to the rear of Comrade Maslennikov's army.

The *front's* Military Council decided to issue orders to Comrade Maslennikov at 1500 hours on 30 August to withdraw his two divisions – 252nd and 243rd RDs –to the Iamishche, Zapadnaia Dvina Station, and Barlovo sector along the Western Dvina River, with the mission – to prevent the enemy from spreading out further to the east. Maslennikov has been ordered to leave forward units in front of the army's front, with the mission to hold back the movement of the enemy's Il'ino grouping. Before the main forces of Maslennikov's army arrive, the crossings along the river will be secured by two motorized regiments transferred there beforehand, and 246th RD will be sent from Staraia Toropa to the crossings across the Western Dvina River at Zheleznovo.

Comrade Khomenko [30th Army] has been ordered to move his army's 134th RD from the Belyi region to the vicinity of Nelidovo Station immediately to seize of the road junction in that region, and 107th TD will shift to the Belyi region, where it will quickly put itself in order.

The Military Council of the Western Front

Source: "Doklad voennogo soveta Zapadnogo fronta ot 30 avgusta 1941 g. Verkhovnomu Glavnokomanduiushchemu o ostavlenii voiskami 22-i Armii gor. Toropets i o reshenii otvesti pravoflangovye soedineniia 29-i Armii za r. Zapadnaia Dvina" [Report by the Military Council of the Western Front of 30 August 1941 to the Supreme High Commander about the abandoning of Toropets by 22nd Army's forces and about the decision to withdraw 29th Army's right flank formations behind the Western Dvina River], *SBDVOV*, issue 41, 103-104.

8. *Stavka* VGK Directive No.001512 to the Commander of the Forces of the Western Front about Measures for Liquidating the Enemy Penetration in 22nd Army's Sector

Copy: To the Commander of the Forces of the Reserve Front
1 September 1941

For liquidating the enemy who has penetrated 22nd Army's front, 133rd and 178th RDs will reach you by railroad from the Reserve Front. The beginning of loading for the 133rd will be 1 September and for the 178th, 2 September. The regions for unloading are Soblago Station for the 133rd and Olenino Station for the 178th. I request you submit a plan for employment of the arriving divisions.

For the *Stavka* of the Supreme High Command,
Chief of the General Staff, B. Shaposhnikov

Source: "Direktiva Stavki VGK No. 001512 komanduiushchemu voiskami Zapadnogo fronta o merakh po likvidatsii proryva protivnika v polose 22-i Armii" [*Stavka* VGK Directive No.001512 to the commander of the forces of the Western Front about measures for liquidating the enemy penetration in 22nd Army's sector], in Zolotarev, "*Stavka* 1941," 154.

9. Combat Order No. 25 of the Commander of the Forces of 22nd Army of 1 September 1941 on Defense of the Mitrosheno, Likhusha, Selino, and Iamishche Line

Individual Combat Order No. 25, Headquarters, 22nd Army,
Martisovo,
1200 hours on 1 September 1941
1:100,000 scale map

1. Large enemy panzer and motorized units have penetrated the front in the Toropets and Staraia Toropa sector and are developing an offensive toward the southeast and northeast.

The enemy's forward units tried to cross over the Western Dvina River in the Zhelezovo region on 30-31 August 1941.

2. 22nd Army, while conducting brief rear-guard fights with the enemy and successfully repelling his units along the entire front on 29 and 30 August, inflicted heavy losses on him, having destroyed more than 4 battalions in the center and on the left wing. On the morning of 30 August, the army's units went on the defense

along the Mitrosheno, Likhusha, Selino, and Iamishche line, while simultaneously preparing main defensive positions along the Andreapol', Western Dvina River, and Iamishche line, with the mission to hold firmly to the intermediate and, in the future, the main defensive line, and prevent an enemy penetration to the northeast and southeast.

3. On the right, 256th RD on 27th Army's left flank is defending positions along the Pog. El'nia, Pikali, and Smykovo front (all points 40-45 kilometers northwest of Toropets).

On the left, 29th Army's units are defending positions from Iamishche to Western Dvina and the system of Lakes Dobresho and Rakomlia.

The boundary line with it: Verkhniaia, Iamishche, and Lake Kodosno.

4. 214th RD will firmly defend the sector from Mitrosheno to the main railroad line (1 kilometer northwest of Novo-Tikhvinskoe), and Kliukunovo [15 kilometers west to 4 kilometers southwest of Andreapol'], while preventing an enemy penetration toward Andreapol'. Fill out the division with the remnants of 48th TD, whose main units will withdraw into the reserve. I am entrusting 214th RD with protecting the army's right flank. Pay special attention to protecting the road junctions leading to the northwest.

The boundary line on the left: Rogovo, Drozdovo, and Martisova.

CP – the woods northeast of Kozhukhova.

5. 179th RD, filled out by 676th March Battalion, will firmly defend the sector from the (incl.) main railroad, (incl.) to Verkhniaia Ol'khovka, and Fomino [10 kilometers west-southwest to 10 kilometers south-southwest of Andreapol'] and prevent an enemy penetration toward the northeast. Relieve 48th TD's units on the night of 1-2 September.

The boundary on the left: Shcherkovishche, (incl.) Verkh. Ol'khovka, and Chernyshevo.

CP – Hill 236.8.

6. 186th RD will firmly defend the sector from Verkh. Ol'khovka to (incl.) Selino and Alekseevo [10 kilometers south-southwest to 15 kilometers south of Andreapol'] and prevent an enemy penetration toward the east.

The boundary on the left: Vel'e, (incl.) Selino, and Ivakhnovo.

CP – Suvorovo.

7. 126th RD will firmly defend the sector from Selino to Iamishche [15-27 kilometers south of Andreapol'] and prevent an enemy penetration toward the east and northeast.

The boundary line on the left: the army's left boundary.

CP – Karpovo.

8. 174th RD will concentrate in the Rozhenko and Korabanovo region, fill out the division with personnel, restore order, and prepare the Andreapol', Koshelevka, and Obrub defensive sector, with the mission, by a stubborn defense, to prevent an enemy penetration toward the east.

Prepare a bridgehead in the Andreapol' and Mishnevo [7 kilometers south of Andreapol'] region.

The Army's reserve – 675th March Battalion will concentrate in the Vasil'evo, Hill 238.5, and Terenino region and prepare a defensive region along the Milavino, Luben'kino, and Terenino front [10-15 kilometers south-southeast of Andreapol'].

9. Artillery – 509th ATR and 56th CAR.

a) Prevent a penetration by enemy tanks toward the Martisovo and Andreapol' railroad, along the Toropets and Andreapol' highway, and at the junction with 29th Army.

b) Destroy enemy motor-mechanized units on the march and prevent them from approaching the forward edge.

c) Destroy enemy artillery and mortar batteries.

d) Support 186th, 214th, and 179th RDs with one ATR each.

10. In accordance with an order of the Western Front's commander-in-chief, withdraw 48th TD, consisting of the division's headquarters, the tank regiments, the motorized rifle battalion, the antiaircraft battalion, reconnaissance and communications – into reserve and send it to the Alabino region (in the MMD [Moscow Military District]).

Transfer [48th TD's] artillery and motorized units to fill out 214th RD.

11. I am entrusting the organizational formation and filling out of 126th and 186th RDs to Major General Samokhin, which, after being reformed, will be placed at the disposal of the army's Military Council. Colonel Kuznetsov will do analogous work with 214th and 179th RDs. Complete the on re-formation work by the morning of 2 September 1941.

12. Division commanders will organize defensive sectors by creating strong battalion and company defensive AT regions echeloned in depth, with orderly systems of fire and necessary AT and anti-infantry barriers and obstacles, chiefly straddling roads and road junctions, between them.

Combat security will be along the Hill 274.2, Shelai-Lokhny, Hill 285.8, Marker 252.8, Minino, Seroe, Gladkii Log, Aristovo, Zakharino, Durakovo, Veselukha, Lopotovo, Mishkovo, Andronovo, and Pavlovo line.

214th, 186th, and 126th RDs will dispatch forward detachments [FDs] in up to company strength and with sappers forward, with the mission to make contact with forward enemy units, organize extensive obstacle systems, and prevent the enemy from advancing to the combat security line. Send the FD's to the Lake Lobno, Prudishninki, Zagory, Kostiukhovo, and Lake Glubovkoe line.

13. Disband the corps headquarters of 29th, 62nd, and 51st RCs, employing their personnel to fill out formation and unit headquarters. I am entrusting the disbanding of 29th RC to Major General Samokhin, and the personnel of 29th RC's headquarters will be used to fill out 126th and 186th RDs' headquarters. Submit a list of the command cadre assigned to the divisions to the army's Military Council for approval by 0800 hours on 2 September 1941. The chief of the Cadres Department will present me with a proposal for using the command cadre of 62nd and 51st RC by 0800 on 2 September 1941. Send 51st and 62nd RCs' enlisted personnel to units designated by the army's headquarters.

14. Send reports: 1st – upon the sending out of the forward detachments and 2nd – upon completing the filling out and full readiness of the defensive sectors.

The Commander of 22nd Army, Major General Iushkevich
The Member of the Military Council, Brigade Commissar Shevchenko
The Chief of Staff of 22nd Army, Colonel Shalin

Source: "Boevoi prikaz komanduiushchego voiskami 22-i Armii No. 25 ot 1 sentiabria 1941 g. na oboronu rubezha Mitrosheno, Likhusha, Selino, Iamishche" [Combat order no. 25 of the commander of the forces of 22nd Army of 1 September 1941 on defense of the Mitrosheno, Likhusha, Selino, and Iamishche line], *SBDVOV*, issue 41, 253-254.

10. Combat Order No. 15 of the Commander of the Forces of 29th Army of 1 September 1941 about the Transition of the Army's Forces to a Firm Defense

Combat Order No. 15, Headquarters, 29th Army,
Dran'kovo,
1530 hours on 1 September 1941
1:100,000 scale map

1. The enemy is conducting an offensive against 22nd Army with large forces and tanks and artillery. Units of up to one ID and one PzD are attacking against 29th Army's front, while displaying some activity in the sector from Iamishche to Zhelezovo. Significant enemy reserves with tanks and artillery have been detected advancing in the general direction of Lake Griadetskoe and Lake Moshno.

2. 29th Army, having completed its regrouping, is going over to a firm defense in the Iamishche, Kotino, Zapadnaia Dvina, and Barlovo sector along the Western Dvina line, while organizing a bridgehead along the Lake Derboesh, Lake Pesno, Lake Ulin, and Lake Rakomle line.

3. On the right, 22nd Army is defending positions at Iamishche and further north along the Western Dvina River.

The boundary with it: Povadino, Iamishche, and Lake Kodosno.

On the left, 30th Army is continuing an offensive in the general direction of Shelepy and Zarech'e.

The boundary with it is as before.

4. The Separate Motorized Brigade (the former Composite Division): will concentrate in the Biberevo and Sheverdino region, prepare defensive positions on Hill 257, with their front toward the north, and on Hill 215.2 – with their front toward the west, and prepare counterstrokes along the [following] axes: Danilovo, Ovinishche, and Koshkino; and Ostrozhko, Shibarevo, and Zapadnaia Dvina.

Protect the junction between 22nd and 29th Armies in the Selino and (incl.) Iamishche sector with one RBn and one btry, and 29th CR will fulfill its previous mission.

The boundary on the left: for the right flank battalion (incl.) Mukhino, (incl.) Iamishche, and (incl.) Pavlovo.

CP – Sheverdino.

5. 243rd RD, with 1st Btry, 309th ATBn, and 5th Btry, 644th CAR, will firmly defend positions in the Iamishche, Kotino, Hill 235.4, and Shemetova sector along the Western Dvina River, with the missions to prevent an enemy penetration toward the east and create an AT region in the Iamishche and Zhelezovo sector.

The boundary on the left: Shemetovo, Khotino, and Abrazkovo.

CP – Borok.

6. 246th RD, with 309th ATBn (without 1st Btry), and 4th and 6th Btrys, 644th CAR, will firmly defend the (incl.) Khotino, Barlovo, Marker 193.3 sector along the Western Dvina River, and the line of the Velesa River. Create a bridgehead on the land between the lakes [as follows]: from the bend in the Western Dvina River (4044) to Lake Derboesh, with its front toward the north; from Lake Derboesh to Lakes Pesno and Ulin – with its front toward the west; from Lake Ulin to Lake Glubokoe, with its front toward the southwest; from Lake Glubokoe to Lake Rakomle, with its front toward the southwest; and from Lake Rakomle to the Western Dvina River.

The boundary on the left: Hill 193.3, Ekhlovo, Shestakovo, and Abakonovo.

CP – forward – Propletkino, and main – Abakonovo.

Group DD-246 [long-range artillery of 246th RD – 1st Bn, 644th CAR.

7. 252nd RD, concentrated in the Mukhino, Spiridovo, Lopatino, and Staroe and Novoe Polutino region in army reserve, will prepare defensive positions in the vicinity of Hill 210.1, with their front toward the north, and Hill 207.3, with their front toward the west, with the mission of protecting the junction between 22nd and 29th Armies in the general direction of Selino. Prepare counterstrokes along the [following] axes: 1) Mukhino and Selino, 2) Spiridovo and Iamishche, and 3) Lopatino and Khotino.

CP – Lopatino.

8. Artillery. Readiness – 2300 hours on 1 September 1941.

Missions:

1) Prevent the enemy from approaching along the [following] axes: Andronovo, Moshnitsa, Griadtsy, Semichino, Staraia Toropa, inflict a defeat with long-range fires during his approach to the forward edge, prevent the enemy from crossing [the river] at Arkhangela, Iamishche, Zhelezovo, Klin, Koshkino, Zapadnaia Dvina Station, and Barlovo, and protect the crossings at Zhelezovo and Klin especially firmly.

2) Organize antitank defenses in the positions you occupy and protect the [following] axes especially firmly: Iamishche, Zhelezovo, Klin, and Koshkino.

3) Suppress enemy artillery, while damaging batteries opposite the defenses' front the most.

4) Protect 252nd RD's counterstrokes toward: Mukhino and Selino; Spiridovo and Iamishche; and Lopatino and Khotino.

9. The army's Chief of Engineer Forces will support the work fortifying the Western Dvina River in an antitank and anti-infantry respect, while constructing strong obstacles in front of the forward edge of the Western Dvina River line and the bridgehead sector.

10. Readiness of the defense – 2300 hours on 1 September 1941. Readiness of work in the 3rd stage – by day's end on 2 September 1941. Readiness of the obstacle – 1200 hours on 3 September 1941.

13. First echelon of the army's headquarters – Dran'kovo.

14. Present reports: 1) for 252nd RD and separate motorized brigade – upon completion of the concentration in designated regions; 2) about the readiness of the

defenses; 3) about the readiness of work to strengthen obstacle line and the completion of work emplacing obstacles in the bridgehead region.

> The Commander of 29th Army, Lieutenant General Maslennikov
> The Member of the Military Council of 29th Army,
>   Divisional Commissar Gurov
> The Chief of Staff of 29th Army, Major General Sharapov

Source: "Boevoi prikaz komanduiushchego voiskami 29-i Armii No. 15 ot 1 sentiabria 1941 g. o perekhode voisk armii k upornoi oborone" [Combat order no. 15 of the commander of the forces of 29th Army of 1 September 1941 about the transition of the army's forces to a firm defense], *SBDVOV*, issue 41, 276-277.

11. Combat Order of the Commander of the Forces of the Western Front of 2 September 1941 to the Commanders of the Forces of 22nd and 29th Armies about Strengthening Defenses along the Andreapol' and Western Dvina Axes

To the Commanders of 22nd and 29th Armies
Copy: To the Chief of the General Staff

I order you to prevent an advance by the enemy east of the Lake Vyt'bino, Lake Otolovo, Mitroshino, Bezdetka River, and Western Dvina River line.

1. 22nd Army, with 133rd RD, which is arriving in the army, will occupy and firmly defend the Lake Vyt'bino, Lake Otolovo, Bazhenovo, Mitroshino, Bezdetka River, and Western Dvina River line to Chizhevo.

Concentrate the defense's main effort in the Bazhenovo, Mitroshino and Gusarovo and Plotomoi sectors.

Maintain contact with 27th Army with strong reconnaissance units.

Destroy enemy reconnaissance units penetrating into the Novaia, Dubino, and Roman'e regions.

Prepare the army's rear line along the Western Dvina River. Have strong army reserves in the Andreapol' region. Accelerate bringing the army to full combat readiness.

2. 29th Army will occupy and firmly defend the line of the Western Dvina River and, further, along the Velesa River.

Pay special attention to defense of the Chizhevo-Selino and Iamishche-Novaia Derevnia sectors and the vicinity of the town of Zapadnaia Dvina. Employ the newly-arrived 178th RD in first echelon along the main axis on the army's right flank.

Have one RD and a motorized brigade in army reserve in the Sopot', Kurovo, Kholm, Zagvozd'e, and Kol'kino region. Subordinate 134th RD, which is situated in the region it occupies, to the army and employ from this region only with my approval.

3. The boundary line between 22nd and 29th Army – Povadino, Vysokoe, Chizhevo, and Toropets, all for 29th Army.

4. Construct the defense with centers of resistance, echeloned, with extensive use of the obstacle services, and with strong forward detachments positioned well forward.

5. Report orders received and defense plans for approval by 2400 hours on 2 September.

Timoshenko, Sokolovsky

Source: "Boevoe rasporiazhenie komanduiushchego voiskami Zapadnogo fronta ot 2 sentiabria 1941 g. komanduiushchim voiskami 22-i i 29-i Armii o usilenii oborony na Andreapol'skom i Zapadnodvinskom napravleniakh" [Combat order of the commander of the forces of the Western Front of 2 September 1941 to the commanders of the forces of 22nd and 29th Armies about strengthening defenses along the Andreapol' and Western Dvina axes], *SBDVOV*, issue 41, 109-110.

12. Individual Combat Order No. 31 of the Commander of the Forces of 22nd Army of 6 September 1941 to the Commander of 133rd Rifle Division on Protection of the Army's Right Flank

Individual Combat Order No. 31, Headquarters, 22nd Army,
Pestovo
1300 hours on 6 September 1941
1:100,000 scale map

1. On 5 September 1941, the movement of an enemy motorized column was discovered at 1630 hours, with its head at Snegiri and its rear at Lake Gorodno. According to reconnaissance information, a small column and group of tanks were observed north of the army's right flank.

2. **22nd Army** will continue to defend the Vit'bino, Lake Okhvat, and Andreapol' line and the line of the Western Dvina River and prevent an enemy advance toward the east.

3. For firm protection of the army's right flank, the commander of 133rd RD will quickly send one rifle battalion from 681st RR, reinforced by a battery, to the Gogol' and Kniazh'evo region, with the mission to defend the indicated sector with separate company defensive regions, cut off all of the road junctions, and prevent the enemy from infiltrating toward the southeast and east. Consider Gogol' to be the main axis. The march-route the battalion should follow – Soblago, Orekhovnia, Bervenets, and Kniazh'evo.

133rd RD's commander will pay special attention to reinforced reconnaissance along every axis – the roads leading to the army's flank and rear and prevent an enemy penetration at all cost, while forcing the fortification of all defensive sectors in the region in readiness for the division's forces to inflict a decisive defeat on the enemy.

The Commander of 22nd Army, Major General Iushkevich
The Member of the Military Council, Brigade Commissar Shevchenko
The Chief of Staff of 22nd Army, Colonel Shalin

Source: "Chastnyi boevoi prikaz komanduiushchego voiskami 22-i Armii No. 31 ot 6 sentiabria 1941 g. komandiru 133-i Strelkovoi Divizii na obespechenie pravogo flange armii" [Individual combat order no. 31 of the commander of the forces of 22nd Army of 6 September 1941 to the commander of 133rd Rifle Division on protection of the right flank of the army], *SBDVOV*, issue 41, 255.

13. Individual Combat Order No. 32 of the Commander of the Forces of 22nd Army of 6 September 1941 to the Commander of 521st Rifle Regiment on the Destruction of the Enemy in the Ramen'e and Korabanovo Region

Individual Combat Order No. 32, Headquarters, 22nd Army,
Pestovo
1300 hours on 6 September 1941
1:100,000 scale map

1. Separate enemy machine-gun groups and groups with automatic weapons are occupying jumping-off positions in the Ramen'e and Karabanovo, Borok, and Dudino region on the approaches to Andreapol', while trying to hold onto a bridgehead and preparing for an attack toward Andreapol' and to the north.

2. 22nd Army's units are continuing to fulfill their previous missions.

3. The army's reserve – 521st RR – will immediately leave its concentration region at Chechetovo and Aleksino by the Aleksino, Kremena, and Chernevo march-route, leave one battalion in the Hill 222.8, Troskino, and Chernevo region as an army reserve, and, having occupied jumping-off positions for an attack in the Mishutino, Kostiushino (northern), and Zagoz'e region with two battalions by 0200 hours on 7 September 1941, will attack toward Mishutino and Ramen'e at first light on 7 September, seize Ramen'e and Korabanovo with a decisive blow toward Ramen'e from the north, while penetrating along the Gorodnia stream, and, having destroyed the enemy's units there, hold on to that line in readiness for an advance westward toward Mitrosheno.

4. A rifle battalion of 174th RD, which is operating on the left from Andreapol', will attack toward Borok, Kliukunovo, Hill 233.1, and Korabanovo at first light on 7 September and assist 521st RR's battalion in destroying the enemy in the Korabanovo and Ramen'e region by an attack from the south.

5. For protection of the surprise attack from Milutino toward Ramen'e, 521st RR's commander will send out reinforced reconnaissance (a reinforced rifle company) from the two battalions which are operating along this axis from jumping-off positions (Troskino), while protecting itself upon reaching Zagoz'e with covering forces from the reconnaissance [company] along the road from Hill 232.0 to ward Dudino.

6. The battalion remaining in army reserve in the Troskino region, will conduct reconnaissance (a rifle company with two machine-guns and one antitank gun) toward Chernevo, Zhabero, and Verkhov'e at first light on 7 September, and, simultaneously, the battalion will prepare defenses in the region indicated.

7. The two battalions of 521st RR operating toward Ramen'e from the north, upon concentrating in the Troskino and Chernevo region, will become operationally subordinate to the commander of 174th RD, who will direct the operation for the seizure of Ramen'e and Korabanovo.

8. The army's Chief of Artillery will provide no fewer than three battalions of artillery for support of the battalions operating toward Ramen'e, the chief of artillery will coordinate signals for cooperation with the commanders of 174th RD and 521st RR, communications with the battalions of 521st RR will be through the commander of 174th RD; and the army's Chief of Communications will provide

regular radio communications, having determined radio call signs and appropriate enciphering of conversations.

9. Send reports: 1st – upon leaving the concentration region; 2nd – upon arrival in the Troskino region; 3rd – after sending out reconnaissance; 4th – upon reaching the Mishutino region; and 5th – upon fulfillment of the missions.

The Commander of 22nd Army, Major General Iushkevich
The Member of the Military Council, Brigade Commissar Shevchenko
The Chief of Staff of 22nd Army, Colonel Shalin

Source: "Chastnyi boevoi prikaz komanduiushchego voiskami 22-i Armii No. 32 ot 6 sentiabria 1941 g. komandiru 521-i Strelkovogo Polka na unichtozhenie protivnika v raione Ramen'e, Korabanovo" [Individual combat order of the commander of the forces of 22nd Army no. 32 of 6 September 1941 to the commander of 521st Rifle Regiment on the destruction of the enemy in the Ramen'e and Korabanovo region], *SBDVOV*, issue 41, 255-256.

14. Report Notes of the Military Council of 22nd Army to the Military Council of the Western Front about the Army's Combat Operations along the Velikie Luki and Toropets Axes from 21 through 25 August 1941

To the Military Council of the Western Front
Report about 22nd Army's Operations from
21 through 25 August 1941
About 7 September 1941

While fulfilling Order No. 17 of the Western Front command, 22nd Army went over to the offensive at 1300 hours on 21 August 1941. The offensive developed normally in the sectors of 126th, 179th, 174th, and 186th RDs. The units advanced 3-5 kilometers by the end of the day. The slowest advance tempo was on 214th RD's left wing and in 170th RD's sector, where the latter encountered strong enemy fortified positions and could not advance.

48th TD had not even one serviceable tank and fought as an infantry division, conducting active reconnaissance in its sector.

98th RD, which had just been reestablished, had no artillery and had up to 50 heavy machine guns. On 19-20 August, it received around 5,000 replacements, which arrived from the Volga Military District, two of its regiments were located in 29th RC's reserve, behind 179th RD, with the mission to develop its success, and the third regiment was located on trucks in the army's reserve in the vicinity of Ushitsy State Farm.

According to intelligence information, 251st, 253rd, 206th and 110th IDs and Detachment Brunning were identified opposite the army's front.

The army's forces continued the offensive on the morning of 22 August 1941.

At 1000 hours an enemy force of up to an infantry regiment with tanks penetrated the front in 186th RD's sector in the direction of Dreki and began a swift advance northward toward Annino [32 kilometers southeast of Velikie Luki]. The army's reserve regiment from 98th RD was sent to support 186th RD's units and entered combat at 1400 hours. Five AT guns were sent to the Abliapushi region

[28 kilometers east-southeast of Velikie Luki] for reinforcing antitank defenses in the Kun'ia region [26 kilometers east of Velikie Luki]. Two battalions of the newly-formed regiment of 112th RD were sent, one to the Vtorinovo region for defense of the approaches to Kun'ia, and the other – to the Vishenka region for protecting the northeastern axis.

By 1400 hours it was apparent that the enemy was attacking with large forces of infantry and tanks. Another two regiments of 98th RD were moved into the Kamenka and Miasovo region for a combined attack with 62nd Rifle Corps' units toward the southeast to liquidate the penetration. The regiments concentrated by the end of the day.

By 2000 hours the enemy captured Ushitsa State Farm, Zhigalovo State Farm, and Velikopol'e Station [16 kilometers east to 18 kilometers east-southeast of Velikie Luki] with forward units and moved their forces into these regions during the night.

On 23 August the situation in 48th TD's and 214th RD's sectors was unchanged, and, in accordance with an order from the army commander, 126th and 179th RDs withdrew to positions they had previously occupied.

On the night of 23-24 August, 179th RD was withdrawn from the front and, without one regiment, received the mission, together with 126th RD, to destroy the enemy grouping in the vicinity of Ushitsy State Farm [18 kilometers east-southeast of Velikie Luki]. 62nd RC's counterattacks and 179th RD's attack were unsuccessful. The commander of 179th RD, Gvozdev, lost control of his regiments (the division's headquarters was cut off from the regiments by tanks).

Enemy aircraft operated successively and massively against our units' combat formations.

On 24 August 1941, 179th and 126th RDs' units once again began an attack toward Ushitsy State Farm, but, under strong pressure from enemy aircraft, tanks, mortar fire, and infantry, 179th RD withdrew behind the Kun'ia River [12 kilometers east-southeast of Velikie Luki], and 126th RD also had no success. At 1400 hours the enemy exerted strong pressure on 174th RD with tanks, the division suffered heavy losses, and its left wing withdrew to an intermediate line, while 170th RD stubbornly continued to hold on to its positions stubbornly.

At 1600 hours air reconnaissance confirmed a concentration of tanks and artillery in the Ushitsy State Farm, Zhigalovo State Farm, Peski, and Zabolot'e region [15-16 kilometers east-southeast of Velikie Luki]. At 1600 hours, the Zabolot'e group (up to 40 tanks and 2 battalions of motorized infantry) advanced toward Velikie Luki. Throughout the duration of 24 August, enemy fighter and bomber aircraft repeatedly pressured our units. Communications were lost with 186th and 98th RDs.

The measures the army command undertook to liquidate the enemy penetration did not produce the desired results chiefly because a single fist was assembled, and there was no organized control and good communication between the units sent to liquidate the penetration and the formations sending the units that were, supposedly, sufficient to liquidate the penetration.

By 1700 hours it had become clear that we had not succeeded in liquidating the penetration, the army's units were encircled, the supply lines had been cut since 22 August, a quarter of the combat load of shells, in 152mm – from 2 to 7 shells per gun, remained, fuel and food was being at an and, and all of the units' combat formations were exposed to artillery fire.

From an order seized from a dead [German] officer on the night of 23 August, it became clear that the enemy was attacking to the west of Lakes Dvin'e and Zhizhitskoe with two corps: 57th Panzer and 40th Army, with the mission of liquidating the Velikie Luki grouping. While evaluating all of these difficult conditions, the army commander, having changed his initial plan for withdrawing toward the northeast, decided to organize a withdrawal from the encirclement to the north, in the direction Bol'shie and Malye Usviaty [30 kilometers northeast of Velikie Luki].

The combat formation during the penetration was organized as follows: 126th RD and 48th TD went in the penetration's first echelon and, in the second echelon – the remnants of 179th RD and 214th RD, behind them 62nd RCs' units, and, finally 170th RD, whose mission was to protect the units' withdrawal from the rear, exited.

During the penetration, 126th RD was ordered to leave a covering force at Ushitsy State Farm and blockade Zabolot'e, and 48th TD and 366th RR were to leave a covering force along the Ovechkino and Ivantsevo line [from 7-25 kilometers east-northeast of Velikie Luki].

The units began moving at 2200 hours on 24 August 1941.

By the evening, the enemy moved 19th PzD along the road from Zabolot'e to Velikie Luki regiment by regiment and occupied populated places and the heights between the high road to Ushitsa Sate Farm and the railroad from Velikie Luki to Velikopol'e Station with firing points. The materiel (artillery and auto-transport) of 214th and 126th RDs and the corps' rears was stretched out on the road along 214th RD's main attack axis, and, on the morning of 25 August 1941, it began moving forward behind the penetrating units. The materiel of 48th, 179th, 170th, and 174th [RDs] moved directly behind their own units.

During the movement, the artillery and auto-transport were subjected to strong pressure from enemy aircraft, artillery, mortar fire, and tanks. As a result, a large quantity of artillery and auto-transport was destroyed on the approach to the penetration, and the units themselves were partially destroyed. The infantry, which penetrated forward, did not take effective measures to support the full evacuation of their materiel.

Questions of Control

From the beginning of 22nd Army's offensive on 21 August, the operational group of the army's headquarters and the Military Council left for a new CP (the woods west of Romanovo [7 kilometers west-northwest of Kun'ia]), having in mind drawing near to the units commanders but by day's end on 22 August, the CP was twice fired upon by enemy aircraft and approaching tanks, and, as a result, the question arose about moving the CP. The Military Council decided to transfer it to 29th RC's CP, from which it could control the combat of the majority of the divisions more successfully.

Upon our arrival at 29th RC on the night of 23 August, its command post was also under attack and, once again, we had to relocate to the next CP in the Mikhal'ki region [11 kilometers east-southeast of Velikie Luki]. In Mikhal'ki we used 29th RC's communications equipment (wire and radio). The army's radios did not reach the new CP and, apparently, perishing en route. On 22, 23, and 24 August, communications relied on telephone, radio, and liaison officers from 61st, 51st, and 29th RCs. On 23 August we lost communications with 98th and 186th RDs.

Before the beginning of the movement into the penetration, the staff commanders of the army's headquarters were distributed among the forces for communications purposes and to check on the fulfillment of orders about the preparations for the penetration. The corps commanders and the commanders of 126th and 214th RDs were summoned to the Military Council, where, in addition to the orders, they personally received instructions regarding the order of organizing and conducting the penetration operation.

When the units' movement into the penetration began, the Military Council, the available part of the army's headquarters, and 29th RC's headquarters moved on foot behind 214th RD's RRs. On the night of 25 August, while crossing a river in the region east of Novosel'e, the army and corps' headquarters group, with accompanying Red Army soldiers, lost touch with the regiment that was moving forward and, as a result, could not overtake either this or any other regiment, and, having fallen under, first, artillery and, then, machine gun fire, slowed their movement and were not able to find the regiments until first light.

The infantry units turned out to be far ahead, and the passage was closed once again by the enemy in the morning. As a result, the Military Council, the Chief of Staff, the Group of headquarters commanders, and up to 100 Red Army soldiers were forced to pass through independently, while sticking to the main axis of movement of the withdrawing forces. As a result, all command and control of the forces was lost after 0200 hours on 25 August.

The Military Council, with a detachment of 546 men, exited from encirclement on 5 September in 133rd RD's sector in the Poliany region.

Personnel Losses

Up to the beginning of the battle – on 20 August, there were 71,613 men in units located at the front, and, according to incomplete data, 20,025 men escaped from the encirclement by 7 September. Deducting the 7,271 men who were wounded from 21 through 27 August, 44,317 [men] did not escape, with those killed also included in this figure.

The withdrawal from the encirclement is continuing up to this time, and many groups and individuals, who fought their way to their units, still remain in the enemy's rear.

Material Losses

According to the state of things on 1 September, 18,091 rifles have been carried out [evacuated], and 42,226 have been lost. The arrival of soldiers with weapons has continued since 1 September; machine pistols carried out – 125 and not carried out – 367; light machine guns carried out – 39 and not carried out – 486; heavy machine guns carried out – 25 and not carried out – 354; mortars of all caliber carried out – 30 and not carried out – 261; and artillery of all calibers evacuated – 39 and not carried out – 264.

Automobiles: there were 1,273 in the forces on 20 August, and 370 came out by 3 September.

Among the quantities of lost weapons are included weapons lost in the fighting during the offensive on 21-22 August.

Conclusions:

1. 22nd Army's command, in the person of the commander, Comrade Ershakov, and the Member of the Military Council, Comrade Leonov, underestimated the danger on the left wing. The measures undertaken after receipt of the order from the Western Front's commander, Marshal of the Soviet Union Timoshenko, turned out to be inadequate (one RR and a destroyer detachment of 250 men were allocated to the left wing's reserve). They did not succeed in detecting the tank group opposite their left wing in timely fashion; as a result, additional measures were not taken to strengthen antitank defenses.

2. At the beginning of the enemy offensive, the grouping of enemy forces which penetrated behind the front lines was not completely clear to army command, and 98th RD, which was assigned to liquidate the penetration, turned out to be inadequate to liquidate the enemy. It would have been more expedient if we had had 98th Division occupy jumping-off positions along the Kun'ia River and the heights to the east of Ushitsy State Farm and brought 179th RD forward to that line by 1200 hours on 23 August and then began to liquidate the penetration with the combined forces.

3. The column with the equipment was organized incorrectly – the mass was concentrated chiefly along one road behind 214th RD. In addition, the infantry, which was penetrating forward, apparently, forgot about their equipment.

4. Command and control was disorganized during the period of the penetration, and the estimate [of the situation] by individual leaders and delegates turned out to be unsuited to the existing situation.

5. The army's most serious mistake was the interval between the army command and the units, which led to the loss of command and control during the most critical period of fighting.

6. The forces have [received] poor training in combat with tanks, and "fear of tanks" among the personnel of many units has not been eliminated, which is one of the main reasons for 186th RD's disorderly withdrawal.

The Commander of 22nd Army, Lieutenant General Ershakov
The Member of the Military Council of 22nd Army,
Corps Commissar Leonov

Source: "Dokladnaia zapiska Voennogo Soveta 22-i Armii Voennomu Sovetu Zapadnaia fronta o boevykh deistviiakh armii na Velikolukskom i Toropetskom napravleniakh s 21 po 25 avgusta 1941 g." [Report notes of the Military Council of 22nd Army to the Military Council of the Western Front about the army's combat operations along the Velikie Luki and Toropets axes from 21 through 25 August 1941], *SBDVOV*, issue 41, 241-244.

15. Report by the Commander of the Forces of the Western Front of 8 September 1941 to the Chief of the General Staff about the Situation in 22nd Army's Forces and the Necessity of Reinforcing it with Two Divisions

General Staff

To the Chief of the General Staff, Marshal Comrade Shaposhnikov

According to reports by 22nd Army's commander and my assistant, Lieutenant General Comrade Boldin, the situation on 22nd Army's front is extremely unstable.

27th Army's left-flank 256th RD is withdrawing toward the east and northeast in separate groups. Its headquarters, having lost command and control of its units, withdrew to the Lake Ershovo region on 8 September. To protect its flank with 22nd Army, I ordered 22nd Army's commander, until further notice, to subordinate 256th RD's withdrawing groups to himself and, together with 133rd RD's units, to protect the southeastern axis toward Penno by occupying the Bitukha, Otonets, and Novoselok line and, simultaneously, to prepare a main defensive line along the Kud' River.

Considering 256th RD's condition and the enemy grouping at the boundary with 27th Army, which numbers up to three divisions, I consider the freeing up of 22nd Army's forces to protect the boundary to be inadequate to secure the Penno region reliably. In addition, I request you send 22nd Army one RD for a firm defense of the Kud' River line and one CD for operations against the rear area of the enemy's Novgorod axis.

The Commander of the Forces of the Western Front,
Marshal of the Soviet Union Timoshenko
The Member of the Military Council of the Western Front (signed)

Source: "Doklad komanduiushchego voiskami Zapadnogo fronta ot 8 sentiabria 1941 g. nachal'niku General'nogo Shtaba o polozhenii voisk 22-i Armii i neobkhodimosti usileniia ee dvumia diviziiami" [Report of the commander of the forces of the Western Front of 8 September 1941 to the chief of the General Staff about the situation in 22nd Army's forces and the necessity of reinforcing it with two divisions], *SBDVOV*, issue 41, 126.

Appendix S

The Third Soviet Counteroffensive: The Western Front's Dukhovshchina Offensive, 25 August-10 September 1941

1. Combat Order No. 045 of the Commander of the Forces of 30th Army of 25 August 1941 on a Continuation of the Offensive

Combat Order No. 045, Headquarters, 30th Army,
the woods 2 kilometers northeast of Podzaitsevo,
0145 hours on 25 August 1941
1:50,000 scale map

1. The enemy is continuing to offer stubborn resistance, while introducing his last reserves into action and trying to hold onto the positions he occupies.

2. Information about the neighbors and the boundaries with them are as before.

3. 30th Army will continue to fulfill the missions assigned by Order No. 044 on 25 August 1941 by delivering its main attack with 162nd RD, reinforced by a rifle regiment and one MRR, toward Shelepy and Hill 230.3. The beginning of the offensive will be at 1400 hours.

4. 242nd RD, while holding firmly to the Staraia Morokhovo and Novoe Morokhovo sector, will support the army's shock group from the right by attacking in the general direction of Churkino and Kostino with its left wing..

5. 250th RD, without 922nd RR, will capture Hill 215.2 and subsequently attack toward Hill 229.6.

6. 162nd RD, with 922nd RR from 250th RD and 237th MRR, will attack in the general direction of Ivkino and Zarech'e, with the immediate mission to capture Malyi Fomenki and Ivkino, while exploiting subsequent success toward Zarech'e, and prevent an enemy withdrawal toward the southwest.

7. 251st RD will relieve 107th TD's 120th MRR with one regiment at 0600 hours on 25 August 1941, with the mission to protect the army shock group's left flank. Be prepared to exploit 162nd RD's success with your right wing in the general direction of Sechenki, Krechets, and Boris'kova.

8. 107th TD, after the relief of 120th MRR and 143rd TR, will concentrate in the woods west of Baranovo, where it will put itself in order and repair and refit its equipment.

9. The boundaries of the divisions are as before.

Artillery. Readiness at 0600 hours

Missions:

351

1) Continue to destroy all identified targets beginning at first light on 25 August 1941.

2) Carry out powerful fire raids from 1350 to 1400 hours against [enemy] firing means [weapons] in the Losinye Iamy, Shelepy, Hill 228.9, the northwestern edge of the woods 1.5 kilometers east of Shelepy, and the northern edge of the woods 300 meters south of Staroe Selo region.

3) Suppress enemy artillery and mortar units in the Kostino, Ivkino, and Shanino Farm region.

11. CP – in their previous places.

The Commander of 30th Army, Lieutenant General Khomenko
The Member of the Military Council of 30th Army,
    Brigade Commissar Abramov
The Chief of Staff of 30th Army, Lieutenant Colonel Vinogradov

Source: "Boevoi prikaz komanduiushchego voiskami 30-i Armii No. 045 ot 25 avgusta 1941 g. na prodolzhenii nastupleniia" [Combat order no. 045 of the commander of the forces of 30th Army of 25 August 1941 on a continuation of the offensive], *SBDVOV*, issue 41, 288-289.

2. Individual Combat Order No. 046 of the Commander of the Forces of 30th Army of 25 August 1941 on a Regrouping of Forces

Individual Combat Order No. 046, Headquarters, 30th Army,
the woods 2 kilometers northeast of Podzaitsevo,
1310 hours on 25 August 1941
1:50,000 scale map

1. Information about the enemy is as before.

2. 134th RD will protect and defend the Ust'e, Sopot', Belyi, Glintsova, Polianova, Liapkino, Khotino, Berezovka, Morozovo, and Moshki line, with the mission to prevent an enemy penetration toward Belyi.

To do so:

a) Relieve 250th RD's 918th RR with one regiment by 0400 hours on 26 August 1941;

b) Concentrate your main forces in the region of prepared positions southwest of Belyi by 0500 hours on 27 August 1941; and

c) Relieve the reconnaissance detachment of 30th Army's headquarters along the Ust'e and Sopot' line by 0600 hours on 28 August.

3. 250th RD's 918th RR, after its relief by 134th RD's units, will concentrate in the Zhidki region by 0500 hours on 27 August in readiness for operations with the division's main forces.

4. The composite reconnaissance detachment of 30th Army's headquarters will be disbanded after its relief by 134th RD, having transferred its personnel and equipment among its establishment [TO&E – *shtat*] units.

Complete the disbanding by 2000 hours on 31 August 1941.

The Commander of 30th Army, Lieutenant General Khomenko

The Member of the Military Council of 30th Army,
    Brigade Commissar Abramov
The Chief of Staff of 30th Army, Lieutenant Colonel Vinogradov

Source: "Chastnyi boevoi prikaz komanduiushchego voiskami 30-i Armii No. 046 ot 25 avgusta 1941 g. na peregruppirovku voisk" [Individual combat order no. 046 of the commander of the forces of 30th Army of 25 August 1941 on a regrouping of forces], *SBDVOV*, issue 41, 289-290.

3. *Stavka* VGK Directive No. 001255 to the Commanders of the Forces of the Briansk and Central Fronts about the Dissolution of the Central Front

0200 hours on 25 August 1941

1. For the purpose of uniting the control of forces operating on the Briansk axis with the forces on the Gomel' axis, disband the Central Front effective at 0000 hours on 26 August 1941, having transferred its forces to the Briansk Front. Effective 0000 hours on 26 August 1941, the Briansk Front will consist of 50th, 3rd, 13th, and 21st Armies.

2. Combine the forces operating along the Gomel' and Mozyr axes, having transferred all 3rd Army's forces to 21st Army.

The commander of Briansk Front will employ 3rd Army's headquarters on the Mglin axis, having transferred to it part of 50th and 13th Armies's divisions at your discretion.

3. Appoint Lieutenant General Efremov, M. G., the commander of the Central Front, as the Briansk Front's deputy commander.

4. Appoint Lieutenant General Kuznetsov, V. I. the commander of 3rd Army, as 21st Army's commander.

Major General Gordov, V. N., the temporary commander of 21st Army, will revert to performing his direct responsibilities as 21st Army's chief of staff.

5. Appoint Major General Kreizer, Ia. G., the commander of 1st MotD, as the 3rd Army's commander.

6. Relieve Major General Golubev, K. D., of his duties as the commander of 13th Army and place him at the disposal of the NKO.

Appoint Major General Gorodniansky, A. M., the commander of 129th [Rifle] Division, as the commander of 13th Army.

7. The commander of the Briansk Front is authorized to use part of the Central Front's command cadre and control elements to fill the Briansk Front's command and control requirements, and the remaining elements will be placed at the disposal of the NKO.

8. Relieve Lieutenant General Sokolov from his duties as the Central Front's chief of staff and place him at the disposal of the High Command.

9. The boundary line between the Briansk and Southwestern Fronts will remain the same as between the Central and Southwestern Fronts.

10. Confirm receipt of this directive and report on its fulfillment.

I. Stalin, B. Shaposhnikov

4. Directive No.001254 of the *Stavka* of the Supreme High Command of 25 August 1941 to the Forces of the Western Front about the Development of an Offensive Operation to Destroy the Enemy's Smolensk Grouping (see Map 9)

0230 hours on 25 August 1941

    1. The enemy, while defending on the Belyi, Viaz'ma, and Spas-Demensk axes, has concentrated his mobile forces against the forces of the Briansk Front, apparently, with the aim to deliver an attack on the Briansk and Zhizdra axis in the near future.

    2. The Western Front's forces will energetically continue the offensive they have begun to destroy the opposing enemy and, in cooperation with forces on the Reserve Front's left wing, reach the Velizh, Demidov, and Smolensk front by 8 September. To that end:

    a) 22nd Army [Ershakov and Iushkevich on 28 August] will liquidate the enemy's mobile units, which have penetrated into the Velikopol'e Station, Nazimovo, Zhizhitsa, and Zamosh'e region and, by exploiting aircraft and tanks and an active and firm defense of the Nasva Station, Velikie Luki, and Lake Velinskoe line to achieve that end, will protect the *front's* attacking forces from the north and from the direction of Opochka. With the advance by 29th and 30th Armies to the Velizh and Demidov front, the army's left wing will advance to the Lake Usmynskoe line.

    b) 29th Army [Maslennikov], while developing the offensive it has begun, will conduct its main attack toward Velizh.

    c) 30th Army [Khomenko] will assist 19th Army's offensive toward Dukhovshchina and further toward Smolensk by an offensive toward Tiukhovitsy, Eliseevichi, and Kholm.

    d) 19th Army [Konev] will develop an offensive with the immediate mission to capture Dukhovshchina and, subsequently, capture the Smolensk region by a blow toward the southwest and without attacking Smolensk frontally.

    e) 16th Army [Rokossovsky] will facilitate 19th and 20th Armies' destruction of the enemy's Smolensk-Iartsevo grouping by a blow toward Kardymov Station and Smolensk.

    f) 20th Army [Lukin] will destroy the enemy's Smolensk grouping, together with 19th and 16th Armies, by an initial blow in the general direction of Klokovo Station and Riabtsevo Station and, thereafter, toward the northwest.

    3. On the right – the Northwestern Front has the mission of halting the enemy on the Lovat' River by an active defense.

    The boundary with it – Likhoslavl', Lake Seliger, and Nasva Station line, all points inclusive for the Western Front.

    On the left – the Reserve Front will launch an offensive on the morning of 30 August, liquidate the enemy's El'nia grouping, and attack with the forces of 24th Army toward Pochinok and with 43rd Army toward Roslavl', with the missions to defeat the enemy, capture these points and reach the Dolgie, Nivy, Khislavichi, and

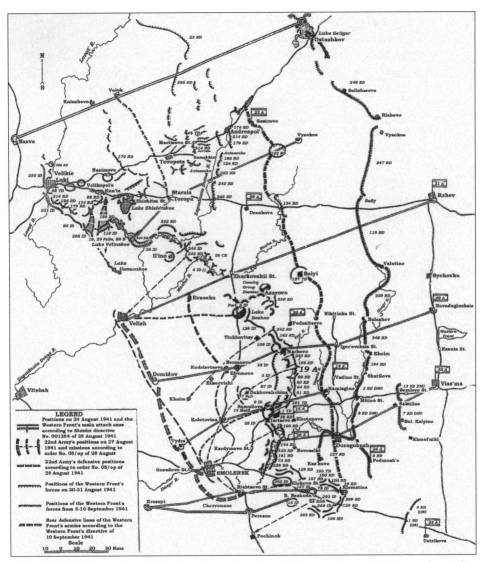

Map 9: The Western Front's Combat Operations from 24 August through 10 September 1941

Petrovichi front by 8 September 1941, and continue to develop a defensive belt along the Ostashkov, Selizharovo, Olenino, Dnepr River (west of Viaz'ma), Spas-Demensk, and Kirov line with its main forces.

The boundary with it – Bol'shaia Nezhoda, Peresna Station, and Krasnyi line, all points inclusive for the Western Front.

4. During the course of the entire operation, eliminate any sort of surprises for the forces by well-organized and systematic intelligence collection at all command levels. Pay special attention to continuous and skillful reconnaissance along open flanks.

5. It is obligatory to fortify all lines and points seized from the enemy, while demanding that your forces immediately erect defensive works.

6. The operations of infantry, artillery, aviation, and tanks must be well coordinated and studied in advance by command cadre. Tank and infantry operations must be anticipated and accompanied by aviation support.

7. Prepare the operation in the utmost secrecy, abstain from telephone conversations and transmissions, and assign missions verbally in person to the responsible party.

8. Confirm receipt.

>   The Supreme High Commander, I. Stalin
>   The Chief of the General Staff, B. Shaposhnikov

Source: "Direktiva Stavki Verkhovnogo Glavnokomandovaniia voiskam Zapadnogo fronta No. 001254 ot 25 avgusta 1941 g. o razvitii nastupatel'noi operatsii s tsel'iu razgroma Smolenskoi gruppirovki protivnika" [Directive No.001254 of the *Stavka* of the Supreme High Command of 25 August 1941 to the forces of the Western Front about the development of an offensive operation to destroy the enemy's Smolensk grouping], *SBDVOV*, issue 41, 7-8.

5. Directive No.001253 of the *Stavka* of the Supreme High Command to the Commander of the Forces of the Reserve Front about Preparation for an Operation to Destroy the Enemy's El'nia Grouping

0235 hours on 25 August 1941

1. The enemy, while defending on the Belyi, Viaz'ma, and Spas-Demensk axes, has concentrated his mobile forces against the forces of the Briansk Front, apparently with the aim to deliver an attack on the Briansk and Zhizdra axis in the near future.

2. The Reserve Front's forces, while continuing to fortify a defensive belt along the Ostashkov, Selizharovo, Olenino, Dnepr River (west of Viaz'ma), Spas-Demensk, and Kirov line with its main forces [31st, 49th, 32nd, and 33rd Armies], will go over to an offensive on 30 August with its left-wing 24th and 43rd Armies, with the missions to finish off the enemy's El'nia grouping, capture El'nia, and, by subsequently attacking toward Pochinok and Roslavl', reach the Dolgie Nivy, Khislavichi, and Petrovichi front by 8 September. To that end:

>   a) 24th Army [Rakutin], consisting of eight RDs, one TD, and one MD – will destroy the enemy's El'nia grouping by concentric attacks and will reach the Bol'shaia Nezhoda Station, Petrovo, and Stroina front by 1 September, and,

subsequently, while developing the offensive, attack toward Pochinok and, having captured the latter, reach the Dolgie Nivy and Khislavichi front by 8 September;

b) 43rd Army [Seleznev], having left 222nd and 53rd RDs on the defensive front they occupy and the army's main forces in defense of positions at Spas-Demensk and Kirov, will go over the an offensive in the general direction of Roslavl' on 30 August with two rifle and two tank divisions and, having captured Roslavl', will reach the (incl.) Khislavichi and (incl.) Petrovichi front by 8 September;

c) 31st [Dolmatov], 49th [Zakharkin], 32nd [Fediuninsky], and 33rd [Onuprienko] Armies, while remaining in place, will continue work to develop the defensive sectors they occupy;

d) Retain one RD per army in *front* reserve at the expense of the reserves of people's militia divisions in order to strengthen the defenses on the Sukhinichi and Zhizdra axes and to protect the boundary with the Briansk Front in the Kirov and Liudinovo regions, and conduct the regrouping by foot-marches; and

e) Transfer 298th RD to the disposal of the commander of the Briansk Front and move it by rail to the Diat'kovo region by 1 September.

3. On the right – the Western Front is continuing to develop an offensive, with the missions to reach the Velizh, Demidov, and Smolensk front by 8 September. Its left-wing 20th Army has the missions – to defeat the enemy's Smolensk grouping and capture the Smolensk region together with 16th and 19th Armies by an initial attack in the general direction of Klokovo and Riabtsevo Stations and, subsequently, toward the northwest.

The boundary line with the Western Front – Bol'shaia Nezhoda Station, Peresna, and Krasnoe, all points except Krasnoe are inclusive for the Reserve Front.

On the left – the Briansk Front will go over to an offensive on 2 September, with the missions to destroy the enemy's groupings concentrated in the Dubrovka, Pochep, and Surazh regions and, subsequently, reach the Petrovichi, Osmolovichi, Belaia Dubrava, and Guta-Koretskaia front.

The boundary line with the Briansk Front – Mtsensk, Zhizdra, Frolovka, Roslavl', and Mstislavl'; all points except Roslavl' are inclusive for the Reserve Front.

4. During the course of the entire operation, conduct well-organized and systematic reconnaissance at all levels of command to eliminate any sort of surprises for the forces. Pay special attention to continuous and careful reconnaissance along all unprotected flanks.

5. It is obligatory to fortify all positions and points seized from the enemy during the operation while demanding that your forces immediately erect defensive works.

6. Operations by infantry, artillery, aviation, and tanks must be well coordinated as to time and place and effectively worked out in advance by command cadre. You must anticipate and accompany infantry and tank operations with air support.

7. Prepare the operation with the utmost secrecy and abstain from telephone conversations and transmissions. Do not issue general orders for all subordinate formations in the operation. Limit the issuance of orders to each army and, within the armies, issue separate orders verbally to each division

8. Confirm receipt.

I. Stalin, B. Shaposhnikov

Source: "Direktiva Stavki VGK No. 001253 komanduiushchemu voiskami Rezervnogo fronta o podgotovke operatsii po razgromu El'eninskoi gruppirovki protivnika" [Directive No.001253 of the *Stavka* of the Supreme High Command to the commander of the forces of the Reserve Front about preparation for an operation to destroy the enemy's El'nia grouping], in Zolotarev, "*Stavka* 1941," 136-137.

6. A Plan for an Offensive Operation of the Forces of the Western Front of 25 August 1941 for the Destruction of the Enemy's Smolensk Grouping

Plan of Operations, Western Front,
in accordance with *Stavka* Directive No. 001254
1:500,000 scale map
25 August 1941

1. The mission of the *front* is, while continuing the offensive which it has begun, simultaneously inflict defeat on the enemy penetrating 22nd Army's front and, in cooperation with the forces on the Reserve Front's left wing, reach the Velikie Luki, Velizh, Demidov, and Smolensk front by 8 September 1941.

2. On the left, the Reserve Front will go over to the offensive on 30 August and, while liquidating the El'nia grouping of enemy, will develop the attack toward Pochinok.

The boundary with it – Bol'shaia Nezhoda, Peresna Station, and Krasnyi (incl.).

3. Envision fulfillment of the operation in three stages:

1st Stage – Halt the enemy's offensive by inflicting defeat on him with aviation and ground forces on 22nd Army's front, fill out and regroup the forces for a decisive attack against the enemy together with the Reserve Front, with the simultaneous continuation of offensives by 19th, 29th, and 30th Armies.

Duration of this stage – 26-29 August.

2nd Stage – Go over to a general offensive, with the mission to smash the opposing enemy units and fulfill the *front's* immediate mission, that is, to penetrate the enemy's tactical defenses.

Duration of this stage – 30 August-5 September, at an offensive tempo of 3-4 kilometers per day.

3rd Stage – The development of success and the armies' arrival at the lines designated by the Supreme High Command's order.

Duration – 6-8 September, at a tempo of 15 kilometers per day.

4. Grouping and missions of the armies:

1) 22nd Army, will strike the enemy with aviation and forward detachments and advance to the Men'shova, Martinovka. Nazimova Station, Artemovo Platform, and Lake Zhizhitskoe line with forward detachments up to 30 August. The army will put itself in order and prepare for a general offensive, while fortifying the lines indicated.

The army will be reinforced with one CD arriving from the Reserve of the High Command and 107th TD from 30th Army, having reinforced it with tanks and 57th MR transferred from the Toropets and Staraia Toropa region by day's end on 29 August. Reinforce the army with artillery weapons.

Go over to a general offensive on 30 August, while delivering the main attack on the direction of Toropets, Kun'ia, and Velikie Luki. The army is to reach the Lovat' River, Velikie Luki, and Lake Usmanskoe line by day's end on 8 September.

The boundary to the left is up to Lake Velinskoe and further to Lake Usmanskoe.

2) 29th Army, in its present configuration, will continue to fulfill its assigned missions, with the Composite Brigade in the army's reserve. While developing an offensive toward Il'ino and Velizh, the army has the mission to reach the Khlebanikha, Lake Usodishche, and Punishche line by 6 September and the Velizh and Demidov line (incl.) by 8 September.

3) Cavalry Group Dovator will continue its mission of arriving in the rear of the enemy's Dukhovshchina grouping and, subsequently, operating toward Rudnia in the enemy's rear.

4) 30th Army, while protecting the Belyi axis with a force of no fewer than two RRs of 250th RD, will continue the offensive with its remaining forces, without 107th TD and 134th RD, with the mission to capture enemy strong points.

30th Army will go over to a general offensive toward Tiukhovitsy, Eliseevichi, and Kholm on 30 August and, while developing success, reach the Dubrovo, Starina, Zviagino, and Spas-Ugly line by 6 September and the Demidov and Kasplia line by 8 September.

The boundary on the left – as before and, further, to Kasplia.

4) 19th Army, consisting of 244th, 166th, 91st, 89th, 64th, and 50th RDs, 101st MD, and 75th CD, will continue its offensive, with the mission to capture Dukhovshchina no later than 3 September. Subsequently, while developing the attack toward the southwest, capture the Smolensk region and reach the Kasplia and Gnezdovo line by 9 September.

The boundary on the left – as before, to Grishino and, further, to Gnezdovo.

5) 16th Army will continue to defend the positions it occupies up to 30 August, and, consisting of 152nd, 38th, 108th, and 144th RDs, go over to a decisive offensive on 30 August, while delivering a main attack with its right wing toward Novosel'e, Mushkovichi, Dukhovshchina, and Smolensk. Revert to *front* reserve when 19th and 20th Armies reach the Smolensk region.

The boundary on the left from 30 August – Dorogobuzh, Zabor'e, and Smolensk.

6) 20th Army will go on the defense up to 30 August and withdraw 153rd and 161st RDs into the army's reserve for rest and refitting.

20th Army, consisting of 153rd, 73rd, 161st, 129th, and 229th RDs, with a grouping on its left wing, will go over to an offensive toward Klokovo Station and Riabtsovo Station on 30 August, capture the Pridneprovskaia Station and Riabtsovo Station regions by 6 September, and, subsequently, turn its attack toward the northwest and reach the Gnezdovo and Pogost' line by 8 September. Constantly keep no fewer than one RD in reserve.

7) The *Front's* reserve: 1st TD and a CD, which will be arriving from the Reserve of the High Command at the junction between 19th and 16th Armies in readiness to exploit 16th Army's success.

127th TB in the Vadino region.

5. To support the plan of operations:

1) Concentrate units attached to reinforce 22nd Army's front in the Toropets and Staraia Toropa region by day's end on 29 August as follows:

134th RD by auto-transport and foot march along the Belyi and Staraia Toropa march-route;

57th MR – from Sychevka through Rzhev to Staraia Toropa (200-300 kilometers);

107th TD on foot, having reinforced it with one ATBn, along the Belyi, Nelidovo, and Toropets march-route (200 kilometers); and

The CD from the Reserve of the High Command by rail to the Toropets region.

2) Fill out 153rd, 161st, and 134th RDs by 29 August;

3) Reinforce 107th TD with 30 tanks, which will arrive from Moscow;

4) Refill 30th Army's units with personnel;

5) Create ammunition reserves on the basis of 4 b/k [combat loads] for 19th and 20th Armies' operations and 3 combat loads for 29th and 30th Armies;

6) Issue all orders about the general offensive no later than 28 August, having reserved 29 August for preparation of the offensive in divisions, regiments, and battalions; and

7) Give all orders verbally.

The Chief of Staff of the Western Front, Lieutenant General Sokolovsky

[On the document were the following notes by the Western Front's chief of staff, Lieutenant General Sokolovsky]

"Order of the High Command: Do not carry out the reinforcement of 22nd Army, and its mission is – defense and reinforced operations by forward detachments.

Provide 20th Army with [river] crossing means and also 29th Army.

Unload the CD, and do not send it to Viaz'ma. Determine the location.

Dovator's cavalry, in the future toward Velizh.

Carry out the grouping on 30 and 31 August and go over to a decisive offensive on 1 September.

1. Request: 1. Tanks for 48th TB and 2 RDs, and artillery equipment from the *Stavka* for 22nd Army.

Additional aviation for the *Stavka* – 2 regiments of IL-2, 2 regiments of LAGG-3 or MIG-3, 2 regiments of PE-2, and 2 reconnaissance squadrons.

Change the boundary with the Reserve Front.

2. [no entry].

3. 1 regiment for antiaircraft defense of Smolensk; machine-guns, medium antiaircraft guns, and so on.

To Rokossovsky, 152nd RD, 1st TD, and 18th TD."

Source: "Plan nastupatel'noi operatsii voisk Zapadnogo fronta ot 25 avgusta 1941 g. po razgromu Smolenskoi gruppirovki protivnika" [A plan for an offensive operation of the forces of the Western Front of 25 August 1941 for the destruction of the enemy's Smolensk grouping], *SBDVOV,* issue 41, 74-76.

7. Operational Summary No. 120 of the Headquarters of the Western Front at 2000 hours on 25 August 1941 about the Combat Operations of the *Front's* Forces

Operational Summary No. 120 at 2000 hours on 25 August 1941,
Headquarters. Western Front
1:500,000 and 100,000 scale maps

First. The Western Front, while continuing the offensive in its center and on its left wing, is organizing on the right wing to liquidate the penetration and destroy the enemy units which have penetrated into the rear.

Second. 22nd Army – no new information received.

Third. 29th Army is fulfilling its previous missions.

252nd RD – positions unchanged.

246th and 243rd RDs have been fighting along their previous lines since 0200 hours on 25 August. The enemy is offering stubborn resistance.

1st and 2nd MRRs, while cooperating with 243rd RD, are attacking Katkovo. Katkovo is burning.

Headquarters of 29th Army – Bentsy; CP – the grove south of Poiarkovo.

Fourth. Cavalry Group Dovator – no information received.

Fifth. 30th Army went over to the offensive from the Novoe Morokhovo, Mikhailovshchina, and Zhukovo line at 1400 hours on 25 August.

The enemy, while holding firmly to the defensive positions he occupies, is resisting our units' offensive with machine gun, mortar, and artillery fire.

242nd RD, while overcoming fierce enemy resistance, occupied the eastern outskirts of Erkhovo by 1700 hours and is fighting to capture this populated point.

250th RD's 926th RR is fighting to capture Hill 215.2.

162nd RD is fighting for possession of Hill 228.0 and Shelepy. The enemy is offering strong fire resistance.

251st RD is fighting to capture Sechenki.

The enemy is offering strong fire resistance but not employing counterattacks.

107th TD is withdrawing to the woods west of Baranovo to put itself in order.

The army's units seized: 3 antitank guns, one antitank rifle, 3 mortar batteries, and 6 heavy machine guns and destroyed 8 sub-machine guns, 5 antitank guns, two mortar batteries, and 8 pillboxes.

Losses: killed and wounded – 118 men.

Sixth. 19th Army resumed its offensive at 0800 hours on 25 August after a 30-minute artillery preparation. While overcoming strong enemy resistance and engineer obstacles on the roads and in the woods, it developed its offensive on its right wing.

By 1700 hours, the army's units were fighting [as follows]:

244th RD, while overcoming intense mortar and artillery fire, captured Novo-Losevo with its forward units.

The enemy withdrew westward in small groups. The enemy abandoned ammunition (quantities being verified) in the vicinity of Zanino 2.

166th RD, having 735th RR in second echelon, is fighting to capture Borniki and Losevo. The division's units seized 3 122mm howitzers, 350 mines, 21 rifles, 4 hand and 1 heavy machine guns, 3,400 bullets, 2 mortars, and 2 of our tanks.

The division discovered 20 graves in its sector, where 200 German soldiers were buried, and 70-80 unburied corpses belonging to 56th IR [5th ID].

91st RD, having captured Hill 190.3 and Muk, is fighting to capture Balashova.

89th RD forced the Loinia River with part of its forces, under heavy enemy machine gun and mortar fire, and is developing its attack toward Hill 220.3.

The commander of 3rd Battalion, Captain Papuashvili, perished heroically in combat.

Units of 14th IR [5th ID] are operating opposite the division's front.

50th RD had no success in its advance because of strong fire resistance from the vicinity of Hills 220.3 and 212.6 and is continuing to fight along its previous lines.

Trophies: one large caliber machine gun, 6 sub-machine guns, and 2 automatic pistols.

Losses for 25 August: dead – 19 and wounded – 57 men.

64th RD, while facing dug in enemy, encountered strong fire resistance and is fighting in its previous positions from Popova to Petrova and Osipova.

The division's units are suffering heavy losses.

Observation detected up to 30 tanks in the woods west of Kokhanovo and other groups of tanks concentrating south of Siniakovo.

101st TD withdrew as a result of four enemy counterattacks and is occupying Hill 228.0 and the church in Skachkovo, and the division's left wing is 1 kilometer northeast of Novosel'e.

During the counterattacks, 9 enemy heavy machine guns, one antitank gun, and 150 men were destroyed.

We seized: 2 prisoners, 11 bicycles, 5 rifles, and 1 mortar.

Losses: killed – 3 men and wounded – 16 men.

45th CD is moving to the Kastalanova region.

Seventh. 16th Army. The positions of the army's units are unchanged.

The enemy is displaying no activity.

Eighth. 20th Army is continuing to fulfill its assigned missions on 25 August.

144th and 73rd RDs are in their previous positions.

The enemy is conducting methodical fires against the crossings and the dispositions of our force in the Ratchino and Pashkovo region.

229th RD and 153rd RD are conducting sustained fighting for Hill 249.9, while repelling strong enemy counterattacks enemy and while overcoming his strong mortar and artillery fire.

The division's units abandoned Hill 249.9 at 0600 hours on 25 August as a result of counterattacks by an enemy force of up to two infantry companies, supported by two tanks and strong artillery and mortar fire. The division resumed its attack at about 1100 hours and captured Hill 249.9 once again by 1300 hours.

161st RD is conducting sustained fighting to capture Vishniaki, the grove north of Pogibilka, and the unnamed hill south of Samodurovka, while meeting with strong enemy fire resistance.

The division's units captured the unnamed hill south of Chuvakhi at 0800 hours, where they discovered many corpses of Germans.

At about 1400 hours, an enemy fire raid on the division's CP disrupted communications between its units.

Trophies: 4 enemy heavy machine guns were taken.

129th RD continued its attack toward Prokhlopovka with two battalions of 343rd and 457th RR, and the attack was met by enemy company-size counterattacks. The counterattacks have been repelled and the enemy thrown back to Gorodok.

The battalions' advance is being held up by strong mortar and machine gun fire.

Ninth. The *front's* reserve – 152nd RD – in the Neelovo state Farm, Drozdovo, and Sergeevskoe State Farm region.

1st TD – in the Kapyrovshchina, Zubovshchina, and Matveenki region.

Tenth. The VVS of the *front* cooperated with the ground forces, conducted reconnaissance since the morning of 25 August, while directing their main efforts at destroying enemy motor-mechanized units which penetrated into 22nd Army's rear.

Overall, a total of 97 aircraft sorties were carried out overnight on 24-25 August and during the first half of the day on 25 August.

23rd BAD bombed penetrating enemy motor-mechanized units in the Peski, Zhigalovo State Farm, and Ushitsy State Farm region and the airfield and enemy headquarters in the Usviaty region on the night of 24-25 August.

The bombing set many centers of fire and several explosions. Velikopol'e Station and Zhigalovo Station are burning. Several fires were set in Usviaty.

43rd MAD bombed centers of resistance in the Il'ino region and artillery positions in the vicinity of Nikol'skoe State Farm on the night of 24-25 August. Results are unknown.

On the morning of 25 August, it cooperated with 19th Army's forces.

46th MAD bombed enemy centers of resistance in the Il'ino region on the night of 24-25 August. It cooperated with 22nd Army's units on the morning of 25 August.

47th MAD cooperated with 22nd Army's units and destroyed enemy motor-mechanized units in the Khramtsovo and Kresty region. As a result of the assault raids, 21 vehicles were destroyed, 3 vehicle cisterns were burned, 4-5 tanks were put out of action, up to 20 carts were smashed, and heavy personnel losses were inflicted.

31st MAD cooperated with 22nd Army's units and conducted reconnaissance in the Velikie Luki and Nevel' region.

Enemy losses: 3 IU-88 aircraft shot down on 24 August.

Our losses: 1 SB aircraft shot down, 1 I-16 suffered an accident, and 1 SB crashed at the airfield while landing.

> The Chief of Staff of the Western Front, Lieutenant General Sokolovsky
> The Military Commissar of the Western Front's headquarters,
>   Regimental Commissar Anan'ev
> The Chief of the Operations Department, Lieutenant General Malandin

Source: "Operativnaia svodka shtaba Zapadnogo fronta No. 120 k 20 chasam 25 avgusta 1941 g. o boevykh deistviiakh voisk fronta" [Operational summary no. 120 of the headquarters of the Western Front at 2000 hours on 25 August 1941 about the combat operations of the *front's* forces], *SBDVOV*, issue 41, 76.77.

8. Combat Order No. 039/op of the Commander of the Forces of 19th Army of 26 August 1941 on the Destruction of the Enemy's Dukhovshchina Grouping between the Loinia and Tsarevich Rivers

Combat Order No. 039/op, CP, Commander, 19th Army,
the woods 1 kilometer east of Vasilisino
0110 hours on 26 August 1941
1:50,000 scale map

1. The enemy on the army's right wing, while suffering a defeat, withdrew to the Novo-Losevo and Stepanidino front with negligible forces of 5th ID, where it is trying to hold back 244th and 166th RDs' attacks with separate centers of defense. The enemy, while bringing new units of about one ID forward, is stubbornly defending the Kazakova, Shishkino, Siniakova, Kokhanovo, and Novosel'e sector, while maneuvering with his mobile reserves (mortar batteries and motorized units) and trying to halt 50th RD's successful attack.

2. Neighbors are fulfilling their previous missions.

3. 19th Army will develop 244th and 166th RDs' success toward Krotovo with night operations on its right wing, while destroying the remnants of 5th ID, and will attack toward Dukhovshchina at 1100 hours on 26 August 1941, with the mission to destroy the enemy's Dukhovshchina grouping between the Loinia and Tsarevich Rivers.

4. 244th RD will destroy the enemy centers of defense in the Kuchina, Levashovo, and Kazarina region [26-30 kilometers north of Iartsevo], attack toward Staraia Kazarina with the division's main forces, and, in cooperation with 166th RD, destroy the opposing enemy and protect the commitment of 45th CD into the penetration in the Novo-Losevo 1 and Novo-Losevo 2 sector. Capture Isakovo Farm (western), Shakhlovo, and Novaia Kazarina by day's end. Firmly protect the army's right flank. Have one battalion in reserve in the Bitiagovo region.

The boundary on the left is as before.

5. 166th RD, with 399th HAR, while continuing the attack toward Krotovo in cooperation with 244th RD, destroy the opposing enemy and, while cutting off its routes of withdrawal to the west, protect the commitment of 45th CD into the penetration in the Borniki sector. Capture the Krotovo, Myshkovo, and Barsuki region [23-26 kilometers north of Iartsevo] by day's end.

6. 91st RD, with its previous reinforcements, will attack toward Balashova and Myshkovo. Capture the Hill 230.0 (0.5 kilometers north of Myshkovo and Hill 226.2 (0.5 kilometers south of Myshkovo) line [20-23 kilometers north of Iartsevo] and seize Rytvino and Ponizov'e with your forward units by day's end. Allocate one RR to my reserve.

The boundary on the left: (incl.) Hill 245.6 (0.5 kilometers north of Novaia Guta), (incl.) Shuklino, (incl.) Pochepova, (incl.) Shchelkina, and Ponizov'e.

7. 89th RD, with present reinforcing units, will attack toward Hill 220.3 and Sel'tso. Capture the Hill 224.9 (0.5 kilometers north of Sel'tso) and Mashutino [18-20 kilometers north of Iartsevo] line by day's end. Seize the crossings at Maleevka and Pavlova with your forward units.

The boundary line on the left: the brickworks (1 kilometer southwest of Novaia Guta), Hill 221.5 (southeast of Sorokaren'ia), Makov'e, Mashutino, and hill 232.9 (1 kilometer east of Afanas'evo).

8. 50th RD, with 202nd TR, 1st Bn, 596th AR and 4th Bn, 302nd AR, while continuing an energetic and precipitous attack toward Kalugino and Mashutino, destroy the opposing enemy and capture Mashutino, Novo-Nikol'skoe State Farm, Sushchevo, and Kalugino [14-18 kilometers north of Iartsevo] by day's end. Have in second echelon – one RR behind the division's left wing.

The boundary on the left is as before.

9. 64th RD, with previous reinforcing units, while carrying out a regrouping to your right wing, attack toward Turishchevo. Capture Masolovo, Navol'nia, and Bortniki [10-14 kilometers north of Iartsevo] by day's end.

The boundary on the left is as before.

10. 101st TD will destroy the opposing enemy and capture the Kokhanovo and Kholm regions [5-10 kilometers north of Iartsevo].

11. 45th CD will enter the penetration in the Novo-Losevo 1 and Borniki sector [25-26 kilometers north of Iartsevo]. Destroy the enemy's rear and reserves by surprise attacks and operate toward Zhukova and Dukhovshchina. Strike out from the Krotovo region toward Shchelkina against the enemy's rear area with part of your forces in order to assist the army's forces attacking from the front.

12. Artillery. Readiness – at 0600 hours on 26 August 1941; and an artillery preparation in the Losevo, Kazakova, Shishkina, Petrova, Kokhanovo, and Chistaia sectors from 1100 until 1130 hours.

Missions:

1) Suppress enemy mortars and personnel by massed raids; and

2) Suppress enemy artillery in the Novoselishche, Krotovo, Barsuki and Sirotinka, Kalugino, Turishchevo, and Shishkino regions.

Attach to the DD [long-range action] group two battalions of 399th HAR and one battalion of 506th HAR.

13. VVS [Air Forces]. Missions:

1) Protect the commitment of 45th CD with fighters.

2) Suppress enemy forces and firing points in the Sirotinka and Hill 218.5 (south of Shishkina) sector with bomber strikes against the forward edge at 1125 hours on 26 August 1941.

3) Destroy concentrations of enemy personnel and tanks in the Shchakhlovo, Berdino, Myshkovo, and Krotovo regions by repeated bombing raids.

4) Assist 45th CD's attack with assault aircraft.

14. CP and headquarters of the army are at their previous points

15. Operational and reconnaissance summaries – at previous times.

The Commander of 19th Army, Lieutenant General Konev

The Member of the Military Council of 19th Army,
    Division Commissar Sheklanov
The Chief of Staff of 19th Army, [Malyshkin]

Source: "Boevoi prikaz komanduiushchego voiskami 19-i Armii No. 039/op ot 26 avgusta 1941 g. na unichtozhenie Dukhovshchinskoi gruppirovki protivnika mezhdu rekami Loinia i Tsarevich" [Combat order no. 039/op of the commander of the forces of 19th Army of 26 August 1941 on the destruction of the enemy's Dukhovshchina Grouping between the Loinia and Tsarevich Rivers], *SBDVOV*, issue 41, 185-187.

9. Combat Order No. 059 of the Commander of the Forces of 20th Army of 26 August 1941 on Defending the Positions They Occupy

Combat Order No. 059, Headquarters, 20th Army,
2210 hours on 26 August 1941
1:50,000 scale map

1. The enemy is defending the Dnepr River in the Zadnia, Zabor'e, and Sopshino sector with a force of up to two IDs and – the Sopshino, Erdetsy, the southern slopes of Hill 259.9, Vishniaki, Hill 228.0, and Klemiatino line and further along the western bank of the Ustrom River to Mar'ino with 263rd ID's units.

2. 20th Army will withdraw 153rd and 161st RDs' units from combat and go over to the defense in the positions it occupies, while preventing an enemy penetration toward the east and northeast.

3. On the right, 16th Army's 108th RD is defending along the Vop' River.
The boundary with it: Dorogobuzh and Zadnia.
On the left, 24th Army's 102nd MR is fighting in the Bataevo region.

4. 144th RD, with 3rd Bn, 592nd GAR (9-122mm guns) and a battery of 872nd ATR, while continuing to defend the Dnepr River in the sector from the mouth of the Vop' River to Ratchino, will hold on to the bridgeheads it occupies on the western bank of the Dnepr River at Makeevo, Pnevo, Mit'kovo, and Ratchino. Pay special attention to protecting the boundary with 16th Army's 108th RD, the responsibility for which has been entrusted to the commander of 144th RD.
The boundary on the left: Usviat'e, Bykovo, Mukhinka, Iaroshenki, the barn (1 kilometer south of Zabor'e), Ratchino, and (incl.) Fedurno.
CP – in its previous location.

5. 73rd RD, while continuing to defend the Dnepr River from Ratchino to Elydnia, will firmly hold on to the bridgehead on the western bank of the Dnepr River at Pashkovo and the woods south of Golovino and the woods at Erdetsy.
The boundary on the left: Peski, Dumamory, Pleshcheevo, Balakirevo, Kucherovo, and Erdetsy.
CP – in its previous location.
The commanders of 144th and 73rd RDs will pay special attention to firmly holding on to the crossings over the Dnepr River.

6. 229th RD, with 666th RR and 153rd RD's AR, 127th Sapper Bn, 592nd GAR (without one battalion), 302nd HAR, and two batteries of 872nd ATR, having relieved 153rd RD's remaining units, 161st RD in full, and 129th RD's subunits on the night of 28-29 August, will firmly defend positions from the southern edge

of the woods south of Motovo to Hill 249.9, Marker 205.9, Hill 221.3, and the southwestern slopes of Hill 224.8, while preventing an enemy penetration toward Kucherovo and Mileevo.

The boundary on the left: Mutyshino, Kuzino, Romodanovo, Mileevo, (incl.) Hill 224.8, and (incl.) Obzhorovka.

Prepare blocking fires of artillery against the exits from the woods west of Prokhlopovka and from the woods south of Volobuevo.

CP – the woods north of Sel'tso.

7. 129th RD, with 129th Light Eng. Bn, 161st RD's AR, two batteries of 872nd ATR, and the cavalry squadron of the army's headquarters, having given up the sector from Chuvakhi to Hill 224.8 to 229th RD on the night of 28-29 August, will firmly defend positions on Hill 224.8 and further along the Ustrom River from the edge of Klemiatino to Mar'ino.

Have up to one regiment in reserve in the Slobodka region to protect the Brykino and Antinino axes.

CP – in its previous location.

8. 153rd RD, without 666th RR and its AR, having given up the positions it occupies to 229th RD on the night of 28-29 August, will concentrate in the Balakirevo, Naidenovo, and Privol'nia region by 0700 hours on 29 August, where, while resting and refitting in the army's reserve, will begin preparing a defensive line along the Ustrom River from Borovka to Vasiuki at 1900 hours on 29 August.

CP – the woods northeast of Samuilovo.

9. 161st RD, without its AR, having given up the positions it occupies to 229th RD on the night of 28-29 August, will concentrate in the Romodanovo, Iurkino, and Borovishche region by 0700 hours on 29 August, where, while resting and refitting in the army's reserve, will begin preparing defensive line from Marker 183.4 to Ekimovo, the woods south of Lunevo, Hill 231.1, and Hill 239.9 at 1900 hours on 29 August..

CP – Borovishche.

10. The commanders of 153rd and 161st RDs will prepare a plan for constructing, first and foremost, antitank obstacles, company strongpoints, and battalion regions. 20th Army's Chief of Engineers will prepare an antitank region along the Iurkino and Gorodok line with the forces of army engineer units.

11. The commanders of 144th, 73rd, 229th, and 129th RDs will continue to fortify the positions they occupy, construct full profile trenches with overhead covers, bunkers, pill boxes, and observation posts, set up barbed wire obstacles and minefields, and make obstructions, abbattis, open escarpments, antitank ditches, and other antitank obstacles.

12. CP –Novoselki.

The Commander of 20th Army, Lieutenant General Lukin
The Member of the Military Council, Corps Commissar Semenovsky
The Chief of Staff of 20th Army, Major General Korneev

Source: "Boevoi prikaz komanduiushchego voiskami 20-i Armii No. 059 ot 26 avgusta 1941 g. na oboronu zanimaemogo rubezha" [Combat order no. 059 of the commander of the forces of 20th Army of 26 August 1941 on defending the positions they occupy], *SBDVOV*, issue 41, 221-222..

10. Operational Summary No. 122 of the Headquarters of the Western Front at 2000 hours on 26 August 1941 about the Combat Operations of the *Front's* Forces

Operational Summary No. 122 at 2000 hours on 26 August 1941,
Headquarters. Western Front
1:500,000 and 100,000 scale maps

First. The Western Front is continuing the offensive in its center and on its left wing and, on the right wing, 22nd Army is trying to fight its way out of encirclement.

Second. 22nd Army – the army's units, while fighting in encirclement, continued to withdraw northeastward from it, while inflicting heavy losses on the enemy.

On the army's left wing, small groups from 62nd RC's units reached the Chernost' River, Pochinok, Barsuki, Terekhov, Lug, and Ranki line on 25-26 August. According to reports from individual commanders, its units are fighting sustained battles in encirclement, while inflicting heavy losses on the enemy.

On the night of 24-25 August, the army's main grouping – 29th RC – in accordance with the corps commander's orders, completed penetrating the encirclement toward the northeast. The penetration was carried out in organized fashion and by a massive blow unexpected by the enemy. As a result, the enemy in the region east of Velikie Luki was dealt a serious blow at 0100 hours on 25 August and withdrew toward the east.

29th RC's units are continuing to fight, while breaking through to the Chernost' River and Pochinok line.

There are no communications with Ershakov. Measures are being taken to establish contact.

22nd Army's withdrawing units, 29th Army's student detachment, and the composite detachment sent by the *front* occupied defenses along the Podolina, Polibino, Iakshino, and Novaia Derevnia line on 25 August, with the aim to prevent an enemy penetration to Toropets and Staraia Toropa.

A separate detachment of the signal regiment, under the command of Major Kadyshev, is occupying the Ekimino, Ozerets, Peski, and Kabanikha line on 25 August.

Captain Latkin's composite detachment is occupying the Pochinok, Barsuki, and Skvortsovo Station region.

Polukhin's composite detachment is defending the Hill 210.9, Hill 216.9 and Loshaedy line.

Antosenko's composite detachment will reach the [following] positions by day's end on 26 August: 9th MRR – Rudino and Savino for combined operations with Polukhin's detachment; and 8th MRR – Savino and Zhizhitsa Station for combined operations with 29th Army's student detachment.

Antosenko has the mission to throw the opposing enemy back and then assist 22nd Army's escape from encirclement.

29th Army's student detachment is in sustained combat at Zhizhitsa Station.

The positions of 22nd Army's remaining units are being verified.

Third. 29th Army (252nd RD) is firmly defending its previous positions on its right wing, and, on the left wing, 248th and 243rd RDs are attacking enemy strong points.

The enemy is stubbornly defending the Sharkovo, Hill 209.6, and Katkovo line.

The offensive is continuing.

Headquarters of 29th Army – Bentsy.

Fourth. Cavalry Group Dovator – no new information received.

Fifth. 30th Army resumed its offensive from the Erkhovo, eastern slope of Hill 215.2, Shanino, and Sechenki line at 1200 hours on 26 August, while concentrating its efforts along the Shelepy and Zarech'e axis.

The enemy, while continuing to offer fire resistance, is attacking our attacking units with dive bombers.

242nd RD, while defending in positions from Staroe Morokhovo to Novoe Morokhovo with its right wing, is attacking toward Churkino from the northeast with its left wing and reached the brushy region (1 kilometer northeast of Churkino) by 1500 hours.

250th RD is attacking toward Churkino, captured Hill 215.2, and was fighting 500 meters west of the hill at 1500 hours.

162nd RD is fighting for possession of Shelepy and Ivkino.

251st RD is fighting to capture Bol'shoe Repino with its right wing. On its left wing, it is protecting the Nazemenki and Torchilovo sector.

107th TD was withdrawn to the Mikhailovshchina region by 1200 hours on 26 August, where it is continuing to put itself in order.

The losses of the army for 26 August: killed and wounded – 182 men.

Trophies: one heavy machine gun, one antitank gun, and one machine pistol were seized.

Sixth. 19th Army, while protecting its right flank with part of 244th RD's forces in the Shupeki and Priglovo sector, continued an offensive on the remainder of its front at 1100 hours on 26 August, while concentrating its main forces along the Krotovo and Dukhovshchina axis.

45th CD is being committed at 1350 hours for developing success on the main attack axis.

The enemy in the Novo-Losevo 1 and Stepanidina sector on the right wing, while withdrawing toward the west, nevertheless offered strong resistance in separate centers.

The enemy in the army's center and along the Kazakova and (incl.) Novosel'e front on its left wing, while defending, are offering strong resistance and going over to counterattacks with infantry supported by tanks along separate axes.

At 1700 hours, the army's units were fighting [as follows]:

244th RD, while defending the Shupeki and Priglovo sector, in the remaining sectors of the front, is attacking toward Staraia Kazarina and reached the western edge of the woods east of Novo-Losevo 1 with its main forces. The division's forward units are continuing to fight along the Novo-Losevo 1 and Novo-Losevo 2 line.

The mined [booby trapped] bodies of 15 Red Army soldiers were discovered in the region north of Bortniki.

166th RD, while overcoming the resistance of enemy covering units, reached the Isakovka, Hill 227.0, western edge of the grove southwest of Bortniki, and Hill 222.3 front with two regiments, with one regiment in second echelon behind its right wing.

91st RD, while pursuing small groups of withdrawing enemy, which were resisting along intermediate lines, reached the Marker 225.1 and separate building in Stepanidina front, where it encountered strong fire from the eastern edge of the grove southwest of Barsuki and the hill to the south.

89th RD, while overcoming stubborn enemy resistance, reached the Pochelovo, western bank of the Loinia River, and eastern slope of Hill 220.3 line.

50th RD successfully repelled 4 counterattacks by enemy infantry, supported by tanks, and is occupying its previous lines.

During the counterattack used flamethrower tanks. While repelling the counterattacks, 11 tanks were put out of action, and 2 tanks were burned.

64th RD. The division's right wing successfully repelled a counterattack by up to a company of enemy infantry supported by tanks, after which, it went over to the attack and is fighting in the woods southwest of Zaitsevo State Farm.

The division's center and left wing are fighting in their previous positions.

101st TD is continuing to exchange fire in ts previous positions.

45th CD was committed into the junction between 244th and 166th RDs at 1350 hours. At 1500 hours one CR is moving to Novoselishche, a second CR is passing through the combat formations on 166th RD's left wing toward Ivaniki. The third CR is in second echelon on the division's left wing.

There has been no further news about the division's progress.

Seventh. 16th Army. The positions of the army's units are unchanged. The enemy is inactive. No new enemy units have been detected.

Eighth. 20th Army. The army's units along the western axis are continuing to defend in their previous positions along the Dnepr River, and those along the southern axis are fortifying their previous positions in positions from the grove south of Motovo to Pogibilka, the stream west of Chuvakhi, Chuvakhi, Hill 224.8 and further along the eastern bank of the Ustrom River to Praslovo.

144th and 73rd RDs are defending the positions they occupy. There is occasional artillery and mortar fire on the division's front. 144th RD destroyed one machine gun and suppressed two enemy batteries in the Skrushevo region by artillery fire.

229th and 153rd RDs conducted sustained fighting for Hill 249.9 all night and on the morning of 26 August, while repelling determined enemy counterattacks, supported by intense artillery and mortar fire.

229th RD's composite regiment abandoned Hill 249.9 at about 1100 hours under strong enemy mortar and machine gun fire and dug in on the northern slopes of that hill.

153rd RD's 435th and 666th RRs were counterattacked twice by enemy infantry supported by 4 tanks and mortars. An answering counterattack by the division drove the enemy back and regained the lost positions.

161st RD's 542nd and 603rd RRs were fighting along their previous lines. 477th Regiment abandoned the unnamed hill south of Chuvakhi under pressure of enemy mortar and machine gun fire and withdrew behind the stream west of Chuvakhi, where it dug in.

129th RD's 457th RR, having left combat security along a line 300 meters east of Prokhlopovka, was withdrawn to the eastern bank of the Ustrom River, where it dug in, with the aim of creating a firmer defense.

438th RR captured the unnamed hill east of Brykino with part of its forces.

Ninth. The *front's* reserve – 152nd RD and 1st TD are in their previous positions, 134th RD is concentrating in the Belyi region by day's end on 26 August, and 18th TD is in the Vadino region.

Tenth. The VVS of the *front* cooperated with armies' ground forces overnight on 25-26 August and during the first half of the day on 26 August, while directing their main efforts at defeating enemy groups which have penetrated into 22nd Army's rear.

Overall, a total of 97 aircraft sorties were carried out.

23rd BAD bombed penetrating enemy units in the Velikopol'e Station, Sertse Station, Morozovo, and Starosel'e; and Artemova, Kresty, Kamenka, and Usviaty regions on the night of 25-26 August. As a result of the bombing, several fires appeared in the regions, and several explosions were observed.

43rd MAD bombed Kardymova Station and concentrations of forces in the Kardymova, Zamiatino, Turishchevo, and Shishkino region on the night of 25-26 August. Observation by the crews noted the bombs fell on their targets. During the first half of the day, cooperated with 19th Army's units and bombed the enemy in the Sirotinka, Turishchevo, and Rakhmanino region. Crew observations noticed a large number of fires in the region of operations.

46th MAD bombed crossings in the Khlebanikha region and troop concentrations east and south of Krutiki on the night of 25-26 August. As a result of the bombing, fires appeared, and strong explosions were observed. It cooperated with 29th Army's units during the first half of the day.

47th MAD conducted reconnaissance on 22nd Army's front and destroyed the enemy in the Kazakova and Afanas'ev region in 19th Army's sector.

31st MAD bombed the Kun'ia Station and Mishovo region. Crew observations in the bombing region detected fires.

There is no information about enemy losses or our losses during the first half of the day.

> The Chief of Staff of the Western Front, Lieutenant General Sokolovsky
> The Military Commissar of the Western Front's headquarters,
>   Regimental Commissar Anan'ev
> For the Chief of the Operations Department,
>   Colonel Belianko, [General Malandin's deputy]

Source: "Operativnaia svodka shtaba Zapadnogo fronta No. 122 k 20 chasam 26 avgusta 1941 g. o boevykh deistviiakh voisk fronta" [Operational summary no. 122 of the headquarters of the Western Front at 2000 hours on 26 August 1941 about the combat operations of the *front's* forces], *SBDVOV*, issue 41, 80-83.

11. Operational Summary No. 124 of the Headquarters of the Western Front at 2000 hours on 27 August 1941 about the Combat Operations of the *Front's* Forces on 27 August 1941

Operational Summary No. 124 at 2000 hours on 27 August 1941,
Headquarters. Western Front
1:500,000 and 100,000 scale maps

First. On the *front's* right wing, 22nd Army is withdrawing from encirclement, in the center, the forces are continuing the offensive, while overcoming stubborn enemy resistance, and, on the *front's* left wing, the forces are fortifying the positions they occupy.

Second. 22nd Army, while continuing its fighting to withdraw from encirclement, occupied a defense along the Ekimino, Kabanikha, Pochinok, and Zhizhitsa Station line with part of its forces which escaped from encirclement and concentrated part of its forces and was putting itself in order in the Ozerets region.

Simultaneously, it is preparing and occupying a rear defensive line – Podolina, Toropets, and Staraia Toropa – with separate detachments.

The main grouping of enemy motorized infantry and tanks in unknown strength were discovered by aviation in the regions east of Velikie Luki, Kun'ia Station, and Lake Kodosno on 27 August.

The enemy attacked toward Ozerets from the west on 27 August with a force of up to a battalion of motorized infantry with 10-12 tanks. With the help of aviation, the attack by the enemy was repelled, and the position was restored by 1500 hours. Four enemy tanks were destroyed.

Up to a battalion of enemy motorized infantry are attacking toward Zhizhitsa Station, but the results of the fighting have not been received.

The condition of the withdrawing units of 22nd Army are being verified.

Third. 29th Army. The army's units, while defending on the right wing, are conducting a successful offensive on the left wing

The enemy is offering stubborn resistance.

252nd RD is defending along its previous lines.

246th RD, while developing its attack successfully, captured the strong points on the hills east of Sharkovo and Hill 209.6. Six enemy machine gun firing points, two guns, 18 mortars, 2 vehicles, and more than 2 platoons of enemy infantry have been destroyed.

243rd RD captured Bol'shoi Borok and fought for Novinka. 906th RR was thrown back to the eastern parts of Novinka by an enemy counterattack from the direction of Tselpino. The fighting for Novinka is continuing.

The Composite Brigade – positions are unchanged.

In these battles, 18 enemy prisoners belonging to 37th and 58th IRs of the enemy's 6th ID were seized by 246th and 243rd RDs' units.

According to additional information, around 90 Germans were destroyed in bayonet attacks in the Glazovo region during the period from 22-24 August by 252nd RD's subunits, which were located on the southern bank of the Western Dvina River.

Reconnaissance of 29th CR killed and wounded up to 45 Germans in fighting in the Ordynka region.

Fourth. Cavalry Group Dovator – According to a report by a representative who arrived from the group of horse-holders [cavalrymen who remained with the horses], as before, the cavalry group has no communications with the "horse-holders." News has not been received about the cavalry group.

Fifth. 30th Army has been pursuing the enemy, who has been rapidly withdrawing from Los'mino and Chernyi Ruchei line, with its reconnaissance detachments since the morning of 27 August. Simultaneously, it has been conducting an offensive since 0900 hours from the Staraia Morokhovo and Sekachi line.

The enemy (supposedly) are withdrawing their units southward from the Los'mino, Okolitsa, and Chernyi Ruchei line under pressure from Cavalry Group Dovator's forces, whose cavalrymen have been penetrating on foot in the Podviaz'e region. The withdrawing enemy units are being protected by a stubborn defense of the Staraia Morokhovo and Gorodno line.

The army's units are fighting [as follows] at 1700 hours on 27 August:

134th RD reached [the following] with its reconnaissance detachments: Detachment No. 1. – 2nd Los'mianka and Detachment No. 2. – Svity. Enemy forces have not been discovered in either point; but they did abandon shells and vehicles in Sutoki. The reconnaissance detachments are continuing their movement.

134th RD's 629th RR and 250th RD's 918th RR are moving toward the southwest. The heads of the columns crossed over the Zaozer'e and Chernyi Ruchei line at 1700 hours.

The army's remaining units are fighting in previous positions, while encountering with stubborn enemy resistance on the Staraia Morokhovo, Shelepy, and Gorodno line.

The army's left wing, having occupied Markovo, established contact with 19th Army's right wing units.

Sixth. 19th Army went over to an offensive along the Novo-Losevo 1, Novoselishche, Ivaniki, Kazakova, Muzhilova, Popova, and Skachkovo line at 1200 hours on 27 August

The enemy is offering stubborn resistance.

The army's units were fighting [as follows] at 1700 hours on 27 August:

244th RD, while concentrating its efforts on its right wing and attacking toward Staraia Morokhovo, captured Markovo, Kuchina, Levashova, and Shakhlovo.

Weak enemy covering forces are operating in the Shupeki and Priglovo sector, but the enemy is offering strong resistance along the remainder of the front.

166th RD. The division's attack is being held up by strong enemy fire. The division has been fighting in its previous positions all day long.

91st RD repulsed an enemy counterattack from the woods north of Semenkovo at 1200 hours, with heavy losses for the enemy, and is continuing to fight in its previous positions. As a result of the counterattack, more than 200 German corpses remained on the battlefield and, in addition, 270 boxes of 82mm mines [mortar shells], rifles, machine pistols, and motorcycles were seized.

89th RD met with strong machine gun and mortar fire during its transition to the attack, and, as a result, its attack was unsuccessful. The division's units are continuing to fight in their previous positions.

50th RD, while attacking toward Hill 216.6, forced the Loinia River with one RR and was fighting of the eastern edge of the woods west of Hill 214.0

64th RD, while attacking, captured Osipovo and is fighting to capture Popova.

101st TD is continuing to fight in its previous positions.

45th CD, while committed into combat from the vicinity of the woods northeast of the village of Panov toward Berdino and Ponizov'e at 1000 hours, was observed by aircraft concentrating in the Staraia Kozarina region by 1500 hours. Information has not been received from the division about the results of the fighting

Seventh. 16th Army. The positions of the army's units are unchanged. The enemy is conducting occasional artillery and mortar fire. No new enemy units have been noticed on the army's front.

Eighth. 20th Army. The army's units were continuing to fortify their occupied positions at 1300 hours on 27 August.

144th and 73rd RDs defended their previous positions, while conducting reconnaissance of the enemy. There is scattered artillery and mortar fire in the divisions' sectors. Our artillery fire suppressed an enemy battery in the Krasnoel' region.

229th and 153rd RDs fortified their previous positions, while repulsing local attacks and attempts by the enemy to infiltrate the division's dispositions with separate groups.

An attack by up to 50 enemy infantry, with accompanying tanks, from Suborovka toward Hill 249.9 was beaten back at 1200 hours.

161st RD – positions unchanged. There is artillery and mortar fire in the sector.

129th RD in doing entrenching work and reconnaissance and exchanging fire with the enemy in its previous positions.

Ninth. The *front's* reserve – 152nd RD and 1st TD are in their previous positions.

Tenth. The VVS of the *front* cooperated with the armies' ground forces, while continuing to direct their main efforts on destroying enemy units which have penetrated into 22nd Army's rear.

Air operations from the morning were limited because of poor weather conditions. Overall, a total of 84 aircraft sorties were carried out.

23rd BAD destroyed enemy forces in the region west of Zhizhitsa Station and Nazimova Station, fulfilled special missions in the Minsk and Grodno regions, and dropped leaflets on the night of 26-27 August.

As a result of the bombing in the Zhizhitsa Station region, the entire region was covered by fires, and we observed several small and two large explosions. In the vicinity of Nazimova Station, a great number of fires and explosions appeared.

43rd MAD conducted reconnaissance of the Demidov, Dukhovshchina, Krasnyi, and Vitebsk roads and the Vitebsk airfield on the night of 26-27 August.

In the morning, it cooperated with 19th Army's units – while destroying enemy personnel and firing points in the Kislova and Shakhlovo region.

46th MAD bombed enemy troop concentrations and vehicles in the Il'ino region. A great number of fires resulted from the bombing.

31st MAD bombed enemy forces in the Kun'ia Station region. Many fires were created by the bombing.

47th, 46th, and 31st MADs did not carry out combat flights on the morning of 27 August because of poor weather conditions.

Our losses: 1 MIG-3 aircraft was shot down by enemy antiaircraft fire.

The Chief of Staff of the Western Front, Lieutenant General Sokolovsky
The Military Commissar of the Western Front's headquarters,
    Regimental Commissar Anan'ev
For the Chief of the Operations Department, Colonel Belianko

Source: "Operativnaia svodka shtaba Zapadnogo fronta No. 124 k 20 chasam 27 avgusta 1941 g. o boevykh deistviiakh voisk fronta v techenie 27 avgusta 1941 g." [Operational summary no. 124 of the headquarters of the Western Front at 2000 hours on 27 August 1941 about the combat operations of the *front's* forces on 27 August 1941], *SBDVOV*, issue 41, 85-86.

12. Combat Order No. 042/op of the Commander of the Forces of 19th Army of 27 August 1941 on a Continuation of an Offensive to Destroy the Enemy's Dukhovshchina Grouping

Combat Order No. 042/op, CP, Commander, 19th Army,
the woods 1 kilometer east of Vasilisino,
2400 hours on 27 August 1941
1:50,000 scale map

1. On 27 August 1941, the enemy, with the same forces as before, continued to offer stubborn resistance to the army's offensive, which was developing successfully on the right wing toward Novo-Losevo 1 and Berdino, with the same forces as before, and, during the second half of the day, the movement of an enemy motorized column with up to a regiment of forces from the Dukhovshchina region was detected.

2. The army will continue the offensive on 28 August 1941, with the aim of destroying the Dukhovshchina grouping by enveloping him with our right wing in the direction of Berdino, Ponizov'e, and Dukhovshchina and cutting off the enemy's routes of withdrawal to the Tsarevich River.

3. The divisions will continue a precipitous offensive by conducting night operations.

4. Boundaries: between 244th RD and 166th RD – up to Novoselishche, as before, and further to Ponkratova, inclusive for 166th RD; and the left boundary of 166th RD, up to Ivaniki, as before, and further, to Myshkovo and Sel'tso. For the remaining divisions, the boundaries are as before.

5. VVS:

a) Protect the army grouping in the Berdino, Muzhilova, and Vasilisino region, and pay special attention to protecting the Berdino and Myshkovo region and along the axis of 45th CD's operations;

b) Bomber aircraft will cooperate with the forces in the destruction of enemy artillery in the Shchelkina, Sushchevo, and Sirotinka region; and

c) Destroy enemy reserves approaching from the direction of Dukhovshchina.

The Commander of 19th Army, Lieutenant General Konev
The Member of the Military Council of 19th Army, Division Commissar
    Sheklanov
The Chief of Staff of 19th Army, [Malyshkin]

Source: "Boevoi prikaz komanduiushchego voiskami 19-i Armii No. 042/op ot 27 avgusta 1941 g. na prodolzhenii nastupleniia s tsel'iu unichtozheniia Dukhovshchinskoi gruppirovki protivnika" [Combat order no. 042/op of the commander of the forces of 19th Army of 27 August 1941 on a continuation of an offensive to destroy the enemy's Dukhovshchina Grouping], *SBDVOV*, issue 41, 188-189.

13. Notes of a Conversation between the Commander of the Forces of the Western Front and the Commander of 19th Army's Forces about the Results of the Army's Combat Operations on the Night of 27 and 28 and during the Day on 28 August 1941
1630 hours on 28 August 1941

Marshal Timoshenko – on the apparatus – Hello, Comrade Konev. About [Colonel Nikolai Mikhailovich] Dreier [commander of 45th CD], I know the region you assigned him was close to the front but, at the first opportunity, he spread out somewhat closer to the river and was, as we will subsequently see, put in check. As concerns the operations over night and in the morning, at present I do not know. Report if you can.

Konev – on the apparatus. Hello, Comrade Marshal. The night operations did not provide any special results. Today, the units have been fighting since dawn and captured Shakhlovo, Hills 240. and 233.4, and, further along the Loinia River to Hill 227.0, fighting is going on for Hill 226.7, one kilometer northwest of Ivaniki, and Hill 225.1 and the village of Stepanidina have been occupied; and, from Stepanidina to the south along the western bank of the Loinia River, [Colonel Arkadii Aleksandrovich] Boreiko [commander of 50th RD] is attacking and has captured the part of the woods west of Muzhilovo, Griasnov, and Mikhailov in the previous location.

The fighting indicated that the enemy's second defensive belt passes through Pavlovshchina and Panov, the woods west of Shakhlovo, further along the Loinia River southeastward to Novoselishche, and further to Hill 220.3, and further again along the Loinia River to its mouth.

The enemy is using anti-infantry and antitank mines extensively in front of the forward edge on the right wing.

The fighting has established the presence of 35th ID's 34th IR. 5th ID, in full composition, is in the Panov region. 28th ID, in full composition, is in the Shakhlovo and Ivaniki region. 83rd, 7th, and 49th IRs – are in the Makov'e sector and further to the south up to the left flank. In addition, 8th ID's 84th IR is in the Makov'e and Bolotino sector, and prisoners from 14th ID's 53rd IR are being seized at Panov. The enemy is stubbornly holding on to this line. Regarding Dreier, according to his report, he chopped up as much as a company of enemy in Panov and up to a company of enemy 2 kilometers north of Morozovo, and his reconnaissance in Pavlovshchina established – no enemy have been discovered, but he abstained from any actions at Pavlovshchina because of the fatigue of Dreier's horses. I have placed him even closer to the river so that he can put himself in order sooner and exploit the nearby forest for camouflage rather than draw him away from the front. My plan is to continue penetrating the enemy's defensive belt and, today, capture Krotovo and destroy the enemy between the Loinia and Tsarevich Rivers. That is all.

I request if only one battalion of tanks, and you see to it that mine detectors are dispatched to us.

Source: "Zapis' peregovora komanduiushchego voiskami Zapadnogo fronta s komanduiushchim voiskami 19-i Armii o rezul'tatakh boevykh deistvii voisk armii v noch' s 27 na 28 i dnem 28 avgusta 1941 g." [Notes of a conversation between the commander of the forces of the Western Front and the commander of 19th Army's forces about the results of the army's combat operations on the night of 27 and 28 and during the day on 28 August 1941], *SDBVOV*, issue 41, 89.

14. Operational Summary No. 126 of the Headquarters of the Western Front at 2000 hours on 28 August 1941 about the Combat Operations of the *Front's* Forces

Operational Summary No. 126 at 2000 hours on 28 August 1941,
Headquarters. Western Front
1:500,000 and 100,000 scale maps

First. On the *front's* right wing, 22nd Army, while continuing to withdraw from encirclement, is in fierce fighting on the Petrovskoe, Skvortsovo Station, and Zhizhitsa Station line, while simultaneously preparing and occupying the Iamy, Man'kovo, Lepekhino, and Sidorovo intermediate line and the rear line – Podolino, Iashkino, Lake Zalikovskoe, and Staraia Toropa.

In the center, the forces are continuing the offensive, while overcoming stubborn enemy resistance, and on the *front's* left wing, the forces are fortifying the positions they occupy.

Second. 22nd Army. The army's forces, which have escaped from encirclement, are putting themselves in order and, while going over the defense along the Petrovskoe, Skvortsovo Station, and Zhizhitsa Station line with part of its forces, are fighting fiercely with numerically superior enemy forces.

The enemy's 57th Panzer Corps, consisting of 19th and 20th PzDs and 30th MotD, are trying to develop an offensive in the general direction of Toropets. At 1200 hours on 28 August, the movement of columns of motor-mechanized units were discovered at: a) head – Kostino, and rear – Levkovo; b) head – Skvortsovo Station, and rear – Pochinok; and c) head – Chukhni, and rear – Artemova.

214th and 112th RD are occupying a defense in positions from Petrovskoe to Davydovo, while protecting 48th TD's withdrawal to the Iamy (12 kilometers northeast of Petrovskoe), Hill 199.5, and Man'kovo line. The division's units are fighting intensely with an enemy panzer division.

126th RD is fighting with units of an enemy panzer division in the Skvortsovo Station region.

Antosenko's Detachment is fighting in the Timurniki and Lake Kodosno sector, while preparing the Lepekhino, Sidorovo, and Hill 197.6 line for defense, with the mission to protect Toropets from the south and southwest.

29th Army's student detachment is fighting with enemy motorized infantry at Zhizhitsa Station. News about the results of the army's combat operations in the second half of the day has not been received.

186th RD, having abandoned its defense positions in the vicinity of Skvortsovo Station at 1430 hours on 28 August, began a disorganized withdrawal toward the east and northeast. Measures are being taken to restore order in the division.

Third. 29th Army. The army's units (252nd RD), while continuing to defend in their previous positions along the right wing, withdrew under strong enemy artillery, machine gun, and mortar fire on the left wing and are fortifying [the following] lines:

246th RD – Trubniki, the northeastern slopes of Hill 199.4, and the eastern slopes of Hill 209.6.

243rd RD – (incl.) Hill 209.6, the woods southwest of Bodnevka, the woods 1 kilometer northeast of Nikolaevskie, and Ias'kovo.

The Composite Brigade (1st and 2nd MRRs) occupies its previous positions, while enveloping Katkovo from the north, northeast, and east and while protecting itself from the south with one battalion in the vicinity of Hill 175.4.

29th CR is fulfilling its previous missions.

Fourth. 30th Army. On the army's right wing, 629th RR (134th RD) and 918th RR (250th RD) are pursuing the enemy toward the southwest on the morning of 28 August, and the army's remaining units are continuing the conduct an offensive from the Staraia Morokhovo, Erkhovo, Sechenki, and Sekachi line since 1300 hours on 28 August.

As of 1700 hours, the army's units were fighting [as follows]:

134th RD – 629th RR, with 250th RD's 918th RR attached – are continuing to pursue the enemy toward the southwest, and the division's remaining regiments are in their previous positions.

Information about the positions of the units is being verified.

In the sector of movement of 134th RD's units, the enemy is extensively mining the roads.

242nd RD. The attack by the division's units had no success. The division is continuing to fight in previous positions.

250th RD. While continuing its attack, the division's units reached positions from the brushy area 400 meters south of Churkino to the northern slopes of Hill 229.6. The division is fighting to capture that hill.

162nd RD, while attacking with its right wing, reached the western slopes of Hill 228.9 an,d with its left wing – the separate house 1 kilometer southwest of Shanino. The division is continuing its attack toward Khomenki.

251st RD captured Bol'shoe Repino in fighting and reached positions from Hill 212.9 to the road junction southwest of Sekachi by 1500 hours, while continuing its attack toward Krechets and Gorodno.

107th TD. 143rd TR – is in the army commander's reserve in the Mikhailovshchina region, and the division's remaining regiments are operating together with 162nd and 251st RDs.

Losses for 28 August: killed and wounded – 453 men.

Trophies: for 27 and 28 August include 4 dug-in tanks, two burned tanks, 2 motorcycles, 15 boxes of shells, 2 mortars, 250 rifles, and 1 heavy and 3 light machine guns seized.

Fifth. 19th Army conducted combat operations, which did not produce essential results, with part of its forces overnight on 27-28 August. The army continued its offensive on the morning of 28 August, while concentrating its main efforts on capturing separate centers of resistance on the army's front.

The enemy on the army's right wing is employing antitank and anti-infantry mines extensively and is offering stubborn fire resistance in the center and on the right wing.

At 1700 hours on 27 August, the army's units were fighting [as follows]:

244th RD is concentrating its efforts on capturing Hill 240.1 and the eastern edge of the grove west of Shakhlovo.

166th RD is fighting to capture Hills 227.0 and 226.7, and the enemy is offering strong fire resistance.

91st RD captured Hill 225.1 and Stepanidina, while continuing to fight for the woods south of Ivaniki and the eastern outskirts of Semenkovo.

89th RD is conducting fire in its previous positions.

50th RD, while attacking toward Hill 211.6, captured part of the woods west of Muzhilova on its left wing.

64th RD and 101st TD are exchanging fire with the enemy in their previous positions.

45th CD. According to additional information from 19th Army's headquarters, it has been verified that the units of 45th CD's main forces were situated in the Panov region during the second half of the day on 28 August. Only reconnaissance units were situated in Staraia Kazarina (the information is being verified). From the Panov region, the division was trying to penetrate toward Berdino, but the division had no success because of the enemy's fire resistance and withdrew to its jumping-off positions, where it was situated all night.

While the division was entering the Panov region, its units chopped up 7 companies in the Morozova region and 4 companies of 14th IR [5th ID] at Panov.

At first light on 28 August, the division's units withdrew from the Panov region to the Zanino, Lopatchiki, and Volkovo region for a rest and to put themselves in order because of the units' fatigue.

The division's units have suffered losses in men and horses (the information is being verified).

Sixth. 16th Army. The positions of the army's units are unchanged. The enemy is inactive and conducting occasional artillery and mortar fire against the army's positions.

Seventh. 20th Army. The positions of the army's units were unchanged.

The army's units are fortifying the positions they occupy and preparing for a partial regrouping.

The enemy is displaying no activity in front of the army and is conducting methodical artillery fire against road junctions and the dispositions of our forces from the Pnevo and Dobromino regions and machine gun and mortar fire from the Dobrikova and Sopshino regions.

Our artillery destroyed 1 mortar, 2 heavy machine guns, and 4 transports [cart]. We suppressed several guns and mortars and one heavy machine gun. Up to a platoon of infantry in the region southwest of Pashkovo and up to a platoon of infantry on trucks in the Vishniaki region were dispersed.

An advance by small groups of enemy toward the crest of Hill 249.9 was repelled by fire.

Trophies [captured] by the army from 23-26 August include: 8 antitank guns, 7 mortars, 4 machine guns, 4 automatic weapons, 25 grenades, more than 200 artillery shells, 2 motorcycles, and other equipment.

Eighth. The *front's* reserve – 1st TD and 152nd RD – are in their previous positions.

Ninth. The VVS of the *front* operated against enemy airfields overnight on 27-28 August. Air operations on the morning of 28 August and during the first half of the day were limited because of poor weather conditions, except for separate flights to reconnoiter the weather.

Overall, a total of 30 aircraft sorties were carried out.

23rd AD operated against enemy airfields in Vitebsk, Kamenka, Rudnia, Zubovo, and Usviaty on the night of 27-28 August. The results of the bombing were not observed because of the cloudiness. Fires appeared at Zubovo airfield.

Of the 25 ships which flew off during the night to fulfill their missions, operational summaries complied up to this time indicate 11 ships returned to their airfields. 9 aircraft landed in various places on their own territory because of the unfavorable weather. There is no information about 5 planes, but measures are being taken to search for them.

31st AD bombed forces on the western bank of Lake Kodosno with one aircraft on the night of 27-28 August. Fires were observed as a result of the bombing.

The remaining aviation divisions did not carry out combat flights.

Our losses: 1 PE-2 aircraft did not return from fulfilling its mission.

During the second half of the day, the VVS of the *front* operated against a column of enemy motor-mechanized units on 22nd Army's front.

> The Chief of Staff of the Western Front, Lieutenant General Sokolovsky
> The Military Commissar of the Western Front's headquarters,
>   Brigade Commissar Kazbintsev
> For the Chief of the Operations Department, Colonel Belianko

Source: "Operativnaia svodka shtaba Zapadnogo fronta No. 126 k 20 chasam 28 avgusta 1941 g. o boevykh deistviiakh voisk fronta" [Operational summary no. 126 of the headquarters of the Western Front at 2000 hours on 28 August 1941 about the combat operations of the *front's* forces], *SBDVOV*, issue 41, 90-92.

15. Combat Order No. 051 of the Commander of the Forces of 30th Army of 28 August 1941 on a Continuation of the Offensive

Combat Order No. 051, Headquarters, 30th Army,
the woods 2 kilometers northeast of Podzaitsevo
2010 hours on 28 August 1941
1:50,000 scale map

1. The enemy is continuing to defend the Staroe Morokhovo, Novoe Morokhovo, Churkino, Shelepy, Hill 211.9, Hill 214.9, Hill 235.1, and Gorodno front stubbornly.

2. 30th Army will attack the enemy along the entire front on the morning of 29 August, with the aim to fulfill the mission assigned by the army's Order No. 047. The infantry attack – at 0900 hours after a five-minute artillery raid against enemy dispositions on order of the division commanders.

3. The commander of 107th TD will transfer one battalion of tanks, consisting of 30 machines and 1st Bn, 120th MRR, at the disposal of the commander of 251st RD, who will concentrate the attached tanks, with 1st Bn, 120th MRR, in the Karpova region.

4. The commander of 251st RD will employ the tanks for an attack toward Gorodno and Novoselki for seizing crossings over the Votra River on the Krechets and Frol'tsovo front.

5. My reserve – 2nd Bn, 120th MRR, which will concentrate in the Guliaevo region.

6. The grouping and missions of the artillery – as before.

9. The boundaries of the divisions – are unchanged.

The Commander of 30th Army, Lieutenant General Khomenko
The Member of the Military Council of 30th Army,
    Brigade Commissar Abramov
The Chief of Staff of 30th Army, Lieutenant Colonel Vinogradov

Source: "Boevoi prikaz komanduiushchego voiskami 30-i Armii No. 051 ot 28 avgusta 1941 g. na prodolzhenii nastupleniia" [Combat order no. 051 of the commander of the forces of 30th Army of 28 August 1941 on a continuation of the offensive], *SBDVOV*, issue 41, 290-291.

16. Combat Order No. 043 of the Commander of the Forces of 19th Army of 28 August 1941 on the Destruction of the Enemy Grouping between the Loinia and Tsarevich Rivers

Combat Order No. 043, CP, Commander, 19th Army,
the woods 1 kilometer east of Vasilisino
2125 hours on 28 August 1941
1:50,000 scale map

1. 5th and 28th IDs in full and units of 35th, 8th, and 14th IDs and 11th PzD are defending opposite the army's front. The forward edge of the defense is along the Pavlovshchina, Panov village, the woods west of Shakhlovo, the woods west of Novoselishche, and the Barsuki line, and further along the western bank of the Loinia River. His closest negligible reserves are in the Kislovo, Mashutino, and Mishino regions.

2. On the right, 30th Army is attacking southwestward from the Staroe Morokhovo, Shelepy, and Sekachi line. On the left, 16th Army is defending the Novosel'e (eastern) line and further along the Vop' River.

The boundaries with them are as before.

3. 19th Army will penetrate the enemy's defenses in the Shakhlovo, Ivaniki, Kazakova, and Myshkovo sectors [22-30 kilometers north of Iartsevo] at 1400 hours on 29 August 1941. It will encircle and destroy the enemy grouping between the

Loinia and Tsarevich Rivers by attacks along the Novoselishche, Krotovo, Myshkovo and Bolotino, and Mashutino axes; and, subsequently, develop the attack toward Dukhovshchina.

4. 244th RD, with 1st Bn, 399th HAR, while protecting the army's right flank in the sector between the Votra River and the wooded mass to the west of it, will penetrate the enemy's defenses in the Novaia Kazarina and Novoselishche sector [25-27 kilometers north of Iartsevo], by delivering the main attack toward Hill 229.4, Staraia Kazarina, and Pankratova [Ponkratova]. Capture the Kislovo and Pankratova line by day's end.

The boundary on the left is as before.

5. 166th RD, with 399th HAR (without 1st Bn), will penetrate the enemy's defenses in the (incl.) Novoselishche and road junction (0.5 kilometers south of Hill 227.0) [23-25 kilometers north of Iartsevo] sector. Deliver the main attack toward the southern outskirts of Krotovo and Myshkovo. Capture the (incl.) Pankratova and Myshkovo line by day's end.

The boundary on the left is as before.

6. 91st RD will attack toward Hill 225.1 and Hill 230.8 and capture the (incl.) Myshkovo and Shchelkina line [21-23 kilometers north of Iartsevo] by day's end.

The boundary on the left is as before.

7. 89th RD will attack toward Hill 220.3 and the southern slopes of Hill 229.8 [19-21 kilometers north of Iartsevo]. Capture the western edge of the woods west of Shchelkina by day's end.

The boundary on the left: (incl.) Makov'e, (incl.) Mishutino, and (incl.) Pavlova.

8. 50th RD, with 202nd TR, 4th Bn, 302nd HAR, and 1st Bn, 596th HAR, will penetrate the enemy's defenses in the Hill 214.0 and (incl.) Ivanovo sector [17-19 kilometers north of Iartsevo]. Deliver the main attack toward Hill 216.1 and Kalugino. Capture the line of the Tun'ka River by day's end.

The boundary on the left: (incl.) Neelova, Miagshevo, (incl.) Ivanovo, Hill 221.8, the House of invalids, and (incl.) Butsevo.

9. 64th RD, with 2nd and 3rd Bns, 596th HAR, will penetrate the enemy's defenses in the sector from Shishkino to the northern edge of the woods 0.5 kilometers east of Turishchevo [15-17 kilometers north of Iartsevo]. Deliver the main attack toward Hill 218.5 and Sushchevo. Capture the Sushchevo region and crossings over the Tsarevich River in the House of Invalids and Sushchevo sector and prevent an enemy withdrawal behind the Tsarevich River.

The boundary on the left: (incl.) Kolkovichi, and further along the Tsarevich River to Hill 213.4 and Kulagino.

10. 101st TD will defend the Petrova, Osipova, Skachkovo, and Chistaia line [7-15 kilometers north of Iartsevo], while protecting the army's left flank and the boundary with 16th Army.

11. Reserve: 613th RR – in the Kastalanova region; and 390th RR – Hill 219.4 and Sel'kovo.

12. Artillery. Readiness by 0600 hours. Artillery preparation from 1330 to 1400 hours [missions missing].

13. VVS [missing].

14. CP and the headquarters of the army – as before.

15. Operational and reconnaissance summaries – as before.

> The Commander of 19th Army, Lieutenant General Konev
> The Member of the Military Council of 19th Army,
> Division Commissar Sheklanov
> The Chief of Staff of 19th Army, [Malyshkin]

Source: "Boevoi prikaz komanduiushchego voiskami 19-i Armii No. 043 ot 28 avgusta 1941 g. na unichtozhenie gruppirovki protivnika mezhdu rekami Loinia i Tsarevich" [Combat order no. 043 of the commander of the forces of 19th Army of 28 August 1941 on the destruction of the enemy grouping between the Loinia and Tsarevich Rivers], *SBDVOV*, issue 41, 189.

17. Order No. 05/op of the Commander of the Forces of the Western Front of 28 August 1941 on Preparation for an Offensive to Capture the City of Smolensk

Order No. 05/op to the Forces of the Western Front,
2330 hours on 28 August 1941
1:500,000 scale map

1. The enemy, while continuing an offensive along the Velikie Luki axis with the forces of up to 10 divisions (including 2 panzer), is stubbornly defending along the remaining sectors of the front, while conducting persistent counterattacks with the aim of halting the offensive by the *front's* armies.

2. On the right, the Northwestern Front has the mission to contain the enemy along the Lovat' River with an active defense.

The boundary with it: Likhoslavl', Lake Seliger, and Nasva Station, all points inclusive for the Western Front.

On the left, the Reserve Front will go over to an offensive on the morning of 30 August, liquidate the enemy's El'nia grouping, deliver a blow with 24th Army toward Pochinok and 43rd Army toward Roslavl', and reach the Dolgie Nivy and Khislovichi front by 8 September.

The boundary with it: Klemiatino Station, Riabtsevo Station, and Krasnyi, all points inclusive for the Western Front.

3. The Western Front's armies will go over to a decisive offensive on 1 September, with the missions to smash the opposing enemy and reach the Lake Velinskoe, Pukhnovo, Baranovo, Velizh, Demidov, Gnezdovo, and Chervonnoe front by day's end on 8 September, while defending actively along the Velikie Luki axis, to which end, I order:

a) 22nd Army will organize a defense in forward positions from Kniazhovo to Lake Zhizhitskoe. Conduct reconnaissance and reinforced operations toward the west with forward detachments. The army's main defensive line is Volok, Toropets, and Staraia Toropa.

Bring the army to combat readiness by 5 September and prepare for an offensive in the direction of Velikie Luki.

The boundary on the left: Vysokoe, Staraia Toropa, and Lake Velinskoe, all points inclusive for 22nd Army.

b) 29th Army – 252nd, 246th, and 243rd RDs and the Special Brigade [NKVD] – go over to the defense along the Western Dvina River, having the forward units in the positions they occupy. Transfer one RD and motorized brigade to the Staraia Toropa region, with the missions to prevent the enemy from spreading out toward Toropets. Prepare an offensive toward Il'ino and Velizh by 5 September.

The boundary on the left: Rzhev, Zharkovskii Station, and Velizh, all points inclusive for 29th Army.

c) Cavalry Group Dovator – 50th and 53rd CDs – continue to fulfill your assigned missions – reach into the rear of the enemy which are operating against 30th Army and, in cooperation with 30th Army, destroy the enemy. Subsequently, plan on operating toward Velizh.

d) 30th Army – 250th, 242nd, 251st, 162nd, and 134th RDs and 107th TD, with present reinforcements – will continue the offensive.

Carry out a necessary regrouping and prepare for a general offensive on 30 and 31 August. Go over to a decisive offensive on 1 September and, while delivering the main attack toward Demidov, smash the opposing enemy and reach the Evseevka and Kudriavtsevo line by 6 September and reach the Velizh and Demidov line exclusively by day's end on 8 September.

The boundary on the left: Igor'evskaia Station, Karpova, Beresnevo, and Demidov, all points inclusive for 30th Army.

e) 19th Army – 244th, 166th, 91st, 89th, 50th, and 64th RDs, 101st TD, 45th CD, and present reinforcements – will continue the offensive. Conduct the necessary regrouping and prepare for a general offensive on 30-31 August.

Go over to a decisive offensive on 1 September, with the missions to smash the enemy's Dukhovshchina grouping. Reach the Efremova and Kolotovina line by 6 September and the Demidov and Vydra line exclusively by day's end on 8 September.

Constantly keep at least one RD in the army's reserve.

The boundary on the left: Komiagino, Samuilova, Kolotovina, and Vydra, all points inclusive for 19th Army.

f) 16th Army – 152nd, 38th, and 108th RDs and 1st and 18th TDs, with present reinforcements – while conducting a necessary regrouping on 30 and 31 August, will go over to a decisive offensive on 1 September and smash the enemy's Iartsevo grouping. Deliver the main attack with the right wing and commit the mobile tank group into the penetration on the army's right wing. Seize Smolensk by enveloping it from the north and west, and do not get involved in a frontal battle for Smolensk. Reach the Vydra and Gnezdovo line exclusively with the main forces by day's end on 8 September.

The boundary on the left: inclusively Viaz'ma, (incl.) Dorogobuzh, and the Solov'evo crossing for 16th Army.

g) 20th Army – 144th, 73rd, 229th, 153rd, 161st, and 129th RDs, with present reinforcements – will continue a stubborn defense on the army's left wing. Create a grouping in the army's center and prepare for an offensive on 30 and 31 August.

Go over to a decisive offensive on 1 September and, while enveloping Smolensk from the south with the main forces, reach the (incl.) Gnezdovo, Bobyri, and Riabtsevo Station line by day's end on 8 September.

h) The *front's* Chief of Engineers will provide crossing means (parks) to 20th and 16th Armies by 30 August.

i) The commander of the VVS of the *front* will attach the aviation divisions for cooperation with the armies. Work out cooperation with aviation, in particular, with the commander of 16th Army and with the mobile group – 1st and 18th TDs.

4. At all cost, conduct well-organized and systematic reconnaissance at all force levels during the course of the entire operation to prevent the forces from being surprised. Pay special attention to constant and careful reconnaissance along open flanks.

5. It is obligatory to fortify [dig in] all positions and points seized from the enemy, while demanding the forces immediately erect defensive works.

6. The operations of infantry, artillery, aircraft, and tanks must be well integrated amongst themselves and studied in advance by the command cadre. It is obligatory to envision and accompany the operations of infantry and tanks with aircraft.

7. Prepare the operation with utmost secrecy and do not permit telephone conversations and messages, while assigning missions to those persons and units fulfilling them orally and in person.

8. Confirm receipt.

> The Commander-in-Chief of the Western Front,
>   Marshal of the Soviet Union Timoshenko
> The Member of the Military Council of the *front*, [signed]
> The Chief of Staff of the *front*, Lieutenant General Sokolovsky

Source: "Prikaz komanduiushchego voiskami Zapadnogo fronta No. 05/op ot 28 avgusta 1941 g. na podgotovku nastupleniia s tsel'iu ovladniia gor. Smolensk" [Order no. 05/op of the commander of the forces of the Western Front of 28 August 1941 on the preparation for an offensive with the aim of capturing the city of Smolensk], *SBDVOV*, issue 41, 93-95.

18. Operational Summary No. 128 of the Headquarters of the Western Front at 2000 hours on 29 August 1941 about the Combat Operations of the *Front's* Forces

Operational Summary No. 128 at 2000 hours on 29 August 1941,
Headquarters. Western Front
1:500,000 and 100,000 scale maps

First. On the *front's* right wing on 29 August, 22nd Army's units, which withdrew from encirclement, are fighting fiercely with enemy tanks and motorized infantry in rear defensive positions from Podolino to Iashkino, Lake Zalikovskoe, and Staraia Toropa.

In the center, the forces are continuing the offensive, while destroying the enemy, which are stubbornly defending strong points.

On the *front's* left wing, the forces are fortifying the positions they occupy while conducting a regrouping.

Second. 22nd Army, while continuing to put itself in order and while occupying a defense in positions from Podolina to Nishevitsy, Lake Zalikovskoe, and Novaia Derevnia, are fighting fiercely with enemy tanks and motorized infantry in separate sectors with part of their forces.

The enemy's main efforts are being directed toward Toropets and northeast of Toropets.

At 1140 hours on 29 August, aircraft detected movement of a column of enemy tanks and vehicles, with its head at Nazimovo and its rear at Kun'ia Station.

At 1300 hours [we detected] movement of a column of up to 300 vehicles, protected by fighters, with its head at Selishche and its rear at Lake Kodosno.

48th TD's and 214th RD's units, which remained in intermediate positions, are conducting sustained fighting with the enemy along the Podroshcha and Man'kovo front.

Positions from Podolina to Iashkino are being defended by units of 709th and 199th ARs, 174th and 186th RDs, and 38th MRBn. Information about the positions in this sector has not been received.

Positions from Iashkino to Lake Zalikovskoe are being defended by126th RD's units.

A group of enemy tanks and motorized infantry penetrated toward Iakshino and Fad'kova at 1000 hours on 29 August. The further movement of the enemy tanks is being hindered by minefields. Measures are being taken to liquidate the penetration.

Since 1200 hours, 186th and 126th RDs' units, together with a detachment of people's militia from Toropets, are fighting stubbornly with enemy on the northwestern, northern, and western outskirts of the town. Street fighting is underway with sub-machine-gunners in the center of the city.

Positions from Shatry to Novaia Derevnia are being defended by 186th RD's units and two ARs.

Antosenko's composite detachment occupied defenses in positions from Ol'khovka to Sidorovo and Mit'kovo.

At 1700 hours, Antosenko's detachment was fighting stubbornly with enemy motorized infantry trying to envelop Ol'khovka from the south.

The enemy attack has been repelled by the detachment's counterattacks, and the front is being held.

29th Army's student detachment is successfully holding on to Zhizhitsa Station.

Information has not been received about the combat operations of the remaining units.

Third. 29th Army is continuing to defend previous positions on its right wing (252nd RD) and carrying out a regrouping in accordance with the commander-in-chief's order with its remaining units.

A reinforced rifle battalion from 252nd RD is holding off an enemy force of more than a battalion, which has penetrated from the Kochegarovo region, in positions from Malye Napolki to Sokhi and Liagushka.

246th RD concentrated one and one half regiments in the Piatiusova region by 1630 hours and repulsed an enemy attack toward Baevo with its remaining forces at 1425 hours.

243rd RD is holding on to the Trubniki and Krysy line with one reinforced RR and occupied defenses in the Belianki and Zui sector along the northern bank of the Western Dvina River with its remaining forces.

The Composite Brigade (1st and 2nd MRRs NKVD) is defending the (incl.) Krysy and Elaga line with one battalion and moving to the Rodino, Shestakovo, and Zaluzh'e region with its remaining units

29th CR – is in its previous region.

Fourth. Cavalry Group Dovator. No new information has been received.

Fifth. 30th Army. The army's units resumed their pursuit of the enemy on the right wing and went over to an offensive from the Novoe Morokhovo, Ivkino, and Sekachi line at 0900 hours on 29 August, while concentrating its efforts on its right wing toward Gorodno and Novoselki.

The enemy on the army's right wing withdrew toward the southwest, while protected by small groups of infantry and while mining the roads and passages through the forests, and offered strong fire resistance along the remainder of the army's front.

134th RD. According to the army's headquarters (requires verification), the division's FD [forward detachment] reached the Lomonosovo Station region, where it determined that there were no enemy or units from Group Dovator in the vicinity of Lomonosovo Station.

918th RR's (attached to 134th RD) FD made contact with enemy covering units in the Zyki region at 1000 hours. After a short fight, the enemy withdrew into the woods southwest of Zyki.

A reconnaissance group of 629th RR consisting of two rifle platoons, which is being sent to establish contact with Group Dovator, left from the Frolova region toward Boiarshchina at 1000 hours on 29 August.

Information has not been received about the positions of 629th RR (134th RD) and 918th RR, which are pursuing the enemy. 30th Army's headquarters has no communications with them.

134th RD's remaining 2 regiments are continuing to rest and refit, one in the Los'mino, Demekhi, and Petrushina region, and the second – in the Belyi region.

242nd, 250th, and 162nd RDs, while going over to the attack, encountered strong enemy fire, mined sectors of terrain, and, in some sectors, barbed wire obstacles. The units' attacks had no success.

251st RD, while encountering heavy enemy fire, reached positions in the western edge of the grove 500 meters east of Hill 214.9, captured Hill 235.1 and the groves southwest of Gorodno, and is fighting to capture Gorodno at 1430 hours.

107th TD (without 237th MRR, 143rd TR, and 119th AR) – is in the army commander's reserve in the Mikhailovshchina region.

Losses of the army's units for 28 August: killed and wounded – 220 men.

Trophies for 29 August (according to incomplete data) – 4 AT guns, 6 heavy and 5 light machine guns, and 10 boxes of 37mm shells seized.

Sixth. 19th Army, while carrying out a partial regrouping and defending on its flanks, went over to an offensive from the Shakhlovo, Stepanidina, and Osipova line at 1400 hours on 29 August.

The enemy on the army's front went over to an organized defense, while offering stubborn resistance to the attacking forces.

244th RD, while protecting the army's right flank in the sector between the Votria River and the forested mass west of Priglovo, went over to the attack from the Shakhlovo and Novoselishche line, while meeting with organized fire from the defending enemy's 56th IR [5th ID]

166th RD, while conducting a regrouping of its units, went over to the attack from the (incl.) Novoselishche and (incl.) Ivaniki line, while meeting organized fire from the enemy's defending 14th IR [5th ID] and mined sectors of terrain.

The division's attack is developing successfully.

91st RD is conducting an attack along the (incl.) Ivaniki and Stepanidina front, while overcoming minefields and clearing the woods south of Ivaniki of small groups of enemy.

89th RD went over to the attack from positions on Hill 220.3 against the enemy's defending 173rd IR [87th ID].

The division's attack is developing successfully. During the initial hour of fighting, the division captured several enemy defensive firing points with both of its wings.

50th RD, reinforced by 202nd TR and two battalions of howitzer artillery, went over to the attack from the Kazakova and Muzhilova line.

64th RD went over to the attack from positions from the western edge of the woods 1 kilometer east of the Zaitsevo State Farm to Popova and Osipova, while concentrating its efforts on its left wing.

101st TD, while carrying out a regrouping of its units to support the army's left wing, went over to a defense in positions from (incl.) Osipova to the church in Skachkovo, and Hill 200.

45th CD has been concentrating in the woods west of Zaovrazh'e and Lopatchiki since 1900 hours on 28 August. The division's losses in the fighting from 27 through 28 August: killed and wounded – up to 200 men and 150 horses.

Trophies of the army's units for 28 August: 45 rifles, 1 heavy machine gun, 5 light machine guns, 3 large caliber machine guns, 8 automatic weapons, 9 pistols, 3 mortars, 3 radio stations, and 20 bicycles.

Seventh. 16th Army. The positions of the army's units are unchanged.

The enemy is displaying no activity, and no new units have been identified on the army's front.

Eighth. 20th Army is continuing to dig in along the Dnepr River line, while completing a regrouping in the center and on the left wing.

144th and 73rd RDs are defending in their previous positions, with scattered artillery and mortar fire along the front.

229th RD, with 435th RR, is defending the front from the northern edge of the grove 1 kilometer northeast of Suborovka to the eastern slopes of Hill 249.9, Hill 205.9, the woods north of Chuvakhi, and (incl.) Hill 224.8. There is occasional mortar firing along the front.

153rd RD (without 435th RR) was concentrating in the vicinity of the grove north of Naidenova, the grove south of Samoilovo, and the woods 2 kilometers east of Samoilovo by 1000 hours on 29 August.

161st RD is fortifying its present positions in readiness to relieve 229th RD's units on the night of 29-30 August and move into the Romodanovo and Iurkino region.

There is occasional firing on the division's front.

129th RD is defending the front from Hill 224.8 to the woods 1 kilometer northeast of Klemiatino, and further along the Ustrom River to the mouth of the Trubel'nia River.

343rd RR concentrated in the Rubezhok and Slobodka region.

There is mortar fire on the division's front.

On the night of 28-29 August, 1 tractor, 1 T-26 tank, and 5 trucks were withdrawn from the western bank of the Dnepr River.

Ninth. The *front's* reserve – 1st TD and 152nd RD – are in their previous positions.

Ninth. The main efforts of the *front's* VVS were directed at detecting and destroying enemy forces along the Toropets axis and assisting the advance of 19th Army's units.

Air operations were limited because of unfavorable weather conditions. Overall, a total of 77 aircraft sorties were carried out.

46th AD conducted reconnaissance along the Toropets-Nazimova, Toropets-Kun'ia, and Toropets-Lake Kodosno axes.

47th AD conducted reconnaissance and destroyed the enemy in the Zhizhitsa Station, Kun'ia Station, Lake Kodosno, and Nazimova Station regions.

As a result of the raids by assault aircraft, up to 10 tanks and 4 vehicles were destroyed, the fires of two field batteries were suppressed, and the enemy suffered personnel losses.

31st AD conducted reconnaissance and destroyed enemy units in the Nazimova, Kun'ia Station, and Velikie Luki regions.

43rd AD operated on 19th Army's front – and bombed enemy artillery positions and concentrations of enemy tanks in the Berdino, Verkhov'e, Zamiatino, Sirotinka, and Shishkino region. Direct hits were noted on targets.

23rd AD and 38th RAS did not conduct combat flights.

> The Chief of Staff of the Western Front, Lieutenant General Sokolovsky
> The Military Commissar of the Western Front's headquarters,
>   Brigade Commissar Kazbintsev
> For the Chief of the Operations Department, Colonel Belianko

Source: "Operativnaia svodka shtaba Zapadnogo fronta No. 128 k 20 chasam 29 avgusta 1941 g. o boevykh deistviiakh voisk fronta" [Operational summary no. 128 of the headquarters of the Western Front at 2000 hours on 29 August 1941 about the combat operations of the *front's* forces], *SBDVOV*, issue 41, 95-99.

19. Combat Order No. 052 of the Commander of the Forces of 30th Army of 29 August 1941 on a Regrouping of the Army's Forces

Combat Order No. 052, Headquarters, 30th Army,

the woods 2 kilometers northeast of Podzaitsevo
2300 hours on 29 August 1941
1:50,000 scale map

1. The army will continue the offensive and simultaneously carry out a regrouping of forces.

2. 134th RD, while firmly holding on to the sector it previously occupied and while protecting the army's right flank, will have forward detachments along the [following] lines:

    a) Ust'e, Bol'shoe Kozlovo, and Borisovo;

    b) Solov'evo, Chichata, and Maksimovka;

    c) In the Mezha region; and

    d) Los'mino, Chernyi Ruchei, and Demekhi.

918th RR will reach the Soshno, P. Arzhavets, Amshara, and Zamosh'e line.

The divisions' main forces will deploy along the Feliukino, El'cheno, Hill 209.0, Cherepy, Karelovo, Baturino, Ladyzheno, Perevozino, and Struevo line.

Relieve 242nd RD's units on the Demekhi and Novoe Morokhovo line.

The boundary on the left: (incl.) Baturino, (incl.) Esinaia, Novoe Morokhovo, and Krivets.

3. The commander of 242nd RD will relieve 250th RD's units in the Hill 215.2 and Shelepy sector, with the immediate missions to capture Churkino, Kostino, and Hill 229.6.

The boundary on the left: (incl.) Dolgoe, Shelepy, and (incl.) Ekhanovo.

4. 162nd RD will capture Hill 230.3, Ploskoe, and Ivkino.

The boundary on the left is as before

5. 251st RD will capture Krechets and Novoselki and protect the army's left flank.

6. 250th RD, without 918th RR, after its relief, will concentrate in the Sukharevo, Vorob'ikha, and Ponomari region.

7. 107th TD will concentrate in the woods east of Novo-Vysokoe Farm by 0800 hours on 30 August 1941.

8. 2nd Bn, 542nd CAR, will occupy a strong point in the Dolgoe, Guliaevo, and Staroe Selo region on the night of 3031 August 1941 and become subordinate to the commander of 542nd CAR.

9. 107th TD's artillery will remain in the old strong point and support 162nd RD.

Report fulfillment in writing. Complete the regrouping by 2400 hours on 30 August 1941.

The Commander of 30th Army, Lieutenant General Khomenko
The Member of the Military Council, Brigade Commissar Abramov
The Chief of Staff of 30th Army, Lieutenant Colonel Vinogradov

Source: "Boevoi prikaz komanduiushchego voiskami 30-i Armii No. 052 ot 29 avgusta 1941 g. na peregruppirovku voisk armii" [Combat order no. 052 of the commander of the forces of 30th Army of 29 August 1941 on a regrouping of the army's forces], *SBDVOV*, issue 41, 291.

20. Combat Order No. 2/op of the Commander of 16th Army of 30 August 1941 on the Destruction of the Enemy's Iartsevo Grouping

Combat Order No. 2/op,
Headquarters, 16th Army,
the woods 1 kilometer northeast of Khotenova
1:100,000 and 50,000 scale maps
1800 hours on 30 August 1941

1. The enemy's reinforced 28th ID is defending along the western bank of the Vop' River, with its forward edge on the Kokhanovo, Novosel'e (eastern), Iartsevo Station, Zubovo, Svishchevo, and Makeevo line. On the forward edge, there are 1 to 3 coils of barbed wire and bunkers in the Khatyni, Pologi, and Bol'shie and Malye Gorki regions. Reserves: in the Samuilova, Semukhina, and Soprykina region, in the woods west of Toropa; and in the Berezuevo, Isakovo, Eiskova and Tresviat'e, Barsuki, and Likhovskoe region.

2. On the right, 19th Army is attacking in the general direction of Dukhovshchina, Samuilova, and (incl.) Kolotovina.

On the left, 20th Army is attacking in the general direction of Dukhovskaia.

The boundary with it: (incl.) Dorogobuzh, Slobodishche, Zadnia, and Kamenka.

3. 16th Army, while holding onto the Iartsevo and Buianovo sector on the eastern bank of the Vop' River with one RR of 38th RD and 108th RD's units, will go over to an offensive with its remaining forces at 0700 hours on 1 September 1941, with the immediate missions to destroy the enemy's Iartsevo group of forces and reach the Mal'tsova, Soprykino, and Pologi front, and subsequently develop the attack toward Stepanovo and Nikola-Edrevichi, while protecting its right flank against an enemy counterattack from Dukhovshchina.

4. 1st TD, with 311th HAR and 587th CAR, will attack the enemy in the (incl.) Chistaia and (incl.) Novosel'e (eastern) sector, with the immediate missions to reach the eastern bank of the unnamed stream (3 kilometers west of Novosel'e (western), and capture the (incl.) Mal'tsova and heights without a marker (0.5 kilometers west of Semukhina) line.

The boundary line on the left: Gridina, (incl.) Novosel'e (eastern), (incl.) Soprykina, and Nikola-Edrevichi.

5. 152nd RD, with 214th AR and 1st and 3rd Bns, 471st GAR, will attack the enemy in the Novosel'e (eastern) and (incl.) Khatyni sector, with the immediate missions to capture the Kudinova, (incl.) Panina, and Khatyni line and reach the southwest outskirts of Soprykina and Hill 234.9 front by day's end on 1 September.

The boundary line on the left: Vyshegor Station, the church in Staroe Suetovo, Sviatets, (incl.) Lake Khatyni, (incl.) Panina, (incl.) Gorodok, and (incl.) Zalesova.

6. 38th RD (without 214th AR), with 2nd Bn, 49th CAR, while holding the eastern bank of the Vop' River in the sector from Iartsevo to the southern edge of the woods 3.5 kilometers south of Iartsevo with one regiment, will attack the enemy in the Lake Khatyni and (incl.) Iartsevo Station sector with its remaining forces, with the immediate missions to capture the Panina, Pervomaiskii village, and Iartsevo region, and, subsequently, by attacking with the division's entire force, to reach the

sector from the (incl.) southeastern slopes of Hill 234.9 to Pologi and the fork in the road 3 kilometers southeast of Pologi by day's end on 1 September 1941.

The boundary line on the left: (incl.) Khotenova, Dar'ino, Shchikino, the southern edge of the woods 3.5 kilometers south of Iartsevo, Zubovo, and Kornilova.

7. 108th RD, with 1st Battalion, 49th CAR, while protecting its left flank and firmly holding onto the sector it occupies from the Lumber Mill, 3.5 kilometers southwest of Starozavop'e, to Buianovo along the eastern bank of the Vop' River, will be prepared to go over to the attack toward Svishchevo and Podroshch'e on the morning of 2 September 1941.

8. 127th Tank Brigade – my reserve.

Jumping-off position – the eastern edge of the woods west of Manchina and Kozhukhova – by 0500 hours on 1 September 1941.

When 1st TD's and 152nd RD's infantry reach the Samuilova and Kudinova line, begin crossing the Vop' River in the sector from the mouth of the Tsarevich River to Dubrovo and reach the assembly area – the forest west of Kholm and southwest of Novosel'e (western).

9. Artillery. Be in readiness – by 2000 hours on 31 August 1941.

Artillery preparation – 30 minutes.

Missions:

    a) Suppress enemy AT guns and strong points along the forward edge;

    b) Prevent enemy flanking fire and counterattacks from the direction of Kokhanovo, Krovopuskovo, and Ivashenka;

    c) Prepare concentrated fires by four battalions against the southeast edge of the woods southwest of Kokhanovo and of three battalions – against the exits from the woods southeast of Krovopuskovo, and of three battalions against the exits from the woods southwest of Krovopuskovo; and

    d) Re-subordinate 214th AR to the commander of 38th RD when the infantry reaches the Samuilova, Kudinova, and Panina line.

    e) The ADD [long-range action] group – 2nd Bn, 471st GAR RGK, and 3rd Bn, 49th CAR; and the commander – the CO of 471st GAR.

Missions: suppress enemy artillery and reserves in the [following] regions: Samuilova, Soprykina, the depression northwest of Pervomaiskii village, and Pologi, and prevent the approach of enemy reserves from the direction of Krovopuskovo and Stogovo.

10. The chief of the army's Engineer Department will support the construction of crossings from on-hand materials for the crossing of medium and heavy tanks over the Vop' River in the sector from the mouth of the Tsarevich to incl.) Dubrovo with the forces and equipment of 243rd and 169th Sep. Sapper Bns, and, after the units cross, rather than taking the bridges down, instead maintain them for communications with the rear and provide security [for them] in accordance with the instructions of the army's chief of staff.

11. Supply station – Dorogobuzh Station. Transport – in accordance with the orders of division and separate units commanders.

12. CP – the woods 1 kilometer northeast of Khotenova. The VPU (auxiliary command post) from 2100 hours on 31 August 1941 – the woods 0.5 kilometers

north of Vyshegor. The subsequent axis of movement of the VPU – along the Moscow-Minsk road.

Attachment: Planning table for 16th Army's combat on 1 September 1941.

The Commander of 16th Army, Major General Rokossovsky
The Member of the Military Council of the army,
    Divisional Commissar Lobachev
The Chief of Staff of 16th Army, Colonel Malinin

Source: "Boevoi prikaz komanduiushchego voiskami 16-i Armii No. 2/op ot 30 avgusta 1941 g. na unichtozhenie Iartsevskoi gruppirovki protivnika" [Combat order no. 2/op of the commander of 16th Army of 30 August 1941 on the destruction of the enemy's Iartsevo grouping], *SBDVOV*, issue 41, 138-139.

21. Combat Order No. 060 of the Commander of the Forces of 20th Army of 30 August 1941 on an Offensive Toward Zapol'e

Combat Order No. 060, Headquarters, 20th Army,
Late on 30 August 1941
1:50,000 scale map

1. The enemy, relying on prepared centers of resistance at Pnevo, Mit'kovo, and Titkovo, is defending on the high ground at Pnevo, Mit'kovo, Liakhovo, and Dubrova and in the woods south of Golovino and Malinovka, with reserves in the Kardymova region. 263rd ID is defending along the Sopshino, Suborovka, Klemiatino, and Iakovlevichi line.

2. On the right, 16th Army will go over to an offensive on the morning of 1 September, with the main attack on its right wing.

The boundary line with it is as before.

On the left, 107th RD is developing an attack toward Sadki and Malaia Nezhoda.

The boundary line with it: Klemiatino and Riabtsevo Station.

3. 20th Army, while firmly defending on its left wing, will go over to an offensive in the general direction of Zapol'e at 1000 hours on 1 September, with the missions to smash the opposing enemy and reach the Khmost' River.

4. 144th RD, with 1st Bn, 592nd GAR, while attacking toward Skrushevo and Pnevo with one regiment, with the mission of seizing them, will attack the enemy in Mit'kovo and Liakhovo with its remaining forces at 1000 hours on 1 September and capture the Mashkino and Fedurno line by day's end, while protecting the army shock group's right flank.

The boundary on the left: (all points inclusive) Klimova, Osovo, Logunovo, Morevo, and Pochinok.

CP   the farm 1.5 kilometers northwest of Osovo.

5. 153rd RD, with 302nd HAR and two batteries of 872nd ATR, having relieved 144th RD's units on the night of 30-31 August, will attack the enemy on the heights west of Ratchino from jumping-off positions – on the heights west of Logunovo and Ratchino, at 1000 hours on 1 September and capture Morevo and dig in by day's end. Subsequently, plan to attack toward Pochinok.

The boundary on the left: Ryzhii Ugol', Platavets Station, the barn (1 kilometer south of Zabor'e), Ratchino, Babeevo, (incl.) Ryzhkovo, and Hill 186.6.

CP – the woods 0.5 kilometers northwest of Zabor'e.

6. 161st RD, with 2nd Bn, 592nd GAR, and one battery of 872nd ATR, will relieve 73rd RD units in the sector from Pashkovo to southeastern edge of the woods south of Pashkovo sector on the night of 30-31 August. Attack the enemy at 1000 hours on 1 September from positions on the western bank of the Dnepr River, while delivering the attack from the right wing, and occupy and fortify Morevo State Farm and Titkovo by day's end. Subsequently, plan to attack toward Zaovrazh'e.

The boundary on the left: Kucherovo, the road intersection 3 kilometers south of Zabor'e, Titkovo, and Remenishche.

CP – the woods west of the Mertvaia River.

7. 73rd RD, after seizing Malinovka and Sopshino with one regiment, attack the enemy with the remaining forces from the bridgehead you occupy on the western bank of the Dnepr River at 1000 hours on 1 September, and, having destroyed him, occupy the western and southern edges of the woods south of Titkovo by day's end. Two battalions of artillery from 129th RD will provide support.

The boundary on the left is as before. Share the road from Kucherovo to Balakirevo with 161st RD. The commander of 73rd RD is entrusted with responsibility for order and security.

CP – the woods in the vicinity of Marker 179.1.

8. 229th RD, with two batteries of 872nd ATR and 127th Sapper Bn, will continue to defend the Suborovka, Hill 249.9, Chuvakhi, and Hill 224.8 line and will capture the southern slopes of Hill 249.9, the woods northwest of Vishniaki, and Hill 221.3 successively by brief attacks.

The boundary lines and CP are as before.

9. 129th RD, with 129th Light Eng. Bn, will continue to defend the Ustrom River from Klemiatino to Mar'ino. Support 73rd RD's attack with two battalions of artillery from the Kucherovo region.

Have a reserve of at least one and one half regiments in the Mileevo and Vasiuki region in readiness to deliver a counterattack toward the southwest and southeast.

The boundary lines and CP are as before.

10. Artillery.

Missions:

a) Suppress enemy artillery in the Skrushevo, Pnevo, Mit'kovo, Morevo, Ryzhkovo, and Remenishche regions;

b) Suppress firing systems and centers of resistance in Mit'kovo, Liakhovo, the heights west of Logunovo, the woods south of Golovino, Mashkino, Morevo, and Fedurno; and

c) Prevent counterattacks from the Pnevo, Mit'kovo, Logunovo, Babeevo, Dubrova, and Ratchino axes and from the woods east of Titkovo and Pashkovo. Group DD – 126th CAR.

Duration of the artillery preparation – 40 minutes. Expenditure of ammunition for the entire day of combat – 1 combat load.

11. The chief of the army's Engineer Forces will construct two bridges each in the sectors of 144th, 153rd, 161st, and 73rd RDs by 0300 hours on 1 September, while ensuring their continuous operations.

12. The Chief of the Air Defense (PVO) Department will protect the crossing from the air from 0300 hours on 1 September.

13. CP – in previous locations. OP from 0800 hours on 1 September – Osovo.

14. I demand: it is obligatory to fortify all positions and points seized from the enemy by means of the immediate erection of defensive works and the organization of systems for machine-gun and artillery fire.

Coordinate the actions of infantry and artillery with one another, having verified matters of coordination on the terrain. Each jump forward by the infantry must be supported by the actions of artillery.

For the de-mining of minefields, sapper with mine detectors will push forward in front of the infantry.

> The Commander of 20th Army, Lieutenant General Lukin
> The Member of the Military Council, Corps Commissar Semenovsky
> The Chief of Staff of 20th Army, Major General Korneev

Source: "Boevoi prikaz komanduiushchego voiskami 20-i Armii No. 060 ot 30 avgusta 1941 g. na nastuplenie v napravlenii Zapol'e" [Combat order no. 060 of the commander of the forces of 20th Army of 30 August 1941 on an offensive toward Zapol'e], *SBDVOV*, issue 41, 222-224.

22. Operational Summary No. 130 of the Headquarters of the Western Front at 2000 hours on 30 August 1941 about the Combat Operations of the *Front's* Forces

Operational Summary No. 130 at 2000 hours on 30 August 1941,
Headquarters. Western Front
1:500,000 and 100,000 scale maps

First. On the *front's* right wing, 22nd Army abandoned Toropets under the onslaught of a numerically superior enemy forces and conducted sustained fighting along the Lake Iassy, Ponizov'ia, and Lake Griadetskoe line all day on 30 August.

In the center, the forces are continuing the offensive, while meeting stubborn enemy resistance.

On the *front's* left wing, the forces are conducting a regrouping and fortifying the positions they have reached.

Second. 22nd Army. The army's units conducted stubborn fighting for possession of Toropets with enemy tanks and motorized infantry along the entire front.

After fierce fighting, which led to hand-to-hand fights in the streets, the enemy captured Toropets by day's end on 29 August and, on 30 August, is developing the offensive toward Lake Griadetskoe (the high road from Toropets toward Nelidovo).

Aircraft established the movement of motor-columns with tanks: a) along the Toropets-Nelidovo high road at 1330 hours on 30 August, with its head – at Lokhovka and its rear – at Toropets; and b) at 1630 hours, with its head – at Selishche and its rear – at Lake Kodosno.

48th TD, with the remnants of 214th RD, while preparing a defensive line along the Zaprud'e and Gavrilovskoe front (10 and 4 kilometers north of Lake Iassy) with part of its forces, attacked toward Toropets from the Zolotilovo, Safonovo, and Zaprud'e region on the morning on 30 August, and the division's forward units reached Berdovo (northwest of Lake Iassy) by 1300 hours.

A detachment consisting of 690th RR and 501st and 589th HARs began an attack toward Toropets from the Vasilevo region (northern bank of Lake Kudinskoe) at 0830 hours on 30 August, and the detachment reached the eastern bank of the Toropa River along the Koldino and Zarech'e front at 1000 hours, but, having encountered strong enemy resistance, could advance no further.

126th RD began an attack toward Toropets from the Ponizov'e region (12 kilometers east of Toropets on the morning of 30 August but, after being outflanked by the enemy from the right, was forced to withdraw to its jumping-off positions.

Antosenko's detachment is being thrown back to the Lokhovka, Sheikino, and Rusanova Gora line (western and southern bank of Lake Gorodetskoe) by penetrating enemy units, having large enemy motor-mechanized units on its front.

29th Army's student detachment is withdrawing to the Staraia Toropa region.

22nd Army's headquarters has no information about the army's remaining units.

Third. 29th Army. The army's units, while defending and repelling enemy attacks on its right wing (252nd RD) and while holding on to the Trubniki, Ias'kovo, and Elaga line, are carrying out a regrouping.

252nd RD, having repelled two enemy attacks from the Rumishche and Vypolzovo region, is fighting along the Sokhi and Pali Farm line with one RR against up to an enemy IR with tanks, supported by a regiment of artillery.

246th RD – is in its previous region.

243rd RD – is in its previous positions, having repelled an attack by up to a company from the direction of Sharkovo and Shelygany.

The Composite Brigade (1st and 2nd MRRs NKVD) moved from the Shestakovo, Pishchevitsa, and Litvinovo region to the vicinity of the town of Zapadnaia Dvina and was moving into Zhelezovo with part of its forces to occupy a defense along the Zhelezovo and Western Dvina line on the eastern bank of the Western Dvina River.

29th CR is fulfilling its previous mission.

The army is preparing to fulfill the *front* commander's Order No. 3950 of 30 August 1941.

Fourth. Cavalry Group Dovator. No additional information has been received about the group during the day.

Fifth. 30th Army. Conducted an offensive at 0900 hours on 30 August, with the mission of capturing the Krivets, Erkhanovo, Nekliudova, Staroe Selo, and Duniki line. Simultaneously, it carried out local regroupings along the army's front to protect the axis toward Belyi.

We received no information about the nature of enemy operations on the army's right wing. The enemy is continuing to offer stubborn resistance to the units attacking along the Ivanovichi, Churkino, Novoselki, and Slavinka front.

At 1700 hours on 30 August, the army's units are fighting at [the following locations]:

134th RD carried out its movement to its defensive positions on the morning of 30 August, with the mission of protecting the Belyi axis. The division's forward detachments are moving forward to the Mezha, Borisovo, Ust'e, Bol'shoe Kozlovo, Solov'evo, Maksimovka, Los'mino, Chernyi Ruchei, and Demekhi line. The main forces are moving into the Feliukino, El'chino, Hill 209.0, Cherepy, Baturino, Ladyzhino, Perevozino, and Struevo defensive region.

918th RR (250th RD), attached to 134th RD, has the mission to move into defensive positions from Soshno to Arzhevets village, Ashmary, and Zamosh'e. Information about the regiment's position has not been received during the day.

242nd RD, having the mission to protect the Demekhi, Novoe Morokhovo, and Krivets front, conducted exchanges of fire along its previous line during the day, while moving units to the Demekhi, and Staraia Morokhovo line.

250th RD exchanged fire from its previous positions, while having the mission to turn over the front it occupies from the western slopes of Hill 215.2 to (incl.) the northern outskirts of Shelepy to 242nd RD's units and to concentrate in the Sukharovo, Ponomari, and Rzhavets region on the night of 31 August.

162nd RD had no success in advancing during the day.

251st RD, while attacking toward Gorodno and Novoselki, captured Gorodno by 1600 hours and is continuing to conduct its attack.

The enemy withdrew from the Gorodno region toward the northwest.

107th TD – the positions of the division's units are unchanged.

Losses and trophies are being verified.

Sixth. 19th Army continued its offensive at 1000 hours on 30 August. The army's units, while encountering strong enemy resistance, had no success.

At 1700 hours on 30 August, the units were fighting in their previous positions.

45th CD is putting itself in order in the vicinity of the woods at Kislaevo, Klimovo State Farm, and Shershiki.

The enemy, having brought reserves forward, reinforced his defensive line with firing weapons and halted our units' advance.

Seventh. 16th Army. The positions of the army's units are unchanged.

Eighth. 20th Army. The army's units fortified their occupied positions, completed their regrouping, and filled out their units.

144th and 73rd RDs – the positions of the units are unchanged, and there is occasional artillery, mortar, and machine gun fire on their front.

The division's artillery suppressed two enemy artillery batteries and a mortar battery in the Krasnoel' region and an enemy observation post in the church at Pnevo on the night of 29-30 August.

229th RD, having relieved 153rd and 161st RDs' units, dug into positions from the southern edge of the grove 1 kilometer northeast of Suborovka to the eastern slopes of Hill 249.9, the northern edge of the grove northwest of Vishniaki, the Borovka River, and Hill 224.8.

There is scattered firing on the division's front.

One enemy tank was set afire on 25 August in the vicinity of Hill 249.9 by new [types of] shells.

129th RD dug into its previous positions.

153rd and 161st RDs are continuing concentration in regions previously indicated.

Ninth. The *front's* reserve – 1st TD and 152nd RD – in their previous positions.

Tenth. The VVS of the *front* cooperated with the armies' forces on the battlefield, operated against approaching enemy reserves, and directed their main efforts along the Toropets axis.

From the morning, combat operations were limited because of unfavorable weather conditions. Overall, a total of 49 aircraft sorties were carried out.

46th AD conducted reconnaissance of the enemy in the Khlebanikha, Sevost'ianovo, and Il'ino region and protected the operations of 29th Army's units.

47th AD destroyed concentrations of enemy infantry, artillery, and tanks in the region east of Lake Zhizhitskoe, Lake Kodosno, and west of Lake Dvin'e. As a result of raids by assault aircraft, 18 vehicles were destroyed, 6 guns were put out of action, and the enemy suffered personnel losses.

31st AD bombed enemy forces on the roads west of Lake Zhizhitskoe and Lake Kodosno on the night of 29-30 August, and many fires appeared as a result of the bombing.

During the first half of the day on 30 August, it conducted reconnaissance in the sector of the Toropets and Velikopol'e Station railroad line.

43rd AD operated with 19th Army's forces.

23rd AD and 38th RAS did not carry out flights because of the poor weather.

Losses of the enemy: 1 Iu.87 aircraft.

Our losses: one IL-2 aircraft did not return.

> The Chief of Staff of the Western Front, Lieutenant General Sokolovsky
> The Military Commissar of the Western Front's headquarters,
>   Brigade Commissar Kazbintsev
> For the Chief of the Operations Department, Colonel Belianko

Source: "Operativnaia svodka shtaba Zapadnogo fronta No. 130 k 20 chasam 30 avgusta 1941 g. o boevykh deistviiakh voisk fronta" [Operational summary no. 130 of the headquarters of the Western Front at 2000 hours on 30 August 1941 about the combat operations of the *front's* forces], *SBDVOV*, issue 41, 100-103.

23. Extracts from a Report by the Commander of the Forces of 20th Army of 31 August 1941 to the Commander of the Forces of the Western Front about Preparations for the Offensive and the Inadequate Provision of Weapons, Ammunition, and Communications Equipment to the Army's Forces

To the Commander-in-Chief of the Western Direction, Marshal Timoshenko
0605 hours on 31 August 1941

I am reporting:

1. In fulfillment of your Order No. 05 of 28 August, the army is conducting a regrouping and occupying jumping-off positions for an offensive toward the west with four divisions and is defending on the left wing with two divisions.

144th RD occupied jumping-off positions from (incl.) the Solov'evskaia crossing to (incl.) Logunovo. On 1 September, the division will seize Skrushevo and Pnevo with one regiment, deliver an attack on Liakhovo and Fedurno with the remaining regiments, and capture Fedurno by day's end. 153rd RD occupied jumping-off positions from Logunov to Ratchino, will attack toward Ratchino and Morevo, and will capture Starinovo by day's end.

161st RD occupied jumping-off positions from Pashkovo to the woods south of Golovino, will attack toward Dubrova and Morevo State Farm, and will capture Morevo and Titkovo by day's end. 73rd RD will seize Malinovka and Sopshino with one regiment on 1 September, occupy jumping-off position on the western bank of the Dnepr River from the barn to the bend [in the river] 1.5 kilometers south of the barn with two regiments, attack toward Kolpino, and capture the western edge of the woods south of Titkovo.

229th RD will firmly defend the sector from Hill 249.9 to Chuvakhi, Hill 224.8, and the ford on the Ustrom River and successively seize the southern slopes of Hill 249.9, the woods ½ a kilometer northwest of Vishniaki, and Hill 221.3, having no fewer than two battalions in reserve: one behind the division's left wing and one behind the right wing.

129th RD will defend the sector of the Ustrom River. the division should be relieved by 24th Army's units. However, 24th Army reports that the boundary line between 20th and 24th Armies is not Klemiatino and Riabtsevo Station, as front order No. 05 indicates, but the previous [boundary], which passed through Bol. Nezhoda. Therefore, 129th RD, while designated as the army's only reserve, will not be relieved by 24th Army's units.

2. Preparations for the army's operation are in full course. Replacements numbering 2,500 soldiers arrived in 229th RD. 153rd and 161st RDs each received 3,000 unarmed soldiers. The replacements for these divisions were brought forward by auto-transport and combined means on 29 and 30 August. The replacements immediately went to occupy jumping-off positions on the western bank of the Dnepr River.

153rd and 161st RDs received replacements of 2,500 rifles each by day's end on 30 August. A portion of these weapons require short-term repairs. Therefore, about 500-700 soldiers in both 153rd and 161st RDs remain unarmed. Around 10% of the replacements, which have arrived in the divisions, are untrained. A part of the replacements will await weapons and have to be trained in the conduct of the simplest forms of combat.

The arriving replacements have not fired and require 1-2 days for familiarization with the weapons given to them, which they will take into combat.

3. By the morning of 31 August, the army had no 107mm shells whatsoever for 7 guns and no 120mm mines [rounds] for 29 mortars, and has still not been given the promised 60 shells for each 152mm gun, the 40 shells for the 24 122mm gun (1938)s, and, in addition, for the light 76mm guns. We have only shrapnel rounds, which are not sufficiently effective for working over the forward edge of a fortified belt.

4. The division's artillery does not have means of communications needed to provide cooperation when in the depths.

592nd and 126th HARs have enough wire to lay to one position. 126th CAR's sound battery does not have special wire, and that is why, in the absence of aircraft for correcting fire from the air, the neutralization of 9-10 newly-discovered enemy batteries cannot be ensured.

302nd HAR has only 22 kilometers of cable for the regiment. The inspectors, which we summoned from the *front* headquarters on 26 August, returned on the 30th, but we have not received even a kilometer of cable, in addition to elements and pliers. Of the 2,000 kilometers of wire designated for the army in August, only 80 kilometers have been received. The receipt of the remaining cable was turned down because of the shortages of it in the *front*.

5. 302nd HAR has only 10 tractors for 18 guns.

All of the things I have noted above have forced me to begin the offensive without sufficient quantities of shells of appropriate calibers and means of communications.

I request [you]:

1. In short order, give orders about the dispatch of shells and wire to the army.
2. Protect the crossings with aircraft.
3. Define the boundary with 24th Army more precisely.

The Commander of 20th Army, Lieutenant General Lukin
The Member of the Military Council, Corps Commissar Semenovsky
The Chief of Staff of 20th Army, Major General Korneev

Source: "Doklad komanduiushchego voiskami 20-i Armii ot 31 avgusta 1941 g. komanduiushchemu voiskami Zapadnogo fronta o podgotovke k nastupleniiu i nedostatochnom obespechenie voisk armii vooruzheniem, boepripasami sredstvami sviazi" [Report of the commander of the forces of 20th Army of 31 August 1941 to the commander of the forces of the Western Front about preparations for the offensive and the inadequate provision of weapons, ammunition, and communications equipment to the army's forces], *SBDVOV,* issue 41, 224-225.

24. Combat Order No. 044 of the Commander of the Forces of 19th Army of 31 August 1941 on Capturing the Kislovo, Sushchevo, Bortniki, and Chistaia Line

Combat Order No. 044, CP, Commander, 19th Army,
the woods 1 kilometer east of Vasilisino,
1130 hours on 31 August 1941
1:50,000 scale map

1. The enemy's 5th and 28th IDs and separate parts of other divisions are defending before the army's front.

The approach of reserves from the direction of Dukhovshchina is possible.

Entrenching work is being detected along the Lomonosovo (21 kilometers north of Dukhovshchina), Bur'kovo, and Spas-Ugly rear line.

2. On the right, 30th Army will go over to a decisive offensive in the general direction on Demidov.

The boundary with it: Igor'evskaia Station, Karpovka, and Berenevo.

On the left, 16th Army will go over to a decisive offensive by delivering its main attack on its right wing.

The boundaries with it: Komiagino Station, Samuilova, Kolotovina.

3. 19th Army will penetrate the enemy's defense along the (incl.) Novoselishche and Zaitseva State Farm front and destroy the enemy's Dukhovshchina grouping.

Reach the Kislova, Myshkovo, Sushchevo, Navol'nia, Bortniki, Kokhanovo, and Chistaia front by day's end, while developing a subsequent offensive toward Ponizov'e and Dukhovshchina.

4. 244th RD will firmly protect the army' right flank by a defense along the edge of the Voskresensk woods to Panov village. Attack toward Staraia Kazarina and Kislovo with your main forces and capture Kislovo and Pankratova by day's end.

The boundary on the left: (all incl.) Shershiki, Bortniki, Krotovo, and Hill 232.1 (1 kilometer north of Ponizov'e).

5. 166th RD, with 399th HAR, will penetrate the enemy's defenses in the (incl.) Novoselishche and Semenkovo sector and, while delivering the main attack with the right wing, capture Pankratova and Myshkovo by day's end. Subsequently, attack toward Ponizov'e. Plan the commitment of 45th CD after the capturing Pankratova and Myshkovo.

The boundary on the left: (incl.) Pechenichino, (incl.) Balashova, Myshkovo, and (incl.) Pavlova.

6. 89th RD, with 120th HAR, two AT batteries, and with the support of a howitzer battalion from 91st RD, will penetrate the enemy's defenses in the Semenkovo and (incl.) Kazakova sector. Capture the "Shchelkina" woods by day's end. Subsequently, attack toward Pavlova.

The boundary on the left: up to Mashutino and further to (incl.) Butsevo.

7. 50th RD, with 596th HAR, 3rd Bn, 311th GAR, one battery of AT guns, and 202nd TR, will penetrate the enemy's defenses in the Kazakova and Hill 216.1 sector and, while developing the attack with your left wing, envelop the "Shchelkina" woods from the south and capture Hill 221.8 and Sushchevo by day's end. Seize crossings [over the Tsarevich River] at the House of Invalids and Sushchevo with your forward units. Plan for the commitment of 45th CD in the division's sector.

The boundary on the left: up to Ivanovo, as before, and further to Sushchevo and Baranova.

8. 64th RD, with 4th Bn, 302nd HAR, and one AT battery, will penetrate the defenses of the enemy in the sector from Ivanovo to the woods west of Zaitseva State Farm. The main attack will be on the right wing toward Turishchevo. Capture Turishchevo and Hill 213.4 (on the southern bank of the Tsarevich River). Assist 50th RD in capturing Sushchevo with part of your force.

The boundary on the left: up to Kolkovichi, as before, and further to (incl.) Popova and (incl.) Khudkova.

9. 101st TD, with one battery of AT guns, will restore the situation on the western bank of the Tsarevich River, capture the Hill 222.8 and Chistaia line, and, while going over on the defense, protect the army's left flank.

10. Artillery. Readiness by 0600 hours on 1 September 1941. Artillery preparation—45 minutes. DD [long-range action] – 1st, 2nd, and 4th Bns, 311th HAR.

Missions:

1) Suppress firing points and mortars on the forward edge of the enemy's defenses.

2) Suppress enemy artillery in the Krotovo, Myshkovo, and Bykovo region and the Shchelkina, Mashutino, Sushchevo, and Rakhmanino region.

3) Prevent enemy counterattacks from the Pankratova, Myshkovo, and "Shchelkina" woods region and from the direction of Sushchevo.

4) Prevent flanking fire from the direction of Navol'nia, Uvarova, and Popova with the fires of 3-4 battalions.

11. VVS:

1) Assist in destroying the enemy along the forward edge of his defense in the Barsuki, Semenovka, Sirotinka, Afanas'eva, and Shishkino sector and the grove 0.75 kilometers west of Muzhilova (Marker 178.8) with strikes by all aviation.

2) Destroy enemy artillery and reserves in the Krotovo, Ponizov'e, and Shchelkina region and the Shchelkina, Pavlova, Sushchevo, and "Shchelkina woods" region.

3) Protect the army's grouping in the Novoselishche, Kolkovichi, and Vasilisino region. Protect the commitment of 45th CD.

12. The army's reserve – 91st RD – leave in the Moteva, Potelitsa, and Zadniaia region in readiness to attack toward Ivaniki, Myshkovo, and Ponizov'e and Bolotino, Kalugino, and Pavlova. Have liaison delegates with the commanders of 166th, 89th, and 50th RDs.

13. 45th CD, while remaining in the Klimovo State Farm, Volkova, and Chudinovo region, be prepared to develop success in 166th and 50th RDs' sectors. Have liaison delegates and reconnaissance organs in 166th, 89th, and 50th RDs' sectors.

14. During the course of the offensive, conduct constant and well-organized reconnaissance at all levels of command to preclude surprises for the forces at all cost. Pay special attention to conducting constant and careful reconnaissance along open flanks.

15. Dig in firmly in positions and points seized from the enemy with the obligation to construct defensive works. These measures should in no way decrease the offensive tempo.

16. I demand careful organization of cooperation between infantry, artillery, tanks, and aviation. I am reminding you once again about the full employment of all types of infantry fire.

17. CP and headquarters of the armies – as before.

18. The time of the attack will be reported by a special order.

19. Confirm receipt. Submit your combat orders and combat planning table to me by 1800 hours on 31 August.

> The Commander of 19th Army, Lieutenant General Konev
> The Member of the Military Council of 19th Army,
>   Division Commissar Sheklanov
> The Chief of Staff of 19th Army, [Malyshkin]

Source: "Boevoi prikaz komanduiushchego voiskami 19-i Armii No. 044 ot 31 avgusta 1941 g. na ovladenie rubezhom Kislovo, Sushchevo, Bortniki, Chistaia" [Combat order no. 044 of the commander of the forces of 19th Army of 31 August 1941 on capturing the Kislovo, Sushchevo, Bortniki, and Chistaia line], *SBDVOV*, issue 41, 193-194.

25. A List of the Trophy [Captured] Property Seized by 19th Army's Formations during the Period from 17 through 30 August 1941

No.	Type of Property	Quantity
I. Artillery Property		
1	Motors	7
2	Antitank guns	16
3	105mm guns	19
4	155mm guns	9
5	75mm antiaircraft guns	11
6	120mm mortars	9
7	150mm guns	3
8	Guns of various calibers	19
9	Mortars	20
10	Heavy machine guns	19
11	Machine pistols	13
12	Pistols, "Parabellum"	10
13	Antitank rifles	21
14	Sub-machine guns	84
15	Base plates for mortars	883
16	Cartridge belts for machine guns and magazines	208
17	Rifles	248
18	Reserve barrels for machine guns	224
19	Periscopes	1
20	Automatic weapons	21
21	Panoramic sights for guns	1
22	Rifle bullets	332,522
23	High caliber bullets	246
24	Hand grenades	531
25	Mines (mortar shells) of various calibers	936
26	Shells of various calibers	5,065
27	Stands with shells	159
28	Optical sights for tanks	2
29	Rockets	93
30	Large caliber machine guns	7
31	Binoculars	4
32	Bullets for machine pistols	2,820
33	Flamethrowers	1
34	Antiaircraft machine guns	1

No.	Type of Property	Quantity
II. Armored Property		
35	Tanks	86
36	Light vehicles and trucks	12
37	Flamethrower tanks	1
38	Ambulances	1
39	Tractors	1
40	Motorcycles	11
41	Bicycles	161
III. Engineer Property		
42	Barbed wire cutters	12
43	Anti-infantry Fougasse mines	129
45	Antitank mines	106
46	Fougasse grenades	6
47	MZP	2
IV. Chemical Property		
48	Gas masks	334
49	Back-pack flamethrowers	1
50	Anti-chemical suits	37
V. Quartermaster Property		
51	Cloth greatcoats	610
52	Jackets of various types	63
53	Steel helmets	231
54	Canvas raincoats	462
55	Cloth blankets	126
56	Jackboots	20pair
57	Leather knapsacks	62
58	Banners [flags]	1
59	Field kitchens	2
60	Headquarters tents	1
VI. Communications Property		
61	Radios	6
62	Telephone apparatuses	14
63	Telephone carts	1
VII. Aviation Property		
64	Aircraft shot down in combat	7
65	Sound locators	1
66	Aircraft machine-guns	2

No.	Type of Property	Quantity
67	Aircraft electronic instruments	2
68	Aircraft engines	1

Notes:

1. Part of the property and weapons have been turned over to the force formations to protect the forces, and the other part – evacuated and given to forward warehouses and repair bases.

2. The quartermaster property is being repaired, after which it will be evacuated.

3. Part of the damaged trophy weapons (more than 30 tanks) and the equipment portion of the artillery property requires evacuation from the battlefield, which was delayed, on the one hand, by the absence of a necessary number of transport means (tractors) and, on the other hand, by the fact that the indicated trophy weapons are still situated under enemy mortar and machine gun fire.

> The Chief of Staff of 19th Army, [Malyshkin]
> The Military Commissar of 19th Army's headquarters,
> Senior Battalion Commissar Vagin

Source: "Vedomost' zakhvachennogo trofeinogo imushchestva soedineniiami 19 A za period s 17 po 30.8.41." [A list of the trophy property seized by 19th Army's formations during the period from 17 through 30 August 1941], *SBDVOV*, issue 41, 191-192.

26. Operational Summary No. 132 of the Headquarters of the Western Front at 2000 hours on 31 August 1941 about the Combat Operations of the *Front's* Forces

Operational Summary No. 132 at 2000 hours on 31 August 1941,
Headquarters. Western Front
1:500,000 and 100,000 scale maps

First. On the *front's* right wing, 22nd Army conducted sustained fighting with enemy motor-mechanized units with part of its forces, while holding up its advance to the Western Dvina River, and its main forces withdrew to a defensive line along the eastern bank of the Western Dvina River.

29th Army withdrew to the eastern bank of the Western Dvina River with its main forces for a defense of the Iamishche, Zapadnaia Dvina, and Barlovo line, while protecting its withdrawal by holding on to the Sokhi, Pali, Beliankin, and Zui defense line.

In the center and on the left wing, the forces are continuing to fortify the positions they have reached, while carrying out a regrouping.

Second. 22nd Army conducted fierce holding actions with enemy motor-mechanized units on 31 August and withdrew to the line of the Western Dvina River with its main forces, having before it the previous enemy grouping, which displayed special activity along the Toropets, Lake Griadetskoe, and Zhelezovo axis.

The remnants of 214th RD and 48th TD fought along the Chernaia and Lake Abramovskoe line with rear guards at 1500 hours and passed through the Lake Lobno, Pospeloe, and Pashkovo line with its main forces.

A composite group made up of 126th and 186th RDs' remnants, under the command of Major General Samokhin, passed through the Danskoe and Proskurino line with its main forces at 1500 hours, while protecting its withdrawal with rear guards units along the Martisovo and Chernyshevo line.

Antosenko's detachment (8th and 9th MRRs), after a series of stubborn battles with superior enemy forces, withdrew to the eastern bank of the Western Dvina River, where it joined with 29th Army's composite brigade, which was defending the crossings over the Western Dvina River in the Zhelezovo region.

Third. 29th Army is withdrawing to the eastern bank of the Western Dvina River with its main forces on 31 August, while it is occupying defenses along the Iamishche, Zapadnaia Dvina, and Barlovo line with part of its forces, and is moving to its indicated defense line with its main forces.

The Composite Brigade (1st and 2nd MRRs, the remnants of 8th and 9th MRRs – and Antosenko's detachment) is defending the crossings over the Western Dvina River in the Zhelezovo region, with up to a regiment of enemy infantry with tanks on its front.

246th RD is occupying the defile between the lakes along the Lakes Pesno, Ulin, and Glubokoe line with two regiments. One regiment is concentrated in the town of Zapadnaia Dvina.

252nd RD passed through Bentsy with the head of its main forces at 1230 hours on 31 August and is fighting with an enemy force of up to an IR with tanks along the Sokhi and Pali Farm line with covering units.

243rd RD approached Shcheboreva with the head of its main forces at 1500 hours, while protecting the movement of 910th RR, which occupied positions along the northern bank of the Western Dvina River in the Beliankin and Zui sector.

29th CR, while protecting the army's left flank with reconnaissance, is concentrating in the Obukhova region.

Iurlov's student battalion was fighting in the Krivkina region (7 kilometers west of Staraia Toropa) at 1600 hours on 30 August.

Fourth. Cavalry Group Dovator. According to radio reports, Cavalry Group Dovator's main forces were concentrated in the forest northeast of Nikulino [10-12 kilometers northwest of the Belyi-Dukhovshchina road and 25 kilometers northwest of Staroe Morokhovo] at 0830 hours on 31 August, while preparing to exit from the raid.

30th Army's headquarters is being ordered to organize communications and cooperation with the group.

The second part of Group Dovator, under the command of 37th CR's commander and with 900 sabers, concentrated in the vicinity of Los'mianka 2, Chichata, Ivashkina, and Ekaterinovka [10-15 kilometers northwest of Chernyi Ruchei on the Belyi-Dukhovshchina road]. It has the mission to penetrate into the region northwest of Nikulino for a link-up on the night of 1 September.

Fifth. 30th Army conducted a regrouping of its forces and 134th RD moved into the Golakovo, Stodolishche, and Nelidovo region, with the aim to protect the Belyi axis from the direction of Toropets to the northwest.

The enemy conducted active air reconnaissance operations on the army's front throughout the day.

Sixth. 19th Army carried out a regrouping of forces on 31 August, while fortifying the positions it reached.

The enemy went over to unsuccessful counterattacks on the morning of 31 August. He did not display special activity during the second half of the day and conducted occasional mortar and artillery firing.

The losses of the army's units, according to verified data for the period from 29-30 August, were killed – 193 men, wounded – 706, and missing in action – 11 men.

45th CD, according to verified data, for the period of 27-28 August, lost: killed and wounded – 100 men and 100 horses, and missing in action – 157 men, with their horses.

Trophies for 31 August: 2 tanks, 1 truck, 1 light vehicle, 1 light machine gun, 1 mortar, and 63 gas masks.

Seventh. 16th and 20th Armies fortified their previous positions, while completing a regrouping of forces in accordance with the *front's* Order No. 05/op.

There was artillery and mortar fire along the armies' fronts.

Eighth. [The *front's* reserve]: 1st TD and 152nd RD – in their previous positions.

Ninth. The main effort of the VVS of the *front* was directed at the identification and destruction of enemy forces along the Toropets axis. The VVS protected the groupings of forces and assisted the advance by 19th Army's units. Overall, a total of 144 aircraft sorties were carried out.

46th AD cooperated with 22nd Army's units and bombed concentrations of enemy tanks, vehicles, and personnel in the Zhelezovo, Klin, Lake Griadetskoe, Lokhovka, Pavlovo, and Shipkovo regions.

Up to 15 enemy vehicles were destroyed, and casualties were inflicted on the enemy.

47th AD destroyed concentrations of enemy motor-mechanized units in the Pavlovo and Lokhovka region with assault operations. As a result of the attacks, up to 45 vehicles and 2-3 tanks were destroyed or put out of action, and considerable personnel casualties were inflicted on the enemy.

31st AD conducted reconnaissance in the Staritsa region, along the Toropets and Nelidovo road, and in the Gorki, Nikitina, and Selishche region and attacked an enemy tank and vehicular column in the vicinity of Zabolot'e.

43rd AD bombed enemy artillery and infantry in the Navol'nia, Sel'tso, Rafenino, and Siniavka region.

The crews noticed direct hits on the targets.

Losses of the enemy: one HE-113 shot down.

Our losses: 1 aircraft shot down, and two aircraft did not return to their airfields, one of which, apparently, made a forced landing on its own territory.

The Chief of Staff of the Western Front, Lieutenant General Sokolovsky
The Military Commissar of the Western Front's headquarters,
    Brigade Commissar Kazbintsev
The Chief of the Operations Department, Lieutenant General Malandin

Source: "Operativnaia svodka shtaba Zapadnogo fronta No. 132 k 20 chasam 31 avgusta 1941 g. o boevykh deistviiakh voisk fronta" [Operational summary no. 132 of the headquarters of the Western Front at 2000 hours on 31 August 1941 about the combat operations of the *front's* forces], *SBDVOV*, issue 41, 104-105.

27. Report of the Headquarters of the Western Front of 31 August 1941 to the Chief of the General Staff about Cavalry Group Dovator's Situation

Notes by direct line
General Staff, to Marshal Comrade Shaposhnikov
2400 hours on 31 August 1941

The Cavalry Group of Comrade Dovator, consisting of 50th and 53rd CDs, had the mission, assigned to Comrade Dovator personally by Marshal Timoshenko, to operate against the rear area in the general direction of Dukhovshchina.

Before the raid, a controlled map, a table of radio signals, and enciphering documents – for communications by radio, were given to the Group's headquarters. Communications with the Cavalry Group before the commitment of its main units into the enemy's rear were continuously by radio, about which was reported in the operational summaries. During Comrade Dovator's commitment into the rear, the horse-holders and radio stations were cut off, and that is why continuous communications with him was lost. The radio stations remained with the horse-holders, the communications with them did not cease, and we had periodic communications with Dovator through them.

Air reconnaissance was conducted of the region of the cavalry group's operations repeatedly, along with photography of the terrain, with the mission to determine the cavalry group's location, but this did not produce favorable results.

Today, a report was received by radiogram at 0830 hours that the Cavalry Group was concentrating in the forests east of Nikulino for a return from the raid. The Group is conducting reconnaissance to determine the route of the strike. They are not asking for ammunition and food supplies.

30th Army's headquarters is being ordered to undertake energetic measures to communicate with the Cavalry Group.

On the night of 31 August-1 September, a detachment consisting of 500 sabers and 130 bayonets, with AT guns, has the mission to penetrate the enemy's front in the direction of the forest east of Nikulino and, by doing so, assist the Cavalry Group's exit from the raid.

Sokolovsky, Kazbintsev, Malandin

Source: "Donesenie shtaba Zapadnogo fronta ot 31 avgusta 1941 g. nachal'niku General'nogo Shtaba o polozhenii Kavaleriiskoi Gruppy Dovatora" [Report of the headquarters of the Western Front of 31 August 1941 to the chief of the General Staff about Cavalry Group Dovator's Situation], *SBDVOV*, issue 41, 106.

28. Operational Summary No. 38 of the Headquarters of 16th Army of 1500 hours on 1 September 1941 about the Positions of the Army's Forces

Operational Summary No. 38, Headquarters, 16th Army,
the woods northeast of Khotenova

1500 hours on 1 September 1941
1:100,000 scale map

1. 16th Army, while defending the eastern bank of the Vop' River on the Iartsevo, Skrushevskie, and Buianovo front and having forced the Vop' River along the Chizhiki, Dubrova, and (incl.) Iartsevo front at 0700 hours on 1 September, went on the offensive in the general direction of Novosel'e, Stepanovo, and Nikola-Edrevichi.

Subunits of 336th IR and units of the enemy's 28th ID are defending opposite the army's front. The enemy is offering stubborn fire resistance and employing mines and engineer obstacles extensively.

2. 1st TD occupies [the following] positions at 1200 hours on 1 September:

a) 175th RR is fighting on the eastern bank of the unnamed stream west of Kholm and Novosel'e (western); and

b) The Novocherkassk RR is in second echelon behind 175th RR on the southwestern outskirts of Chistaia. The enemy's 2nd Bn, 336th IR, is defending opposite 175th RR's front (according to prisoner testimony, 1st Bn, 336th IR, is being withdrawn to the rear to receive replacements).

Losses of 1st Tank Division by 0830 hours – killed or wounded – 25 men.

Headquarters of 1st TD – the woods 1 kilometer west of Manchina.

152nd RD occupies [the following] positions at 1200 hours:

a) 544th RR captured the unnamed heights 1.5 kilometers north of Khatyni;

b) 480th RR is fighting along the line from the eastern slopes of Hill 217.9 to the eastern outskirts of Khatyni; and

c) 646th RR – is in second echelon in the grove east of Dubrovo. Losses and trophies are being verified, and 14 prisoners were seized.

Headquarters of 152nd RD – the grove 2 kilometers southeast of Ozerishche.

38th RD, while defending the Iartsevo and Marker 169.9 front on the eastern bank of the Vop' River with 48th RR, [the following] reached [the following] fronts:

a) 29th RR – from the southern bank of Lake Khatyni to the eastern outskirts of Iartsevo and Iartsevo Station: and

b) 343rd RR – in second echelon on the western bank of the Vop' River behind 29th RR.

There are no trophies or prisoners, and losses are being verified.

108th RD is defending the Marker 169.9, Skrushevskie Farm, and Buianovo sector on the eastern bank of the Vop' River.

127th TB – the commander's reserve – is concentrated in the Ozerishche region and not committed to combat.

3. Neighbor on the right – 101st TD – is fighting along the Osipova and Skachkovo line.

Communications with it is by liaison officer.

Neighbor on the left – 144th RD – is defending the Korovniki and Zabor'e sector on the eastern bank of the Dnepr River.

Communications with it is by delegate.

4. Roads in the army's sector are in satisfactory conditions and suitable for the movement of all types of wheeled transport.

Communications with the units is by radio, telephone, and liaison officers.

Bottles with flammable mixtures "KS" were not used on the army's front on 1 September.

5. Headquarters of the army – the woods 1 kilometer northeast of Khotenovo. The auxiliary command post is in the woods 0.5 kilometer north of Vyshegor.

Malinin, Sedenkov

Source: "Operativnaia svodka shtaba 16-i Armii No. 38 k 15 chasam 1 sentiabria 1941 g. o polozhenii voisk armii" [Operational summary no. 38 of the headquarters of 16th Army of 1500 hours on 1 September 1941 about the positions of the army's forces], *SBDVOV*, issue 41, 142-143.

29. Operational Summary No. 1 of 16th Army's Department of Auto-Armored Forces of 1 September 1941 about the Offensive by the Army's Auto-Armored Forces and their Situation and Condition at 2000 hours on 1 September 1941

Operational Summary No.1, Department ABT, 16th Army,
1 kilometer north of Vyshegor,
2000 hours on 1 September 1941
1:100,000 scale map

1. 16th Army's units attacked the enemy on the Chistaia, Novosel'e, Khatyni, and Iartsevo Station front at 0700 hours on 1 September 1941 and are attacking in the general direction of Stepanovo and Grishino. The enemy, while offering strong fire resistance, is conducting a fighting withdrawal toward the west. Enemy tanks have not been discovered during the day.

2. 1st TD, having attacked the enemy on the Chistaia and Novosel'e (eastern) front, reached positions from the eastern edge of the woods, 1 kilometer west of Kholm, to Novosel'e (western) and, subsequently, is continuing to fulfill the order by 16th Army's commander to reach the Mal'tsevo and Semiaosina line.

   a) 175th MRR (with 2nd Platoon of KVs, 1st and 2nd Companies of T-34s less one platoon, and 1st Company of BTs), having attacked the enemy on the Chistaia and Novosel'e (eastern) line, captured Novosel'e (western) at 2000 hours.

   b) 6th MRR, (with 1st Platoon of KVs, a company of T-34s, and a company of BTs), while operating in second echelon and developing the attack from behind 175thMRR's right wing, captured the eastern edge of the grove 1 kilometer west of Kholm.

   c) The division commander's reserve – 3rd Bn, 6th MRR, a company of T-26s, a company of T-40s, 2 platoons of BT-7s, and a platoon of T-34s – began crossing to the western bank of the Vop' River but were not committed to combat.

   d) The RVR [tank repair point] is in the vicinity of the Vorotynovo woods.

   e) The headquarters of 1st TD -– the woods 1 kilometer west of Manchina.

3. 127th TB – the army commander's reserve – is in the vicinity of the woods east of Ozerishche.

4. Advanced Warehouse 1739 is in the vicinity of the woods 1 kilometer southeast of Anokhovo.

5. 22nd ABT Workshop – Nikolo-Pogorelovo.

6. Losses in personnel and equipment will be verified and reported separately.

Senior Assistant Chief of the Operations Department, ABTV 16,
Captain Ovsiannikov

Source: "Operativnaia otdela avtobronetankovykh voisk 16-i Armii No. 1 ot 1 sentiabria 1941 g. o nastuplenii avtobronetankovykh voisk armii i ikh polozhenii po sostoianiiu na 20 chasov 1 sentiabria 1941 g." [Operational summary no. 1 of 16th Army's Department of Auto-Armored Forces of 1 September 1941 about the offensive by the army's auto-armored forces and their situation and condition at 2000 hours on 1 September 1941], *SBDVOV*, issue 41, 143-144.

30. Operational Summary No. 92 of the Headquarters of 30th Army at 1700 hours on 1 September 1941 about the Positions of the Army's Forces

Operational Summary No. 92, Headquarters, 30th Army,
the woods 2 kilometers northeast of Podzaitsevo
1700 hours on 1 September 1941

1. The army's units went on the offensive at 0900 hours on 1 September 1941, while delivering the main attack with its left wing and protecting the axis toward Belyi with its right wing.

The enemy is offering organized fire resistance and employing roaming systems of mortar fire.

2. The army's units reached the [following] lines by 1700 hours:

107th TD is occupying its previous positions, and there are no changes in its dispositions.

242nd RD attacked at 0900 hours on 1 September and by 1535 reached:

997th RR – 500 meters from the northeastern outskirts of Churkino;

903rd RR reached the eastern outskirts of Shelepy; and

900th RR is in second echelon behind 903rd RR. The enemy is conducting strong machine-gun fire, while opposing the offensive.

162nd RD, while attacking toward Fomenki and Marker 230.3, had no success. The division's units are located in their previous positions, while striking enemy strong points with artillery fire.

251st RD began its attack at 0900 hours. By 1630 hours it reached:

919th RR occupied Hill 214.9 and is continuing its attack on Krechets; and

223rd RR entered the brushy area 500 meters east of Ivanovo and is continuing its attack toward Ivanino.

250th RD – the army's reserve – is located in its previous region, putting itself into order, and engaged with combat training.

3. We have no news about Group Dovator.

4. The weather is cloudy, with intermittent rain, and the roads are passable for transport.

The Chief of Staff
The Military Commissar of the headquarters,
The Chief of the Operations Department

Note. No signatures present, but with the annotation, "Transmitted by [Captain V. P.] Gribanov [Assistant Chief of 30th Army's Operations Department]. Accepted 1800 hours 1 September 1941 by [Major F. G.] Rybakov [Assistant Chief of the Western Front's Operations Department]"

Source: "Operativnaia svodka shtaba 30-i Armii No. 92 k 17 chasam 1 sentiabria 1941 g. o polozhenii voisk armii" [Operational summary no. 92 of the headquarters of 30th Army at 1700 hours on 1 September 1941 about the positions of the forces of the army], *SBDVOV*, issue 41, 292.

31. Combat Order No. 056 of the Commander of the Forces of 30th Army of 1 September 1941 about Shortcomings in the Offensive by the Army's Forces on 1 September 1941 and the Missions on 2 September 1941

Combat Order No. 056,
Headquarters, 30th Army,
The woods 2 kilometers northeast of Podzaitsevo
1:100,000 scale map
2340 hours on 1 September 1941

The offensive operations of the army's units on 1 September 1941 were sluggish in nature and lacking in initiative. Skillful maneuver by the troops and a strengthening of efforts along the axes were absent where we intended to achieve success. Furthermore, 162nd RD's 501st RR continued to "lay down" throughout the day under weak machine gun and mortar fire, and the commander of that regiment displayed his inactivity under the influence of enemy flanking fire and did not envision maneuver for a decisive attack in another direction.

I order: the army's units to fulfill Order No. 053.

1. **250th RD,** having subordinated to itself 1st Bn, 515th RR on the Orlova and Erkhovo line and Maiorov's reconnaissance detachment in the Ust'e sector, will leave one RR in my reserve in the Sukharevo, Vorob'ikha, and Ponomari region, relieve 629th RR's units along the Bor, Chernyi Ruchei, and Okolitsa line with one regiment (the 922nd) by 0400 hours on 2 September 1941, and continue its attack with 918th RR toward Novoselki and Vorontsovo, while employing an enveloping maneuver against the enemy's centers of resistance.

Simultaneously, protect the army's right flank from the west and southwest, with forward detachments in the [following] regions: a) Verkhnyi Karakovo, b) Frolovo; and c) Ust'e. Conduct reconnaissance with Maiorov's reconnaissance detachment toward Lake Shchuch'e, Lake Velisto, and Lake Soshno.

2. **242nd RD** will concentrate its main efforts toward Hill 215.2 and Churkino, and leave fire cover [protection] and demonstrate actively with firing means [weapons] in the remaining sectors.

3. **162nd RD** will occupy a narrow front overnight for an attack toward Shanino and Fomenki. Do not permit deeply-echeloned combat formations. Conduct a secondary attack toward Hill 229.1 and 241.2, together with 242nd RD, and conducted demonstrative fires actively along the remaining front.

4. **251st RD** will regroup its main forces to its left wing overnight and, while establishing communications with 244th RD, will capture the road junction at

Dorofeevo and seize crossings over the Votra River in the Krechets and Dorofeevo sector.

5. 107th TD will have its main forces in accordance with the order of 31 August 1941 and, simultaneously, while protecting the army's right flank from the west and northwest, will have forward detachments in the Shumily, Kitaevo, and Borisovo regions. Pay special attention to maintaining constant communications with 134th RD's headquarters and inform the army's headquarters about all information.

6. Begin the offensive at 0800 hours on 2 September 1941.

The Commander of 30th Army, Lieutenant General Khomenko
The Member of the Military Council of 30th Army,
    Brigade Commissar Abramov
The Chief of Staff of 30th Army, Lieutenant Colonel Vinogradov

Source: "Boevoi prikaz komanduiushchego voiskami 30-i Armii No. 056 ot 1 sentiabria 1941 g. o nedostatkakh v nastuplenii voisk armii 1 sentiabria 1941 g. i zadachakh na 2 sentiabria 1941 g." [Combat order no. 056 of the commander of the forces of 30th Army of 1 September 1941 about shortcomings in the offensive by the army's forces on 1 September 1941 and the missions on 2 September 1941], *SBDVOV*, issue 41, 293.

32. Combat Report of the Headquarters of 16th Army to the Chief of Staff of the Western Front of 1 September about the Positions of the Army's Forces at Day's End on 1 September

To the Chief of Staff of the Western Front
To the Chiefs of Staff of 19th and 20th Armies
1:50,000 scale map
2400 hours on 1 September 1941

First. 16th Army, while destroying the units of the enemy 161st and 28th IDs, reached [the following] front with its divisions by day's end on 1 September 1941:

1st TD – the eastern bank of the stream south of Samuilova;

152nd RD –the eastern bank of the stream south of Samuilova; and

38th RD – Hill 209.2, Iartsevo Station, and Marker 174.7.

108th RD is defending in the Marker 169.9 and Buianovo sector on the eastern bank of the Vop' River.

127th TB – the army commander's reserve – the Ozerishche region.

Second. The army's headquarters has been sent 47 prisoners and 1 officer. The prisoners are continuing to come in. The quantity of trophies seized is being verified.

Third. The army's units will continue the offensive on the morning of 2 September, with its previous missions

Malinin, Sedenkov

Source: "Boevoe donesenie shtaba 16-i Armii nachal'niku shtaba Zapadnogo fronta ot 1-sentiabria 1941 g. o polozhenii voisk armii k iskhodu 1 sentiabria 1941 g." [Combat report of the headquarters of 16th Army to the chief of staff of the Western Front of 1 September about the positions of the army's forces at day's end on 1 September 1941], *SBDVOV*, 144.

33. Combat Order No. 048 of the Commander of the Forces of 19th Army of 2 September 1941 on a Continuation of the Army's Offensive

Combat Order No. 048, CP, Commander, 19th Army,
the woods 1 kilometer east of Vasilisino
0040 hours on 2 September 1941
1:50,000 scale map

1. I order 91st RD, with 120th HAR, to concentrate in the Kolkovichi, Miagchenki, and Prisel'e region by the morning of 2 September. Go over to the attack in the Osipova and Kokhanova sector [9-14 kilometers north of Iartsevo] toward Stepanovka at 0900 hours on 2 September 1941. Capture Stepankova (northern) and Borki [13-16 kilometers north-northwest of Iartsevo] by the end of the day. Cut the Dukhovshchina and Iartsevo road in the Rakhmankova region with forward units.

The boundary on the left: Kudinovo, Padylishche, Miagchenki, Kokhanova, and the farm south of Borki.

2. 101st TD, with 91st RD's arriving units, will regroup to the left wing and, in cooperation with 1st TD and 91st RD, will develop an attack toward Ivashenka and Petrykina. Capture (incl.) Borki, Vorotysheva, and Mkhovka by day's end. Cut the Dukhovshchina and Iartsevo road in the vicinity of Nizovo Selo with your forward units.

3. 166th RD will continue its attack toward Myshkovo, while fulfilling the missions assigned in Order No. 044 of 31 August 1941. Withdraw one RR into my reserve in the Hill 220.5 and Potelitsa region by the morning of 2 September 1941. Subordinate one battalion of 399th HAR to the commander of 89th RD.

4. 244th, 89th, 50th, and 64th RDs will continue their attacks, fulfilling the missions assigned in Order No. 044 of 31 August 1941.

5. 45th CD, while remaining in my reserves in the Maslikhi and Matveenki region, will organize an AT defense in the Pechenichino, Kapyrovshchina, and Khachenki sector along the line of the Vop' River.

6. Artillery. Readiness by 0600 hours. Artillery preparation—15 minute fire raid. Missions:

1) Suppress enemy artillery in the Rakhmanino, Kulagino, Sushchevo, and Turishchevo region and the Navol'nia, Khutkovo, and Osinovki region.

2) As the offensive develops, support 91st RD's attack with two battalions from 311th GAR.

11. VVS: Missions:

1) Protect the army's grouping in the Ivaniki, Chistaia, and Vasilisino region.

2) Assist 91st RD's and 101st TD's attacks with assault aircraft. Attack Sen'kova, Kokhanovo, and Krovopuskovo along the forward edge – at 0850 hours on 2 September 1941.

3) Conduct reconnaissance along the axes: a) Otria and Dmitrovka; b) Krotovo and Dukhovshchina; and c) Kolkovichi and Dukhovshchina.

The Commander of 19th Army, Lieutenant General Konev
The Member of the Military Council of 19th Army,
    Division Commissar Sheklanov

The Chief of Staff of 19th Army, [Malyshkin]

Source: "Boevoi prikaz komanduiushchego voiskami 19-i Armii No. 048 ot 2 sentiabria 1941 g. na prodolzhenii nastupleniia voisk armii" [Combat order no. 048 of the commander of the forces of 19th Army of 2 September 1941 on a continuation of the army's offensive], *SBDVOV*, issue 41, 196-197.

34. Operational Summary No. 135 of the Headquarters of the Western Front at 0800 hours on 2 September 1941 about the Combat Operations of the *Front's* Forces

Operational Summary No. 135 at 0800 hours on 2 September 1941,
Headquarters. Western Front
1:500,000 and 100,000 scale maps

First. 22nd and 29th Armies continued to dig in on the Likhusha defensive line and further along the eastern bank of the Western Dvina River, having small enemy reconnaissance groups of motorized infantry and tanks on their fronts.

In the center and on the left wing, overnight on 1-2 September, the *front's* forces carried out preparations for an offensive on the morning of 2 September.

Second. 22nd Army, while continuing to put itself in order during the second half of the day on 1 September, 214th RD fought with enemy motorized infantry, supported by tanks and armored vehicles, along the Novaia and Ramen'e line and [the army] continued to fortify the positions it occupies in its center and on its left wing.

Information has not been received about the army's operations on the night of 1-2 September.

Third. 29th Army. The positions of the army's units are essentially unchanged as of 0500 hours on 2 September.

The enemy is not active opposite the army's front.

243rd RD is digging in on the Iamishche and Khotino sector on the eastern bank of the Western Dvina River.

246th RD is holding on to the defile between the lakes in the Solonkino, Kaliukhova, Glubokoe, Dorokhova, and Mel'nitsa sector with two RRs, and one RR is continuing to prepare a defensive line in the Sotino and Barlovo sector on the eastern bank of the western Dvina River.

252nd RD – the army commander's reserve – is in the Mukhino, Spiridovo, and Novoe Polutino region in readiness to operate toward Selino, Iamishche, and Khotino.

The Motorized Brigade is occupying defenses in the Selino and Savino sector with RBn.

29th CR is defending positions from Lake Plovnoe to Lake Emlen', while protecting the army against attack from the south and southwest.

The Motorized Brigade's remaining units are in the Bibirevo and Bukhovitsy region in readiness for operations toward Zapadnaia Dvina.

Fourth. Cavalry Group Dovator reached the Filino region [20 kilometers northwest of Los'mino and the Belyi-Dukhovshchina road] during the night. A representative of the army headquarters [30th Army] has been sent to the region of the group's dispositions to clarify its condition, as well as four trucks with foodstuffs and supplies.

Fifth. 30th Army continued its offensive during the second half of the day. It captured Shelepy by 2000 hours, and the army's units continued fighting in their previous positions along the remainder of the front.

The enemy, defending opposite the army's front, offered stubborn resistance. During the second half of the day on 1 September, the enemy conducted artillery fire from the Panas'kino, Rekta, Kostino, and Fomenki region with batteries of heavy artillery.

The army's units occupy [the following positions] at 0500 hours on 2 September:

134th RD, in its previous composition, occupies defenses in the Golanovo, Stodolishche, and Nelidovo region [45-60 kilometers north of Belyi].

134th RD's 629th RR (without one battalion) occupies defenses in the Bor and Chernyi Ruchei sector [20 kilometers south-southwest of Belyi].

250th RD's 918th RR, while encountering strong resistance, is fighting along the Svinkovo, Shcheglovo, and Sutoki line [10 kilometers south-southwest of Chernyi Ruchei].

107th TD, while reinforced by two battalions from 629th RR, continues to occupy all-round defenses in the Belyi region.

242nd RD captured Shelepy at 1900 hours on 1 September and is continuing its attack.

162nd RD – the attacks by the division's units achieved no success. The division is continuing to fight in its previous positions,

251st RD is digging into positions from Hill 214.9 to Novoselki and the southwestern outskirts of Gorodno.

Losses of the army's units for 1 September: killed and wounded – 248 men.

Trophies: 5 light machine guns, 2 mortars, and 15 rifles seized and 5 pillboxes and 18 firing points destroyed.

Sixth. 19th Army. The offensive by the units on the army's right wing and in its center during the second half of the day on 1 September were unsuccessful.

The army's left wing, while attacking toward Kokhanovo, slowly continued to develop the offensive. The army's reserve – 91st RD, is concentrating in the Kolkovichi, Miagchenki, and Prisel'e region to exploit success on the army's left wing.

The army's units will continue the offensive at 0900 hours on 2 September, while exploiting success on the left wing.

The enemy occupies defensive positions from Pavlovshchina to Panov, Novoselishche, Barsuki, Sirotinka, Popova, and Kokhanovo and is offering stubborn resistance to the offensive on the army's right wing and in its center. On the left wing, south of the Tsarevich River, he is withdrawing westward under pressure by 101st TD.

The positions of 244th, 166th, 89th, 50th, and 64th RDs were unchanged as of 0500 hours on 2 September.

101st TD occupies a front from the eastern outskirts of Osipova to the eastern outskirts of Skachkovo and from the individual buildings south of Kokhanovo to the eastern outskirts of Kholm.

During the offensive on 1 September, the division's units captured 15 prisoners belonging to 14th ID's 336th IR.

Information has not been received about losses and trophies.

Seventh. 16th Army, while destroying units of the enemy's 161st and 28th IDs during the second half of the day on 1 September, reached the front from the eastern bank of the stream south of Samuilova to the eastern bank of the stream west of Kudinovo and Iartsevo Station by day's end.

The advance by the army's units was halted by mine fields, barbed wire entanglements, and flanking fire by artillery and mortars from the Krovopuskovo region.

The enemy, while suffering heavy losses, threw away their guns, artillery, machine guns, mortars, ammunition, and other equipment in separate sectors.

The army's units reached [the following] front:

1st TD – the eastern bank of the stream south of Samuilova;

152nd RD – the eastern bank of the stream west of Kudinovo; and

38th RD – Iartsevo Station and Marker 174.7;

108th RD is defending the Marker 169.9 and Buianovo sector on the eastern bank of the Vop' River; and

127th TB is in the army commander's reserve in the Ozerishche region.

48 prisoners have been taken, including 1 officer.

The quantity of trophies seized has not been verified.

The army's units will continue the offensive on the morning of 2 September, with its previous missions.

Eighth. 20th Army. The army's units continued their offensive during the second half of the day on 1 September, while fulfilling their previous missions. They dug into the positions they reached on the night of 1-2 September.

144th RD, having encountered strong enemy fire resistance from the direction of Pnevo, and, as a result of a stubborn battle in Liakhovo, had no success and dug in along into positions from 1 kilometer east of Skrushevo to 200 meters east of Pnevo and to 1 kilometer northeast of Mit'kovo and Liakhovo.

153rd RD, having encountered heavy fire and barbed wire entanglements on the unnamed heights north of Dubrova, dug into positions from 600-800 meters west of Logunovo to 600-800 meters west of Ratchino.

161st RD, while developing the offensive, advanced 300-400 meters west of Dubrova on its right wing by day's end and fought for the forest south of Golovino on its left wing, but, having encountered barbed wire entanglements and blockhouses, had no further success and dug into the positions it reached.

73rd RD, while developing the offensive on its right wing, advanced 1 kilometer west of the barn and, having encountered strong fire from bunkers, dug into the positions it reached.

229th RD, while firmly defending its occupied positions, drove the enemy out of the woods northwest of Vishniaki by a brief strike toward Hill 249.9 at 1700 hours on 1 September and captured Hill 249.9 and advanced 500 meters to the south by day's end. A further advance by the division was halted by strong enemy fire from the direction of the grove northeast of Suborovka.

129th RD is defending the positions it occupies.

The army's units will continue the offensive on the morning of 2 September, with their previous missions.

Ninth. 133rd RD is moving from Viaz'ma to Sychevka by two trains at 0800 hours on 2 September. The division's remaining units are loading or ready for loading.

178th RD (equipment) – one train left from Viaz'ma Station at 0620 hours on 2 September. The positions of the division's units, which are being transported by trucks, are being verified.

Our losses of ground forces are being verified.

Tenth. The VVS of the *front* supported the offensives by 16th and 19th Armies's units during the first half of the day on 2 September. Overall, a total of 75 aircraft sorties were carried out.

43rd AD protected concentrations of forces in the Prisel'e, Skachkovo, Iartsevo Station region and the unloading at Viaz'ma, Semtsevo, and Izdeshkovo and attacked centers of enemy resistance in the Morevo and Babaevo region.

47th AD assaulted enemy motor-mechanized units, artillery, and infantry in the Krotovo, Myshkovo, Bykova, Shchelkina, Shishkovo, and Sushchevo region and conducted reconnaissance and re-basing in new airfields.

As a result of the assault operations, up to 8 enemy tanks, up to 32 vehicles, 12 motorcycles, and 2 armored vehicles were destroyed or put out of actions, and the enemy suffered heavy losses in personnel.

46th and 31st AD did not carry out combat flights in light of the unfavorable weather conditions.

38th RAS conducted reconnaissance in the Safonovo, Dukhovshchina, Iartsevo, and Smolensk region.

Our losses: 1 PE-2 aircraft did not return to its airfield.

> The Chief of Staff of the Western Front, Lieutenant General Sokolovsky
> The Military Commissar of the Western Front's headquarters,
>   Brigade Commissar Kazbintsev
> The Chief of the Operations Department, Lieutenant General Malandin

Source: "Operativnaia svodka shtaba Zapadnogo fronta No. 135 k 8 chasam 2 sentiabria 1941 g. o boevykh deistviiakh voisk fronta" [Operational summary no. 135 of the headquarters of the Western Front at 0800 hours on 2 September 1941 about the combat operations of the *front's* forces], *SBDVOV*, issue 41, 106-109.

35. Combat Order of the Commander of the Forces of 16th Army of 2 September 1941 on Capturing the Nikitino, Luk'ianiki, and Trekhsviat'e Line

To the Commanders of 1st TD and 152nd, 38th, and 108th RDs, and 127th TB

16th Army will go on the offensive at 1000 hours on 2 September 1941, with the missions to capture the Nikitino, Grishino, Luk'ianiki, Maliavshchina, and Trekhsviat'e line and, subsequently, reach the line of the Khmost' River.

1st TD – Immediate mission – capture Nikitino and Grishino, and subsequently attack toward Khmost'.

152nd RD – Immediate mission – capture the (incl.) Grishino and (incl.) Gorodok line; and subsequently attack toward Medvedeva.

38th RD – Immediate mission – capture the Gorodok and Lopatkina line (southern), and subsequently attack toward Borodino.

108th RD – Immediate mission—capture the Minino and Chadovishchi line, and subsequently attack toward Kartyshi.

127th TB – my reserve: plan to move into and operate in 1st TD for exploiting success.

All divisions will operate within their previous boundary line in accordance with Order No. 2/op.

The Commander of 16th Army, Major General Rokossovsky
The Member of the Military Council, Division Commissar Lobachev

Source: "Boevoe rasporiazhenie komanduiushchego voiskami 16-i Armii ot 2 sentiabria 1941 g. na ovladenie rubezhom Nikitino, Luk'ianiki, Trekhsviat'e" [Combat order of the commander of the forces of 16th Army of 2 September 1941 on capturing the Nikitino, Luk'ianiki, and Trekhsviat'e line], *SBDVOV*, issue 42, 145.

36. Combat Report of the Headquarters of 16th Army to the Chief of Staff of the Western Front of 2 September about the Army's Combat Operations and Positions at 1700 hours on 2 September 1941

To the Chief of Staff of the Western Front
To the Chiefs of Staff of 19th and 20th Armies
1:50,000 scale map
1900 hours on 2 September 1941

First. The enemy is offering stubborn resistance along the army's entire front.

Second. 16th Army's units, while continuing the offensive, were fighting along [the following] line at 1700 hours on 2 September:

152nd RD – the western outskirts of Soprykina and the eastern slopes of Hill 234.9, and attacked Hill 234.9 repeatedly;

38th RD – the western slopes of Hill 209.2, the eastern outskirts of Pervomaiskii village, and the eastern outskirts of Pologi;

108th RD is conducting sustained fighting in the Svishchevo and Zadnia sector on the western bank of the Vop' River.

1st TD's positions are being verified, and I will report additionally about conditions on the division's front.

To the first point. The enemy displayed greater activity all day on 2 September than was the case on 1 September 1941. The enemy noticeably strengthened the strength of artillery and mortar fire along the army's entire front. Flanking fire by artillery and mortars continued in the Krovopuskovo region and in the woods to the west.

Malinin, Sedenkov

Source: "Boevoe donesenie shtaba 16-i Armii nachal'niku shtaba Zapadnogo fronta ot 2-sentiabria 1941 g. o boevykh deistviiakh i polozhenii voisk armii k 17 chasam 2 sentiabria 1941 g." [Combat report of the headquarters of 16th Army to the chief of staff of the Western Front of 2 September about the army's combat operations and positions at 1700 hours on 2 September 1941], *SBDVOV*, 145.

37. Operational Summary No. 94 of the Headquarters of 30th Army at 1700 hours on 2 September 1941 about the Positions of the Army's Forces

Operational Summary No. 94, Headquarters, 30th Army,
1700 hours on 2 September 1941

1. The army's units have been continuing the offensive and exchanging fire with the enemy since 0800 hours on 2 September 1941. We have had no success by 1700 hours. The enemy is offering strong fire resistance, while committing large caliber mortars and heavy artillery, and is conducting fire from the Krivets, Rekta, Kostino, Fomenki, Pochinok, and Zarech'e regions.

134th RD's 629th RR, having given up the positions it occupies from Bor to Okolitsa to 250th RD's 922nd RR, has been completing its march to 134th RD's concentration region since 0800 hours on 2 September 1941.

2. The army's units have not advanced by 1700 hours. They are located in their previous positions, while exchanging fire with the enemy.

Losses: killed or wounded – 48 men.

3. Heavy rain is passing through the army's sector, and the roads are passable for auto-transport only with difficulty.

Communications with the divisions is intermittent.

Communications with the *front's* headquarters was only by radio from 1300 hours to 1630 hours.

The Chief of Staff
The Military Commissar,
The Chief of the Operations Department

Source: "Operativnaia svodka shtaba 30-i Armii No. 94 k 17 chasam 2 sentiabria 1941 g. o polozhenii voisk armii" [Operational summary no. 94 of the headquarters of 30th Army at 1700 hours on 2 September 1941 about the positions of the army's forces], *SBDVOV*, issue 41, 294.

38. Operational Summary No. 136 of the Headquarters of the Western Front at 2000 hours on 2 September 1941 about the Combat Operations of the *Front's* Forces

Operational Summary No. 136 at 2000 hours on 2 September 1941,
Headquarters. Western Front
1:500,000 and 100,000 scale maps

First. On the *front's* right wing, 22nd Army is fighting on the western outskirts of Andreapol' with its right wing,

In the center and on the left wing, 22nd Army and 29th Army's forces were continuing to fortify the positions they occupy along the eastern bank of the Western Dvina River, with small enemy reconnaissance groups on their front.

In the *front's* center and on its left wing, 30th, 19th, 16h, and 20th Armies' forces were continuing the offensive.

Second. 22nd Army, while continuing to restore order, conducted sustained fighting with enemy motorized infantry and tanks on the western outskirts of

Andreapol' with its right wing (214th RD) on 2 September and continued to fortify the positions it occupies in its center and on its left wing.

214th RD, under heavy pressure from up to two battalions of enemy infantry, supported by 30 tanks, attacking from the direction of Ramen'e, withdrew its right wing to the western outskirts of Andreapol' and Karabanovo by 1200 hours on 2 September, where it is now fighting. The division's units on the northern and southern outskirts of Andreapol' launched counterattacks at 1200 hours on 2 September and drove the enemy back to the west. The positions are being verified.

A detachment of 300 men is being dispatched toward Kozhulovo and Stolbino for an attack against the rear of the attacking enemy groups.

The positions of the army's remaining units are unchanged.

The enemy is not displaying any activity, while conducting occasional artillery and mortar fire.

Third. 29th Army. The positions of the army's units are unchanged, and enemy units are digging into the positions they occupy.

The enemy is not displaying any activity on the army's front. The enemy is conducting entrenching work and concentrating motorized infantry and tanks in the Zhelezovo region on the western bank of the Western Dvina River.

Fourth. Cavalry Group Dovator. The Cavalry Group, numbering 2,500 men, reached and linked up with its horse-holders (about 1,500 men) and is concentrating in the Filino region.

Fifth. 30th Army, while carrying out a partial regrouping, went on the attack along the Novoe Morokhovo and Gorodno front at 0900 hours on 2 September.

The army's offensive failed to achieve success in a single sector of the front. At 1700 hours on 2 September, the army's units exchanged fire from their previous positions.

The enemy, while committing heavy artillery and heavy mortars into the battle, resisted stubbornly, while continuing to defend on the army's front.

134th RD's 629th RR was relieved in its defensive sector from Bor to Okolitsa by 922nd RR (250th RD) and has been on the march to 134th RD's defensive region since 0800 hours on 2 September.

226th RR (250th RD) – is in the army's reserve – in the Sukharevo, Vorob'ikha, and Ponomari region.

Sixth. 19th Army went on the offensive at 0900 hours on 2 September after a 15-minute artillery preparation. The army's right wing fought in its previous positions all day. The center and left wing slowly advanced. The army's reserve, 91st RD, was committed to combat on the army's left wing at 1400 hours for developing success.

The enemy, while defending on the army's front is offering strong resistance.

At 1700 hours on 2 September, the army's units are fighting [in the following locations]:

244th, 166th, 89th, and 50th RDs, while encountering strong fire resistance in the enemy's defense, had no success in advancing and are fighting in their previous positions.

64th RD, while conducting an attack toward Maslovo, advanced 200-300 meters by 1400 hours, and the division's left wing forced the Tsarevich River. The division's units are continuing the attack under intense enemy mortar, machine gun, and artillery fire.

91st RD (the army commander's reserve), having relieved 101st TD's units in the Osipova and Hill 222.8 sector, has been attacking toward Koz'mina and Stepankova (northern) since 1400 hours.

101st TD, in cooperation with 1st TD's right wing (16th Army), is continuing to develop the offensive, while advancing slowly toward the west. The division's left wing advanced 700-1,000 meters to the west of Kholm by 1700 hours. The attacks by the division's units are continuing. In the division's sector, an enemy "Fokke-Vul'f" aircraft has been shot down by machine gun fire, and the aircraft's crew of 3 men has been taken prisoner.

45th CD is in its previous region prepared to develop the offensive in the army's center and on its left wing.

Seventh. 16th Army continued the offensive with its right wing at 1000 hours on 2 September, with previous missions, while encountered strong enemy fire resistance along the entire front. The left wing is defending its previous positions.

Units of enemy 28th ID's 336th IR are defending on the army's front. The enemy is employing mining and engineer obstacles extensively.

The army's units were fighting [as follows] at 1230 hours:

1st TD – in positions on the eastern bank of the stream south of Samuilova, while having forward units in the woods 1.5-2 kilometers west of the stream;

152nd RD – on the eastern bank of the unnamed stream west and southwest of Kudinovo; and

38th RD –on the eastern outskirts of Pervomaiskii village and the eastern outskirts of Pologi.

108th RD is continuing to defend its previous lines.

127th TB is in the army commander's reserve in the Ozerishche region.

Trophies: 2 guns, 2 mortars, and 20 rifles.

Losses: 1st TD – killed or wounded – 25 men, 152nd RD – killed or wounded – 150 men,; and being verified in the army's remaining units.

The offensive is continuing.

Eighth. 20th Army continued to develop the offensive with its right wing, with previous missions, on the morning of 2 September. It encountered strong enemy fire resistance along the entire front and repelled local enemy counterattacks.

144th, 161st, 153rd, and 73rd RDs conducted fire from their previous positions, with insignificant advances in separate sectors, while repelling local enemy counterattacks.

229th and 129th RDs are continuing to defend their previous positions.

Ninth. 133rd RD – has loaded and dispatched out 6 trains by rail, and 3 trains are loading.

178th RD: of the equipment and supplies following by rail, 7 trains have been loaded and sent out, and one train is being loaded. Of those already dispatched, one train is unloading at Nelidovo Station.

The units being transferred by auto-transport – 38th RR concentrated in the woods south of Nelidovo by 2000 hours on 2 September; and the main forces – 709th and 639th RRs – had their lead elements at Bosino (13 kilometers southeast of Belyi) at 1730 hours.

Tenth. The VVS of the *front* did not carry out flights on the night of 1-2 September and the first half of the day on 2 September because of poor weather conditions.

The 1 PE-2 aircraft that did not return on 1 September has been discovered. The aircraft is in full operating condition and will return to its airfield when weather conditions are favorable.

> The Chief of Staff of the Western Front, Lieutenant General Sokolovsky
> The Military Commissar of the Western Front's headquarters,
> > Brigade Commissar Kazbintsev
> The Chief of the Operations Department,
> > Lieutenant General Malandin [signed by Colonel Belianko]

Source: "Operativnaia svodka shtaba Zapadnogo fronta No. 136 k 20 chasam 2 sentiabria 1941 g. o boevykh deistviiakh voisk fronta" [Operational summary no. 136 of the headquarters of the Western Front at 2000 hours on 2 September 1941 about the combat operations of the *front's* forces], *SBDVOV*, issue 41, 110-112.

39. Report by the Headquarters of the Western Front about Cavalry Group Dovator's Operations in the Enemy's Rear from 23 August through 2 September 1941

To the Chief of the RKKA's General Staff, Marshal of the Soviet Union Comrade Shaposhnikov

A Report
About the Operations of Comrade Dovator's Cavalry Group
(50th and 53rd RDs) in the Belyi, Demidov, and Dukhovshchina Regions
in the Enemy's Rear from 23 August through 2 September 1941

I. On 10 August 1941, the Military Council of the Western Front personally assigned the cavalry group the [following] missions:

> a) Enter the enemy's rear in the Demidov and Dukhovshchina region;

> b) Paralyze enemy communications, while destroying transport, warehouses, headquarters, and communications means; and

> c) Clarify the attitudes of the population to the Red Army in the territory occupied by the enemy.

II. During the course of 11 and 12 August, the cavalry group prepared itself for the fulfillment of its assigned missions and, after a 50-kilometer march through forested swampy terrain, concentrated in the Nizhne Karakovo, Budnitsa, and Shveikin region with a force of 3,000 sabers and 30 heavy machine guns on 14 August.

A reconnaissance group established the presence the enemy in Filino, Boiarshchino, Rozhino, and Kotovo.

The enemy was thrown back to the Krestovaia, Podviaz'e, and Ust'e (northern) line by the actions of the cavalry group's forward detachments.

The enemy, while defending positions from Shikhtovo to Krestovaia, Podviaz'e, and Ust'e, offered very strong resistance, and the cavalry group conducted unsuccessful fighting from 15 through 22 August, while striving to penetrate the enemy's defenses, with the aim of entering the rear.

The group conducted a regrouping on 22 August 1941 and, having concentrated its main forces in the Mit'kovo region at 0400 hours on 23 August and having smashed the 9th Battalion of the enemy's 9th ID's 430th IR in the Ust'e region, penetrated the enemy's defenses east of Podviaz'e and entered the Turnaeva region with 5 cavalry regiments and one composite regiment.

From 23 through 30 August, the group operated in the Zhemokhova, Rybsheva, and Zabor'e region, where it destroyed enemy headquarters, transports, and warehouses and demolished enemy communications installations on the Demidov and Belyi and Demidov and Dukhovshchina communications routes.

III. Having fulfilled its assigned missions, the cavalry group returned to its own forces in the Chichata region on 2 September.

At the present time, the cavalry group is concentrated in the Smorodovka, Sholakhovka, and Vas'kova region, where it is putting itself in order.

IV. As a result of the energetic operations by Dovator's cavalry in the enemy's rear area from 23 August through 2 September, the cavalry group destroyed: up to 3,000 German soldiers, 19 officers, 150 vehicles of various types, 4 armored personnel carriers, 2 tanks, 4 guns, 6 mortars, and 3 heavy machine guns; seized 65 light machine guns, 67 horses, and many rifles and automatic weapons, burned: 3 warehouses with ammunition and several fuel cisterns [tanks], and smashed two battalion headquarters and one regimental headquarters.

The cavalry group brought back from the rear 400 [enemy] soldiers and commanders.

During its stay in the enemy's rear, the cavalry group determined:

a) The vast majority of the population in enemy-occupied territory relates well to the Red Army and waits impatiently for the Red Army's return;

b) An absence of enemy reserves in the Demidov and Dukhovshchina region; and

c) The enemy's great attention to harvesting crops in the fields.

Experience demonstrates that, while organizing raids into the enemy's rear by similar cavalry groups, it is necessary to include in these groups small-caliber artillery, AT guns, a small number of light tanks, and powerful radio sets.

V. A more detailed report about the cavalry group's operations will be submitted by the Military Council of the Western Front directly to the Supreme High Commander on 5 September 1941.

> The Chief of Staff of the Western Front, Lieutenant General Sokolovsky
> The Military Commissar of the Western Front's headquarters,
>   Brigade Commissar Kazbintsev
> The Chief of the Operations Department, Lieutenant General Malandin

Source: "Doklad shtaba Zapadnogo front nachal'niku General'nogo Shtaba o deistviiakh Kavaleriiskoi Gruppy Dovatora v tylu protivnika s 23 avgusta po 2 sentiabria 1941 g." [Report by the headquarters of the Western Front about Cavalry Group Dovator's operations in the enemy's rear from 23 August through 2 September 1941], *SBDVOV*, issue 41, 67-68.

40. Combat Order No. 049 of the Commander of the Forces of 19th Army of 3 September 1941 on a Continuation of the Offensive toward Dukhovshchina

Combat Order No. 049, CP, Commander, 19th Army,
the woods 1 kilometer east of Vasilisino
0240 hours on 3 September 1941
1:50,000 scale map

1. On the right wing and in the army's center, the enemy is defending, while offering resistance with organized machine gun and mortar fire. On the left wing, he is withdrawing to the Skachkova and Chistaia line.

2. The neighbors are fulfilling their previous missions.

3. 19th Army, while defending on the Pavlovshchina and Novoselishche front, will continue the offensive in the general direction of Dukhovshchina in its center and on its left wing at 0800 hours on 3 September 1941.

4. 244th, 166th, 89th, and 50th RDs – missions as before.

5. 64th RD, with its reinforcing units and 2nd and 3rd Bns, 596th HAR, will attack, while conducting a main attack toward Sloboda and Sel'tso [20 kilometers north of Iartsevo]. In cooperation with 91st RD, destroy the enemy in the Sloboda, Osinovki, and Khutkova region and capture crossings over the Tsarevich River at Sushchevo with part of your force by an attack along the southern bank of the Tsarevich River. Reach the Sushchevo, Kulagino, and Stepankova (northern) line [8-16 kilometers north-northwest of Iartsevo] by day's end.

The boundary on the left: up to Popova, as before, and further to – Rafenina, (incl.) Stepankova (northern), and (incl.) Griaznoki.

6. 91st RD, while delivering a main attack toward Kokhanova sand Makeeva, in cooperation with 64th RD and 101st TD, destroy the enemy in the Rafenina, Stepankova (southern), Borki, Potapova, and Kokhanovo region. Capture the Hill 215.8 and Borki line by day's end and cut the Iartsevo and Dukhovshchina road at Tret'iakovo [15 kilometers northwest of Iartsevo] with forward units.

The boundary on the left is as before.

7. 101st TD will continue to develop success, while delivering an attack toward Mkhovka. Capture the Borki and Vorotyshino line [8-12 kilometers north-northwest of Iartsevo] by day's end. Cut the Iartsevo and Dukhovshchina road in the Nizovo Selo region with forward units.

8. 45th CD will be prepared to enter the penetration in 91st RD's and 101 TD's sectors to estroy the enemy's rear area and headquarters in the Dukhovshchina region. Concentrate in the woods west of Dukhovshchina by day's end for subsequent operations in the enemy's rear.

9. Reserve – 735th RR – in its present positions.

10. Artillery. Readiness by 0600 hours on 3 September 1941.
Missions:

1) Suppress enemy artillery in the [following] regions:
a) Rakhmanino, Mashutino, Sushchevo, and Turishchevo; and
b) Navol'nia, Khutkova, Osinovka, and Siniakova.

2) Prevent enemy counterattacks from the Potapova region.

11. VVS: Missions:

1) Protect the army's grouping in the Sushchevo, Kokhanovo, and Vasilisino region.

2) Assist 64th and 91st RDs and 101st TD in the destruction of the enemy in the Stepankova, Petrykina, and Potapova region. Destroy enemy reserves approaching from Dukhovshchina.

3) Conduct reconnaissance along the axes: a) Berdino and Dmitrovka; b) Ponizov'e and Otriadnoe; c) Lukshino and Dukhovshchina; and d) observe enemy groupings in the Stepankova, Petrykina, and Potapova region.

12. CP and the headquarters of the army – in their previous points.

13. Operational and reconnaissance summaries – at the previous times.

The Commander of 19th Army, Lieutenant General Konev
The Member of the Military Council of 19th Army,
    Division Commissar Sheklanov
The Chief of Staff of 19th Army, [Malyshkin]

Source: "Boevoi prikaz komanduiushchego voiskami 19-i Armii No. 049 ot 3 September 1941 g. na prodolzhenii nastupleniia v napravlenii Dukhovshchina" [Combat order no. 049 of the commander of the forces of 19th Army of 3 September 1941 on a continuation of the offensive toward Dukhovshchina], *SBDVOV*, issue 41, 197-198.

41. Operational Summary No. 40 of the Headquarters of 16th Army of 0300 hours on 3 September 1941 about the Positions of the Army's Forces

Operational Summary No. 40, Headquarters, 16th Army,
the woods northeast of Khotenova
0300 hours on 3 September 1941
1:100,000 scale map

1. 16th Army is continuing to develop an offensive in the general direction of Stepanovo and Nikola-Edrevichi at 1000 hours on 2 September 1941.

The enemy's 336th IR and 28th ID's units are continuing to operate on the army's front. The enemy is offering stubborn fire resistance, while using mines and engineer obstacles extensively. The enemy attacked 1st TD's right flank at 1730 hours on 2 September 1941 and captured Novosel'e (eastern) at 1800 hours. The situation on the 1st TD's front was restored by 2100 hours by an attack with 127th TB on Novosel'e (eastern).

2. 1st TD dug into the [following] positions by 2400 hours on 2 September 1941:

a) 6th MRR – the western outskirts of Kholm; and

b) 175th MRR – the western edge of the grove of woods, 1.5 kilometers west of Novosel'e (western).

152nd RD dug into positions from the northwestern edge of the woods east of Kudinova to Hill 234.9.

a) 544th RR is digging into positions from the edge of the woods east of Kudinova to Kudinovo, with its front facing northwest;

b) 480th RR is digging in on Hill 234.9; and

c) 646th RR is digging in on the northern edge of the woods 1.5 kilometers north of Khatyni.

Trophies: 105mm battery, 6 tanks, and many mortars and other weapons.

38th RD dug into positions from the eastern outskirts of Panina to the northwestern outskirts of Iartsevo and the southeastern outskirts of Pologi. The division has the mission during the night to reach the Hill 234.9 and Pologi front. Losses for 2 September 1941: killed – 9 men and wounded – 259. Seven men were taken prisoner.

Trophies: 4 large caliber machine guns, 24 rifles, and 1 telephone apparatus.

108th RD is conducting heavy fighting in the Alferova and Zadnia sector on the western bank of the Vop' River.

127th TB attacked the enemy along the Novosel'e (eastern) and Krovopuskovo axis at 1800 hours on 2 September 1941. As a result of the attack, the situation on 1st TD's front was restored by 2200 hours on 2 September 1941.

The brigade crushed the enemy's 11th Separate Infantry Battalion.

15 AT guns, 5 field guns, and 12 mortars were destroyed.

The brigade concentrated in the Novosel'e (eastern) region by 2100 hours, where it is restoring order and replenishing its ammunition.

3. Neighbor on the right – 101st TD is fighting on the Osipova, Skachkovo, and northeastern outskirts of Kholm front. Communications with it are by liaison officer.

Neighbor on the left – 144th RD is fighting along the Makeevo and Liakhovo front on the western bank of the Dnepr River. Communications with it are by liaison officer.

4. The roads in the army's sector are being washed away by rain and are impassable for auto-transport.

Communications with the army's units is by radio, telephone, and liaison officers.

Bottles with mixtures of "KS" were not employed on the army's front on 2 September 1941.

5. Headquarters of the army – the woods 1 kilometer northeast of Khotenova.

CP of the army commander – the woods 1 kilometer north of Vyshegor.

> The Chief of Staff of 16th Army, Colonel Malinin
> The Military Commissar of the Headquarters,
>   Regimental Commissar Sedenkov
> The Chief of the Operations Department, Colonel Bulanov

Source: "Operativnaia svodka shtaba 16-i Armii No. 40 k 3 chasam 3 sentiabria 1941 g. o polozhenii voisk armii" [Operational summary no. 40 of the headquarters of 16th Army of 0300 hours on 3 September 1941 about the positions of the army's forces], *SBDVOV*, issue 41, 146-147.

42. Operational Summary No. 96 of the Headquarters of 30th Army at 1700 hours on 3 September 1941 about the Combat Operations of the Army's Forces

Operational Summary No. 96, Headquarters, 30th Army,
the woods 2 kilometers northeast of Podzaitsevo,
1700 hours on 3 September 1941

1:100,000 and 50,000 scale maps

The army's units have been continuing to conduct an offensive unsuccessfully since 1200 hours on 3 September and are conducting defensive work on the right wing

The enemy is offering fire resistance, while striving to hold on to his main centers of resistance.

2. The army's [are doing the following] at 1700 hours:

134th RD is conducting defensive work on the positions it occupies. The division's units are occupying their previous positions.

107th TD, while protecting the Belyi axis, is continuing defensive work.

250th RD (without 926th RR).

922nd RR occupies defenses in the Bor and Okolitsa region.

918th RR is conducting a fire fight for Kiriakino and Lake Sutoki.

242nd RD, while continuing its attack, encircled Churkino from the north, south, and east by 1700 hours and is fighting to capture Churkino.

162nd RD is attacking toward Ivkino, while encountering strong enemy fire resistance.

251st RD, while advancing on Kerets, Novoselki, and Mamonovo, is fighting in positions from Muk to Novoselki and road junction 40 meters east of Mamonovo.

250th RD's 926th RR – the commander's reserve – is located in its previous positions.

The weather is cloudy. The roads are difficult for the passage by auto-transport. Communications with the divisions is working without interruption.

The Chief of Staff
The Military Commissar
The Chief of the Operations Department

Source: "Operativnaia svodka shtaba 30-i Armii No. 96 k 17 chasam 3 sentiabria 1941 g. o boevykh deistviiakh voisk armii" [Operational summary no. 96 of the headquarters of 30th Army at 1700 hours on 3 September 1941 about the combat operations of the army's forces], *SBDVOV*, issue 41, 294-295.

43. Combat Order No. 063 of the Commander of the Forces of 20th Army of 3 September 1941 on an Offensive toward Slotovo

Combat Order No. 063, Headquarters, 20th Army,
OP of the army commander, Osovo,
1830 hours on 3 September 1941
1:50,000 scale map

1. The enemy, having suffered the defeat of 8th ID's by two rifle regiments, is continuing to defend the Makeevo, Pnevo, Mit'kovo, Liakhovo, Dubrova, the woods south of Golovino, Novaia Malinovka and Sopshino front and 263rd ID – from Sopshino, Suborovka, Klemiatino, and Ustrom River front.

2. 20th Army, while fortifying the positions it has reached, will continue the offensive in the general direction of Slotovo with its left wing, in its center, and with its right wing, with the missions to smash the opposing enemy and reach the Mashkino

and Nadva River line by day's end on 4 September, having seized crossings over the Khmost' River with its forward units.

3. On the right, 16th Army's units are conducting a successful offensive toward the west.

The boundary line with it is as before.

On the left, 24th Army is conducting a successful offensive toward El'nia.

The boundary line with it is as before.

4. 144th RD (without 449th RR), while firmly holding on to the positions it occupies with one battalion, seize Pnevo with two battalions, and while attacking from the east and northeast, seize Mit'kovo with one regiment, while protecting the army's shock group from the right flank. Subsequently, plan to attack toward Mashkino.

The boundary on the left: the Dnepr River 1.5 kilometers north of Zabor'e, (incl.) Liakhovo, (incl.) Morevo, and (incl.) Pochinok.

5. 153rd RD, with 144th RD's 449th RR, and 302nd HAR, will occupy jumping-off positions from 200 meters east of Liakhovo to the road intersection 0.5 kilometers south of Liakhovo by 0500 hours on 4 September.

Begin an offensive on Liakhovo and Morevo at 1200 hours on 4 September and seize Morevo by day's end. Move a forward detachment forward into Pochinok. The division's combat formation on the western bank of the Dnepr River – is two regiments in first echelon and two regiments in second echelon.

The boundary on the left: (incl.) Osovo, Logunovo, and the northern outskirts of Morevo.

6. 161st RD, with 592nd GAR, having relieved 153rd RD's units and having occupied jumping-off positions 200 meters from the enemy on the heights west of Ratchino, will begin an attack toward Babeevo and Morevo State Farm at 1200 hours and capture Morevo State Farm by day's end, having moved a forward detachment forward to the Khmost' River west of Hill 186.6.

The division's combat formation on the western bank of the Dnepr River – is two regiments in first echelon and one – in second echelon on the right wing north of Ratchino.

The boundary [on the left]: (incl.) the barn 1 kilometer south of Zabor'e, the southern outskirts of Ratchino, and Morevo State Farm.

7. 73rd RD, having relieving 161st RD's units in the sector from Pashkovo to the woods to the south by 2400 hours on 3 September and while protecting the left flank of the army's grouping, will attack toward the southern outskirts of Dubrova and Titkovo with one regiment at 1200 hours on 4 September and seize Titkovo by day's end. While holding on to the front you occupy, assist the attack by the army's shock group by seizing the woods south of Titkovo and Novaia and Staraia Malinovka ith the remaining units. Upon seizing Titkovo, move a forward detachment forward to the Khmost' River and Riabinino Collective Farm.

The boundary on the left is as before.

8. 229th RD and 129th RD will continue to defend the lines they occupy firmly.

Prevent the enemy from taking units and transferring them from the division's front to other sectors.

9. The army's Chief of Artillery [will]:

a) Support the attack and advance by 153rd and 161st RDs' infantry up to positions from the grove 1 kilometer southwest of Liakhovo to the western outskirts of Babeevo – by barrage fire; and subsequently by successive concentrations of fire against the objectives of the infantry;

b) Support the advance by 153rd and 161st RDs' infantry by blocking fires and cutting-off fires from the direction of Mit'kovo, Morevo, Morevo State Farm, and the woods south of Dubrovo;

c) I am designating 126th CAR as DD [long-range] artillery, with the missions: to suppress enemy artillery and, first and foremost, enemy mortar batteries in the Pnevo and Pnevskaia Sloboda, Mashkino, Vachkovo State Farm, and Morevo, and Morevo State Farm and Titkovo regions; and

d) Conduct the artillery preparation by methodical aimed fire from 1100 to 1200 hours on 4 September 1941.

10. Begin the general attack at 1200 hours in accordance with the general signal – a series of green rockets from the OPs of the division commanders.

11. Ammunition expenditure on 4 September will be no more than 0.75 combat loads.

12. My CP – the hill west of Osovo.

The Commander of 20th Army, Lieutenant General Lukin
The Member of the Military Council, Corps Commissar Semenovsky
The Chief of Staff of 20th Army, Major General Korneev

Source: "Boevoi prikaz komanduiushchego voiskami 20-i Armii No. 063 ot 3 sentiabria 1941 g. na prodolzhenii nastupleniia v napravlenii Slotovo" [Combat order no. 063 of the commander of the forces of 20th Army of 3 September 1941 on an offensive toward Slotovo], *SBDVOV*, issue 41, 226-227.

44. Operational Summary No. 138 of the Headquarters of the Western Front at 2000 hours on 3 September 1941 about the Combat Operations of the *Front's* Forces

Operational Summary No. 138 at 2000 hours on 3 September 1941,
Headquarters. Western Front
1:500,000 and 100,000 scale maps

First. On the *front's* right wing, 22nd Army is continuing to fight with enemy infantry and tanks on the western outskirts of Andreapol', and there are artillery exchanges on the Benovo and Plotomoi line; 29th Army, while continuing to fortify the positions its occupies, has the mission to destroy the up to an infantry regiment of enemy, with tanks, which has penetrated to the eastern bank of the Western Dvina River in the Suvorovo and Ivanova Gora region, with the forces of 22nd Army's 252nd and 126th RDs.

In the center and on the *front's* left wing, 30th, 19th, 16h, and 20th Armies' forces were continuing the offensive.

Second. 22nd Army is conducting fighting with enemy infantry and tanks on the western outskirts of Andreapol' on its right wing at 1430 hours on 3 September.

In 186th RD's sector in the center, there is fighting to liquidate the up to a regiment of enemy infantry, which has penetrated into the Suvorovo and Ivanova Gora region.

On its left wing (126th RD), it successfully repulsed enemy attempts to force the Western Dvina River from positions at Arkhangely and Pavlovo [28 kilometers south of Andreapol'].

174th RD, while occupying the northwestern, western, and southern outskirts of Andreapol', has been fighting with a regiment of enemy infantry with tanks since 0900 hours on 3 September.

214th RD occupies defenses along the eastern bank of the Western Dvina River south of Andreapol'.

179th RD, while occupying its previous positions, is conducting strong artillery and mortar fire.

186th RD is fighting with an enemy force of up to a regiment, which has penetrated into the Suvorovo and Ivanova Gora region [18 kilometers south of Andreapol'].

126th RD has the mission to liquidate the enemy, which have penetrated into the Suvorovo region, by combined operations with 29thArmy's 186th and 252nd RDs.

Information has not been received about the operations of the detachments at Novaia and Dudino.

Third. 29th Army is continuing to dig into the positions it occupies along the eastern bank of the Western Dvina River.

243rd RD – the units' positions are unchanged. The units of an enemy PzD are operating on the division's front, and the enemy is conducting strong artillery and mortar fire.

246th RD – positions are unchanged. The enemy is conducting artillery and mortar fire.

252nd RD left the region it occupied region at 0300 hours of 3 September, with the mission, together with 22nd Army's 126th RD, to destroy the enemy in 186th RD's sector,. ˙

The Motorized Brigade – is in its previous positions.

Information has not been received about 29th CR's positions.

Fourth. Cavalry Group Dovator. The positions of the group are unchanged. The group's units are putting themselves in order.

Fifth. 30th Army, while defending on its right wing, went on the offensive from the Novoe Morokhovo and Gorodno line at 1200 hours on 3 September with part of the forces of 250th, 242nd, 162nd, and 251st RDs.

The offensive by the army's units during the day were unsuccessful, and by 1700 hours the army's units were fighting in their previous positions.

The enemy, while continuing to hold onto its centers of resistance, offered stubborn resistance.

107th TD occupies the Belyi region as before.

Sixth. 19th Army continued its offensive at 0800 hours on 3 September in its center and on its right wing.

The offensive by the army's units provided no important results.

The units advanced only 100-200 meters in separate sectors of the front by 1700 hours.

The enemy, having strengthened his defensive sectors on the army's front with mined obstacles and barbed wire, is meeting the offensive by the army's units with automatic weapons, mortar, and artillery fire.

The army's units, while concentrating their efforts on the left wing, conducted a decisive offensive at 1800 hours, with the mission to destroy the enemy in the Petrova, the woods west of Kokhanova, and Osinovka region.

The positions of the divisions are unchanged.

Losses and trophies of 144th RD for 2 September:

Losses: killed – 13 killed – 75 wounded.

Trophies: 210 rifles, 3 heavy machine guns, 8 light machine guns, 3 mortars, 3 bicycles, 131 gas masks, and 8,500 small-arms rounds.

Seventh. 16th Army continued to develop the offensive with its right wing at 1400 hours on 3 September, while fulfilling previous missions.

1st TD – reached positions on the eastern bank of the stream south of Samuilova with its forward units by 1630 hours. At the same time, its main forces reached positions from the western outskirts of Novosel'e to the western edge of the woods north of Kudinovo.

152nd RD is fighting in its previous positions.

38th RD is fighting stubbornly for Panino, Pervomaiskii village and Pologi, while enveloping these points from the south and southwest.

108th RD is fighting in its previous lines.

According to verified information, during the fighting on 2 September, 127th TB destroyed 15 antitank guns, 5 field guns, and 12 mortars. One 105mm battery, 6 tanks, 4 large caliber machine guns, and 24 rifles were seized.

Eighth. 20th Army continued the offensive with its right wing at 0900 hours on 3 September, and is fighting sustained battles along the Pnevo and Sopshino front in the enemy's defensive belt. The left wing is defending its previous positions.

Repeated attacks by 144th and 153rd RDs on Mit'kovo and the Liakhovo region had no success. The division's units are fighting in their previous positions.

161st RD went on the attack toward Dubrova and Morevo State Farm at 1400 hours after a 30-minute artillery preparation.

The results are being verified.

73rd RD is fighting west of the barn, while blockading enemy pillboxes. 392nd RR is fighting in its previous positions.

229th and 129th RDs are defending their previous positions. There are occasional artillery exchanges along their front.

Ninth. 133rd RD – has loaded and sent out 19 trains by 2000 hours on 3 September, 2 trains are loading, and 9 trains have reached the unloading stations.

178th RD: of the equipment and supplies following by rail, 15 trains have been loaded and sent out, and 11 trains have arrived at the unloading station and are being unloaded.

The units being sent by auto-transport have arrived in full and are being unloaded in the Nelidovo region.

Tenth. The VVS of the *front*. The activities of the VVS during the first half of the day were limited to only reconnaissance flights because of poor weather conditions. A total of 10 aircraft sorties were carried out.

Reconnaissance was conducted [as follows]: 46th AD – in the Il'ino region, 31st AD – Toropets and Belyi Lug; and 43rd AD – Dukhovshchina.

23rd and 47th ADs and 38th RAS did not carry out flights.

Enemy losses: 1 KhSh-126 aircraft shot down.

Our losses: 1 I-16 aircraft did not return to its airfield. The one IaK-4 aircraft that did not return from fulfilling its mission of 30 August returned to its airfield.

The Chief of Staff of the Western Front, Lieutenant General Sokolovsky
The Military Commissar of the Western Front's headquarters,
  Brigade Commissar Kazbintsev
The Chief of the Operations Department, Lieutenant General Malandin

Source: "Operativnaia svodka shtaba Zapadnogo fronta No. 138 k 20 chasam 3 sentiabria 1941 g. o boevykh deistviiakh voisk fronta" [Operational summary no. 138 of the headquarters of the Western Front at 2000 hours on 3 September 1941 about the combat operations of the *front's* forces], *SBDVOV*, issue 41, 114-116.

45. Combat Order No. 050 of the Commander of the Forces of 19th Army of 3 September 1941 on a Continuation of the Army's Offensive toward Dukhovshchina

Combat Order No. 050, CP, Commander, 19th Army,
The woods 1 kilometer east of Vasilisino,
2330 hours on 3 September 1941

1:50,000 scale map

1. The enemy is holding on to the Mamonova, Panovo village, the woods with Marker 280.9 (1 kilometer northeast of Krotovo), Ivaniki, Zamiatino, and Shishkino line with stubborn resistance and abandoned Osipova and Kokhanovo under pressure of 91st RD and 101st TD.

Aircraft noticed the movement of enemy reserves northeastward from the Dukhovshchina by road at 1330 hours on 3 September 1941.

2. The neighbors are continuing to fulfill their previous missions.

3. The army will continue to fulfill the mission for the destruction of the enemy's Dukhovshchina grouping.

4. 244th RD, while firmly protecting the army's right flank on the Voskresensk, Shakhlovo, and Hill 229.3 front, will penetrate the enemy's defenses in the (incl.) Hill 229.7 and Novoselishche sector.

Immediate mission – capture Staraia Kazarina and (incl.) Krotovo and subsequently attack toward Kiseleva.

The boundary on the left is as before.

5. 166th RD (without 735th RR) will penetrate the enemy's defenses in the Ivaniki and grove at Marker 225.1 sector. Immediate mission – capture Hill 226.9 and (incl.) Bykova. Subsequently attack toward Myshkovo.

The boundary on the left is as before.

6. 89th RD will penetrate the enemy's defenses in the Semenkovo and Hill 213.6 sector, with the immediate mission to capture Bykovo and Sirotinka. Subsequently, attack toward Sel'tso to envelop the "Shchelkina" woods from the north. Provide assistance to 50th RD for the destruction of enemy strong point in Kazakova with part of your forces.

The boundary on the left is as before.

7. 50th RD (2nd RR) will destroy the enemy who are occupying Kazakova. Penetrate the enemy's defenses in the Hill 214.0 and (incl.) Ivanova sector.

Immediate mission – capture the Hill 211.6 region. Subsequently, attack toward Sushchevo.

The boundary on the left is as before.

8. 64th RD will penetrate the enemy's defenses on the Seviakova and Sloboda front on the southern bank of the Tsarevich River and, while attacking toward Khutkova, Rafenina, Bortniki, and Osinovka, will reach the Kulagino and Stepanovka (northern) front by day's end.

The boundary on the left is as before.

9. 91st RD will penetrate the enemy's defenses in the Petrova and woods west of Kokhanova sector and attack toward Osinovka and Potapova. Destroy the enemy in the Rafenina, (incl.) Krovopuskovo, and Osinovka region in cooperation with 64th RD and 101st TD. Reach the Stepanovka (southern) and Borki region by day's end.

Cut the road in the Krestovka region [17 kilometers northwest of Iartsevo] with your forward units.

The boundary on the left is as before.

10. 101st TD will reach the (incl.) Borki and Vorotyshino front [8-12 kilometers north-northwest of Iartsevo] by day's end. Attack with part of your forces toward Krovopuskovo and Osinovka and, in cooperation with 91st RD, destroy the enemy in the Osinovka and Krovopuskovo region.

Cut the road in the Nizovo Selo region with your forward units.

The boundary on the left is as before.

11. Artillery. Readiness by 0500 hours. Duration of the artillery preparation will be 15 minutes against firm targets (enemy firing points and mortars).

Mass the fires of all types of weapons on a narrow front in the penetration sector, while supporting the attack with machine gun, mortar, and artillery fire. In particular, employ 45mm guns and regimental artillery in direct fire against firm targets.

I demand that division commanders deal relentlessly with commanders and chiefs who do not exploit small-caliber and regimental artillery.

DD [long-range artillery] – a) Suppress enemy artillery in the Navol'nia, Stepkovo, and Rafenino regions; and b) Strike approaching enemy reserves in the Kalugino, Stepanovka, Potapova, and Vorotyshino regions.

12. The VVS of the army:

1) Attack enemy firing points and infantry on the forward edge of his defense in the Siniakova, Sloboda, Bortniki, Osinovka, and Krovopuskovo sector at 1000 hours on 4 September 1941 with all aircraft.

2) Destroy approaching enemy reserves and groupings in the Stepanovka, Borki, Vorotyshino, Samuilova, and Rafenino region with successive strikes.

3) Protect the army's grouping in the Ivaniki, Samuilova, and Vasilisino region.

4) Detect enemy movement on the roads by air reconnaissance [along the following routes]:

    a) Otria and Bortniki;

    b) Dukhovshchina and Krotovo;

    c) Dukhovshchina and Stranshevo; and

    d) Dukhovshchina and Samuilova.

13. The army's **reserve**: 735th RR – in the Posiagaelitsa and Hill 230.5 region; 2nd RR – in the Sel'kovo region, 2 kilometers east of Bolotino; and 45th CD – in its previous region and with its previous mission.

14. CP and the headquarters of the armies are in their previous points.

The Commander of 19th Army, Lieutenant General Konev
The Member of the Military Council of 19th Army,
    Division Commissar Sheklanov
The Chief of Staff of 19th Army, [Malyshkin]

Source: "Boevoi prikaz komanduiushchego voiskami 19-i Armii No. 050 ot 3 September 1941 g. na prodolzhenii nastupleniia voisk armii na Dukhovshchinskom napravlenii" [Combat order no. 50 of the commander of the forces of 19th Army of 3 September 1941 on a continuation of the army's offensive toward Dukhovshchina], *SBDVOV*, issue 41, 198-200.

46. Combat Order No. 03/op of the Commander of the Forces of 16th Army of 4 September 1941 on the Destruction of the Enemy Grouping in Krovopuskovo, Vorotyshino, and Semukhina

Combat Order No. 03/op, Headquarters, 16th Army,
the woods 0.5 kilometer north of Vyshegor
0610 hours on 4 September 1941
1:100,000 and 50,000 scale maps

1. Units of enemy 161st and 28th IDs, while offering resistance on the Kokhanovo, Kholm, Semukhina, Marker 231.0, Kuz'minaka, Pologi, Sel'tso, and Zadnia front, are bringing reserves forward to the Krovopuskovo and Samuilova region.

2. On the right, 19th Army's 101st TD is fighting on the front from Kokhanovo to the northeastern outskirts of Kholm and attacking toward the northwest.

On the left, 20th Army's 144th RD is fighting on the Makeevo and Pnevo front.

3. 16th Army will continue the offensive at 1200 hours on 4 September 1941, with the mission, together with 19th Army's units, to destroy the enemy's Dukhovshchina grouping in the Krovopuskovo, Vorotyshino, and Semukhina region and, while protecting the left flank of the army's shock group from the west, to develop the attack toward Uzval'e.

4. 127th TB, while attacking toward Novosel'e (eastern), Kholm, and Krovopuskovo, together with 101st TD, will destroy the enemy in the Kholm and Krovopuskovo region; and subsequently attack toward Makeeva and Stepankova (northern).

5. 1st TD, with 1st Bn, 18th AR, and 587th CAR: immediate mission – destroy the enemy in the Samuilova and Ivishenka region, and subsequently attack toward the southwestern outskirts of Makeeva and Stepankova (southern).

6. 152nd RD, with 214th AR and 1st Bn, 471st GAR RGK, while protecting yourself along the Semukhina, Soprykino, and Hill 234.9 front from the west with one RR, attack toward Hill 221.3 and Mkhovka with the remaining forces and reach the Mkhovka and Vorotyshino front by day's end.

7. 38th RD (without 214th AR), while delivering the main attack toward Panina and the southern slopes of Hill 234.9, capture the Hill 231.0, Kuz'mina, and Pologi line by day's end on 4 September 1941, with the mission to protect the shock group of the army against a counterattack by the enemy from the south and southwest.

8. 108th RD, with 2nd Bn, 49th CAR, while firmly defending the Skrushevskie Farm and Buianovo sector on the eastern bank of the Vop' River with one RR, attack with the remaining forces, with the mission to capture the Svishchevo and Bol'shie Gorki line; and subsequently attack toward Podrosh'e.

9. Artillery. Artillery preparation of 15 minutes from 1145 to1200 hours, with the missions:

a) Suppress enemy antitank guns and firing points in the Kholm, southern part of Samuilova, Semukhina, Hill 231.0, Kuz'mina, Mizinovo, and Bol'shie Gorki region;

b) Support 127th TB's attack with four battalions; and

c) Prevent enemy counterattacks from [the following] regions: the woods west of Krovopuskovo, Ivishenka toward Kholm, from the woods southeast of Mal'tsova toward Semukhina, and from the woods southeast of Kuz'mina toward Hill 234.9.

d) ADD -16 [long-range artillery group of 16th Army] – 2nd and 3rd Bns, 471st GAR RGK, and 1st and 3rd Bns, 49th CAR. Commander – 471st GAR RGK.

Missions: Suppress enemy artillery in the [following] regions: Ostashevka, Iushina, Dedeshina, Zubovo, and Alferovo.

10. Supply station – Dorogobuzh Station.

11. CP – the woods 1 kilometer northeast of Khotenova; and VPU [auxiliary command post] – the woods 0.5 kilometers north of Vyshegor.

The Commander of 16th Army, Major General Rokossovsky
The Member of the Military Council, Divisional Commissar Lobachev
The Chief of Staff of 16th Army, Colonel Malinin

Source: "Boevoi prikaz komanduiushchego voiskami 16-i Armii No. 03/op ot 4 sentiabria 1941 g. na unichtozhenie gruppirovki protivnika v raione Krovopuskovo, Vorotyshino, Semukhina" [Combat order no. 03/op of the commander of the forces of 16th Army of 4 September 1941 on the destruction of the enemy grouping in Krovopuskovo, Vorotyshino, and Semukhina], *SBDVOV*, issue 41, 147-148.

47. Operational Summary No. 140 of the Headquarters of the Western Front at 2000 hours on 4 September 1941 about the Combat Operations of the *Front's* Forces

Operational Summary No. 140 at 2000 hours on 4 September 1941,

Headquarters. Western Front

1:500,000 and 100,000 scale maps

First. The armies on the *front's* right wing, while continuing to hold on to Andreapol', fought to liquidate the enemy force of up to two regiments, which penetrated to the eastern bank of the Western Dvina River.

In the *front's* center and on its left wing, our forces are continuing the offensive.

Second. 22nd Army continued to hold on to its previous positions with its right wing and in its center at 1700 hours 4 September. It is continuing to fight with enemy forces that have penetrated into the Ivanova Gora and Suvorovo region with its left wing.

174th, 214th, and 179th RDs – positions are unchanged. The enemy is displaying no activity.

126th and 186th RDs repelled an enemy counterattack toward the west and captured the Ivanova Gora and Suvorovo region with their combined forces at 1200 hours on 4 September.

In fierce counterattacks, Ivanova Gora changed hands three times, and, as a result of the fighting, it remains under control of 186th RD.

Third. 29th Army drove the enemy on its right wing back toward the west by the combined efforts of 243rd and 252nd RDs, it is fighting for Iamishche and the woods northwest of Shatry, and the situation is unchanged along the remainder of the army's front.

252nd RD threw up to two regiments of enemy infantry back toward the west and captured Zubovo, with the combined efforts of 243rd RD; and fighting is underway for Iamishche.

243rd RD, while throwing the enemy back tooward the west, captured Shatry and Hills 235.4, 203.7, and 205.8.

246th RD is continuing to hold on to its previous positions.

Fourth. Cavalry Group Dovator. Is concentrated in the Chichata region for rest and to put itself in order.

Fifth. 30th Army, while attacking, is struggling to capture separate enemy centers of resistance, and the divisions' positions are unchanged.

Sixth. 19th Army, while concentrating its efforts toward Uviaz'e on its left wing, on 4 September continued to fulfill its mission for the destruction of the enemy's Dukhovshchina grouping in cooperation with 16th Army's right wing..

The enemy, while defending the Pavlovshchina, Shakhlovo, Zamiatino, Popova, and Krovopuskovo line, is offering stubborn resistance by an organized system of machine gun, mortar, and artillery fire.

The presence of sectors of minefields and barbed wire entanglements has been confirmed in the enemy's defensive positions in front of the army's right wing.

244th, 166th, 89th, 50th, 64th, and 91st RDs, while attacking, were unsuccessful and are continuing to fight in their previous positions at 1700 hours on 4 September.

101st TD, while attacking toward Ivashinki, advanced forward and captured the western edge of the grove 1 kilometer east of Hill 221.6 at 1400 hours. At 1500 hours it successfully repelled an enemy counterattack from the direction of the grove west of Krovopuskovo and is continuing to fight to capture Hill 221.6.

The army reserve is concentrated [as follows]: 735th RR – in the Potelitsa region, 2nd RR – in Sel'kovo, and 45th CD – in Maslikhi.

Seventh. 16th Army. The offensive on the army's right wing on 4 September toward Novosel'e (western) and Krovopuskovo was unsuccessful.

1st TD abandoned Novosel'e (western) and withdrew to the Chistaia, Novosel'e (eastern), and the hollow north of Khatyni as a result of a counterattack by up to two enemy battalions.

The division is preparing for an attack to restore its situation.

152nd RD, while holding on to the woods north of Khatyni with its right wing, captured positions from the bridge over the stream north of Kudinovo to the eastern outskirts of Semukhina.

The division's left-wing units are holding onto the western slopes of Hill 234.9.

38th and 108th RDs are fighting in their previous positions.

Eighth. 20th Army. The offensive on the army's right wing on 4 September was unsuccessful.

144th RD conducted fire from its jumping-off positions on the approaches to Skrushevo, Pnevo, and Mit'kovo.

153rd RD, having advanced 100-150 meters, faltered in front of the enemy's barbed wire on the eastern outskirts of Liakhovo and is preparing passages through the wire.

161st RD conducted fire from positions from the woods north of Pashkovo to the western edge of Pashkovo.

73rd RD is fighting in positions from the southeastern outskirts of Pashkovo to the northern edge of the woods south of Golovino with one RR and in positions from the mouth of the ravine 2 kilometers east of Malinovka to the northwestern edge of the grove at Erdetsy with its remaining units.

229th RD is defending its previous positions, with occasional firing on its front.

129th RD fought its way across the Ustrom River with one RBn and, after determining that the enemy had destroyed the crossing at Shiparevy, is fighting for the woods east of that point. The positions of the division's remaining units are unchanged.

128th TB is on the march from the Kakushkino region to the Peski, Bykovo, and Vygor' region.

Ninth. 133rd RD – has loaded and sent out 30 trains by 1900 hours on 4 September, 1 train is loading, 17 trains have unloaded, and 13 trains are moving.

178th RD: of the equipment and supplies following by rail, 19 trains have been loaded and sent out, 16 trains are being unloaded, and 3 trains are moving.

The headquarters of 44th Rifle Corps has loaded and sent out 3 trains, 1 train is being unloaded, and 2 trains are moving.

Tenth. The VVS of the *front* did not carry out combat flights during the first half of the day because of poor weather conditions.

According to additional information, one MIG-3 aircraft was lost in an accident and burned.

The Chief of Staff of the Western Front, Lieutenant General Sokolovsky
The Military Commissar of the Western Front's headquarters,
   Brigade Commissar Kazbintsev
The Chief of the Operations Department, Lieutenant General Malandin

Source: "Operativnaia svodka shtaba Zapadnogo fronta No. 140 k 20 chasam 4 sentiabria 1941 g. o boevykh deistviiakh voisk fronta" [Operational summary no. 140 of the headquarters of the Western Front at 2000 hours on 4 September 1941 about the combat operations of the *front's* forces], *SBDVOV*, issue 41, 116-118.

48. Combat Order No. 051 of the Commander of the Forces of 19th Army of 5 September 1941 on the Destruction of the Enemy's Dukhovshchina Grouping in the Krovopuskovo, Stepanovka, and Uzval'e Region

Combat Order No. 051, CP, Commander, 19th Army,
the woods 1 kilometer east of Vasilisino,
0215 hours on 5 September 1941
1:50,000 scale map

1. The enemy is striving to stop our offensive with an organized defense along the entire front and counterattacks toward Krovopuskovo and Kholm.

2. The neighbors are continuing to fulfill their previous missions.

3. 19th Army will tie down the enemy along the Voskresensk and Zaitseva State Farm front with an active defense, while preventing the shifting of units from this or that sector of the front. On the right wing, it will continue its offensive in the general direction of Dukhovshchina at 1200 hours on 5 September and, in cooperation with 16th Army, destroy the enemy's Dukhovshchina grouping in the Krovopuskovo, Stepanovka, and Uzval'e region.

4. 244th RD will firmly defend the Voskresensk and Novoselishche front and prevent an enemy penetration along the Voskresensk and Kuchino and Shakhlovo and Zanino axes.

The boundary on the left is as before.

5. 166th RD, with 3rd Bn, 399th HAR, will relieve 89th RD's units in the Balashova and Stepanidina sector on the night of 5 September 1941 and actively defend the (incl.) Novoselishche and Stepanidina sector. Prevent an enemy penetration toward Potelitsa.

The boundary on the left: Vasilisino, Pochepova, Shchelkina, and Utkino.

6. 89th RD, with 1st and 2nd Bns, 399th HAR and 1st, 2nd, and 4th Batteries of 874th ATR, will relive the units of 50th RD in its sector and firmly defend the (incl.) Stepanidina, Hill 220.3, Hill 214.0, and Ivanova sector and prevent a penetration by the enemy toward Novaia Korov'ia. Conduct the relief on the night of 5 September 1941.

The boundary on the left: Neelova, Miagshevo, Ivanova, and Sushchevo.

7. 64th RD, with 4th Bn, 302nd HAR and 5th and 6th Batteries, 874th ATR, while protecting its right flank with part of its force, will attack toward Sloboda and

Kulagino with its main forces. Capture the Kulagino and north Mikheikovo line and seize crossings over the Tsarevich River in the Navol'nia and Sushchevo region from the south by day's end.

The boundary on the left: up to Rafenino -— as before, and further to Hill 225.2 (1.5 kilometers southeast of Kulagino) and Baranova.

8. 91st RD, with 596th GAR and 3rd Battery, 874th ATR, will attack toward Kokhanovo, Khudkovo, and Griaznoki. In cooperation with 64th RD and 101st TD, destroy the enemy in the Stepankova and Krovopuskovo regions and capture the (incl.) Mikheikovo and Hill 215.8 (south of Stepankova) line by day's end.

The boundary on the left: Miagchenki, Kokhanovo, Potapova, and Hill 236.7 (north of Uzval'e).

9. 101st TD will attack toward Krovopuskovo and Uzval'e. Capture the (incl.) Stepankova (southern), Uzval'e, and Borki region by day's end. 50th RD's 202nd AR will support the division from the morning of 5 September.

10. 50th RD will move 2nd RR for protecting the Kolkovichi and Miagchenki sector of the Tsarevich River line and concentrate 202nd AR for supporting 101st TD in the (incl.) Miagchenki and Balykina region on the night of 5 September 1941. Upon their relief by 89th RD, on the morning of 6 September 1941, the division's remaining units will concentrate in the Sel'kovo, (incl.) Kolkovichi, (incl.) Prisel'e, and Borodulino region as my reserve. Be prepared to attack in 101st TD's sector and at the boundary with 16th Army.

11. 45th CD will remain in the region it occupies. Its mission is as before.

12. Artillery. Readiness by 0800 hours on 5 September 1941 (excepting 50th RD's artillery). Artillery preparation of 15 minutes.

The main mission of all artillery – accompany the infantry, while suppressing enemy machine guns and mortars and preventing counterattacks.

Missions of ADD [long-range artillery]: 1) Suppress enemy artillery in the Navol'nia, Stepanova, Mkhovka, Krovopuskovo, and Osinovka regions; and 2) Strike enemy reserves approaching from the Dukhovshchina region toward the Kulagino, Stepanovka, Potapova, and Vorotyshino regions with long range fires.

13. CP and the headquarters of the armies – in their previous points.

> The Commander of 19th Army, Lieutenant General Konev
> The Member of the Military Council of 19th Army,
>   Division Commissar Sheklanov
> The Chief of Staff of 19th Army, [Malyshkin]

Source: "Boevoi prikaz komanduiushchego voiskami 19-i Armii No. 051 ot 5 September 1941 g. na unichtozhenie Dukhovshchinskoi gruppirovki protivnika v raione Krovopuskovo, Stepanovka, Uzval'e" [Combat order no. 051 of the commander of the forces of 19th Army of 5 September 1941 on the destruction of the enemy's Dukhovshchina Grouping in the Krovopuskovo, Stepanovka, and Uzval'e region], *SBDVOV*, issue 41, 200-201.

49. Combat Order No. 81/op of the Commander of the Forces of the Western Front of 5 September 1941 to the Commander of 30th Army about Fortifying the Positions You Have Reached

To the Commander of 30th Army
1:100,000 scale map
0230 hours on 5 September 1941

To create a stable front and afford necessary rest to the forces, I order:

1) While continuing fulfillment of the missions assigned by me for the operations of strong detachments, chiefly at night, the army will fortify the positions it has reached with its main forces.

2) 250th RD will throw the enemy back from the Sutoki region and capture the Savostino, Vorontsovo, and Nivy region with part of its forces, where it will fortify itself.

3) Withdraw 162nd RD into the army's reserve and concentrate it in the Lukashevo, Krapivna, and Pochinok region on 6 September.

4) While fortifying the units in the positions they have reached, have in each regiment no fewer than two lines of strong points echeloned in depth, prepared full-profile trenches with protection for machine guns, communications trenches, and antitank and anti-infantry obstacles. The engineer works will be fully prepared – by 12 September.

5) Submit an operational plan and a plan for engineer works in the positions to me for approval on 7 September.

Timoshenko, Sokolovsky

Source: "Boevoe rasporiazhenie komanduiushchego voiskami Zapadnogo fronta No. 81/op ot 5 sentiabria 1941 g. komanduiushchemu voiskami 30-i Armii o zakreplenii na dostignutom rubezhe" [Combat order No. 81/op of the commander of the forces of the Western Front of 5 September 1941 to the commander of 30th Army about fortifying the positions you have reached], *SBDVOV*, issue 41, 118.

50. Combat Order No. 79/op of the Commander of the Forces of the Western Front of 5 September 1941 to the Commander of 20th Army about Fortifying the Positions You Have Reached

To the Commander of 20th Army
1:100,000 scale map
0230 hours on 5 September 1941

To create a stable front for 20th Army and successively restore order in the army and affording rest to its units, I order:

1) Withdraw two rifle divisions into the army's reserve and concentrate them by day's end [in the following regions]: 161st RD – in the Krasnyi Kholm, Smorodinka, and Fedorovskoe region, and 153rd RD – in the Repushki, Klimova, and Samodurovka region.

2) The army will go on defense on 5 September, having its main defensive belt along the eastern bank of the Dnepr River and further along the positions occupied

by its left wing divisions. Along the western bank of the Dnepr River, have forward units on the lines reached by the forces in the offensive.

3) Organize a defense echeloned in depth and immediately set about preparing the positions; have in the regiments no fewer than two lines of strong points with full-profile trenches, protection for machine guns, communications trenches, and antitank and anti-infantry obstacles. Pay special attention to defense of your left flank.

4) Continue preparing the already begun army line and have it ready by 15 September.

5) Submit an operational plan and a plan for engineer works in the army's belt to me for approval by day's end on 7 September.

Timoshenko, Sokolovsky

Source: "Boevoe rasporiazhenie komanduiushchego voiskami Zapadnogo fronta No. 79/op ot 5 sentiabria 1941 g. komanduiushchemu voiskami 20-i Armii o zakreplenii na dostignutom rubezhe" [Combat order No. 79/op of the commander of the forces of the Western Front of 5 September 1941 to the commander of 20th Army about digging into the positions you have reached], *SBDVOV*, issue 41, 118-119.

51. Combat Order No. 04/op of the Commander of the Forces of 16th Army of 5 September 1941 on Capturing the Makeevo, Mkhovka, and Vorotyshino Line

Combat Order No. 04/op, Headquarters, 16th Army,
the woods 0.5 kilometer north of Vyshegor
0400 hours on 5 September 1941
1:100,000 and 50,000 scale maps

1. Units of the enemy's 161st, 250th, and 28th IDs are offering stubborn resistance in positions from the eastern edge of the woods west of Kokhanovo to Kholm, Samuilova, Semukhina, Hill 231.0, Kuz'mina, Pologi, Alferovo, and Bol'shie Gorkie. Reserves are in the [following] regions: the woods west of Krovopuskovo, Petrykina, Chernyshova, and the woods west of Khudotino.

2. On the right, 19th Army's 101st TD is attacking from the Kholm and Kokhanova line in the general direction of Krovopuskovo.

On the left, 20th Army's 144th RD is fighting along the Makeevo, Pnevo, and Mit'kovo line.

3. 16th Army, while defending the Starozavop'e and Buianovo sector on the eastern bank of the Vop' River, will continue the offensive in the general direction of Samuilova, Ivishenka, and Borki with its main forces, with the mission, in cooperation with 19th Army's left wing divisions, to destroy the enemy's Iartsevo grouping of forces in the Kholm, Krovopuskovo, Ivishenka, and Semukhina region and reach the Makeeva, Mkhovka, and Vorotyshino front by day's end on 5 September 1941.

Begin the offensive at 1200 hours on 5 September 1941.

4. 1st TD, with 38th RD's 48th RR, a motorized battalion of 127th TB, 2nd Bn, 18th HAR, 375th HAR RGK, and 587th CAR, will attack the enemy in the sector from the grove (1.5 kilometers northwest of Novosel'e (eastern)) to Novosel'e (western), with the immediate missions to capture the Kholm, Marker 221.6, and

the eastern outskirts of Samuilova region. Subsequently, while developing the attack toward Makeeva, reach the front from Potapova to the western edge of the woods (1.5 kilometers southwest of Potapova) by day's end on 5 September 1941.

5. 152nd RD, with 127th TB's 35th TR, 214th AR, and 1st and 2nd Bns, 471st GAR RGK, while protecting your left wing along the Semukhina, Soprykina, and Hill 234.9 line against a counterattack by the enemy from the southwest with one RR, will attack the enemy with the remaining forces, with the immediate mission to capture the Samuilova, the southern part of Ivishenka, and the Hill 221.3 region and, subsequently, by attacking toward Mkhovka, reach the front from (incl.) the western edge of the woods (1.5 kilometers southwest of Potapova) to Vorotyshino, having cut the Dukhovshchina-Iartsevo road at the road junction 1 kilometer southwest of Vorotyshino.

6. 38th RD, without 48th RR and without 214th AR, will attack the enemy in the Panina and Pervomaiskii village sector to improve its positions and seize and fortify positions from Hill 234.9 to the unnamed hill (0.5 kilometers west of Pervomaiskii) and Pervomaiskii village.

7. 108th RD without one rifle battalion and with 2nd Bn, 49th CAR, will go on the defense, while having its forward edge along the eastern bank of the Vop' River in the sector from the northern edge of the woods (2.5 kilometers northwest of Starozavop'e) to Skrushevskie and Buianovo. Leave reinforced combat security on the western bank of the Vop' River.

8. Artillery: Readiness – by 0800 hours on 5 September 1941. Artillery preparation – 15 minutes.

Missions

a) Suppress enemy AT guns and firing points on 1st TD's and 152nd and 38th RDs' front; and

b) Prevent enemy flanking fire and counterattacks from the woods west of Krovopuskovo, north of Ivishenka, southwest of Mal'tsova, and the woods southwest of Kuz'mina.

ADD [long-range artillery] – 3rd Bn, 471st AR and 1st and 3rd Bns, 49th CAR. Commander – 471st GAR. Missions: suppress enemy artillery in the [following] regions: Krovopuskovo, Samuilova, Ostashevka, Iushino, and reserves in the woods west of Krovopuskovo.

Prepare concentrations of fires by three battalions against the exits from Vorotyshino and the woods southwest of Mal'tsova.

9. 43rd AD will suppress enemy artillery and reserves in the [following] region by groups of aircraft (5-6 planes) in the periods [indicated]: 1045-1100 hours and 1115-1130 hours: Krovopuskovo, Potapova, and Ivishenka and Ostashevka, Iushino, and Dedeshina.

During the day on 5 September 1941, prevent enemy reserves from approaching along the roads from Dukhovshchina to Semukhina and from Smolensk to Pervomaiskii village.

10. The commander of 127th TB will concentrate 35th TR in the Khatyni and Kudinovo region by 0600 hours of 9 September 1941 and subordinate it to the commander of 152nd RD. At the same time, transfer the headquarters of 127th TB

to the vicinity of the woods 1 kilometer east of Gorodok. I am entrusting the material and technical support of 35th TR to the commander of 127th TB and his staff.

11. The commander of 108th RD will allocate one rifle battalion into my reserve and concentrate it in the Ozerishche region by 1300 hours on 9 September 1941.

12. Supply station – Dorogobuzh Station. Transport – in accordance with the orders of the commanders of divisions and separate units.

13. CP – the woods (0.5 kilometers north of Vyshegor).

> The Commander of 16th Army, Major General Rokossovsky
> The Member of the Military Council of the army,
>   Divisional Commissar Lobachev
> The Chief of Staff of 16th Army, Colonel Malinin

Source: "Boevoi prikaz komanduiushchego voiskami 16-i Armii No. 04/op ot 5 sentiabria 1941 g. na ovladenie rubezhom Makeevo, Mkhovka, Vorotyshino" [Combat order no. 04/op of the commander of the forces of 16th Army of 5 September 1941 on capturing the Makeevo, Mkhovka, and Vorotyshino line], *SBDVOV*, issue 41, 148-149.

52. Combat Order No. 064 of the Commander of the Forces of 20th Army of 5 September 1941 on Defense of the Erdetsy, Chuvakhi, and Prasolovo Line

Combat Order No. 064, Headquarters, 20th Army,
1600 hours on 5 September 1941
1:50,000 scale map

1. The enemy, while relying on prepared centers of resistance with 8th ID's units, is defending on the heights of Pnevo, Mit'kovo, Liakhovo, Dubrova, the woods south of Golovino and Malinovka.

Positions from Sopshino to Suborovka, Klemiatino, and Novaia Iakovlevichi are being defended by 263rd ID.

2. 20th Army, while withdrawing part of its forces into army's reserve, will on the defense in positions on the eastern bank of the Dnepr River from Erdetsy to Hill 249.9, Chuvakhi, and Hill 224.8 and further along the Ustrom River to Prasolovo, with forward positions on the western bank of the Dnepr River

3. 144th RD, with one regiment of 153rd RD, 1st and 3rd Bns, 592nd GAR, and two batteries of 872nd ATR, having relieved 153rd RD's units by 0100 hours on 6 September, will occupy for defense the eastern bank of the Dnepr River from the mouth of the Vop' River to Ratchino (incl.).

Pay special attention to defense of the Solov'evo and Korovniki axis. I am entrusting the commander of 144th RD with responsibility for the boundary with 16th Army.

Hold onto the positions you occupy on the western bank of the Dnepr River with forward detachments, having occupied strong points and the heights. Fortify the intervals between them with strong obstacles.

The boundary on the left: Bykovo, Ryzhii Ugol, Iaroshenki, Zabor'e, (incl.) Ratchino, and (incl.) Babeevo.

CP – Kushkovo.

4. 153rd RD, having transferred one rifle regiment and the sector you occupy to 144th RD by 0100 hours on 6 September, will concentrate in the Repushki, Klimovo, and Samodurovka region in the army's reserve by 0500 hours on 6 September.

March-route of movement: Osovo and Iaroshenki.

5. 73rd RD, with one regiment of 161st RD and 2nd Bn, 592nd GAR, having relieved 161st RD's units by 0100 hours on 6 September, will continue defense of the eastern bank of the Dnepr River from Ratchino to Sopshino. Hold onto the positions you occupy on the western bank of the Dnepr River with strong forward detachments. Fortify the intervals between them with strong obstacles.

I am entrusting the commander of 73rd RD with responsibility for the boundary with 144th RD.

The boundary on the left: Dumamory, Balakirevo, Kucherovo, and Erdetsy.

6. 161st RD, having transferred one regiment and the sector you occupy to 73rd RD by 0100 hours of 6 September, will concentrate in the Shegaki, Smorodinka, Privol'nia, and Krasnyi Kholm region in the army's reserve by 0700 hours.

March-route of movement: Kucherovo, Balakirevo, and Smorodinka.

7. 229th RD, with 126th CAR, 1st Bn, 302nd HAR, one battery of 872nd ATR, and 127th Sapper Bn, while continuing to defend the positions you occupy from the woods south of Motovo to Hill 249.9 and Chuvakhi, will capture the southern slopes of Hill 249.9, the woods northwest of Vishniaki, and Hill 221.3, successively, by brief attacks.

The boundary [on the left]: Mutyshino, Kuzino, Mileevo, Chuvakhi, and Kholmetsy.

8. 129th RD, with 2nd Bn, 302nd HAR, two batteries of 872nd ATR, and 129th Light Eng. Bn, while continuing defense of the positions you occupy, will tie the enemy down with brief attacks on Iakovlevo, while preventing the regrouping of forces to the El'nia axis.

The boundary line on the left: Rozhdestvo Station and Glinka Station.

9. 128th TB will remain in the region it occupies as my reserve.

10. The commanders of 144th and 73rd RDs will prepare to relieve the attached rifle regiments on the night of 7-8 September and send them to the concentration regions of their respective divisions.

11. Division commanders will organize defenses echeloned in depth and immediately set about outfitting their positions. In the regiments, have no fewer than two lines of strong points, not counting the forward positions on the western bank of the Dnepr River, with full profile trenches, bunkers, pillboxes, overhead cover for machine guns, communications trenches, and antitank and anti-infantry obstacles.

Submit a plan for the defense and of the engineer preparations of the defensive belt to me for approval by 1900 hours on 6 September.

Have a fully complete and developed defense by 15 September 1941.

Report daily at 2000 hours about the course of the work

12. CP – Novoselki.

The Commander of 20th Army, Lieutenant General Lukin
The Member of the Military Council, Corps Commissar Semenovsky
The Chief of Staff of 20th Army, Major General Korneev

Source: "Boevoi prikaz komanduiushchego voiskami 20-i Armii No. 064 ot 5 sentiabria 1941 g. na oboronu rubezha Erdetsy, Chuvakhi, Prasolovo" [Combat order no. 064 of the commander of the forces of 20th Army of 5 September 1941 on defense of the Erdetsy, Chuvakhi, and Prasolovo line], *SBDVOV*, issue 41, 227-229.

53. Operational Summary No. 142 of the Headquarters of the Western Front at 2000 hours on 5 September 1941 about the Combat Operations of the *Front's* Forces

Operational Summary No. 142 at 2000 hours on 5 September 1941,
Headquarters. Western Front
1:500,000 and 100,000 scale maps

First. The armies of the *front's* right wing, while continuing to hold onto Andreapol', are continuing to fight to destroy the two enemy regiments which penetrated to the eastern bank of the Western Dvina River.

In the center, 30th, 19th, and 16th Armies continued their offensive. On the *front's* left wing, 20th Army is digging into the positions it has reached.

Second. 22nd Army was continuing to dig into its previous positions with its right wing at 1500 hours on 5 September 1941.

In its center and on its left wing, it attacked repeatedly with the forces of Antosenko's detachment and 126th and 186th RDs from positions in the woods 2 kilometers east of Suvorovo to Hill 236.2, Frolovo, and Ialdy at 1815 hours on 5 September. The results of the attack are being verified.

133rd RD, while securing the boundary with 27th Army, occupies centers of resistance in the Lake Vitbino, Lake Krivoe, and Lake Okhvat region with four battalions and a regiment of artillery. The division's remaining units are continuing to concentrate.

Losses: 214th RD for the period from 2 through 4 September – killed or wounded – 148 men.

Third. 29th Army continued to fight with the enemy in the Iamishche, Zhelezovo, and Borok region along the eastern bank of the Western Dvina River with its right wing. The army fortified its previous positions with its right wing, while fighting with enemy infantry in the defile between the lakes.

252nd RD occupied a defense 1 kilometer south of Serezhino at 1300 hours, with one regiment facing toward the north. The remaining regiments are fighting in their previous positions, while repelling enemy counterattacks.

243rd RD, after an unsuccessful attack, occupies a defense along the Borok and Novaia Derevnia line.

178th RD completed its concentration in the Mukhino, Zhivilka, and Zuevo region by 1300 hours.

246th RD continued to fortify its previous positions with two regiments, and one regiment fought with up to two battalions of enemy infantry with tanks in the Trofimovo region within the defile between the lakes.

The regiment withdrew part of its forces to Zapen'kov'e by 1300 hours.

Trophies: 1 light machine gun, 1 automatic weapon, 3 rifles, 3 bicycles, 2 gas masks, 800 bullets of various size, and 175 enemy men killed.

Losses are being verified.

Fourth. Cavalry Group Dovator. Positions are unchanged.

Fifth. 30th Army continued its offensive at 0800 hours of 5 September with 250th, 242nd, 162nd, and 251st RDs' forces. The offensive by the army's units was unsuccessful.

The units' positions were unchanged at 100 hours on 5 September.

Losses: killed and wounded – 131 men.

Sixth. 19th Army, while defending the Voskresensk and Zaitsevo State Farm line and conducting a partial regrouping, continued the offensive toward Dukhovshchina with its left wing at 1200 hours.

The enemy conducted intense mortar and artillery fire along the army's entire front all day long.

On 101st TD's front, an enemy force of up to a regiment of infantry, supported by a great number of mortars and artillery fire, launched a counterattack from the grove west of Kokhanovo and the Krovopuskovo region at 0700 hours of 5 September.

The enemy attack was repulsed.

The army's units occupied [the following positions] at 1700 hours:

244th RD – a defensive belt on the (incl.) Voskresensk, (incl.) Shakhlovo, (incl.) Novoselishche front.

166th RD is defending the front from (incl.) the grove 1 kilometer south of Novoselishche to (incl.) Ivaniki and is conducting a relief of 89th RD's units in the Bolasheva and (incl.) Stepanidina sector.

89th RD is defending the Stepanidina and Hill 220.3 sector on the morning of 5 September and carried out a relief of 50th RD's units on the (incl.) Hill 220.3 and Ivanova front.

50th RD is continuing to fight along its previous lines with part of its forces and simultaneously transferred its sector to 89th RD's units. The division will enter the army's reserve and concentrate in the Sel'kovo, Kolkovichi, and Baradulino region on the morning of 6 September.

64th RD, while protecting its right flank with part of its forces, has been conducting an attack toward Siniakovo with its main forces since 1200 hours. The positions of its units are being verified.

91st RD, while attacking toward Bortniki, captured Petrova by 1300 hours and is continuing to fight for the grove west of Skachkova.

101st TD, while conducting an attack from positions from the grove one half kilometer southwest of Skachkova to the heights 1.5 kilometer northeast of Kholm, was attacked from the grove west of Kokhanovo and the Krovopuskovo region by an enemy force of up to a regiment of infantry, supported by a great number of mortars and artillery fire. As a result of the counterattack, the division's units withdrew to positions on the heights 1.5 kilometers northeast of Kholm. The enemy counterattack was beaten back by 1200 hours with heavy losses to him, and at 1300 hours the enemy began to withdraw toward Krovopuskovo pressured by the division's units, reinforced with tanks.

The army's reserve: 45th CD – in its previous positions; and 2nd RR, without one battalion, occupies a defense along the western bank of the Tsarevich River in the sector from Skachkovo to the inscription [on the map] "Skachikhino."

Seventh. 16th Army, while conducting a partial regrouping, continued to develop the offensive toward Samuilovo and Ivishenka [5-7 kilometers north of Iartsevo] with its right wing on 5 September, with the aim of destroying the enemy in the Kholm, Krovopuskovo, Ivishenka, and Samukhina region.

The left wing is defending positions on the Staro Zavop'e and Buianovo front on the eastern bank of the Vop' River, with combat security on the western bank.

The enemy's 761st Lithuanian and 400th Infantry Regiments, offering stubborn resistance, are slowly withdrawing toward Samuilovo and Uzval'e.

1st TD, with part of 127th TB's forces, while overcoming enemy resistance, captured the western outskirts of Chistaia and Novosel'e (western) line by 1630 hours.

152nd RD, with part of 127th TB's forces, while throwing units of the enemy's 761st and 400th Infantry Regiment back toward the north and northwest, captured positions from the stream east of Samuilovo to Marker 221.3 by 1530 hours. The attack is continuing.

38th RD fought in its previous positions.

108th RD, having left combat security on the western bank of the Vop' River, went over to the defense in the Starozavol'e and Buianovo sector on the eastern bank of the Vop' River.

Trophies: 1st TD's antiaircraft artillery shot down one enemy aircraft on 3 September.

38th RD seized three mortars and 1 heavy and two light machine guns. Two men were taken prisoner.

127th TB destroyed two companies of infantry, 17 AT guns, and 10 enemy mortars on 4 September.

Losses: 1st Tank Division – for 4 September, killed – 13 men and wounded – 185 men. Overall, for the period 1-4 September, the division lost 396 men killed and 1,622 men wounded.

152nd RD – losses reached 30%, but the quantity is being verified.

38th RD – for 4 September, killed – 113 killed and wounded – 337 men.

127th TB – lost 24 tanks on 4 September.

Eighth. 20th Army is fortifying the positions it has reached on 5 September. The units' positions are unchanged.

There is occasional artillery fire along the army's front.

Ninth. The VVS of the *front*. Operations were limited to flights for reconnaissance in light of the unfavorable weather conditions during the first half of the day. A total of 10 aircraft sorties were carried out.

31st AD carried out 5 aircraft sorties to reconnoiter the weather and enemy forces in the Andreapol' and Zapadnaia Dvina region.

46th AD conducted 5 aircraft sorties; two aircraft conducted reconnaissance of the weather in the Nelidovo and Zapadnaia Dvina region, and three aircraft conducted reconnaissance of the enemy in the Andreapol' and Danilovo region.

The Chief of Staff of the Western Front, Lieutenant General Sokolovsky
The Military Commissar of the Western Front's headquarters,
    Brigade Commissar Kazbintsev
The Chief of the Operations Department, Lieutenant General Malandin

Source: "Operativnaia svodka shtaba Zapadnogo fronta No. 142 k 20 chasam 5 sentiabria 1941 g. o boevykh deistviiakh voisk fronta" [Operational summary no. 142 of the headquarters of the Western Front at 2000 hours on 5 September 1941 about the combat operations of the *front's* forces], *SBDVOV*, issue 41, 120-122.

54. Combat Order No. 052 of the Commander of the Forces of 19th Army of 5 September 1941 to the Commanders of 64th and 91st Rifle and 101st Tank Divisions on the Encirclement and Destruction of the Enemy in the Krovopuskovo Region

To the Commanders of 64th RD, 91st RD, and 101st TD
Copies: To the Commanders of divisions – 244th RD, 166th RD, 89th RD, 50th RD, and 45th CD
Combat Order No. 052, CP, Commander, 19th Army,
the woods 1 kilometer east of Vasilisino,
2330 hours on 5 September 1941
1:50,000 scale map

64th RD, 91st RD, and 101st TD will continue fulfilling the missions for the encirclement and destruction of the enemy in the Krovopuskovo region.

Begin operations on 6 September 1941 at 0500 hours in order to deny the enemy time for regrouping and to escape from under the blow.

Konev, Sheklanov

Source: "Boevoi prikaz komanduiushchego voiskami 19-i Armii No. 052 ot 5 sentiabria 1941 g. komandiram 64-i i 91-i Strelkovykh i 101-i Tankovoi Divizii na okruzhenie i unichtozhenie protivnika v raione Krovopuskovo" [Combat order no. 052 of the commander of the forces of 19th Army of 5 September 1941 to the commanders of 64th and 91st Rifle and 101st Tank Divisions on the encirclement and destruction of the enemy in the Krovopuskovo region], *SBDVOV*, issue 41, 201.

55. Combat Order No. 05/op of the Commander of the Forces of 16th Army of 5 September 1941 on Capturing the Potapova, Mkhovka, and Vorotyshino Line

Combat Order No. 05/op, Headquarters, 16th Army,
the woods 0.5 kilometer north of Vyshegor,
2345 hours on 5 September 1941
1:100,000 and 50,000 scale maps

1. Units of the enemy's 161st, 250th, and 28th IDs, while suffering heavy losses, are being thrown back to positions from the eastern edge of the woods west of Bortniki to the woods west of Kokhanovo, Kholm, the northern edge of the woods west of Novosel'e (western), Hill 221.3, the northern part of Semukhina, Dedeshina, Kuz'mina, and Pologi.

2. On the right, 19th Army's left-wing units, while attacking toward the west, reached the Bortniki, Kokhanovo, and the grove 1.5 kilometers southwest of Kokhanovo front by day's end on 5 September 1941 and will continue the offensive toward Krovopuskovo on the morning of 6 September 1941.

On the left, 20th Army's 144th RD is fighting on the Makeeva and Pnevo front.

3. 16th Army, while defending positions in the Starozavop'e and Buianovo sector on the eastern bank of the Vop' River, will continue the offensive with its main forces at 1000 hours on 6 September 1941, with the mission, in cooperation with 19th Army, to encircle and destroy the enemy in the Osinovka, Ivishenka, Hill 221.3, and Kholm region and reach the Potapova, Mkhovka, and Vorotyshino front by day's end on 6 September 1941

4. 1st TD, with attached units, will continue the offensive, with the missions to capture the Kholm, Marker 221.6, and the eastern outskirts of Samuilova region and, subsequently, while developing the attack toward Makeeva, reach the front from Potapova to the northwestern edge of the woods 1.5 kilometers southwest of Potapova by day's end on 6 September 1941.

5. 152nd RD, with attached units, while protecting your left wing against enemy counterattacks from the west and southwest with one RR, will attack the enemy with the remaining forces, with the missions to capture the Ivishenka, Hill 221.3, and western part of Samuilova region, and, subsequently, by attacking toward Mkhovka, reach the Mkhovka and Hill 238.7 front by day's end on 6 September 1941.

6. 38th RD, without 48th RR and 214th AR, will continue the offensive, with the missions to capture and fortify the Hill 234.9 and Pervomaiskii village line.

7. 108th RD, with attached units, will continue to defend the Starozavop'e and Buianovo sector on the eastern bank of the Vop' River, with reinforced combat security on the western bank of the Vop' River.

8. Artillery: Readiness at 0600 hours on 5 September 1941. Artillery preparation – 30 minutes, from 0930-1000 hours.

Missions

a) Suppress enemy antitank guns and firing points on the forward edge of the enemy; and.

b) Prevent enemy flanking fire and counterattacks from the woods east and west of Krovopuskovo, north of Ivishenka, and the woods southwest of Mal'tsova.

ADD-16 [16th Army's long-range artillery] – 3rd Bn, 471st AR and 1st and 3rd Bns, 49th CAR. Commander – 471st GAR.

Missions:

a) Suppress enemy artillery in the [following] regions: Krovopuskovo, Ivishenka, Hill 234.4, and Ostashevka and reserves in the woods west of Krovopuskovo; and

b) Prepare concentrations of fires by three battalions against the road junction 1.5 kilometers southwest of Vorotyshino.

9. 43rd AD will suppress enemy artillery and reserves in the Krovopuskovo, Makeeva, Mkhovka, Ostashevka, Iushino, and Dedeshina region by groups of aircraft (5-6 planes) in the periods: 0830-0845 hours and 0900-0915 hours, and, during the day on 6 September 1941, prevent enemy reserves from approaching along the roads from Dukhovshchina and Smolensk to Iartsevo.

10. Supply station – Dorogobuzh Station. Transport – in accordance with the orders of division and separate unit commanders.

11. CP – the woods 0.5 kilometers north of Vyshegor.

The Commander of 16th Army, Major General Rokossovsky
The Member of the Military Council, Divisional Commissar Lobachev
The Chief of Staff of the army, Colonel Malinin

Source: "Boevoi prikaz komanduiushchego voiskami 16-i Armii No. 05/op ot 5 sentiabria 1941 g. na ovladenie rubezhom Potapova, Mkhovka, Vorotyshino" [Combat order no. 05/op of the commander of the forces of 16th Army of 5 September 1941 on capturing the Potapova, Mkhovka, and Vorotyshino line], *SBDVOV*, issue 41, 150-151.

56. Combat Order No. 053 of the Commander of the Forces of 19th Army of 7 September 1941 on Capturing Individual Enemy Centers of Resistance

Combat Order No. 053, CP, Commander, 19th Army,
the woods 1 kilometer east of Vasilisino,
0030 hours on 7 September 1941
1:50,000 scale map

1. The enemy, after suffering heavy losses in counterattacks from 4-6 September 1941, has gone on the defense on the army's entire front.

2. The neighbors are fulfilling their previous missions.

3. 19th Army will actively defend on its right wing and in its center and, from 1145 hours on 7 September, will destroy the enemy by active operations and capture separate centers of defense, while denying the enemy an opportunity to strengthen his defensive system and exhausting his forces.

4. 244th, 166th, and 89th RDs will actively defend the positions they occupy and, while destroying the enemy, capture [the following] separate centers of resistance of his defense:

244th RD – Novoselishche; 166th RD – Semenkovo and Hill 213.6; and 89th Rifle Division – Kazakova.

5. 64th RD will continue its attack and capture Popova and Sloboda by day's end.

6. 91st RD, while carrying out a regrouping to its right wing, will capture Bortniki and liquidate the enemy in the forests of Kokhanovo by envelopment.

7. 101st TD will continue its attack and capture Krovopuskovo and Hill 221.6 by the end of the day.

8. 45th CD and 50th RD – missions as before.

9. Artillery. Readiness by 0800 hours on 7 September 1941.

Mission – the suppression of enemy mortars along the forward edge and work over the attack objectives assigned to the divisions.

Suppress firm [positively identified] firing points by 5-10-minute raids and prevent enemy counterattacks. The plan for conducting the fire is given with special instructions from the army's Chief of Artillery.

ADD. Missions:

1) Suppress enemy artillery in [the following] regions: a) Masolovo and Kulagino; b) Rafenina, Osinovka, and Koz'mina; and c) Khudkova and Potapova.

2) Suppress approaching enemy reserves with long-range fires.

10. CP and headquarters of the army – in their previous points.

The Commander of 19th Army, Lieutenant General Konev
The Member of the Military Council of 19th Army,
    Division Commissar Sheklanov
The Chief of Staff of 19th Army, [Malyshkin]

Source: "Boevoi prikaz komanduiushchego voiskami 19-i Armii No. 053 ot 7 sentiabria 1941 g. na ovladenie otdel'nymi uzlami oborony protivnika " [Combat order no. 053 of the commander of the forces of 19th Army of 5 September 1941 on capturing separate enemy centers of resistance], *SBDVOV*, issue 41, 203-204.

57. Combat Order No. 054 of the Commander of the Forces of 19th Army of 7 September 1941 to the Commander of 89th Rifle Division about Outfitting New Defensive Regions

Combat Order No. 054, CP, Commander, 19th Army,
the woods 1 kilometer east of Vasilisino,
1330 hours on 7 September 1941
1:50,000 scale map

1. Simultaneously with developing of defensive work on the positions you occupy from the western slopes of Hill 220.3 to the western slopes of Hill 214.0, set about fortifying [the following] regions:

1) (incl.) Pochepova, the grove northeast of Kazakova, and the western outskirts of Makov'e;

2) The oblong grove, 0.5 kilometers west of Makov'e, the grove south of Makov'e State Farm, and Hill 220.3; and

3) Bolotino and the grove south of Bolotino.

The first and third regions – on the basis of defense by a battalion, and the second – by a reinforced company.

2. Erect cut-off positions on [the following] lines:

1) The northeastern bank of the unnamed stream from the southeastern outskirts of Pochepova, inclusive of the grove north of Hill 216.7, with its front toward the southwest;

2) The northeastern bank of the stream in the Makov'e and (incl.) Bulanina sector, with its front toward the southwest; and

3) The northwestern slopes of Hill 216.7 and Makov'e, with its front toward the northwest.

3. Echelon the artillery for antitank missions along the [following] lines:

1) BA and PA [battalion and regimental artillery] – along the eastern bank of the Loinia River, and, in the vicinity of Hills 220.3 and 214.0, leave from 2-4 guns; and

2) DA [division artillery] and artillery reinforcements on the [following] lines: a) the western edge of the grove west of Hill 217.9, Hill 216.7, Hill 220.3 (southeast of Makov'e), and Hill 219.4; and b) Hill 217.9, Hill 217.0, and Bulanina.

4. Hold onto the occupied forward edge of the defense, having improved it by seizing Kazakova and the unnamed hill west of Kazakova, as a bridgehead for a transition to the future offensive.

The Commander of 19th Army, Lieutenant General Konev
The Member of the Military Council of 19th Army,
    Division Commissar Sheklanov
The Chief of Staff of 19th Army, [Malyshkin]

Source: "Boevoi rasporiazhenie komanduiushchego voiskami 19-i Armii No. 054 ot 7 sentiabria 1941 g. komandiru 89-i Strelkovoi Divizii ob oborudovanii novykh oboronitel'nykh raionov" [Combat order no. 054 of the commander of the forces of 19th Army of 7 September 1941 to the commander of 89th Rifle Division about outfitting new defensive regions], *SBDVOV*, issue 41, 204.

58. Combat Order No. 057 of the Commander of the Forces of 19th Army of 8 September 1941 about Creating an Army Mobile Antitank Reserve

To the Commander of 166th RD
To the Commander of 1st Bn, 735th RR
Combat Order No. 057, CP, Commander, 19th Army,
the woods 1 kilometer east of Vasilisino,
2245 hours on 8 September 1941
1:50,000 scale map

1. Create an army mobile antitank reserve consisting of 1st Bn, 735th RR, 2nd and 5th Batteries, 874th ATR, 25 GAZ trucks (from 166th RD), and a sapper detachment (obstacle detachment) by 1000 hours on 9 September 1941.

2. I am appointing the commander of 1st Bn, 735th RR, as the chief of the reserve.
The reserve will concentrate in the Zubovo and Potelitsa region by 1000 hours on 9 September 1941.
CP of the commander of the reserve – Potelitsa.

3. The chief of the reserve will set about outfitting the Zaovrazh'e, Hill 220.8, and Potelitsa line in an antitank respect at 1200 hours on 9 September 1941.

4. The commander of 166th RD will concentrate 1st Bn, 735th RR, in full, in the Potelitsa region by 1000 hours on 9 September 1941.

5. At the same time, the Chief of Auto-Armored Forces, Colonel Sirota, will concentrate 25 GAZ trucks, prepared for transporting 1st Bn, 735th RR's personnel, in the woods northeast of Potelitsa.

6. The army's Chief of Engineers will support the AT reserve with positioned antitank equipment. Ensure control over and assist in outfitting the lines.

7. The army's Chief of Communications will support by direct communications with 1st Bn, 735th RR's commander..

The Commander of 19th Army, Lieutenant General Konev
The Member of the Military Council of 19th Army,
    Division Commissar Sheklanov
The Chief of Staff of 19th Army, [Malyshkin]

Source: "Boevoi rasporiazhenie komanduiushchego voiskami 19-i Armii No. 057 ot 8 sentiabria 1941 g. o sozdanii armeiskogo podvizhnogo protivotankovogo rezerva" [Combat order no. 057 of the commander of the forces of 19th Army of 8 September 1941 about creating an army mobile antitank reserve], *SBDVOV*, issue 41, 205.

59. Combat Order No. 058 of the Commander of the Forces of 19th Army of 8 September 1941 to the Commanders of 64th and 91st Rifle and 101st Tank Divisions about Capturing Enemy Centers of Resistance

To the Commanders of 64th, 91st, and 101st Divisions
Copies: To the Commanders of 24th, 166th, 89th, and 50th Divisions
Combat Order No. 058, CP, Commander, 19th Army,
the woods 1 kilometer east of Vasilisino,
2400 hours on 8 September 1941
1:50,000 scale map

1. Continue destroying the enemy on 9 September 1941. After a careful and well-organized 15-20-minute artillery preparation, capture the enemy centers of resistance at Popova, the woods west of Kokhanovo, and Krovopuskovo.

2. The commander of 101st TD will transfer 4 additional tanks to the commander of 91st RD.

3. I demand the infantry move skillfully in the attack 300 meters behind the explosions of their artillery shells in order to deny the enemy the opportunity to prepare himself to repel our attacks.

4. Begin operations at 1230 hours of 9 September 1941.

The Commander of 19th Army, Lieutenant General Konev
The Member of the Military Council of 19th Army,
    Division Commissar Sheklanov
The Chief of Staff of 19th Army [Malyshkin]

Source: "Boevoi rasporiazhenie komanduiushchego voiskami 19-i Armii No. 058 ot 8 sentiabria 1941 g. komandiram 64-i, 91-i Strelkovykh i 101-i Tankovoi Divizii na ovladenie uzlami soprotivleniia protivnika" [Combat order no. 058 of the commander of the forces of 19th Army of 8 September 1941 to the commanders of 64th and 91st Rifle and 101st Tank Divisions about capturing enemy centers of resistance], *SBDVOV*, issue 41, 205.

60. Combat Order No. 06/op of the Commander of the Forces of 16th Army of 9 September 1941 on Defending the Positions it Occupies

Combat Order No. 06/op, Headquarters, 16th Army,
the woods 1.5 kilometer north of Vyshegor
0135 hours on 9 September 1941
1:100,000 and 50,000 scale maps

1. The enemy are offering stubborn resistance to the army's attacking units in positions from the Kholm to Samuilova, Semukhina, the northeastern edge of the woods southwest of Soprykina, Panina, Iartsevo Station, Pologi, the northeastern edge of the woods north of Alferova, Khatyni, Bol'shie Gorki, and Zadnia with units

of 161st, 250th, and 28th IDs and is continuing to bring up reserves from the depths in the Krovopuskovo and Pologi regions.

2. On the right, 19th Army's 101st TD is fighting in positions on the southeastern edge of the woods east of Krovopuskovo.

On the left, 20th Army's 144th RD is defending in the Buianovo and Osova sector on the eastern bank of the Dnepr River.

3. 16th Army will continue the offensive with 38th RD's units and part of 152nd RD's forces at 1100 hours on 9 September 1941, with the mission to capture positions from Hill 234.9 to Pervomaiskii village. It will dig into the positions it occupies with its remaining force, while conducting reconnaissance.

4. 1st TD and 152nd RD, with attached units and reinforcements, will fortify the positions they reach, while conducting combat reconnaissance on their fronts.

5. 38th RD, with 1st and 2nd Bns, 49th CAR, will attack at 1100 hours on 9 September, with the missions to capture and fortify positions from Hill 234.9 to Pervomaiskii village.

6. The commander of 152nd RD will organize an attack by one battalion from Hill 234.9 into the flank and rear of the enemy along the road to Pervomaiskii village, in cooperation with 38th RD's attack. The battalion's attack will be coordinated with 38th RD's commander.

7. 108th RD, with attached units, will defend the Starozavop'e and Buianovo sector on the eastern bank of the Vop' River, while having reinforced combat security on the western bank of the Vop' River for the purpose of establishing the presence of enemy regroupings and movements in front of the division's front, especially on its right wing.

8. Artillery: Readiness at 0900 hours on 9 September 1941. A fire raid of 10 minutes.

Missions

    a) Suppress enemy firing points, AT guns, and mortars in the Panina, Pervomaiskii village, and brush 0.5 kilometers southwest of Panina region;

    b) Prevent enemy flanking fire and counterattacks from the eastern edge of the woods south of Hill 234.9 and from Pologi;

    c) Suppress enemy artillery in the Ostashevka, Kurtsovo, Pologi, and Dedeshina region; and

    d) Prepare [the following] concentrations of fires: a) by four battalions upon exiting from the woods southwest of Mal'tsevo; b) by four battalions against edge of the woods 1 kilometer southwest of Semukhina; and c) by five battalions against the edge of the woods southwest of Kuz'mina.

9. 43rd AD. Missions:

    a) Suppress the enemy's infantry combat formations in the Kuz'mina, Pologi, and Pervomaiskii village region with groups of 3-5 aircraft in the periods: 0950-1000 hours and 1030-1040 hours;

    b) Support 152nd and 38th RDs' attack in the Samuilova, Soprykina, Pologi, and Iartsevo region from 1000-1400 hours; and

    c) During the day on 9 September, prevent enemy reserves from approaching on the roads from Dukhovshchina, Smolensk, and Iartsevo and the enemy regrouping and movement on the army's front.

10. Supply station – Dorogobuzh Station. Transport – in accordance with the orders of division and separate unit commanders.

11. CP – the woods 1.5 kilometer north of Vyshegor.

> The Commander of 16th Army, Major General Rokossovsky
> The Member of the Military Council of the army,
>   Divisional Commissar Lobachev
> The Chief of Staff of 16th Army, Colonel Malinin

Source: "Boevoi prikaz komanduiushchego voiskami 16-i Armii No. 06/op ot 9 sentiabria 1941 g. na oborony" [Combat order no. 06/op of the commander of the forces of 16th Army of 9 September 1941 on defending the positions it occupies], *SBDVOV*, issue 41, 151-152.

61. Report by the Headquarters of the Western Front of 10 September 1941 to the Chief of the General Staff's Operations Directorate about the Enemy's Grouping Before the *Front* and Measures for Repelling a Possible Enemy Offensive

Special Importance
Headquarters, Western Front
1:100,000 and 500,000 map
1400 hours on 10 September 1941

To the Chief of the General Staff's Operations Directorate, General Comrade Vasilevsky

1. There are four main grouping before the *front*. The first enemy grouping, which is operating at the boundary between 27th and 22nd Armies – is up to three divisions, one division of which is pushing 256th RD toward Penno. The second enemy grouping is up to five divisions operating toward Zapadnaia Dvina and Nelidovo (102nd, 256th, 110th, and 26th IDs and 20th PzD). This grouping is offering resistance to Maslennikov's army [29th Army]. The third grouping on 30th Army's front includes up to three IDs in the Novoselki, Zamosh'e, and Dubovitsa region, apparently with the aim of striking toward Belyi. The fourth grouping on 19th and 16th Armies' fronts has a total of 7-8 divisions, including one PzD and one MotD in the Zadnia, Dukhovshchina, and Iartsevo region. The appearance in this region of one or two more IDs, whose transfer from the Smolensk region has been detected during the period 7-10 September, is possible. The densest mass of enemy forces in this grouping is at the boundary between 19th and 16th Armies. The aim of this grouping, apparently, is a short attack toward Iartsevo.

2. For the purpose of opposing a possible enemy transition to a counteroffensive, the commander-in-chief orders:

1) The *front's* armies to go on the defense in the positions they occupy. Dig firmly into the ground. Create reliable strong points, with extensive employment of obstacles.

2) Each army will allocate no less than one division to the army's reserve at the expense of secondary axes.

3) The armies will immediately begin to prepare army rear defensive positions on the Zhukopa River, Nelidovo, and Belyi line and further to the south along the Sveta and Vopets Rivers through Dorogobuzh Station and Mantrovo to Beliavina.

3. On the Viaz'ma axis, a rear defensive line will be created in the Kuz'mino, Neelvo Station, and Dorogobuzh sector along the Vopets River, which is already 50% prepared. Its development will continue.

4. Let the armies know about the enemy groupings. Measures will be taken for echeloning AT weapons and for bringing the units to combat readiness.

5. In addition to 134th RD in the Nelidovo region, we have in the *front's* reserve 107th TD in the Belyi region and 128th TB in the Bykovo region and, in accordance with the commander-in-chief's orders, we intend to withdraw an additional two RDs (64th and 152nd) and two TDs (101st and 1st) into the *front's* reserve and position 64th RD and 101st TD in the Vadino region and 152nd RD and 1st TD in the Kakushkino region.

Sokolovsky, Kazbintsev

Source: "Doklad shtaba Zapadnogo fronta ot 10 sentiabria 1941 g. nachal'niku Operativnogo Upravleniia General'nogo Shtaba o gruppirovke protivnika pered frontom i merakh po otrazheniiu vozmozhnogo nastupleniia protivnika" [Report by the headquarters of the Western Front of 10 September 1941 to the chief of the General Staff's Operations Directorate about the enemy grouping before the *front* and measures for repelling a possible enemy offensive], *SBDVOV*, issue 41, 127.

62. *Stavka* VGK Directive No. 001805 to the Commander of the Forces of the Western Front about a Transition to the Defense
0335 hours on 10 September 1941

The prolonged offensive by the *front's* forces against a well-dug in enemy is leading to heavy losses. The enemy has withdrawn to previously-prepared defensive positions, and our units are being forced to gnaw their way through them.

The *Stavka* orders you to cease further attacks on the enemy, go over to the defense, firmly dig in, and, at the expense of secondary axes and the firm defense, withdraw six to seven divisions into reserve in order to create a powerful maneuver group for an offensive in the future.

By order of the *Stavka* of the Supreme High Command
Chief of the General Staff, B. Shaposhnikov

Source: "Direktiva Stavki No. 001805 komanduiushchcmu voiskami Zapadnogo Fronta o perekhode k oborony" [*Stavka* VGK Directive No. 001805 the commander of the forces of the Western Front concerning a transition to the defense], in Zolotarev, "*Stavka* 1941," 171.

63. Directive of the Commander of the Forces of the Western Front of 10 September 1941 about a Transition of the *Front's* Forces to the Defense
To the Commanders of 22nd, 29th, 30th, 19th, 16th, and 20th Armies

Copies: To the Chief of the General Staff, the Chief of Staff of the Reserve Front, the Chief of the Directorate for the *Front's* Rear, and the Chief of the *Front's* Political Directorate
1:500,000 and 100,000 scale maps
1850 hours on 10 September 1941

1. The enemy is operating along the Penno and Nelidovo axes with a force of 8-9 infantry divisions. Along the remaining front, while relying on previously-prepared defensive positions, he is concentrating new forces in the Dukhovshchina and Kardymovo Station region.

2. The *front's* forces will go on the defense and firmly dig in to the ground, having allocated a reserve in each army of at least a division at the expense of secondary axes.

3. 22nd Army will organize a firm defense on the basis of positions along the Kud' River, Kolpino, and Sukhany and Zhabero, and Andreapol' lines and further along the Western Dvina River, while having forward positions on the Pronino, Mishurino, and Petrovo line and along the Lakes Vitbino and Otolovo line.

The army's main mission – prevent an enemy penetration toward the east or northeast. Create an army reserve in the Penno region.

The boundaries on the right and left are as before.

4. 29th Army will firmly defend the front along the Western Dvina River, while holding onto the town of Zapadnaia Dvina.

The boundary on the left – Rzhev, Baturino, Mezha River, Zharkovskii Station, and Velizh (all points inclusive for 29th Army).

5. 30th Army will firmly defend the positions it occupies, with the mission to prevent an enemy penetration toward Belyi and Kaniutino Station.

For the protection of Belyi from the northwest, have a battalion center of resistance in the Borisovo region.

The boundary on the left is as before.

6. 19th Army will on the defense in the positions it has reached, with the mission to prevent an enemy penetration toward Vadino. Pay special attention to the strength of the defense on your left wing.

The boundary on the left is as before.

7. 16th Army will go over to the defense and dig into the positions you have reached. Have a deep defense and your reserve along the Iartsevo axis.

The boundary to the left is as before.

8. 20th Army will firmly defend the positions it occupies. Devote special attention to the sector of the Solov'evo crossing and your left wing.

The boundary on the left is as before.

9. On the instructions of the armies' commanders, prepare army rear positions along the Zhukopa River, Nelidovo, and Belyi line and further to the south along the Sveta and Vopets Rivers, Dorogobuzh Station, Mantrovo, and Leviavina line.

10. The *front's* reserves:

134th RD – in the Nelidovo region. Prepare an antitank line in the Nelidovo region.

107th TD – in the Belyi region. Hold onto the antitank line prepared in the Belyi region.

Once again, withdraw [the following] into the *front's* reserve and concentrate then in [the following locations]:

64th RD – in the region southwest of Vadino on 12 September, prepare to occupy a defensive line in the Pirogovo and Kamiagino sector along the Vopets River.

152nd RD – upon its relief by 112th RD, move to the Kakushkino region;

101st TD – in the woods northwest of Vadino of 14 September; and

1st MD – in the Kakushkino region on 13 September.

45th CD will reach the Shverevo region on 15 September, while planning fulfillment of my special mission [in a separate order].

> The Commander of the Forces of the Western Front,
> Marshal of the Soviet Union S. Timoshenko
> The Member of the Military Council of the Western Front, Lestev
> The Chief of Staff of the Western Front, Lieutenant General Sokolovsky

Source: "Direktiva komanduiushchego voiskami Zapadnogo fronta ot 10 sentiabria 1941 g. o perekhod voisk fronta k oborone" [Directive of the commander of the forces of the Western Front of 10 September 1941 about a transition of the *front's* forces to the defense], *SBDVOV*, issue 41, 128-129.

64. Combat Order No. 055 of the Commander of the Forces of 19th Army of 11 September 1941 on Defense of the Positions It Occupies

Combat Order No. 055, CP, Commander, 19th Army,
the woods 1 kilometer east of Vasilisino,
0305 hours on 11 September 1941
1:50,000 scale map

1. The enemy, relying on prepared defensive positions, is concentrating new forces in the Dukhovshchina and Kardymova region.

2. The neighbors are going over the defense in the positions they have reached. The boundaries with them as as before.

3. 19th Army will go on the defense in the positions it has reached, with the mission to prevent an enemy penetration toward Vadino.

To fulfill this missions prepare [the following] lines:

1) Voskresensk, the western edge of the large forest, Ivaniki, Stepanidina, (incl.) Kazakova, Muzhilova, Zaitseva State Farm, Kokhanova, and Chistaia; and

2) The Votra and Vop' Rivers.

The Votra River is within the army's boundaries.

Prepare the 1st line in an engineer respect, with full profile trenches for no less than a platoon, communications trenches, CPs and OPs, and slit trenches and dug outs.

Employ mining extensively against enemy infantry and tanks as well as engineer obstacles, in the [following] sectors: 1) Osipova and Chistaia; 2) Muzhilova and Zaitseva State Farm; 3) Kazakova; and 4) the large forest.

The army's Chief of Engineers will create bridgehead fortifications at crossing sites over the Vop' River with army engineer units, having paid special attention to fortifying the eastern bank of the Vop' River in the sector from Kapyrovshchina to the army's left boundary.

4. 244th RD will firmly defend the sector it occupies. Prevent enemy penetrations along the [following] axes:

a) Voskresensk and Krasnitsa; and b) Shakhlovo and Zanino.

The boundary on the left: Dedova, Ust'e, Borniki, and (incl.) Klipiki.

5. 166th RD, with 399th HAR, will defend the Hill 227.0 (1.5 kilometers southeast of Novoselishche), western edge of the grove (.5 kilometers northeast of Ivaniki), Stepanidina, Hill 220.3, Turovo, and Lopatchinki sector.

The boundary on the left: Hill 241.5 (north of Gavrilovo), Zavozni, (incl.) Kazakova, and Pavlovo.

6. 89th RD, with 163rd AR, 4th Bn, 302nd AR, and 1st and 4th Batteries of 874th ATR, will defend the Kazakova, (incl.) Kolkovichi, Dubrovka, and Kharina sector. Have the main defensive sector's forward edge in positions from Hill 214.0 to Hill 211.6 and the grove 1 kilometer south of Zaitseva State Farm.

The boundary on the left: Shamova, (incl.) Kolkovichi, Tsarevich River, the bend (2 kilometers southwest of Zaitseva State Farm), and Dukhovshchina.

7. 50th RD, with 596th HAR, 120th HAR, and 3rd Battery, 374th AR, will defend the Osipova, Chistaia, Borodulino, and Balykina sector. Have the main defensive sector's forward edge in positions from the western outskirts of Osipova to Hill 222.8 and western outskirts of Chistaia.

8. 64th RD will concentrate in the Gavrilov, Repishche, and Vedosa region by 0800 hours on 12 September 1941 and reach the Pakei, Mikhalevo, and Plos region by 2300 hours on 12 September, where it will enter the *front's* reserve in readiness to occupy a defense in the Pirogovo and Kamiagino sector along the Vopets River.

9. 101st TD will concentrate in the Medvedev, Kukhareva, and Ianova region by 0800 hours on 12 September 1941. Subsequently, move by night march to the Rzhava, Neelovo, and (incl.) Rzhava Station region by the morning of 14 September 1941 – in the *front's* reserve.

10. 91st RD – in my reserve. Concentrate in the Kapyrovshchina, Blagodatnoe, and Novoselki region by 0800 hours on 12 September 1941, in readiness for the occupation and outfitting of a defensive line in the Blagodatnoe and Padylishche sector along the Vop' River.

11. The commanders of 166th and 50th RDs will relieve 64th and 91st RDs' and 101st TD's units by 0200 hours on 12 September 1941.

12. The army's mobile antitank reserve – consists of 2nd and 5th Batteries, 874th ATR, and a sapper detachment. The chief of the reserve – is the commander of 874th ATR. In its present region.

13. Artillery.

1) ADD [long-range artillery] – 311th GAR, with 4th Bn, 302nd HAR attached – prepare DONs [preplanned concentrations] against approaching enemy force in the [following] regions: a) Ponizov'e, Zhukova, and Pavlova; b) Novo-Nikol'skoe State Farm and Sushchevo (against the crossings); c) Kulagino; d) Khudkovo, Stepanova, and Potapova; and e) Vorotyshino, and suppress enemy artillery in the Shchelkino and Krovopuskovo sector.

2) Prevent concentrations of enemy infantry and tanks and their occupation of jumping-off positions for an attack in the [following] regions: a) Berdino, and Novaia and Staraia Kazarina; b) Krotovo, Bykova, and Pankratova; c)

Semenkovo, Sirotinka, and Shchelkino; d) Afanas'eva, Shishkino, and Kalugino; and e) Bortniki, the woods west of Kokhanovo, and Krovopuskovo.

3) Prepare the fires of ten battalions to prevent enemy infantry and tanks from approaching in the Sloboda, Osinovka, and Krovopuskovo sector.

4) The commanders of 89th and 50th RDs will prepare a plan for an artillery counter-preparation.

5) The army's Chief of Artillery will organize AT defenses along the Vop' River line. Division commanders will submit plans for deeply echeloned antitank defenses by the morning of 12 September 1941.

14. Division commanders will take the strictest measures to ensure that all personnel, horses, and equipment have been dug into the ground. As the divisions develop their designated sectors, extensively use false trenches and carefully camouflage the division's entire combat formation. Prepare reserve positions for firing means [weapons] and reserve command posts.

15. CP and the headquarters of the army – in their previous points.

16. Operational and intelligence summaries at the previous times.

The Commander of 19th Army, Lieutenant General Konev
The Member of the Military Council of 19th Army,
    Division Commissar Sheklanov
The Chief of Staff of 19th Army, [Malyshkin]

Source: "Boevoi prikaz komanduiushchego voiskami 19-i Armii No. 055 ot 11 September 1941 g. na oboronu zanimaemogo rubezha" [Combat order no. 055 of the commander of the forces of 19th Army of 11 September 1941 on defense of the positions it occupies], *SBDVOV*, issue 41, 206-207.

65. Combat Order No. 058 of the Commander of the Forces of 30th Army of 11 September 1941 on Defending the Positions it Occupies

Combat order No. 058, Headquarters, 30th Army,
the woods 2 kilometers northeast of Podzaitsevo
2400 hours on 11 September 1941
1:50,000 scale map

1. The enemy is continuing to defend stubbornly the Griada, Morzino, Podviaz'e, Ust'e, Berlezovo, Torchek, Zamosh'e, Staroe Morokhovo, Churkino, and Novoselki line with the units of 6th and 129th RDs and the remnants of 106th ID and, simultaneously, bringing new forces forward in the Dukhovshchina region. A 2nd defensive position is being prepared along the Pashkovo, Zabolotskoe, Surovtsevo, the eastern bank of Lake Soshno, Vorontsovo, Iakovtsevo, Novoe Sochnevo, and Kostino line.

2. On the right, 29th Army is going on the defense along the Western Dvina River. Its left-flank division occupies the Barlovo, Efimovo, and Mokryshchi front.

The boundary with it: Rzhev, Baturino, Mezha River, Zharkovskii Station, and Velizh. (all points inclusive for 30th Army).

On the left, 19th Army is defending the positions it occupies.

On 11 September 1941, 244th RD is digging in on the Voskresensk, Panovo, and Shakhlovo line.

3. The army will go over to a firm defense of the positions it occupies, while continuing to fortify strong points, antitank, rear and cut-off positions in accordance with Order No. 057, and entrench deeply into the ground, with the main missions to prevent an enemy penetration with infantry and tanks in the general direction of Belyi and Kaniutino.

To which end:

a) Colonel Dovator's Cavalry Group, while remaining in its previous region, will continue to put its units in order. It will firmly hold onto the Ust'e, Makarovo, and Kotov region with one cavalry regiment and prevent an enemy penetration toward Chichata. Conduct reconnaissance in accordance with previous instructions.

b) 107th TD (the *front's* reserve), henceforth, will continue to fulfill missions for protecting the army's right flank from the north and from the west until special instruction from the *front* headquarters,

c) 250th RD, with 118th AR, without one battalion, will occupy and firmly defend the Rzhat' River line along the Chichata, Ostroluki, Malinovka, Koshelevo, Sutoki, and Zyki front. Prepare a rear line and create AT regions at Lake Chichatskoe, 1st Los'mianka, Bor, and Chernyi Ruchei. Main mission – prevent an enemy penetration toward Chichata, Bor, Belyi, and Sutoki, Chernyi Ruchei, and Belyi.

For protecting the left flank against infiltration by small enemy groups through the isolated Boloto Svitskii Mokh [Svitskii Mokh Swamp], occupy Morozovo and Usty Romanovskie with a rifle platoon and prepare routes for movement to Svity and Kliny.

The boundary on the left is as before.

d) 242nd RD, with its previous reinforcements, will firmly defend the Hill 200.8, Orlovo, Shelepy, and Shestaki region, while having strong combat security along the Orlovo, Staraia Morokhovo, Novoe Morokhovo, 500 meters west of Erkhovo, and Shelepy line and the forward edge – from Spiricheno to Esennaia, Hill 220.0. Losinye Iamy and grove west of Pochinok 2. The main mission – to prevent a penetration by enemy infantry and tanks toward Dolgoe and firmly protect the junction with 251st RD.

The boundary on the left is as before.

e) 251st RD, with previous reinforcements, will firmly defend the Hill 228.0, Ol'khovka, and Il'ina Farm region, while having combat security along the Shelepy, Shanino Farm, 1 kilometer west of Sechenki, and western outskirts of Gorodno line and the main defensive belt's forward edge – from the northern edge of the woods south of Pochinok 2 to the western slopes of Hill 220.0, Sechenki, Bol'shaia Repina, and Ol'khovka. Mission – prevent a penetration by enemy infantry and tanks toward Gordeenki from the direction of Savinka and Karpovo and protect the junction with 244th RD.

The boundary on the left is as before.

f) 162nd RD, without one RR, – in reserve. While protecting the army's left flank, continue fortifying the Hill 216.3, Pod'ezzhalovo, Kropivnia, and

Lukashevo line. In cooperation with 251st Rifle Division, prepare counterstrokes toward Kropivnia and Gordeenki and Poloviki Farm and L'vovo.

g) The army's ORB [separate reconnaissance battalion] of the army – in the army's reserve – complete filling out by 15 September 1941 and be prepared to fulfill combat missions.

4. Division commanders will have no less than a reinforced rifle battalion in their reserve.

5. The army's Chief of Engineers will place 1,000 anti-infantry mines at the disposal of 251st RD for strengthening the antitank defenses on the army's left flank. Prepare dams in the Pogorel'tsy region along the Votra River and the Lelimovo region on the Ositnia River.

6. Division, regimental, and battalion commanders will pay special attention to the outfitting of observation and command posts (reliable concealment and the capability to conduct observation and command and control in any conditions of the combat situation).

Carry out entrenchment and camouflaging combat equipment (transport, horses, field kitchens, vehicles, and cartridge boxes), for which make and outfit separate specialized slit trenches.

7. The missions of artillery – (see Order no. 057).

8. CP – 2 kilometers northeast of Podzaitsevo.

The Commander of 30th Army, Lieutenant General Khomenko
The Member of the Military Council of 30th Army,
    Brigade Commissar Abramov
The Chief of Staff of 30th Army, Lieutenant Colonel Vinogradov

Source: "Boevoi prikaz komanduiushchego voiskami 30-i Armii No. 058 ot 11 sentiabria 1941 g. na oboronu zanimaemogo rubezha" [Combat order no. 058 of the commander of the forces of 30th Army of 11 September 1941 on defending the positions it occupies], *SBDVOV*, issue 41, 297-298.

66. Decree of the Military Council of 30th Army No. VS/0064 of 6 September 1941 about Measures for Eliminating Shortcomings in the Organization and Conduct of Force Intelligence [Reconnaissance]
8 September 1941   The Operating Army

Despite an entire series of completely exceptional orders and instructions regarding the organization and conduct of constant force intelligence [reconnaissance] and observation of the enemy (behind the battlefield), up to this time, the state of force intelligence in units and formations continues to be unsatisfactory.

Moreover, there have been instances when a whole series of facts speak about failures in the work of intelligence organs, which borders on betrayal of the Motherland and perfidy (242nd and 251st RDs).

In the divisions, as a rule, instead of laborious everyday work on the selecting personnel for intelligence organs, on their education and well-thought out hourly employment, with the constant aim of determining the enemy's condition and his intentions, there are people here who treat intelligence matters very lightly.

Intelligence organs and scouts [*razvedchikov*] are being employed like any other infantry subunit within this or that regiment. Such a situation – in essence, amounts to bankruptcy in the intelligence realm – and can be explained only by:

1. The passivity of division commanders and commissars, the division headquarters' chiefs of staff and commissars, and those leading figures who immediately direct the reconnaissance services, in regard to making the business of intelligence a matter of principle. Without well-organized intelligence, whatever the type of operation and whatever the form of fighting (offense or defense), it will always lead to blindness and, most frequently, condemnation to failures, from which senseless losses flow.

2. An underestimation of the importance of force agent intelligence in the Operating Army on the part of commanders and commissars, as well as political organs, in headquarters at all levels.

The Military Council of the Army, while warning unit and formation commanders and commissars and headquarters' chiefs of staff and military commissars, unconditionally demand you put an end to this laxity.

The Military Council has decided:

1. To require the army's chief of staff, Colonel Vinogradov, the military commissars of the army's headquarters, and unit and formation commanders and commissars to change fundamentally their attitude toward the matter of organizing and conducting intelligence and leading the intelligence services. During the next three days, formulate a concrete plan with measures for improving the state of force reconnaissance and agent intelligence in the army. Present the army headquarters' to the Military Council for approval. The army's chief of staff and the army headquarters' military commissars will examine and approve the division headquarters plans. The divisions' plans must be signed by the divisions' commanders, commissars, and chiefs of staff, and, in regard to the regiments, – [signed] by the regiments' commanders and chiefs of staff.

During the month of September, the matter of force and agent intelligence in regiments, in divisions, and in the army must be elevated to a matter of principle.

In the first instance, it is necessary:

a) To select a cadre of intelligence/reconnaissance men [*razvedchiki*] immediately. Expel all of those incapable of fulfilling this important function in the Operating Army from intelligence organ.

b) To organize daily systematic training for *razvedchiki* at all levels.

c) To make those answerable in each separate instance of a negligent attitude to the matter of intelligence and criminal treatment of *razvedchik*i, which has led to a work failure, right up to judgment by a military tribunal.

2. The Military Council of the Army is warning the commander of 242nd Division, Major General Kovalenko, the division's military commissar, Regimental Commissar Kabichkin, the division's chief of staff, Major Glebov, and the military commissar of the division's headquarters, Senior Political Worker, Khrapunov, the commander of 251st Division, Colonel Stenin, the division's military commissar, Regimental Commissar Pisarenko, the division's chief of staff, Colonel Dubrovsky, and the military commissar of the division's headquarters, Battalion Commissar Zaitsev, that, henceforth, the attitudes toward intelligence on the part of the division's

leadership, which have existed up to this time, will be viewed as ignoring the most important branch of work, with consequences flowing from it concerning personal responsibility for these matters.

3. The Military Council of the Army is taking notice of the unsatisfactory state of the intelligence services of the chief of the army's Intelligence Department, Major Lebedev.

4. The Military Procurator will immediately conduct an investigation, based on the facts, of the failures in the work of 242nd RD's and 251st RD's intelligence organs, for the purpose of instituting criminals proceeding against those guilty. Present the results of the investigation to the Military Council no later than 8 September 1941.

5. Upon receipt, announce this decree of the Military Council to division and regimental commanders and commissars, headquarters' chiefs and commissars, and the chiefs of unit and formation intelligence organs.

6. The Chief of the army's Political Department [PU] and the Chief of the army's Special Department [OO] will provide effective assistance to commands and headquarters in verifying and selecting personnel for intelligence organs.

> The Commander of 30th Army, Major General Khomenko
> The Member of the Military Council of the army,
> Brigade Commissar Abramov

Source: "Postanovlenie Voennogo Soveta 30-i Armii No. VS/0064 ot 6 sentiabria 1941 g. o merakh po likvidatsii nedostatkov v organizatsii i vvedenii voiskovoi razvedki" [Decree of the Military Council of 30th Army no. VS/0064 of 6 September 1941 about measures for eliminating shortcomings in organizing and conducting force reconnaissance], *SBDVOV*, issue 41, 295-296.

67. Directive No. 2171s of the Headquarters of the Western Front's Artillery of 7 September 1941 about Eliminating Shortcomings in the Employment of Artillery in Combat

To the Chiefs of Artillery of 19th, 16th, 20th, 22nd, 29th, and 30th Armies
Copy: To the Chief of Artillery of the Red Army

As a result of the 2 months of combat operations, our *front's* artillery has inflicted huge losses on the enemy. This is confirmed by the bodies the enemy has left on the battlefield and the testimony of prisoners who confirmed the great losses from our artillery fire.

The effect of our artillery's operations can be even more significant with the elimination of existing deficiencies in the combat employment and work of artillery.

The basic shortcomings are:

1. Reconnaissance and Observation

Reconnaissance of the enemy stands at a low level in all levels of artillery. The strength and groupings of the enemy's firing means (observation posts, firing points, antitank guns, etc.) in the forward edge of the enemy's defenses, for the most part, remain undetected. Such a situation can only exist where intelligence does not assign concrete missions on the ground, constant observation over the field of battle is absent, flank and forward points are not being selected, and observation is not being organized from them. Commanders themselves seldom observe the battlefield. As a result, reconnaissance is not generalized, and conclusions are not reached.

Finally, this can be only when senior artillery chiefs and their staffs themselves do not organize reconnaissance, they do not control the work of reconnaissance organs, and they do not teach their subordinates the organization and conduct of reconnaissance.

2. The Grouping of Artillery and the Dispositions of Observation Posts and Operational Posts

The grouping of artillery often does not correspond to the missions assigned to formations and the artillery itself. The desire to be strong everywhere leads only to the dispersal of weapons. Observation posts [OPs] and firing positions [FPs] are huddled together. The distance of OPs and FPs from the forward edge is very great, which complicates observation over the fires and enemy, especially when developing offensives and the great distance of the FPs lessens the effectiveness of the fires. Reserve FPS are seldom prepared and outfitted.

3. Cooperation of Artillery with Infantry

During the organization of an offensive, higher chiefs and their staffs, as a rule, do not assign concrete missions to their subordinate units and subunits on the ground and, in many instancese, do not grant the hours of daylight necessary for the organization of cooperation of the regiment – [with the] group, battalion – artillery battalion, and company – battery. Control by seniors and higher chiefs and their staffs over familiarizing subordinates with their missions on the ground is, as a rule, absent. Cooperation of infantry fire with artillery [fire] is not being harmonized and coordinated. Mortars, as a rule, do not participate in artillery preparations. With the completion of the artillery preparation and the beginning of the infantry attacks, their firing means (machine-guns, mortars, and regimental artillery) do not protect their movement.

With the development of the offensive, the observation posts of the command group and artillery battalions and batteries continue to remain at great distances and, because of this, are not able to view the battlefield personally. Because of this, when the artillery commanders are asked the question, "Why is the artillery silent?" they answer, "There are no requests from the infantry," and the majority of forward posts serve as a formal indicator of cooperation, since the correction of fire from them is a rare phenomenon. The commanders of batteries themselves poorly observe the field of battle and do not display initiative in opening fire. A unified system of orientation between the infantry and the artillery is almost totally absent.

Target designation from the infantry to the artillery in the developing fighting is crude; the regions are indicated to which the fire should be directed and the artillery chiefs open fire according to maps, while enlisting the efforts of corps artillery to this end. Such disgraces entail only unjustifiable expenditures of shells and can lead to unfortunate instance of firing on one's own, which occurred in 19th Army's 50th and 166th RDs, and these scandalous facts were not investigated and the guilty were not called to account.

4. Firing

The techniques of firing of all types of artillery still do not remain at the highest level.

Adjustment of fire is poorly conducted, the boundaries [limits] of brackets are not provided for, and firing for destruction is not being corrected, and, as a result, in frequent cases, even after a great expenditure of ammunition, the target remains unsuppressed. The sense of careful and economical expenditure of ammunition is not being inculcated. Firing with shrapnel is to one's credit. Attempts to excuse by the lack of targets – is false and incorrect – and frequently, in cases when the enemy goes over to a counterattack, there are no shells other than shrapnel that can and will inflict a deadly blow on the enemy.

The most effective type of fire is ricochet shell fire, but despite special instructions, it is not being employed. Timed firing [with range clocks] for the suppression of enemy batteries is also poorly employed. Harassing fire (fire for exhaustion) at night from temporary firing positions in almost never organized.

Target designation from reference points and from theoretical lines is conducted with a great number of mistakes.

5. The Exploitation of Equipment and Expenditure of Ammunition

There have been instances when guns are being put out of action because of the illiteracy of command cadre. In 73rd RD – a 122mm howitzer was put out of action thanks to the fact that they continued to conduct fire at an abnormally high rate.

In 38th RD – a gun went out of action because firing regimes [techniques] were ignored. There are frequent instances of the premature explosion of shells thanks to wasteful firing.

The allocation of quantities of shells between the guns is absent, and, thanks to this, the losses of muzzle velocity of the main guns seldom differ from the remaining guns.

Shells are being expended uneconomically, and the nature of the targets is not being considered. The unjustified expenditure of shells by corps systems is especially great – this borders on an unconscious crime. There are units which have used up as many as 1,120 shells per gun over the short period of time. Perhaps the mediocre artilleryman does not know that there is a limit to the stress placed on the guns and that, with preposterous exploitation, the weapons will go out of action prematurely.

6. Combat Training

Despite the inadequate training of individual specialists, the periods of quiet are seldom exploited for improving the combat training of both individual specialists (especially scouts and topographers), as well as the sub-units as a whole.

The command cadre are paying very little attention to their own training, as well the training of their sub-units.

I order:

1. While deploying into combat formations, do not permit congested placement of OP, and FPs. During an offensive the artillery's combat formation will occupy [positions] as close as possible to the enemy.

Remember that the long-range guns do not exist to be positioned further back than they can fire.

2. When organizing an offensive, artillery chiefs and senior commanders will aim for the concept of exploiting day light for organizing cooperation at the levels of battalion and artillery battalion and company and battery.

I oblige all senior chiefs and their staffs to check up on the familiarization of subordinates with their missions on the ground [terrain], the readiness of units and sub-units to fulfill their prepared missions, and, in the event they are not ready, to report to the combined-arms commander about the necessity for altering the time for beginning the offensive. Report about the all attacks without organized cooperation.

I demand that all forward posts have infantry in the first line, and the posts of battery and battalion commanders, as a rule, be co-located with the commanders of battalions and companies.

Develop tactical roundtables for battery commanders, and encourage initiative on the part of battery commanders for skillful and timely fires, especially with the development of the fighting, in every way possible.

Eradicate such situations as when the commander of a battery (artillery battalion) does not observe the actions of the companies (battalions) which he is supporting and continue to await fire request from the infantry with indifference.

3. Actively and correctly achieve the organization of a system of reconnaissance [intelligence], whereby, in timely fashion, the firing means and the combat formation are established within the limits of visibility.

Use forward and flank [observation] posts extensively.

4. Increase the quality of firing and destructive fire. Use ricochet and shrapnel fire extensively and timed range firing for suppressing enemy batteries at night

5. Exploit every period of quiet for organizing combat training, paying special attention to the training of scouts, calculators of fire, and battery commanders.

6. Cease the aimless expenditure of shells and especially of heavy caliber.

I demand all army chiefs of artillery take personal control of the expenditure of ammunition by corps systems and forbid the use of that type of artillery to fulfill missions which can be successfully resolved by divisional artillery and infantry weapons.

7. Require uniform exploitation of guns by rearranging [equalizing] the number of guns in the batteries.

8. Take the strictest measures with those who are guilty of putting guns out of action.

The Chiefs of Artillery of the armies will report what they have done to eliminate these deficiencies by 20 September. Inspect at least two divisions personally.

> The Chief of Artillery of the Western Front, Major General of Artillery Kamera
> The Military Commissar of the Western Front's Artillery Directorate, Regimental Commissar Shurupov
> The Chief of Staff of the Western Front's Artillery, Colonel Bykov

Source: "Direktiva shtaba artillerii Zapadnogo fronta no. 2171s ot 7 sentiabria 1941 g. ob ustranenii nedochetov v ispol'zovanii artillerii v boiu" [Directive no. 2171s of the headquarters of the Western Front's artillery of 7 September 1941 about eliminating shortcomings in the employment of artillery in combat], *SBDVOV*, issue 41, 123-126.

Appendix T

The Third Soviet Counteroffensive: The Reserve Front's El'nia Offensive, 30 August-10 September 1941

1. Notes of a Conversation by Direct Line between the Supreme High Commander and the Commander of the Forces of the Reserve Front

Completed at 2304 hours on 29 August 1941

    Zhukov – on the apparatus.

    Stalin – is here – Hello. It seems as if they have damaged you. You have temporarily called for the use of aviation. Is this true?

    Zhukov – Yes, they want to summon it on 30 and 31 [August]; and request it be left, if this could be arranged.

    Stalin – Precisely what aviation do you want to take and how much?

    Zhukov – The intention is to take all of the combat aviation, that is, the bombers and fighters, and a quantity of 120 to 130.

    Stalin – This aviation is very much needed in the south. I would ask you to let then go to the south, and I can send you a regiment of IaK-1. They are very good aircraft – and a day later – a regiment of bombers. In two more days, you will be a very rich man. As for tomorrow's matter, you must, for all that, do what you must do. I ask you to agree.

    Zhukov – Agreed. I only request that you leave me twenty aircraft for correction of artillery and for the protection of the aerostatic balloon observation detachments for reconnaissance. I am requesting 20 aircraft of various types, such as three Pe-2s and MiGs, and the remainder – I-153s and IaK-1 s, for a total of 20 aircraft.

    Stalin – I will leave a total of 20 aircraft for you, but no more. All remaining aircraft will go to the south. Where should I send the IaKs to, and where are they needed? Tell me which aircraft to send to you?

    Zhukov – The IaKs are very good aircraft. I request, if they are available, two regiments of IaK-1 and one regiment of Il-2s. I ask you to provide these aircraft for the reinforcement of 24th Army. It would not be bad if we could receive one bomber regiment for 43rd Army. I would also urgently request you provide one fighter regiment and one bomber for Rzhevsky's [31st] army in four to five days. It seems to me that the Rzhev axis is about to have a need for aviation. Those are all of my requests.

    Stalin – I cannot fulfill all of your requests immediately, but they will be fulfilled gradually. I will begin tomorrow with the regiment of IaK's. The remainder will be later. Goodbye. That is all.

Zhukov – All is clear. Your mission will be fulfilled. I am directing the aircraft to the south. I will keep 20 aircraft of various types for myself. I will expect the remaining promised aircraft from you. Be healthy. Zhukov.

Source: "Zapis' peregovorov po priamomu provodu Verkhovnogo Glavnokomanduiushchego s komanduiushchim voiskami Rezervnogo Fronta" [Notes of a conversation by direct line of the Supreme High Commander with the commander of the forces of the Reserve Front], in Zolotarev, "*Stavka* 1941," 147-148.

2. Notes of a Conversation by Direct Line between A. N. Poskrebyshev and G. K. Zhukov
1 September 1941

Army General Zhukov – on the apparatus.

Poskrebyshev – on the apparatus. Hello. I am transmitting a request to you from Comrade Stalin. Can you immediately come to Moscow? I wish very much, if it is at all possible, for you to come to Moscow, after handing off matters during the time of your absence to Rakutin or Bogdanov. That is all.

Zhukov – Hello, Comrade Poskrebyshev. I just now received unpleasant news about 211th [Rifle] Division, which was operating toward Roslavl'. It, this division which yielded to panic during the night, jumped back 3-6 kilometers and, by that flight, created an unfavorable situation for another rifle division – for the 149th. In light of the difficult situation, I would like to go down to 211th Division's sector tonight to restore order and take whoever is responsible in hand; therefore, I ask you, if it is possible, to postpone my trip, and, if I cannot postpone it, I can leave in 15 minutes.

At El'nia, matters are developing not badly. The enemy will be completely squeezed into a ring in a maximum of two days. We have now reached the El'nia-Smolensk railroad line. If I am ordered to go, I will leave my deputy Bogdanov himself, and then I will order Bogdanov to transfer supervision of the group along the Roslavl' axis to Sobennikov. I will await Comrade Stalin's instructions, whether to go to Moscow or down to the forward positions. That is all.

Poskrebyshev – Comrade Stalin's answer is, "In this instance you can postpone the trip to Moscow and go down to the position. I. Stalin."

Zhukov – I have one question for you. Do I need to be ready to travel to Moscow in the immediate future or can I work on my plan in the immediate future?

Poskrebyshev – You may work on your plan.

Zhukov – All is clear. Be healthy. Regards to Comrade Stalin.

Source: "Zapis' peregovorov po priamomu provodu A. N. Poskrebysheva s G. k. Zhukovym" [Notes of a conversation by direct line of A. N. Poskrebyshev with G. K. Zhukov], in Zolotarev, "*Stavka* 1941," 155.

3. Notes of a Conversation by Direct Line between the Supreme High Commander, the Chief of the General Staff, and the Commander of the Forces of the Reserve Front

4 September 1941
Beginning 0345 hours
Ending 0430 hours

Zhukov – on the apparatus.

Stalin and **Shaposhnikov** – on the apparatus. Hello. After liquidating El'nia, it seems you plan to send your forces to Smolensk, leaving Roslavl' in its present unpleasant situation. I think you should conduct the operation in the Smolensk region only after eliminating Roslavl'. It would be better still to postpone Smolensk, liquidate Roslavl' together with Eremenko, and then sit on Guderian's tail by moving some of your divisions to the south. The main thing is to defeat Guderian, and then Smolensk will not escape us. That is all.

Zhukov – I wish you good health, Comrade Stalin. Comrade Stalin, I am not thinking about the operation along the Smolensk axis, and I believe Timoshenko must attend to that matter. I would now like to attack with [43rd Army's] 109th [Tank], 149th [Rifle], and 104th [Tank] Divisions to hasten the destruction of the enemy's El'nia Group. After it is liquidated, I will have seven-eight more divisions to send to the Pochinok region [50 kilometers southeast of Smolensk], and, after protecting myself against threats from the Smolensk region, I can attack toward Roslavl' and westward into the rear of Guderian with a powerful group. As experience indicates, to conduct a deep attack with three-four divisions will lead to trouble, since the enemy's mobile units will quickly envelop such a small group. This is why I am asking you to permit such a maneuver. If you order me to advance along the Roslavl' axis, I can do so. However, it would be better if I first liquidated El'nia. Today, our El'nia grouping's right wing captured Sofievka by day's end. The enemy's [escape] corridor is only six kilometers wide. I believe we will complete the tactical encirclement tomorrow. That is all.

Stalin – I fear that the terrain along the Pochinok axis is forested and swampy, and your tanks will become bogged down there.

Zhukov – I report. The attack intended through Poguliaevka and to the south of the Khmara River to reach the Storino and Bas'kovo region, 30 kilometers northwest of Roslavl' and 10 kilometers south of Pochinok, is through better terrain. Furthermore, we should avoid attacking along the previous axis. Today, a German soldier who deserted to our side indicated that 267th ID will relieve the defeated 23rd ID this evening, and he also observed SS units. The attack toward the north is still advantageous because it will strike the boundary between two divisions. That is all

Stalin – Do not place too much faith in prisoners-of-war. Interrogate him under torture and then shoot him. We do not object to your proposed maneuver 10 kilometers south of Pochinok. You can act. In particular, concentrate air strikes and also employ multiple rocket launchers. When do you think you can begin? That is all.

Zhukov– We will carry out the regrouping by 7 September, we will be ready on 7 September, and will attack on 8 September. I urgently request you provide 76mm rocket ammunition, 152mm 09/30 [rounds], and 120mm shells, and, in addition, if possible, one regiment of "Ils" [*Shturmovik* assault aircraft], one regiment of Pe-2s [light bombers], and 10 KV and 15 T-34 tanks. That is all I need. That is all.

Stalin – Unfortunately, we have no reserves of multiple rocket launchers – when we do, I will provide them. You have already received multiple rocket launchers. It is just a shame Eremenko has to operate against Roslavl' alone. Why can't we organize an attack against Roslavl' from the northwest? That is all.

Zhukov – It is no use, no use, Comrade Stalin. I can only do so with separate detachments reinforced by artillery, but this will only be a holding action, and I will conduct my main attack at first light on 8 September. Perhaps I will try to do so at first light on 7 September. Eremenko is still far from Roslavl', and I think, Comrade Stalin, that an attack on 7 or 8 September will not be too late. That is all.

Stalin – And will the illustrious 211th [Rifle] Division "sleep" for long?

Zhukov – I hear you. I will organize for 7 September. The 211th is now re-forming and will be ready no earlier than 10 September. I will use it as a reserve and not let it "sleep." I request you permit me to arrest and condemn all of the scaremongers to which you refer. That is all.

Stalin. The 7th will be better than the 8th. We gladly permit you to judge them with full severity. That is all. Goodbye.

Zhukov. Be healthy.

Source: "Zapis' peregovorov po priamomu provodu Verkhovnogo Glavnokomanduiushchego i nachal'nika General'nogo Shtaba s komanduiushchim voiskami Rezervnogo Fronta" [Notes of a conversation by direct line of the Supreme High Commander, the chief of the General Staff, and the commander of the forces of the Reserve Front], in Zolotarev, "*Stavka* 1941," 162-163.

4. *Stavka* VGK Directive No. 001736 to the Commander of the Forces of the Reserve Front about the Withdrawal from Combat of 127th and 100th Rifle Divisions

Copy: To the Chief of the Main Directorate for the Forming and Filling-Out of Forces 1820 hours on 7 September 1941

The Supreme High Commander has ordered:

Immediately withdraw 127th and 100th RD from combat into the rear, and prepare them for dispatch by railroad to another region.

Carry out the withdrawal of the divisions from the front in secret, exploiting the night for that purpose.

Report the loading stations and time the loading begins to the General Staff of the Red Army.

Submit requests for the transfer of 100th and 127th RDs to the Military Communications (VOSO) Directorate of the Red Army no later than 8 September 1941.

By Order of the *Stavka* of the Supreme High Command
Chief of the General Staff, B. Shaposhnikov

Source: "Direktiva Stavki VGK No. 001736 komanduiushchemu voiskami Rezervnogo Fronta o vyvode iz boia 127-i i 100-i Strelkovykh divizii" [*Stavka* VGK Directive No. 001736 to the commander of the forces of the Reserve Front about the withdrawal from combat of 127th and 100th Rifle Divisions], in Zolotarev, "*Stavka* 1941," 166.

5. *Stavka* VGK Directive No. 001941 to the Commander of the Forces of the Reserve Front about Shortcomings in the Organization of the Offensive
0600 hours on 13 September

The recent offensives by 24th and 43rd Armies did not provide completely positive results and led only to excessive losses both in personnel and in equipment.

The main reasons for the lack of success – were the absence of required shock groupings and attempts to attack along the entire front of the armies and the insufficiently strong, overly short, and disgracefully organized aviation and artillery preparation for the infantry and tank attacks.

Henceforth, it is necessary to cease and not tolerate disorganized and weakly prepared artillery and aviation support of infantry and tank attacks unsupported by required reserves.

B. Shaposhnikov

Source: "Direktiva Stavki VGK No. 001941 komanduiushchemu voiskami Rezervnogo Fronta o nedostatkakh v organizatsii nastupleniia" [*Stavka* VGK Directive No. 001941 to the commander of the forces of the Reserve Front concerning shortcomings in the organization of the offensive], in Zolotarev, "*Stavka* 1941," 181-182.

Appendix U (Part 1)

Armeegruppe Guderian's Jockeying for Position along the Desna River, 22-25 August 1941

German 12. The Supreme High Command of the Armed Forces (OKW) Order to the High Command of the Ground Forces (OKH), 21 August 1941

21 August 1941

Order from the Supreme High Command of the Armed Forces
to the High Command of the Ground Forces

The OKH's 18 August considerations regarding the further conduct of operations in the East do not agree with my intentions.

I order:

1. The most important missions before the onset of winter are to seize the Crimea and the industrial and coal regions of the Don, deprive the Russians of the opportunity to obtain oil from the Caucasus, and, in the north, to encircle Leningrad and link up with the Finns rather than capture Moscow.

2. The favorable operational situation, which has resulted from reaching the Gomel' and Pochep line, must be exploited immediately by conducting an operation along concentric axes with the joined flanks of Army Groups South and Center. Our objective is not to push the Russian 5th Army back beyond the Dnepr by the Sixth Army's local attacks. Instead, [it is] to destroy the enemy before he can withdraw to the Desna River, Konotop, and Sula line.

Army Group South can do so only by digging in in the region east of the middle reached of the Dnepr and continuing operations toward Khar'kov and Rostov with the forces operating in its center and on its left flank.

3. Army Group Center is to allocate sufficient forces to that offensive to ensure the destruction of the Russian 5th Army's forces, and, at the same time, it will be prepared to repel enemy counterattacks in the central sector of its front.

The decision to advance Army Group Center's left flank to the hills in the Toropets region and tie it in with Army Group North's right flank is unchanged.

4. The seizure of the Crimean peninsula has colossal importance for the protection of oil supplies from Rumania. Therefore, it is necessary to employ all available means, including mobile formations, to force the lower reaches of the Dnepr rapidly before the enemy is able to reinforce its forces.

5. Only by encircling Leningrad, linking-up with the Finns, and destroying the Russian 5th Army can we free up forces and create prerequisites for fulfilling the missions contained in the 12 August addendum to Directive No. 34, that is, a successful offensive and the destruction of Group Timoshenko.

[signed] Hitler

Source: *Sbornik voenno-istoricheskikh materialov Velikoi Otechestvennoi voiny, vypusk 18* [Collection of military-historical materials of the Great Patriotic War, issue 18] (Moscow: Voenizdat, 1960), 241-242. Prepared by the Military-Historical Department of the Military-Scientific Directorate of the Red Army General Staff and classified secret.

1. Combat Order No. 01 of the Commander of the Forces of 50th Army of 16 August 1941 about the Army's Formation and Combat Missions

Combat Order No. 01, Headquarters, 50th Army
Chaikovichi,
2000 hours on 16 August 1941
1:500,000 and 100,000 scale maps

First. The Briansk Front has been created in accordance with an order of the Supreme High Command. Lieutenant General Eremenko has been appointed as the commander of the *front*. Division Commissar Mazepov and the First Secretary of the Orel oblast' [provincial] committee of the VKP (B) [All-Russian Communist Party (Bolshevik)], Comrade Boitsov, have been appointed as members of the Military Council.

50th Army, consisting of 217th, 279th, 258th, 260th, 290th, 269th, and 280th RDs, 55th CD, 2nd and 20th RCs' artillery regiments, 761st and 763rd ATRs, 86th Sep.AABn, 10th Sep. Armored Car Bn, and 5th Sep. Sapper Bn, has been created by this order.

I have been appointed as the army's commander and Brigade Commissar Miftakhov as the Member of the Military Council. The army's headquarters is being formed on the base of 2nd RC.

Second. 43rd Army is operating on the right. The boundary with it is: (incl.) Zhizdra, Pochinok, and (incl.) Smolensk.

13th Army is operating on the left. The boundary with it is: Trubchevsk, Zhudilovo Station, Khotovizh, and (incl.) Moliatichi.

Third. 217th and 279th RDs will remain in their current deployment regions until receipt of information about their combat dispositions. The left boundary with 258th RD is – Borovka, (incl.) Zhukovka, (incl.) Seshcha, and (incl.) Roslavl'. Conduct reconnaissance up to the Baranovka, Ratovskaia, and Kokhanovo line.

Fourth. 258th RD, with 761st and 753rd ATRs, will defend the Zhukovka and (incl.) Stolby line. The boundary on the left is: Briansk, (incl.) Stolby, Iudin (20 kilometers southwest of Seshcha), and Krivoles.

Conduct reconnaissance up to the Seshcha and Iudin line.

I entrust the commander of 258th RD with responsibility for the boundary on the right.

Fifth. 260th RD will organize reconnaissance along the Pestrikovka, Lutna (8-10 kilometers northwest of Kletnia), Kamenets (15 kilometers southwest Kletnia), Bolotnia, and Lugovka line at first light on 17 August and, after transferring its defensive positions to 280th RD, will occupy the line indicated above by the morning of 18 August, while locating one rifle regiment in the Pestrikovka and Lutna sector and two rifle regiments in the Kamenets, Bolotnia, and Lukavitsa sector.

For the transfer of the sectors to 280th RD, leave operational workers [staff officers] in each regiment.

Conduct reconnaissance up to the Rukhan' and Khotimcha (25 kilometers northwest of Khotimsk) line.

Sixth. 280th RD will occupy and defend 260th RD's sector from Stolby to Dmitrovo. Organize familiarization of the sector you are to occupy at first light on 17 August. Occupy the sector by the morning of 18 August.

The boundary on the left is: Panikovitsa, Malka, Dmitrovo, and Duvovka.

Conduct reconnaissance along the [following] axes:

a) Vysokoe and Sal'nikovo;

b) Kul'nevo and Muzhinovo;

c) Rudnia and Starosel'skaia Sloboda; and

d) Dmitrovo and Divovka.

Seventh. 290th RD will remain in its current positions, while defending the (incl.) Dmitrovo and Pochep sector with one regiment (878th) and the Goliazh'e, Temenichi, and Paluzh'e sector with two regiments.

378th RR will conduct reconnaissance toward Pochep and Zapol'e and [conduct] reconnaissance up to the Kotovka and Iakovskaia line with the remaining forces.

Eighth. 55th CD will concentrate in the Shelud'ki and Zhudilovo Station region by the morning of 17 August. The mission of the division is – to conduct reconnaissance along the [following] axes:

a) Zhudilovo, Mglin, and Kostiukevichi; and

b) Zhudilovo and Unecha.

The division will establish communications with 13th Army's headquarters and forces at all cost.

Ninth. The corps artillery and remaining units – missions assigned in separate orders.

Tenth. My reserve – 278th RD will concentrate in the woods directly north of Goliazh'e and Zastavishche.

The headquarters of the division – Zastavishche.

Eleventh. 269th RD will remain in its previous region, (incl.) Bol'shoe Polpino and the woods east of Briansk.

The headquarters of the division – 1 kilometer north of Snezhen'skaia Station.

Twelfth. The headquarters of the army will be in the Vygonichi region from 2300 hours on 17 August.

With the aim of doubling technical communications, I demand that each division send two delegates [liaison officers] of the commander, with vehicles and security, to the army's headquarters. The delegates will be at Chaikovichi (at the headquarters of the cooperative on the northern outskirts) by 0400 hours on 17 August.

The Commander of 50th Army, Major General Petrov
The Member of the Military Council, Brigade Commissar Miftakhov
For the Chief of Staff, Colonel Pern

Source: "Boevoi prikaz komanduiushchego voiskami 50-i Armii No. 01 ot 16 avgusta 1941 g. o sformirovanii i boevykh zadachakh armii" [Combat order no. 01 of the commander of the forces of 50th Army of 16 August 1941 about the army's formation and combat missions], *SBDVOV*, issue 43, 351-352.

2. Combat Order No. 02 of the Commander of the Forces of 50th Army of 19 August 1941 on Defense of the Positions they Occupy

Combat Order No. 2, Headquarters, 50th Army
Deminteevka,
1100 hours on 19 August 1941
1:500,000 scale map

First. The enemy on the army's front is in accordance with Intelligence Summary No. 4. Along the Mglin and Unecha axis, an enemy force of up to one motorized division with tanks is striving to cut the communications from Briansk to Gomel', and his forward units captured Unecha and Starodub on 18 August.

Second. As before, 43rd Army's units are defending on the right. On the left, 13th Army, in cooperation with 55th CD, is destroying the enemy which penetrated into the Unecha region and is digging in along the Shelud'ki, Pavlovka, Peschanka, Klintsy, and Ushcherp'e line.

Third. 217th, 279th, 258th, 260th, 278th, and 290th RDs are defending their previous sectors, while conducting active reconnaissance directly opposite its front.

Fourth. 269th RD, while remaining in its previous region, will seize, with strong forward detachments, crossings over the Desna River in the Iakovskaia, Liubozhichi, Arel'sk, Ostraia Luka, and Trubchevsk regions.

Fifth. 55th CD will establish close communications with the units of 13th Army's units on 19 August at all cost, with the aim of inflicting a powerful attack and smashing the enemy in the general direction of Mglin, while fulfilling the missions assigned to you in my separate order.

Sixth. The commander of 269th RD, Colonel Khokhlov, is personally responsible for establishing communications with 55th CD by sending reinforced detachments toward Kletnia and Akulichi on 19 August, while simultaneously holding onto the defensive positions it occupies.

Seventh. 280th RD will occupy firmly the previously-prepared defensive sector along the (incl.) Pil'shino, Krasnoe, Khmelevo, and Sosnovka front by first light on 20 August.

Eighth. The VVS of the army, in cooperation with 50th and 13th Armies, will destroy the enemy which penetrates to Unecha.

Ninth. All division commanders, and especially 258th, 260th, 290th, 169th and 55th, will determine the enemy's grouping by combat reconnaissance, with the aim of smashing his main forces by bomber aviation on the night of 19-20 August.

Submit reconnaissance information to me by no later than 1700 hours on 19 August.

The Commander of 50th Army, Major General Petrov
The Member of the Military Council, Brigade Commissar Miftakhov
The Chief of Staff of 50th Army, Colonel Pern

Source: "Boevoi prikaz komanduiushchego voiskami 50-i Armii No. 02 ot 19 avgusta 1941 g. na oboronu zanumaemykh rubezhei" [Combat order no. 02 of the commander of the forces of 50th Army of 19 August 1941 on defense of the positions they occupy], *SBDVOV*, issue 43, 352-353.

3. Combat Order No. 056 of the Commander of the Forces of 13th Army of 21 August 1941 on Defense of the Romassukha, Pogar, and Vorob'evka Line

Combat Order No. 056, Headquarters, 13th Army,
1520 hours on 21 August 1941
1:500,000 scale map

1. A large enemy grouping has concentrated in the Unecha, Starodub, and Staropochep'e region.

2. On the right, 50th Army is defending, and the boundary with it is: Trubchevsk, Zhudilovo Station, and (incl.) Khatovizh.

On the left is 21st Army, and the boundary with it is: Novgorod-Severskii and (incl.) Gaishin.

3. 13th Army will organize a firm defense along the Romassukha, Valuets, Baklan', Pogar, Kister, and Vorob'evka line, while creating mobile reserves, and be prepared in the future to make the transitionto the offensive.

4. 45th RC (155th and 282nd RDs), with 378th HAR and 420th CAR, will defend the Sentsy, Kalacheva, Baklan', and Posudichi line. Have one regiment of 282nd RD for the defense of Trubchevsk. 137th RD, after 282nd RD's concentration, will be relieved and withdraw into army reserve in the woods south of Trubchevsk, while receiving the mission of protecting the crossings at Trubchevsk.

The boundary on the left: Kholopets, Isaevka, Znob', and Setnoe.

5. 4th AbnC, with 6th and 307th RDs and 462nd CAR, will defend the Pogar, Kister, Buchki, and Vorob'evka line.

Have your CP in Naprasnovka.

6. 4th CD will concentrate in the Arel'sk region and the woods to the south in readiness for an attack toward Pochep.

Place your headquarters in Arel'sk.

7. 50th TD, after relief by 282nd RD's units in the Baklan' region, will concentrate in the Pobeda Station region in army reserve in readiness for an attack toward the [following] directions:

1) Pobeda Station and Vitemlia; and

2) Pobeda Station and Novgorod-Severskii.

8. 137th RD, after its relief by 282nd RD's units, will enter the army reserve and protect the crossing over the Desna River south of Trubchevsk.

Have the division's headquarters in the woods south of Trubchevsk.

9. 132nd RD will form in the Negino region.

10. 143rd RD will defend the front it occupies.

The headquarters of the division – in the woods south of Sagut'eva, where it will fill out and rearm the division.

11. 148th RD will withdraw for reconstitution in the Suzemka region and all of its units will return to their places for their assignments.

12. 121st RD's rear will withdraw to the Suzemka region. 21st and 52nd CDs will concentrate in the woods southeast of Koleevka.

13. The reserve regiment will be placed in Sevsk.

The Chief of the Department for Forming Units will organize a collection point for single persons, those detained, stragglers, and the like in the woods north of Seredina Buda.

14. The CP of the army headquarters will be in the woods 1 kilometer north of Staraia Guta. The 2nd echelon of the army headquarters – Gorozhanka.

15. Submit operational and intelligence summaries daily at 0400 and 2200 hours. Combat reports at 1200 and 1800 hours daily.

> The Commander of 13th Army, Major General Golubev
> The Member of the Military Council, Brigade Commissar Ganenko
> The Deputy Chief of Staff of 13th Army, Lieutenant Colonel Ivanov

Source: "Boevoi prikaz komanduiushchego voiskami 13-i Armii No. 056 ot 21 avgusta 1941 g. na oboronu rubezha Romassukha, Pogar, Vorob'evka" [Combat order no. 056 of the commander of the forces of 13th Army of 21 August 1941 on defense of the Romassukha, Pogar, and Vorob'evka line], *SBDVOV*, issue 43, 296-297.

4. Individual Combat Order No. 057 of the Commander of the Forces of 13th Army of 21 August 1941 on Creating an All-round Defense in the Semenovka and Novgorod-Severskii Region with 143rd Rifle Division

Individual Combat Order No. 057, Headquarters, 13th Army
1920 hours on 21 August 1941
1:500,000 scale map

1. The enemy's Starodub grouping is posing the threat of spreading out toward the south and southeast, while threatening our left flank at the boundary with 21st Army.

2. For liquidating this threat, as a supplement and change to Order No. 056, 143rd RD, with 699th ATR and 12th Sep. AABn (located in Novgorod-Severskii) will move to and create an all-round defense in the Semenovka and Novgorod-Severskii regions by day's end on 22 August 1941.

For strengthening the division, include in it the remnants of 148th RD, which is located in Novgorod-Severskii, and one march-battalion of 1,000 bayonets, which is being transferred by railroad to Pirogovka Station.

> The Commander of 13th Army, Major General Golubev
> The Member of the Military Council, Brigade Commissar Furt
> The Chief of Staff of the army, *Kombrig* Petrushevsky

Source: "Chastnyi boevoi prikaz komanduiushchego voiskami 13-i Armii No. 057 ot 21 avgusta 1941 g. na sozdanii krugovoi oborony 143-i Strelkovoi Divizlei v raione Semenovka, Novgorod-Severskii [Individual combat order no. 057 of the commander of the forces of 13th Army of 21 August 1941 on creating an all-round defense in the Semenovka and Novgorod-Severskii region with 143rd Rifle Division], *SBDVOV*, issue 43, 297.

5. Individual Combat Order No. 03 of the Commander of the Forces of 50th Army of 22 August 1941 to the Commanders of 280th and 269th Rifle Division on Recapturing and Retaining Routes of Communications from Pochep to P'ianyi Rog, Krasnyi Rog, Kotovka, and Semtsy

To the Commanders of 280th and 269th RDs

Copy: To the Chief of Staff of the Briansk Front

Individual Combat Order No. 03, Headquarters, 50th Army,

Deminteevka,

1100 hours on 22 August 1941

1:500,000 scale map

     1. During the course of 21 August, enemy motor-mechanized units conducted active combat reconnaissance in the (incl.) Azarovo and Pochep sector. In this sector, 878th RR withdrew from the western bank of the Sudost' River to the eastern bank, where it went on the defense by the morning of 21 August. On the left, a march-battalion of 13th Army is operating in the vicinity of Semtsy.

     2. The commander of 280th RD will immediately send out no fewer than two battalions of infantry on vehicles, having reinforced them with antitank weapons, for recapturing and retaining the routes leading from Pochep [43 kilometers north-northwest of Trubchevsk] to P'ianyi Rog [Pervomaiskoe] [10 kilometers east-southeast of Pochep] and Krasnyi Rog [20 kilometers east of Pochep]. Have a special group in the Krasnyi Rog region and a reinforced detachment in the P'ianyi Rog region.

     3. The commander of 269th RD will send out a reinforced rifle regiment on auto-transport (while employing a combined march) for recapturing the routes leading from Pochep to Kotovka [12 kilometers south-southeast of Pochep] and Semtsy [12 kilometers south of Pochep]. Reinforce the regiment with a battalion of artillery. Have a special group in the Kotovka and Krasnaia Slobodka [15 kilometers south-southeast of Pochep] region.

     4. While division commanders will pay special attention to the operations of reliable communications, strive to get into positions so as to have information from them about the situation at the front at any moment. The commander of 269th RD will establish communications with the march-battalion in Semtsy. The commander of 280th RD [will do likewise] with 878th RR, which is operating in the Pochep region.

       The Commander of 50th Army, Major General Petrov

       The Member of the Military Council, Brigade Commissar Miftakhov

       The Chief of Staff of 50th Army, Colonel Pern

Source: "Chastnyi boevoi prikaz komanduiushchego voiskami 50-i Armii No. 03 ot 22 avgusta 1941 g. komandiram 280-i i 269-i Strelkovykh Divizii na perekhvat i uderzhanie putei soobshcheniia iz Pochep na P'ianyi Rog, Krasnyi Rog, Kotovka i Semtsy" [Individual combat order no. 03 of the commander of the forces of 50th Army of 22 August 1941 to the commanders of 280th and 269th Rifle Division on recapturing and retaining routes of communications from Pochep to P'ianyi Rog, Krasnyi Rog, Kotovka, and Semtsy], *SBDVOV*, issue 43, 354-355.

6. Combat Order of the Commander of the Forces of 13th Army of 22 August 1941 to the Commander of 307th RD on Occupying Starodub

To the Commander of 307th RD

Copy: To the Commander of 4th AbnC

Upon having information there is no enemy in the Starodub region,

I order:

1. Immediately move a reinforced rifle battalion on vehicles with a battery for occupying Starodub by day's end on 22 August and organize them into an all-round defense, with the aim of holding onto it, while organizing reconnaissance toward Klintsy.

2. For strengthening this detachment, I am sending a company of tanks with 6 BT [tanks] by railroad, which you will unload and direct to Starodub at the disposal of the battalion's commander.

3. I am sending 10 automobiles for your use. Organize their dispatch before they arrive.

4. Report fulfillment, indicating the beginning of operations and the time you occupy Starodub.

5. Occupy Unecha with a battalion from 45th RC.

The Commander of 13th Army, Major General Golubev

The Member of the Military Council, Brigade Commissar Furt

The Chief of Staff of the army, *Kombrig* Petrushevsky

Source: "Boevoe rasporiazhenie komanduiushchego voiskami 13-i Armii ot 22 avgusta 1941 g. komandiru 307-i Strelkovoi Diviziei na zaniatie Starodub [Combat order of the commander of the forces of 13th Army of 22 August 1941 to the commander of 307th RD on occupying Starodub], *SBDVOV*, issue 43, 297-298.

7. Combat Order of the Commander of the Forces of 13th Army of 22 August 1941 to the Commander of 45th RC on Occupying Unecha

To the Commander of 45th RC

Upon having information there is no enemy in the Starodub region, a battalion of 307th RD is being sent to Starodub.

I order:

1. Organize careful reconnaissance toward Unecha and, having allocated a battalion with a battery, occupy Unecha by the morning of 23 August 1941 and organize them into an all-round defense, while dispatching reconnaissance toward Surazh.

2. Report the time on movement toward and occupation of Unecha.

The Commander of 13th Army, Major General Golubev

The Member of the Military Council, Brigade Commissar Furt

The Chief of Staff of 13th Army, *Kombrig* Petrushevsky

Source: "Boevoe rasporiazhenie komanduiushchego voiskami 13-i Armii ot 22 avgusta 1941 g. komandiru 45-i Strelkovogo Korpusa na zaniatie Unecha [Combat order of the commander of the forces of 13th Army of 22 August 1941 to the commander of 45th RS on occupying Unecha], *SBDVOV*, issue 43, 298.

8. Individual Combat Order No. 059 of the Commander of the Forces of 13th Army of 22 August 1941 on Concentrating 50th Tank Division in the Vorob'evka Region

Individual Combat Order No. 059, Headquarters, 13th Army
2000 hours on 22 August 1941
1:500,000 scale map

    1. 4th AbnC is defending the Pogar, Borshchevo, and Voronok front, while protecting the boundary with 21st Army.

    2. On the left, 21st Army's left wing is withdrawing along the Solovo and Borshchevo line.

    3. 50th TD, while constituting the army's reserve, will concentrate in the Vorob'evka region and prepare counterattacks toward:

        a) Vorob'evka and Starodub; and

        b) Vorob'evka and Semenovka.

    The Commander of 13th Army, Major General Golubev
    The Member of the Military Council, Brigade Commissar Furt
    The Chief of Staff of 13th Army, *Kombrig* Petrushevsky

Source: "Chastnyi boevoi prikaz komanduiushchego voiskami 13-i Armii No. 059 ot 22 avgusta 1941 g. na sosredotochenie 50-i Tankovoi Divizii v raione Vorob'evka" [Individual combat order no. 059 of the commander of the forces of 13th Army of 22 August 1941 on concentrating 50th Tank Division in the Vorob'evka region], *SBDVOV*, issue 43, 299.

9. Directive No. 1339 of the General Staff of the Red Army of 22 August 1941 to the Commander of the Forces of the Briansk Front about Withdrawing 13th Army's Left Wing to the Solova, Borisshchovo, Pogar, and Sudost' River Line

To the Commander of the Briansk Front

    According to a report by Colonel Argunov, 13th Army is withdrawing to occupy defensive positions along the Sudost' River.

    I am calling 13th Army's attention to the threat being created from the direction of Starodub and your special attention to protecting the junction with the Central Front.

    Withdraw the right wing of Central Front's 21st Army to the Lyzhskie, Lobanovka, and Zamyshevo line. In this connection, withdraw 13th Army's left wing to the Solova, Borisshchovo, and Pogar line and further along the Sudost' River. Have a reserve at the boundary between the *fronts*.

    Shaposhnikov

Source: "Direktiva General'nogo Shtaba Krasnoi Armii No. 1339 ot 22 avgusta 1941 g. komanduiushchemu voiskami Brianskogo fronta ob otvode levogo kryla 13-i Armii na rubezh Solova, Borisshchovo, Pogar i r. Sudost'" [Directive no. 1339 of the General Staff of the Red Army] of 22 August 1941 to the commander of the forces of the Briansk Front about withdrawing 13th Army's left wing to the Solova, Borisshchovo, Pogar, and Sudost' River line], *SBDVOV*, issue 43, 8.

10. Individual Combat Order No. 04 of the Commander of the Forces of 50th Army of 23 August 1941 on Capturing Pochep with 280th Rifle Division

Individual Combat Order No. 04, Headquarters, 50th Army,
Deminteevka,
1630 hours on 23 August 1941
1:500,000 scale map

First. According to unverified information we have, only small enemy subunits are situated Pochep.

Second. The commander of 280th RD, having subordinated 878th RR to himself, will reach the eastern bank of the Sudost' River with one RR and an artillery battalion by first light on 24 August and occupy the town of Pochep, by doing so, restoring its previously occupied positions.

Establish, by reconnaissance with the obligatory seizure of prisoners, what enemy units are operating in the Pochep region.

The boundary on the right is: (incl.) Panikovitsa, (incl.) Marfa, (incl.) Dmitrovo, and (incl.) Duvovka. The boundary on the left is: Sosnovka, Sosnovoe Boloto, P'ianyi Rog, Pochep, and Podbelovo.

Third. The commander of 269th RD will occupy and defend the eastern bank of the Sudost' River in the (incl.) Pochep and mouth of the Rozhok River sector with one RR and artillery battalion by first light on 24 August. Occupy Kalachevo [20 kilometers south-southwest of Pochep] with a reinforced detachment.

The units of 13th Army's 155th RD are defending in the Baklan' region [27 kilometers south-southwest of Pochep], with which you will establish communications.

The boundary on the left is: Trubchevsk and Zhudilovo Station.

Fourth. 878th RR, with its artillery, will remain operationally subordinate to the commander of 280th RD, and all of its remaining units will be subordinate to the commander of 290th RD.

> The Commander of 50th Army, Major General Petrov
> The Member of the Military Council, Brigade Commissar Miftakhov
> The Chief of Staff of 50th Army, Colonel Pern

Source: "Chastnyi boevoi prikaz komanduiushchego voiskami 50-i Armii No. 04 ot 23 avgusta 1941 g. na ovladenii 280- Strelkovoi Divizii Pochep" [Individual combat order no. 04 of the commander of the forces of 50th Army of 23 August 1941 on capturing Pochep with 280th Rifle Division], *SBDVOV*, issue 43, 355.

11. Combat Order No. 03/op of the Commander of the Forces of the Briansk Front of 23 August 1941 on Defending the Betlitsa Station, Zhukovka, Vysokoe, Eastern Bank of the Sudost' River, Pogar, Borshchovo, and Luzhki Line

Combat Order No. 03/op to the Forces of the Briansk Front,
Sven',
2000 hours on 23 August 1941
1:500,000 scale map

1. Units of the enemy's 47th Panzer Corps, consisting of 29th Motorized Division, 3rd, 4th, and 17th Panzer Divisions, and the remnants of 18th Panzer Division, which make up Group Guderian, are operating opposite the Briansk Front's forces.

Enemy tank and motorized units are displaying the greatest activity in the Pochep, Mglin, and Unecha region, while simultaneously carrying out an assembly of forces along the Roslavl' and Briansk axis and while conducting active reconnaissance on the entire front.

2. On the right is 43rd Army, and the boundary with it is: (incl.) Mtsensk, (incl.) Zhizdra, Frolovka, Kazaki, Pochinok, (incl.) Smolensk.

On the left – are 21st Army's units along the Luzhki, Lobanovka, Zamyshevo, and Novozybkov line. The boundary with it is as before.

3. The Briansk Front's forces will firmly hold onto the Betlitsa Station, Zhukovka, Vysokoe, eastern bank of the Sudost' River, Pogar, Borshchovo, and Luzhki line and destroy the enemy with all systems of fire and counterstrokes in cooperation with the VVS [Air Forces], while conducting active reconnaissance along the entire front.

4. 50th Army, consisting of 217th, 279th, 258th, 260th, 280th, 290th, and 278th Rifle Divisions, 55th CD, 2nd and 20th RCs' corps artillery regiments, and 761st and 753rd AT Artillery Regiments, will firmly defend the Betlitsa Station, Zhukovka, and Vysokoe front and the eastern bank of the Sudost' River to Pochep, inclusively, having one division in a prepared antitank defensive region on the immediate approaches to the city of Briansk from the west and no fewer than one RD in army reserve.

Special attention to the [following] axes:

a) Roslavl' and Briansk; and

b) Unecha, Pochep, and Briansk.

The boundary on the left: (incl.) Efratovo, (incl.) Uty, Pochep, Khotimsk, Khotovishch, and (incl.) Moliatichi.

5. 13th Army, consisting of 269th, 155th, 282nd, 307th, 137th, 148th, 143rd, 6th, 132nd, 121st, and 283rd Rifle Divisions, 4th, 21st, and 52nd Cavalry Divisions, and 50th Tank Division, will firmly hold onto the (incl.) Pochep, eastern bank of the Sudost' River, Pogar, Borshchovo, and Luzhki line.

Concentrate special attention on the (incl.) Pochep, Baklan', and Semtsy fortified regions.

Prepare a cut-off position in the Uty and P'ianyi Rog sector.

I entrust responsibility for securing the boundary with 50th Army to 13th Army.

Have one rifle division (283rd RD) in the Novgorod-Severskii region on the left flank. Seize Starodub and have in it at least a reinforced rifle regiment.

Withdraw the airborne corps from combat and concentrate it in the woods north of Suzemka.

6. The *front's* reserve:

a) 299th RD will concentrate in the woods directly north of Sel'tso.

b) 287th RD – in the Sinezerki Station region.

c) 108th TD – in the woods directly south of Ol'khovka.

d) 1st Guards-Mortar Regiment – in the woods 10 kilometers south of Belye Berega.

7. The army commanders will create army mobile reserves for which they will use auto-transport and horse-drawn transport. Also create mobile reserves in each division.

8. The commander of 50th Army will continue to fortify the first defensive line and concentrate special attention on the development of 2nd and 3rd lines.

The commander of 13th Army will fortify and develop a 1st line with the forces of the army. Prepare the [following] cut-off positions [at]:

a) Uty, P'ianyi Rog, and Semtsy; and

b) Pogar, Borshchovo, Kister, and Ugly Station – factory.

The Desna River line and [the following] cut-off positions will be prepared by the *front's* forces.

Create bridgeheads in the [following] regions along the western bank of the Desna River:

a) Uty,

b) Mantsurovka,

c) Arel'sk,

d) Ostraia Luka,

e) Trubchevsk,

f) Saguteeva,

g) Vitimlia,

h) Kasmeskaia Sloboda,

i) Mamechkino, and the strongest – in the Novgorod-Severskii region.

9. Concentrate your main attention on preparing antitank barriers with all-round defense along all defensive lines and cut-off positions, while constructing antitank artillery positions with flanking fire.

Have reserves of antitank artillery, mines, and "KS" [flammable] bottles along likely axes for the movement of enemy tanks.

10. The VVS of the *front* and armies:

a) Direct the main attack of aviation against enemy groupings and columns, while employing them en masse, while protecting their actions with fighter aviation, and while tying them in with the ground forces.

b) Discover regroupings and concentrations of enemy forces by systematic reconnaissance.

c) Protect 299th, 287th, and 283rd RDs' arrival and concentration in the Briansk region.

11. The army's Military Council will nip in the bud any attempt to withdraw without permission of the senior chief, and take "Not a step back" – as is demanded by our Supreme High Commander, Comrade Stalin.

12. Changes of CPs will occur only with the permission of the higher headquarters.

13. CP of 50th Army – the Poluzh'e region.

CP of 13th Army – in the Guta Station region.

> The Commander of the Briansk Front, Lieutenant General Eremenko
> The Member of the Military Council, Division Commissar Mazepov
> The Chief of Staff of the *front*, Zakharov

Source: "Boevoi prikaz komanduiushchego voiskami Brianskogo Fronta No. 03/op ot 23 avgusta 1941 g. na oboronu rubezha stantsiia Betlitsa, Zhukovka, Vysokoe, vostochnyi bereg r. Sudost', Pogar, Borshchovo, Luzhki" [Combat order no. 03/op of the commander of the forces on the Briansk Front of 23 August 1941 on defending the Betlitsa Station, Zhukovka, Vysokoe, eastern bank of the Sudost' River, Pogar, Borshchovo, and Luzhki line], *SBDVOV*, issue 43, 39-40.

12. Combat Order No. 060 of the Commander of the Forces of 13th Army of 24 August 1941 on Defending the Pochep, Pogar, Kister, and Luzhki Line

Combat Order No. 60, Headquarters, 13th Army
1800 hours on 24 August 1941
1:500,000 scale map

First. The enemy (motorized infantry and tanks) has concentrated his main grouping in the Pochep, Mglin, and Unecha regions on the army's front, with up to a motorized regiment with tanks in the Starodub region, and his reconnaissance units are operating along the army's entire front.

Second. On the right, 50th Army is defending the Zhukovka and Zhiriatino front and further along the Sudost' River to Pochep.

The boundary with it is: Efratovo, Uty, (incl.) Pochep, (incl.) Khotimsk, and (incl.) Khotovizh.

On the left, 21st Army is defending the Luzhki, Lobanovka, Zamyshevo, and Novozybkov line.

The boundary with it is: (incl.) Glukhov, Novgorod-Severskii, and (incl.) Gaishin.

Third. 13th Army will firmly defend the line of the Sudost' River along the (incl.) Pochep, Pogar, Kister, Ponurovka, Voronok, and Luzhki front.

Destroy the enemy with all systems of fire and counterattacks, in cooperation of all types of forces, while conducting active and constant reconnaissance.

Fourth. 45th RC (269th, 282nd, and 155th RDs), with 420th CAR and 387th HAR, will defend the line of the Sudost' River along the (incl.) Pochep, Kozorezovka, Rogovo, Baklan', Posudichi, and (incl.) Pogar front.

269th RD will have one regiment on the (incl.) Pochep and (incl.) Rogovo front and two other regiments disposed in a line of cut-off positions – Uty, P'ianyi Rog, and the Rozhok River.

Leave one of 282nd RD's regiments in Trubchevsk as the corps' reserve. I entrust the commander of 45th RC with responsibility for the junction with the neighbor on the right in the Pochep region.

Have your CP in the Ramassukha region.

The boundary on the left: Unecha, Kholopets, Aleshinka, Pogoshch' Station, Novoe Iamskoe, and Dmitriev-L'govskii.

Fifth. 307th RD, with 462nd CAR, will defend the Pogar, Borshchevo, and Kister front, having especially strengthened Pogar and Kister for a firm all-round defense, and will prepare a defensive line along the Sudost' River on the Pogar and Gremiach' front.

The boundary on the left: Starodub, Kister, Kamen', Rudnia, Setnoe, and Novoe.

Sixth. 6th RD will defend the (incl.) Kister, Bol'shie Andreikovichi, and Ponurovka front and simultaneously prepare a defensive line along the streams on the Kister, Buchki, and Buda front.

Have your headquarters in Buchki.

The boundary line on the left: Kamen', Ponurovka, Buda, Leskonogi, Koleevka, and Belitsa.

Seventh. 143rd RD, having moved forward, will defend a line along the (incl.) Ponurovka, Voronok, and Luzhki front. Occupy the defense on 25 August 1941. Transfer the defense of Novgorod-Severskii and Semenovka to 283rd RD. Place the headquarters of the division in Lomakovka.

Eighth. 4th AbnC's units – the paratroopers will go into reserve in the woods north of Suzemka Station only after 6th and 143rd RDs' units have occupied their defenses.

Ninth. 283rd RD constitutes the army's reserve. Locate it in Novgorod-Severskii. Have a mobile group of no less than a battalion on automobiles. Prepare counterattacks toward:

1. Novgorod-Severskii and Pogar; and
2. Novgorod-Severskii, Ponurovka, and Luzhki.

Prepare Novgorod-Severskii for defense.

The headquarters of the division – Novgorod-Severskii.

Tenth. 50th TD – the army's reserve in the Vorob'evka region.

Be prepared for attacks toward:

1. Vorob'evka, Kister, and Pogar; and
2. Vorob'evka, Kosobor, and Luzhki.

The headquarters of the division – Vorob'evka.

Eleventh. 52nd CD – is the army's reserve located in the woods of Koleevka. Be prepared for operations toward Starodub, Klintsy, and Semenovka independently or for a counterattack together with 50th TD. Conduct reconnaissance toward Semenovka and Radomys and prepare for defending the eastern bank of the Desna River along the Pirogovka and Chepleevka front.

Twelfth. 4th CD will concentrate in the Vzdruzhnoe, Liubovichi, and Arel'sk region and protect the crossings over the Desna River in that region.

Have forward detachments in the Ryzhskii and Fomchino region.

Conduct reconnaissance toward P'ianyi Rog, Krasnaia Sloboda, and Kotovka.

Thirteenth. All remaining formations and units will train and fill out in accordance with previous Order No. 056.

In the first instance, reconstitute 6th, 143rd, 155th, and 137th RDs.

Fourteenth. All units will immediately begin work organizing defenses, first and foremost, constructing antitank barriers by exploiting the local population, and constructing cut-off positions.

The Chief of Engineer Services will prepare a detailed plan for engineer work, while using the forces and local population.

Fifteenth. The VVS of the army will:

1) Conduct systematic reconnaissance to reveal the regroupings and concentration of enemy forces.

2) Bomb concentrations of enemy infantry, transports, and tanks both in place and moving.

3) Protect 283rd RD's unloading in the Novgorod-Severskii region on 26 August 1941.

Sixteenth. Cut short any and all attempts to retreat without the orders of the senior chief – "Not a step back," as demanded by our Supreme High Commander, Comrade Stalin.

Seventeenth. Carry out displacement of CPs only with permission from higher headquarters.

Eighteenth. Distribution Station – L'gov.

Nineteenth. Submit any changes to previously issued operational orders and intelligence summaries to 13th Army's headquarters at 1200 and 2200 hours.

Combat reports daily at 0400 and 1700 hours.

Twentieth. CP of the army's headquarters – Staraia Guta.

The Commander of 13th Army, Major General Golubev
The Member of the Military Council, Brigade Commissar Furt
The Chief of Staff of 13th Zrmy, *Kombrig* Petrushevsky

Source: "Boevoi prikaz komanduiushchego voiskami 13-i Armii No. 060 ot 24 avgusta 1941 g. na oboronu rubezha Pochep, Pogar, Kister, Luzhki" [Combat order no. 060 of the commander of the forces of 13th Army of 24 August 1941 on defending the Pochep, Pogar, Kister, and Luzhki line], *SBDVOV*, issue 43, 299-301.

13. Combat Order No. 07 of the Commander of the Forces of 50th Army of 24 August 1941 on Defending the Frolovka, Zhukovka, Stolby, and Pochep Line

Individual Combat Order No. 74, Headquarters, 50th Army,
Deminteevka
2300 hours on 24 August 1941
1:500,000 scale map

First. The units of 29th MotD, 17th PzD, and a panzer division whose number has not been established are operating on the army's front.

The enemy is conducting active reconnaissance along the army's entire front and is displaying special activity on 258th and 260th RDs' fronts.

Second. 43rd Army's units are defending on the right. The boundary with it is: (incl.) Mtsensk, (incl.) Zhizdra, Frolovka, Kazaki, Pochinok, and (incl.) Smolensk. On the left, 13th Army's units are going on the defense in the Semtsy, Vorob'evka, and Semenovka sector. The boundary with it is: (incl.) Efratovo, (incl.) Uty, Pochep, Khotimsk, Khotovizh, and (incl.) Moliatichi.

Third. 50th Army (217th, 279th, 258th, 260th, 280th, 290th, and 278th RDs, 55th CD, 151st and 645th CARs, 761st and 753rd ATRs, and 207th HAR) will continue to defend the Frolovka (9034), Zhukovka, Stolby, along the eastern bank of the Sudost' River, and Pochep front firmly, while having one division in the army's reserve in the Darkovichi, Chaikovichi, and (incl.) Galiazh'e region.

Pay special attention to the Roslavl' and Briansk and Pochep and Briansk axes.

Fourth. 217th RD, with 207th HAR, will defend positions along the eastern bank of the Snopot' River and Desna River in the sector from Bol'shaia Lutna (8248) to the 1st of May State Farm. After its relief by 43rd Army's units, 766th RR will withdraw into reserve behind its right wing.

The boundary on the left is: Sel'tso (5668), Kholopenkovy Farm, (incl.) Iablon', and Zubovo (26 kilometers southeast of Roslavl'), while conducting active combat reconnaissance in its sector. I entrust 217th RD with responsibility for protecting the junction with 43rd Army.

The headquarters of the division until the morning of 26 August will be in Kosevat village.

Fifth. 279th RD, while remaining in its previous positions, will firmly defend positions along the Desna River in the (incl.) Kholopenkovy Farm, (incl.) and Zhukovka sector. The boundary on the left is: Borovka (22 kilometers north of Briansk), (incl.) Zhukovka, Zhukova, and (incl.) Den'gubovka (27 kilometers north of Kletnia).

Conduct active reconnaissance up to the Radichi and Staraia Kocheva line.

The headquarters of the division – Pogorelovka.

Sixth. 258th RD, with 761st ATR and 151st CAR, while remaining in its previous positions, will firmly defend positions in the Zhukovka and (incl.) Stolby sector. Pay special attention to the Briansk-Roslavl' road and Ovstug, Uprussy, and Sal'nikovo axes. The boundary on the left is: Briansk, (incl.) Stolby, and (incl.) Kletnia, while conducting active reconnaissance up to the Staraia Kocheva and Kletnia line. I entrust responsibility for the junction with the neighbor on the left to 258th RD.

The headquarters of the division – Ovstug.

Seventh. 260th RD, with two batteries of 753rd ATR and 645th CAR, will firmly defend the positions it occupies in the Stolby and Dmitrovo sector. Pay special attention to the Stolby and Kletnia and Zhiriatino and Vorobeinia axes. The boundary to the left: Panikovitsa (15 kilometers northeast of Krasnoe), Dmitrovo, (incl.) Shmotovka, and (incl.) Akulichi. I entrust responsibility for protection of the junction with the neighbor on the left to 260th RD.

The headquarters of the division – Krasnyi Pakhar'.

Eighth. 280th RD, with 753rd ATR (without two batteries), 878th RR, with an artillery battalion of 290th RD, and 1020th RR, with an artillery battalion of 269th RD, temporarily subordinate to it operationally, while remaining in its previous positions with its main forces and while continuing to improve its defensive positions in the Pil'shino and Sosnovka sector in an antitank respect, will destroy the opposing enemy with three rifle regiments (1031st, 878th, and 1020th) and capture Pochep by day's end on 25 August, having restored its previous positions. Subsequently, defend positions along the eastern bank of the Sudost' River, Pochep and to the south along the Sudost' River to Rogovo (8 kilometers southwest of Pochep). Conduct active combat reconnaissance up to the Akulichi, Deremna, and Starosel'e line. Pay special attention to the Pochep and Akulichi axis and to the Pochep and Unecha road. I entrust responsibility for protection of the junction with 13th Army to the commander of 280th RD

The headquarters of the division – Miakishevo (Shatikhina).

Ninth. 290th RD (without 878th RR and 2nd Bn, 827th AR), while remaining in your old positions, continue to improve antitank defenses in the Goliazh'e and Paluzh'e sector.

The headquarters of the division – Tolmachevo.

Tenth. 278th RD – the army's reserve, while remaining in the positions it occupies and while continuing to fortify its positions in the Shibenets and (incl.) Goliazh'e sector, will study the axis and be prepared for delivering a powerful attack in the event of an enemy penetration along the Darkovichi and Diat'kovo, Chaikovichi and Kabalichi (the Briansk-Roslavl' road), and Ordzhonikidze and Paluzh'e axes.

The headquarters of the division – the woods north of Zastavishche.

Eleventh. 55th CD, in cooperation with *frontal* aviation and on 24-24 August, while operating on a broad front and while conducting daring attacks against the enemy's rear and communications toward Ormino, Mglin, and Severnaia Rassukha [35 kilometers west of Pochep], will concentrate in the region of the woods at Valuets and Berezovka (28 kilometers south of Pochep) by the morning of 26 August, where it will establish communications with 13th Army.

The headquarters of the division – Valuets from the morning of 26 August.

Twelfth. 269th RD (without 1020th RR) will transfer to 13th Army effective 24 August. 1020th RR, with 1st Bn, 836th AR, will remain operationally subordinate to the commander of 280th RD until special instructions.

Thirteenth. The army's artillery.

I establish the main missions of artillery [as follows]:

1. 217th RD will protect the boundary between the neighboring division on the right and the boundary between 217th and 279th RDs in the Zhukova and Zalenskii village with artillery fire.

2. 279th RD will protect the boundary between 279th and 258th RDs in the Vyshkovichi and Korobki sector with artillery fire.

3. 258th RD will protect the approaches to the Roslavl' road in the Ugost' and Krasnoe Znamia sector with fire and protect the boundary between 258th and 260th RDs in the Uprussy and Stolby sector with artillery fire,

4. 260th RD will protect the approaches to the Boguchevo and Sin'kovo sector on the Marfa axis with artillery fire and protect the boundary between 260th RD and 878th RR in Dmitrovo and Leninskii.

5. 280th RD will protect the approaches to Marfa, Krasnoe, Nikol'skii, Borodino, Uruch'e, and Sosnovka.

6. The commander of 753rd ATR will conduct a personal reconnaissance on the ground and prepare firing positions in the Merkul'evo, Tiganovo, and Slobodka region, with the mission to cover the approaches to Briansk from

the direction of Roslavl' and Pochep. Simultaneously, the regiment will be my mobile reserve.

7. 290th RD will protect the approaches to Briansk in the Kabalichi, Sevrikovo, Deminteevka, and Novaia Sloboda sectors.

Fourteenth. Division commanders will create divisional mobile reserves, each consisting of a rifle battalion with a battery of divisional artillery and an antitank battery. For this purpose, use automobile and horse transport (of the forces and local population). Have similar reserves in each rifle regiment.

Fifteenth. My mobile reserve is two battalions of 855th RR (278th RD), a battalion of divisional artillery, and three batteries of 753rd ATR. The commander of the mobile group – is the commander of 855th RR. For this purpose: the commander of 278th RD will always have one battalion of mobile means (automobiles or horse transport), and the one battalion will have the army auto-company ready, which the Chief of the Rear, Colonel Volkov, will position in the woods southwest of Zastavishche by the morning of 25 August.

Maintain all of the auto-transport, which is free from transporting, close to the maneuver group at night time.

Sixteenth. Division commanders will continue to fortify and improve their defensive lines and pay special attention to the development of second and third lines (280th, 290th, and 278th RDs).

Create firm antitank centers with mobile antitank artillery and a sufficient quantity of ammunition and bottles of "KS" along likely axes for the movement of tanks. Open traps for tanks (snares) and emplace antitank mines, having protected them with security. Have well-prepared and hand-picked groups of destroyers of tanks in antitank regions.

Seventeenth. The army's Chief of Communications will establish technical communications with 217th and 279th RDs by the morning of 26 August, after creating an additional communications center in Diat'kovo. Take all measures so that technical communications and communications with liaison works precisely and without a hitch in any combat condition. Prepare radio data with the divisions and establish signal junctions in the work of radio stations.

Eighteenth. Observe instances of systematic tardiness (from 2 to 6 hours) of [reports] by operational and intelligence representatives, and other reports by lower level headquarters. Frequently, those which are exhaustive do not cast light on the actual situation and do not provide exact characteristics and the time of enemy actions.

Division commanders must guarantee timely submission of periodic and non-periodic reports and summaries. Henceforth, the Military Council will undertake the most decisive measures against those guilty for the late submission of summaries.

Nineteenth. Nip in the bud any attempts to withdraw without the permission of the senior chief. For willful withdrawal of a subunit or units, the commanders and commissars of these units will be immediately handed over for judgment by a military tribunal.

Twentieth. Carry out moving CPs only with the permission of higher headquarters and in the presence of a working communications net with the new CP.

Twenty-first. Submit all summaries at the time established by the headquarters, and combat reports every three hours, regardless of the situation.

The Commander of 50th Army, Major General Petrov
The Member of the army's Military Council,
    Brigade Commissar Miftakhov
The Chief of Staff, Colonel Pern

Source: "Boevoi prikaz komanduiushchego voiskami 50-i Armii No. 07 ot 24 avgusta 1941 g. na oboronu rubezha Frolovka, Zhukovka, Stolby, Pochep" [Combat order no. 07 of the commander of the forces of 50th Army of 24 August 1941 on defending the Frolovka, Zhukovka, Stolby, and Pochep line], *SBDVOV*, issue 43, 356-358.

14. Notes of a Conversation between the Supreme High Commander, the Chief of the General Staff, and the Commander of the Forces of the Briansk Front on 24 August 1941 about the Situation in the Briansk Front's Sector

Eremenko – Lieutenant General Eremenko on the apparatus.
Shaposhnikov – Chief of the General Staff, Marshal Shaposhnikov, on the apparatus.
Hello Comrade Eremenko! Report briefly on the situation in your *front*. Respond.
Eremenko – Lieutenant General Eremenko on the apparatus.
Hello, Comrade Marshal! I am reporting the enemy's situation on the front.
First: On 50th Army's front, the enemy's 29th Motorized Division has been precisely identified in the Dubrovka and Rognedino region; and the enemy's 18th Motorized Division in the Peklino and Leliatino region. Prisoners were seized from these units, and the locations of these divisions were determined based on the testimony of these prisoners. The prisoners reported that 17th Panzer Division is operating north of the Osovik region, but we have seized no prisoners from it. The 18th Panzer Division and 10th Motorized Division are operating in the Akulichi and Pochep sector, and, although we have no prisoners from these units, this was twice revealed by non-commissioned officers seized from 3rd Panzer Division, who revealed that 4th Panzer and 10th Motorized Divisions were operating to the north of 3rd Panzer Division, and 3rd Panzer Division has been confirmed three times by prisoners that it was located in the Starodub and Unecha region and had the mission, as one of the non-commissioned officers who overheard a conversation of his officers testified, that 3rd Panzer Division had as its mission to operate toward the south and to cut off Budenny. This report had some basis to it, since, at first, on 19 August 3rd Panzer Division began moving from Starodub toward the south, but then turned toward the west and appeared somewhat to the north of Starodub. The prisoners confirmed that it turned because someone was enveloping its rear.
Enemy operations on 24 August in the Zhukovka Station region – The enemy conducted an artillery preparation and tried to percolate into the vicinity of the defensive belt with small groups. The enemy's most active operations developed along the Ishova and Pochep front. In the Ishova, Kolodnia, and Sen'kovo region, the enemy conducted an attack with tanks and motorized infantry, and pushed our left flank units back. The 260th RD is now fighting in the Makarovo, Eliseevichi, and Hill 166.1 region. In the meantime, the tanks did not cross through the antitank ditches. A concentration of tanks has been observed in the Vorobeinia region and

to the south, and there are about 300 different vehicles in the Kolodnia region. In addition, in the Azarovo region, a force of up to two enemy battalions with tanks pushed our 1st Battalion, 878th Regiment, back and was approaching Fedorovichi and the Pochep region by the evening. The enemy already captured Pochep yesterday. Now, fighting is underway along the Vitovka line. Motorized infantry with artillery and small groups of 30-40 tanks have been noticed in that region both yesterday and today.

In the Starodub region, detachments sent out along with an armored train for seizing Starodub joined battle with the enemy along the Mishkovka line. On the enemy's side, 4 batteries, motorized infantry, and 17-20 tanks were operating in that region. Our aviation took on enemy aircraft in the Seshcha region. 15 enemy planes were destroyed by the first flight, but the results of the second flight have still not been reported.

I have ordered the commander of 260th RD to liquidate the enemy forces that have penetrated into the Kolodnia, Boguchevo, and Sin'kovo region. The 269th RD, together with 280th RD's and 260th RD's units, is being ordered to move up to the Sudost' River line, with the mission to destroy the penetrating enemy. In addition, the tank division, which has been deployed behind the antitank ditch in the region 10 kilometers north of Krasnoe, will be prepared for launching an attack against the enemy with its artillery and tanks, depending on the situation, either directly toward the west or toward the southwest.

Besides, one battalion of 1st Guards-Mortar Regiment [*Katiushas*] is to move into the same region.

Overall conclusion: I believe that the enemy is conducting active reconnaissance with strong forward units, supported by a significant number of tanks, and, apparently, any day now, but not tomorrow – the day after tomorrow, [he] will conduct an offensive along the entire front.

I am reporting about 55th CD's operations. It is located 20 kilometers somewhat to the north of Mglin, and its headquarters – is in the vicinity of Hill 202.7. I ordered it to operate audaciously and skillfully on a broad front – to conduct an attack against the enemy's rear in the general direction toward the south, with the mission to reach the region north of Rassukha, 20 kilometers east of Unecha, and subsequently operate – to go southeast with its units.

I received a request from Kalmykov [Major General Konstantin Gavrilovich Kalmykov, commander 55th CD], which asked for permission to turn to partisan operations. I have still not resolved this matter. I wish to ask your opinion. A squadron of 52nd CD, which withdrew northwestward, has linked up with Comrade Kalmykov, and a group of infantry, more than 200 men from a defeated division, has also linked up.

Now I am reporting on a second matter. The 287th and 283rd RDs are being taken from their transports until further notice. I received such a telegram signed by Kovalev and Kvashin. That is all I have.

Shaposhnikov – What sort of plan are you undertaking if an attack by Guderian follows tomorrow or the day after tomorrow? Bear in mind that his main grouping is aimed against 217th and 279th RDs. Therefore, it is necessary to strengthen the second echelon here and scatter mines in order to prevent him from exploiting his offensive toward Zhizdra and from enveloping Briansk from the north. That is all.

Eremenko – If the enemy conducts an attack on the Pochep front and to the north, then, having 3 antitank belts here, at first, I am thinking of defeating him in these antitank positions and then finishing him off with a counterattack with three rifle divisions and one tank brigade. With regard to the north, that is, in 217th and 219th RDs' sectors, I am now taking measures to dispatch sappers, and I will direct the division which has concentrated in the Sel'tso region in that direction.

Shaposhnikov – Are you now reinforcing 13th Army? It needs to be restored immediately. With regard to 287th and 283rd RDs, they are being held up for several days so as to complete their filling out.

Eremenko – Concerning 13th Army, I am taking every measure for its restoration. I have already sent 10,000 replacements and two divisions, which arrived and have been included it is composition. Four cavalry divisions have also been included in its composition. I have transferred 17 tanks to them, which arrived to restore 50th TD.

Shaposhnikov – You have not answered my question as to how you view the operations of 55th CD?

Eremenko – Good. The 55th CD can turn to partisan operations, but only Kalmykov himself can strike while the iron is hot I would like to ask one more question regarding dive bombers because enemy mobile forces are operating on the front, and dive bombers can hinder their maneuvers. They are great, chiefly for actions against bridges and narrow defiles. I know this from experience, since the enemy hindered us at Smolensk with their dive bombers; therefore, I request you provide me with one regiment of P-2s, preferably 244th Red Banner Regiment. In addition, give me one squadron of TB-3s for systematic night operations against the enemy, and I also request you provide 10 U-2 planes for communications.

Stalin – Stalin on the apparatus. Hello!

You have already been sent the U-2s. You will receive the TB-3s. I can send two P-2 regiments or even 3 to you immediately.

I have several questions for you.

1. Should we not disband the Central Front, combine 3rd Army with the 21st [Army], and transfer 21st Army's formations to your subordination? I am asking you about this because Moscow is dissatisfied with Efremov's work.

2. You require many personnel replacements and weapons. From your requests, I see that you are basing this on the old *shtat* [tables of organization] of 17,000 men in a division. But we have now decided not to have 17,000 in a division in light of the unwieldiness of the rear services, but [instead] have 11,000 in a division. If the old divisions maintained both regiments of artillery, it could have up to 13,000 in a division – as a last resort, up to 15,000 men, but no more. I request you follow these considerations when compiling your requests.

3. We can send to you in days, tomorrow, or, in the last resort, the day after tomorrow, 2 tank brigades with some quantity of KVs in them and 2-3 tank battalions. Do you need them?

4. If you promise to defeat the scoundrel Guderian, then we can send you another several regiments of aviation and several batteries of RS [multiple rocket launchers –*Katiushas*].

Your answer?

Eremenko – I am answering.

1. My opinion about the disbanding of the Central Front is such; because I wish to defeat Guderian and unquestionably smash him, then we need to protect the axis from the south strongly and this means to cooperate firmly with the shock group which will be operating from the Briansk region. Therefore, I request you subordinate 21st Army, combined with 3rd Army, to me. Regarding the replacements: here, apparently, some mistakes have crept in. On the contrary, I assigned the mission to those divisions which are being restored in 13th Army to fill them out, at first, if only up to 6,000 [men] and did not require 17,000. Here, apparently, our inexperienced workers simply made a hash of it.

I thank you very much, Comrade Stalin, for the fact that you are reinforcing me with tanks and aircraft. I only request that you speed up their dispatch. They are very much needed. And about that scoundrel Guderian, it goes without saying we will do the utmost to fulfill the mission you have put before us, that is, smash him.

Stalin – We can take Comrade Efremov from the *front* and make him your deputy if you wish this and then appoint Kuznetsov, the former commander of 3rd Army, as commander of 21st Army, with 3rd Army joining it. In the General Staff, it is said that Comrade Kuznetsov is more energetic and capable than Efremov. I say that 21st Army had already received or will receive 27,000 replacements. We think that you could use the workers of 3rd Army to reinforce your *front* staff. As concerns the *front* staff of the Central Front, we would wish to receive them in Moscow.

One question. How are your Il-2 assault aircraft [*shturmoviki*] working? That is all.

I have no further questions for you, unless you have questions for me.

Eremenko – I am answering your former question. I have no objections to the appointment of Efremov as deputy commander of the Briansk Front. With regards to the staff of 3rd Army, I would ask to use them as the staff of an army placed along the front between 50th and 13th Armies, with 3 rifle divisions and one cavalry division subordinate to it, because there are 10-11 formations per army, and it is now difficult for me to manage things in the armies, and appoint Major General Kreizer, who has proven himself to me and displays exceptional command qualities, as the commander of this army. He now commands the Western Front's 10th Motorized Division.

The second question. Today, I sent you an enciphered report with a request that you appoint Major General Gorodniansky, the commander of 129th [Rifle] Division, as the commander of 13th Army. He too has proven himself in battle and displays great tactical skills and an unbending will to victory. Concerning the IL-2 assault aircraft, the pilots and all of the commanders are delighted with their operations. As a matter of fact, they alone inflicted a significant defeat on the enemy and compelled Group Guderian to mark time in place for two days.

Stalin – Good. We will do as you suggest.

The Chief of the General Staff wants to continue the conversation with you. Goodbye! I wish you success.

Eremenko – Goodbye, Comrade Stalin! Good. I will wait.

Shaposhnikov – Comrade Eremenko!

Tomorrow, on 25 August 1941, you will receive an order about your future operations. The order will be sent to you from the General Staff by a special courier in an automobile. Upon receipt of the order, I request you telegraph me about its delivery to you. That is all.

Source: "Zapis' peregovora Verkhovnogo Glavnokomanduiushchego i nachal'nika General'nogo Shtaba s komanduiushchim voiskami Brianskogo Fronta 24 avgusta 1941 g. ob obstanovke v poloce Brianskogo Fronta" [Notes of a conversation between the Supreme High Commander, the chief of the General Staff, and the commander of the forces of the Briansk Front on 24 August 1941 about the situation in the Briansk Front's sector], *SBDVOV*, issue 43, 8-11.

15. Report by the Commander-in-Chief of the Forces of the Southwestern Direction to the Supreme High Commander on a Proposal to Reorganize the Central and Southwestern Fronts

25 August 1941

In connection with the withdrawal of the Central Front's forces toward the south, a situation has been created in which two separate *fronts* are occupying positions, one in relation to the other, with their rears at right angles; in which case the Central Front, in fact, does not have its own rear.

The absence of unified command and control along the Gomel' and Chernigov axes can create a muddle and confusion.

I propose two variants for resolving this matter.

1. Include 5th Army in the Southwestern Front and establish the [following] boundary between the fronts: Ovruch, the mouth of the Pripiat' River, Nezhin, Vorozhba, and further to the rear.

2. Transfer the Central Front's 21st and 3rd Armies to the Southwestern Front. Relocate the Central Front's headquarters to Lubny to provide command and control for 26th and 38th Armies.

I request your resolution of this matter.

S. Budenny
A. Pokrovsky

Source: "Doklad Glavnokomanduiushchego voiskami Iugo-Zapadnogo Napravleniia Verkhovnomu Glavnokomanduiushchemu predlozhenii po reorganizatsii Tsental'nogo i Iugo-Zapadnogo frontov" [Report by the commander-in-chief of the forces of the Southwestern Direction to the Supreme High Commander on a proposal to reorganize the Central and Southwestern Fronts], in Zolotarev, "*Stavka* 1941," 367.

16. Combat Order No. 04/op of the Commander of the Forces of the Briansk Front of 25 August 1941 about Including the Central Front's Forces in the Briansk Front's Composition

Order No. 04/op to the Forces of the Briansk Front,
Sven',

1800 hours on 25 August 1941
1:500,000 scale map

1. By a decision of the Supreme High Command of 25 August 1941, transmitted in enciphered telegram No. 001255, the Central Front's forces will be transferred to the Briansk Front's subordination effective at 0000 hours on 26 August 1941.

2. I establish the following compositions for the Briansk Front's armies effective at 0000 hours on 28 August 1941.

3. 50th Army: 217th, 279th, 258th, 260th, 290th, and 278th RDs and 55th CD.

The boundary on the right: (incl.) Mtsensk, (incl.) Zhizdra, Frolovka, Kazaki, Pochinok, and (incl.) Smolensk.

The boundary on the left: (incl.) Kromy, Btre, Lopush', Dmitrovo, Razrytoe, and Mstislavl'.

Headquarters of the army – the Poluzh'e region.

4. 3rd Army: 280th, 269th, 155th, 137th, and 148th RDs and 4th CD.

The boundary on the left: Belitsa Station, Sevsk, Suzemka, Selets, Nabichi, and Vokhor.

Headquarters of the army – Vzdruzhnoe region.

5. 13th Army: 282nd, 307th, 143rd, 6th, 132nd, 121st, and 283rd RD, 21st CD, 52nd CD, and 50th TD.

The boundary on the left: Vorozhba, Voronezh-Glukhov, Luzhki, and Mogilev.

Headquarters of the army – the Guta Staraia region.

6. 21st Army: include all of 21st Army's and former 3rd Army's forces, excluding 3rd Army's headquarters, with its communications and security equipment.

The boundary on the left: the Central Front's left boundary.

7. The Briansk Front's left boundary – the former Central Front's left boundary.

8. Transfer 3rd Army's headquarters, with its communications and security equipment, to the Vzdruzhnoe region by the morning of 27 August 1941, having transferring its forces to 21st Army.

9. The commanders of 50th, 3rd, and 13th Armies will organize command and control over their new forces by day's end on 27 August, and in 21st Army – upon receipt of this order.

10. The Supreme High Command appoints:

The commander of the Central Front, Lieutenant General Efremov, M. G. – as my deputy.

The commander of 3rd Army, Lieutenant General Kuznetsov, V.I. – as commander of 21st Army.

The commander of 21st Army, Major General Gordov, will revert to fulfilling his direct duties in the position of chief of staff of 21st Army.

The commander of 1st Motorized Division – Major General Kreizer, Ia. G., is designated as commander of 3rd Army.

The commander of 13th Army, Major General Golubev, is freed from the duties he performs and placed at the disposal of the People's Commissariat of Defense of the USSR.

The commander of 129th RD, Major General Gorodniansky, A. I., is designated as commander of 13th Army.

The chief of staff of the Central Front, Lieutenant General Zakharov, is freed from the duties he performs and placed at the disposal of the High Command.

11. I have decided to use the Central Front's headquarters for filling out the Briansk Front's headquarters.

The Commander of the Briansk Front, Lieutenant General Eremenko
The Member of the Military Council, Division Commissar Mazepov
The Chief of Staff of the *front*, Zakharov

Source: "Boevoi prikaz komanduiushchego voiskami Brianskogo Fronta No. 04/op ot 25 avgusta 1941 g. o vkliuchenii voisk Tsentral'nogo Fronta v sostav voisk Brianskogo Fronts" [Combat order no. 04/op of the commander of the forces of the Briansk Front of 25 August 1941 about including the Central Front's forces in the Briansk Front's composition], *SBDVOV*, issue 43, 42-43.

Appendix U (Part 2)

Armeegruppe Guderian's Advance across the Desna River, 25-28 August 1941

17. Operational Summary No. 014 of the Headquarters of the Briansk Front at 2000 hours on 25 August 1941 about the Combat Operations of the *Front's* Forces

Operational Summary No. 014 by 2000 hours,
Headquarters, Briansk Front,
1900 hours on 25 August 1941
1: 100,000 and 50,000 scale maps

First. The *front's* armies are continuing to defend their positions, while fortifying them in an engineer sense and conducting reconnaissance on the entire front.

Second. 50th Army is continuing to defend the Frolovka, Zhukovka, Stolby, along the eastern bank of the Sudost' River, and Pochep front firmly, while having one division in the army's reserve in the Darkovichi, Chaikovichi, and (inc.) Goriazh'e region.

Third. 217th RD, with 207th HAR, is defending positions along the eastern bank of the Sudost' River in the Bol'shaia Lutna, and 1 May State Farm sector.

Fourth. 279th RD is defending positions along the Desna River in the (incl.) Kholopenkovy Farm, (incl.) Zhukovka, Zhukova, and (incl.) Len'gubovka sector.

Fifth. 258th RD, with 761st AR and 151st CAR, is defending the Zhukovka and (incl.) Stolby line.

Sixth. 260th RD, with two batteries of 753rd ATR and 645th CAR, is defending the Stolby and Dmitrovo line.

Seventh. [Missing]

Eighth. 280th RD, with 753rd ATR (without two batteries) and 878th RR, is defending the Pil'shino and Sosnovka line and attacking toward Pochep with three rifle regiments.

Ninth. 290th RD (without 878th RR) is defending the Goliazh'e and Paluzh'e sector.

Tenth. 278th RD – the army's reserve in the Shibenets and (incl.) Goliazh'e region.

Eleventh. 55th CD, while operating in cooperation with aviation toward Ormino and Mglin against the enemy's rear north of Rassukha region, is concentrating in the vicinity of the woods at Valuets and Berezovka (28 kilometers south of Pochep) by the morning of 26 August.

Twelfth. 269th RD (without 1020th RR) was transferred to 13th Army on 24 August.

Thirteenth. 13th Army is defending positions along the Sudost' River on the (incl.) Pochep, Pogar, Kister, Ponurovka, Voronok, and Luzhki front.

Fourteenth. 45th RC (269th, 282nd, and 155th RD) is defending the (incl.) Pochep, Kozorezovka, Rogovo, Baklan', Posudichi, and (incl.) Pogar front.

Fifteenth. 307th RD, with 462nd CAR, is defending the Pogar, Borshchovo, and Kister line.

Sixteenth. 6th RD is defending the Kister, B. Andreikovichi, and Ponurovka line.

Seventeenth. 143rd RD is defending the (incl.) Ponurovka, Voronok, and Luzhki line.

Eighteenth. 283rd RD is in the army's reserve in the Novgorod-Severskii region.

Nineteenth. 50th TD – is in the army's reserve in the Vorob'evka region.

Twentieth. 52nd CD – is in the army's reserve in the Koleevka region.

Twenty-first. 4th CD is concentrated in the Vzdruzhnoe, Liubozhichi, and Arel'sk region.

Twenty-second. 108th TD is in the Ol'khovka region.

Twenty-third. 1st Guards-Mortar Regiment is in the Frolovka region.

Twenty-fourth. The VVS of the *front* carried out reconnaissance and destroyed enemy columns, which were moving from Seshcha toward the south and from Mglin toward Starodub.

They carried out bombing and dropped bottles with the flammable mixture "KS".

The Chief of Staff of the Briansk Front, Major General Zakharov
The Commissar of the *front's* headquarters,
    Battalion Commissar Kuznetsov
The Chief of the Operations Department, Colonel Argunov

Source: "Operativnaia svodka shtaba Brianskogo Fronta No. 014 k 20 chasam 25 avgusta 1941 g. o boevykh deistviiakh voisk fronta" [Operational summary no. 014 by 2000 hours on 25 August 1941 about the combat operations of the *front's* forces], *SBDVOV*, issue 43, 43-44.

18. Combat Order No. 08 of the Commander of the Forces of 50th Army of 26 August 1941 about the Army's Missions and Boundary Lines in Connection with Changes in its Combat Composition

Combat Order No. 08, Headquarters, 50th Army,
Deminteevka,
1315 hours on 26 August 1941
1:500,000 and 100,000 scale maps

1. According to the Briansk Front's Order No. 03/op of 25 August 1941, effective at 0000 hours on 28 August, 217th, 279th, 258th, 260th, 290th, and 278th RDs, 55th CD, and previous reinforcing units will enter 50th Army's composition.

2. 43rd Army is operating on the right. The boundary with it is: (incl.) Mtsensk, (incl.) Zhizdra, Frolovka, Kazaki, Pochinok, and (incl.) Smolensk

To the left of (incl.) Pochep and to the south, 3rd Army is going on the defense, to whose subordination 269th and 280th RDs will be transferred from 50th Army at 0000 hours on 28 August. The boundary with it is: (incl.) Kromy, Butre, Lopush', Dmitrovo, Razrytoe, and Mstislavl'.

Headquarters of 3rd Army – the Vzdruzhnoe region.

3. 217th, 279th, 258th, 260th, 290th, and 278th RDs will remain in their previous regions and strictly fulfill the instructions in my Combat Order No. 07 of 24 August 1941.

4. The commander of 290th RD, after being relieved by 878th RR and 280th RD's units, will deploy a regiment, with 2nd Bn, 827th AR attached, for defense of the Krasnoe, Khmelevo, and Kiselevka sector, while having a reinforced company in the Sosnovka region.

5. The commander of 280th RD will relieve 878th RR by the morning of 27 August and firmly occupy the (incl.) Dmitrovo and Pochep sector with the division. Immediately communicate with 3rd Army's headquarters.

6. The commander of 269th RD, while fulfilling his previously assigned mission, will become subordinate to 3rd Army. Before establishing communications with 3rd Army's headquarters, have close combat communications with 280th RD's headquarters.

7. 753rd ATR, while remaining is in its previous firing positions, will become subordinate to 290th RD (the headquarters of the division – Slobodka, 4 kilometers southwest of Ordzhonikidze) at 0600 hours on 27 August.

> The Commander of 50th Army, Major General Petrov
> The Member of the Military Council, Brigade Commissar Miftakhov
> The Chief of Staff of 50th Army, Colonel Pern

Source: "Boevoi prikaz komanduiushchego voiskami 50-i Armii No. 08 ot 26 avgusta 1941 g. o zadachakh i razgranichitel'nykh liniiakh voisk armii v sviazi s izmeneniem v ee boevom sostave" [Combat order no. 08 of the commander of the forces of 50th Army of 26 August 1941 about the army's missions and boundary lines in connection with changes in its combat composition], *SBDVOV*, issue 43, 359.

19. Report by the Commander-in-Chief of the Forces of the Southwestern Direction to the Supreme High Commander about the Necessity for More Precisely Defining the Briansk and Southwestern Fronts' Defensive Sectors

1935 hours on 26 August 1941

For a second time, I am reporting about the abnormal mutual positions of the former forces of the Central, but now of the Briansk and Southwestern Fronts.

21st Army's divisions, which are withdrawing southward from the Gomel' region, are situated a total of 20 kilometers to the north of the Repki region, where the Southwestern Front's 200th RD is organizing a defense. The question arises of uniting the commands.

The Briansk Front's command, with its Order No. 04/op, allotted the 13th Army's left boundary within the Southwestern Front's sector.

It is necessary to introduce clarity immediately in the Briansk and Southwestern Fronts' positions; otherwise, confusion can arise in terms of command and control and responsibilities in the event of 21st Army's further withdrawal.

S. Budenny
A. Pokrovsky

Source: "Doklad Glavnokomanduiushchego voiskami Iugo-Zapadnogo Napravleniia No. 205 Verkhovnomu Glavnokomanduiushchemu predlozhenii o neobkhodimosti utochneniia polos oborony Brianskogo i Iugo-Zapadnogo frontov" [Report by the commander-in-chief of the forces of the Southwestern Direction to the Supreme High Commander about the necessity for clarifying the Briansk and Southwestern Fronts' defensive sectors], in Zolotarev, "Stavka 1941," 367-368.

20. Stavka VGK Directive No. 001296 to the Commander of the Forces of the Briansk Front about Destroying the Enemy in the Starodub Region
0400 hours on 26 August 1941

The enemy has one motorized regiment, supported by tanks, in the Starodub region, and, west of Starodub, the enemy has still not spread to the south along the Unecha-Klintsy-Novozybkov railroad. 21st Army's 55th RD is located in the Klimovo region. It seems possible to envelop the Starodub position, destroy the enemy in Starodub, and close up the flanks of 13th and 21st Armies. The Supreme High Command considers the conduct of such an operation completely feasible and capable of yielding good results.

Report results achieved.

For the Stavka of the Supreme High Command
Chief of the General Staff B. Shaposhnikov

Source: "Direktiva Stavki VGK No. 001296 komanduiushchemu voiskami Brianskogo Fronta o razgrome protivnika v raione Staroduba" [Stavka VGK Directive No. 001296 to the commander of the forces of the Briansk Front about destroying the enemy in the Starodub region], in Zolotarev, "Stavka 1941," 138.

21. Combat Order No. 061 of the Commander of the Forces of 13th Army of 26 August 1941 on Capturing Starodub
Combat Order No. 061, Headquarters, 13th Army
2000 hours on 26 August 1941
1:500,000 scale map

1. A large grouping of enemy motorized infantry, with artillery and tanks, is developing an offensive from Starodub toward Novgorod-Severskii.
2. On the right, 50th Army is defending along the Sudost' River. The boundary with it is as before. On the left, 21st Army is attacking from the Klimovo and Novozybkov line toward Starodub with its right wing.

3. 13th Army will attack toward Starodub on the morning of 27 August 1941, and, having captured Starodub, will attack into the rear of the penetrating enemy and destroying him northwest of Novgorod-Severskii.

The beginning of the offensive will be 1000 hours on 27 August 1941.

4. 45th RC (282nd, 155th, and 269th RDs), with previous means of reinforcements, while protecting its right flank from the direction of Pochep and defending with 269th RD along the P'ianyi Rog, Kotovka, and Semtsy line, will attack toward Starodub. Mission – reach the Starodub and Kartyshino line by day's end on 27 August 1941.

The boundary on the left: Kholopets, Kalinovka, and Kartyshino.

5. 307th RD will attack toward Tarasovka, with the mission – to reach the Kartyshino and Bol'shie Andreikovichi line by the end of the day.

The boundary on the left: Kister, (incl.) Bol'shie Andreikovichi, Ponurovka, and Lomakovka.

6. 6th RD, with previous reinforcing units, will defend the Bol'shie Andreikovichi, Poliany, and Buda-Vorob'evskaia line, while protecting the shock group from the left.

The boundary on the left: Buda-Vorob'evskaia, Kostobobr, and Arkhipovka.

7. 50th TD will advance into the Vorob'evka, Chaikin, and Smiach'e region, while protecting the junction between 6th and 143rd RDs.

The boundary on the left: Leskonogi, Smiach'e, and Ivanovka.

8. 143rd RD will contain the enemy offensive with its active operations and prevent him from spreading out further to the Smiach'e, Sheptaki, and Forostovichi line.

9. 52nd CD will protect the army's left flank along the Desna River southeast of Novgorod-Severskii along the (incl.) Novgorod-Severskii and Kurilovka line.

10. 137th RD will occupy and defend the bridgehead at Trubchevsk from the direction of Pochep by the morning of 27 August 1941, while protecting the crossings over the Desna River.

11. 132nd RD will advance for defense of the Desna River line along the Och'kin and (incl.) Novgorod-Severskii front.

Place the headquarters of the division at Khil'chitsy.

12. 4th CD will move into the Zarech'e and Chekhovka region by forced march, with the mission to attack toward Ivanteiki and Galinsk, while protecting the shock group from the right.

The headquarters of the division in its jumping-off positions – Karbovka.

13. The VVS of the army.

    1) Ensure observation of the enemy by reconnaissance on the field of battles and for approaching columns.

    2) Protect the offensive from the air.

    3) Prevent enemy reserves from approaching Starodub.

14. I will be with the operational group in Trubchevsk.

The Commander of 13th Army, Major General Golubev
The Member of the Military Council, Brigade Commissar Furt
The Chief of Staff of 13th Army, *Kombrig* Petrushevsky

Source: "Boevoi prikaz komanduiushchego voiskami 13-i Armii No. 061 ot 26 avgusta 1941 g. na ovladenie Starodub" [Combat order no. 061 of the commander of the forces of 13th Army of 26 August 1941 on capturing Starodub], *SBDVOV*, issue 43, 301-302.

22. Notes of a Conversation by Direct Line between the Supreme High Commander and the Commander of the Forces of the Briansk Front
0240-0250 hours on 27 August 1941

> **Briansk** – Eremenko on the apparatus.
> **Moscow** – Stalin on the apparatus, Hello.
> **Eremenko** – Hello, Comrade Stalin. I can hear you.
> **Stalin** – I am called you for two minutes. The High Command's Reserve Aviation Group No. 1 is in the Bogodukhov region northwest of Khar'kov. There are 4 regiments in the group. The commander of the group is Trifonov. It is subordinate to me. Communicate with the group's commander and inform him on my behalf that, from this day, that is, 27 August, he and his aviation group will temporarily transfer to your disposition. What do you know about this aviation group?
> **Eremenko** – I know nothing about this group. Now I will establish communications with it through the General Staff and by aircraft. I will employ it, together with *frontal* aviation and a counterstroke by the ground forces, on the Novgorod-Severskii and Starodub axis in order to destroy the enemy's Starodub and Novgorod-Severskii group. I will deliver a concentric blow against Starodub tomorrow morning, with the aim to cut off and destroy the enemy group from Starodub to the south. Today, our aircraft destroyed up to 200 vehicles. It was clear to me all of this involved aviation. What other instructions do you have? I have no questions.
> **Stalin** – I have no further instructions for you. You yourself know what needs to be done. Off you go to hand the order to the commander of the aviation group, Trifonov, so that he can become subordinate to you in timely fashion. I wish you success. All the best.
> **Eremenko** – Goodbye Comrade Stalin.

Source: "Zapis' peregovorov po priamomu provodu Verkhovnogo Glavnokomanduiushchego s komanduiushchim voiskami Brianskogo fronta" [Notes of a conversation by direct line between the Supreme High Commander and the Commander of the forces of the Briansk Front], Zolotarev, "*Stavka* 1941," 143-144.

23. *Stavka* VGK Directive No. 001325 to the Commander of the VVS of the Red Army, 1st Aviation Group, and the Forces of the Briansk Front about the Temporary Re-subordination of 1st Aviation Group
0340 hours on 27 August 1941

> The Supreme High Commander orders:
> Subordinate 1st Reserve Aviation Group temporarily to the commander of the Briansk Front.
> Carry out the transfer the aviation group by air on 27 August 1941 to airfields designated by the commander of the Briansk Front. Organize maintenance and allowances in accordance with the instructions of the commander of the Briansk Front.

For the Supreme High Commander
Chief of the General Staff,
B. Shaposhnikov

Source: "Direktiva Stavki VGK No. 001325 komanduiushchemu VVS Krasnoi Armii, 1-i Rezervnoi Aviagruppoi, voiskami Brianskogo fronta o vremennom perepodchinenii 1-i Rezervnoi Aviagruppy" [*Stavka* VGK Directive No. 001325 to the commander of the VVS of the Red Army, 1st Aviation Group, and the forces of the Briansk Front about the temporary re-subordination of 1st Aviation Group], in Zolotarev, "*Stavka* 1941," 144-145.

24. Operational Summary No. 017 of the Headquarters of the Briansk Front at 0600 hours on 27 August 1941 about the Combat Operations of the *Front's* Forces

Operational Summary No. 017 by 0600 hours,
Headquarters, Briansk Front,
0700 hours on 27 August 1941
1: 100,000 and 50,000 scale maps

First. On the *front's* right wing toward Roslavl', fighting took place with enemy reconnaissance groups on 26 August and the night of 26-27 August. On the left wing toward Starodub and Novgorod-Severskii, fierce fighting was going on with the enemy who were making the transition to the offensive. The enemy captured Novgorod-Severskii during the second half of the day and is continuing to develop the offensive toward the south.

Second. On 50th Army's front, the situation is unchanged. On the right wing, active operations by enemy artillery are being noted in 217th RD's sector.

Third. Along the Zhukovka and Roslavl' axis, small groups of enemy are operating in 279th and 258th RDs' sectors. The positions of the units – are unchanged.

Fourth. On the left flank, fighting occurred with groups of enemy which were trying to penetrate into our units' defensive dispositions in 260th and 280th RDs' sectors. At 1630 hours up to two companies of enemy infantry supported by 15 tanks attacked toward Kovalevka. 280th RD's artillery repelled the attack, and the enemy was scattered.

At 1900 hours the enemy launched an attack from the direction of Vitovka toward Kalinovka for a second time. Simultaneously, up to two companies of infantry with tanks spread out from the Ol'khovka region toward Hill 171.3. The fighting is continuing.

Fifth. On the right wing of 13th Army's front, an enemy force of up to two battalions of infantry supported by tanks went over to the attack at 1530 hours and captured Semtsy. The enemy was thrown back by a counterattack by our units, and Semtsy was occupied by our units at 2200 hours. The situation at the front was restored.

Sixth. In the Baklan' and Pogar sector, there are operations by small enemy reconnaissance groups. The positions on the front – are unchanged.

Seventh. On the army's left wing toward Starodub, Mishko, and Novgorod-Severskii, during the second half of the day on 26 August, the enemy penetrated the defensive front with large forces (one panzer and one motorized division) and occupied Novgorod-Severskii, while continuing to develop the offensive toward the south.

Eighth. The VVS of the *front* continued to bomb, with successive strikes, enemy columns detected enemy moving toward Starodub and Novgorod-Severskii during the day on 26 August.

Ninth. 108th TD has been concentrated in the woods immediately to the south of Ol'khovka in the *front's* reserve.

Tenth. 299th RD was concentrated in the woods in the Sel'tso region – in the *front's* reserve.

Eleventh. Communications with 50th Army – telephone, telegraph, and liaison officers worked without interruption.

Communications with 13th Army – telephone and telegraph – worked with interruptions.

> The Chief of Staff of the Briansk Front, Major General Zakharov
> The Commissar of the *front* headquarters,
>   Battalion Commissar Kuznetsov
> The Deputy Chief of the Operations Department, Colonel Revunenkov

Source: "Operativnaia svodka shtaba Brianskogo Fronta No. 017 k 6 chasam 27 avgusta 1941 g. o boevykh deistviiakh voisk fronta" [Operational summary no. 017 by 0600 hours on 27 August 1941 about the combat operations of the *front's* forces], *SBDVOV*, issue 43, 46.

25. Combat Report of the Headquarters of 21st Army No. 031 of 27 August 1941 to the Headquarters of the Briansk Front about the Positions of the Army's Forces

Combat Report No. 031, Headquarters, 21st Army
(south of Androniki)
1200 hours on 27 August 1941
1:100,000 and 500,000 scale maps

1. The enemy, while continuing an offensive, is trying to close the ring from the Semenovka and Novgorod-Severskii and Gomel', Dobrianka, and Mena axes, with the objective to encircle 21st Army's right wing and center.

The enemy's forward units occupied Sosnitsa (20 kilometers east of Mena). We have detected an airborne assault by 50-60 men, 2 tankettes, and motorcyclists in the Avdeevka region (35 kilometers northeast of Sosnitsa).

2. The army's units are conducting sustained fighting in [the following] positions at 1000 hours:

187th RD – Kliusy and Glinishche.

117th RD, while penetrating the ring, is escaping from encirclement and fighting in the Ivanovka and Starye Iurkovichi region at 0800 hours.

219th MD – Gorodok and Sen'kovka.

55th RD – Lemeshevka and Perepis.

232nd and 75th RDs are holding onto the Gornostaevka Station, Iankovka, and Skitok line.

24th RD, together with the cavalry group, has the mission to restore the situation in the Verbovka and Dobrianka region.

42nd RD is moving to the Shchors region by auto-transport.

277th RD is occupying Siadrina, Luposovo, Beloshitskaia Sloboda, and Mokryi Oles.

Reserve: 852nd RR – in Naumovka.

3. The army commander has decided: while holding onto the general Gutka Studenetskaia, Elino, Moshenka, Korobichi, Aleksandrovka, and Starye Iarylovichi line, to destroy the enemy in the Vladimirovka and Dobrianka region with active operations by the cavalry group and 24th RD and to deliver an attack against the main enemy grouping, which is moving in the direction of Semenovka and Novgorod-Severskii, with 277th and 42nd RDs..

4. I request you speed up the movement and re-subordination of 200th RD to 21st Army's commander and prevent the further advance by the enemy's Semenovka grouping and destroy his groupings in the Churovichi, Krugovets, Dobrianka, and Rudnia (southeast of Savinki) region with *frontal* aviation.

> The Chief of Staff of 21st Army, Major General Gordov
> The Commissar of the army's headquarters,
>   Regimental Commissar Mandrik
> The Chief of the Operations Department, Lieutenant Colonel Posiakin

Source: "Boevoe donesenie shtaba 21-i Armii No. 031 ot 27 avgusta 1941 g. shtabu Brianskogo Fronta o polozhenii voisk armii" [Combat report of the headquarters of 21st Army No. 031 of 27 August 1941 to the headquarters of the Briansk Front about the positions of the army's forces], *SBDVOV*, issue 43, 339-340.

26. *Stavka* VGK Directive No. 001355 to the Commander-in-Chief of the Forces of the Southwestern Direction about Protecting the Starodub and Shostka Axes
0350 hours on 28 August 1941

Measures have been taken for liquidating of the enemy penetration from Starodub toward Novgorod-Severskii and Shostka, but this does not exclude the necessity for the Southwestern Front to take the most urgent measures for protecting these axes. The temporary use of airborne units is permitted for this aim. You cannot count on the *front* being reinforced by tank units in the near future.

The Supreme High Commander has not permitted 21st Army's transfer from the Briansk Front to the Southwestern.

> B. Shaposhnikov

Source: "Direktiva Stavki VGK No. 001355 Glavnokomanduiushchemu voiskami Iugo-Zapadnogo Napravleniia o prikritii napravleniia Starodub, Shostka" [*Stavka* VGK Directive No. 001355 to the commander-in-chief of the forces of the Southwestern Direction about protecting the Starodub and Shostka axes], in Zolotarev, "*Stavka* 1941," 145.

27. Report No. 2107 of the Commander of 21st Army to the Commander of the Forces of the Briansk Front about the Situation and Measures for Preventing the Army's Encirclement

0440 hours on 28 August 1941

The enemy penetrated the army's front along the Khorobichi and Shchors axis and reached the Moshchenka, Gorodnia, and Drozdovitsy region, and, on the right wing, an enemy motor-mechanized group reached the Makova region. This has created a threat of rupturing the army and encircling it in piecemeal fashion.

I request once again that you immediately subordinate 200th and 62nd RDs to me, along with the headquarters of 15th Rifle Corps, or allow the commitment 66th Rifle Corps and the cavalry group on the right flank of the army, after designating Gorodnia as the junction between the two armies (21st and 5th).

Kuznetsov, Kolonin, Gordov

Source: "Doklad komanduiushchego 21-i Armiei No. 2107 komanduiushchemu voiskami Brianskogo fronta ob obstanovke i merakh po nedopushcheniiu okruzheniia armii" [Report No. 2107 of the commander of 21st Army to the commander of the forces of the Briansk Front about the situation and measures for the preventing the army's encirclement], in Zolotarev, "*Stavka* VGK 1941," 368.

28. Combat Order No. 041 of the Headquarters of the Briansk Front of 28 August 1941 to the Commander of the Forces of 21st Army on an Offensive toward Starodub

To the Commander of 21st Army
Order No. 041, Headquarters, Briansk Front,
1000 hours on 28 August 1941
1:500,000 scale map

1. The enemy, with around two panzer divisions, has penetrated into Novgorod-Severskii and is spreading out toward Shostka and Iampol'.
2. 13th Army is attack toward Starodub.
The *front* commander orders:
    a) This confirms your order about 21st Army's offensive toward Starodub with a force of no fewer than 3 RDs and the creation of reserves for your right flank in the Semenovka region.
    b) Maintain communications with the operational post in the Khutor Mikhailovskii region and with us by radio, while using the notebook [code book] which I am sending to you with this order.

The Chief of Staff of the Briansk Front, Major General Zakharov
The Commissar of the *front's* headquarters,
    Battalion Commissar Kuznetsov

Source: "Boevoi rasporiazhenie shtaba Brianskogo Fronta No. 041 ot 28 avgusta 1941 g. komanduiushchemu voiskami 21-i Armii na nastuplenie v napravlenii Starodub" [Combat order no. 041 of the headquarters of the Briansk Front of 28 August 1941 to the commander of the forces of 21st Army on an offensive toward Starodub], *SBDVOV*, issue 43, 47.

29. *Stavka* VGK Directive No. 001374 to the Commander of 21st Army about Liquidating the Enemy Penetration in the Gorodnyi Region
1645 hours on 28 August 1941

Your request about permission to commit 66th Rifle Corps and the cavalry group on the army's right flank is incomprehensible. The situation has obliged you to do so for a long time. Employing all forces as is possible, immediately organize an attack toward the northeast to link up with Golubev [13th Army], with the objective of liquidating the penetrating enemy group.

Your left flank will be protected by the Southwestern Front's 15th RC along the Pekurovka and Grabovo line.

B. Shaposhnikov

Source: "Direktiva Stavki VGK No. 001374 komanduiushchemu 21-i Armiei o merakh po likvidatsii proryva protivnika v raione Gorodnyi" [*Stavka* VGK Directive No. 001374 to the commander of 21st Army about liquidating the enemy penetration in the Gorodnyi region], in Zolotarev, "*Stavka* 1941," 145.

30. Operational Summary No. 020 of the Headquarters of the Briansk Front at 1800 hours on 28 August 1941 about the Combat Operations of the *Front's* Forces
Operational Summary No. 020 by 1800 hours,
Headquarters, Briansk Front,
1800 hours on 28 August 1941
1: 100,000 and 50,000 scale maps

First. The Briansk Front is continuing to defend along the Roslavl' axis on its right wing and, on its left wing, is organizing the liquidation of the penetration by enemy motor-mechanized units which have penetrated toward Novgorod-Severskii and Iampol'.

Second. 50th Army is continuing to hold onto its previous defensive positions. Combat operations by reconnaissance units and artillery exchanges have developed along its flanks.

Third. 217th RD is continuing to occupy defenses along the eastern bank of the Desna River on the Buda and (incl.) Kholopenkovy front.

On the division's front, up to two enemy IRs and up to 130 tanks dislodged the division's combat security at 1000 hours on 28 August and reached the Lozitsy, Krasnyi Shchipal', Pavlova Sloboda, and (incl.) Molot'kovo front, and, while trying to approach the forward edge of the defense, was beaten back everywhere.

The division is holding onto it's the positions it occupy's.

Fourth. 279th RD is along the eastern bank of the Desna River on the Zelenskovo, Lake Orekhovoe, Sviatki, Berestovskii, and (incl.) Zhukovka front.

The division's positions are unchanged on the front.

Fifth. 258th RD is occupying the Zhukovka and (incl.) Stolby front. The enemy is displaying no activity on the division's front.

Sixth. 260th RD – Stolby, Sheika, Malye Koski, Morochevo, (incl.) Kashevo, and Dmitrovo. The enemy is displaying no activity on the division's front.

Seventh. 280th RD, with 1031st RR, 269th RD, and 290th RD's 878th RR are fighting stubbornly to capture Pochep. At 1200 hours they were fighting along the Putilovskii, Zelenaia Roshcha, Kalinovka, and Vitovka line, and, by this time, 269th RD's 1020th RR was fighting to capture Rechitsa State Farm. The enemy is defending stubbornly, while protecting himself actively with aviation.

Trophies: 4 officers have been taken prisoner and 7 vehicles, 2 motorcycles, and a headquarters with important documents have been seized. Losses are being verified.

Eighth. 278th RD occupies the Darkovichi, Glaenka, and Buda (15 kilometers north of Ordzhonikidze) region with two regiments, and one is advancing in the Krasnoe region.

Ninth. 290th RD, without 878th RR, occupies defenses: from Goliazh'e to Poluzh'e and Eliseevichi. No information has been received about 55th CD.

Tenth. 13th Army – sustained fighting continued on its entire front.

On its right wing, the enemy continued active operations and captured Pokrovskii, Romanovka, and Chekhovka.

On its left wing, fighting continued with enemy forces penetrating into Novgorod-Severskii.

Eleventh. Information has not been received about the positions of 21st Army's units as of the time this summary was prepared.

Twelfth. 298th RD is fully concentrated in the vicinity of Diat'kovo Station.

Thirteenth. 299th RD is fully concentrated in the Sel'tso region.

Fourteenth. 108th TD is in the *front's* reserve in the woods south of Ol'khovka.

Fifteenth. 121st RD is fully concentrated in the *front's* reserve in the Dorozhevo region.

Sixteenth. 141st TB is fully concentrated in the Gololobovo region.

Seventeenth. Communications with 50th Army are working without interruption. Communications with 13th Army – are [working] with great interruptions, except for radio. With 21st Army – only by radio.

The Chief of Staff of the Briansk Front, Major General Zakharov
The Commissar of the *front's* headquarters,
    Battalion Commissar Kuznetsov
The Deputy Chief of the Operations Department, Colonel Revunenkov

Source: "Operativnaia svodka shtaba Brianskogo Fronta No. 020 k 18 chasam 28 avgusta 1941 g. o boevykh deistviiakh voisk fronta" [Operational summary no. 020 by 1800 hours on 28 August 1941 about the combat operations of the *front's* forces], *SBDVOV*, issue 43, 47-48.

31. Extracts from, Combat Orders of the Headquarters of the Briansk Front of 28 August 1941 to the Commanders of 4th Cavalry Division and 141st Tank Brigade

No. 042 on 28 August – to 4th Cavalry Division

The enemy was moving toward the Karbovka, Pokrovskii, and Romanovka line with forward units

The *front* commander orders:

1. Move into and occupy the Mostochnaia, Semiachki, and Voiborovo region by 0300 hours on 29 August 1941, having thrown forward detachments out to the Karbovka, Romanovka, and Griazivets line.

2. Establish communication with the tank subunits that will be moving into the vicinity of the woods west of Vershan' and the Radinsk region by the morning of 29 August ...

Un-numbered at 1915 hours on 28 August 1941 – to 141st Tank Brigade

The enemy is occupying Semtsy, Valuets, and Romanovka.

The *front* commander oders:

1. You will force the Desna River in the Sovrasovka and Vzdruzhnoe sector and concentrate in the Komiagino, Radinsk, Sloboda, and Subbotovo region by 0300 hours on 29 August 1941.

2. Establish communications with 108th Tank Division in the Dol'sk, Polovetskii, and Vershan' region.

3. Conduct reconnaissance toward Porovichi, Sosnovka, Issaevka, and Goritsy ...

> The Chief of Staff of the Briansk Front, Major General Zakharov
> The Commissar of the *front's* headquarters,
>   Battalion Commissar Kuznetsov
> The Chief of the Operations Department, Colonel Argunov

Source: "Boevye rasporiazheniia shtaba Brianskogo Fronta ot 28 avgusta 1941 g. komandiram 4-i Kavaleriiskoi Divizii i 141-i Tankovoi Brigady" [Combat orders of 28 August 1941 to the commanders of 4th Cavalry Division and 141st Tank Brigade], *SBDVOV*, issue 43, 49.

32. Supreme High Command Order No. 0077 to the Commanders of the Forces of the Briansk and Reserve Fronts about Conducting an Air Operation to Destroy the Enemy's Tank Grouping

28 August 1941

1. With the aim of disrupting the operations of the enemy's tank grouping on the Briansk axis, conduct an operation with the forces of the *front's* VVS and aviation of the High Command's Reserve from 28-31 August 1941.

2. Employ the Briansk and Reserve Fronts' VVS, 1st Reserve Aviation Group, and no fewer than 100 DB-3 aircraft for the operation to destroy the enemy's tank grouping.

In all, 450 combat aircraft should participate in the operation.

Begin the operation at dawn on 29 August or 30 August and complete it by day's end on 31 August 1941.

3. I am entrusting the organization and conduct of the operation to the Military Council and headquarters of the Red Army's VVS.

4. Report on the course of the operation at 2200 hours on 29, 30, and 31 August 1941.

> The Supreme High Commander, I. Stalin
> The Chief of the General Staff, B. Shaposhnikov

Source: "Prikaz Verkhovnogo Glavnokomanduiushchego No. 0077 komanduiushchim voiskami Brianskogo i Rezervnogo Frontov o provedenii vozdushnoi operatsii po razgromu tankovoi gruppirovki protivnika" [Supreme High Command Order No. 0077 to the commanders of the forces of the Briansk and Reserve Fronts about conducting an air operation to destroy the enemy tank grouping], in Zolotarev, "*Stavka* 1941," 146.

Appendix U (Part 3)

The Third Soviet Counteroffensive: The Briansk Front's Roslavl'-Novozybkov Offensive, 29 August-14 September 1941

German 13. Führer Directive No. 35, 6 September 1941
The Führer and Supreme High Command
of the Armed Forces (OKW).
Führer headquarters
OKW, Headquarters of the Operations Directorate.
6 September 1941
Department for the Defense of the Country (1st Dept.).
No. 441492/41. Top Secret

Directive No. 35

The initial successes in operations against enemy forces located between the adjoining flanks of Army Groups South and Center, combined with further successes in the encirclement of enemy forces in the Leningrad region, have created prerequisites for the conduct of a decisive operation against Army Group Timoshenko, which is unsuccessfully conducting offensive operations in front of Army Group Center. It must be destroyed decisively before the onset of winter within the limited time indicated in existing orders.

To this end, we must concentrate all of the efforts of ground and air forces earmarked for the operation, including those that can be freed up from the flanks and transferred in timely fashion.

On the basis of the OKH's report, I am issuing the following orders for the preparation and conduct of this operation:

1. **On the southern wing of the Eastern Front** – destroy the enemy located in the Kremenchug, Kiev, and Konotop triangle with the forces of Army Group South, which have crossed the Dnepr to the north, in cooperation with the attacking forces of Army Group Center's southern flank. As soon as the situation permits, freed up formations of Second and Sixth Armies and also the Second Panzer Group should be regrouped to carry out new operations.

No later than 10 September, mobile formations on Army Group South's front, reinforced with infantry and supported along the main axes by the Fourth Air Fleet, are to begin a surprise offensive northwestward through Lubna from the bridgehead created by the Seventeenth Army. At the same time, the Seventeenth Army will advance along the Poltava and Khar'kov axis.

Continue the offensive along the lower course of the Dnepr toward the Crimea supported by the Fourth Air Fleet. (Simultaneously, depending on what forces you have at your disposal, undertake an offensive from the bridgehead in the Dnepropetrovsk region.)

Movement of mobile forces southward from the lower course of the Dnepr to Melitopol' will considerably assist the Eleventh Army fulfill its missions.

2. **In the sector of Army Group Center** – Prepare an operation against Army Group Timoshenko as quickly as possible so that we can launch an offensive in the general direction of Viaz'ma and destroy the enemy located in the region east of Smolensk by a double envelopment by powerful panzer forces against his flanks.

To that end, form two shock groups:

The first – on the southern flank, presumably in the region southeast of Roslavl', with an attack axis to the northeast. The composition of the group [will include] forces subordinate to Army Group Center and the 5th and 2d Panzer Divisions, which will be freed up to fulfill that mission.

The second – in the sector of Ninth Army, with its attack axis presumably through Belyi. In so far as possible, this group will consist of large Army Group Center formations.

After destroying the main mass of Timoshenko's group of forces in this decisive encirclement and destruction operation, Army Group Center is to begin pursuing enemy forces along the Moscow axis while protecting its right flank on the Oka River and its left on the upper reaches of the Volga River. The Second Air Fleet, reinforced in timely fashion by transferred formations, especially from the northern sector of the front, will provide air support for the offensive. While doing so, it will concentrate its main forces on the flanks while employing the principal bomber formations (Eighth Air Corps) for support of the mobile formations in both attacking flank groupings.

3. **In the northern sector of the Eastern Front**. Encircle enemy forces operating in the Leningrad region (and capture Shlissel'burg) in cooperation with Finnish forces attacking on the Karelian Isthmus so that a considerable number of the mobile formations and the First Air Fleet's formations, particularly the VIII Air Corps, can be transferred to Army Group Center no later than 15 September. First and foremost, however, it is necessary to strive to encircle Leningrad completely, at least from the east, and, if weather conditions permit, conduct a large-scale air offensive against Leningrad. It is especially important to destroy the water supply stations.

As soon as possible, Army Group North's forces must begin an offensive northward in the Neva River sector to help the Finns overcome the fortifications along the old Soviet-Finnish border, and also to shorten the front lines and deprive the enemy of the ability to use his air bases. In cooperation with the Finns, prevent enemy naval forces from exiting Kronshtadt into the Baltic Sea (Hango and the Moonzund Islands) by using mine obstacles and artillery fire.

Also isolate the region of combat operations at Leningrad from the sector along the lower course of the Volkhov as soon forces necessary to perform this mission become available. Link up with the Army of Karelia on the Svir River only after enemy forces in the Leningrad region have been destroyed.

4. During the further conduct of operations, ensure that the southern flank of Army Group Center's offensive along the Moscow axis is protected by an advance to the northeast by a flank protection grouping in Army Group South's sector created from available mobile formations. [Also ensure] that Army Group North's forces be directed to protect Army Group Center's northern flank and also the advance along both sides of Lake Il'men' to link up with the Army of Karelia.

5. Any curtailment of the period for preparing and acceleration of the operation's beginning will accompany the preparation and conduct of the entire operation.

[signed] Hitler

Addendum: In as much as the Fourth Air Fleet has not allocated forces to support the offensive from the Dnepropetrovsk bridgehead, the Führer considers it desirable that all of the motorized divisions participate in the First Panzer Group's offensive from the Kremenchug bridgehead.

The 198th Infantry Division and also Italian or Hungarian forces are holding on to the bridgehead.

The Chief of Staff of the Supreme High Command
of the Armed Forces [OKW]

Source: *Sbornik voenno-istoricheskikh materialov Velikoi Otechestvennoi voiny, vypusk 18* [Collection of military-historical materials of the Great Patriotic War, issue 18] (Moscow: Voenizdat, 1960), 242-244. Prepared by the Military-Historical Department of the Military-Scientific Directorate of the Red Army General Staff and classified secret.

33. Combat Report by the Commander of the Forces of 13th Army to the Commander of the Forces of the Briansk Front of 29 August 1941 about the Positions of the Army's Forces and the Necessity for Withdrawing It to the Eastern Bank of the Desna River

To the Commander of the Briansk Front, Lieutenant General Eremenko
Copy: To the *Stavka* of the Supreme High Command
0945 hours on 29 August 1941

1. The enemy is operating on both of our army's wings and at the boundaries of 50th Army and 21st Army, with two large mobile groups.

On the left wing, as many as two panzer divisions and an army corps [are operating] toward Pogar and Novgorod-Severskii.

On the right wing, 47th PzC's units [are operating] toward Semtsy, Valuets, and Romanovka, with possible attacks toward Trubchevsk or to link up with the enemy's Novgorod-Severskii group.

2. 13th Army's units, while fulfilling the *front's* order for capturing Starodub, occupy the following positions:

3. 269th RD is defending Usozhki, P'ianyi Rog, and Kotovka with two regiments (1018th and 1022nd) and has repelled attacks by up to two motorized regiments and forty tanks. 1020th RR has suffered up to 40% losses.

The division has been subjected to raids by 34 bombers.

The division has the mission to attack toward Semtsy and Valuets into the penetrating enemy's rear.

4. 282nd RD fought fierce battles for Semtsy, and, on 27 August 1941, the enemy penetrated its front with the forces of about an infantry division and 63rd and 40th IRs, with tanks. On 28 August the division fought for separate places in the Kalachevka and Baklan' region, and 877th RR successfully repulsed attempts by enemy tank and motorized infantry [to penetrate] from the direction of Ramassukha toward Trubchevsk.

282nd RD did not represent a controlled organism by the evening of 28 August. I have called for order to be restored, with the right to replace the division's commander, and, in the event it is necessary, to check on the division commander's fighting. It has the mission, while protecting the Trubchevsk road at Ramassukha and having assembled its remaining forces, to hit the enemy in his flank toward Kambovka.

5. 155th RD reached Zaduben'e and Galinsk by 1300 hours on 27 August, and on 28 August, under the pressure of enemy tanks, it withdrew to the eastern bank of the Sudost' River and dug in on the Kazilovka and Belevaia front.

6. 4th CD conducted sustained combat in the Karbovka, Khamovshchina, and Pokrovskii region on 28 August and, by day's end, pressed the enemy back to the Semiachki and Uzha front, where it is now putting itself in order, while having the mission to attack toward Baklan'

7. 307th RD was fighting along the Khotkin, Borshchevo, and Kister front at 1300 hours on 28 August, while facing up to 50 tanks and motorized infantry. The division abandoned Pogar by day's end.

8. 6th RD withdrew to positions in the woods east of Kamen' on the eastern bank of the Desna River during the day. Having halted its withdrawal, the division has the mission to capture its previous positions. Gremiach has been occupied by around 100 enemy tanks.

9. 50th TD, because of 6th RD's withdrawal, began to withdraw from the Vorob'evka and Rogovka line to the eastern bank of the Desna River and has halted its withdrawal, with the mission to restore its positions.

10. 132nd RD is fighting with motorized infantry and tanks from the enemy's 3rd AC and 3rd PzD along the Birin and Prokopovka line.

11. 52nd CD, as a result of the fighting, went on the defense in the western outskirts of Antonovka and the woods to the southwest. It has been ordered to continue to attack, with the aim of reaching the Desna River south of Novgorod-Severskii.

12. 143rd RD – There is no news about 800th and 383rd RRs. 635th RR is being assembled in the Mikhailovskii Farm region with about 600 unarmed men.

13. 137th RD is protecting the approaches to Trubchevsk with one composite battalion.

Conclusions:

With its present forces, the army is not in a condition to destroy the penetrating enemy.

Given the difficult conditions that have been created, as I already reported in my combat report of 27 August, a withdrawal of the army to the eastern bank of the

Desna River for a firm defense and the preparation for a more solid offensive, would be most expedient, for which, I once again request your decision.

The existing situation is creating the threat of the army's destruction in piecemeal fashion.

> The Commander of 13th Army, Major General Golubev
> The Member of the Military Council, Brigade Commissar Furt
> The chief of staff of 13th Army, *Kombrig* Petrushevsky

Source: "Boevoi donesenie komanduiushchego voiskami 13-i Armii komanduiushchemu voiskami Brianskogo Fronta ot 29 avgusta 1941 g. o polozhenii voisk i neobkhodimosti otvoda ikh na vostochnyi bereg r. Desna" [Combat report of the commander of the forces of 13th Army to the commander of the forces of the Briansk Front of 29 August 1941 about the positions of the army's forces and the impossibility of withdrawing it to the eastern bank of the Desna River], *SBDVOV*, issue 43, 303-304.

34. Combat Order of the Commander of the Forces of 21st Army No. 014 of 29 August 1941 on Continuing the Offensive toward Semenovka

To the chief of staff of the Briansk Front
Combat Order No. 014, Headquarters, 21st Army,
Mena,
29 August 1941
1: 100,000 and 500,000 scale maps

1. The enemy is continuing attacks across the army's entire front. The enemy's Starodub grouping has been identified, with its forward units along the Semenovka, Korop, Kholmy, and Avdeevka line.

2. On the right, the Kostobobr and Kister line is being defended by 13th Army's left flank units.

On the left, 15th RC is on the Burovka and Danichi line.

3. The army's mission is to defend the northern axis firmly, while delivering its main attack against the Starodub grouping.

4. 67th RC (42nd and 277th RD) will continue its offensive in the general direction of Semenovka on the morning of 30 August, with the mission to reach the Radichev, Avdeevka, Radomka, and Pogorel'tsy line by day's end.

The boundary on the left: Tikhonovichi, Shishkovka, and (incl.) Bleshnia.

The corps' commander will organize cooperation between the divisions and prevent a gap between them at all cost, while protecting 42nd and 277th RDs' flanks.

5. 28th RC (187th, 219th, and 117th RDs) will firmly defend the Gutka Studenetskaia, Mostki, Elino, Bezuglovka, and Novye Borovichi line, while having a reserve of – one RR –in the Luka region. Create a maneuverable antitank reserve.

The boundary on the left: The Snov River and Churovichi.

6. 66th RC (55th, 266th, 75th, and 232nd RDs, 20th MotR, 65th FR, and 49th and 50th BEPOs) will occupy and firmly defend the Borovichi Station, Kamka, Petrovka, Dubrovnoe, and (incl.) Burovka line. Relieve the cavalry group in the Zaimishche and Novye Mliny sector.

The boundary on the left: Sednev, Tupichev, and Varonichi.

7. The Cavalry Group, upon relief by 66th RC's units, will concentrate in the grove northwest of Makoshino.

8. 24th RD and 214th AbnB – my reserve, will concentrate in the region of the southwestern outskirts of Mena in readiness to attack toward Semenovka behind 42nd RD.

9. The commanders of 28th and 66th RCs will bring their positions to a state of defense, construct trenches for every platoon, and organize AT defenses, while employing part regimental and divisional artillery in the infantry's forward positions. Organize coordination with the artillery.

10. Immediately refill all reserves. Bring ammunition up to the norms.

The Commander of 21st Army, Lieutenant General Kuznetsov
The Member of the Military Council, Division Commissar Kolonin
The Chief of Staff of 21st Army, Major General Gordov.

Source: "Boevoi prikaz komanduiushchego voiskami 21-i Armii No. 014 ot 29 avgusta 1941 g. na prodolzhenii nastupleniia v napravlenii Semenovka" [Combat order of the commander of the forces of 21st Army No. 014 of 29 August 1941 on continuing the offensive toward Semenovka], *SBDVOV*, issue 43, 340.

35. Combat Order No. 07 of the Commander of the Forces of the Briansk Front of 29 August 1941 on an Offensive toward Pogar, Starodub, and Novgorod-Severskii

Combat Order No. 07 to the Forces of the Briansk Front,
0700 hours on 29 August 1941

1. The enemy (3rd PzD with motorized units) penetrated 13th Army's left wing, forced the Desna River in the Novgorod-Severskii region, and spread out in the direction of Iampol' and Sosnitsa on 26 August 1941, while simultaneously developing an attack toward Semenovka and Shchors in an attempt to envelop 13th and 21st Armies' flanks.

2. 50th Army is holding onto its previous positions, while conducting intense fighting in the Pochep region.

3. The commander of 13th Army [Gorodniansky] will develop an energetic offensive following directly behind the mobile group in the general direction of Pogar and Starodub and, while protecting itself from the north and northwest, destroy the opposing enemy.

Reach the line of the Sudost' River by day's end on 30 August and reach the Gartsevo, Gridenki, and Dokhnovichi line by the morning of 1 September 1941.

4. The Mobile Group (108th TD, 141st TB, and 4th CD), under the overall command of Major General Comrade Ermakov, will attack toward Gruzdova, Sosnovka, Pogar, Tarasovka, Voronok, Zheleznyi Most', Mashevo, and Novgorod-Severskii, with the aim of destroying the enemy which have penetrated towards Novgorod-Severskii.

Reach the Dokhnovichi, Tarasovka, and Grinevo line by day's end on 30 August 1941.

Reach the Novgorod-Severskii region by day's end on 31 August 1941.

5. 108th TD, with a sapper platoon, will attack toward Mostochnaia, Romanovka, Pogar, Grinevo, Dokhnovichi, Novo-Mlynka, Voronok, Zheleznyi Most', Mashevo, Arapovichi, and Shostka.

Force the Sudost' River in the Posudichi and Pogar sector.

6. 141st TB, with a sapper platoon, will attack toward Il'ino, Glybochka, Peregon, Andreikovichi, Azarovka, Kostobobr, Novgorod-Severskii, and Iampol'.

Force the Sudost' River in the Suvorovo and Lukin sector.

7. 4th CD, while attacking in second echelon behind the tank group, will destroy the enemy in cooperation with the tanks.

8. Aviation (*frontal*) – during the course of 29, 30, and 31 August 1941:

a). From 0500 to 1100 hours on 29 August, protect 141st TB's march along the Gololobovo, Sidorovka, Komiagino, Sloboda, and Subbotovo march-route and its crossings over the Desna River in the Uty and Mantsurovka sector and the concentrations of the entire mobile group in the Pliuskovo, Mostochnaia, and Radinsk region.

b). On 30 August 1941, protect the mobile group's march into the Pogar region. Pay special attention – during the forcing of the Sudost' River in the Pogar region.

c). The mission of assault and bomber aviation [is]: to destroy the opposing enemy in cooperation with the mobile group, while forestalling the movement of its mobile groups with its strikes.

9. Command and control

a). Have radio centers, with cipher clerks of the army commander, in 108th TD, 141st TB, and 4th CD.

b). The commander of the *front's* VVS will allocate one U-2 aircraft each directly to each operational commander in 108th TD and 141st TB.

c). The *front's* Chief of Communications will create a radio center in the Trubchevsk region by 1200 hours on 29 August.

The Commander of the Briansk Front, Lieutenant General Eremenko
The Member of the *front's* Military Council,
    Division Commissar Mazepov
The Chief of Staff of the *front*, Major General Zakharov

Source: "Boevoi prikaz komanduiushchego voiskami Brianskogo fronta No. 07 ot 29 avgusta 1941 g. na nastuplenie v napravlenii Pogar, Starodub, and Novgorod-Severskii" [Combat order no. 07 of the commander of the forces of the Briansk Front of 29 August 1941 on an offensive toward Pogar, Starodub, and Novgorod-Severskii], *SBDVOV*, issue 43, 50-51.

36. *Stavka* VGK Directive No. 001428 to the Commander of the Forces of the Briansk Front about an Offensive Operation along the Roslavl'-Briansk Axis
0610 hours on 30 August 1941

1. The enemy, while defending on the Belyi, Viaz'ma, and Spas-Demensk axes, has concentrated his mobile forces against the Briansk Front's forces, with the aim

of developing a penetration from Novgorod-Severskii to Vorozhba [120 kilometers southeast of Novgorod-Severskii].

2. The Briansk Front's forces will go on the offensive and, while delivering a blow toward Roslavl' and Starodub, will destroy the enemy grouping in the Pochep, Novgorod-Severskii, and Novozybkov region. Subsequently, develop the offensive in the general direction of Krichev and Propoisk and reach the Petrovichi, Klimovichi, Belaia Dubrava, Guta-Koretskaia, Novozybkov, and Shchors front by 15 September; to which end:

a) 50th Army [Petrov], having left 217th, 279th, 258th, and 290th RDs to defend their positions, will go on the offensive on 3 September and, together with the Reserve Front's 43rd Army, destroy the enemy grouping in the Zhukovka and Dubrovka region with an attack by four RDs with tanks from the Viazovsk and Vereshovskii front [from 15 kilometers north to 12 kilometers south of Zhukovka] toward Peklina, Novyi Krupets, and Roslavl', and, subsequently, capture the Roslavl' region and reach the Petrovichi and Klimovichi front by 13 September.

b) 3rd Army [Kreizer] will conduct a blow from the Lipki, Vitovka, and Semtsy front toward Starodub and Novozybkov with an attack by no fewer than two RDs, reinforced by tanks, and, together with 13th Army, will smash the enemy's mobile grouping in the Starodub, Novgorod-Severskii, and Trubchevsk region. The army will reach the (incl.) Klimovichi and Belaia Dubrovka front by 15 September.

c) 13th Army [Gorodniansky], consisting of five divisions with tanks, will continue its offensive, and, while delivering its attack in the general direction of Zheleznyi Most and Semenovka, will, together with 3rd Army, destroy the enemy's Novgorod-Severskii grouping. Reach the (incl.) Belaia Dubrovka and Guta-Koretskaia front by 15 September.

d) 21st Army [V. I. Kuznetsov], while firmly defending on its left wing, will continue its offensive, while delivering a main attack from the Koriukovka, Pereliub, and Novye Borovichi front toward Semenovka and Starodub and, together with 13th Army, destroy the enemy in the Semenovka, Starodub, and Novgorod-Severskii region;

e) Have 298th RD in the *front's* reserve in the Diat'kovo region to protect the boundary with the Reserve Front.

3. On the right – the Reserve Front will go on the offensive on 30 August 1941, with the missions to destroy the enemy's grouping in the Pochinok and Roslavl' region, capture Roslavl', and reach the Dolgie Nivy, (incl.) Khislovichi, and Petrovichi front. The boundary line with it – Mtsensk, Zhizdra, Frolovka, and Roslavl'; all points are inclusive for the Briansk Front.

On the left – the Southwestern Front will conduct an active defense along the Makishin, Repki, and Lopatin line and further along the Dnepr River. The boundary line with it – Krolevets, Gorodnia, and Rechitsa; all points are inclusive for the Briansk Front.

4. During the course of the entire operation, eliminate any sort of surprises for the forces by well-organized and systematic intelligence collection at all command levels. Pay special attention to continuous and skillful reconnaissance along open flanks.

5. It is obligatory to fortify all lines and points seized from the enemy, while demanding that the forces immediately erect defensive works.

6. It is obligatory that you anticipate operations by infantry and tanks and accompany them with massive and concentrated actions of aviation.

7. Before the beginning of the operation, subject the enemy's mobile groupings to constant air operations.

8. Conduct preparations for the operation with utmost secrecy and abstain from telephone conversations and transmissions.

9. Confirm receipt.

I. Stalin
B. Shaposhnikov

Source: See *SBDVOV,* Issue 41, 12-13 and "Direktiva Stavki VGK No. 001428 komanduiushchemu voiskami Brianskogo fronta o nastupatel'noi operatsii na Roslavl'sko-Starodubskom napravlenii" [*Stavka* VGK Directive no. 001428 to the commander of the forces of the Briansk Front about an offensive operation along the Roslavl'-Briansk axis], in Zolotarev, "*Stavka* 1941," 148-149.

37. Operational Summary No. 022 of the Headquarters of the Briansk Front at 1800 hours on 29 August 1941 about the Combat Operations of the *Front's* Forces

Operational Summary No. 022 by 1800 hours,
Headquarters, Briansk Front,
1800 hours on 29 August 1941
1: 100,000 and 50,000 scale maps

First. The Briansk Front's units are continuing to conduct sustained defensive fighting on the right and left wings and offensive fighting in the Pochep region to restore the situation and seize Pochep.

The enemy is displaying active offensive operations on his left and right wings from the directions of Roslavl', Briansk, and Novgorod-Severskii, while defending stubbornly and conducting counterattacks in the Pochep region. According to information from aviation, concentrations of enemy have been occurring in the Vorob'evka, Buda, Dmitrovo, and Krasnaia Sloboda region and from the direction of Kletnia toward Vorob'evka since the morning of 29 August 1941.

Second. 50th Army's 217th RD is firmly holding on to its occupied position, while repelling and destroying attacking enemy units in the Snopot and Piatnitskoe region with artillery, mortar, and machine gun fire. The division's positions are unchanged.

Third. 279th, 258th, and 260th RD did not conduct active combat operations. They continue to occupy their previous positions, while fortifying them in an engineer respect. The enemy is displaying no activity on the division's front.

Fourth. 280th RD, with 878th RR, and 1020th RR, is fighting continuously to destroy the enemy's Pochep grouping and seize Pochep.

The division went on the attack on the morning of 29 August, drove the enemy out of the P'ianyi Gog region, and captured Putilovskii, Zelenaia Roshcha,

Ol'khovka, and Vitovka at 1200 hours. 1020th RR fought to capture the railroad station at Pochep. At 1350 hours two battalions of enemy infantry, supported by 50 tanks and a large number of aircraft, conducted a counterattack on Vitovka, and, at that time, the enemy tanks penetrated into P'ianyi Rog. The infantry were cut off from the tanks. Under pressure from aircraft bombing and the tanks, 280th RD's left wing in Vitovka suffered heavy losses. Communications with it was lost at 1530 hours. All measures are being taken to clarify the situation and verify the positions of the units in Pochep.

Fifth. 278th and 290th RDs are not participating directly in the fighting, and their positions are unchanged.

Sixth. 13th Army's units conducted sustained fighting with the enemy across the entire front on 29 August.

Seventh. 269th RD is fighting with numerically superior forces from the enemy 53rd and 41st MotRs with tanks in the Semtsy region. The division's commander, [Colonel Nikolai Fedorovich] Garnich, has been severely wounded in the fighting.

Eighth. 45th CD's units conducted sustained fighting with the enemy during the day on 29 August and withdrew from the Kozievka and Bileevo line, but the enemy anticipated this and occupied Sagut'evo and Vitemlia with reconnaissance units.

155th and 307th RDs were in the Liubets, Krasnyi Ugol, and Evdokol' region during the second half of the day on 29 August.

Ninth. 6th RD is defending on the Murav'i and Kamen' front along the eastern bank of the Desna River.

Tenth. 50th Tank Division occupies positions from (incl.) Murav'i to Ochkino.

Eleventh. 132nd RD is along the Ochkino and Birin line.

Twelfth. 143rd RD occupies Vovki.

Thirteenth. 52nd CD is located in the Antonovka and Poleevka region.

Fourteenth. The positions of the remaining units are unchanged.

Fifteenth. 298th RD is moving to Liudinovo Station and will concentrate in the Diat'kovo region. All units will be concentrated by 30 August.

Sixteenth. 108th TD is marching to the Dol'sk, Polovetskie, and Vershan' region.

Seventeenth. 141st TB is marching to the Komiagino, Radinsk, and Subbotovo region.

4th CD is concentrating in the Mostochnaia, Semiachova, and Voiborovo region.

Eighteenth. 299th RD is in its previous positions in the *front's* reserve.

Nineteenth. Information has not been received about the positions of 21st Army's units as of the time this summary was prepared.

> The Chief of Staff of the Briansk Front, Major General Zakharov
> The Commissar of the *front's* headquarters,
>   Battalion Commissar Kuznetsov
> The Chief of the Operations Department, Colonel Argunov

Source: "Operativnaia svodka shtaba Brianskogo Fronta No. 022/op k 18 chasam 29 avgusta 1941 g. o boevykh deistviiakh voisk fronta" [Operational summary no. 022 at 1800 hours on 29 August 1941 about the combat operations of the *front's* forces], *SBDVOV*, issue 43, 51-53.

38. Combat Order No. 01 of the Commander of the Briansk Front's VVS of 30 August 1941 on the Conduct of Strikes against Enemy Motor-Mechanized Groupings

Combat Order No. 1, Headquarters, VVS of the Briansk Front
0400 hours on 30 August 1941
1:500,000 scale map

1. The enemy occupied the Pochep, Dmitrovo and Stechnia, Vasil'evka, Aleshenka, and Uzha region (all points 15-20 kilometers west of Trubchevsk) with his motor-mechanized units by day's end on 29 August 1941. Heavy movement of auto-transport has been identified along sectors of the Roslavl', Zhukovka, Peklino and Vysokoselishche, Divovka, Deremna, as well as the Starodub, Pogar and Starodub, Sheptaki dirt roads.

2. The VVS of the Briansk Front will destroy the discovered enemy motor-mechanized groupings on the morning of 30 August 1941 by consecutive strikes.

3. The VVS of 13th Army

a) 11th MAD [Mixed Aviation Division], protected in the target area by 12 fighters from 162nd FAR, will assault and bomb enemy motor-mechanized columns in the Stechnia, Vasil'evka, Aleshenka, and Uzha region from 0705 to 0710 hours. The fighters will provide escort to the targets and protection to landing.

During the daylight, beginning from 0600 on 30 August 1941 and every three hours thereafter, disrupt movement of enemy columns along the Starodub, Grinev, Pogar and Starodub, Ponurovka, Kostobobr, Sheptaki roads with attacks by individual Il-2 aircraft.

Reconnoiter the results of the attacks by our aviation in the [following] regions by single fighters: at Stechnia, Vasil'evka, Aleshenka, and Uzha at 0730 hours and to a radius of 10 kilometers in the Novgorod-Severskii region at 0800 hours.

b) 61st MAD, with an attack wing of Il-2 from 237th AAR attached to cooperate, will destroy enemy motor-mechanized forces in the Pochep and Dmitrovo region by assault strikes and bombing. Protect the flights with the fighters. The landing region of 162nd FAR is Olekhino and Mertvaia. Determine the results of the bombing at 0830 hours with individual fighters.

c) 60th MAD – 12 MiG-3s will strike antiaircraft in the Stechnia, Vasil'evka, and Uzha region and protect the assault and bombing operations of 11th MAD in the same region at 0700 hours. Determine the results of the strikes by our aircraft in the Seshcha, Volkovshchina, Vyshkovichi, and Vladimirovka region with individual fighters at 0700 hours. During daylight on 30 August 1941, beginning at 0600 hours and every three hours thereafter, disrupt movement of enemy columns along the Roslavl', Dubrovka, Lugovets, Mglin, and Divovka roads with attacks by individual Il-2 aircraft of 237th AAR. Immediately report the results of the assault strikes and bombing operation as determined by the crews to the headquarters of the VVS by indicating the name of the executor [the pilot].

d) Readiness for the recurring flights of all formations and units at 1130 hours on 30 August 1941.

The Commander of the VVS of the Briansk Front,
    Major General of Aviation, Polynin
The Military Commissar of the VVS of the Briansk Front,
    Regimental Commissar Romazanov

Source: "Boevoi prikaz komanduiushchego Voenno-Vozdushnymi Silami Brianskogo Fronta No. 01 ot 30 avgusta 1941 g. na nanesenii udarov po motomekhanizirovannym gruppirovkam protivnika" [Combat order no. 01 of the commander of the Briansk Front's VVS of 30 August 1941 on the conduct of strikes against enemy motor-mechanized groupings], *SBDVOV*, issue 43, 53-54.

39. Operational Summary No. 023 of the Headquarters of the Briansk Front at 0800 hours on 30 August 1941 about the Combat Operations of the *Front's* Forces

Operational Summary No. 023 by 0700 hours,
Headquarters, Briansk Front,
0800 hours on 30 August 1941
1: 100,000 and 50,000 scale maps

First. The Briansk Front's units are continuing to conduct defensive fighting on the right wing and especially intense fighting in the center – along the Pochep and Novgorod-Severskii axes.

Second. 50th Army. No changes occurred in the positions along the front. The army's units are occupying their previous positions.

Third. On the right wing of 217th RD's front, enemy attempts to near the forward edge were repulsed by artillery and machine gun fire.

Fourth. On 279th, 258th, and 260th RDs' fronts, there were no changes. The enemy displays no activity, and their units occupy their previous positions.

Fifth. On 280th RD's front, heavy fighting is continuing along the Pochep axis. At 1330 hours on 29 August, up to two enemy battalions with 50 tanks launched a counterattack toward Vitovka.

The tanks penetrated to P'ianyi Rog. The fighting is continuing.

Sixth. 13th Army continued to conduct sustained fighting with the attacking enemy. Especially intense fighting occurred in the Semtsy and Valovets sector on its right wing during the day on 28 August.

Seventh. 269th RD is defending Usoshki, P'ianyi Rog, and Kotovka. It was attacked by up to two enemy motorized regiments with 40 tanks and was subjected to raids by 34 bombers. The enemy tank attack was repelled, and the units are occupying their previous positions.

Eighth. 282nd RD fought in several places in the Kalachevka, Baklan', and Ramassukha regions during the day on 28 August. As a result of the fighting with superior enemy forces, supported by a large number of tanks and aircraft, the division did not constitute a controlled organism by the end of the day.

Ninth. 155th RD reached Zaduben'e and Galinsk on 27 August, but, under pressure from enemy tanks, it was forced to withdraw to the eastern bank of the Sudost' River and dig in along the Kazilovka and Velevaia front by day's end.

Tenth. 4th CD, after fighting in the Karmovka, Khamovshchina, and Pokrovskii region, withdrew to the Semiachki and Uzha region by day's end on 28 August.

Eleventh. 307th RD fought along the Borshchovo and Kister front from 1300 hours on 28 August, while having a force of up to 50 tanks and motorized infantry on its front. It abandoned Pogar by the end of the day on 28 August.

Twelfth. 6th RD withdrew into the woods east of Kamen' on the eastern bank of the Desna River on 28 August.

Thirteenth. 50th TD withdrew to the Krivonosovka and Borovichi region on the eastern bank of the Desna River on 28 August.

Fourteenth. 132nd RD is fighting with enemy motorized infantry and tanks (3rd Motorized Corps and 3rd PzD) on the Birin and Prokopovka line.

Fifteenth. 52nd CD is defending on the western outskirts of Antonovka and the woods to the southwest.

Sixteenth. 137th RD is protecting the approaches to Trubchevsk with a composite battalion.

No information has been received about 143rd RD.

Seventeenth. 21st Army. The army's units are in fierce fighting along the [following] lines:

227th RD – Matveevka and Mokryi woods.

219th RD was holding onto the Gorodok and Glinishche line. It was pushed back to the Sin'kovka line by the enemy by day's end on 28 August.

55th TD is fighting along the Zhabchichi and Gorodets line.

24th RD was fighting for Brekhunovka and Suslovka. It had the mission to concentrate in the Shchors region by day's end on 28 August.

75th and 232nd RDs were concentrating and fighting in Politichi and Chudovka.

62nd RD, while subordinated to the orders of 21st Army's commander, it was being moved to the Gorodnia and Nevklia line

Eighteenth. 299th and 298th RDs and 125th TB are in the *front's* reserve in their previous regions.

Nineteenth. 108th TD concentrated in the Vershan', Dol'sk, and Orekhovskoe region on 29 August.

Twentieth. 141st TB concentrated in the Komiagino, Radchinsk, and Subbotovo region.

Twenty-first. The VVS of the *front* carried out attacks on enemy columns and concentrations during the day on 29 August. They conducted 113 aircraft sorties. 15 enemy aircraft were destroyed at airfields and up to 40 tanks.

The Chief of Staff of the Briansk Front, Major General Zakharov
The Commissar of the *front* headquarters,
    Battalion Commissar Kuznetsov
The Chief of the Operations Department, Colonel Argunov

Source: "Operativnaia svodka shtaba Brianskogo Fronta No. 023 k 8 chasam 30 avgusta 1941 g. o boevykh deistviiakh voisk fronta" [Operational summary no. 023 at 0800 hours on 30 August 1941 about the combat operations of the *front's* forces], *SBDVOV*, issue 43, 55-56.

40. Combat Order of the Headquarters of the Briansk Front of 30 August 1941 on Destroying the Enemy East of Pochep

To the Commander of 50th Army
1320 hours on 30 August 1941

Eremenko has ordered:
1. Liquidate the enemy to the east of Pochep by the morning of 31 August 1941.
2. Report on the course of the battle every 3 hours.
3. Draw in the neighbor on the left.
4. Eremenko is paying special attention to the fulfillment of this mission.
5. Submit an encoded plan of operations no later than 1700 hours

The Chief of Staff of the Briansk Front, Major General Zakharov
The Commissar of the *front's* headquarters,
Battalion Commissar Kuznetsov

Source: "Boevoi rasporiazhenie shtaba Brianskogo fronta ot 30 avgusta 1941 g. komanduiushchemu voiskami 50-i Armii na unichtozhenie protivnika vostochnee Pochep" [Combat order of the headquarters of the Briansk Front of 30 August 1941 on destroying the enemy to the east of Pochep], *SBDVOV*, issue 43, 56.

41. Individual Combat Order No. 06 of the Commander of the Forces of 50th Army of 30 August 1941 on Capturing the Eastern Bank of the Sudost' River with 280th and 269th Rifle Divisions

Individual Combat Order No. 6, Headquarters, 50th Army,
Deminteevka,
1700 hours on 30 August 1941
1:100,000 scale map

First. The enemy is not displaying special activity on the army's front. Only on the left flank in the Pochep region, infantry with tanks are in possession of the eastern bank of the Sudost' River, while holding on to Kalinovka, Vitovka, and the woods 2 kilometers east of Kozorezovka.

Second. On the right, 43rd Army went on the offensive on the morning of 30 August. On the left, the *front's* mobile group also inflicted a crippling attack on the enemy which has penetrated into the Novgorod-Severskii region.

Third. 280th RD, while exploiting the powerful fire of a guards-mortar battalion and artillery, will encircle the enemy in the Roshcha, Veselyi Farm, and Vitovka region at first light on 31 August and, having occupied the (incl.) Dmitrovo and Pochep line, will capture the eastern bank of the Sudost' River during the first half of the day, in cooperation with 269th RD.

The boundary on the left: Usoshki and Pochep.

Fourth. 269th RD, having protected itself in the Semtsy region, will attack the enemy with two regiments from the Zelenyi Rog and Vysokii Stan line and, in cooperation with 280th RD, will reach the eastern bank of the Sudost' River in the Fabrika, the western edge of the grove 1 kilometer east of Peschanka, and Marker 144.9 (3 kilometers north of Semtsy) line.

Fifth. The commander of 280th RD will establish reliable communications with 269th RD no later than 2400 hours on 30 August.

By this time, the army's Chief of Staff will have wire communications with the headquarters of 280th RD.

The commander of 280th RD will report every 2 hours about the course of fulfilling this order.

The Commander of 50th Army, Major General Petrov
The Member of the Military Council, Brigade Commissar Miftakhov
The Chief of Staff of 50th Army, Colonel Pern

Source: "Chastnyi boevoi prikaz komanduiushchego voiskami 50-i Armii No. 06 ot 30 avgusta 1941 g. na ovladenie 280-i i 269-i Strelkovymi Diviziiami vostochnym beregom r. Sudost'" [Individual combat order no. 06 of the commander of the forces of 50th Army of 30 August 1941 on capturing the eastern bank of the Sudost' River with 280th and 269th Rifle Divisions], *SBDVOV*, issue 43, 361.

42. Report No. 349 by the Commander of the Forces of the Briansk Front to the Supreme High Commander on an Operational Plan for Destroying the Enemy in the Pochep, Trubchevsk, Novo-Severskii, and Novozybkov Region

2400 hours on 30 August 1941

1. Period of the operation – from 30 August through 15 September 1941.

2. Mission – to destroy the opposing enemy (17th, 18th, and 3rd PzDs and 29th MotD) and reach the Petrovichi, Klimovichi, Belaia Dubrava, Guts-Koretskaia, Novozybkov, and Shchors front by 15 September.

3. Conduct the attack along two axes:

a) Along the Roslavl' axis, with the mission of destroying the enemy in the Zhukovka and Dubrovka region; and

b) Southwestward toward Starodub, with the mission of destroying the enemy in the Pochep, Starodub, and Novgorod-Severskii region.

4. Composition of the forces:

a) On 50th Army's [Petrov] front:

For delivering the blow from the Viazovsk and Vereshovskii front [from 12 kilometers north to 15 kilometers south of Zhukovka] toward Roslavl', allocate 299th, 278th, 290th, and 279th RDs, 121st TB, and one TBn [113th] and from Diat'kovo – two RGK [High Command Reserve] regiments and one guards-mortar regiment

b) On 3rd Army's [Kreizer] front:

For delivering the blow from the Pochep and Semtsy front toward Starodub, allocate 269th and 282nd RDs, 108th TD, 4th CD, one battalion of guards-mortars, and one RGK regiment.

c) On 13th Army's [Gorodniansky] front:

For delivering the blow from the Pogar, Gremiach, and Pushkari front toward Semenovskii, allocate 155th, 307th, and 6th RDs, 141st TB, 50th TD (without tanks), and two RGK regiments

d) On 21st Army's [V. I. Kuznetsov] front:

While firmly defending the Karpovichi and Gorodnia front along the line of the Snov River, deliver a blow from the Sidorkin and Pereliub front toward Semenovka with three divisions.

5. Stages of the operation:

I. First stage – from 30 August through 2 September:

a) Regrouping of forces; and

b) Preparation of material, replenishment of fuel and ammunition, and so forth.

The armies on the main attack axes will be provided with no fewer than 5 combat loads;

c) Preparation of artillery, bore-sighting of tanks, and the working out of cooperation; and

d) The compilation of operational plans in the armies.

Aviation: during the period from 30-31 August 1941 and 1-2 September 1941, will destroy and demoralize the enemy both during the day and at night by systematic successive strikes against force groupings and columns.

The main air strikes will be along the following axes:

a) Dubrovka and Roslavl';

b) Pochep and Mglin; and

c) Starodub and Novgorod-Severskii.

II. Second Stage.

Contents of the stage – penetration and destruction of the opposing enemy and an advance to a depth of 12-15 kilometers.

Period – from 3 September through 6 September.

Artillery missions – conduct a two-hour artillery preparation employing artillery remaining in the first line of RDs.

Aviation.

Missions – work over the attack region.

Method – aviation raids prior to the artillery preparation and, subsequently, suppression of enemy firing systems and personnel by successive, uninterrupted strikes immediately in front of the combat formations of the advancing infantry and tanks. To do so, operating aviation must communicate closely with the command posts of the attacking units.

Protect the army's main grouping from the air.

III. Third stage.

Period – from 6 September through 15 September.

Contents of the stage – pursuit of the enemy and reaching the Petrovichi, Klimovichi, Belaia Dubrova, Guta Koretskaia, Novozybkov, and Shchors line, with conducting necessary regroupings:

a) To move up reserves, and

b) To shift forces.

Missions of the VVS – destroy withdrawing enemy units, destroy bridges, and protect [cover] our own units.

Do not permit the movement of fresh enemy reserves.

Conduct deep reconnaissance and reconnaissance along the flanks.

Eremenko, Mazepov, Zakharov

Source: "Doklad komanduiushchego voiskami Brianskogo Fronta No. 349 Verkhovnomu Glavnokomanduiushchemu plana operatsii po razgromu protivnika v raione Pochep, Trubchevsk, Novgorod-Severskii, Novozybkov" [Report No. 349 of the commander of the forces of the Briansk Front to the Supreme High Commander on an operational plan for destroying the enemy in the Pochep, Trubchevsk, Novo-Severskii, and Novozybkov region], in Zolotarev, "*Stavka* VGK 1941," 369, is erroneously dated 0610 hours on 2 September, when it was actually issued at 2400 hours on 30 August. It also misidentifies 13th Army's 141st Tank Brigade as 147th Tank Division. However, a copy of the same order included in *SBDVOV*, issue 43, 57-58, entitled "Plan komanduiushchego voiskami Brianskogo fronta na provedenie nastupatel'noi operatsii s 30 avgusta po 15 sentiabria 1941 g. po unichtozheniiu protivnika na Roslavl'skom i Starodubskom napravleniakh" [Plan of the commander of the forces of the Briansk Front on the conduct of an offensive operation from 30 August through 15 September 1941 for destroying the enemy on the Roslavl' and Starodub axes], properly dated as 2400 hours on 30 August 1941 improperly includes 108th Tank Division and 4th Cavalry Division in 13th Army. The conflicting versions of these orders indicate that there was confusion over whether the mobile group was to be subordinate to 3rd or 13th Armies.

43. Combat Report No. 034 of the Headquarters of 21st Army of 31 August 1941 about the Results of the Offensive toward Semenovka

Combat Report No. 034, Headquarters, 21st Army

Mena,

The afternoon of 31 August 1941

1:100,000 and 500,000 scale maps

1. The enemy continued his offensive along the entire front during the day on 30 August 1941 and directed his main attack toward Bezuglovka and Sloboda Borovitskaia and the boundary between 66th and 15th RC at Makushin and Sednev.

2. The army's units, while holding on to the Gutka Studenetskaia, Elino, Shchors, Novye Mlyny, Ias'kovo, Begach, and Borki line, continued to attack toward Semenovka with the right wing (67th RC) and, by day's end [on 30 August], reached:

42nd RD – Osmaki and Rudnia; and

277th RD – Zhadov and attacking Semenovka.

The Cavalry Group is approaching its concentration area in the woods near Domashlin, with the mission to attack toward Orlovka and Demidovo Station.

28th RC is firmly holding on to the positions it occupies along the southern bank and east of the Snov River with two RDs, while repelling attacks by up to 2 enemy IRs in the Bezuglovka and Sloboda region.

66th RC. 155th RD defended the (incl.) Borovichi Station, Shchors, and Novye Mlyny sector

232nd and 75th RD reached the (incl.) Novye Mlyny, Ias'kovo, Begach, and Borki line.

The corps has the mission to capture the Novye Borovichi, Gorodnia, and Tupichev line by the morning of 31 August, in cooperation with 15th RC.

24th RD – the army commander's reserve, which concentrated in Velichkovka at 1200 hours, will enter the Rudnia region (40 kilometers northeast of Mena) in accordance with orders.

214th AbnB concentrated in Mena.

3. The army's commander has decided: to hold the positions in 28th RC's center firmly, to capture Semenovka and link up with 13th Army's units with the right wing (67th RC), and, in cooperation with 15th RC, to reach the Novye Borovichi, Gorodnia, and Tupichev line with the left wing (66th RC).

4. I request you point out to me where 13th Army's units are located and direct their efforts toward Semenovka.

> The Chief of Staff of 21st Army, Major General Gordov
> The Commissar of the army's headquarters,
>   Regimental Commissar Mandrik
> The Chief of the Operations Department, Lieutenant Colonel Posiakin

Source: "Boevoe donesenie shtaba 21-i Armii No. 034 ot 31 avgusta 1941 g. o rezul'tatakh nastupleniia v napravlenii Semenovka" [Combat report of the headquarters of 21st Army No. 034 of 31 August 1941 about the results of the offensive toward Semenovka], *SBDVOV*, issue 43, 341.

44. Combat Report No. 035 of the Headquarters of 21st Army of 31 August 1941 about the Results of the Offensive toward Semenovka

Combat Report No. 035, Headquarters, 21st Army
Mena,
Late on 31 August 1941
1:100,000 and 500,000 scale maps

1. The enemy continued an offensive along the army's entire front and, while directing his main efforts toward the boundary between 66th RC and 5th Army's 15th RC, is operating actively toward Elino, Bezuglovka and Novye Borovichi.

Attempts to break through the army's units in the Novye Borovichi region have been repelled.

2. The army's forces, while continuing to hold firmly to the Gutka Studenetskaia, (incl.) Elino, (incl.) Sloboda Borovitskaia, Shchors, Leninovka, and Begach defense line and while attacking toward Semenovka with its right wing, reached the [following] positions [late on 31 August]:

67th RC. 42nd RD occupied Obolon'e and Osmaki and is fighting intense battles in the woods west of Rudnia.

277th RD captured Ivanovka, Semenovka, Krasnaia Zaria, and Bleshnia.

24th RD reached the Rudnia region, while having the mission of moving into Kholmy to close the gap with one RR.

28th RC fought to liquidate the enemy, which have penetrated into Bezuglovka and Novyi Borovichi, during the day. The remaining units are unchanged.

66th RC. 55th RD, having crossed over the Snov River, fought for and captured Gvozdikovka Griazna, and the fighting is continuing.

232nd RD, having relieved the Cavalry Group's units, occupied Novyi Mlyny, (incl.) Ias'kovo, and the southern outskirts of Leninovka, while holding off a strong onslaught by two enemy IRs toward Leninovka.

75th RD repelled an enemy attack from the direction of Malyi Sednev during the day.

The Cavalry Group, leaving the combat sector, is putting itself in order in the Loseva Sloboda region.

3. I have decided: In connection with the passive neighbors on the left, 5th Army's 15th RC, to continue the offensive with the right wing, while fulfilling the mission of the joint destruction of the enemy in the Semenovka, Starodub, and Novgorod-Severskii with 13th Army's units, and to hold on to the defense line firmly.

4. I request a more energetic advance by 13th Army's units toward Novgorod-Severskii and Semenovka for the combined destruction of the enemy penetrating southward from Starodub.

Require 15th RC to cease withdrawing its right wing and go on the offensive with it, with the mission to reach the Tupichev and Ripki line; and require the commander of 5th [Army] to protect the boundary between 5th and 21st Armies, arising from the fact that 21st Army is fulfilling its mission – destroying the enemy's Semenovka grouping and withdrawing within its boundaries for a link-up with 13th Army.

Strike the enemy's Starodub, and Novgorod-Severskii group with *frontal* aviation.

> The Commander of 21st Army, Lieutenant General Kuznetsov
> The Member of the Military Council, Division Commissar Kolonin
> The Chief of Staff of 21st Army, Major General Gordov

Source: "Boevoe donesenie shtaba 21-i Armii No. 035 ot 31 avgusta 1941 g. o rezul'tatakh nastupleniia v napravlenii Semenovka" [Combat report of the headquarters of 21st Army No. 035 of 31 August 1941 about the results of the offensive toward Semenovka], *SBDVOV*, issue 43, 342.

45. *Stavka* VGK Directive No. 001482 to the Commander of the Forces of the Briansk Front about Accelerating Preparations for 50th Army's Offensive

1700 hours on 31 August 1941

1. The offensive by the Reserve Front's 43rd Army along the Roslavl' axis is developing successfully. However, the enemy is bringing forces up for an attack from the south.

Consequently, it is necessary to speed up preparations for 50th Army's offensive and to begin it on 1 September or, in case of special emergency, on 2 September, in order to assist 43rd Army's offensive and prevent the enemy from concentrating forces against it.

50th Army must continue uninterrupted and energetic reconnaissance along its front with reinforced battalions.

2. There is an entirely intolerable interruption of communications with you and no transmission of reports by radio. The Supreme High Commander warns that the

front's chief of communications and chief of staff will be prosecuted for not submitting reports in timely fashion. It is necessary to always have reserve communications centers and to carry out reliable communications by radio.

3. Confirm receipt and report fulfillment.

For the *Stavka* of the Supreme High Command,
Chief of the General Staff, B. Shaposhnikov.

Source: "Direktiva Stavki VGK No. 001482 komanduiushchemu voiskami Brianskogo fronta ob uskorenii podgotovki nastupleniia 50-i Armii" [*Stavka* VGK Directive no. 001482 to the commander of the forces of the Briansk Front about accelerating preparations for 50th Army's offensive], in Zolotarev, "*Stavka* 1941," 151.

46. Directive No. 0068 of the Commander of the Forces of the Briansk Front of 31 August 1941 to the Commander of the Forces of 50th Army on an Offensive along the Roslavl' Axis

Top secret

Directive No. 0068 to the Forces of the Briansk Front,
1900 hours on 31 August 1941
1:100,000 and 500,000 scale maps
Only: To the Commander of 50th Army

1. Enemy mobile forces, consisting of 24th PzC (3rd and 4th PzDs and 10th MotD) penetrated at the boundary between 13th and 21st Armies and are operating in the general direction of Novgorod-Severskii and Vorozhba and, simultaneously, 47th PzC (17th and 18th PzDs and 29th MotD) are moving from the Roslavl' region toward the Pochep region and to the south.

2. On the right, 43rd Army has been attacking since 30 August, with the objective of destroying the enemy in the Roslavl' region.

The boundary line with it – Mtsensk, Zhizdra, Frolovka, and Roslavl'. All points inclusively for 50th Army.

3. On the left, 3rd Army will go on the offensive on the morning of 2 September in the general direction of Pochep and Starodub.

The boundary line with 3rd Army – (incl.) Kromy, Butria, Lopush', Dmitrovo, Razrytoe, and Klimovichi.

4. 50th Army, with a shock group consisting of 279th, 278th, 299th, and 290th RDs, 121st TB, one separate tank battalion, two artillery regiments RGK, and one guards-mortar regiment, will go on the offensive from the Viazovsk and Vereshovskii front on the morning of 2 September 1941 and destroy the grouping of enemy in the Rekovichi, Seshcha, Gorodets, and Leliatino region by a blow toward Peklina, Novyi Krupets, and Roslavl' in cooperation with 43rd Army.

Subsequently, capture the Roslavl' region and reach the Petrovichi and Klimovichi front by 13 September 1941.

5. Leave 217th, 258th, and 260th RD in the positions they are defending. Place 137th RD along the third defensive line instead of 290th RD.

6. Position 298th RD in the *front's* reserve in the Diat'kovo region for protecting the boundary with 43rd Army.

7. During the preparatory period for the offensive, it is necessary to take the following measures from 30 August through 1 September:

a) Complete the regrouping of forces by day's end on 1 September 1941.

b) Prepare equipment and material, top off fuel and ammunition, etc. Provide no fewer than five combat loads on the army's main attack axis.

c) Prepare artillery, bore-sight tanks, and work out questions of cooperation.

d) Compile a plan of army measures.

8. The missions of aviation.

During the period from 30 August through 2 September, destroy and demoralize the enemy in both day and night by systematic and consecutive strikes against groupings and columns. The main axis for airstrikes is Dubrovka and Roslavl'.

9. Second stage of the operation – from 2 through 6 September 1941.

Penetration and destruction of the opposing enemy and reaching 12-15 kilometers into the depth.

The mission of artillery – conduct a two-hour artillery preparation employing all of the artillery remaining in the first defensive line of RDs.

The mission of aviation – work over the attack regions.

Method – a raid by aviation before the beginning of the artillery preparation and, subsequently, inflict defeat on enemy firing weapons and personnel immediately in front of the combat formations of the attacking infantry and tanks by successive and continuous strikes, to which end aviation must operate closely coordinated with the command posts of the attacking units.

Protect the army's main grouping from the air.

10. Third stage – from 6 through 13 September 1941.

Pursuit of the enemy with arrival at the Petrovichi and Klimovichi line and the conduct of necessary regroupings.

a) Bringing reserves forward; and

b) Rebasing.

The missions of aviation – destruction of withdrawing enemy units, destruction of bridges, and protection of our own forces from the air.

Prevent fresh enemy reserves from moving forward.

Deep reconnaissance and reconnaissance on the flanks, especially along the Buda and Beloglavaia Station line.

11. Conduct well-organized and systematic reconnaissance at all force levels during the operation to exclude any sort of surprise. Pay special attention to constant and careful reconnaissance of open flanks.

12. It is obligatory to fortify all lines and points seized from the enemy during the process of the operation, while demanding the troops immediately construct defensive works.

13. Conduct preparations for the operation in a strict regime of secrecy, while abstaining from telephone conversations and correspondence.

Do not give overall orders on the operation to all subordinate formations, limit assigned missions to each division, and, in the divisions, to each regiment by separate partial orders.

14. Confirm receipt.

15. Submit army operational plans and specific division orders to the *front's* headquarters by 2000 hours on 1 September 1941.

The Commander of the Forces of the Briansk Front,
    Lieutenant General Eremenko
The Member of the Military Council of the *front,*
    Division Commissar Mazepov
The Chief of Staff of the *front*, Zakharov

Source: "Direktiva komanduiushchego voiskami Brianskogo fronta No. 0068 ot 31 avgusta 1941 g. komanduiushchemu voiskami 50-i Armii na nastuplenie v Roslavl'skom napravlenii" [Directive no. 0068 of the commander of the forces of the Briansk Front of 31 August 1941 to the commander of the forces of 50th Army on an offensive along the Roslavl' axis], *SBDVOV*, issue 43, 60-62.

47. Operational Summary No. 025/op of the Headquarters of the Briansk Front at 1800 hours on 31 August 1941 about the Combat Operations of the *Front's* Forces

Operational Summary No. 025/op by 1800 hours,
Headquarters, Briansk Front,
1900 hours on 31 August 1941
1: 100,000 and 50,000 scale maps

First. The Briansk Front's units are continuing to conduct defensive fighting and partially went on the offensive on the Pochep axis. Especially sustained fighting is going on in the center and in the Pochep, Trubchevsk, and Novgorod-Severskii region on the *front's* left wing.

The enemy is continuing to develop active offensive operations toward Novgorod-Severskii and Glukhov.

Second. 50th Army is holding onto its previous defensive lines. The enemy did not display any special activity on 31 August. Small reconnaissance groups from both sides are operating in front of the *front*.

Third. 217th RD, while holding onto its defensive sector, is conducting reconnaissance on its front.

Fourth. 279th, 258th, and 260th RDs are defending their sectors, while conducting reconnaissance actions before their fronts. A corporal from 31st ISD's 12th IR has been taken prisoner on 260th RD's front.

Fifth. 280th RD began an attack on Vitovka at 0630 hours, and by 1200 hours the division's units reached the western edge of the grove (north of Ol'govka), Korolevka, Kovalevka, and Zelenyi Rog line. At 1300 hours our infantry occupied Veselyi.

Sixth. 278th RD and 290th RD, as before, are occupying the second defensive line and are not conducting combat operations.

Seventh. 55th CD began to withdraw from encirclement on 29 August 1941 and concentrated in the Leninskii and Klevernyi region by 31 August 1941.

Eighth. 269th RD, while conducting stubborn fighting in the Pochep region and to the south and suffering heavy losses, occupies a line along the northeastern bank of the Rozhov River and along the (incl.) Usoshki, and Krasnyi Bor line by 31 August. 1020th RR lost two-thirds of its personnel in the fighting for Pochep. The regimental commander, the chief of staff, all of the battalion commanders, and the commander of the regiment's headquarters perished, and the division commander was wounded.

Ninth. 13th Army conducted a stubborn holding action along the army's entire front all day on 30 and 31 August 1941.

Tenth. 292nd RD is continuing to put itself in order in the Galevskaia, Il'ino, and Vlasovo region.

Headquarters of the division – Progress.

Eleventh. 137th RD is defending the approaches to Trubchevsk with a composite battalion.

Headquarters of the 137th – the woods south of Trubchevsk.

Twelfth. 45th RC

a) 155th RD passed across the Desna River in the Vitemlia and Sagut'eva sector with separate groups during the day. The units are putting themselves in order.

b) 307th RD crossed the Desna River in the Vitemlia River during the day. The conditions of its units are being verified.

c) 6th RD is defending the Novo-Vasil'evskii and Marker 123.0 line, while holding on to the western edge of the grove north of Kamen', Titchenkov Bugor, and grove southwest of Kamenskaia Sloboda line.

The headquarters of the division is in the woods southeast of Chervonnyi.

Thirteenth. 50th TD is defending the Ochkino, Borovichi, and Rogovka line.

Headquarters of the 50th – the woods west of Zhuravka.

Fourteenth. 52nd CD dug into the woods 4 kilometers west of Antonovka.

Headquarters of the 52nd – the woods east of Antonovka.

Fifteenth. 132nd RD is fighting intensely along the Birin, the woods north of Prokopovka, and Hill 139.7 line.

Headquarters of the 132nd – Khil'chitsy.

Sixteenth. 143rd RD's 635th RR occupied Vovki and Gudka with its remaining forces, and the unarmed part is in Mikhailovskii Farm.

Headquarters of the 143rd – Gudka.

Seventeenth. 21st CD – the woods south of Denisovka.

Headquarters of the 21st – Denisovka.

Eighteenth. The mobile group:

a) 108th TD occupies the Chekhovka (15 kilometers northwest of Trubchevsk) line and fought with enemy tanks and motorized infantry during its movement, and seized prisoners from 17th PzD.

b) 4th CD is moving behind 108th TD.

c) 141st TB occupies Selets and Glybochka. It was subjected to bombing by enemy aircraft two times while on its movement route. The results of the bombing are not clear, but it is not fighting with enemy ground units.

Nineteenth. 298th and 299th RDs and 121st TB are in their previous regions in the *front's* reserve. They are conducting combat training.

Twentieth. 113th Separate Tank Battalion arrived and is unloading at Diat'kovo Station.

114th Tank Battalion is at Vygonichi Station and was subordinated to the commander of 260th RD at 1500 hours on 30 August 1941.

Twenty-first. The *front's* communications with the armies is only by radio and liaison officers and telephone and telegraph are not working. The wire has been broken by enemy aircraft.

> The Chief of Staff of the Briansk Front, Major General Zakharov
> The Commissar of the *front's* headquarters,
>   Battalion Commissar Kuznetsov
> The Chief of the Operations Department, Colonel Argunov

Source: "Operativnaia svodka shtaba Brianskogo Fronta No. 025/op k 18 chasam 31 avgusta 1941 g. o boevykh deistviiakh voisk fronta" [Operational summary no. 025 of the headquarters of the Briansk Front at 1800 hours on 31 August 1941 about the combat operations of the *front's* forces], *SBDVOV*, issue 43, 55-56.

48. *Stavka* VGK Directive No. 001502 to the Commander of the Forces of the Briansk Front and the Deputy Commander of the Red Army's VVS about Measures to Destroy the Enemy's Tank Grouping
0210 hours on 1 September 1941

The Supreme High Commander has ordered that it is obligatory to settle with Guderian's group and smash it, to which end, up to 5 September, the offensive by the Briansk Front's ground forces must be supported, inclusively, by all aviation assembled under the command of Comrade Petrov. Comrade Petrov can inquire about his future work after 5 September.

> For the *Stavka* of the Supreme High Command,
> Chief of the General Staff, B. Shaposhnikov.

Source: "Direktiva Stavki VGK No. 001502 komanduiushchemu voiskami Brianskogo fronta, zamestiteliu komanduiushchego VVS Krasnoi Armii o merakh po razgromu tankovoi gruppirovki protivnika" [*Stavka* VGK Directive no. 001502 to the commander of the forces of the Briansk Front and the deputy commander of the Red Army's VVS about measures to destroy the enemy's tank grouping], in Zolotarev, "*Stavka* 1941," 152.

49. Directive No. 0069 of the Commander of the Forces of the Briansk Front of 1 September 1941 to the Commander of the Forces of 3rdArmy on an Offensive by the Army toward Zhudilovo Station and Rassukha
Directive No. 0069 to the Forces of the Briansk Front,
Headquarters, Briansk Front,
1:100,000 and 500,000 scale maps
Only: To the Commander of 3rd Army

1. The enemy's mobile forces, consisting of 24th PzC (3rd and 4th PzDs and 10th MotD), penetrated at the boundary of 13th and 21st Armies and are operating in the general direction of Novgorod-Severskii and Vorozhba. Simultaneously, 47th

PzC (17th and 18th PzDs and 29th MotD) is moving from the Roslavl' region to the Pochep region and to the south.

2. On the right – 50th Army will attack along the Roslavl' axis on the morning of 2 September 1941, with the aim of destroying the Roslavl' grouping of enemy.

The boundary line with it: Kromy, (incl.) Butre, (incl.) Lopush', (incl.) Dmitrovo, (incl.) Razrytoe, and (incl.) Klimovichi.

On the left – 13th Army will go over to an offensive in the direction of Semenovka on the morning of 3 September 1941.

The boundary line with it: Sevsk, Suzemka, Berezovka, (incl.) Surazh, and Belaia Dubrava.

3. 3rd Army will go on the attack on the morning of 3 September 1941 from the Pochep and Semtsy front with a shock group consisting of 269th and 282nd RDs, 108th TD, 4th CD, one AR RGK, and one guards-mortar regiment to destroy the enemy in the Pochep, Dunaevskii, Zhukova, and Baklan' region by a strike toward Zhudilovo Station and Rassukha, in cooperation with 13th Army.

Subsequently, capture the line of the Iput' River and reach the (incl.) Klimovichi and Belaia Dubrava front by 15 September 1941.

Leave 280th RD in its defensive positions and operate with strong reconnaissance detachments in its sector. Immediately fill out 148th RD and keep it as a reserve.

4. To the commander of the VVS of the *front*.

During the period from 30 August through 2 September, destroy and demoralize the enemy during both day and night by systematic and successive strikes against groupings and columns. Subsequently, support the offensive with no fewer than 2 aviation regiments.

The main axis for aviation: Pochep, Unecha, and Starodub.

5. During the operation, [conduct] well-organized and systematic reconnaissance at all force levels to exclude surprise at all cost. Pay special attention to constant and careful reconnaissance on open flanks.

6. You must dig in [fortify] all positions and points seized from the enemy during the operation, while demanding the forces immediately construct defensive works.

7. Conduct preparations for the operation in strict secrecy and abstain from telephone conversations and transmissions. Do not issue general orders on the operation for all subordinate formations, limit the missions assigned for each division, and, in the divisions, give [missions] for each regiment by individual personal orders

8. Confirm receipt. Present the army's operational plan and individual orders to the divisions to the *front's* headquarters by 2000 hours on 2 September 1941.

> The Commander of the Forces of the Briansk Front,
> Lieutenant General Eremenko
> The Member of the Military Council of the *front*,
> Division Commissar Mazepov
> The Chief of Staff of the *front*, Major General Zakharov

Source: "Direktiva komanduiushchego voiskami Brianskogo fronta No. 0069 ot 1 sentiabria 1941 g. komanduiushchemu voiskami 3-i armii na nastuplenie armii v napravlenii st. Zhudilovo, Rassukha" [Directive No. 0069 of the commander of the forces of the Briansk Front of 1 September 1941 to the commander of the forces of 3rd Army on an offensive by the army toward Zhudilovo Station and Rassukha], in *SBDVOV*, issue 43, 66-67.

50. Directive No. 0071 of the Commander of the Forces of the Briansk Front of 1 September 1941 to the Commander of the Forces of 13th Army on an Offensive by the Army toward Kister, Zheleznyi Most', and Semenovka

Directive No. 0069 to the Forces of the Briansk Front,
Headquarters, Briansk Front,
1:100,000 and 500,000 scale maps
Only: To the commander of 13th Army

1. The enemy's mobile forces, consisting of 24th PzC (3rd and 4th PzDs and 10th MotD) penetrated at the boundary of 13th and 21st Armies and are operating in the general direction of Novgorod-Severskii and Vorozhba. Simultaneously, 47th PzC (17th and 18th PzDs and 29th MotD) is moving from the Roslavl' region to the Pochep region and to the south.

2. On the right – 3rd Army will go on the offensive and deliver a blow along the Zhudilovo Station and Rassukha axis on the morning of 3 September 1941.

The boundary line with it: (incl.) Suzemka, (incl.) Berezovka, Surazh, and (incl.) Belaia Dubrava.

On the left – 21st Army will attack toward Preliub and Semenovka on the morning of 3 September 1941.

The boundary line with it: Shostka, Luzhki, Guta-Koretskaia, and Propoisk.

3. 13th Army will go on a more decisive attack on the morning of 3 September 1941 from the Pogar, Gremiach, and Pushkari front with a shock group consisting of 155th, 307th, and 6th RDs, 50th TD (without tanks), 141st TB, and 2 RGK ARs to destroy the enemy in the Pogar, Starodub, Zheleznyi Most', and Vorob'evka region, in cooperation with 3rd Army.

Subsequently, capture the Unecha and Klintsy region and reach the (incl.) Belaia Dubrava and Guta-Koretskaia front by 15 September 1941.

For protecting the boundary with 40th Army [then fielding forward], leave 121st and 143rd RDs and 52nd and 21st CDs in the positions they occupy to tie down the enemy with strong reconnaissance detachments.

4. The mission of aviation during the entire operation is to destroy and demoralize the enemy in both day and night by systematic and successive strikes against groupings, columns, and combat formations on the battlefield.

The main axis for aviation – Pogar and Semenovka and to protect the main grouping from the air.

Prevent fresh enemy reserves from moving forward.

[Conduct] deep reconnaissance and reconnaissance on the flanks.

5. During the operation, [conduct] well-organized and systematic reconnaissance at all force levels to exclude surprise at all cost. Pay special attention to constant and careful reconnaissance on open flanks.

6. You must dig in [fortify] all positions and points seized from the enemy during the operation, while demanding the forces immediately construct defensive works.

7. Conduct preparations for the operation in strict secrecy and abstain from telephone conversations and transmissions.

Do not issue general orders on the operation to all subordinate formations, limit the missions assigned to each division, and, in the divisions, give [missions] to each regiment by individual personal orders.

8. Confirm receipt. Present the army's operational plan and the individual orders to divisions to the *front's* headquarters by 2400 hours on 2 September 1941.

> The Commander of the Forces of the Briansk Front,
>   Lieutenant General Eremenko
> The Member of the Military Council of the *front*,
>   Division Commissar Mazepov
> The Chief of Staff of the *front*, Major General Zakharov

Source: "Direktiva komanduiushchego voiskami Brianskogo fronta No. 0071 ot 1 sentiabria 1941 g. komanduiushchemu voiskami 13-i armii na nastuplenie armii v napravlenii Kister, Zheleznyi Most', Semenovka" [Directive No. 0071 of the commander of the forces of the Briansk Front of 1 September 1941 to the commander of the forces of 13th Army on an offensive by the army toward Kister, Zheleznyi Most', and Semenovka], in *SBDVOV*, issue 43, 67-68

51. Combat Order No. 065 of the Commander of the Forces of 13th Army of 1 September 1941 on Capturing the Town of Novgorod-Severskii

Combat Order No. 065, Headquarters, 13th Army
1450 hours on 1 September 1941
1:100,000 scale map

1. The enemy 3rd and 4th PzDs and 10th MotD, while holding on to a bridgehead east of Novgorod-Severskii, are bringing forward reserves from the north, while trying to develop an offensive toward Glukhov and Krolevets.

The enemy has seized crossings in the Vitemlia region and is concentrating new units there.

2. 3rd Army is operating on the right.

The boundary with it is: (incl.) Belitsa Station, (incl.) Sevsk, (incl.) Suzemka, Selets, and (incl.) Kanichi.

The mobile group (108th TD, 141st TB, and 4th CD) is attacking toward Pogar and Novgorod-Severskii, with the mission of smashing the enemy along this axis and occupying Novgorod-Severskii. By the morning of 1 September 1941, it was located along the Chekhovka, Romanovka, and Kvetun' line.

On the left is 21st Army. The boundary with it is: Vorozhba, Voronezh-Glukhov, Luzhki, and Shirki.

3. 13th Army will defend on its right wing and in its center. It is to destroy the enemy on the eastern bank of the Desna River with its left wing and capture the city of Novgorod-Severskii. The offensive will be on the morning of 2 September 1941.

4. 45th RC, with 462nd CAR, and consisting of 155th, 307th, and 6th RDs, will defend the line of the Desna River on the (incl.) Selets and Rogovka front. 155th and 6th RDs and one regiment of 307th RD will occupy the indicated line. Withdraw

307th RD's headquarters and remaining units to the vicinity of the woods north of Zhikhov for rest and refitting. Plan for the possibility of a counterattack toward Trubchevsk, Khil'chichi, and Dubrovka.

Locate the headquarters of the corps in the woods north of Ulitsa.

The boundary on the left is: (incl.) Dubrovka, Glazov, Smiach', and Semenovka.

5. 50th TD will attack southward along the Desna River. It has the mission to reach the Desna River on the (incl.) Domotkanov and (incl.) Ostroushki front on 2 September 1941.

The boundary on the left is: Zhuravka, (incl.) Birin, and (incl.) Ostroushki.

6. 132nd RD, with 420th CAR, will attack toward Novgorod-Severskii on the morning of 2 September 1941, with the mission to reach the line of the Desna River along the Ostroushki and Pogrebki front.

The boundary on the left is: Glazov, Prokopovka, Svirzh, and Pogrebki.

7. 143rd RD will attack toward Kolievka and Ivot. The division's mission is to seize Ivot, and subsequently reach the Desna River along the (incl.) Pogrebki and mouth of the Ivotka River front.

The boundary on the left is: Spartak, Gudovshchina, Ivot, and the Ivotka River.

8. 52nd CD, while cooperating with 143rd RD, will capture Ivot, and subsequently attack toward Obrazhevka and Pirogovka, with the mission to reach the Desna River on the Drobyshevo, Pirogovka, and Sobach front.

9. 21st CD will concentrate in the woods east of Zhikhov, place the headquarters of the division – in Zhikhov, conduct reconnaissance toward Iampol' and Paleevka, and continue to fill out the division.

10. 121st RD will continue to form in the Suzemka region.

11. CP of the army's headquarters – Staraia Guta.

> The Commander of 13th Army, Major General Gorodniansky
> The Member of the Military Council, Brigade Commissar Furt
> The Chief of Staff of 13th Army, *Kombrig* Petrushevsky

Source: "Boevoi prikaz komanduiushchego voiskami 13-i Armii no. 065 ot 1 sentiabria 1941 g. na ovladenie gor. Novgorod-Severskii [Combat order of the commander of the forces of 13th Army no. 065 of 1 September 1941 on capturing the town of Novgorod-Severskii], *SBDVOV*, issue 43, 304-305.

52. Combat Order No. 09 of the Commander of the Forces of 50th Army of 1 September 1941 on an Offensive toward Pochep and Starodub

Combat Order No. 09, Headquarters, 50th Army,
Deminteevka,
1000 hours on 1 September 1941
1:100,000 scale map

First. Units of the enemy's 34th ID have been identified on the army's front. Up to two enemy regiments (253rd and 107th IRs) have gone on the defense in the Viazovsk (12 kilometers north of Zhukovka) and Letoshniki sector along the eastern edge of the grove west of the Desna River.

Second. On the right, 43rd Army began an offensive on the morning of 30 August, with the aim of destroying the enemy in the Roslavl' region.

The boundary line with it is: Mtsensk, Zhizdra, Frolovka, and Roslavl'. All point are inclusive for 43rd Army.

Third. On the left, 3rd Army will go on the offense on the morning of 2 September in the general direction of Pochep and Starodub.

The boundary line with it is: (incl.) Kromy, Butre, Lopush', Dmitrovo, Razrytoe, and Klimovichi.

Fourth. 50th Army, while defending on its external flanks, will attack the enemy from the Viazovsk, Zhukovka, and Letoshniki line [12 kilometers north of Zhukovka to 12 kilometers south of Zhukovka] on the morning of 2 September (the hour of the attack by separate order) and, in cooperation with 43rd Army, will destroy him in the Davydchichi (7 kilometers southeast of Seshcha), Zhabovo, and Riabchichi [17 kilometers southeast of Seshcha] region. Subsequently, reach the Seshcha, Staraia Kocheva, and Grabovka region (28 kilometers west of Zhukovka).

Fifth. 217th RD, with 1st and 2nd Bns, 207th CAR, will firmly defend positions from Frolovka along the eastern bank of the Desna to the mouth of the Seshcha River (4642). Seize and hold on to the Lipovka (5232) and Dubrovka (5032) region [22-25 kilometers northwest of Zhukovka] by day's end on 2 September.

The boundary line with 279th RD is: Star' (15 kilometers west of Diat'kovo), Pogorelovka, Rekovichi, Dubrovka (4832), and Seshcha. All points besides Dubrovka are exclusively for 217th RD.

Sixth. 279th RD, with 3rd Bn, 207th CAR, will attack the enemy in the Viazovsk and Korobki sector and, while delivering an attack toward Berestok and Zhabovo with the left wing, capture Khlistovka (4632), Aleshnia, Liubimovka, and Sloboda (3834) by day's end on 2 September.

Subsequently, be prepared to attack along the road toward Roslavl'.

The boundary line with 278th RD is: Sosnovka (6 kilometers south of Diat'kovo), Grishina Sloboda, Riabchichi, and Zhabovo. All points except Riabchichi are exclusively for 279th RD. Locate the headquarters of the division in Petukhovka.

Seventh. 278th RD will attack the opposing enemy and capture the Riabchichi, Peklina, and Sergeevka region by day's end on 2 September.

Upon capturing the woods west of Vyshkovichi, have the main grouping cooperate with 299th RD on the left flank.

Subsequently, be prepared to attack in the general direction of Staraia Kocheva (10 kilometers southwest of Seshcha).

The boundary line with 299th RD is: Dorozhova (20 kilometers northwest of Ordzhonikidze), Zhukovka, Ol'khovka, and Zobovka (6 kilometers south of Riabchichi). All points are exclusively for 278th RD. Locate the headquarters of the division in Skrabovka.

Eighth. 299th RD, with a guards (-mortar) battalion, will attack the opposing enemy and capture the Sharovka, Tureiskie, and Oleshenskii village region by day's end on 2 September. Seize and hold Bodogliadovka (12 kilometers south of Riabchichi) and Oleshenka with a reinforced battalion.

Subsequently, be ready to attack in the general direction of Grabovka (20 kilometers southwest of Seshcha). Locate the headquarters of the division in the western outskirts of Poliakova.

Ninth. 258th RD, with 761st ATR, while conducting reinforced reconnaissance up to the Grabovka and Kletnia line, firmly hold the positions from the mouth of the Seshcha River to Zhukovka and Stolby.

With the beginning of 299th RD's offensive, attack the enemy in the Letoshniki and Hill 183.6 region with a reinforced battalion and occupy and hold the woods (3 kilometers west of Leliatino) and Marker 206.9.

The boundary line with 260th RD is: Briansk, (incl.) Stolby, (incl.) Kletnia, and Razrytoe.

Tenth. 260th RD, with one battalion of 645th CAR, while conducting reinforced reconnaissance up to the Kletnia and Akulino line, will firmly hold on to its occupied positions from Stolby to Dmitrovo.

The boundary line on the left – the army's left boundary.

Eleventh. 55th CD will occupy and defend the Krasnoe, Khmelevo, and Sosnovka sector by 2000 hours on 1 September. Pay special attention to protecting the Uruch'e, Lopush', Krasnyi Rog, and Krasnoe road. Locate the headquarters of the division in the Miakishevo region.

Twelfth. 121st TB will concentrate in the Negotino, Ovstug, and Rechitsa region by first light on 2 September and, when the infantry reach the Novaia Buda and Krasnoe Znamia line, commit the brigade on 299th RD's left wing, with the mission of destroying the enemy in the direction of the Roslavl' road.

Concentrate in the Krasnaia Poliana, Oleshenskii village, and Kochevskii region by the end of the day.

Thirteenth. 290th RD, having concentrated in the Diad'kovichi, Spinka, and Shamordina region and constituting my reserve, will be ready to protect the army shock group's left flank. Situate the headquarters of the division in Novyi Put'.

Fourteenth. Artillery – readiness at 2000 hours on 1 September 1941 and an artillery preparation of two hours (begin the artillery preparation on special orders).

a) 217th, 258th, and 260th RDs' artillery, while remaining in the first defensive line, will suppress revealed enemy firing points and assemblages on their divisions' fronts during the artillery preparation.

b) 1st and 2nd Bns, 207th CAR, while remaining subordinate to the commander of 217th RD, will protect the boundary with the neighbor on the left in the Rekovichi and Kazanova sector.

c) 151st CAR will suppress revealed enemy firing points on 999th RR's front during the artillery preparation. When 290th RD reaches the Letoshniki line, establish communications with it and anticipate supporting its operations.

d) 753rd ATR is in my mobile reserve. Occupy firing positions in the Kostyli, Krasnyi Kurgan, and Pesochnia region, while protecting the shock group's offensive against possible enemy tank attack from the direction of Belogolovl' and Bykovichi. Maintain communications with the commander of 290th RD.

e) 645th CAR, while remaining at the disposal of the commander of 260th RD, protect the boundary between 258th and 260th RDs in the Uprusy and Stolby region.

Fifteenth. Allow only a limited number of operational workers in the headquarters to work out combat documents and, at all cost, do not permit the disclosure of the forthcoming offensive among the entire command cadre.

Establish a strict regime of custody for all operational documents associated with the forthcoming offensive.

Issue orders down to battalions at 6 hours before the offensive begins. Begin preparing sub-units for the offensive immediately.

Sixteenth. Have reliable commanders and liaison officers with means of movement for communications with the army's headquarters and with regimental headquarters. In the event communications is lost, these [liaison officers] will be obliged to seek out contacts not only from above but also from below. Do not change command posts without permission from the higher level headquarters,

Seventeenth. The army's headquarters from 2000 hours on 1 September: the operational group – Zastavishche and, subsequently, Lipovskie. The second echelon from 0800 hours on 1 September – Chaikovichi.

> The Commander of 50th Army, Major General Petrov
> The Member of the Military Council, Brigade Commissar Shliapin
> The Chief of Staff, Colonel Pern

Source: "Boevoi prikaz komanduiushchego voiskami 50-i Armii No. 09 ot 1 sentiabria 1941 g. na nastuplenie v napravlenii Pochep, Starodub'" [Combat order no. 09 of the commander of the forces of 50th Army of 1 September 1941 on an offensive toward Pochep and Starodub], *SBDVOV*, issue 43, 361-363.

53. Combat Report of the Commander of the Forces of 21st Army of 1 September 1941 about the Positions of the Army's Forces and Necessary Measures for Ensuring its Successful Offensive

To the Commander of the *front*, Eremenko
To the *Stavka*, Shaposhnikov
Headquarters, 21st Army,
Mena,
2300 hours on 1 September 1941
1:100,000 scale map

1. During the course of 31 August and 1 September, the enemy has been conducting intense attacks along the entire front of the army.

At 1500 hours on 1 September, the enemy, supported by strong artillery with tanks, crossed over the Snov River in the Elino, Bezuglovka, Novyi Borovichi, Smiach, Malyi Dyrchin, and Begach sector.

All of our units' efforts to liquidate the penetrating enemy have not produce positive results, and, at the points indicated, the enemy has remained on the eastern bank of the Snov River on the night of 1-2 September.

2. 67th RC, on the army's right wing, while fulfilling its assigned mission to attack toward Semenovka to link up with 13th Army's units, is fighting in difficult conditions along the Obolon'e, Verba, Rudnia, and Oborki line for the second day, and its 277th RD, having captured the Semenovka and Bleshnia line on 31 August, had to turn toward the east and southeast on 1 September to protect its right flank and ended up in a position isolated from the corps' units.

67th RC's attacks toward Semenovka have become very bitter. Obolon'e and Rudnia changed hands several times on 1 September.

It has been determined that 10th MotD's units, with a machine gun regiment, have sufficiently fortified this line in an engineer sense

3. We cannot exclude the possibility that we will encounter fresh forces along this axis.

It was determined at 1100 hours on 31 August that a column with its head at Kostobobr and its tail at Starodub and a concentration of infantry with tanks at Vorob'evka could turn out on to be on 21st Army's front.

4. Repeated requests to 5th Army's units to hold onto their positions and protect the boundary between the armies has also not produced positive results. 62nd RD withdrew behind the Desna Rover by day's end on 1 September. By day's end on 1 September, the flanks of both armies were open, and 28th and 66th RCs are being tied down by enemy attacks and have been deprived of maneuver.

5. I will continue the offensive on the morning of 2 September toward the southeast for a link up with 13th Army, and I am committing the cavalry group.

I request you demand energetic operations by 13th Army toward Semenovka, liquidation of the enemy in the Korop region and an arrival at the Desna River by 40th Army, and the cessation of 5th Army's withdrawal and an advance northward by it to unite the flanks.

The absence of these measures and a further withdrawal by 5th Army could compel 21st Army to withdraw behind the Desna River.

I await your orders.

> The Commander of 21st Army, Lieutenant General Kuznetsov
> The Member of the Military Council, Division Commissar Kolonin
> The Chief of Staff of 21st Army, Major General Gordov

Source: "Boevoe donesenie komanduiushchego voiskami 21-i Armii ot 1 sentiabria 1941 g. komanduiushchemu voiskami Brianskogo Fronta o polozhenii voisk armii i neobkhodimykh merakh po obespecheniiu ikh uspeshnogo nastupleniia [Combat report of the commander of the forces of 21st Army of 1 September 1941 about the positions of the army's forces and necessary measures for ensuring its successful offensive], *SBDVOV*, issue 43, 343.

54. *Stavka* VGK Directive No. 001540 to the Commander of the Forces of the Briansk Front and the Deputy Commander of the Red Army's VVS about the Unsatisfactory Results of Operations to Destroy Group Guderian and the Missions of Aviation

0250 hours on 2 September 1941

The entire *Stavka* is entirely dissatisfied with your work. Despite the work of aviation and the ground units, Pochep and Starodub are still in the enemy's hands. This means that you nibbled away at the enemy a little but did not succeed in budging him.

The *Stavka* demands that the ground forces operate in cooperation with aviation, knock him out of the Starodub and Pochep region, and properly destroy him. Until you do so, all conversations will remain empty words.

The *Stavka* orders Petrov [the commander of the VVS] to remain in place and assist the decisive success of the ground forces with all of the VVS's formations. You must smash Guderian and his entire group to smithereens. Until you do so, all of your assurances of success will be worthless. We await your reports about the destruction of Group Guderian.

> Stalin
> Shaposhnikov

Source: "Direktiva Stavki VGK No. 001540 komanduiushchemu voiskami Brianskogo Fronta, zamestiteliu komanduiushchego VVS Krasnoi Armii o neudovletvoritel'nykh resultatakh deistvii po razgromu gruppy Guderiana i zadachakh aviatsii" [*Stavka* VGK Directive No. 001540 to the commander of the forces of the Briansk Front and the deputy commander of the Red Army's VVS about the unsatisfactory results of operations to destroy Group Guderian and the missions of aviation], in Zolotarev, "*Stavka* 1941," 155.

55. *Stavka* VGK Directive No. 001556 to the Commander of the Forces of the Western [should read Briansk] Front on the Necessity for Holding onto Chernigov
2 September 1941

    1. The Supreme High Commander has ordered me to confirm that 21st Army will not be transferred to the Southwestern Front.

    2. With the capture of Vibli by the enemy, a clear danger has been created to Chernigov and the boundary between the *fronts*. Report immediately about the measures you have taken along that axis. Chernigov must be held at all cost.

> For the *Stavka* of the Supreme High Command,
> Chief of the General Staff, B. Shaposhnikov

Source: "Direktiva Stavki VGK No. 001556 komanduiushchemu voiskami Zapadnogo [should read Brianskogo] Fronta o obiazatel'nom uderzhanii Chernigova" [*Stavka* VGK Directive No. 001556 to the commander of the forces of the Western [should read Briansk] Front on the necessity for holding onto Chernigov], in Zolotarev, "*Stavka* 1941," 156.

56. Plan for Employing the Briansk Front's Aviation and Organizing its Cooperation with the Ground Forces on the Night of 1-2 and 2 September
Plan for Employing Aviation and its Cooperation with the Ground Forces
on the night of 1-2 September and on 2 September 1914

1. Inflict a defeat on and exhaust the enemy's forces in the Dubrovka, Solyn' Station, Malaia Solyn', Peklino, and west of Pervomaiskii region with night operations throughout the entire night.

2. Aviation will work over the [following] regions from 0700-0800 hours on 2 September:

    1) Rekovichi, Krasnyi, Maiak Farm, and Devochkino;

    2) Berestok, Solyn' Station, and Bubnov;

    3) Krasnaia Sloboda, northwestern Zhukovka, and Vyshkovichi;

    4) The woods 2 kilometers west of Vyshkovichi; and

    5) Nikol'skaia Sloboda and Novaia Buda: the artillery in firing positions (inflict a strike by *front* aviation from 0700 to 0730 hours and with Long-Range aviation from 0730 to 0800 hours).

Conduct an artillery preparation from 0800 to 1000 hours, and, during this period, fighter aircraft will protect our own grouping from artillery and destroy enemy artillery. During the artillery pause, from 1000 to 1010 hours, assault aircraft will strike the enemy's forward edge.

Subsequently, during the day aviation will destroy the enemy and his firing means with successive strikes directly in front of the attacking infantry and tanks by orienting on the [following] lines:

    1) Devochkino, Berestok, Vyshkovichi, and Krasnoe from 1000 to 1100 hours;

    2) Rekovichi, Sobolevo, Summa, Nikol'skaia Sloboda, and Pervomaiskii from 1200 hours; and

    3) Rzhavets, Solyn' Station, Peklino, Kochevskii, and Irinskii village from 1400 hours.

While summoning the aircraft to their targets from the CP, use the numbered quadrants on the maps.

Land two U-2 aircraft at the army commander's forward CP.

    The Commander of the Forces of the Briansk Front,
       Lieutenant General Eremenko
    The Member of the Military Council of the *front*,
       Division Commissar Mazepov
    The Chief of Staff of the *front*, Major General Zakharov

Source: "Plan ispol'zovaniia aviatsii Brianskogo Fronta i organizatsii vzaimodeistviia ee s nazemnymi voiskami v noch' 2 i 2 sentiabria 1941." [Plan for employing the Briansk Front's aviation and organizing its cooperation with the ground forces on the night of 1-2 and 2 September], *SBDVOV*, issue 43, 68-69.

57. Operational Summary No. 029 of the Headquarters of the Briansk Front at 1800 hours on 2 September 1941 about the Combat Operations of the *Front's* Forces

Operational Summary No. 029 at 1800 hours on 2 September 1941,
Headquarters, Briansk Front,
1: 100,000 and 50,000 scale maps

First. On the *front's* right wing, 50th Army conducted offensive fighting to destroy the enemy in the Davydchintsy, Zhabovo, and Riabchitsy region.

In the *front's* central sector, fighting is underway to destroy the enemy tank group which has penetrated into the Semiachki, Potapovo, and Uzha region.

On the left wing, 13th and 21st Armies' units are fighting to destroy the enemy in the Novgorod-Severskii, Shostka, and Glukhov region.

Second. 50th Army, while continuing to hold onto its previous defensive lines, went on the offensive from the Viasovsk and Bereshovskii line in the general direction of Roslavl' with four rifle divisions and one tank brigade at 1400 hours on 2 September.

217th RD conducted a partial regrouping and is occupying the Frolovka and mouth of the Seshcha River line.

Headquarters of the division – Kosevat.

279th RD went on the attack toward Berestok at 1400 hours on 2 September. No news has been received about the course of the attack by day's end.

278th RD went on the attack toward Peklina at 1400 hours on 2 September and captured Bubnov, Lipovka, and Hill 193.7 by 1800 hours. The enemy is withdrawing toward the west, while resisting with small groups.

299th RD, with a guards battalion [presumably guards-mortar – *Katiusha*], went on the attack at 1400 hours on 2 September and, having captured Petukhovka at 1800 hours, while fighting with its left wing toward Ol'khovka, is fighting in the woods 2 kilometers west of Gostilovka State Farm with its right wing.

290th RD, in second echelon, is moving into the Diad'kovichi, Kostyli, and Viznok region.

121st TB – No information has been received about the results of its attack.

258th RD carried out a regrouping to its right wing and occupies a defense along the (incl.) mouth of the Seshcha River and (incl.) Stolby line. A reinforced company conducted combat reconnaissance on the morning of 1 September and reached the edge of the woods south of Gostilovka State Farm by day's end.

Losses – 19 killed, 43 wounded, and 8 missing in action.

260th RD is defending the Stolby, Ratnaia, Boguchevo, and Dmitrovo line.

55th CD concentrated in the Krasnoe and Sosnovka region.

Headquarters of the army – Zastavishche.

Third. 3rd Army repelled enemy attacks on its right wing and is holding onto the Mashki, P'ianyi Rog, and Vlasovo line.

On its left wing, the operational group (108th RD, 141st TB, and 4th CD) is fighting to destroy the enemy tank group in the Semiachki, Potapovo, and Uzha region.

280th RD and 269th RD were fighting defensive battles along the Mashki, Putilovskii, Sloboda, Popsueva, and Korolevka line by day's end on 2 September. News has not been received about the results of the fighting.

282nd RD is defending the Golevskaia, Vlasovo, and Kvetun' line.

Headquarters of the division – The MTS [Motor Tractor Station] at Trubchevsk.

137th RD's 771st RR is defending the southwestern outskirts of Trubchevsk and further along the Desna River. Separate units and the division's headquarters are in the woods southeast of Trubchevsk.

148th RD – no news received.

Fourth. The Operational Group fought to destroy the enemy tank group in the Semiachki, Potapovo, and Uzha region on 2 September.

108th TD, as a result of the fighting, was half encircled in the Karbovka region, and its communications with the remaining units has been interrupted.

4th CD, having completed a march-maneuver to assist 108th TD, was attacked by 15 enemy tanks in the Mostochnaia and Bobovnia region. While suffering heavy losses, the division withdrew from the fighting and concentrated in the Magor region by day's end.

141st TB attacked from the Tishino and Korovichi region toward Semiachki, Potapovo, and Karbovka at 1330 hours, with the mission to destroy the penetrating enemy tanks and link up with 108th TD.

Fifth. 13th Army was holding on to its previous defensive positions by the end of the day on 2 September, while repelling enemy attacks in the Birin region.

21st CD is defending the eastern bank of the Desna River in the Chrub and Benzonka sector with a detachment of 260 men. The remaining forces are being concentrated in the Denisovka region. On 2 September the division's commander, Colonel [Iakob Kulievich] Kuliev, and the division's military commissar, Battalion Commissar Ul'ianov, escaped from the encirclement.

Headquarters of the division – Denisovka.

45th RC is defending the Benzonka, Kholmy, and (incl.) Novyi Vasil'evskii line. In the Murav'i region, having forced the Desna River on the morning of 1 September, the enemy seized the grove northwest of Novyi Vasil'evskii and Marker 139.0.

155th RD is defending the Benzonka and Kholmy line.

Headquarters of the division – Melichi.

307th RD is defending the (incl.) Kholmy and (incl.) Novyi Vasil'evskii line.

Headquarters of the division – the woods southeast of Znob' Station.

Headquarters of the corps – the grove north of Ulitsa.

6th RD is defending the Novyi Vasil'evskii and (incl.) Ochkino line. Part of the force is holding onto a bridgehead on the western bank of the Desna River along the Delevki, Kamen', Kamenskaia Sloboda, and Krymskii Bugor line.

Headquarters of the division – the woods east of Zhuravka.

50th TD (without tanks) repelled fierce enemy counterattacks during the course of the day along the Ochkino and woods south of Borovichi line.

Headquarters of the division – the woods east of Zhuravka.

132nd RD fought stubbornly with approaching enemy reserves in the Birin region on 1 September. By day's end on 1 September, it was holding onto positions from the cutting in the forest 1.5 kilometers south of Marker 133.1 to the peat bog southeast of Birin. From 31 August through 1 September, the division destroyed 281 enemy and shot down 4 enemy aircraft with antiaircraft artillery.

Headquarters of the division – the woods north of Birin.

143rd RD's 635th and 800th RR (around 400 men) once again captured Kashevka on the morning of 2 September. After an unsuccessful attack on Ivot, the composite battalion was withdrawn to the Zhikhov region. The unarmed part of the division – 287th RR, 166th AA Bn, 186th AT Bn, and 135th Sep. Recon Bn, were concentrated in the woods north of Seredina Buda.

Headquarters of the division – Zhikhov.

52nd CD is defending positions 500 meters east of Ivot.

Headquarters of the division – Staraia Guta.

Sixth. 21st Army. The army's units repelled attacks by the enemy toward Guta Studenetskaia, Shchors, and Novye Mliny on 1 September. On the right wing, 67th RC continued its attack toward Obolon'e, Orlovka, and Semenovka.

67th RC occupied the [following] by day's end on 1 September:

42nd RD, while overcoming stubborn enemy resistance, captured Obolon'e.

24th RD, while throwing the enemy back, reached the Liashkovichi, Sverok, and Rudnia line.

277th RD is fighting along the line from the northern and northeastern outskirts of Semenovka, to Krasnaia Zaria and Bleshnia, with one regiment in the Zhadov region.

Losses for 31 August and 1 September:

42nd RD – 67 men killed and wounded.

24th RD – 18 men killed and wounded.

277th RD – 75 men killed and wounded.

Trophies: 10 automobiles, 3 guns, 3 heavy machine guns, 4 mortars, 8 submachine guns, 25 barrels of fuel, clothing and other property. 12 prisoners were seized, more than 100 dead and wounded remained on the battlefield, and 2 enemy aircraft were shot down by antiaircraft artillery fire.

Headquarters of the corps – Volynka.

28th RC fought sustained defensive battles along the [following] lines:

187th RD – Guta Studenetskaia and (incl.) Mostki.

219th RD, after repeated attacks on Bezuglovka, went on the defense along the (incl.) Mostki, Kim Farm, and Marker 127.2 line.

Losses – 50 men killed and 223 wounded.

117th RD assisted 219th RD in destroying the enemy in Bezuglovka with two regiments and defending the Sloboda and Borovitskaia region with its remaining forces.

Losses – 200 men killed and wounded.

Headquarters of the corps – Androniki.

66th RC fought to liquidate the enemy who penetrated to the eastern bank of the Snov River in the Malyi Dyrchin, Krasnye Gory, and Begach region, but the attacks produced no results.

55th RD occupies the Marker 117.0 and (incl.) Novye Mliny line.

232nd RD occupies the Novye Mliny, Pisarevshchina Farm, and Ias'kovo line.

75th RD – Leninovka, Begach, and (incl.) Borki line.

20th MotR – Bork and Lake Ziabok.

Losses from enemy bombing: 30 men and 12 horses killed and wounded.

The Cavalry Group concentrated in the Domashlin, Naumovchikovy, and Mokrets region by day's end on 1 September.

BEPO Nos. 46 and 52 are in the Shchors region. Nos. 50 and 51 – in the Makoshino and Bondarevka region.

Seventh. The VVS of the *front* carried out reconnaissance of the enemy and inflicted strikes with bombers and assault aircraft against enemy concentrations in the [following] regions: Voronovo, Rakovichi, Novaia Buda, Mokraia, and Zhirovka; Semiachki, Potapovo, Uzha, Pochep, and Pogar; and Novgorod-Severskii, Shostka, and Voronezh-Glukhov and protected the offensive by 50th Army's and the Operational Group's forces.

The results of aircraft operations during the day have not been received.

A total of 214 aircraft sorties were carried out on 1 September. 1066 bombs were dropped.

Losses – 1 Pe-2 and 3 Il-2.

Destroyed: 45 tanks and 130 automobiles and suppressed: up to 50 enemy guns.

Eighth. Communications with the armies – wire worked with interruptions and radio – uninterrupted.

> The Chief of Staff of the Briansk Front, Major General Zakharov
> The Commissar of the *front's* headquarters,
>   Battalion Commissar Kuznetsov
> The Chief of the Operations Department, Colonel Argunov

Source: "Operativnaia svodka shtaba Brianskogo Fronta No. 029 k 18 chasam 2 sentiabria 1941 g. o boevykh deistviiakh voisk fronta" [Operational summary no. 029 of the headquarters of the Briansk Front at 1800 hours on 2 September 1941 about the combat operations of the *front's* forces], *SBDVOV*, issue 43, 69-70.

58. Individual Order of the Commander of the Forces of 3rd Army of 2 September 1941 on Destroying the Enemy in the Pochep, Zhukovka, and Baklany Region

Individual Order No. 1, Headquarters, 3rd Army
2000 hours on 2 September 1941
1:100,000 scale map

1. The enemy's 29th MotD and separate battered units of 18th PzD, which are especially energetic along the Kotovka and Karbovka axis, are operating on 3rd Army's front.

2. On the right, 260th RD (50th Army) is attacking in the general direction of Zaria Kommunizma.

The boundary line with it: (incl.) Lapushi, (incl.) Leninskii, and (incl.) Muzhilova.

On the left, 269th RD is attacking toward Zelenyi Gai and Lizagubovka.

3. 3rd Army will go on the attack toward Pochep and Sin'ki with its right wing on 3 September 1941 and destroy the enemy in the Pochep, Zhukova, and Baklany region by attacking toward Zhudilovo Station and Rassukha in cooperation with 13th Army in readiness for an offensive toward Struzhenka, while continuing to defend the positions it occupies with part of its forces. Begin the offensive at 1600 hours.

4. 280th RD, with a mortar battalion of a guards regiment and a separate tank battalion – jumping-off positions at Fedorovka, Shlengovka, and Boiuri – while delivering an attack with its right wing toward Igrushkina and Staroroshep'e, will destroy the enemy in the Shmotova, Pochep, and Azerovo region, in cooperation with 269th RD, and reach the Geleshi, Damanishi, and Pochep line by day's end

on 3 September 1941. The boundary line to the left: Sosnovoe, Boloto, Usoshki, Pochep, and (incl.) Milasheva.

    5. Artillery:

        1) A two-hour artillery preparation i cooperation with bomber aviation to suppress enemy firing means and personnel in the forward edge of the defenses.

        2) Suppress artillery in the [following] regions:

            a) Pochep; and

            b) Malinovskii, Nabinskii, and Razdel.

        3) Prevent counterattacking enemy tanks from penetrating through the attacking infantry's combat formations.

    6. Headquarters of the army – the woods 6 kilometers east of Vzdruzhnoe.

The Commander of 3rd Army, Major General Kreizer

The Member of the Military Council of 3rd Army,

    Division Commissar Shlykov

The Chief of Staff of 3rd Army, Major General Zhidov

Source: "Chastnyi boevoi prikaz komanduiushchego voiskami 3-i Armii no. 1 ot 2 sentiabria 1941 g. na unichtozhenie protivnika v raione Pochep, Zhukovka, Baklany" [Individual order of the commander of the forces of 3rd Army of 2 September 1941 on destroying the enemy in the Pochep, Zhukovka, and Baklany region], *SBDVOV*, issue 43, 281-282.

59. Combat Order No. 01 of the Commander of the Forces of 50th Army of 2 September 1941 on Continuing the Offensive toward Pochep and Starodub

Combat Order No. 01, Operational Group, Commander, 50th Army,

Poliakovy,

2400 hours on 2 September 1941

1:100,000 scale map

    First. The divisions and 121st TB will continue to fulfill the mission set forth by Order No. 09 of 2 September 1941 at 0600 hours on 3 September 1941.

    Second. Achieve outflanking and enveloping of the enemy's subunits and their piecemeal destruction by rapid and decisive operations.

    Third. Conduct the offensive by the divisions and the units on the basis of cooperation between the types of forces and their neighbors. It is obligatory to have not only technical but also fire communications with your neighbor and liaison officers with vehicles in their headquarters.

    Fourth. The sluggish operations on 2 September permitted the enemy to evacuate all of his wounded and all of his equipment.

    I demand that commanders at all levels cut off and destroy the enemy's subunits by skillful operations, while seizing prisoners and equipment.

    Fifth. Division commanders will warn unit commanders that, on 3 September, attacks by large enemy units are possible. The artillery must be ready to repel enemy attacks with infantry and tanks with their own power. The infantry must be ready for combat with their own means of struggle.

Sixth. As the units move forward, protect and cover artillery and tank movements from the air.

Seventh. Organize and constantly conduct reconnaissance of the enemy on the front and also on the flanks and, in particular, carefully organize night "snatches" [searches and seizures].

Eighth. After the fighting and especially at night, organize rest for the units, while allocating no less than one-third of the forces to combat security and while systematically conducting the performance of execution of BO [combat observation] services.

Ninth. The commander of 121st TB will continue its advance behind the infantry and be prepared for active operations in front of its own infantry and to repel enemy tank attacks.

Tenth. The commander of 290th RD, while following behind 299th RD's left wing, will be prepared to exploit success and repel enemy tank attacks.

Eleventh. During the period of the offensive, in addition to the operational summary, I am prescribing the submission of combat reports from the division commanders twice a day, at 0900 and 2200 hours. Besides descriptions of the fighting, indicate in these reports their positions at the moment of the submissions of the report and the losses and trophies.

The Commander of 50th Army, Major General Petrov
The Member of the Military Council, Brigade Commissar Shliapin
The Deputy Chief of the Operations Department, Major Garan

Source: "Boevoi rasporiazhenie komanduiushchego voiskami 50-i Armii No. 01 ot 2 sentiabria 1941 g. na prodolzhenii nastupleniia v napravlenii Pochep, Starodub'" [Combat order no. 01 of the commander of the forces of 50th Army of 2 September 1941 on continuing the offensive toward Pochep and Starodub], *SBDVOV*, issue 43, 364.

60. Individual Combat Order No. OG [Operational Group]/1 of the Commander of the Forces of 50th Army of 3 September 1941 on an Attack by 121st Tank Brigade toward the Briansk and Roslavl' Road

Individual Combat Order No. OG/1, Headquarters, 50th Army,
Poliakovy
0730 hours on 3 September 1941
1:100,000 scale map

First. Up to a regiment of enemy infantry is withdrawing on the front of the army's shock group.

Second. 279th, 278th, 299th, and 290th RDs will continue to fulfill Order No. 09.

Third. 121st TB will conduct a decisive attack toward the Briansk and Roslavl' road, while destroying firing points and personnel on the attacking divisions' fronts. Attack at 0900 hours on 3 September 1941.

Fourth. The commanders of 299th and 278th RDs will support [protect] the tank brigade's attack with operations by its own artillery and infantry.

Fifth. The commander of 121st TB will have his liaison officers with 290th and 299th RDs. Report about the results of the fighting to me every two hours by means of the liaison officers.

> The Commander of 50th Army, Major General Petrov
> The Member of the Military Council, Brigade Commissar Shliapin
> The Deputy Chief of the Operations Department, Major Garan

Source: "Chastnyi boevoi prikaz komanduiushchego voiskami 50-i Armii No. OG/1 ot 3 sentiabria 1941 g. na nastuplenie 121-i Tankovoi Brigady v napravlenii shosse Briansk, Roslavl'" [Individual combat order no. OG/1 of the commander of the forces of 50th Army of 3 September 1941 on an attack by 121st Tank Brigade toward the Bransk and Roslavl' road], *SBDVOV*, issue 43, 365.

61. Combat Order of the Commander of the Forces of 21st Army No. 062 of 3 September 1941 on Destroying the Enemy's Avdeevka-Obolon'e Grouping

Combat Order No. 062, Headquarters, 21st Army,
Mena,
3 September 1941
1:100,000 and 500,000 scale maps

1. The enemy, while bringing reserves forward, is continuing his offensive along the entire front, and the most active operations are occurring along the Naumovka, Shchors, Sokhnovka, and Begach axes.

2. The army is continuing to destroy the enemy's Avdeevka-Obolon'e grouping and is repelling attack in the Okhomeevichi, Naumovka, Shchors, Novyi Mlyny, Begach, and Borki sectors.

3. 67th RC. 42nd and 24th RDs, together with the cavalry group, will complete destroying the enemy in the Ivan'kovo, Osmaki, and Obolon'e regions, with the subsequent mission to reach the Cherniavka, Ivan'kovo, Avdeevka, and Zhuklia line by day's end on 4 September.

Upon fulfilling this mission, 24th RD will withdraw into reserve in the Rudnia, Chernotochi, and Kudrovka region.

277th RD will defend the Zhuklia, Chenchiki, Siadrina, and Spichevatovo line, and have one regiment in reserve in the Samotugi, Ozeredy, and Oborki region.

The boundaries are as before.

4. The Cavalry Group will continue to fulfill its assigned mission by combined operations with 67th RC's units and, upon fulfillment, will withdraw to the Karasevka, Slobodka, and Pokoshichi region and conduct reconnaissance toward Sobichi, Novgorod-Severskii, and Mashevo.

5. 28th RC will firmly dig in along the (incl.) Spichevatovo, Naumovka, and (incl.) Shchors line, and withdraw one RR into reserve behind its left wing.

The boundaries are as before.

6. 66th RC will restore the situation at Shchors, Leninovka, Begach, and Borki and firmly defend the line of the Snov River.

7. The VVS of the army will support 66th RC's attack to liquidate the enemy in the Shchors, Leninovka, Begach, and Borki regions.

Assist the liquidation of the enemy by 67th RC in the Ivan'kovo, Osmaki, and Obolon'e region.

8. CP – Mena; and reserve CP – Borzna.

The Commander of 21st Army, Lieutenant General Kuznetsov
The Member of the Military Council, Division Commissar Kolonin
The Chief of Staff of 21st Army, Major General Gordov

Source: "Boevoe rasporiazhenie komanduiushchego voiskami 21-i Armii No. 062 ot 3 sentiabria 1941 g. na unichtozhenie Avdeevsko-Obolon'enskoi gruppirovki protivnika" [Combat order of the commander of the forces of 21st Army No. 062 of 3 September 1941 on destroying the enemy's Avdeevka-Obolon'e grouping], *SBDVOV*, issue 43, 344.

62. Operational Summary No. 031 of the Headquarters of the Briansk Front at 1800 hours on 3 September 1941 about the Combat Operations of the *Front's* Forces

Operational Summary No. 031 at 1800 hours on 3 September 1941,
Headquarters, Briansk Front,
1: 100,000 and 50,000 scale maps

First. The Briansk Front's forces continued to develop an offensive from the Dubrovets (10 kilometers northwest of Zhukovka), Korobki, Ol'khovka, and Novaia Buda line toward Peklina and Beloglavaia Station on the right wing with 50th Army's shock group during the day on 3 September.

In the *front's* central sector, the mobile group continued fighting to destroy the enemy's tank group in the Potapovo, Uzha, and Sosnovka region.

On the left wing, 21st Army's units continued an offensive toward Avdeevka and Semenovka with the mission, in cooperation with 13th Army, of defeating the enemy grouping which has wedged into the gap between 13th and 21st Armies along the Novgorod-Severskii and Glukhov axis.

Second. 50th Army is firmly defending its previous positions with its right and left wings, while continuing an offensive with its central grouping toward Peklina and Beloglavaia Station.

217th RD is occupying its previous defensive region along the Frolovka and mouth of the Seshcha River line at 1800 hours on 3 September 1941. The enemy is displaying no activity.

Headquarters of the division – Kosevat.

279th RD continued an attack toward Zarech'e on the morning of 3 September. The division's units captured Kazanovka and Berestok by 1200 hours on 3 September.

278th RD, while continuing its attack on the morning of 3 September, was fighting for Malaia Solyn', Sumy, and Novosel'e at 1200 hours. Offering stubborn resistance, the enemy is withdrawing to Peklina.

299th RD completely captured Novaia Buda by 1200 hours on 3 September and was fighting along the approaches to Kochevskii.

121st TB went on the attack along the Briansk-Roslavl' main road at 0600 hours on 3 September and reached the Ol'khovka and Nikol'skaia Sloboda line by 1200 hours on 3 September.

290th RD, by a decision of the *front* commander, was not committed into combat but instead remained in the Ded'kovichi, Kostyli, and Vshchizh region. One reinforced rifle battalion arrived in the Legoshniki region in readiness to protect the left flank of 50th Army's attacking grouping.

258th RD and 260th RDs are defending the (incl.) Zhukovka, Stolby, Ratnaia, and Dmitrovo line. The enemy is displaying no activity.

55th CD concentrated in the Krasnoe, Sosnovka, and Subbotovo region.

Third. 3rd Army, while repelling enemy attacks toward Vitovka, P'ianyi Rog, and Kotovka, continued regrouping and filling out of units, while preparing for active offensive operations.

280th RD, while repelling attacks by enemy forces of up to two IRs and a battalion of tanks from 29th MotD, occupied the Sloboda, Pozhuevo, Putilovskii, Ol'govka, Kovalevka, Dyriavyi, Ganzha, and Chernoe Ruch'e line by the morning of 3 September.

Headquarters of the division – the woods 1 kilometer northeast of Krasnyi Rog.

269th RD, under pressure of a regiment of enemy infantry with 30-40 tanks, abandoned P'ianyi Rog by 2400 hours on 2 September and is occupying positions from the southern bank of the Rozhok River (south of P'ianyi Rog) to Krasnyi Stiag.

Two march-battalions with 2,100 men are being sent to the division.

Headquarters of the division – the woods 1 kilometer northeast of Kotovka.

282nd RD, while attacking together with 141st TB, reached the Parovichi, Alad'ino, Kartashova, Filippovichi, and Kvetun' line by day's end on 2 September but, while having up to 150 enemy tanks (47th MotC) on its front in the Gruzdovtsy, Borshnia, and Sosnovka region, and, while being attacked by a part of the tanks, exited from the fighting and withdrew to the Popovka, Temnaia, and Telets region on the morning of 3 September.

Headquarters of the division – Popovka.

137th RD is defending the southern outskirts of Trubchevsk with one regiment, and the division's remaining forces and headquarters are concentrated in the woods southeast of Trubchevsk.

148th RD (headquarters and rear) concentrated in the woods southwest of Saltanovka by the morning of 3 September, where it is being sent three battalions of replacements.

Fourth. The Mobile Group was fighting with a group of up to 150 tanks (47th PzC) in the Koruzha, Bobovnia, and Uzha region during the day on 3 September.

108th TD, after fighting in the Karbovka region, concentrated in the woods south of Brusnichnyi at 1500 hours on 3 September, from which it attacked toward Bobovnia.

141st TB fought with enemy tanks in the Verkhniaia Potapovo and Seleno region at 1400 hours on 3 September.

Losses: 1 KV tank and 3 T-34 tanks.

4th CD concentrated and put itself into order in the Radinsk region.

Headquarters of the group – Trubchevsk.

Fifth. 13th Army is fighting to destroy the enemy in the Novye Vasil'evskii region. In the remaining sectors, the enemy is displaying no activity.

21st CD is continuing to defend the eastern bank of the Desna River in the Poruba and Borzovka sector with a detachment of 260 men, and the division's remaining forces moved from the Denisovka region to the vicinity of the woods east of Zhikhov by the morning of 3 September.

45th RC, while repelling enemy attacks from Novyi Vasil'evskii, held onto the Benzonka and Kholmy line with 155th RD.

Headquarters of the division – Melichi.

307th RD – (incl.) Kholmy and (incl.) Novyi Vasil'evskii line.

Headquarters of the division – the woods southeast of Znob' Station.

The corps' units gathered up the [following] weapons by day's end on 3 September: 17 heavy machine guns, 4 120mm mortars, 5 82mmm mortars, 2 50mm mortars, 20 sub-machine guns, 16 antitank rifles, 754 rifles, and 4 revolvers.

Headquarters of the corps – Melichi.

6th RD, having left covering units on the Delevki, Kamenskaia Sloboda, and Krymskii Bor line, went on the attack toward Novyi Vasil'evskii on the morning of 2 September. The results of the attack are unknown.

Headquarters of the division – the woods northwest of Chervonyi.

50th TD, having left covering units on the Ochkino and Kholsty line, went on the attack toward Novyi Vasil'evskii on the morning of 3 September and captured the northern edge of the woods south of Ukrainskii by day's end.

132nd RD dug in along the Marker 133.1 (4 kilometers southeast of Birin) and the grove south of Prokopovka line during the day on 2 September, and, on 1 September, 1st Bn, 498th RR, was encircled by 9 enemy tanks in the woods west of Podgornyi, the battalion was cut off and assembled only 100 men, but one tank was destroyed.

Headquarters of the division – the woods north of Birin.

143rd RD and 52nd CD – no information received.

121st RD is filling out in the Suzemka region.

Sixth. 21st Army. No information received because of the absence of wire communications and reliable radio communications. The positions of the army's forces on 1 September are in accordance with Summary No. 029.

Seventh. Neighbors – 40th Army was fighting along the [following] lines on 31 August:

10th MotD – Slout and Pisarevshchina.

293rd RD – Pogorelovka and Zhernovka.

Headquarters of the division – Krolevets.

135th RD – Korop and Maksaki.

Headquarters of the division – Galaibin.

107th RD – moving from the Glukhov region to the Altynovka region.

Eighth. The VVS of the *front* – Summary of operations on 3 September:

Carried out 183 aircraft sorties and dropped 2,182 bombs.

Losses – 7 Il-2s, 5 SU-2s, 1 Pe-2, and 1 Iak-1.

Shot down: two KHe-125 and one ME-109.

Destroyed 14 enemy tanks, 10 automobiles, and one antiaircraft battery.

Ninth. Communications – wire with the armies worked with interruptions.

The Chief of Staff of the Briansk Front, Major General Zakharov
The Commissar of the *front's* headquarters,
  Battalion Commissar Kuznetsov
For the Chief of the Operations Department, Major Grigor'ev

Source: "Operativnaia svodka shtaba Brianskogo Fronta No. 031 k 18 chasam 3 sentiabria 1941 g. o boevykh deistviiakh voisk fronta" [Operational summary no. 031 of the headquarters of the Briansk Front at 1800 hours on 3 September 1941 about the combat operations of the *front's* forces], *SBDVOV*, issue 43, 72-74.

63. Operational Summary No. 032 of the Headquarters of the Briansk Front at 0600 hours on 4 September 1941 about the Combat Operations of the *Front's* Forces

Operational Summary No. 032 at 0600 hours on 4 September 1941,
Headquarters, Briansk Front,
1: 100,000 and 50,000 scale maps

First. The Briansk Front's forces continued to develop an offensive toward Aleshnia, Volkovshchina, and Roslavl' on the right wing with 50th Army's shock group during the day on 3 September.

In the *front's* central sector, 3rd Army's units fought fierce battles to liquidate the enemy who have captured P'ianyi Rog and Seleno.

On the left wing, 21st Army's forces and the forces of the Southwestern Front's 40th Army, while holding off the enemy's offensive in the Slout, Pogorelovka, and Korop region, continued their offensive toward Avdeevka and Semenovka, with the mission of destroying the enemy grouping attacking toward Glukhov and Krolevets and linking up with 13th Army's forces.

Second. 50th Army is firmly defending its previous positions with its right and left wings, while continuing an offensive with its central grouping.

The army's units, while repulsing enemy counterattacks in sustained combat, reached the Kazakova, Berestok, Suma, Nikol'skaia Sloboda, and Krasnoe Znamia line by day's end on 3 September.

217th RD occupied a defense in its previous positions from Frolovka to the mouth of the Seshcha River line, while having a battalion of 740th RR in Piatnitskoe and a second battalion of 740th RR 1.5 kilometers northwest of Viazovsk.

Headquarters of the division – Kosevat.

279th RD, having repelled a counterattack by an enemy force of up to two battalions, captured (incl.) Rekovichi Platform, Hill 235.6, and Berestok with two regiments in intense fighting. The third regiment concentrated in the Berestovskii region in second echelon.

21 prisoners were seized from 107th IR.

278th RD (without one RR) is occupying cut-off positions in the Krasnoe region – and captured Bubnov, Peklina, and Marker 196.7 region by day's end.

Headquarters of the division – Lipovka.

299th RD, while overcoming stubborn enemy resistance, captured Nikol'skaia Sloboda and Krasnoe by the end of the day.

Headquarters of the division – the depot 3 kilometers south of Zhukovka.

121st TB, while operating along the Briansk-Roslavl' main road, destroyed up to two artillery batteries, one mortar battery, and a company of infantry in the Sharovka and Dutseevka region, while suffering insignificant losses. The brigade concentrated behind 299th RD's right wing

290th RD (without one regiment) is being concentrated in the Bereshovskii region and the woods to the northeast.

258th RD and 260th RDs are defending the (incl.) Zhukovka, Stolby, Ratnaia, and Dmitrovo line. The enemy is displaying no activity.

55th CD is concentrated in the Krasnoe, Sosnovka, and Subbotovo region.

Third. 3rd Army, while repelling enemy attacks toward Vitovka, P'ianyi Rog, and Kotovka, continued regrouping and filling out units on 3 September, while preparing for active offensive operations.

280th RD, while repelling attacks by an enemy force of up to two IRs and a battalion of tanks and having abandoned P'ianyi Rog, occupies the Sloboda, Pozhuevo, Putilovskii, Ol'govka, Kovalevka, and Smelyi line.

Headquarters of the division – the woods 1 kilometer northwest of Krasnyi Rog.

269th RD, while repelling enemy attacks from the direction of P'ianyi Rog, occupied defenses along the southern bank of the Rozhok River (south of P'ianyi Rog) and Krasnyi Stiag by day's end on 3 September.

Headquarters of the division – the woods 1 kilometer northeast of Kotovka.

282nd RD was fighting along the Parovichi, Alad'ino, Filippovichi, and Kartashevskii line by day's end on 3 September.

137th RD is defending the southeastern outskirts of Trubchevsk with one regiment, and the division's remaining forces and headquarters are concentrated in the woods southeast of Trubchevsk.

148th RD is filling out in the Saltanovka region.

Fourth. The Mobile Group fought with an enemy tank group in the Koruzha, Bobovnia, and Uzha region during the day on 3 September.

108th TD, while fighting in isolation from other formations in the Karbovka region on 2 and 3 September, concentrated in the woods south of Brusnichnyi by day's end on 3 September, from which it went on the attack toward Gruzdovtsy and Kartashevskii at 2300 hours on 3 September, with the mission of destroying the enemy and linking up with 141st TB. The results of the fighting are unknown.

141st TB, while assisting 108th TD's withdrawal from combat, was fighting with enemy tanks in the Gruzdovtsy, Seleno, and Kartashova region at day's end on 3 September.

4th CD is putting itself into order in the Radinsk region.

Detailed reports have not been received from the group about the course of the fighting, losses, and trophies as of the morning of 4 September.

The group was transferred to the subordination of 3rd Army's commander.

Fifth. 13th Army is fighting to destroy the enemy group, which occupied Novyi Vasil'evskii and has been developing an offensive toward Znob Station, and, in the remaining sectors, the enemy is displaying no activity.

21st CD is continuing to defend the eastern bank of the Desna River in the Poruba and Borzovka sector with a detachment of 260 men, and the division's remaining forces concentrated in the woods east of Zhikhov on 3 September.

155th RD – up to a battalion of enemy infantry pushed the division's units from Kholmy by day's end on 2 September, but the enemy was driven from Kholmy by a night attack. The division occupied Bonzonka and Kholmy by day's end on 3 September.

Headquarters of the division – Melichi.

307th RD was defending the Karnaukhovka, Znob Station, and northern outskirts of Znob-Trubchevskaia line by day's end on 3 September.

6th RD, having protected the Delevki, Kamenskaia Sloboda, and Krymskii Bor line, went on the attack toward Novyi Vasil'evskii on the morning of 2 September, but news has not been received about the division's positions by day's end on 3 September.

50th TD, after the battle for Novyi Vasil'evskii, withdrew to the Liubakhov and Vasil'evskaia line under the pressure of heavy enemy fire, while preparing to go on the attack, together with 6th RD, toward Novyi Vasil'evskii on the morning of 4 September.

Headquarters of the division – the woods south of Kusten'.

132nd RD went on the defense in positions from Marker 133.1 to the grove 4 kilometers south of Birin.

Headquarters of the division – the woods north of Birin.

143rd RD, having received 608 replacement bayonets, occupied defenses from Marker 161.8 to Kalievka, Dubovka, and Marker 149.0, and the unarmed personnel of the division are being concentrated in the woods north of Seredina Buda.

Headquarters of the division – Dubrovka.

52nd CD – no information received.

121st RD – filling out in the Suzemka region.

Sixth. 21st Army continued its offensive toward Avdeevka and Semenovka with its right wing, with the mission of defeating the opposing enemy and reaching link up with 13th Army with its left wing.

On the left wing, part of the force is withdrawing toward Lozovka under heavy enemy pressure.

The Cavalry Group – 32nd, 43rd, and 47th CDs, in cooperation with 67th RC, attacked toward Orlovka and captured Lusiki and Zhuklia by the morning of 3 September.

67th RC – there is no information about the results of its attack.

28th RC, under heavy enemy pressure, withdrew to the woods 2 kilometers southeast of Sloboda, Trifonovichi, and Gutishche Station line by the morning of 3 September.

187th RD went over to the defense in positions from the woods 2 kilometers southeast of Sloboda to Tikhonovichi.

217th RD went on the defense in positions from (incl.) Tikhonovichi to (incl.) Lozovka.

117th RD went on the defense on the Lozovka and Gutishche Station line.

66th RC, while repelling enemy attacks, is holding onto the Shchors, Novyi Mliny, Rogozka 2, Morgulichi, and Borki line.

No detailed information has been received about the results of the fighting or the losses and trophies for 3 September.

Headquarters of the army – Mena.

Seventh. The VVS of the *front* – information has not been received about the operations by aviation on 3 September:

Ninth. Communications – wire is working with interruptions because of the destruction of wire by enemy aircraft.

> The Chief of Staff of the Briansk Front, Major General Zakharov
> The Commissar of the *front's* headquarters,
>   Battalion Commissar Kuznetsov
> For the Chief of the Operations Department, Major Grigor'ev

Source: "Operativnaia svodka shtaba Brianskogo Fronta No. 032 k 6 chasam 4 sentiabria 1941 g. o boevykh deistviiakh voisk fronta" [Operational summary no. 032 of the headquarters of the Briansk Front at 0600 hours on 4 September 1941 about the combat operations of the *front's* forces], *SBDVOV*, issue 43, 74-77.

64. Combat Report No. 038 of the Headquarters of 21st Army to the Headquarters of the Briansk Front of 4 September 1941 about the Reasons for Abandoning Semenovka and the Necessity for Supporting the Army with Weapons and Ammunition

To the Chief of Staff of the Briansk Front
Combat Report No. 038, Headquarters, 21st Army,
Mena,
1025 hours on 4 September 1941
1:100,000 scale map

1. In accordance with your order to attack toward Semenovka with no fewer than three divisions for a link up with 13th Army, a regrouping of the army's units to the right wing was carried out.

42nd, 24th, and 277th RDs were allocated for fulfilling this mission, and the Cavalry Group (47th, 43rd, and 32nd CDs) was committed toward Semenovka.

The units went on the attack on 29 August 1941 and were fighting on the Kudrovka, Rudnia, and Gutishche line (24th and 42nd RDs) by day's end on 30 August.

277th RD captured Semenovka on 30 August and held onto it for three days. The enemy went on the attack with large forces (10th MotD and 3rd and 4th PzDs' units) along 67th RC's front on 2 September 1941, and the corps' units began to withdraw under enemy pressure. The fighting here was intense and prolonged in nature. As a result, 277th RD turned out to be isolated, with superior enemy forces on their front, and occupied unfavorable positions. Thus, the link up with 13th Army's units in the Semenovka region did not occur, and, while being counterattacked by SS units, 277th RD abandoned Semenovka on the night of 2-3 September and was forced to withdraw to the Zhuklia, Chenniki, Siadrina, and Spichevatovo line.

2. The army is continuing its offensive on the morning of 4 September from the Hill 185.5, Os'maki, and Avdeevka line, and, in the center and on the left wing, has

the mission to restore the situation and firmly hold on to the Zhuklia, Chenniki, Siadrina, Spichevatovo, Naumovka, Shchors, Leninovka, Begach, and Borki line.

3. I am reporting that, in connection with the scattering of the units, the vastly expanded front, the absence of reserves, and the heavy losses which the units have suffered in the recent fighting, a situation exists which, in the event of the smallest penetration, the units, which are extended along the front without supporting reserves, will be forced to withdraw.

4. I request you speed up 13th Army's offensive toward Semenovka, support the army's offensive with aviation, provide the army with ammunition and equipment, especially automatic weapons and mortars, and define the army's operational boundaries and the army's rear area.

> The Chief of Staff of 21st Army, Major General Gordov
> The Commissar of 21st Army's headquarters,
>   Regimental Commissar Mandrik
> The Chief of the Operations Department, Lieutenant Colonel Posiakin

Source: "Boevoe donesenie shtaba 21-i Armii shtabu Brianskogo Fronta No. 038 ot 4 sentiabria 1941 g. o prichinakh ostavleniia Semenovka i neobkhodimosti obespecheniia armii vooruzheniem i boepripasami [Combat report No. 038 of the headquarters of 21st Army to the headquarters of the Briansk Front of 4 September 1941 about the reasons for abandoning Semenovka and the necessity for supporting the army with weapons and ammunition], *SBDVOV*, issue 43, 345.

65. *Stavka* VGK Directive No. 001643 of 4 September 1941 about Leaving Petrov's Aviation Group at the Disposal of the Briansk Front's Commander until the Final Destruction of Group Guderian

To Briansk, to Eremenko for Petrov

The aviation is operating well, but it would operate even better if the scouts [*razvedchiki*] could summon bombers quickly by radio and not when they land at their airfields.

You must remain in the Briansk Front until the completion of the *front's* operations to destroy Guderian.

I wish you success.

My regards to all of the pilots.

> I. Stalin

Source: "Direktiva Stavki VGK No. 001643 ot 4 sentiabria 1941 g. ob ostavlenii aviatsionnoi gruppy Petrova v rasporiazhenii komanduiushchego voiskami Brianskogo Fronta do okonchaniia razgroma gruppy Guderiana" [*Stavka* VGK Directive No. 001643 of 4 September 1941 about leaving Petrov's aviation group at the disposal of the Briansk Front's commander until the final destruction of Group Guderian], *SBDVOV*, issue 43, 14.

66. Combat Order of the Commander of the Forces of 21st Army No. 065 of 5 September 1941 on Withdrawing the Army's Forces to the Southern Bank of the Desna River

Combat Order No. 065, Headquarters, 21st Army,

Borzna,

1300 hours on 5 September 1941

1:100,000 and 500,000 scale maps

1. The army is going on the defense with its forward edge on the Shabalinovo, Staraia Butovka, Volovitsa, Saltykova Devitsa, and Kovchin front on the southern bank of the Desna River, with the mission of regrouping the army's units to the right wing and a subsequent offensive.

2. On the right, 40th Army's units are fighting on the Altynovka, Korop, and Iakovlinichi line.

On the left, 5th Army's units are fighting along the Iatsevo, Pevtsy, and Novyi Belous line.

3. 67th RC will occupy and firmly defend the Shabalinovo and Novaia Butovka line. [Have] forward detachments in the Progony, Novosel'e, and Slobodka sector on the northern bank of the Desna River. Have one rifle division in reserve in the Baturin, Novyi Mlyny, and Trostanka region.

The boundary on the left: Shapovalovka, Novaia Butovka, and (incl.) Domashlin.

CP of 67th RC – Galaibin.

4. 28th RC will occupy and firmly defend the (incl.) Novaia Butovka and (incl.) Volovitsa line. [Have] forward detachments in the Baba, Leski, and Os'maki sector on the northern bank of the Desna River. Have one rifle division in corps reserve in the Zabolotovo, Adamovka, and the woods (3 kilometers south of Zabolotovo) region.

The boundary on the left: Komarovka, (incl.) Ushnia, and (incl.) Siniavka.

CP of 28th RC – Krasnostav.

5. 66th RC will occupy and firmly defend the Volovitsa, Saltykova Devitsa, Kovchin, and Gorobov line.

[Have] forward detachments in Burkovka, Gusavka, and Borki.

Have one RR in reserve in the Vershina Muraveika region.

The boundary on the left: Drozdovka, Vershina Muraveika, Brusilovo, and Vykhvostovo.

CP of 66th RC – Veresoch'.

6. The Cavalry Group will concentrate in the Karatsubin, Atiusha, and Matievka region in readiness to attack toward the east and southeast.

CP of the Cavalry Group – Matievka.

7. 266th RD, with 696th ATR – my reserve, concentrated in the Koshmalev, Strel'niki, and Ukrainskii village regions.

8. 214th AbnB, after being relieved by 67th RC's units, will concentrate in my reserve in the Shapovalovka region.

9. Corps commanders, within the boundariies of the Zmetnev, Lavy, Baba, Mena, Voloskovichi, Berezna, and Borki line, will hold out with strong forward detachments until the complete evacuation of the units to the southern bank of the

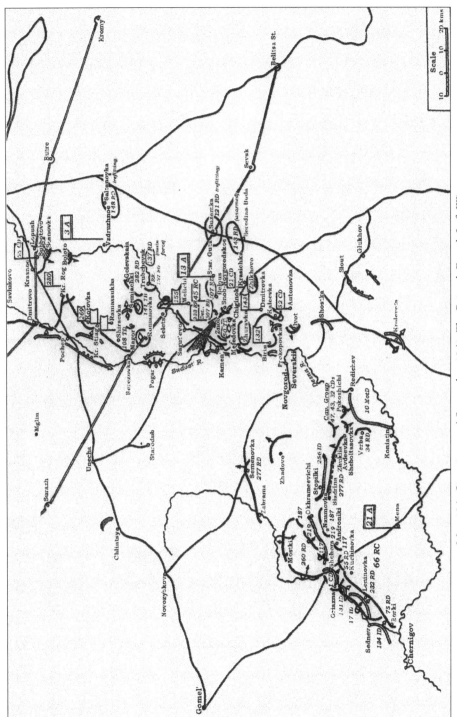

Map 10A: Situation on 4 September 1941. The Briansk Front's Left Wing.

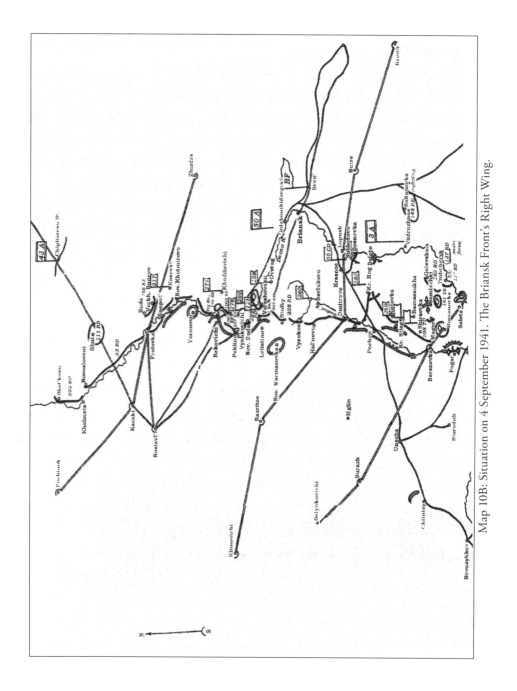

Map 10B: Situation on 4 September 1941. The Briansk Front's Right Wing.

Desna River and [until] the organization of defenses. Any withdrawals by units from this line will be only with my permission.

10. Appoint commandants for each crossing and compile graphics [plans] for the crossings of the transports and units.

Completely eliminate concentrations of forces and transports at the crossings. After the complete evacuation, demolish the bridges on the instructions of corps and division commanders. The commander of 28th RC will demolish the railroad bridge at Makoshino only with my permission.

11. While organizing defenses on the forward edge, plan to occupy all islets by the units in order to prevent the enemy from crossing the Desna River.

Set about strengthening the [defense] line in an engineer sense, and prepare full-profile trenches for platoons and companies.

12. Submit orders of battle of the units by 0600 hours on 6 September.

13. The protection of the boundary with 40th Army is entrusted to 67th RC and with 5th Army to 66th RC.

14. Headquarters of the army – Borzna, and reserve headquarters – Ivangorod.

> The Commander of 21st Army, Lieutenant General Kuznetsov
> The Member of the Military Council, Division Commissar Kolonin
> The Chief of Staff of 21st Army, Major General Gordov

Source: "Boevoe rasporiazhenie komanduiushchego voiskami 21-i Armii No. 065 ot 5 sentiabria 1941 g. na otvod voisk armii na iuzhnyi bereg r Desna [Combat order of the commander of the forces of 21st Army No. 065 of 5 September 1941 on withdrawing the army's forces to the southern bank of the Desna River], *SBDVOV*, issue 43, 346-347.

67. Combat Report of the Commander of the Forces of 21st Army No. 040 of 5 September 1941 about the Results of the Army's Combat Operations and its Decision to Withdraw Behind the Desna River

Combat Report No. 040, Headquarters, 21st Army,
Borzna
5 September 1941
1:100,000 and 500,000 scale maps

1. The enemy resumed his offensive along the entire front on the morning of 5 September and delivered his main attack toward Rudnia, Chernotichi, Lavy, Naumovka, Kopiukovka, Boromyki, and Berezna.

Enemy motorized infantry, with the support of tanks, captured Sosnitsa at 1800 hours and is trying to reach the crossings at Maloe Uste and Makoshino. Up to two RRs are advancing from Siniavka towards Mena.

2. The army conducted sustained fighting during the day, while repelling enemy attacks along the Zmetnev, Kudrovka, Matveevka, Siadrina, Alekseevka, Nizkovka, Berezna, and Begach line.

The units occupied [the following] by 2100 hours:

67th RC was fighting with enemy which have penetrated toward Chernotichi and Volynka with separate groups, and part of the corps' forces was holding off an enemy onslaught in the Matveevka region.

Units of 10th MotD and the SS and tank groups from 3rd and 4th PzDs are operating on the corps' front.

The Cavalry Group, together with 277th RD, cut off the enemy's Chernotichi group from the crossing at Rudnia by a blow along the Ubed' River at 1600 hours on 5 September.

28th RC fought along the Budennovka, Koriukovka, and Buda-Tovstolesova line, and, as a result of a strong enemy attack, the corps was forced to abandon these points and withdraw to the Liubenets, Tiutnitsa, Aleksandrovka, and Siniavka line.

66th RC, after a fierce battle along the Gorodishche, Berezna, and Boromyki line, withdrew under enemy pressure and occupied Os'maki, Podin Farm, and Lake Ol'shanoe.

3. In connection with the enemy's penetration of the army's front and his arrival at the crossing over the Desna River, we decided: to withdraw the army behind the Desna River and carry out a regrouping to its right wing, with the aim of resisting the enemy's Novgorod-Severskii, Korop, and Sosnovka grouping, while at the same time destroying the penetrating enemy.

> The Commander of 21st Army, Lieutenant General Kuznetsov
> The Member of the Military Council, Division Commissar Kolonin
> The Chief of Staff of 21st Army, Major General Gordov

Source: "Boevoe donesenie komanduiushchego voiskami 21-i Armii No. 040 ot 5 sentiabria 1941 g. o rezul'tatakh boevykh deistvii voisk armii i priniatom reshenii na ikh otvod za r. Desna [Combat report of the commander of the forces of 21st Army No. 040 of 5 September 1941 about the results of the army's combat operations and its decision to withdraw behind the Desna River], *SBDVOV*, issue 43, 347-348.

68. Operational Summary No. 035 of the Headquarters of the Briansk Front at 2000 hours on 5 September 1941 about the Combat Operations of the *Front's* Forces

Operational Summary No. 035 at 2000 hours on 5 September 1941,
Headquarters, Briansk Front, (**see Map 10**)
1: 100,000 and 50,000 scale maps

First. On the *front's* right wing, in the process of attacking, 50th Army's shock group had no success on 5 September, having encountered organized enemy resistance and counterattacks.

In the *front's* central sector, 3rd and 13th Armies' forces fought fierce battles from 3-5 September to destroy the enemy in the [following] regions:
1) P'ianyi Rog, Semtsy, and Krasnaia Sloboda;
2) Semiachki, Uzha, and Sosnovka; and
3) Znob Station and Novyi Vasil'evskii.

On the *front's* left wing, 21st Army's forces are fighting to destroy the enemy's Semenovka-Korop Grouping, with the mission to reach and unite with 13th Army's forces.

Second. 50th Army is continuing to defend its previous positions firmly with its right and left wings.

The central grouping fought all day on 5 September, while encountering stubborn resistance and counterattacks by the enemy, who brought fresh forces forward (presumably, 78th ID). By day's end, the forces remained in the positions they reached by day's end on 4 September.

217th RD continues to defend positions from Frolovka to Sviatki, 5 kilometers northeast of Rekovichi. The enemy is not displaying active resistance.

Headquarters of the division – Kosevat.

279th RD, while repelling a counterattack by an enemy force of up to one IR, supported by 4-5 batteries of artillery, from the Salyn' Station and Malaia Salyn' axis, captured the Rekovichi Platform, Vilki, and Berestok line at 1400 hours on 5 September.

Headquarters of the division – Brubachi.

278th RD (without one RR) was counterattacked on its left wing by an enemy force of up to an IR, supported by 7-8 artillery and 7-8 mortar batteries, from Peklino on the morning of 5 September, and, after repelling the counterattack, the division occupied the Bubnov, Baranovka, Hill 187.0, and Suma line by 1400 hours on 5 September. Its 855th RR has transferred to the control of the commander of 3rd Army and shifted to the Sloboda Popsueva region.

The division suffered up to 1,280 men lost from 2-5 September.

299th RD conducted sustained fighting with the enemy along the northeastern outskirts of Ol'khovka, Novaia Buda, and Krasnoe line.

290th RD, while repelling enemy counterattacks, occupies positions from the woods 1 kilometer north of Sileevka to Antoshkin and to the western edge of the woods 1 kilometer east of Pervomaiskii by day's end.

121st TB did not conduct active operations during the day. There is no information about its losses. By day's end on 5 September, the brigade was situated in the woods southeast of Letoshniki.

258th RD is defending the Stolby and Dmitrovo line. It is moving a reinforced battalion to positions on Hill 178.8 (2 kilometers west of Dmitrovo) to protect the boundary between 50th and 3rd Armies.

55th CD is concentrated in the Krasnoe, Sosnovka, and Subbotovo region.

Headquarters of 50th Army – Paikovichi.

Third. 3rd Army has been fighting on 4 and 5 September to destroy the enemy's 17th PzD, which has been attacking from Pochep toward Trubchevsk.

280th RD is fighting to destroy the enemy in the Volzhino, Ustinovo, and Boriki region and occupied the Sloboda Popsueva, Muravka, Podluzh'e, Korolevka, and Dyriavyi Ganzha line by the end of the day.

Headquarters of the division – Krasnyi Rog.

269th RD is fighting to destroy the enemy west of P'ianyi Rog with its right wing and occupied the P'ianyi Rog, Zelenyi Rog, Hill 164.6, and Krasnyi Bor line by day's end on 5 September.

Headquarters of the division – the woods north of Kotovka.

4th CD went on the attack toward Shchetinino on the morning of 4 September and, while counterattacked by enemy tanks from Molchanovo, occupied the Radchino and Radinsk line by day's end on 5 September.

282nd RD, while repelling an enemy counterattack from the direction of Semiachki and Kalachovka, occupied the Parovichi and Vlasova line by day's end on 5 September.

141st TB, while repelling counterattacks by enemy tanks from the direction of Emel'ianovka, Sosnovka, and Khot'ianovka, is fighting along the Kartashova, Filippovichi, and Kvetun' front.

137th RD had no success in its attack, and, while counterattacked by the enemy, it withdrew to the Perednie, Progress, and Hill 187.0 line by day's end on 5 September.

108th TD is fighting in the region southwest of Brusnichnyi and Pokrovskii encircled by enemy tanks.

Headquarters of 3rd Army – Vzdruzhnoe.

Fourth. 13th Army is fighting local battles to destroy the enemy in the Znob Station and Novyi Vasil'evskii region.

45th RC is fighting to destroy the Novyi Vasil'evskii group of enemy.

155th RD, with a battalion of 307th RD subordinated to it, is attacking toward Znob Station, having repelled an enemy counterattack from Znob Station and was fighting for Znob Station at day's end on 5 September.

Losses: 23 men wounded.

Headquarters of the division – Melichi.

50th TD, while repelling enemy counterattacks, withdrew to the Liubakhov and Vasil'evskii line by day's end on 5 September.

Losses: 78 killed and 200 wounded.

Trophies: 12 vehicles and 4 motorcycles burned and two enemy batteries put out of action.

6th RD, while repelling enemy counterattacks, was fighting for the Chervonyi and mouth of the Znobovka River line by the end of the day on 5 September.

Losses – 117 men wounded.

Headquarters of the division – Chervonyi.

Headquarters of the corps – the woods north of Belousovka.

132nd RD is continuing to dig into defensive positions from the woods southwest of Birin to the woods north of Prokopovka.

Losses – 22 men wounded.

Headquarters of the division – the woods north of Birin.

143rd RD's 635th RR is preparing a defense along the Marker 159.5 (2 kilometers south of Kolievka) and Marker 161.4 line. 800th RR is defending along the Marker 137.5 (3 kilometers east of Glazov) and Marker 149.0 line (2 kilometers southeast of Ivot).

52nd CD – is defending the Marker 161.5 and Pen'k (2 kilometers southeast of Ivot) line.

Headquarters of the division – the woods east of Antonovka.

121st RD – filling out in the woods south of Suzemka.

21st CD is preparing cut-off positions along the Lesnoe and Rudnia line.

Headquarters of the division – the woods south of Efaniia.

Headquarters of 13th Army – Staraia Guta.

Fifth. 21st Army – No news received about the positions of its forces.

Sixth. 298th RD reserve – in the Diat'kovo region.

Seventh. The VVS of the *front* – information has not been received about aviation operations on 5 September:

Eighth. Communications – wire with 50th, 3rd, and 13th Armies is reliable, and only radio with 21st Army.

> The Chief of Staff of the Briansk Front, Major General Zakharov
> The Commissar of the *front's* headquarters,
>   Battalion Commissar Kuznetsov
> The Deputy Chief of the Operations Department, Colonel Dolgov

Source: "Operativnaia svodka shtaba Brianskogo Fronta No. 035 k 20 chasam 5 sentiabria 1941 g. o boevykh deistviiakh voisk fronta" [Operational summary no. 035 of the headquarters of the Briansk Front at 2000 hours on 5 September 1941 about the combat operations of the *front's* forces], *SBDVOV*, issue 43, 77-79.

69. *Stavka* VGK Directive No. 001650 to the Commander of the Forces of the Briansk Front Permitting the Creation of Blocking Detachments

5 September 1941

The *Stavka* has familiarized itself with your memorandum and permits you to create blocking detachments in those divisions, which, by their behavior, seem to be unsteady. The aim of the blocking detachments is to prevent willful withdrawal of units and, in instances of flight [running away] – is to stop it by using all necessary weapons.

The matter of attaching artillery battalions to rifle companies is being discussed, and the *Stavka's* decision will be reported to you additionally.

> For the *Stavka* of the Supreme High Command,
> Chief of the General Staff, B. Shaposhnikov

Source: "Direktiva Stavki VGK No. 001650 komanduiushchemu voiskami Brianskogo fronta, razreshaiushchaia sozdanii zagraditel'nykh otriadov" [*Stavka* VGK Directive no. 001650 to the commander of the forces of the Briansk Front permitting the creation of blocking detachments], in Zolotarev, "*Stavka* 1941," 164.

70. *Stavka* VGK Directive No. 001661 to the Commander of the Forces of the Briansk Front and the Deputy Commander of the Red Army's VVS about Strengthening the *Front* with Aviation and Creating Reserves

0700 hours on 5 September 1941

The Supreme High Commander has ordered:

1. Two regiments of Ils – one from Rzhev and the other from Voronezh, and two regiments of fighters – one from Kursk and one from Moscow, are being transferred to our disposal today, 5 September.

2. It aircraft reinforcements are being given to you exclusively with the mission to smash and destroy Guderian into the ground.

3. 298th RD will follow to remain in reserve, for one cannot fight without a reserve. The fresh division, which will be sent to Kursk, must also remain in reserve in the Briansk region so that it can be brought up to a full combat condition.

4. 21st Army will remain at your disposal, but it is necessary to control it firmly, have good communications with it, and help it mainly with aviation while it is fulfilling the missions you assign to it.

> For the *Stavka* of the Supreme High Command,
> Chief of the General Staff, B. Shaposhnikov

Source: "Direktiva Stavki VGK No. 001661 komanduiushchemu voiskami Brianskogo Fronta, zamestiteliu komanduiushchego VVS Krasnoi Armii ob usilenii fronta aviatsiei i sozdanii rezervov" [*Stavka* VGK Directive No. 001661 to the commander of the forces of the Briansk Front and the deputy commander of the Red Army's VVS about strengthening the *front* with aviation and creating reserves], in Zolotarev, "*Stavka* 1941," 164.

71. *Stavka* VGK Directive No. 001697 to the Commanders of the Forces of the Briansk and Southwestern Fronts about Re-subordinating 21st Army
0400 hours on 6 September 1941

By order of the Supreme High Command, the Briansk Front's 21st Army is transferred to the subordination of the Southwestern Front's commander effective 1400 hours on 6 September.

21st Army will retain the mission to attack toward the northeast with the forces of three RDs and the cavalry group for destroying the rear areas of the enemy 3rd and 4th PzDs.

The boundary line between the Briansk and Southwestern Fronts will be established along the Kursk, L'gov, Glukhov, Tereshchenskaia Station, and Novozybkov line. All points are inclusive for the Briansk Front.

Confirm receipt of this order.

> For the *Stavka* of the Supreme High Command,
> Chief of the General Staff, B. Shaposhnikov

Source: "Direktiva Stavki VGK No. 001697 komanduiushchemu voiskami Brianskogo I Iugo-Zapadnogo frontov o perepodchinenii 21-i Armii" [*Stavka* VGK Directive No. 001697 to the commanders of the forces of the Briansk and Southwestern Fronts about re-subordinating 21st Army], in Zolotarev, "*Stavka* 1941," 165.

72. Supreme High Command Order to the Commander of the Forces of the Briansk Front about Improving the Organization of Combat Operations and Withdrawing 108th Tank Division from Encirclement
0600 hours on 6 September 1941

I know that 108th Tank Division has fallen into encirclement and has lost many tanks and crews. This could have occurred only because of bad management on your part, [because] you must not launch a division into the attack by itself having not protected its flanks or having not supported it with aircraft. If aircraft could not fly in light of bad weather, you should have postponed the tank division's attack until the weather improved and aircraft were available to support the tank division. Henceforth, I oblige you not to tolerate such rash actions. I also oblige you to find a way to rescue the *tankists* and as many of the tanks as possible from the encirclement. Also consider that the reference to pilots in bad weather is not always correct. *Shturmoviki* [assault aircraft] can fly even during bad weather if the visibility is not less than 100-150 meters. Tell Comrade Petrov that I oblige him to refer to bad weather less, and that it is a little better to employ *Shturmoviki* [assault aircraft] for flights in bad weather.

> I. Stalin
> B. Shaposhnikov

Source: "Rasporiazhenie Verkhovnogo Glavnokomanduiushchego komanduiushchemu voiskami Brianskogo Fronta ob uluchshenii organizatsii boevykh deistvii i vyvode iz okruzheniia 108-i tankovoi divizii" [Supreme High Command order to the commander of the forces of the Briansk Front about improving the organization of combat operations and withdrawing 108th Tank Division from encirclement] in Zolotarev, "*Stavka* 1941," 165.

73. Combat Order No. 068 of the Commander of the Forces of 13th Army of 6 September 1941 on Destroying the Enemy in the Vicinity of Znob Station, Novyi Vasil'evskii, Podgornyi, and Svirzh

Combat Order No. 068, Headquarters, 13th Army
0745 hours on 6 September 1941
1:100,000 scale

1. The enemy at the boundary between 13th and 21st Armies along the Glukhov and Konotop axes is continuing to bring his forces forward, and, simultaneously, 29th MotD is firmly holding on to the bridgehead it seized on the eastern bank of the Desna River at Novyi Vasil'evskii and Znob Station.

Protection [covering forces] has been left in front of 13th Army's left wing.

2. On the right, 3rd Army is fighting on the approaches to Pochep.

On the left, 21st Army is conducting an offensive toward Semenovka with its right wing. The boundaries with them are as before.

3. 13th Army, while defending on its right wing, will destroy the enemy at Novyi Vasil'evskii and Znob Station and destroy the enemy covering forces in the Prokopovka, Podgornyi, and Svirzh region with its left wing.

4. 45th RC, while firmly holding onto the line of the Desna River on the Porubo and Karnaukhovka front, will destroy the enemy's 29th MotD, which has penetrated to the eastern bank of the Desna River in the vicinity of Znob Station, Novyi Vasil'evskii, and Ukrainskii, with the forces of one regiment of 307th RD, and 155th RD, 50th TD, and 6th RD.

Contain the enemy at Znob Station with one regiment of 307th RD.

Direct 155th RD's efforts from the line of the Chern' River and Znob-Trubchevskaia through the woods toward the railroad and Novyi Vasil'evskii, and attack from south to north with your remaining forces.

The infantry attack will be at 1500 hours on 6 September 1941.

5. 132nd RD will continue to destroy the covering forces of the enemy's main forces in the woods southeast of Birin and to the south of Prokopovka more actively, unit by unit. It has the mission, in cooperation with 143rd RD, to destroy the enemy in the Podgornyi, Hill 153.2, and Prokopovka region by day's end on 6 September 1941.

6. 143rd RD will direct the efforts of the division's forces to assist in destroying the enemy south of Prokopovka.

It has the mission, in cooperation with 132nd RD, to capture Svirzh.

7. 52nd CD will continue to tie down the enemy at Ivot and conduct active reconnaissance toward Gamaleevka, Usok, and Iampol'.

8. 21st CD will continue to improve its defense and increase the number of obstacles in its previous positions.

9. 307th RD, without one regiment, which is operating toward Znob, will withdrew into the woods east of Stiarailovka, where it will continue to put itself in order.

10. 121st RD will fill out in its present region.

11. The Chief of Artillery will suppress enemy firing point with all of the army's artillery in front of 155th RD's, 50th RD's, and 6th RD's defensive front during the day.

Conduct a powerful fire raid before the attack.

During the period of the offensive, constantly support 45th RC's attacking units with fire and maneuver [of fire].

12. The VVS of the army.

1) Conduct reconnaissance of the enemy in the Sagut'evo, Pogar, and Starodub, and Novgorod-Severskii region during the day, with the mission of revealing enemy movements and concentrations.

2) During the course of the day, suppress the enemy along the southern edge of the woods southwest of Znob-Trubchevskaia, from the crossroads and the railroad to Znob Station, with methodical raids by assault and bomber aircraft; and, with the approach of infantry, direct the VVS's efforts at destroying the enemy at Novyi Vasil'evskii and the crossings.

3) Smash the headquarters of enemy groups in the monastery in Novgorod-Severskii.

13. Report about the course of fulfilling this order to the army's headquarters every hour.

14. CP of the army's headquarters is in its previous location.

The Commander of 13th Army, Major General Gorodniansky
The Member of the Military Council, Brigade Commissar Furt
The Chief of Staff of 13th Army, *Kombrig* Petrushevsky

Source: "Boevoi prikaz komanduiushchego voiskami 13-i Armii No. 068 ot 6 sentiabria 1941 g. na unichtozhenie protivnika v raione Stantsii Znob, Novyi Vasil'evskii, Podgornyi, Svirzh" [Combat order no. 068 of the commander of the forces of 13th Army of 6 September 1941 on destroying the enemy in the vicinity of Znob Station, Novyi Vasil'evskii, Podgornyi, and Svirzh], *SBDVOV*, issue 43, 305-306.

74. Operational Summary No. 037 of the Headquarters of the Briansk Front at 2000 hours on 6 September 1941 about the Combat Operations of the *Front's* Forces

Operational Summary No. 037 at 2000 hours on 6 September 1941,

Headquarters, Briansk Front,

1: 100,000 and 50,000 scale maps

First. The *front's* armies are continuing an offensive toward Novyi Vasil'evskii and P'ianyi Rog on the Roslavl' axis and are fortifying the positions they occupy in the remaining sectors of the front.

Second. 50th Army, while defending on its flanks, continued an offensive toward Roslavl' on the morning of 6 September.

217th RD is defending positions along the eastern bank of the Desna River on the Rozhnia, Moksheevo, and Sviatki front. The units of the [enemy] 258th ID are not conducting active operations on the division's front.

Headquarters of the division – Kosevat.

279th RD, while continuing its attack, captured Rekovichi by 0900 hours on 6 September and, failing to achieve success in its center and on its left wing, occupies positions from Rekovichi to Marker 193.4 (1 kilometer south of Rekovichi Station), and Berestok at 1400 hours on 6 September, while having the enemy's 107th IR on its front.

Headquarters of the division – Trubachi.

278th RD failed to achieve success in its attack and, at 1400 hours on 6 September, occupies positions from Bubnov, (incl.) to Peklina, and (incl.) Novosel'e. Units of the enemy's 34th ID are on its front.

Headquarters of the division – the woods 2 kilometers northwest of Vyshkovichi.

299th RD, after going on the attack, occupies the Ol'khovka, Nikolaevskaia Sloboda, "Muk" (at Novaia Buda), and (incl.) Krasnoe line, while having 34th and 78th IDs' units on its front.

Headquarters of the division – the woods 3-4 kilometers southwest of Zhukovka.

121st TB is operating in cooperation with 299th RD at 1330 hours on 6 September and is situated in the woods southeast of Letoshniki.

290th RD is fortifying the positions it occupies along the Antoshkin and Pervomaiskii line.

Headquarters of the division – the woods 1.5 kilometers southeast of Letoshniki.

258th RD is defending the Komsomol'skii, (incl.) Mokraia, and (incl.) Stolby line, while having 78th ID's units on its front.

Headquarters of the division – Ovstug.

260th RD is defending the Stolby, Ishchova, and Boguchevo front, while having the enemy's 82nd IR on its front.

Headquarters of the division – Krasnyi Pakhar'.

55th CD occupies the region of cut-off positions [at]: Pokrovka, Khmelevo, and Sosnovka.

Headquarters of the division – Miakishevo.

Third. 3rd Army put itself into order during the day and is preparing for an offensive during the might.

280th RD and 269th RD – positions are unchanged.

Trophies in 280th RD: 2 light vehicles, 2 motorcycles, 1 heavy machine gun, 3 tractors, and 4 prisoners.

282nd RD occupies the Kalachevka, Seleno, Kolodezki, and Kvetun' line.

Trophies: 4 mortars, 5 rifles, 2 automatic weapons, and 1 prisoner.

Destroyed artillery: 21 enemy tanks, 1 armored vehicle, one mortar battery, 1 battery of 75mm guns.

Losses: 1 man killed and 21 men wounded.

141st TB is in the Kartasheva region.

The brigade has: tanks KV – 3, T-34 – 14, and BT – 21 tanks and BA-10 [armored car] – 1.

Tanks lost in combat on 5 September – 10.

108th TD reached the woods southeast of Orekhovskii with part of its forces.

The division has: KVs – 2, T-34 – 10, and T-40 – 4 and BA-10 – 3 and BA -20 [armored cars] – 2, for a total of 21 machines.

In addition, the motorized rifle regiment has 16 vehicles and 700 men. GEP and TEP [fuel and lubricants] are fully maintained.

137th RD is occupying the Tishino and Ozhigovo line.

Trophies: 4 mortars and 2 automatic weapons.

4th CD – reached the Polovetskie region, 4 kilometers north of Karun'.

148th RD – positions as before.

The same enemy units as before are continuing to operate against 3rd Army.

According to information from the VVS, a motorized column 12 kilometers in length was moving from Semtsy toward Mostochnoe at 1800 hours.

Headquarters of 3rd Army – Orlinka.

Fourth. 13th Army's forces fortified their positions on the morning of 6 September and conducted preparations for an offensive which will begin at 1500 hours on 6 September.

155th RD, with a battalion of 307th RD, after two unsuccessful attacks on Znob Station, withdrew to its jumping-off positions. Losses: 16 men wounded.

Headquarters of the division – the woods north of Ulitsa.

50th TD, having occupied Liubakhov, continued its attack toward the north. The enemy withdrew northward opposite the division's front. There are many enemy bodies in Liubakhov.

Losses: 37 men wounded.

Headquarters of the division – the woods south of Kusten'.

6th RD occupied Ukrainskii and Vasil'evskii by the morning of 6 September. The enemy is resisting stubbornly on the division's front and has tanks in the Ukrainskii region.

Losses for 4-5 September: 35 killed and 102 wounded.

Headquarters of the division – Chervonyi.

Headquarters of 45th RC – the woods north of Belousovka.

132nd RD is fortifying its positions from the southern edge of the woods southwest of Birin to the grove north of Prokopovka on the morning of 6 September, while having 3rd PzD's 12th MotR and 17th Reserve Regiment on its front.

Trophies for 2-3 September 1941: 2 rifles, 2 RPs, 1 heavy machine gun, 1 37mm gun, 6 automatic weapons, 5 pistols, and 5 gas masks, and, on 4 September, 2 guns, 6 machine guns, 6 pistols, and 1 truck were seized.

Headquarters of the division – the woods north of Birin.

143rd RD's 635th RR occupies positions along the line of hills between Kalievka and Antonovka.

One battalion of 800th RR is preparing a line along the northern bank of the Bychikha River.

Headquarters of the division – the woods north of Dubrovka.

52nd CD is defending the Marker 161.5 (2 kilometers west of Antonovka) and "Pen'ki" (1.5 kilometers southeast of Ivot) sector.

Headquarters of the division – Antonovka.

21st CD is preparing the Lesnoe and Rudnia line.

Headquarters of the division – the woods south of Efaniia.

121st RD is filling out in the Suzemka region.

Fifth. The *front's* reserve – 298th RD in the woods west of Diat'kovo.

154th RD is filling out in the Briansk region.

Sixth. The VVS of the *front*: [conducted] a total of 139 flights, including 24 assault, 63 for bombarding columns and targets, 18 for reconnaissance, and 43 to protect the [ground] forces.

The regions of operations [were] Dubrovka, Pochep, and Trubchevsk, and reconnaissance was across the entire front.

Losses for the day – consider as unverified – one MIG-, two IAKs, 4 Ils, and one Pe-2 for a total of 8. About 80% of the bombers and assault aircraft worked in the Trubchevsk region, that is, all of the work today was concentrated in the two regions of Pochep and Mostochnaia and Trubchevsk.

Enemy shot down: one ME-109 – by ramming and one bomber by antiaircraft artillery in the Briansk region.

Seventh. There is no news about the operations of our neighbors.

21st Army was subordinated to the Southwestern Front at 1400 hours on 6 September. The left boundary of the *front*: Kursk, L'gov, Tereshchenskaia Station, and Novozybkov.

Eighth. Communications with the armies is by telephone and radios, and wire communications was disrupted at 1750 hours by enemy bombing of the communications center at Briansk.

The Chief of Staff of the Briansk Front, Major General Zakharov
The Commissar of the *front's* headquarters,
    Battalion Commissar Kuznetsov
The Chief of the Operations Department, Colonel Sandalov

Source: "Operativnaia svodka shtaba Brianskogo Fronta No. 037 k 20 chasam 6 sentiabria 1941 g. o boevykh deistviiakh voisk fronta" [Operational summary no. 037 of the headquarters of the Briansk Front at 2000 hours on 6 September 1941 about the combat operations of the *front's* forces], *SBDVOV*, issue 43, 81-83.

75. Combat Order No. 10 of the Commander of the Forces of 50th Army of 6 September 1941 on Capturing the Rekovichi, Klopotnia, Peklina, and Oleshenskii Village Line

Combat Order No. 10, Headquarters, 50th Army,
Lipovskie,
2400 hours on 6 September 1941
1:100,000 scale map

First. The enemy's 34th ID and a significant portion of 78th ID are defending in front of the shock group.

Despite the weakness of the enemy's defense and the shortcomings in his artillery, the divisions have not exploited their superiority in powerful artillery and mortar fire, they have operated sluggishly, and, although the enemy has suffered heavy losses, they have not succeeded in fully destroying the enemy's 34th ID. The 299th RD, which has been reinforced by the guards [-mortar] battalion and supported by 121st TB, operated especially unsatisfactorily. In the presence of enemy air superiority, the division's commander did not exploit those times when the aircraft were absent (twilight, first light, and night).

The group's units reached the Rekovichi Platform, Soboleva, Malaia Salyn', Hill 202.5, the eastern outskirts of Peklina, Suma, the eastern outskirts of Novaia Buda, and the grove 1 kilometer east of Pervomaiskii line by day's end on 6 September 1941.

Second. The army's shock group will continue the attack along the axes and within the limits in accordance with Order No. 09, and the divisions will reach the Rekovichi, Klopotnia, Sloboda, Peklina, and Oleshenskii village line by day's end on 7 September1941.

Third. 217th RD will protect 279th RD's right flank with one reinforced battalion, to which end it will capture and hold onto the northern outskirts of Rekovichi. The division's remaining units will fulfill their previous missions.

The boundary lines are as before.

Fourth. 279th RD, with 3rd Bn, 207th AR, while having it main grouping on its left wing, will capture and dig in along the Hill 198.4, Klopotnia, and Sloboda line. Capture Rekovichi together with the battalion from 217th RD.

The boundary line on the left is as before.

Fifth. 278th RD will capture and dig in along the Hill 200.7, Peklina, and Sergeevka line. Link up with 299th RD with your left flank and prevent the infiltration of the boundary by small enemy units.

The boundary line on the left is as before.

Sixth. 299th RD, together with 121st TB, while having its main grouping on its left wing, will destroy the enemy's 80th IR by decisive operations and capture and dig in along the Sharovka, and Oleshenskii village line.

Seventh. 258th RD will protected 299th RD's left flank with a reinforced battalion, while following echeloned behind the left wing and while extending this battalion's combat formation toward the southwest.

Eighth. 290th RD will concentrate its main forces in the vicinity of the Platform (2 kilometers southeast of Novaia Buda), Krasnoe Znamia, and Vereshovskii and, while remaining my reserve, will be prepared to repel attacks by enemy infantry and tanks from Girinski village and Leliatino and protect the group's left flank.

Have one battalion at my disposal in the Vyshkovichi and Zhukovka region.

Ninth. 121st TB will operate together with 299th RD for destroying the enemy's 80th IR and be prepared to repel attacks by enemy tanks against the group's left flank. Have the MRB [motorized rifle battalion] in second echelon for developing the success of the infantry and tanks.

Tenth. My CP – Lipovskie, and, subsequently – Zhukovka, and the headquarters of the army – Zastavishche. Submit combat reports to me by 2400 on 7 September 1941 by liaison officers.

> The Commander of 50th Army, Major General Petrov
> The Member of the Military Council, Brigade Commissar Shliapin
> The Deputy Chief of the Operations Department, Major Garan

Source: "Boevoi prikaz komanduiushchego voiskami 50-i Armii No. 10 ot 6 sentiabria 1941 g. na ovladenie rubezhom Rekovichi, Klopotnia, Peklina, Poselok Oleshenskii" [Combat order no. 10 of the commander of the forces of 50th Army of 6 September 1941 on capturing the Rekovichi, Klopotnia, Peklina, and Oleshenskii village line], *SBDVOV*, issue 43, 365-366.

76. Combat Report of the Commander of the Forces of the Briansk Front to the *Stavka* of the Supreme High Command of 7 September 1941 about the Results of the *Front's* Combat Operations in the Trubchevsk Region from 29 August through 7 September 1941

To the Supreme High Commander, Comrade Stalin
To the Chief of the Red Army's General Staff, Marshal Comrade Shaposhnikov
Combat Report No. [unnumbered],
Headquarters, Briansk Front
7 September 1941
1:100,000 and 500,000 scale maps

1) The enemy's 47th PzC (17th and 18th PzDs, 29th MotD, and 2 armored detachments, 70th and 88th) conducted an offensive in the general direction of Trubchevsk and to the south on 28 August, while delivering a concentrated attack with their main forces toward Pochep, Semtsy, and Mostochnaia and while enveloping from the Pogar and Gremiach front from the south toward Sagut'evo and Trubchevsk and a secondary attack from the direction of Vitemlia toward Znob Station.

By this time, the units, which have been conducting the offensive along the Starodub axis joined in a meeting engagement with 269th, 282nd, 155th, and 307th RDs along the line of the Sudost' River and, having been unable to withstand the attack by the enemy panzer corps, they began a disorderly withdrawal behind the Desna River, while suffering significant losses.

2) With the objective of restoring the situation and destroying the enemy's 47th PzC, on 29 August I moved 108th TD, 141st TB (which, after unloading, went into battle from the march), and 4th CD in the general direction of Pogar. Only this maneuver and advance saved a situation whereby the units of the enemy panzer corps, which were pursuing on the heels of our withdrawing units, neither completely crushed these divisions nor occupied Trubchevsk, which they could have still occupied on 29 August, by doing so creating a threat to the Briansk grouping, and this advance provided an opportunity for the withdrawing forces to put themselves in order behind the Desna River and then turn back to participate in the fighting with the tanks units.

Beginning on 31 August 1941, a tank battle broke out in the region 20 kilometers west of Trubchevsk, where up to 300 tanks took part in the fighting on the enemy's side. As a matter of fact, that tank battle is continuing now.

The weather on these days, especially 1-3 September, was not favorable for our employment of aviation, which complicated the tank units' fighting, but, despite this fact, we could not tarry and fail to join battle.

We suffered considerable losses as a result of this tank encounter [meeting] battle, but the enemy suffered even more; the main thing is that we disrupted the enemy's plan for seizing Trubchevsk and smashing the newly-organized 3rd Army, which, at that time, was not yet strong and lacked a fully-functioning headquarters.

According to official data, the enemy suffered the [following] losses in this region:

1. In personnel – no fewer than 2,500 men;
2. In tanks – no fewer than 110-115 tanks;
3. In guns – no fewer than 45 guns;
4. Various vehicles – no fewer than 140; and
5. Several aircraft were shot down by the ground forces on the battlefield and a great number of heavy machine guns and mortars were destroyed.

The enemy has halted his offensive in this sector.

In addition, in 13th Army's sector, in the vicinity of Znob' Station, where the enemy's 29th Motorized Division crossed the Desna River, he also suffered significant losses from our counterattacks, and those points which were occupied by him, Znob' Station and Novo-Vasil'evskii, were occupied by us in return, and our units are continuing the offensive.

Just now, the news has been received that the eastern bank of the Desna River has been cleared of enemy.

According to preliminary data, the enemy's losses in 13th Army's sector for the last three days, including 6 September, are as follows:

Destroyed:

1. Tanks	38
2. Armored personnel carriers	5
3. Guns	11
4. Machine-guns	20
5. Mortars	6
6. Aircraft	11

        7. Vehicles   96

In the Liubakhov region, 15th Motorized Regiment's headquarters was smashed, 12 officers were killed, and 5 guns, 16 machine guns, 32 automatic weapons, 6 vehicles, and documents were seized on 6 September. Complete information about trophies for 6 September along the army's entire front is being verified. This information about the enemy's losses includes only the losses suffered by the ground forces. The strikes delivered by our aircraft will be reported in subsequent summaries.

According to the prisoner testimony and our agent intelligence, the enemy has suffered colossal losses in recent days. Large transports are flying daily with his wounded. According to our calculations, no fewer than 10,000 enemy have been destroyed along the entire front.

3) Our losses for the period of the tank battle in the Trubchevsk region [are];
    1. In 108th TD:
        a) Persons killed and wounded – 500 men;
        b) Destroyed tanks: KV – 3, T-34 – 20, T-40 – 30, and BA – 10;
        c) Guns – 30; and
        d) Transport vehicles – 60.
    2. In 141st TB:
        a) Persons killed and wounded – 80; and
        b) Destroyed tanks – KV – 1, T-34 – 4, ands BT – 19.

The division's and brigade's forward and rear echelon parks are intact.

4) Sustained fighting is underway in 50th Army's sector and in the Pochep region on 3rd Army's right wing. Fresh forces are being fed in by the enemy, but all of his counterattacks are being repulsed.

The enemy threw in strong aviation and actively bombed the Briansk and Karachev region, while employing night bombing, on 6 September and overnight of 6-7 September.

Our aviation also conducted active bombing and especially beginning in the second half of the day.

Intense fighting is continuing in all of the *front's* sectors.

        The Commander of the Forces of the Briansk Front,
            Lieutenant General Eremenko
        The Member of the Military Council of the *front,*
            Division Commissar Mazepov
        The Chief of Staff of the *front*, Major General Zakharov

Source: "Boevoe donesenie komanduiushchego voiskami Brianskogo Fronta Stavke Verkhovnogo Glavnokomandovaniia ot 7 sentiabria 1941 g. o rezul'tatakh boevykh deistvii voisk fronta v raione Trubchevsk s 29 avgusta po 7 sentiabria 1941 g." [Combat report of the commander of the forces of the Briansk Front to the *Stavka* of the Supreme High Command of 7 September 1941 about the results of the *front's* combat operations in the Trubchevsk region from 29 August through 7 September 1941], *SBDVOV*, issue 43, 83-85.

77. Excerpts from the Briansk Front's Operational Summaries, 7-8 September 1941

No. 039 at 2000 hours on 7 September 1941

50th TD captured Novyi Vasil'evskii and continued its attack northwestward toward the crossings and was approaching the Desna River west of Novyi Vasil'evskii on the morning of 7 September ... .

Losses for 6 September: 26 men killed and 160 wounded.

Trophies: picked up 50 German bodies ... . and in the Kamenskaia Sloboda region [found] 9 tanks, 1 armored personnel carrier, and one vehicle with enemy soldiers blown up in mine fields.

Losses of 13th Army for 5 September 1941: wounded: 6th RD – 218 men, 307th RD – 126 men, 155th RD – 82 men, 132nd RD – 42 men, 50th TD – 104 men, and 52nd CD – 7 men.

No. 041 at 2000 hours on 8 September 1941

121st TB concentrated in the region of woods 3 kilometers west of Letoshniki ... .

Losses for 7 September: 49 killed, 79 wounded, and 43 missing in action ... .

45th RC. 307th RD's 1021st RR ... .. Losses for 5 September: 110 men ... .

155th RD ... .Losses for 5 September: 43 men wounded ... .

50th TD has been withdrawn into the [3rd] army's reserve in the Kusten' region ... .. Losses – 37 men wounded ... .

6th RD ... . Losses for 5 September: 115 men wounded.

Source: "Operativnye svodki shtaba Brianskogo Fronta o boevykh deistviiakh voisk fronta" [Operational summaries of the headquarters of the Briansk Front 7-8 September 1941 about the combat operations of the front's forces], SBDVOV, issue 43, 87, 89-90.

78. Directive of the General Staff of the Red Army of 9 September 1941 to the Commander of the Forces of the Briansk Front about Creating a Shock Group for an Offensive in 50th Army's Sector

9 September 1941

To achieve decisive results in 50th Army's offensive, the chief of the General Staff believes it necessary to conduct the following:

1) Do not disperse the army's efforts along the entire front, but [instead] create a strong grouping from 50th Army's units along the main attack axis and deliver a massive blow with the aim of decisively smashing the opposing enemy.

2) Support the shock group with the quantity of artillery weapons necessary for ensuring a successful offensive by the army.

3) Protect the army's offensive on the main attack axis with strong aviation support.

4) Organize and plan cooperation among all of the types of forces in the army according to time and location.

5) Organize assistance and control of 50th Army from the army's headquarters.

In the Name of the Chief of the General Staff, Sharokhin

Source: "Direktiva General'nogo Shtaba Krasnoi Armii ot 9 sentiabria 1941 g komanduiushchemu voiskami Brianskogo Fronta o sozdanii udarnoi gruppirovki dlia nastupleniia v polose 50i Armii" [Directive of the General Staff of the Red Army of 9 September 1941 to the commander of the forces of the Briansk Front about creating a shock group for an offensive in 50th Army's sector], *SBDVOV*, issue 43, 14-15.

79. *Stavka* VGK Directive No. 001918 to the Commander of the Forces of the Briansk Front about Liquidating the Penetration by the Enemy 2nd Panzer Group

2250 hours on 12 September 1941

The *Stavka* of the Supreme High Command orders:

1. Finish off the enemy grouping in the Shostka, Glukhov, Putivl', and Konotop region in a most firm and decisive manner and link up with the Southwestern Front's forces, to which end you are authorized to halt your offensive along the Roslavl' axis and reinforce 13th Army at the expense of 50th Army by attaching its tank units to 13th Army.

2. Begin the operation on 14 September, after exploiting all of the *front's* aviation for its preparation.

3. It is desirable that you complete the operation and completely eliminate the gap between the Briansk and Southwestern Fronts by no later than 18 September.

For the Supreme High Commander,
Chief of the General Staff, B. Shaposhnikov

Source: "Direktiva Stavki VGK No. 001918 komanduiushchemu voiskami Brianskogo Fronta o likvidatsii proryva 2-i tankovoi gruppy protivnika" [*Stavka* VGK Directive No. 001918 to the commander of the forces of the Briansk Front about liquidating the penetration by the enemy 2nd Panzer Group], in Zolotarev, "*Stavka* 1941," 179-180.

Appendix V

The Roslavl'-Novozybkov Offensive: The Records of 108th Tank Division and 40th Army's 10th Tank Division, 28 August-14 September 1941

1. Combat Report No. 25 of the Commander of 10th Tank Division of 31 August 1941 on the March and Arrival in the Concentration Region [not in the narrative]

Combat Order No. 25, Commander, 10th Tank Division,
Slout,
0530 hours on 31 August 1941
1:100,000 scale map

1. The enemy, while committing up to 100 tanks into combat in 10th Motorized Rifle Regiment's sector, pushed it back and reached positions from Hill 173.4 to Devichi and the railroad junction 2 kilometers southwest of Makov by day's end on 30 August 1941.

Enemy motor-mechanized units are in the Korop, Altynovka, and Krolevets region.

2. On the right – 293rd RD. There are no neighbors on the left.

3. 10th Tank Division will reach the region of the woods southeast of Altynovka with two columns by 1700 hours on 31 August 1941, with the mission to destroy the enemy's motor-mechanized units in the Altynovka and Korop region in cooperation with 293rd Rifle Division and 2nd Airborne Corps.

Jumping-off positions – Hill 199.0 and the southern outskirts of Slout – the head of the main force's column will pass through at 0900 hours on 31 August 1941.

Regulating line No. 1 – Oblozhki and Shchebry – 1030 hours on 31 August 1941

Regulating line No. 2 – Krolevets and Solomashin – 1300 hours on 31 August 1941.

4. Forward detachment. Chief – the commander of 20th Tank Regiment. Composition: 20th Tank Regiment and a motorized rifle company, a battery of antitank guns, and a mortar battery from the motorized rifle regiment.

Mission – occupy the western outskirts of Altynovka by 1500 hours on 31 August and hold onto it until the main forces arrive.

March-route – Slout, Chertorigi, Oblizhki, Tuligolovo, Krolevets, and Altynovka. Jumping-off point – the southern outskirts of Slout – pass through at 0700 hours on 31 August 1941.

5. The right column. 19th Tank Regiment, 338th Artillery Regiment, and 5th Antitank Brigade; will move along the forward detachment's march-route. Concentration region – the southwestern corner of the woods southeast of Altynovka, Hill 164.0, and the barn.

6. The left column. Chief – the commander of 10th Motorized Rifle Regiment. Composition: the motorized rifle regiment, two mortar batteries, a battalion from 5th Antitank Brigade, the second echelon of the division's headquarters, 10th Artillery Regiment (without one battalion), and the reconnaissance battalion.

March-route – Slout, Glukhov, Shchebry, Iaroslavets, Kiselia, Solomashin, Khomenkov, Prasolov, Chervonnyi Ranok, and Leninskoe.

Concentration regions: the motorized rifle regiment – the northern corner of the woods, the barn, and Hill 172.6; 10th Artillery Regiment – the grove south of Leninskoe; the headquarters' second echelon – the southeastern corner of the woods west of Liubitov; and the reconnaissance battalion – Liubitov and the grove to the south.

7. 10th Separate Antiaircraft Artillery Battalion will protect the forward detachment's march-route with one battery, protect the march-route of the right column with one battery, protect the left column's march-route with one battery; and protect the operational group of the division's headquarters with one platoon of antiaircraft machine guns.

Upon reaching the concentration region, occupy firing positions in the vicinity of Hills 164.0, 167.4, and 172.6, the barn, and 2 kilometers west of Hill 172.6.

8. The lead echelons of the units' parks [rears] (without kitchens) will follow behind the units. The remainder of the units' rears will concentrate in the woods 6 kilometers west of Putivl' under the protection of 10th Artillery Regiment.

9. I, with the operational group, will be at the head of 19th Tank Regiment.

Submit reports upon passing through the jumping-off points and the regulating lines, upon reaching the concentration region, when there are aircraft raids, and upon contact with the enemy.

The Commander of 10th Tank Division, Major General Semenchenko
The Military Commissar of 10th Tank Division,
    Regimental Commissar Greznev
The Chief of Staff of the division, Lieutenant Colonel Semchuk.

Source: "Boevoi prikaz komandira 10-I Tankovoi Divizii No. 25 ot 31 Avgusta 1941 g. na marsh i vykhod v raion sosredotocheniia" [Combat report no. 25 of the commander of 10th Tank Division of 31 August 1941 on the march and arrival in the concentration region], *SBDVOV*, issue 33, 248-249.

584   BARBAROSSA DERAILED, VOLUME 3

2. Combat Order No. 28 of the Commander of 10th Tank Division of 1 September 1941 on an offensive toward Raigorodok, Vol'noe, and Korop [not in the narrative]

Combat Order No. 28, Headquarters, 10th Tank Division,
Reutitsy,
0700 hours on 1 September 1941
1: 100,000 scale map

1. The remnants of a defeated enemy infantry division, with a force of up to a regiment and mortars, is defending in the Zhernovki, Vol'noe, and Korop region. Up to a regiment of enemy infantry, with 20 guns on mechanized tractors, is in the Okriabr'skoe and Atiusha region.

2. On the right – 293rd Rifle Division.

On the left – 135th Rifle Division is attacking from the Sokhachi region toward Rybotin and the western outskirts of Korop, and 2nd Airborne Corps is attacking in the general direction of Oktiabr'skoe and Korop.

3. 10th Tank Division, with 5th Antitank Brigade and two battalions of 32nd Rifle Regiment, will attack toward Raigoroodok, Vol'noe, and Korop, with the mission to destroy the enemy in the Zhernovki, Korop, and Vol'noe region in cooperation with 293rd and 135th Rifle Divisions.

Readiness to attack – 1000 hours on 1 September 1941. Attack – upon radio signal 515 and three red rockets from the northern outskirts of Luknov.

4. 19th Tank Regiment (without one platoon), with 338th Artillery Regiment, two battalions from 32nd Artillery Regiment, and two mortar batteries, will attack toward Raigorodok, Zhernovki, the northern outskirts of Vol'noe, and the northeastern outskirts of Korop. Jumping-off positions – Hill 135.4 and the brushy area to the north. Assembly region – the southeastern outskirts of Korop.

5. 20th Tank Regiment (without a platoon of medium tanks), with a battalion from the motorized rifle regiment, 661st Artillery Regiment, and two mortar batteries, will attack toward Luknov, the southern outskirts of Vol'noe, the southern slopes of Hill 131.8, and the southern outskirts of Korop. Jumping-off positions – the grove 1 kilometer west of Luknov. Assembly region – the grove south of Vol'noe.

6. Artillery. The region of firing positions – Hill 139.2, the woods 2 kilometers west of Luknov and Luknov. Mission: suppress antitank guns in the Zhernovki and Vol'noe region and accompany the tank regiments' attacks toward Zhernovki, Vol'noe, and Korop.

7. 10th Separate Antiaircraft Artillery Battalion will protect the tank regiments' arrival in the jumping-off positions for the attack. Firing positions – in the vicinity of Hill 139.2, the southern outskirts of Luknov, and Hill 139.8.

8. My reserve: 10th Artillery Regiment, the reconnaissance battalion, two T-34 tanks from 20th Tank Regiment, and three BT-7 tanks from 19th Tank Regiment. Concentrate 10th Artillery Regiment – Krasnopol'e and the reconnaissance battalion and tanks – the eastern outskirts of Luknov.

9. Throw a tank platoon from 19th Tank Regiment, with a platoon from the motorized rifle regiment, under the command of 19th Tank Regiment's commander, forward to the crossings over the Seim River at Baturin and Matievka

10. The division's exchange point – in the Putivl' region.

11. I, with the operational group of the division's headquarters, will be – in the northern outskirts of Luknov, and subsequently – behind 20th Tank Regiment's combat formation.

12. The second echelon of the division's headquarters – the woods southwest of Andreevka.

> The Commander of 10th Tank Division, Major General Semenchenko
> The Military Commissar of 10th Tank Division,
> > Regimental Commissar Greznev
> The Chief of Staff of the division, Lieutenant Colonel Semchuk.

Source: "Boevoi prikaz komadira 10-i Tankovoi Divizii No. 28 ot 1 sentiabria 1941 g. na nastuplenie v napravlenii Raigorodok, Vol'noe, Korop" [Combat Order No. 28 of the commander of 10th Tank Division of 1 September 1941 on an offensive toward Raigorodok, Vol'noe, and Korop], SBDVOV, issue 33, 250-251.

3. (former V. 1) Combat Report No. 6 of the Headquarters of 10th Tank Division of 2 September 1941 about Capturing Korop

To the Chief of Staff of 40th Army
Combat Report No. 6, Headquarters, 10th Tank Division,
Korop
1450 hours on 2 September 1941
1:100,000 scale map

1. The division's units, in cooperation with 3rd Airborne Brigade, captured Korop in heavy fighting at 1130 hours on 2 September 1941.

The Korop, Vol'noe, and Mikhailovka region has been cleared of German remnants.

There are prisoners and many trophies.

2. According to prisoner testimony, 10th Motorized Division (41st and 20th Motorized Regiments, 10th Artillery Regiment, and 10th Antitank Battalion) was operating in the Korop region.

3. A detailed report with information on the enemy's losses and casualties will be provided after the final operations to clear the region of enemy.

> The Chief of Staff of 10th Tank Division, Lieutenant Colonel Semchuk
> The Military Commissar of the headquarters,
> > 10th Tank Division, Senior Political Worker Krivitsky

Source: "Boevoe donesenie shtaba 10-i Tankovoi Divizii No. 6 ot 2 sentiabria 1941 g. ob ovladenii Korop" [Combat report no. 6 of the headquarters of 10th Tank Division of 2 September 1941 about capturing Korop], *SBDVOV,* issue 33, 251.

4. (former V.2) Combat Order No. 30 of the Commander of 10th Tank Division of 3 September 1941 about Defending the Tarasovka and Krasnopol'e Region

Combat Order No. 30, Headquarters, 10th Tank Division,
the western outskirts of Krasnopol'e,
0130 hours on 3 September 1941
1:100,000 scale map

1. Up to 50 enemy tanks with motorized infantry and motorcyclists are in the Dobrotovo region [17 kilometers east of Korop] and the woods 2 kilometers south of Obtovo (Optovo) [18 kilometers east-northeast of Korop], and small enemy reconnaissance groups are being detected in the eastern outskirts of Luknov [12 kilometers east of Korop] and the eastern outskirts of Krasnopol'e [10 kilometers east of Korop]. Separate enemy groups with tanks are moving from the Dobrotovo region toward Altynovka. Small enemy groups from the Obolon'e region are conducting a crossing over the Desna River and attacking toward Lysaia Gora and Korop.

2. On the right – 3rd Airborne Brigade is holding onto the Korop region.

On the left – 293rd Rifle Division is defending the southern bank of the Esman' River [20-30 kilometers northeast of Korop].

3. 10th Tank Division will occupy defenses in the Tarasovka and Krasnopol'e region [from 5 kilometers east to 10 kilometers southeast of Korop], with the mission to protect the Korop axis from the east and southeast, with a subsequent transition to an offensive for destroying the enemy tank and motorized infantry in the Dobrotovo region.

4. 10th Motorized Rifle Regiment, with three mortar batteries, will occupy defensive positions on the eastern and southeastern outskirts of Karyl'skoe (Koryl'skoe) [7 kilometers south-southeast of Korop]. Conduct combat reconnaissance toward Budennovka [13 kilometers southeast of Korop].

5. 32nd Rifle Regiment will continue to defend the Raigorodok and Zaitsev line [10-12 kilometers northeast of Korop] and prepare defensive positions from Raigorodok to the woods 3 kilometers south of Raigorodok. Concentrate the regiment's shock group in Zhernovka [10 kilometers northeast of Korop].

6. 5th Antitank Brigade will create an antitank region in the Tarasovka, Smeloe, Hill 133.4, and Berezentsev sector [5-14 kilometers east of Korop] along the southern bank of the Strizhen River.

7. 10th Artillery Regiment will organize an all-round defense in the Krasnopol'e region.

8. 19th Tank Regiment will concentrate in the Tarasovka region and be prepared for operations [southeastward] toward Krasnopol'e and Altynovka.

9. 20th Tank Regiment will concentrate in the woods east of Tarasovka and be prepared for operations [southeastward] toward Krasnopol'e and Altynovka.

10. 10th Separate Reconnaissance Battalion will concentrate in the eastern outskirts of Tarasovka. Conduct reconnaissance toward: 1) Smeloe, Luknov, and Optovo; 2) Krasnopol'e, Dobrotovo, and Reutintsy; and 3) Krasnopol'e, Altynovka, and Leninskoe.

11. 10th Separate Antiaircraft Artillery Battalion will occupy firing positions in the Tarasovka and Smeloe regions and the western outskirts of Krasnopol'e.

12. The division's exchange point – in the Putivl' region [70 kilometers southeast of Korop].

13. I, with the operational group of the division's headquarters – in Tarasovka.

14. The second echelon of the division's headquarters – in Putivl'.

The Commander of 10th Tank Division, Major General Semenchenko
The Military Commissar of 10th Tank Division,
    Regimental Commissar Greznev
The Chief of Staff of the division, Lieutenant Colonel Semchuk.

Source: "Boevoi prikaz komandira 10-i Tankovoi Divizii No. 30 ot 3 sentiabria 1941. na oboronu raiona Tarasovka, Krasnopol'e" [Combat order no. 30 of the commander of 10th Tank Division of 3 September 1941 about defending the Tarasovka and Krasnopol'e region], *SBDVOV*, issue 33, 252-253.

5. (former V.3). Report by the Commander of 108th Tank Division to the Commander of the Forces of the Briansk Front of 17 September 1941 about the Division's Combat Operations in the Period from 28 August through 4 September 1941

To the Commander of the Briansk Front, Lieutenant General Eremenko

1. At 1930 hours on 28 August 1941, we received the *front* commander's order under the signature of the *front's* chief of staff, Major General Zakharov; the division was to concentrate in the woods in the Orekhovskii, Polovetskii, and Kalinovskii region [14-17 kilometers north of Trubchevsk] by a night march.

The division set out at 2100 hours on 28 August and concentrated in the designated region at 1600 hours on 29 August.

2. At 1800 hours on 29 August 1941, we received the written order of the *front* commander on the fulfilling of a combat mission as part of the Mobile Group (141st Tank Brigade, 108th Tank Division, and 4th Cavalry Division), under the overall command of Major General Ermakov.

Captain Baizbant handed us the order and then said orally, "For communicating with aviation, a representative from the *front's* VVS will arrive at your headquarters on a U-2 aircraft. On questions of cooperation with your neighbors, you will be given additional information while on the march. There will be no order from the group's commander."

At 2400 hours on 29 August 1941, I was given an order to march, provisionally, at 0430 hours on 30 August. The division began its movement at 0600 hours on 30 August 1941 because the battalion, which had been deployed in defenses, was late in assembling.

My decision [order], arising from your concept of operations, was to conduct my main attack [southwestward toward Semenovka] in the general direction of Gruzdova, Romanovka, Pogar, Grinevo, Dokhnovichi, Novo-Mlynka, Voronok, Zheleznyi Most, Mashevo, and Shostka. I decided, while protecting myself from the north with the motorized rifle regiment (without one motorized rifle battalion), to follow along the Karuzha, Mostochnaia, Magor, Karbovka, Chekhovka, Belevaia, Posudichi, Zhuravikhi, the northern outskirts of Grinevo, and Dokhnovichi march-route, having forced the Sudost' River in the Belevaia region [7 kilometers north of Pogar] – with two battalions of the artillery regiment and a company of T-40 tanks.

The main forces (shock group), consisting of 216th Tank Regiment (5 KV, 32 T-34, and 25 T-40 tanks and the advanced evacuation point), were to follow along the eastern outskirts of Polovetskii, the eastern outskirts of Karuzha, Mostochnaia, Bobovnia, Ogorodnia, Brusnichnyi, Pokrovskii, Romanovka, the northern outskirts of Pogar, Kalinovka, the southern outskirts of Grinevo, and the southern outskirts of Dokhnovichi [30 kilometers west of Pogar] march-route. The assembly region was – the woods south of Dokhnovichi.

The crossing of the main forces [over the Sudost' River] was planned in the Posudichi region [8 kilometers north of Pogar].

3. The division set out at 0600 hours on 30 August 1941 in accordance with my decision. When the right column approached the western outskirts of Karbovka and the left column – Pokrovskii [24-26 kilometers west-northwest of Trubchevsk], enemy aircraft carried out a 50-minute bombing strike against both columns, as a result of which the artillery regiment (two battalions) and motorized rifle regiment's 3rd Rifle Battalion were cut off from the right column and one rifle company of 1st Rifle Battalion and the advanced evacuation point were cut off from the left column.

After the enemy air attack, the right column's units (1st Rifle Battalion, the artillery regiment without its 1st Battalion, and 3rd Rifle Battalion) joined battle individually with units of the enemy's 17th Panzer Division in the Chekhovka and Karbovka region.

The left column (the forward detachment), consisting of a rifle company, two 76mm guns, and a platoon of T-40 tanks, while approaching Romanovka at 1600 hours, engaged in fighting with units of the enemy's 17th Panzer Division. The [left column's] main force (all of 216th Tank Regiment, consisting of 3 KV, 32 T-34, and 20 T-40 tanks) was concentrated in the brushy region 2 kilometers north of Romanovka, awaiting the results of the fighting.

At 1800 hours on 30 August 1941, I reached a decision to attack the enemy with two platoons of tanks (3 KV and 3 T-34 tanks), together with the forward detachment, with the aim to capture Romanovka.

The attack was unsuccessful and Romanovka remained in enemy hands. At 1800 hours on 30 August 1941, the main force (all of 216th Tank Regiment) was transferred to the vicinity of the woods at Hill 182.8, northwest of Romanovka.

At 1900 hours on 30 August 1941, the enemy launched a counterattack. The rifle company (forward detachment), which was subjected to an air strike before the counterattack, began to withdraw. While having the command post and division headquarters 2 to 2.5 kilometers north of Romanovka and seeing the danger for the division's headquarters and command post, I, with the division's commissar, Brigade Commissar Grishin, and the chief of staff, Lieutenant Colonel Lashenchuk, who was with him, launched an attack. The enemy's counterattack was repulsed.

At that time (1900-2000 hours), aircraft bombed our tanks, and, as a result, the tanks of the division's commander and commissar were driven into a swamp.

Enemy losses for 30 August 1941 were: the headquarters of an SS regiment was smashed, 12 headquarters' vehicles were destroyed, six men were taken prisoner, 8 guns and documents were captured, and 500-600 enemy soldiers were killed and 4 tanks knocked out.

Our losses: enemy aircraft damaged 50 % of our artillery and 9 transport vehicles, and enemy artillery fire burned 1 KV tank, 3 T-34 tanks, and 5 T-40 tanks.

On the night of 30-31 August 1941, the motorized rifle regiment, without one rifle battalion and one and one half companies of its 1st Rifle Battalion, occupied a front on the western edge of the woods east of Chekhovka, and 216th Tank Regiment was deployed in the woods near Hill 182.8, northwest of Romanovka. The division's headquarters was located in Pokrovskii.

4. Beginning on the morning of 31 August 1941, the enemy conducted an attack on the motorized rifle regiment toward Chekhovka and Karbovka and a tank attack (up to 150 tanks) from Romanovka toward the woods near Hill 182.8 (heavy and medium tanks).

Before the tank attack, the enemy attacked the division from the air. My decision: (there were no communications with the motorized rifle regiment) was to send the Chief of the Operations Section, Major Bokarev, to the motorized rifle regiment, with the mission to hold onto the positions it occupied and verify the situation. The tank regiment engaged the tank attack by fire from their positions. The withdrawal was upon my signal. The assembly area was – the northern edge of the woods 600-700 meters south of Karbovka.

After 30-minutes of artillery fire (for the purpose of protecting the tanks) and verifying the situation, I gave the signal to the tank regiment's commander to withdraw to the designated assembly region. During the course of the day, the motorized rifle regiment continued to repulse the enemy's attacks toward Chekhovka and Karbovka.

The enemy's losses for 31 August 1941: 22 tanks, 6 antitank guns, and 8 medium caliber guns were destroyed.

Our losses: 1 KV tank, 11 T-34 tanks, and 8 T-40 tanks. Personnel losses were not determined.

5. 1 September 1941, the division's units fought in encirclement. The enemy attacked, successively, from the Chekhovka, Karbovka, and Krutoi Rov axes.

The enemy's offensive was accompanied by three tank attacks and four to five air attacks. The enemy's attacks were repulsed by the division's units. The enemy's losses for 1 September 1941: 23 tanks (burned), 5 guns, 4 motorcycles, and 11 vehicles destroyed, and 700-800 men killed.

Our losses: 4 T-40 and 7 T-40 tanks burned and 5 guns destroyed by aircraft.

6. 2 September 1941, the division's units occupied defenses in encirclement on a front from the western edge of the woods east of Chekhovka to the eastern edge of the woods west of Karbovka.

During the day, the enemy conducted active attacks with tanks and aircraft. The enemy's attacks were repulsed.

The enemy's losses for 2 September 1941: 18 tanks destroyed (6 of these were burned) and 500-600 motorized infantrymen killed and 5 guns and 7 mortars knocked out. Our losses: 6 T-34 tanks (3 burned), 2 guns knocked out, and 4 tractors burned by flamethrower tanks. Personnel losses have not been determined.

7. 3 September 1941. On the night of 2-3 September, the division's units moved to the woods south of Karbovka and occupied defenses from the northern edge of the woods north of Karbovka to the eastern edge of the woods west of Pokrovskii.

The division's units were subjected to air strikes from 1500-1600 hours, after which at 1700 hours the enemy launched an offensive from the Karbovka region and an attack with tanks and motorized infantry from the direction of Pokrovskii. As a result of carefully organized defenses, both attacks were repelled.

The enemy's losses for 3 September 1941: 12 tanks, 500 motorized infantrymen, and several guns and mortars.

Our losses: 2 76mm guns.

8. 4 September 1941. Overnight on 3-4 September, because the division's units were running out of ammunition and fuel (the rear services were cut off and food supplies were also used up), I decided to withdraw the division's units [southeastward] from encirclement and enter the rear areas of our combined-arms units in the direction of Brusnichnyi, Magor, the woods (north of the road to Shiriaevka), and Hill 182.7 and then eastward to the woods in the Orekhovskii region. We brought [the following] out of the encirclement: 2 KV, 8 T-34, and 6 T-40 tanks, 6 BA-10 [armored cars], 7 guns, a battalion of motorized infantry, and automobile transports with 100 wounded.

A march [column] was organized with: a forward detachment consisting of a rifle company, a platoon of T-34 tanks, and 2 76mm guns; the main forces – one column – with tanks [KV and T-34s] forward, then infantry, artillery, armored cars, and T-40 tanks; and, for protection, one-fifth of a rifle company. The tanks (KV and T-34), with the motorized infantry, passed through the enemy's defenses along the Brusnichnyi and Pokrovskii line and made it through without any opposition. The second echelon (artillery, auto-transport with the wounded, machine guns, mortars, and two covering rifle companies) were met by the enemy in the Brusnichnyi region. The enemy was smashed by an energetic attack here in the Brusnichnyi region. A regimental headquarters was smashed, 16 trucks and 3 light vehicles were seized and destroyed, 1 medium tank was seized, and 6 motorcycles and 2 tanks were destroyed, and various documents, property, and foodstuffs were seized, and 15 officers and many soldiers were killed.

Our losses: 3 armored cars, 4 T-40 tanks, 3 heavy machine guns, and 20 men.

Because of heavy rains on 4 September 1941, the transport, which was moving in the second echelon, lagged behind the tanks and motorized infantry, and reached only the brushy region north of Brusnichnyi.

The enemy attacked the second echelon from the direction of Magor at 1500 hours on 4 September 1941. As a result of the criminal organization of that echelon's security and defenses by the division's chief of artillery, Colonel Seletkov, and other commanders, the enemy, with an insignificant force of 3 to 5 tanks, smashed and burned this echelon. Our losses after this fight were: 7 guns, 4 T-40 tanks, 3 BA-10 armored cars, an unknown quantity of heavy machine guns, the trucks with the wounded, the tractors, and a large number of killed and wounded. The seriously wounded were shot by the enemy.

During the passage through the Briansk forest, we left four T-34 tanks behind in the vicinity of Hill 169.3 because of the fuel shortage and mechanical breakdowns, one KV tank in the vicinity of Hill 182.7 (which ran over a Fougasse [incendiary] mine), and two armored cars in the woods west of Podlesnyi.

The division escaped with: 17 combat vehicles (2 KV, 7 T-34, 2 T-40, 3 BA-10, and 3 BA-20), 3 76mm guns, 8 antiaircraft guns, and 1,200 men. The division's rear services remain intact.

I request, as a consequence of the extreme fatigue of the personnel who participated in the division's fight in encirclement, you withdraw the division's units into the *front's* rear area for rest and refitting and provide three-four days of rest for the personnel and for refilling the weapons and personnel, after which, I believe the division can once again fulfill the combat missions you assign.

The majority of the personnel (enlisted and command cadre) of the division's sub-units and units displayed steadfastness, courage, and bravery in the fighting, whom I request you recommend for the highest governmental awards; however, there were instances of cowardice and panic, and I believe it necessary to call the cowards and panic-mongers to account for their behavior and turn them over to Military Tribunals for judgment.

Attachment: 1:50,000 scale map [see Map]

The Commander of 108th Tank Division, Colonel Ivanov
The Military Commissar of the division, Brigade Commissar Grishin

Source: "Donesenie komandira 108-i Tankovoi Divizii komanduiushchemu voiskami Brianskim frontom ot 17 sentiabria 1941 g. o boevykh deistviiakh divizii v period s 28 avgusta po 4 sentiabria 1941 g." [Report by the commander of 108th Tank Division to the commander of the forces of the Briansk Front of 17 September 1941 about the division's combat operations in the period from 28 August through 4 September 1941], in *SBDVOV*, issue 33, 121-125.

Appendix W

Excerpts from the Southwestern Front's Daily Operational Directives and Summaries about 40th Army's Positions and Situation, 28 August-10 September 1941 [not in the narrative]

1. Operational Directive No. 00322 of the Southwestern Front at 1600 hours on 28 August 1941 on a Defense along the Dnepr River

1. On the front of the Southwestern Front's armies, the enemy is conducting preparations to force the Dnepr River in several sectors. A concentration of enemy forces and crossing equipment has been detected in the vicinity of the woods at Dymer, Cherkassy, Buzhin and south of Kremenchug. The group of enemy who penetrated at Okuninovo is being destroyed.

A large enemy motor-mechanized group advanced from the Starodub region toward Pogar and Novgorod-Severskii on 27 August. Simultaneously, the enemy, while delivering his main blow along the Gomel' and Chernigov road, pushed 21st Army back to the Solov'evka, Iurkovichi, Gorodnia, Budishche, and Loev front.

. The Southwestern Front's armies, while continuing to hold onto the Dnepr River line and conduct a struggle to destroy the enemy's Okuninovo group, will protect against possible enemy strikes from the north along the Desna River.

Boundaries: on the right – Kursk, L'gov, Glukhov, Gorodnia, Love, Iurevichi, and Stolin (all points for the Briansk Front); on the left – Zmiev, Krasnograd, Perevolochnaia, Aleksandriia, and Kirovograd.

3. 40th Army (293rd and 135th RDs, 10th TD, 2nd AbnC, and 5th ATB), having occupied the Korop and Maloe Ust'e sector with units of 2nd AbnC, which has moved forward on vehicles, is continuing to occupy the southern bank of the Desna River on the Pirogovka Station and Stepanovka front.

The army's mission – is to prevent an enemy penetration toward Krolevets, Vorozhba, and Konotop and firmly defend the *front's* right wing against an attack from the north

Headquarters of the army – Konotop.

Boundary on the left – Sumy, Bakhmach, Ol'godorf, and Shchorsk.

Source: "Operativnaia direktiva komanduiushchego voiskami Iugo-Zapadnogo fronta No. 00322 ot 28 avgusta 1941 g. na oboronu po r. Dnepr" [Operational directive no. 00322 of the commander of the forces of the Southwestern Front of 28 August 1941 on a defense along the Dnepr River], in *SBDVOV*, Issue 40, 133.

2. Operational Summary No. 00117 of the Southwestern Front at 2200 hours on 28 August 1941

1. 40th Army.

293rd RD is defending its previous positions. During the course of 27 August the division's units repelled attacks by the enemy, who was operating toward Sobych' and Klishki. 8 enemy tankettes were destroyed. In the Korop region, an enemy force of up to a company of infantry with three tankettes crossed to the left bank of the Desna River. Detachments from the division conducted fighting to destroy the enemy in that region.

10th TD concentrated in the Poloshki, Shcherby, and Dunaets region.

135th RD occupied the Bol. Ust'e and Volovitsa line, while having separate detachments on the southern bank of the Desna River west of Korop.

5th ATB passed through Baturin on the morning of 28 August. Reports about its arrival in Krolovets have not been submitted.

2nd AbnC – on the march (on vehicles) to its concentration region … .

Source: "Operativnaia svodka shtaba Iugo-Zapadnogo fronta No. 00117 k 2200 chasam 28 avgusta 1941 g. o boevykh deistviiakh voisk fronta" [Operational summary of the headquarters of the Southwestern Front no. 00117 at 2200 hours on 28 August 1941 about the combat operations of the *front's* forces], in *SBDVOV*, issue 40, 125.

3. Operational Summary No. 00119 of the Southwestern Front at 2200 hours on 29 August 1941

1. 40th Army (293rd and 135th RDs, 10th TD, 2nd AbnC, and 5th ATB).

10th TD attacked the enemy in the direction of Voronezh-Glukhov and Shostka with one MRR and 6 tanks in the morning. In the Voronezh-Glukhov region, an enemy command-observation point, 5 AT guns, 6 machine guns, and 3 mortars were destroyed by three tanks. In the Shostka region, the enemy were defending with a force of up to a battalion. There is no information about the capturing of the indicated regions. The results of the offensive are unknown.

293rd RD fought with the enemy in the Pirogovka and Korop region. At 1500 hours an enemy force of up top a regiment of infantry with 15 tanks and tankettes conducted an attack toward Altynovka.

By a decision of the commander, the army will counterattack the enemy toward Korop with the forces of 10th TD, 293rd RD, and units of 2nd AbnC. No information has arrived about the beginning of the attack.

135th RD has had no contact with the enemy.

5th ARB is operating together with 10th TD.

Headquarters of 40th Army – Konotop.

Source: "Operativnaia svodka shtaba Iugo-Zapadnogo fronta No. 00119 k 2200 chasam 29 avgusta 1941 g. o boevykh deistviiakh voisk fronta" [Operational summary of the headquarters of the Southwestern Front no. 00119 at 2200 hours on 29 August 1941 about the combat operations of the *front's* forces], in *SBDVOV*, issue 40, 125

4. Operational Summary No. 00121 of the Southwestern Front at 2200 hours on 30 August 1941

The Southwestern Front's forces are conducting holding actions with its right wing against enemy motor-mechanized units, which are attacking from the north toward Chernigov and Basmach, continuing to combat the enemy, which have penetrated into the Okuninovo region, and improving defenses on the eastern bank of the Dnepr River.

The enemy, while developing an offensive toward Chernigov, is holding onto a bridgehead at Okunionovo and preparing to force the river in the Cherkassy and Kremenchug regions.

1. 40th Army conducted sustained fighting with enemy motor-mechanized units, which are attacking toward Basmach.

10th TD – the division's MRBn, being counterattacked at Shostka by an enemy force of no less than a battalion of infantry with tanks, abandoned Shostka and occupies the woods 2 kilometers east of Shostka. The division's main forces were located in the Voronezh-Glukhov region, which is occupied by 28 MRR NKVD.

293rd RD, having beaten off an enemy attack against its right wing, held onto its previous positions.

2nd AbnC, while developing an attack begun on the morning of 30 September to the north, occupied Koryl'skoe and Nekhaevka.

135th RD, while attacking toward Korop with part of its forces, occupied Sukhachi and is continuing its advance.

42nd RD (Briansk Front) attacked toward Volynka and Avdeevka on the morning of 30 August.

52nd CD (Briansk Front) attacked toward Novgorod-Severskii.

Headquarters of 40th Army – Konotop.

Source: "Operativnaia svodka shtaba Iugo-Zapadnogo fronta No. 00121 k 2200 chasam 30 avgusta 1941 g. o boevykh deistviiakh voisk fronta severo-vostochnee Kieva" [Operational summary of the headquarters of the Southwestern Front no. 00119 at 2200 hours on 29 August 1941 about the combat operations of the *front's* forces northeast of Kiev], in *SBDVOV*, issue 40, 141.

5. Operational Summary No. 00125 of the Southwestern Front at 2200 hours on 1 September 1941

The Southwestern Front's forces, while defending the eastern bank of the Dnepr River with the fortified positions of the Kiev Fortified Region, are continuing to fight along the Chernigov and Oster [50 kilometers north of Kiev] axes and, since the morning of 31 August, have been fighting on their left wing with enemy forces which have crossed the Dnepr River at Derievka [near Kremenchug, 260 kilometers southeast of Kiev].

The enemy, while holding on to the Okuninovo region [on the Dnepr's eastern bank, 30 kilometers north of Kiev], is trying to broaden the bridgehead he seized at Grigor-Briganirovka and develop an offensive toward Bakhmach and Chernigov from the north.

1. 40th Army – is fighting to encircle the enemy grouping in the vicinity of Korop in conditions of a possible envelopment of its right wing toward Glukhov.

293rd RD (with 28th MRR NKVD attached) – while withdrawing its right wing toward the south, went on the defense at 1800 hours along in positions from the northern edge of the woods northwest of Dubovichi to the Esman' River [15 kilometers south-southeast to 15 kilometers southwest of Voronezh-Glukhov], the northern outskirts of Chepelevka [18 kilometers west-southwest of Voronezh-Glukhov] and the left bank of the Desna River to Raigorodok [30 kilometers southwest of Voronezh-Glukhov and 13 kilometers east of Korop]. There are up to two regiments of enemy motorized infantry and a battalion of enemy tanks on the division's front.

2nd AbnC (with 10th TD's 19th TR) – fighting successfully in the Korop region since 1400 hours with an enemy force of up to two motorized infantry regiments of 10th MotD.

10th TD [20th TR] – captured Tsarevka [Tarasovka] [6 kilometers east to 6 kilometers southeast of Korop]. 3rd AbnB – [after capturing Koryl'skoe on 31 August] is fighting on the western and northern outskirts of Koryl'skoe [6 kilometers south of Korop], while repelling an enemy attack from Korop. 4th AbnB [with 10th TD's 19th TR] is fighting on the southern outskirts of Atiusha and Pusto Greblia [15-16 kilometers south of Korop]. 2nd AbnB captured Egorovka [6 kilometers south-southwest of Korop] and is fighting on the western and southern outskirts of Oktiabr'skoe [10 kilometers south-southeast of Korop].

135th RD's 791st RR captured Sukhachi [Sokhachi] [7 kilometers west of Korop] and is fighting on the western outskirts of Rybotin [3 kilometers west of Korop].

The remaining units of 135th RD are defending the Bol'shoe Ust'e and Volovitsa line [10-68 kilometers west-southwest of Korop].

Headquarters of 40th Army – Konotop [40 kilometers south-southeast of Korop].

Source: "Operativnaia svodka shtaba Iugo-Zapadnogo fronta No. 00125 k 22 chasam 1 sentiabria 1941 g. o boevykh deistviiakh voisk fronta" [Operational summary no. 00125 of the headquarters of the Southwestern Front at 2200 hours on 1 September 1941 about the combat operations of the forces of the *front*], in *SBDVOV*, issue 40, 145

6. Operational Summary No. 00129 of the Southwestern Front at 2200 hours on 3 September 1941

1. 40th Army (1:100,000 map)..

293rd RD (with 28th MRR NKVD attached) withdrew under the pressure of two enemy motorized infantry regiments with 50 tanks and dug in, with one group along the Solomashin [7 kilometers southeast of Krolevets] and Buivolovo [6 kilometers south of Krolevets] line and the 2nd group along the Altynovka and Mikhailovshchina line [17 kilometers southwest to 8 kilometers south-southwest of Krolevets], while having 10th TD in the Krasnopol'e region [18 kilometers west of Krolevets]. The division has suffered significant losses, the quantity of which is being verified.

2nd AbnC, after destroying the enemy in Korop, dug in along the Zaitsev, Korop, Sukhachi, and Duchi line [10 kilometers east to 10 kilometers west of Korop], while repelling enemy attempts to cross the Desna River from Obolon'e [9 kilometers north of Korop].

135th RD's 791st RR is moving [eastward] to the Krasnopol'e region [10 kilometers east-southeast of Korop] in the morning.

3rd AbnC – the [Southwestern] *front's* reserve, was transferred to the subordination of 40th Army's commander and occupied positions in the Khizhki, Novosel'skii, Zholdaki, and Lizorubovskii sector [10 kilometers north to 30 kilometers northeast of Konotop] along the Seim River, with the mission of holding onto the crossings over the river.

Headquarters of 40th Army – Konotop.

Source: "Operativnaia svodka shtaba Iugo-Zapadnogo fronta No. 00129 k 22 chasam 3 sentiabria 1941 g. o boevykh deistviiakh voisk fronta" [Operational summary no. 00129 of the headquarters of the Southwestern Front at 2200 hours on 3 September 1941 about the combat operations of the *front's* forces], in *SBDVOV*, issue 40, 148.

7. Operational Summary No. 00133 of the Southwestern Front at 2200 hours on 5 September 1941

The Southwestern Front's armies are in sustained fighting along the Konotop, Chernigov, and Kremenchug axes and defending the eastern bank of the Dnepr River with the fortified lines of the Kiev Fortified Region.

1. 40th Army is fighting with enemy motor-mechanized units (10th MotD and 4th PzD) along its entire front.

293rd RD, with 28th MRR NKVD, while attacked by the enemy, withdrew to the southern bank of the Seim River and concentrated in the Volchik region [24-26 kilometers northeast of Konotop] by day's end on 5 September. On order of the army's commander, after putting itself in order, it will constitute the army's reserve.

During the course of several days of constant fighting, 293rd conducted a fighting withdrawal southward. The division's commander lost communications with his units, and 1032nd RR's position has not been determined. According to a report by 40th Army's headquarters, the regiment remained in the Raigorodok and Zhernovka region [9-12 kilometers northeast of Korop]. A forward detachment from 10th TD has been sent toward Zhernovka to determine 1032nd RR's position.

10th TD, with 5th ATB, is continuing to fight in positions from Altynovka to Budennovka [15-20 kilometers southeast of Korop]. The division's right wing is protected by a battery of 10th AR, two batteries of 5th ATB, and a machine gun sub-unit.

19th TR and 10th TD's reconnaissance battalion have been sent to the Mariental' and Proletarskoe region [20 kilometers south of Korop] to constitute the division commander's reserve.

2nd AbnC restored its position in the Korop region by an attack.

791st RR (subordinate to the 2nd AbnC's commander) is fighting on the northeastern outskirts of Karyl'skoe (Koryl'skoe) [7 kilometers south of Korop].

4th AbnB has been withdrawn from the Shkuraevka and Siniutin line [17-25 kilometers west-southwest of Korop], with the mission of attacking toward Korop. The brigade captured Korop by day's end.

2nd AbnB – having thrown the enemy back, captured Egorovka [6 kilometers south of Korop] and is continuing its attack toward the northeast.

3rd AbnB is occupying the Rybotin, Sokhachi, and Novoselok line [5-15 kilometers west of Korop].

3rd AbnC continues to occupy defenses along the Novosel'e Mutino, Zheldaki, and Taranskii line [along the southern bank of the Seim River 12 kilometers north-northwest to 25 kilometers northeast of Konotop].

21st GAR RGK – is at a strong point in the Novosel'e Mutino, and Volchik region [24-26 kilometers northeast of Konotop], supporting 293rd RD's fighting.

An RGK AT regiment arrived to reinforce the army and occupied a strong point along the Ozarichi and Mel'nia front [14 kilometers north-northeast to 13 kilometers north of Konotop]. 227th RD and remaining reinforcing units have not yet arrived.

Headquarters of 40th Army – Konotop.

Source: "Operativnaia svodka shtaba Iugo-Zapadnogo fronta No. 00133 k 22 chasam 5 sentiabria 1941 g. o boevykh deistviiakh voisk fronta" [Operational summary no. 00133 of the headquarters of the Southwestern Front at 2200 hours on 5 September 1941 about the combat operations of the *front's* forces], in *SBDVOV*, issue 40, 151-152.

8. Operational Summary No. 00135 of the Southwestern Front at 2200 hours on 6 September 1941

The Southwestern Front's forces are conducting sustained fighting with enemy motor-mechanized units along the Konotop-Bakhmach, Chernigov, Oster, and Kremenchug axes, while defending the Dnepr River on the Chernin, Kiev Fortified Region, and Kremenchug front with its center.

1. 40th Army (1:100,000 map)

The army's units held off an offensive by enemy tanks and infantry across the entire front during the day.

3rd AbnC is defending the Khizhki, Zheldaki, and Taranskii line [along the southern bank of the Seim River from 30 kilometers northeast to 12 kilometers north-northeast of Konotop].

6th AbnB is fighting with small groups of enemy which have crossed to the southern bank of the Seim River at Mutino [30 kilometers north-northeast of Konotop]. The enemy is being driven back to the northern bank of the river.

212th and 5th AbnBs had no contact with the enemy.

10th TD, with 5th ATB, conducted holding actions along the Leninskoe, Altynovka, Budennovka, and Atiusha line [27 kilometers southeast to 16 kilometers south of Korop]. Two enemy motorized regiments with 50 tanks (half of them heavy models) attacked the division at 1700 hours. Simultaneously, enemy infantry with 30 tanks attacked the right-wing 2nd AbnB at Atiusha [16 kilometers south of Korop]. The army commander decided to withdraw 2nd AbnC to the southern bank of the Seim River on the night of 6-7 September. After protecting 2nd AbnC's withdrawal, 10th TD will withdraw into the army's reserve in the Konotop region.

Source: "Operativnaia svodka shtaba Iugo-Zapadnogo fronta No. 00135 k 22 chasam 6 sentiabria 1941 g. o boevykh deistviiakh voisk fronta" [Operational summary no. 00135 of the headquarters of the Southwestern Front at 2200 hours on 6 September 1941 about the combat operations of the *front's* forces], in *SBDVOV*, issue 40, 157-158.

9. Operational Summary No. 00137 of the Southwestern Front at 2200 hours on 7 September 1941

The Southwestern Front's forces are conducting sustained fighting with attacking enemy motor-mechanized units and infantry on the Konotop, Chernigov, Oster, and Kremenchug axes, while defending the eastern bank of the Dnepr River on the Chernin and Kiev Fortified Region front and further along the eastern bank to the mouth of the Psel' River.

1. 40th Army.

The army's units are conducting a fighting withdrawal to the southern bank of the Seim River.

During the day, the enemy repeatedly tried to force the Seim River along the Khizhki and Mel'nia line [14 kilometers north-northwest to 30 kilometers northeast of Konotop] but was driven back by artillery fire.

In the second half of the day, the enemy succeeded in crossing the river on a broad front in the Mel'nia region [14 kilometers north-northwest of Konotop] with up to an infantry regiment, supported by strong artillery fire.

To resist the enemy's offensive developing toward Konotop, the army commander decided to use the *front's* reserve – 227th RD.

Konotop was subjected to air strikes by 61 enemy aircraft.

The situation of the army's units at day's end was unclear. There are no communications.

Source: "Operativnaia svodka shtaba Iugo-Zapadnogo fronta No. 00137 k 22 chasam 7 sentiabria 1941 g. o boevykh deistviiakh voisk fronta" [Operational summary no. 00137 of the headquarters of the Southwestern Front at 2200 hours on 7 September 1941 about the combat operations of the *front's* forces], in *SBDVOV*, issue 40, 163-164.

10. Operational Summary No. 00139 of the Southwestern Front at 2200 hours on 8 September 1941

The Southwestern Front's forces are conducting fighting on the line of the Seim and Desna Rivers and on the Kremenchug axis, while defending the eastern bank of the Dnepr on the Chernin, Kiev Fortified Region, and Kremenchug front.

The enemy, while attacking from the north against 40th 21st, and the right wing of 5th Army with large forces, captured crossings over the Seim River at Mel'na and across the Desna river at Butovka, Makoshino, Saltykova, Devitsa, Kovchin, Avdeevka, Brusilovo, and Morovsk and is developing the offensive, especially actively on the Konotop and Chernigov axes. On the Kremenchug axis, the enemy, having broadened his bridgehead, is developing an offensive toward Kozel'shchina.

1. 40th Army.

On 40th Army's front, the enemy forced the Seim River at Mel'na, committed 40 tanks at 1600 hours, and pushed the army's units toward the south. Fighting is underway on the northeastern outskirts of Konotop. About 50 German sub-machine gunners cut the railroad at Bakhmach and are advancing toward Kokhanovka.

10th TD and 227th RD are being committed to combat.

Glukhov is occupied by an enemy tank subunit. Sosnitsa has been abandoned by our units under pressure of an enemy force of 60-70 tanks.

Source: "Operativnaia svodka shtaba Iugo-Zapadnogo fronta No. 00139 k 22 chasam 8 sentiabria 1941 g. o boevykh deistviiakh voisk fronta" [Operational summary no. 00139 of the headquarters of the Southwestern Front at 2200 hours on 8 September 1941 about the combat operations of the *front's* forces], in *SBDVOV*, issue 40, 166-167.

11. Operational Summary No. 00141 of the Southwestern Front at 2200 hours on 9 September 1941 (see Map 11)

The Southwestern Front's forces conducted heavy fighting on 40th, 21st, and 5th Armies' fronts, on 37th Army's right wing, and on the Kremenchug axis.

The enemy is continuing to attack southward toward Konotop and Bakhmach and on the Chernigov and Oster axes. On the Kremenchug axis, the enemy displayed no activity during the day, and one must assume [he] is conducting preparations for an offensive.

1. 40th Army. Fighting is going on in Konotop and Bakhmach. There is no information about the units' positions.

Source: "Operativnaia svodka shtaba Iugo-Zapadnogo fronta No. 00141 k 22 chasam 9 sentiabria 1941 g. o boevykh deistviiakh voisk fronta" [Operational summary no. 00141 of the headquarters of the Southwestern Front at 2200 hours on 9 September 1941 about the combat operations of the *front's* forces], in *SBDVOV*, issue 40, 170.

12. Operational Summary No. 00142 of the Southwestern Front at 1000 hours on 10 September 1941

1. 40th Army. The positions of the army's units at day's end on 9 September: 227th RD is holding onto Konotop, with its front toward the west.

10th TD is in the Mitchenki region, with its front toward the east.

2nd AbnC, 3rd AbnC, and 293rd RD – positions as before.

Enemy tank units and infantry are continuing an offensive toward Bakhmach, Konotop, and to the south, where a gap has formed in our units.

Source: "Operativnaia svodka shtaba Iugo-Zapadnogo fronta No. 00142 k 10 chasam 10 sentiabria 1941 g. o boevykh deistviiakh voisk fronta" [Operational summary no. 00142 of the headquarters of the Southwestern Front at 1000 hours on 10 September 1941 about the combat operations of the *front's* forces], in *SBDVOV*, issue 40, 172.

13. Operational Summary No. 00143 of the Southwestern Front at 2200 hours on 10 September 1941

The Southwestern Front is being penetrated on the Konotop axis by enemy attacking toward the south, and his forward motor-mechanized units reached Gaivoron and Romny in the second half of the day. Our forces are conducting

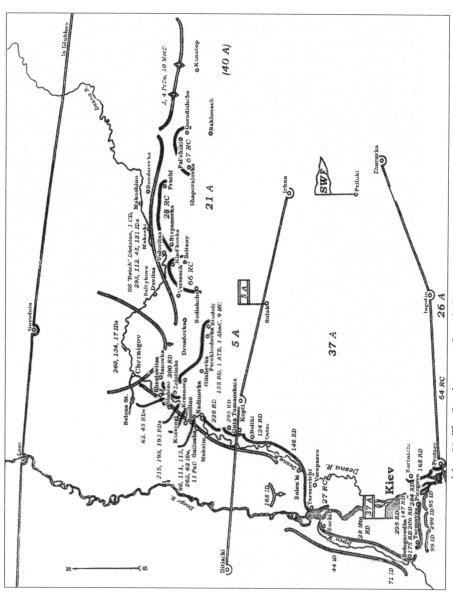

Map 11: The Southwestern Front's Situation Late on 9 September 1941

holding actions on the Nezhin, Chernigov, and Kozelets axes. Our units are going on the offensive on the Kremenchug axis.

1. 40th Army. There is no exact information about the positions of 40th Army's units. The enemy is developing an offensive with 4th PzD and one motorized division toward the south between Bakhmach and Konotop and with 3rd PzD toward Glukhov and Vorozhba.

As of 1000 hours, the army's units were holding onto Konotop and Bakhmach, who preventing the widening of the penetration between those two points. There is no new information.

According to a report from the army's chief of staff, up to 90 enemy tanks have been destroyed by the army's units in the fighting from 6 September through 9 September.

Source: "Operativnaia svodka shtaba Iugo-Zapadnogo fronta No. 00143 k 22 chasam 10 sentiabria 1941 g. o boevykh deistviiakh voisk fronta" [Operational summary no. 00143 of the headquarters of the Southwestern Front at 2200 hours on 10 September 1941 about the combat operations of the *front's* forces], in *SBDVOV,* issue 40, 176.

Index to Documents and Tables

(German orders in **bold italics**)

Related titles published by Helion & Company

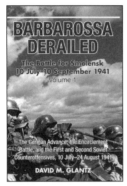

Barbarossa Derailed. The Battle for
Smolensk 10 July-10 September Volume 1
The German Advance, the Encirclement
Battle, and the First and Second Soviet
Counteroffensives, 10 July-24 August 1941
David M. Glantz
ISBN 978-1-906033-72-9 (Hardback)
ISBN 978-1-907677-50-2 (eBook)

Barbarossa Derailed. The Battle for
Smolensk 10 July-10 September Volume 2
The German Advance on the Flanks
and the Third Soviet Counteroffensive,
25 August–10 September 1941
David M. Glantz
ISBN 978-1-906033-90-3 (Hardback)
ISBN 978-1-908916-78-5 (eBook)

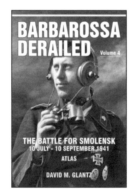

Barbarossa Derailed. The Battle for
Smolensk 10 July-10 September Volume 4
Atlas
David M. Glantz
ISBN 978-1-909982-83-3 (Hardback)

HELION & COMPANY
26 Willow Road, Solihull, West Midlands B91 1UE, England
Telephone 0121 705 3393   Fax 0121 711 4075
Website: http://www.helion.co.uk
Twitter: @helionbooks | Visit our blog http://blog.helion.co.uk